timeout.com

Published by Time Out Guides Ltd, a wholly owned subsidiary of Time Out Group Ltd.
Time Out and the Time Out logo are trademarks of Time Out Group Ltd.

© **Time Out Group Ltd 2008**
Previous edition 2006.

10 9 8 7 6 5 4 3 2 1

This edition first published in Great Britain in 2008 by Ebury Publishing
A Random House Group Company
20 Vauxhall Bridge Road, London SW1V 2SA

Random House Australia Pty Limited 20 Alfred Street, Milsons Point, Sydney,
New South Wales 2061, Australia
Random House New Zealand Limited 18 Poland Road, Glenfield, Auckland 10, New Zealand
Random House South Africa (Pty) Limited Isle of Houghton, Corner Boundary Road &
Carse O'Gowrie, Houghton 2198, South Africa

Random House UK Limited Reg. No. 954009

For further distribution details, see www.timeout.com

ISBN 978-1-84670-056-9

A CIP catalogue record for this book is available from the British Library

Printed and bound by Firmengruppe APPL, aprinta druck, Wemding, Germany

The Random House Group Limited supports The Forest Stewardship Council (FSC), the leading international
forest certification organisation. All our titles that are printed on Greenpeace approved FSC certified paper
carry the FSC logo. Our paper procurement policy can be found at www.rbooks.co.uk/environment.

WHEN YOU VISIT LONDON YOU WILL ALREADY HAVE BEEN TOLD NOT TO MISS THE WAPPING PROJECT.

SO DON'T.

THE WAPPING PROJECT
WAPPING HYDRAULIC POWER STATION
WAPPING WALL, LONDON E1W 3SG

00 44 207 680 2080
WWW.THEWAPPINGPROJECT.COM   DLR: Shadwell

PHOTO CREDIT: STAIRWAYS AND REFLECTIONS BY SHED 54. COMMISSIONED BY
THE WAPPING PROJECT ON BEHALF OF VEUVE CLICQUOT. PHOTO: THOMAS ZANON-LARCHER, 2007.

Time Out Guides Limited
Universal House
251 Tottenham Court Road
London W1T 7AB
Tel + 44 (0)20 7813 3000
Fax + 44 (0)20 7813 6001
Email guides@timeout.com
www.timeout.com

Editorial
Editor Emma Howarth
Copy Editor Simon Coppock
Listings Editor Cathy Limb
Listings Researchers Alex Brown, Gemma Pritchard
Proofreader Tamsin Shelton
Indexer Jackie Brind

Managing Director Peter Fiennes
Financial Director Gareth Garner
Editorial Director Sarah Guy
Series Editor Cath Phillips
Editorial Manager Holly Pick
Assistant Management Accountant Ija Krasnikova

Design
Art Director Scott Moore
Art Editor Pinelope Kourmouzoglou
Senior Designer Henry Elphick
Graphic Designer Gemma Doyle
Junior Graphic Designer Kei Ishimaru
Digital Imaging Simon Foster
Advertising Designer Jodi Sher

Picture Desk
Picture Editor Jael Marschner
Deputy Picture Editor Katie Morris
Picture Researcher Helen McFarland
Picture Desk Assistant Troy Bailey

Advertising
Commercial Director Mark Phillips
Sales Manager Alison Wallen
Advertising Sales Ben Holt, Alex Matthews, Jason Trotman
Advertising Assistant Kate Staddon
Copy Controller Declan Symington

Marketing
Head of Marketing Catherine Demajo
Marketing Manager Yvonne Poon
Sales & Marketing Director North America Lisa Levinson

Production
Group Production Director Mark Lamond
Production Manager Brendan McKeown
Production Controller Caroline Bradford
Production Coordinator Julie Pallot

Time Out Group
Chairman Tony Elliott
Financial Director Richard Waterlow
Group General Manager/Director Nichola Coulthard
Time Out Magazine Ltd MD Richard Waterlow
Time Out Communications Ltd MD David Pepper
Time Out International MD Cathy Runciman
Group Art Director John Oakey
Group IT Director Simon Chappell

Contributors
Neighbourhoods, Restaurants & cafés, Bars & pubs and Shops written by Joe Barry, Joseph Bindloss, Jessica Cargill-Thompson, Simon Coppock, Peterjon Cresswell, Alexi Duggins, Dominic Earle, Paul Edwards, Charlie Godfrey-Fausett, Sarah Guy, Arwa Haider, Emma Howarth, Ronnie Haydon, Tom Lamont, Jenny Linford, Sally Long, Chris Moss, Cath Phillips, Gemma Pritchard, Lisa Ritchie, Cyrus Shahrad, Andrew Shields, Elizabeth Winding.
Additional writing, interviews and research by Alex Brown, Cathy Limb, Nana Ocran, Gemma Pritchard.
The Editor would like to thank Amul Batra, Daniel Smith, Simon Munk and all the estate agents, parents and Londoners who agreed to give their comments and tips.

Maps by JS Graphics (john@jsgraphics.co.uk).

Cover photography Columbia Road Flower Market by Piers Allardyce.
Photography pages 3, 8, 9, 27, 43, 46, 55, 59, 213, 229, 245, 259, 271, 279 Nigel Tradewell; pages 7, 20, 29, 64, 82, 83, 148, 164, 175, 178, 254 Ming Tang Evans; pages 12, 71, 91, 95, 103, 106, 115, 121, 135, 136, 141, 153, 293, 302 Jonathan Perugia; page 17 Christina Theisen; page 33 Gordon Rainsford; pages 60, 209, 263 Abigail Lelliott; page 62 Alys Tomlinson; pages 74, 116, 145, 327 Britta Jaschinski; page 77 Amanda C Edwards; pages 86, 232, 266 Nick Ballon; pages 111, 129, 337 Tricia de Courcy Ling; pages 125, 126, 203 Andrew Blackenbury; pages 128, 132 Heloise Bergman; pages 157, 171, 185, 188, 335 Charlie Pinder; pages 161, 216, 217 Olivia Rutherford; pages 167, 181, 250 Rob Greig; pages 194, 196, 223 Gemma Day; page 238 Jitka Hynkova; page 251 Rogan Macdonald; page 274 Michael Franke; pages 289, 312 Scott Wishart; page 322 Simon Leigh.

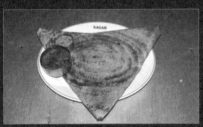

Contents

A river runs through it

Few people think of London's famous river and network of urban waterways when looking for a place to live. Yet with a fast-growing population and ever-increasing demand for affordable housing in the capital, this is a resource of which we could make much better use. **Joe Barry** and **Emma Howarth** find out which ideas hold water.

Take a stroll along the Thames or one of London's canals and it won't be long before you come across a pocket of boat life. From the prestigious – and sought-after – moorings at Chelsea's Cheyne Walk and Wandsworth's Lightermans Walk to the bohemian communities of Downings Roads near Tower Bridge, Little Venice or Battersea's Albion Quay, the capital's waterways are scattered with narrowboats, converted barges and tugboats that Londoners have decided to call home.

It's easy to see the appeal. Why pay £2 million for a Thames-side apartment in Butler's Wharf when, just a few minutes' walk along the river at the Downings Roads moorings, fresh air, nature, community spirit and the best views in London can be yours for something like a tenth of the price. 'The Thames is definitely the last great real estate frontier in the capital,' says James Roeber, owner of Dutch barge *Cathalina*, previously at Downings Roads and now at Docklands' Blackwall Basin Marina.

John Evans of Riverhomes (www.river homes.co.uk), a niche estate agent that specialises in riverside homes and houseboats, couldn't agree more. 'The Thames is a huge resource,' he says. 'It's just a case of finding a good residential mooring. Though it's also important to remember that it's not always a cheaper option – there are mooring fees to be paid.'

Compared with cities such as Amsterdam and Antwerp, however, our waterways are massively underused. One of the reasons for this is logistics – London's tidal range is as much as seven metres, which means a greater infrastructure is necessary to enable boats to moor. Paris's bateaux-lined Seine, meanwhile, has no tide to trouble those who wish to make it their home.

Another reason is the lack of available moorings for residential use. British Waterways (BW), which maintains the nation's 2,000-mile network of canals and inland waterways, admits that 'demand for moorings in London has soared in recent years and now outstrips supply'. BW operates 940 berths in the capital, though only 128 of these are officially residential. In addition, private operators run 1,750 berths on BW's network and around 2,500 berths on non-BW waterways – the Port of London Authority (PLA) manages the tidal Thames, though the moorings on it are privately owned – but, again, only a small proportion of these are residential.

Figures could, and should, be higher. BW's strategy is to create between 30 and 40 new moorings a year in London, 'with a proportion being residential'. It also makes a point of encouraging private-sector developers to create moorings and so-called 'off-line' basins as part of land-based developments, as in the case of the Grand Union Village, a partnership with Taylor Wimpey in Northholt on the Grand Union Canal, which will have 23 berths with residential permission. Such schemes are essential in maintaining London's historic relationship between city and water.

Unsurprisingly, finding a mooring is usually the biggest obstacle faced by those wanting to embark on a life on the river waves. Approach BW or any of the publications (*Canal Boat* or *Canals & Rivers*, for example) and websites (www.waterscape.com) aimed at boat enthusiasts for advice and they all say the same thing: 'Buy a boat but find somewhere to park it first.' Few boats for sale come with a mooring already attached, so it's essential to get your name on BW's waiting lists and contact private moorings (a list of residential moorings on the Thames can be found on the PLA site, www.portoflondon.co.uk) before you even think about purchasing your dream vessel.

> 'Boat living is like London life but with added appeal – and the community spirit is amazing.'

Buying a houseboat is relatively easy (they are legally considered 'chattels' and can be purchased in much the same way one might buy a car); financing one is more difficult. The main reason for this is that 'marine mortgages' (provided by companies such as Collidge & Partners,

Houseboat style: *Cathalina.*

www.collidgeandpartners.co.uk) can be hard to come by and are usually payable over shorter periods than a conventional mortgage (anything from five to 15 years). As a result, the best way to finance a boat is often to remortgage something else – your parents' house, perhaps – and pay that off instead. If your folks are unlikely to find this an amenable proposition, you'll have to pay cash: expect to stump up £40,000 on average for a narrowboat and £150,000 for a well-maintained barge, although you could pay anything up to £300,000 and beyond for a flash conversion. You'll also need to add on the cost of a survey (around £600), a licence (around £400), a boat safety certificate (£60-£180) and mooring fees (£4,000-£10,000 a year depending on the size of the boat and location of the mooring) before you can start living that life-afloat dream. On the plus side, most houseboats (though not all) are exempt from the likes of council tax and water rates.

Though many boat-dwellers joke that the best two days of boat ownership are the day you buy it and the day you sell it, few have any complaints about life aboard. Chris Pierre, owner of Dutch barge *Ringvaart 3*, has lived at Battersea's Albion Quay for just under a year. 'I adore it,' he says. 'Boat living feels like London life but with added appeal – and the community spirit is amazing. Of course that also means that every "quiet drink on deck" becomes some sort of party.'

Una Flynn, who lives on barge *Selby Margaret* at Blackwall Basin, agrees. 'It's a brilliant, laid-back way of life – perfect for stressed-out professionals,' she says. 'Though when people find out you live on a boat they automatically assume you're eccentric, arty or a hippie.'

To the uninitiated it's usually the stereotype of boats being cramped and cold with ominous chemical toilets that's most off-putting. Sam Bemrose, who has converted and sold two barges to Londoners, is quick to dispel the myth: 'Living on a boat isn't all that different, but it is potentially cheaper. And you can have all the facilities you want.' Amenities vary from mooring to mooring, but most include pump-out facilities for sewage as well as water and electricity. Some go as far as toilet/shower blocks and communal

FIVE STEPS TO LIVING ON THE WATER

1. Get a survey

No matter how nice the vendor, no matter how solid the boat looks above the water line, no matter what the last survey said, get the boat out of the water and get someone to give it an ultrasonic inspection. Otherwise you might find you've just bought a very expensive colander. London boatyards are listed on the PLA site (www.portoflondon.co.uk).

2. Find a place to put it

London has very few official residential moorings and almost all have long waiting lists. The bigger the boat, the harder (and more expensive) it is to park. Contact British Waterways (7985 7200, www.britishwaterways. co.uk), private mooring operators (there is a list of Thames moorings on the PLA site) and ask other boat owners for advice.

3. Buy a converted boat

Few boats are ever 'finished' to their owners' satisfaction, but it will save you time, money and sanity if you can live aboard straight away in reasonable comfort. Unless you're a DIY genius forget buying an unconverted barge. And remember, whatever you buy you'll need to get your hands dirty – boats take a lot of maintaining.

4. Don't expect profit

Investing in steel, wood and fibreglass isn't like investing in bricks and mortar – it isn't really an investment at all. Unless you do a lot of work to the boat, or manage to get it into a good mooring where you can sell it, your new home is not going to accrue greatly in value, no matter what the housing market does.

5. Go for a sail

All too many boat engines sit idly while the river waits. You'll have to check your insurance and you might need to hire a qualified skipper, but nothing beats the joy of literally moving house.

Cheyne Walk is the ultimate boat-living location – but waiting lists are long.

washing machines, others have stunning garden barges (Downings Roads) or even access to an indoor swimming pool (Lightermans Walk).

And while it's true that space can be an issue, visitors with *Rosie & Jim* visions are often surprised by the sheer size of living space that's possible on a boat. It's very easy to end up with far more square footage than your average London flat. True narrowboats may well be just six feet wide, but people also live on huge converted barges, tugboats, ice breakers, coal lighters, pilot ships, lighthouse ships – in fact, just about any vessel that's ever floated has houseboat potential.

Small can be beautiful too, though – especially if you're organised. Dick has lived at the privately run Three Mills mooring in Newham on his narrowboat, *Coco*, for two years. 'Everything has its place,' he says. 'You just can't be untidy. But there's nothing I miss.'

Regardless of size, anyone considering a watery life should be prepared to embark on some serious DIY. Even smarter live-aboards tend to have an element of the unfinished project about them and life on a boat is one long round of painting, plumbing and greasing. If you decide to convert a barge from scratch yourself, the maintenance story will definitely become an epic. Even if you buy a lovingly restored

vessel, if you're not handy with a power drill before you buy it, you soon will be. You'll have to be. All this, though, is what living on the water is all about. Boat life offers an alternative lifestyle, one that isn't easily comparable with living on dry land.

Common misconceptions about the kinds of people who live on boats are best ignored too. While waterborne celebrities past and present – Keith Allen, Rhys Ifans, Damien Hirst, Nick Cave, Andy Cato of Groove Armada, Pink Floyd's David Gilmour – have raised the profile of boat living, boat owners are often still regarded by landlubbers as 'dropouts'. Visit any London mooring, though, and you'll find a whole cross-section of society – professionals, families and students all living aboard. If we made full use of the capital's watery resources many more could join them.

So what of the future? Many people would like to see the Thames opened up, with lots more berths for boats, but this would almost certainly mean a rise in rules and regulations. For many boat owners the whole appeal of life aboard is the opportunity to avoid the restrictions that land-ownership brings. They prefer to be almost unseen, quietly existing in idyllic communities on canals and backwaters across the capital. Whatever happens, one thing is certain – London's liquid history lives on.

About the Guide

How the guide is arranged

Thanks to centuries of haphazard growth and various changes in the division and administration of the capital's districts, London is a defiantly disordered city. To cope with contradictory postcode lines, electoral wards and borough boundaries, we've divided this guide into 25 chapters, each focusing on one borough. For this second edition, we've added a new chapter on Kingston upon Thames, and have extended neighbourhood coverage in several boroughs.

The most central boroughs (City of Westminster, City of London, Tower Hamlets, Hackney, Islington, Camden, Kensington & Chelsea, Hammersmith & Fulham, Lambeth, Wandsworth, Southwark and Lewisham) are covered in their entirety; in slightly more outlying boroughs, such as Greenwich and Brent, neighbourhoods closest to central London are covered; in outer boroughs such as Waltham Forest and Redbridge only key areas are covered. Each chapter is broken down by neighbourhood, with guides to restaurants and cafés, bars and pubs, shops and other essentials within the borough.

Neighbourhoods

Inevitably, neighbourhoods don't neatly follow borough boundaries. In cases where one district straddles two or more boroughs, we have included it in the most suitable chapter. Knightsbridge, for example, straddles both Kensington & Chelsea and Westminster, but is included in the former. We've provided a map of each borough, plus an overview map (on page 14) of all the boroughs covered in the guide.

Amenities & essentials

No guide to London's amenities can be completely comprehensive: we have tried to select the best each borough has to offer. Addresses, telephone numbers and websites were all correct as we went to press; most listings for large chains are omitted.

Sport & fitness covers all publicly funded sports centres plus key private facilities. Schools covers all state secondary schools plus landmark private schools. Local estate agents are listed within each chapter.

While every effort has been made to ensure the accuracy of information in this guide, the publishers cannot accept responsibility for any errors it may contain.

Statistics

Our statistics come from a variety of sources. Borough populations are from an Office of National Statistics (ONS) 2006 survey (www.statistics.gov.uk); average property prices from the Land Registry Standard Report April-June 2007; ethnic origins from experimental population estimates from the ONS for 2004/2005; student and retiree figures from the 2001 Census (www.statistics.gov.uk); housing stock figures from the DEFRA municipal waste management survey 2003-2004 (www.capitalwastefacts.com); average weekly earnings from the ONS 'Annual Survey of Hours and Earnings'; crime figures from the 'Recorded Crime for Key Offences 2006/07' report by the Research Development & Statistics Directorate (RDS, www.homeoffice.gov.uk/rds); recycling statistics from the DEFRA household waste recycling audited figures for 2005-2006 (www.defra.gov.uk) and www.capitalwastefacts.com; and CPA (Comprehensive Performance Assessment) ratings from the Audit Commission's 'Harder Test' published in August 2007 (www.audit-commission.gov.uk/cpa/postcode.asp).

Let us know what you think

We hope you enjoy this book and we'd like to know what you think of it. Email us at guides@timeout.com.

London Boroughs

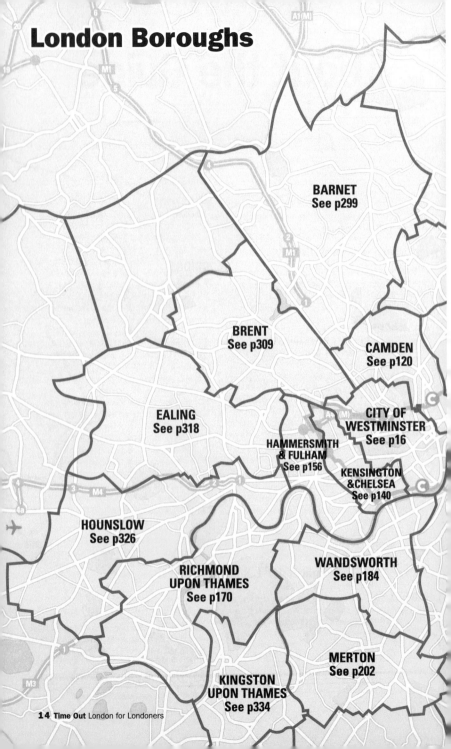

BARNET
See p299

BRENT
See p309

CAMDEN
See p120

EALING
See p318

CITY OF WESTMINSTER
See p16

HAMMERSMITH & FULHAM
See p156

KENSINGTON & CHELSEA
See p140

HOUNSLOW
See p326

WANDSWORTH
See p184

RICHMOND UPON THAMES
See p170

MERTON
See p202

KINGSTON UPON THAMES
See p334

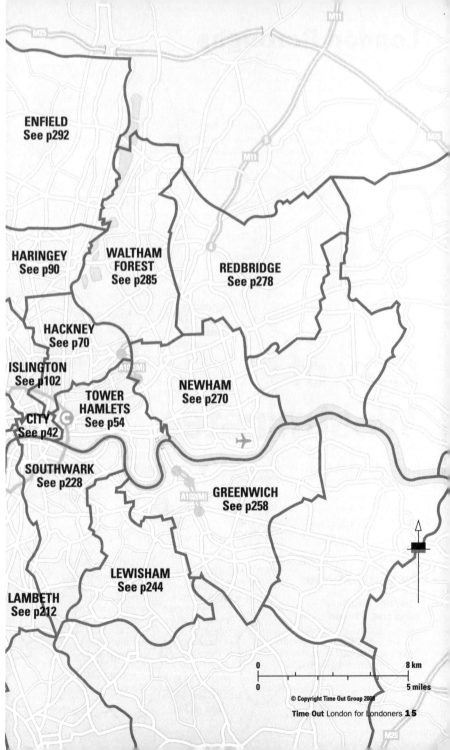

ENFIELD
See p292

HARINGEY
See p90

WALTHAM
FOREST
See p285

REDBRIDGE
See p278

HACKNEY
See p70

ISLINGTON
See p102

NEWHAM
See p270

TOWER
HAMLETS
See p54

CITY
See p42

SOUTHWARK
See p228

GREENWICH
See p258

LEWISHAM
See p244

LAMBETH
See p212

0   8 km

0   5 miles

© Copyright Time Out Group 2008

'I walk down Old Compton Street most mornings with a stupid grin on my face – Soho! London! It's like winning the lottery every day.'

Andrew Humphreys, writer and Soho resident for ten years

City of Westminster

Power, wealth and fame in their most concentrated forms shape the City of Westminster's landscape. Set against a backdrop of much-snapped tourist sights is the busily working, living city, its creative centre earning more than £15 billion a year. Beyond the West End and the corridors of power lies the hectic transport hub of Victoria, along with airy Hyde Park, historic Paddington and, just along the canal, poetic Little Venice.

Neighbourhoods

Covent Garden and the Strand

Though high on every tourist's visiting agenda, Covent Garden is more than an entertainment centre. True, the area is synonymous with the Royal Opera House, hosts daily alfresco entertainment on its central piazza, is surrounded by theatres

and has one of London's most popular museums (the Transport Museum reopened with a fanfare in November 2007 after a two-year revamp). True too, it is always thronged with shoppers and merrymakers. Yet there's a big residential community as well, and many independent businesses.

Thirty-five years ago, Covent Garden was still a busy fruit and veg market (to see what it was like watch Hitchcock's 1972 thriller *Frenzy*). When the wholesale market

City of Westminster

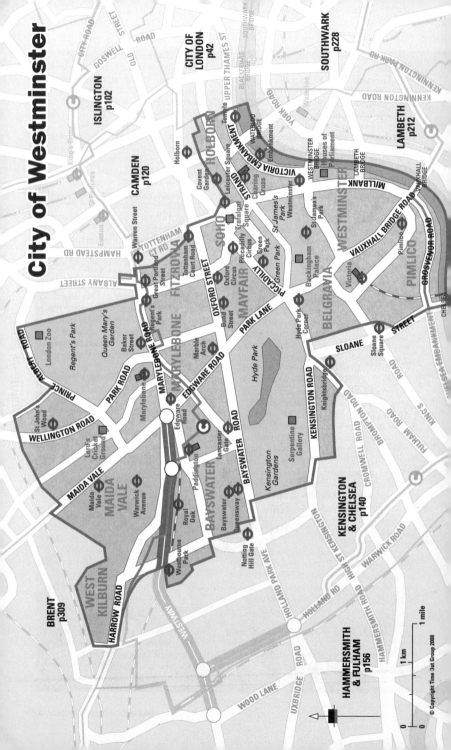

was moved to Nine Elms, this prime site was in line for redevelopment – roads, office blocks and business hotels were planned. Fortunately, the locals demonstrated and squatted properties, kicking up such a fuss that the area was saved. Today the residents are a pleasant mix of people. Sure, there's the odd £3 million apartment for sale, but the denizens of such places share amenities with long-term residents and those living in the local Peabody Trust housing, such as Daveys Court on Bedfordbury. More desirable residential areas can be found at Ching Court, off Shelton Street, and the flats opposite Phoenix Garden, a delightful wildlife garden built on an old car park on Stacey Street (enter from St Giles Passage).

Away from the largely pedestrianised streets and community squares, towards Charing Cross Road, the lights of Theatreland meld into the neon of Leicester Square, only worth a visit if you want cheap same-day theatre tickets from the tkts booth, or to catch a film at the only cinema right-minded folk can afford hereabouts, the Prince Charles. By night the square is like the seventh circle of hell – full of inebriated daytrippers missing the last train to Basingstoke.

Covent Garden's southern border, the Strand, is rather dull by comparison. Connecting Westminster to the City, the area's saving grace is Somerset House, whose galleries are a peaceful antidote to the overcrowded ice rink that becomes its centrepiece every winter. The Savoy hotel (currently closed for a £100 million restoration project; due to reopen early 2009) has always attracted rich tourists and expense-accounters, but, come dusk, the homeless still bed down in doorways along the Strand. Villiers Street, at the Charing Cross end, leads down to the Embankment, built in the 1860s when the riverside Strand proved too thin for its attractions. The newest draw here is Craven Street's quirky performing museum piece Benjamin Franklin House.

Soho and Chinatown

Slippery Soho is a hard place to pin down. Its outline is marked in boisterous fashion by four Circuses: Oxford, St Giles, Cambridge and Piccadilly. The district within – and its southern subsection Chinatown – is residential, touristy, intellectual and historically complex all at the same time.

You'll need to mug up on it. Many Londoners still think it's all about sex and sleaze. Fact is, Soho is a historically diverse part of the West End that has always been more notable for its hostelries than its sexual favours. Certainly, since censorship laws were relaxed and licensed lap-dancing and strip clubs became more widespread, Soho's sex industry has petered out. It now consists of a few hardy venues around Berwick Street, which is much more popular for its daily street market than its 'fresh new models'. Talking of which, Westminster City Council has plans for the regeneration of the Berwick Street area. Recent 'I love Soho' campaigns instigated by the Mayor's office and the council have emphasised the district's more cultural attractions.

Soho also never lost its hardy residential community. Many residents live above shops and restaurants, which means they must live with challenging levels of noise. Their young children are educated at Soho Parish School, on Great Windmill Street, which sits innocently among shuttered lap-dancing clubs.

South of Shaftesbury Avenue is the domain of the LCCA (London Chinatown Chinese Association), centred on Gerrard Street; you can't miss its ersatz oriental street trimmings. The Chinese community first opened restaurants and shops here in the 1950s, with Chinatown another part of Soho whose way of life was established in the halcyon days of cheap rents and slummy streets. Today these streets are valuable real estate; plans are already under way to redevelop the eastern edge of Chinatown, near Charing Cross Road.

Yet another big regeneration plan that's going ahead is the restoration of the old (1852) Marshall Street baths in Soho. A purpose-built leisure centre is promised for 2009. The decision means the Grade II-listed building, with its famous barrel-vaulted roof, will be taken off English Heritage's 'Buildings at Risk' register. Marshall Street will be the third new leisure facility to open in as many years in Westminster – good for the borough's sporty souls. There's planning for 52 homes to be built alongside the centre, 15 of which, we are assured, will be affordable. Time will tell.

Holborn

Camden and the City of London muscle in on this purposeful area of central London, where a short walk can take you to the heart of the British legal system (the Inns of Court), to the West End (Covent Garden is but a block away) or to some of London's great museums and seats of learning (the Hunterian Museum, the British Museum, the London School of Economics).

Residential Holborn is not. There are student halls of residence on High Holborn, where apartment blocks and conversions also yield affordable private homes of the two-bed, one bath variety. Near High Holborn, the Bourne Estate, local-authority-owned but Grade II listed, can sometimes offer one-bed flats around the £350,000 mark, but they're snapped up quickly. Most of Holborn's more affordable property tends to be on the Covent Garden side of Kingsway. Here expensive flats, often in big Victorian buildings such as decommissioned primary schools, make up the stock. Minutes from Holborn tube, crossing the border into Camden borough, quiet Macklin Street and Newton Street have a number of such conversions. Queen Square, north of High Holborn, is also a favoured (expensive) residential area. Mostly, however, property around here – especially anywhere near beautiful Lincoln's Inn Fields – is likely to cost around £1 million, and there are very few unconverted houses.

Amusingly, given the price of property, nearby Carey Street provides its own euphemism for being in debt ('on Carey Street'), which comes from the fact that the back entrance to the Royal Courts of Justice is on it. Debtors were clearly expected to shuffle in through the back door. On a brighter, even twinkly note, Carey Street is home to the Seven Stars pub, legendary for its food, atmosphere and glamorous proprietor, the one and only Roxy Beaujolais.

Mayfair

In 2007 everyone heard about the sub-prime market and the havoc it was causing in money markets across the world. Here, the super-prime market holds sway: you have to be ultra-rich to afford to buy a home in Mayfair, London's most blue-blooded district. Properties went up by about 40 per cent over 2007, which means

Buzzing **Chinatown**. *See p19.*

your average two-bed apartment might cost about £3 million. If you're not into looks, or cat-swinging, there are some modern red-brick blocks around Shepherd Market, where a studio would cost about £400,000.

Bordered by the weighty thoroughfares of Piccadilly, Park Lane and Oxford Street, Mayfair's posh squares and salubrious streets seem by turns hushed and imperious. No nightingales sing in Berkeley Square, but the historic Guinea pub, a delightfully unpretentious drinking den on the north-east corner of Bruton Place, will put a song in your heart. Shepherd Market is Mayfair's real-life bit, still dealing in the pleasures of life. It's named after an early 18th-century food market and famed for its prostitutes (although there are fewer here than when Jeffrey Archer met Monica Coghlan). There are chocolate shops, good restaurants and a couple of nice little boozers. Nearby Farm Street is the kind of residential area most Londoners, if they're truthful, would admit to aspiring to.

The pretty local library, on South Audley Street, speaks of a lucky, literate residential community. There's even a bridge club.

West of Park Lane is the wonderful expanse of Hyde Park. Here you'll find Speakers' Corner, beloved of loons and free speech advocates, and the Serpentine Gallery, host of adventurous modern art and architecture. As Hyde Park becomes Kensington Gardens, it enters the Royal Borough of Kensington & Chelsea.

Marylebone

Only about six years ago, Marylebone was a reasonably affordable part of Westminster. You could pick up a two-bedroom flat for about £300,000. Today Marylebone rents and property prices match those of its expensive neighbours. The successful rebranding of the pretty High Street – despite having Oxford Street just to the south, it could belong to an affluent provincial town – into desirable 'Marylebone Village' has been the success of the decade. Now everyone wants a piece of Marylebone and its lovely quiet squares.

The area isn't all luxury cashmere babywear and Nigella's favourite cheese shop, though. Radiating out from the village are less appealing streets. When it first grew up, this parish – St Mary by the Bourn – was known for its criminal population, many of whom ended up swinging from Tyburn gallows, where Marble Arch is now. Although nowhere is exactly rough round here, the thunderingly busy Marylebone Road is not a particularly pleasant place to linger. However, it does have a splendid old town hall – Westminster Council House – which is both the local library and a classic London wedding venue, its steps always strewn with rose petals and rice.

Lisson Grove, which heads north-west from here, was once all slums: 'it wasn't fit for a pig to live in!' (*Pygmalion*). Much of the housing stock is ex-council. While the large Lisson Green Estate overlooking the canal can be intimidating, the streets between Lisson Grove and Edgware Road are more enticing. There are bargains to be had, but visit the area at different times of day so you know what you're getting into. Still on the Grove (but at the other end of the market), the gated Belvedere development has two-bed flats for £400,000, and there's a small supply of bijou Georgian houses.

Otherwise, you might want to look into buying one of the houseboats on the canal.

Bell Street is one of the more interesting roads hereabouts, with the area's only art gallery (the Lisson) plus a couple of second-hand bookshops. The other standout is Church Street, which has a weekend market but is otherwise almost completely given over to antiques shops, drawn by Alfie's Antique Market with its fine rooftop café.

New building in the as-yet-unprettified quarter of Baker Street, such as the redevelopment of the old Marks & Spencer building, is throwing more housing into the Marylebone mix. The development on Rodmarten Street, just behind Baker Street, promises a mixture of luxury and affordable housing. On the other hand, the gracious Portland building, where Baker Street meets Regent's Park, will become luxury homes, with prices at about £3,500 a square foot when we checked. Still, you would be living next to the formal flower beds, waterfowl lakes and playing fields of Regent's Park, and close to London Zoo.

Fitzrovia

Portland Place, the home of BBC News, separates Marylebone from medialand. Fitzrovia is a district that raises a number of questions among Londoners, 'Where is it?' being a common one. Fitzrovia could also be described as north Soho, although that makes it sound a lot more exciting than it is. Roughly speaking, it lies east of Great Portland Street, bordered by Euston Road to the north, Oxford Street to the south and Charlotte Street to the east. The name comes from Fitzroy Square (on the Camden side), built by one Honourable Charles Fitzroy in the 18th century.

Unlike its neighbours, Marylebone and Bloomsbury, in which lofty terraces, crescents and squares were created by empire-building wealthy landowners, Fitzrovia was developed on a smaller scale by minor landowners. This left the streets feeling less well organised, but the area has a low-key, arty, crafty and business-like vibe. There are a few fashion wholesale businesses, various former departments of the old Middlesex Hospital (now moved to University College Hospital on Euston Road), BT and other communications offices under the famous BT Tower, and loads of restaurants, cafés and pubs.

City of Westminster

DO WONDERS

FOUNTAINS, RIVER VIEWS, WORKSHOPS, AND PLAY

FREE AT SOMERSET HOUSE

Open daily. Admission to Somerset House is free.
Entry fees apply to the Embankment Galleries and events.
Tel: 020 7845 4600 Strand, London WC2 www.somersethouse.org.uk
⊖ Temple, Charing Cross, Embankment, Covent Garden

SOMERSET
HOUSE

The Fitzrovia Neighbourhood Association (39 Tottenham Street, 7580 4576) is used by local organisations for meetings. The association was established (with the battle cry 'The people live here') in the 1970s when the area's residents stood up against would-be developers. It still works for the neighbourhood, affordable housing its main concern. This is possible to find: between expensive mews houses and some chichi housing developments, there are flats available above businesses and hidden down little alleys.

Westminster and St James's

The wider borough is called the City of Westminster, but this inner circle, built up around the Abbey, takes the Westminster name for itself. Happily snapping tourists throng around Parliament Square and its star sights year round, with the latest subject for their viewfinders a new statue of Nelson Mandela that was unveiled in autumn 2007. There could be no better place, of course, for anti-war campaigner Brian Haw to set up his camp. He has been here for the past seven years, despite various (ongoing) efforts to eject him. His makeshift home is a standout residence in a conservation area designated by the UN as a World Heritage Site.

Peace camp notwithstanding, central Westminster is kept spick and span for guests. Its tube station is clean and impressively modern, and the made-over and traffic-calmed central precinct, Trafalgar Square, is London's 'best room', site of the Mayor of London's series of free seasonal festivals and events. Here the famous Norwegian spruce is put up before much ceremony every winter before Christmas, and a very slowly changing art exhibition is hosted on Sir Charles Barry's statuelesss Fourth Plinth: exhibits stay for about 18 months, with the current piece, *Model for a Hotel 2007*, constructed from layers of coloured glass by German artist Thomas Schütte.

Connecting the two public squares is Whitehall, where tourists derive huge pleasure from photographing themselves with Household Cavalry troopers. This is a po-faced land of civil servants, but the ministries that line the road (as well as the heavily guarded, security-gated Downing Street) are strictly off-limits.

Going west from here, gorgeous St James's Park, famed for its waterfowl (notably the pelicans), is far prettier than Green Park, which provides a pleasant walk to a seat of privilege, rather than power: Buckingham Palace. The network of elderly streets bounded by the parks, Millbank and Vauxhall Bridge Road (on which you'll find the Secret Intelligence Service, formerly MI6, building), are peaceful, atmospheric and largely residential. You can tell if someone important lives in one of the houses if there's an armed policeman sitting outside.

Moving through Peter Street, Old Pye Street and Marsham Street returns you to community Westminster. There are Peabody estates for low-paid key workers round here – it can't be bad having Westminster Abbey as your local church.

Highs & Lows

▲ **Internet on the move** Westminster is Europe's biggest wireless internet hotspot. The network spans the West End, Whitehall and Soho, and takes in two council estates: Lisson Grove in Marylebone and Churchill Garden in Pimlico. The council plans to keep extending the network
Accessibility The City of Westminster has more tube stations than any other London borough – 30 in all
Cutting-edge libraries Busy borrowers in Westminster libraries can use self-service checkouts that read your library card, allowing you to take out books without dealing with cardigan-wearing librarians

Noise levels People living in Soho or Covent Garden have always had to contend with late-night shenanigans, but since the law forced smokers outside the problem has become much louder
Big money for titchy flats You'll have to search long and hard to find anything approaching a bargain
Refuse collectors The lorries seem to be out 24/7. There's an awful lot of rubbish to pick up every day in this part of town, and Westminster City Council is conscientious about ▼ its collection

City of Westminster

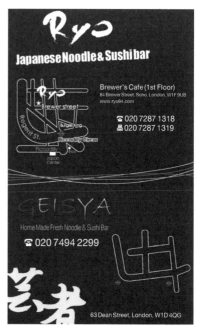

Victoria

Like many areas in Zone 1, Victoria is defined by its transport terminuses. The streets around them are crowded, dominated by backpackers, package tourists, commuters and various other scuttlers on their way somewhere else. The transitory nature of the area has long encouraged residents to insist they live in less frenetic-sounding neighbouring areas – Pimlico, Belgravia, even Westminster – but things seem to be changing.

Victoria Street, once a sorry collection of not terribly satisfying shops and run-down office blocks, where only the 1903 Catholic cathedral offered interest (to Catholics and those looking to enjoy fab views from the campanile), has been rejuvenated. The smart complex of shops and restaurants known as Cardinal Place has done much to cheer office workers and residents. In line with many other London honeypots, Cardinal Place has its own highly priced and rather titchy outdoor ice rink for the Christmas season.

Now the City of Westminster in association with Transport for London, Network Rail and Land Securities (owners of many of those tired 1950s office blocks) are all in on the proposed regeneration of the areas around the station and Buckingham Palace Road. The tube station is in dire need of attention, as crowds can reach dangerous levels down there. The redevelopment should improve life for pedestrians in Victoria's main streets too. Completion is depressingly distant, though: 2014. So for at least another six years, people arriving at London Victoria face a messy introduction to the capital.

Pimlico

Pimlico started off very smartly, with Thomas Cubitt building white stucco dwellings and garden squares for Lord Grosvenor in 1825. When land was sold off and charitable housing project the Peabody Trust built estates for the poor here, the smart money lost interest. After World War II, large public housing estates were built on the area's bombsites and fine houses were converted into flats, so all pretence to exclusivity was lost for decades.

Still, Pimlico is central and pockets of Zone 1 smartness give the whole district panache. In fact, property of any calibre is expensive here. Pimlico's extensive Westminster Council housing stock, all managed by Citywest Homes, includes the Lillington Gardens Estate. Off Tachbrook Street, this high-density, low-rise, red-brick estate, built in the 1970s, has Grade II-listed status. Hide Tower, on Regency Street, was built in the late 1950s and is run by a tenant management organisation. Its flats have fantastic views over London and attract high prices. Hide competes with nearby Tate Britain and the beleaguered, brutalist Pimlico School for the title of Pimlico's most recognisable building.

Down by the river is Dolphin Square, a self-contained village of pieds-à-terre for important people. The fortress-like, red-brick 1930s block has a health club, smart restaurant and a little art deco parade of shops. Such exclusivity is absent in the Westminster Boating Base, with headquarters on the river, just across Grosvenor Road. This charitable trust has been teaching urban youth the joys of watersports for more than 30 years.

Belgravia

Pimlico and Victoria folk enjoy the reflected glory their proximity to Belgravia affords them. Belgravia, however, remains aloof. Like Mayfair, it gets its blue blood from the aristocratic Grosvenor family who still own much of it. Richard Grosvenor, second Marquess of Westminster, commissioned Thomas Cubitt to develop it in the 1820s; Belgrave and Eaton Squares, with their white stucco mansions, are the result. Today the responsibility for managing the estate falls to Gerald, sixth Duke of Westminster, and Grosvenor is an international property group.

The area has never been anything other than posh. When World War II initiated the decline of whacking great Belgravian homes, the mansions were simply converted for use as embassies and institutes. Today the super-prime market that sent property prices in the swankiest parts of London into the stratosphere has attracted the super-rich back to Belgravia. They are now reclaiming the stucco palaces as desirable homes, with many of the properties worth more than £15 million.

It's a refined, rarefied area, and the shops, restaurants, mews houses and garden squares all reflect this. Around Elizabeth

Street, toward Ebury Street and the Sloaney end of Pimlico Road, are shops of privilege, but Peabody social housing also has a foothold – in the shape of a gorgeously picturesque balconied terrace: Lumley Flats on the Pimlico Road. Otherwise, anything vaguely vulgar, such as supermarkets, office blocks and entertainment venues, has been kept firmly out of the enchanted garden. One advantage of Belgravia's refusal to join the real world is the fact that pubs originally built as modest affairs (for servants of the resident aristocracy) have not been superseded by big chain boozers.

Bayswater

Westminster's most multifaceted district, Bayswater is a pleasing mix of once grand mansions, hotels, architecturally significant pleasure palaces and great places to eat and drink. Being Westminster, there's nowhere really cheap to live, although the odd run-down bedsit in some of the scruffier terraces around Queensborough Terrace might represent good value. Bayswater's big council estate, Hallfield, designed by Sir Denys Lasdun, gives its residents spectacular views over west London from top-floor flats that are very much in demand on the private market.

Queensway is Bayswater's backbone and is one big, noisy conservation area. The splendid Edwardian Whiteleys Shopping Centre (www.whiteleys.com), the largest in central London, is located here. The rest of the street is full of Middle Eastern cafés and restaurants. To the south, just opposite the memorabilia-filled Diana Café on the Bayswater Road, lie Kensington Gardens and the excellent playground built to the memory of the late Princess of Wales. The built-up areas of Paddington and Bayswater both benefit from their proximity to these royal green acres, which merge to the east with Hyde Park. At the northern end of Queensway lies the beautiful Porchester Centre, one of the few surviving examples of the Victorian Turkish baths that once proliferated in Britain. West of Queensway, on Moscow Road, the Greek Orthodox Cathedral of St Sophia, with its Byzantine icons and golden mosaics, is another reason for this area's cosmopolitan charm.

North of Bayswater lies Westbourne Green, a high priority area for Westminster Council's regeneration plans. Its challenging position between Harrow Road and the Westway does the place few favours, but impressive new openings, such as the Westminster Academy secondary school and Stowe Community Centre, are bringing new hope to an area dominated by high-rise council homes.

Paddington

Strange as it may seem, only a few years ago the most noteworthy aspect of chaotic Paddington was its station, a lofty example of Victorian engineering, built to the specifications of Isambard Kingdom Brunel, the glazed roof giving shelter thousands of commuters and a small bronze statue of a certain bear.

Today all the excitement is beyond the station. The swankily rejuvenated Paddington Basin, once a neglected body of water forming the terminus of the Grand Junction Canal, is now desirable real estate. It has walkways, pedestrian-friendly towpaths and new bridges that allow strollers to circumnavigate the whole basin for the first time in its history. One of many wonders is the Rolling Bridge, built in eight triangular sections that can be curled up to allow water traffic to pass. (This happens every Friday at noon.) The whole area is surrounded by gorgeous, gleaming new-builds, one of which is the new Marks & Spencer headquarters.

Away from this 21st-century ideal of waterside living, inland Paddington, once deplored for its overcrowding and vice, is still plagued by traffic chaos and a preponderance of rather down-at-heel terraces. The northern edge of the district has the Westway roaring through it (as well as Paddington Green high-security police station, where terrorist suspects are questioned). North of the Westway, the Paddington Green conservation area is centred on St Mary's Church and the children's hospital. The surrounding streets have some 19th-century stucco houses and well-tended mansion flats that date from the mid 20th century.

Going south, Westbourne Terrace, towards Bayswater, was hailed as the finest street in London in its heyday. It still has some fantastically handsome houses that, in common with those on many of the roads running from Paddington to Hyde Park, command high prices.

Modern waterside living at once-derelict **Paddington Basin**.

Maida Vale

When Robert Browning coined the term
'Little Venice', he was describing the point
where the Paddington arm of the Grand
Union Canal meets the Regent's Canal.
South Maida Vale's most poetic citizen is
remembered forever at friendly Browning's
Pool, where pelargonium-adorned
narrowboats contain cafés, galleries and
(during winter) the Puppet Theatre Barge.
Continuing west on the canal path leads
the unwary to the rather less attractive
Westbourne Green and its tower blocks.
Instead stroll east along the towpath,
which will bring you to Regent's Park.

Around Little Venice and Clifton
Gardens, this is an affluent part of London.
The houses are tall, white stucco and the
shops are geared to the luxury market.
More affordable accommodation is available
north-west towards Paddington Recreation
Ground, at Maida Vale's northerly extreme.
Here Kilburn craic starts to impinge on
Maida Vale's sanity. Elgin Avenue bisects
the district west to east, and the pretty,
residential roads that lead off it are lined
by solid Victorian terraces with wrought-
iron balconies and by handsome blocks
of well-proportioned mansion flats. It's a
quiet, cosy part of the world, with few
shops and businesses. The handsome flats
of Westside Court and pretty Delaware
Road are much sought after.

St John's Wood

Smart, desirable and pricey, St John's
Wood is a northerly outpost of Westminster
that's just too quirky to be labelled a mere
suburb. Although its stucco villas, spacious
19th-century housing and well-maintained
purpose-built apartment buildings, the
latter dating from careful 1950s
redevelopment, all reek of provincial
prosperity, the Wood has global appeal.
The biggest attraction is Lord's Cricket
Ground, which keeps the through-traffic
coming all summer. The second biggest is
the Fab Four association: the famous Abbey
Road recording studios and that zebra
crossing. St John's Wood High Street has
a good number of independent stores, as
well as top-end chains. The area has always
been wealthy, and its proximity to gracious
Regent's Park keeps house prices high.
More affordable property can be found in
the apartment blocks along busy St John's
Wood Road, but these are more often
available as short-term rents.

West Kilburn

Travelling north, the City of Westminster's
furthest-flung district seems too ordinary to
be of the same borough; indeed, road signs
announce the imminent onset of Brent.
At West Kilburn's heart is the Queen's
Park Estate, built from 1874 as dwellings
for labourers. It is now extremely popular

with people who feel the need to be associated, by postcode, with trendy Ladbroke Grove and Notting Hill in the Royal Borough of Kensington & Chelsea. The houses on the estate are small, but the exteriors are ornate and they are beautifully put together. Some heartache ensues when children happen along and residents have to move to bigger, still more expensive houses around Kensal Rise. At least here, young families are near enough to the large, family-friendly Corporation of London park of the same name on the other side of the railway tracks. Elsewhere in West Kilburn, there are tall blocks of council flats, which save the district from excessive IKEA-interiored ponciness.

Restaurants & cafés

Westminster locals have some of the capital's finest dining on their doorstep. For starters check out what's below; for the whole menu, see the *Time Out London Eating & Drinking Guide* or, for the latest openings, check out *Time Out* magazine.

Soho's restaurants run the gamut from sleek and chic (dim sum specialist Yauatcha) to heartily fuss-free (sausage, pie and mash merchant Mother Mash), covering countless cuisines and specialities along the way. Stalwarts include L'Escargot Marco Pierre White (classic French), Andrew Edmunds (Modern European) and Richard Corrigan's Lindsay House (Irish). Newer ventures such as Arbutus (Modern European) and Bar Shu (Sichuan) have also made their mark on the neighbourhood. Laid-back breakfast, lunch and snack options are provided by the likes of Breakfast Club, Hummus Bros and tiny sandwich bar Fernandez & Wells.

Escalating overheads and redevelopment plans forced classic Italian caff the New Piccadilly to shut up shop in September 2007, but Soho retains its share of Italian style. Upmarket Vasco & Piero's Pavilion is great for earthy Umbrian dishes, while pizza and pasta joint Italian Graffiti deserves its many fans. Other communities are also represented: Caribbean (Jerk City), Korean (Myung Ga), American (Bodean's, the Diner), Hungarian (Gay Hussar) and Indian (Masala Zone for value, Red Fort for class). Japanese cafés populate Brewer Street (including sushi joint Kulu Kulu).

Many more oriental choices lie south of Shaftesbury Avenue. Chinatown cannot lay claim to producing London's best Chinese food, but locals have the likes of dim sum specialist Imperial China and newcomers Haozhan and Crispy Duck at their disposal.

Along Long Acre and into Covent Garden tourist traps abound, although there are plenty of quality places to eat if you know where to look: unpretentious British restaurant Great Queen Street, for starters. For a handy lunchtime pit-stop Portuguese/Brazilian café Canela is the ticket, while Rock & Sole Plaice and Food for Thought serve up fish and chips and veggie fare respectively. You'll find celeb hangouts J Sheekey (fish) and the Ivy (Modern European) on suitably discreet backstreets. Newcomers include the Carluccio's flagship on Garrick Street and modern Mexican restaurant Wahaca. Near the river and excellently located in Somerset House is the handsome Admiralty (French). For relaxed summer dining, head north towards Lincoln's Inn Fields, where the Terrace provides Modern European food with a Caribbean twist. The National Dining Rooms (Best British Restaurant in *Time Out*'s 2007 Eating & Drinking Awards) is the place to head near Trafalgar Square.

Upmarket Mayfair hosts some of Britain's most celebrated chefs: Gordon Ramsay at Claridge's, Michel Roux at Le Gavroche. Other excellent examples of haute cuisine here include the inventive Greenhouse restaurant and Gordon Ramsay-owned Maze. Mayfair is also where to find recently refurbished Scott's (fish), Wild Honey (Best New Restaurant in the 2007 Awards) and classy Japanese (Nobu), Indian (Tamarind) and Chinese (China Tang) restaurants. Towards Piccadilly the swanky must-visits include Bentley's Oyster Bar & Grill and glam grand-café the Wolseley.

Marylebone is less showy, but there's plenty of excellent (and far more affordable) eating to be had. Cafés are a forte, with brilliant cheese at La Fromagerie (*see p37*), Quiet Revolution's organic stop-off and, in Regent's Park, the retro-chic Garden Café. A branch of Thai canteen Busaba Eathai and vegetarian diner Eat & Two Veg also provide quick bites. Top Italian Locanda Locatelli is on Seymour Street; other highlights include smashing fish and chips at the Golden Hind, two decent

kosher restaurants (Reuben's, Six-13)
and Oliver Peyton's gallery restaurant
the Wallace. Towards Marble Arch, in
the Cumberland Hotel, is Gary Rhodes's
fine-dining restaurant Rhodes W1.

Fitzrovia's dining district is centred on
Charlotte Street, on the border between
Westminster and Camden. Away from
Charlotte Street but firmly in the City of
Westminster, fish-lovers should try Back
to Basics; nearby is Özer (classy Turkish).
Heading towards Marylebone, you'll find
restaurant-bar-deli Villandry.

Westminster contains a few choice
venues. Cinnamon Club is one of London's
best posh Indian restaurants; Bank
Westminster (flying solo following the
closure of its Aldwych sibling) is good
for crowd-pleasing Modern European fare.
St James's, meanwhile, has a rarefied vibe,
as exemplified by the very grand Wiltons;
Green's is in a similar upmarket vein. Inn
The Park is a sleek breakfast-to-dinner
British restaurant in St James's Park.

Primarily a residential area, Pimlico
nonetheless has a smattering of restaurants,
including Seafresh (fish and chips), Rex
Whistler Restaurant at Tate Britain
(Mod Euro) and buzzy Goya (Spanish).
In Belgravia, restaurants have a quietly
sophisticated appeal. Fabulous Sardinian-
influenced fish restaurant Olivomare is a
choice destination, as is first-rate Chinese
venue Hunan. Close by is classic French
eaterie Roussillon, while further up towards
Eccleston Street are Olivo (sister to
Olivomare) and gastropub the Ebury.

Gastropubs are also big in Bayswater,
with celeb-favourite the Cow (on the edge
of Notting Hill) officially in the City of
Westminster. Queensway, meanwhile, holds
some superb Chinese restaurants, including
the flagship venue of dim sum specialist
Royal China. There are trendy Italians
too, such as Sardinian-accented Assaggi.

The development of Paddington Basin
has given the area's dining a much-needed
boost in the form of beautiful Chinese
restaurant Pearl Liang. Malaysian venue
Satay House is another excellent eaterie. For
further choices, head for the Edgware Road,
where Middle Eastern is the gastronomic
forte: try Lebanese restaurant Sidi Maarouf
or late-night kebabery Ranoush Juice Bar.
Also here is Mandalay, London's only
Burmese restaurant.

Great grub at **Great Queen Street**.

Maida Vale's restaurants cater to affluent
locals. Try Raoul's (daytime brunch, night-
time Mediterranean) or Red Pepper (pizzae
and pasta). There's also a branch of bakery
Baker & Spice. Eateries along St John's
Wood High Street feed well-heeled shoppers,
who ogle pastries at Maison Blanc or tuck
into Jewish dishes at Harry Morgan's.

Admiralty *Somerset House, Strand, WC2R
1LA (7845 4646/www.somerset-house.org.uk).*
Andrew Edmunds *46 Lexington Street,
W1F 0LW (7437 5708).*
Arbutus *63-64 Frith Street, W1D 3JW
(7734 4545/www.arbutusrestaurant.co.uk).*
Assaggi *1st floor, 39 Chepstow Place, W2 4TS
(7792 5501).*
Back to Basics *21A Foley Street, W1W 6DS
(7436 2181/www.backtobasics.uk.com).*
Baker & Spice *20 Clifton Gardens, W9 1SU
(7266 1122).*
Bank Westminster *45 Buckingham
Gate, SW1E 6BS (7379 9797/www.bank
restaurants.com).*
Bar Shu *28 Frith Street, W1D 5LF
(7287 6688).*
Bentley's Oyster Bar & Grill *11-15 Swallow
Street, W1B 4DG (7734 4756/www.bentleys
oysterbarandgrill.co.uk).*
Bodean's *10 Poland Street, W1F 8PZ
(7287 7575/www.bodeansbbq.com).*
Breakfast Club *33 D'Arblay Street, W1F 8EU
(7434 2571).*
Busaba Eathai *8-13 Bird Street, W1U 1BU
(7518 8080).*
Canela *33 Earlham Street, WC2H 9LS
(7240 6926/www.canelacafe.com).*
Carluccio's Caffè *26 Garrick Street, WC2E
8JE (7836 0990/www.carluccios.com).*

China Tang *The Dorchester, 53 Park Lane, W1K 1QA (7629 9988/www.thedorchester.com).*
Cinnamon Club *The Old Westminster Library, 30-32 Great Smith Street, SW1P 3BU (7222 2555/www.cinnamonclub.com).*
The Cow *89 Westbourne Park Road, W2 5QH (7221 0021).*
Crispy Duck *27 Wardour Street, W1D 6PR (7287 6578).*
The Diner *18-20 Ganton Street, W1F 7BU (7287 8962/www.thedinersoho.com).*
Eat & Two Veg *50 Marylebone High Street, W1U 5HN (7258 8595/www.eatandtwoveg.com).*
Ebury *11 Pimlico Road, SW1W 8NA (7730 6784/www.theebury.co.uk).*
L'Escargot Marco Pierre White *48 Greek Street, W1D 4EF (7437 2679/www.whitestar line.org.uk).*
Fernandez & Wells *73 Beak Street, W1F 9RS (7287 8124).*
Food for Thought *31 Neal Street, WC2H 9PR (7836 9072).*
Garden Café *Inner Circle, Regent's Park, NW1 4NU (7935 5729/www.thegardencafe.co.uk).*
Le Gavroche *43 Upper Brook Street, W1K 7QR (7408 0881/www.le-gavroche.co.uk).*
Gay Hussar *2 Greek Street, W1D 4NB (7437 0973/www.gayhussar.co.uk).*
Golden Hind *73 Marylebone Lane, W1U 2PN (7486 3644).*
Gordon Ramsay at Claridge's *Claridge's Hotel, Brook Street, W1A 2JQ (7499 0099/www.gordonramsay.com).*
Goya *34 Lupus Street, SW1V 3EB (7976 5309/www.goyarestaurant.co.uk).*
Great Queen Street *32 Great Queen Street, WC2B 5AA (742 0622).*
Greenhouse *27A Hay's Mews, W1J 5NX (7499 3331/www.greenhouserestaurant.co.uk).*
Green's *36 Duke Street, SW1Y 6DF (7930 4566/www.greens.org.uk).*
Harry Morgan's *31 St John's Wood High Street, NW8 7NH (7722 1869/www.harryms.co.uk).*
Haozhan *8 Gerrard Street, W1D 5PJ (7434 3838).*
Hummus Bros *88 Wardour Street, W1F 0TJ (7734 1311/www.hbros.co.uk).*
Hunan *51 Pimlico Road, SW1W 8NE (7730 5712).*
Imperial China *White Bear Yard, 25A Lisle Street, WC2H 7BA (7734 3388/www.imperial-china.co.uk).*
Inn The Park *St James's Park, SW1A 2BJ (7451 9999/www.innthepark.co.uk).*
Italian Graffiti *163-165 Wardour Street, W1F 8WN (7439 4668/www.italiangraffiti.co.uk).*
The Ivy *1 West Street, WC2H 9NQ (7836 4751/www.the-ivy.co.uk).*
Jerk City *189 Wardour Street, W1F 8ZD (7287 2878/www.jerkcity.co.uk).*
J Sheekey *28-32 St Martin's Court, WC2N 4AL (7240 2565/www.j-sheekey.co.uk).*
Kulu Kulu *76 Brewer Street, W1F 9TX (7734 7316).*

Lindsay House *21 Romilly Street, W1D 5AF (7439 0450/www.lindsayhouse.co.uk).*
Locanda Locatelli *8 Seymour Street, W1H 7JZ (7935 9088/www.locandalocatelli.com).*
Maison Blanc *37 St John's Wood High Street, NW8 7NG (7586 1982/www.maison blanc.co.uk).*
Mandalay *444 Edgware Road, W2 1EG (7258 3696/www.mandalayway.com).*
Masala Zone *9 Marshall Street, W1F 7ER (7287 9966/www.realindianfood.com).*
Maze *10-13 Grosvenor Square, W1K 6JP (7107 0000/www.gordonramsay.com).*
Mother Mash *26 Ganton Street, W1F 7QZ (7494 9644/www.mothermash.co.uk).*
Myung Ga *1 Kingly Street, W1B 5PA (7734 8220/www.myungga.co.uk).*
National Dining Rooms *Sainsbury Wing, National Gallery, Trafalgar Square, WC2N 5DN (7747 2525/www.nationalgallery.co.uk).*
Nobu *Metropolitan Hotel, 19 Old Park Lane, W1K 1LB (7447 4747/www.noburestaurants.com).*
Olivo *21 Eccleston Street, SW1W 9LX (7730 2505).*
Olivomare *10 Lower Belgrave Street, SW1W 0LJ (7730 9022).*
Özer *5 Langham Place, W1B 3DG (7323 0505/www.sofra.co.uk).*
Pearl Liang *8 Sheldon Square, W2 6EZ (7289 7000/www.pearlliang.co.uk).*
Quiet Revolution *1st floor, Inn 1888, 21A Devonshire Street, W1G 6PG (7486 7420).*
Ranoush Juice Bar *43 Edgware Road, W2 2JR (7723 5929).*
Raoul's *13 Clifton Road, W9 1SZ (7289 7313).*
Red Fort *77 Dean Street, W1D 3SH (7437 2115/www.redfort.co.uk).*
Red Pepper *8 Formosa Street, W9 1EE (7266 2708).*
Reuben's *79 Baker Street, W1U 6RG (7486 0035).*
Rex Whistler Restaurant at Tate Britain *Tate Britain, Millbank, SW1P 4RG (7887 8825/www.tate.org.uk).*
Rhodes W1 *The Cumberland, Great Cumberland Place, W1A 4RF (7479 3737/www.garyrhodes.co.uk).*
Rock & Sole Plaice *47 Endell Street, WC2H 9AJ (7836 3785).*
Roussillon *16 St Barnabas Street, SW1W 8PE (7730 5550/www.roussillon.co.uk).*
Royal China *13 Queensway, W2 4QJ (7221 2535/www.royalchinagroup.co.uk).*
Satay House *13 Sale Place, W2 1PX (7723 6763/www.satay-house.co.uk).*
Scott's *20 Mount Street, W1K 2HE (7495 7309/www.caprice-holdings.co.uk).*
Seafresh Fish Restaurant *80-81 Wilton Road, SW1V 1DL (7828 0747).*
Sidi Maarouf *56-58 Edgware Road, W2 2JE (7724 0525).*
Six-13 *19 Wigmore Street, W1U 1PH (7629 6133/www.six13.com).*
Tamarind *20 Queen Street, W1J 5PR (7629 3561/www.tamarindrestaurant.com).*

The Terrace *Lincoln's Inn Fields, WC2A 3LJ (7430 1234/www.theterrace.info).*
Vasco & Piero's Pavilion *15 Poland Street, W1F 8QE (7437 8774/www.vascosfood.com).*
Villandry *170 Great Portland Street, W1W 5QB (7631 3131/www.villandry.com).*
Wahaca *66 Chandos Place, WC2N 4HG (7240 1883/www.wahaca.co.uk).*
Wallace *Wallace Collection, Hertford House, Manchester Square, W1U 3BN (7563 9505/ www.thewallacerestaurant.com).*
Wild Honey *12 St George Street, W1S 2FB (7758 9160/www.wildhoneyrestaurant.co.uk).*
Wiltons *55 Jermyn Street, SW1Y 6LX (7629 9955/www.wiltons.co.uk).*
Wolseley *160 Piccadilly, W1J 9EB (7499 6996/www.thewolseley.com).*
Yauatcha *15 Broadwick Street, W1F 0DL (7494 8888).*

Bars & pubs

Westminster attracts a massive influx of revellers – provincials, tourists and local workers; club kids, bar-crawlers and gay-scene posers – and for residents the dream of a cosy local where everyone knows your name can seem destined to remain just that. It doesn't take too much surface-scratching to sort the wheat from the chaff, though. Below are a few essentials, for more consult the *Time Out London Bars, Pubs & Clubs Guide*.

Out-of-towners flock to the big-name locations – Covent Garden, Leicester Square, Soho – with predictable crowd-inducing, nitrokeg-downing results. Venture just a few streets from the Piazza, however, and there are plenty of drinking holes worth sinking into for the evening. Traditional old boozers like the Lamb & Flag (packed to its bare beams after 5pm) and the ultra-cosy Cross Keys are good places to start. Benelux bar Lowlander has a relaxed vibe and great beers, while just off the Strand are two newer subterranean venues – Bedford & Strand (sophisticated wine bar) and CellarDoor (tiny, mirrored bar in a converted public toilet). Also near the Strand are friendly pub the Nell Gwynne and subterranean wine bar Gordon's. Near Leicester Square, basement wine bar the Cork & Bottle is a good escape from the hordes, as is Gallic venue Le Beaujolais.

Soho draws hedonists from across London, the UK and beyond – and it's diverse enough to accommodate the lot. The gay scene is focused on the west end of Old Compton Street, around the Admiral Duncan, Comptons of Soho and, north up Wardour Street, Village Soho; lesbians have the Candy Bar. Barflies should try the likes of Milk & Honey (non-members need to book ahead), 22 Below and Two Floors; pub fans will enjoy historic old boozers the French House, the Old Coffee House and the lovely little Dog & Duck. For something a bit different, try basement bar the Black Gardenia or show off your talents in one of the private karaoke rooms at Lucky Voice.

Holborn has several drinking dens to be proud of, including the gorgeous Seven Stars and gastropub the Bountiful Cow (both owned by local name Roxy Beaujolais). Former journalists' pub the Edgar Wallace has great real ales, or there's the low-key Polish vodka den Bar Polski. For something slicker, try the dramatic Lobby Bar in One Aldwych hotel.

In Mayfair, swanky hotel bars rule: try Claridge's Bar, the Donovan Bar, the David Collins-designed Connaught Bar (due to open in May 2008) or Galvin at Windows. Alternatively, join young royals and trustafarians at pricey Hawaiian club Mahiki. Champagne-cocktailed out? Hide out in a snug corner at the Red Lion on Waverton Street.

Marylebone residents have plenty to choose from; notable choices include the patriotic Windsor Castle on Crawford Place (one of two such named pubs in the vicinity) or the traditional Golden Eagle (complete with round-the-piano pub singalongs). For a touch of swank, try the Langham Hotel's Artesian. Happy-hour bargains abound at ski-lodge-style Moose.

Some of Fitzrovia's best bars are officially in Camden, but among those in the City of Westminster are the Sanderson's Long Bar and DJ bar the Social. Alternatively, sink a pint at the cosy Newman Arms or bargain Sam Smith's boozers the Cock Tavern and Champion.

In Westminster, politicians cram into Parliament Street's Red Lion, complete with a (currently broken) division bell, while the bar at the Cinnamon Club (*see p31*) offers a sophisticated place to unwind. Bank Westminster's Zander Bar is also worth a look. St James's has the old-school pub vibe sewn up with three Lions to its name – two Red (on Crown Passage and Duke of York Street) and one Golden. On the Mall, the ICA Bar serves up a slice of contemporary culture with its drinks.

Pimlico pubs are quiet affairs, frequented by affluent locals and office workers: typical is the Morpeth Arms. Chimes bar-restaurant has a laudable choice of ciders, while Millbank Lounge offers a surprising oasis of calm in hotel-bar form. In Belgravia, the Lanesborough's Library Bar is a classy place to sip a cocktail before you head off to a first-rate boozer like charming time-warp pub the Nag's Head.

The fast regenerating Bayswater and Paddington area offers tiny Fuller's pub the Victoria and the cosy Mitre. Over in Little Venice, don't miss the fabulous Bridge House. Across the water, the beautiful Prince Alfred has great food and drink, while, near Warwick Avenue tube, the Warrington was due to reopen as Gordon Ramsay's third gastropub as we went to press. St John's Wood also houses a few prime drinking establishments. Among them, bucolic hangout the Clifton is down-to-earth and welcoming. Westminster's West Kilburn enclave is best served by Little Venice venues, or the drinking dens of Kensal Green and Queen's Park.

Gay hangout **Comptons of Soho**.

Admiral Duncan *54 Old Compton Street, W1D 5PA (7437 5300).*
Artesian *Langham Hotel, 1C Portland Place, W1B 1JA (7636 1000/www.artesian-bar.co.uk).*
Bar Polski *11 Little Turnstile, WC1V 7DX (7831 9679).*
Bedford & Strand *1A Bedford Street, WC2E 9HH (7836 3033/www.bedford-strand.com).*
Le Beaujolais *25 Litchfield Street, WC2H 9NJ (7240 3776).*
Black Gardenia *93 Dean Street, W1D 3SZ (7494 4955/www.myspace.com/black gardenia93).*
Bountiful Cow *51 Eagle Street, WC1R 4AP (7404 0200).*
Bridge House *13 Westbourne Terrace Road, W2 6NG (7432 1361).*
Candy Bar *4 Carlisle Street, W1D 3BJ (7494 4041/www.candybarsoho.com).*
CellarDoor *Zero Aldwych, WC2E 7DN (7240 8848).*
Champion *12-13 Wells Street, W1T 3PA (7323 1228).*
Chimes *26 Churton Street, SW1V 2LP (7821 7456/www.chimes-of-pimlico.co.uk).*
Claridge's Bar *Claridge's, 49 Brook Street, W1A 4HR (7629 8860/www.claridges.co.uk).*
Clifton *96 Clifton Hill, NW8 0JT (7372 3427/www.capitalpubcompany2.com).*
Cock Tavern *27 Great Portland Street, W1W 8QE (7631 5002).*
Comptons of Soho *51-53 Old Compton Street, W1D 6HJ (7479 7961/www.comptons-of-soho.co.uk).*
Connaught Bar *Connaught, Carlos Place, W1K 2AL (7499 7070/www.theconnaught hotellondon.com).*
Cork & Bottle *44-46 Cranbourn Street, WC2H 7AN (7734 7807).*
Cross Keys *31 Endell Street, WC2H 9EB (7836 5185).*
Dog & Duck *18 Bateman Street, W1D 3AJ (7494 0697).*
Donovan Bar *Brown's Hotel, 33-34 Albemarle Street, W1S 4BP (7493 6020/www.roccoforte hotels.com).*
Edgar Wallace *40 Essex Street, WC2R 3JF (7353 3120/www.edgarwallacepub.com).*
French House *49 Dean Street, W1D 5BG (7437 2799/www.frenchhousesoho.com).*
Galvin at Windows *28th floor, London Hilton, 22 Park Lane, W1K 1BE (7208 4021/www.galvinatwindows.com).*
Golden Eagle *59 Marylebone Lane, W1U 2NY (7935 3228).*
Golden Lion *25 King Street, SW1Y 6QY (7925 0007).*
Gordon's *47 Villiers Street, WC2N 6NE (7930 1408/www.gordonswinebar.com).*
ICA Bar *The Mall, SW1Y 5AH (7930 3647/www.ica.org.uk).*
Lamb & Flag *33 Rose Street, WC2E 9EB (7497 9504).*
Library Bar *Lanesborough, 1 Lanesborough Place, Hyde Park Corner, SW1X 7TA (7259 5599/www.lanesborough.com).*

Lobby Bar *One Aldwych, Aldwych, WC2B 4RH (7300 1070/www.onealdwych.com).*
Long Bar *Sanderson, 50 Berners Street, W1T 3NG (7300 1400/www.sandersonlondon.com).*
Lowlander *36 Drury Lane, WC2B 5RR (7379 7446/www.lowlander.com).*
Lucky Voice *52 Poland Street, W1F 7NH (7439 3660/www.luckyvoice.co.uk).*
Mahiki *1 Dover Street, W1S 4LD (7493 9529/www.mahiki.com).*
Millbank Lounge *City Inn Hotel, 30 John Islip Street, SW1P 4DD (7932 4700/www.cityinn.com).*
Milk & Honey *61 Poland Street, W1F 7NU (7292 9949/www.mlkhny.com).*
Mitre *24 Craven Terrace, W2 3QH (7262 5240).*
Morpeth Arms *58 Millbank, SW1P 4RW (7834 6442).*
Moose *31 Duke Street, W1U 1LG (7224 3452/www.vpmg.net).*
Nag's Head *53 Kinnerton Street, SW1X 8ED (7235 1135).*
Nell Gwynne *1-2 Bull Inn Court, WC2R 0NP (7240 5579).*
Newman Arms *23 Rathbone Street, W1T 1NG (7636 1127/www.newmanarms.co.uk).*
Old Coffee House *49 Beak Street, W1F 9SF (7437 2197).*
Prince Alfred & Formosa Dining Rooms *5A Formosa Street, W9 1EE (7286 3287).*
Red Lion *23 Crown Passage, off Pall Mall, SW1Y 6PP (7930 4141).*
Red Lion *2 Duke of York Street, SW1Y 6JP (7321 0782).*
Red Lion *48 Parliament Street, SW1A 2NH (7930 5826).*
Red Lion *1 Waverton Street, W1J 5QN (7499 1307).*
Seven Stars *53 Carey Street, WC2A 2JB (7242 8521).*
Social *5 Little Portland Street, W1W 7JD (7636 4992/www.thesocial.com).*
22 Below *22 Great Marlborough Street, W1F 7HU (7437 4106/www.22below.co.uk).*
Two Floors *3 Kingly Street, W1B 5PD (7439 1007/www.barworks.co.uk).*
Victoria *10A Strathern Place, W2 2NH (7724 1191).*
Village Soho *81 Wardour Street, W1D 6QD (7434 2124/www.village-soho.co.uk).*
Warrington *93 Warrington Crescent, W9 1EH (7286 2929/www.gordonramsay.com).*
Windsor Castle *29 Crawford Place, W1H 4LJ (7723 4371).*
Zander Bar *Bank Westminster, 45 Buckingham Gate, SW1E 6BS (7379 9797/www.bankrestaurants.com).*

Shops

Westminster wins out as London's all-embracing shopping centre. Below are the highlights; consult the *Time Out London Shops & Services Guide* for more ideas.

Jostling, maddening Oxford Street is the unlovely but convenient retail backbone of the city. The Centre Point end is dominated by cheap clothes shops and tacky gift emporia, but move west towards Oxford Circus and the choice improves. The massive Topshop flagship squats on the north-eastern corner of the Circus, sharing premises with its smaller sister Miss Selfridge. The line-up of global and national fashion chains continues towards Marble Arch. Pedestrianised St Christopher's Place, with its upmarket chains and designer shops, is a welcome respite from the crush. It emerges at Wigmore Street, brimming with swanky kitchen, bathroom and furniture showrooms; don't miss exquisite modern interiors shop Mint.

While most of the city's department stores congregate on Oxford Street, petite Fenwick, known for its accessories and lingerie, perches demurely on nearby Bond Street, and Fortnum & Mason, whose 300th birthday nip-and-tuck in 2007 included the expansion of its famous food hall, is on Piccadilly. John Lewis is king for homeware, haberdashery and other basics, but Selfridges wins hands-down for its exciting displays and all-encompassing selection of clothes, food and gadgets. Down on Regent Street, Liberty may have physically downsized, losing its annex, but its stock has gone from strength to strength, especially in menswear.

Formerly dowdy Regent Street has been revitalised by the arrival of the Apple Store and an influx of new mid-range fashion chains, such as H&M's offshoot COS, great for luxurious basics. Carnaby Street has also undergone a gradual transformation. A few years back, the iconic strip had descended into tacky studded collar/novelty hat territory. Now it's a decent destination for branded streetwear. Don't miss Kingly Court – the small shopping centre houses numerous one-off boutiques and is notable for vintage fashion. There are more small shops on cobbled Newburgh Street, running parallel to Carnaby Street to the east.

In Soho, Berwick Street Market's traders hawk fruit and veg alongside cut-price fabric, household goods and the less wholesome wares of the bordering red-light district. The area is still known for indie record stores, although there have been recent closures. A smattering of fashion in Soho includes Shop at Maison Bertaux, a cache of cutting-edge clothing beneath the iconic cake shop, and designer boutique Souvenir. The original Broadwick Street outpost of luxury lingerie chain Agent Provocateur is at home in its slightly louche locale. On the home front, lifestyle shop Do has a 'Muji with attitude' vibe.

Continuing east towards Covent Garden, Neal Street and the streets radiating off Seven Dials heave with streetwear and limited-edition trainers. Monmouth Street is great for a browse, with Kiehl's skincare, Koh Samui for designer womenswear, print queen Orla Kiely's flagship and London's chicest erotic emporium, Coco de Mer.

LOCALS' TIPS

The most peaceful picnicking place in the West End, Phoenix Garden, is a lovely alternative to the rather more frantic garden of St Paul's Church, which is too near the Piazza to escape the crowds of lunchers that gather there as soon as the sun comes out.
Visit Soho before midday at weekends to experience village life West End style. The streets temporarily return to the locals, who rush around to get their shopping and socialising done before it gets busy.
Hit Berwick Street Market at around 4.30pm to pick up the best fruit and veg bargains.
Westminster is depressingly urban, right? Wrong. You can walk for an hour from Trafalgar Square to Notting Hill with greenery all the way: St James's Park, Green Park, Hyde Park.
For a coffee break or snack lunch in Covent Garden, avoid the high-street chains. Instead try the excellent Bullet, hidden on the third floor of Snow + Rock (4 Mercer Street, WC2H 9QA, 7836 4922, www.bullet-coffee.com).
For respite from thronging crowds or inclement weather, the Westminster Reference Library has a fine reading room with the day's papers and tons of magazines.
Expensive Westminster actually boasts some of the city's best bargains: get cheap cinema tickets at the Prince Charles and (from 10am daily) first-comer £10 tickets for the English National Opera.

Nearby, Neal's Yard Dairy is pungent [with] farmhouse cheeses, while the yard itself has organic pioneers Neal's Yard Reme[dies]. Locals tend to avoid Covent Garden Mark[et] itself, as it offers little beyond mainstream names and tourist trinkets, although parents like Benjamin Pollock's Toyshop for its wonderful model theatres.

While for most people Charing Cross Road is inextricably linked with books, due to the famous Foyles and several dusty second-hand stores, not everyone is aware of Cecil Court (www.cecilcourt.co.uk). A pedestrian alley connecting Charing Cross Road and St Martin's Lane, it is lined with specialist book and print dealers.

Mayfair is the traditional home of tailors (Savile Row) and shirtmakers (Jermyn Street), and there are posh jewellers and designer names galore on Bond Street and environs. Our pick of the flagships include Stella McCartney's elegant townhouse, cult favourite for drainpipes and minidresses PPQ, and Luella's first stand-alone store, Rupert Sanderson's elegant footwear is also worth seeking out. Browns, five interconnecting shops on South Molton Street, has showcased its mix of big-league labels and rising stars for nearly 40 years (see also its sale shop, Labels for Less). For avant-garde fashion just up the road from Savile Row's august tailors, try b store.

The old arcades aren't just for the tourists. Burlington Arcade, off Piccadilly, has been restored to its Regency glory and is attracting hip new residents such as classy indie shoe designer Beatrix Ong. The smaller Piccadilly Arcade houses Jeffery-West, the footwear of choice for modern dandies, while the Royal Arcade, off Old Bond Street, boasts perfumer Ormonde Jayne. Nearby is Rei Kawakubo's 21st-century take on London's old covered markets, Dover Street Market, where all 14 Comme collections join über-designer concessions. Venerable specialists survive in St James's Street, including Swaine Adeney Brigg, purveyor of upper-crust accessories, and lovely traditional toiletries at old-fashioned chemist DR Harris.

To the west, a few notable shops have colonised Shepherd Market, including innovative shoe designer Georgina Goodman. South-west in Belgravia, charming Elizabeth Street offers delicious breads (Poilâne), rare perfumes (Les

...ts (Philip Treacy)
...que (Mungo & Maud).
..., is the London offshoot
...mford's Cotswold farm
...d Organic.
...d wasteland, Victoria now has
...ce shopping centre. Its shops,
...d with lunch options, seem
...wards well-groomed local office
... Zara, L'Occitane, Hawes & Curtis
...akers. Bayswater boasts Edwardian
...ping centre Whiteleys, which retains
...utiful original features, but its 50-odd
...ail spaces are mainly used by chains
...here's also an Odeon and a branch of
bowling bar All Star Lanes). A few isolated
gems – Crimson for well-priced women's
clothes, for example – are tucked behind
Edgware Road's Middle Eastern food stores.
North-west of Bayswater, near the border
with Kensington & Chelsea, boutiques
proliferate around Westbourne Grove.

To the north, Marylebone High Street has
become an established shopping enclave
and weekend hangout for well-heeled
denizens and non-residents alike. Foodies
are well catered for by rustic deli-cum-
cheese specialist La Fromagerie, rare-breed
butcher Ginger Pig and quality choc shop
Rococo, plus a Sunday morning farmers'
market in the car park behind Waitrose.
There's a lovely old bookshop (Daunt) and,
among the middle-to-upmarket clothing
chains, an interesting designer boutique,
Sixty 6. The contemporary jewellery at
Cox & Power and Kabiri dazzles, Fresh
and Aveda satisfy beauty needs, and the
Conran Shop and Skandium provide chic
furnishings. On Saturdays, Cabbages &
Frocks (a small general market) sets up in
the cobbled yard of St Marylebone Parish
Church. Don't bypass Marylebone Lane,
where interesting shops include retro-
influenced Saltwater womenswear, Tracey
Neuls's iconoclastic footwear, laid-back
boutique KJ's Laundry and century-old
deli Paul Rothe & Son.

North of Marylebone Road, at the eastern
end of Church Street, Alfie's Antique
Market has stalls selling 20th-century
Italian furniture and glam vintage fashion.
The number of surrounding antiques shops
has grown, making this one of London's
best hunting grounds. There's also a large
general street market that's at its best
on Saturday. Around the corner is the
delightful Weardowney Get-Up Boutique,
HQ of the high-fashion knitwear label.

In St John's Wood, the High Street has
a pleasant, villagey atmosphere and high-
class food stores, including quality butcher
Kent & Sons and branches of Carluccio's
and Maison Blanc. As well as the usual
upmarket fashion chains, there is an outpost
of Primrose Hill boutique Press. Maida
Vale's shops mainly cater to (affluent)
domestic needs. Some of the best are Raoul's
Deli, Sheepdrove Organic Farm Family
Butcher and superior wine merchants the
Winery, plus venerable Clifton Nurseries,
which has a Daylesford Organic café.

STATISTICS

BOROUGH MAKE-UP
Population 231,900 (during the day,
it exceeds 1,000,000)
Average weekly pay £735.20
Ethnic origins
White 71.17%
Mixed 4.33%
Asian or Asian British 10.54%
Black or Black British 6.65%
Chinese or other 7.31%
Students 11.88%
Retirees 7.88%

HOUSING STOCK
Borough size 22km²
No. of households 113,759
Detached 1%
Semi-detached 1.9%
Terraced 8%
Flats (purpose-built) 59.2%
Flats (converted) 27.9%
Flats (both) 87.1%

CRIME PER 1,000 OF POPULATION
(average for England and Wales in
brackets)
Burglary 6 (5)
Robbery 7 (2)
Theft of vehicle 3 (4)
Theft from vehicle 15 (9)
Violence against the person 34 (19)
Sexual offences 2 (1)

MPs & COUNCIL
MPs *Cities of London & Westminster*
Mark Field (Conservative); *Holborn &
St Pancras* Frank Dobson (Labour);
Regent's Park & Kensington North
Karen Buck (Labour)
CPA 4 stars, improving strongly

Agent Provocateur 6 Broadwick Street, W1V 1FH (7439 0229/www.agentprovocateur.com).

Alfie's Antique Market 13-25 Church Street, NW8 8DT (7723 6066/www.alfies antiques.com).

Apple Store 235 Regent Street, W1B 2EL (7153 9000/www.apple.com).

Aveda 28-29 Marylebone High Street, W1U 4PL (7224 3157/www.aveda.com).

Beatrix Ong 4 Burlington Arcade, Piccadilly, W1J 0PD (7499 4089/0480/ www.beatrixong.com).

Benjamin Pollock's Toyshop 44 The Market, WC2E 8RF (7379 7866/www.pollocks-coventgarden.co.uk).

Browns 23-27 South Molton Street, W1K 5RD (7514 0000/www.brownsfashion.com).

Browns Labels for Less 50 South Molton Street, W1K 5RD (7514 0052/www.browns fashion.com).

b store 24A Savile Row, W1S 3PR (7734 6846/www.bstorelondon.com).

Cabbages & Frocks Market St Marylebone Parish Church Grounds, Marylebone High Street, W1 (7794 1636/www.cabbagesand frocks.co.uk).

Cardinal Place Victoria Street, SW1 (www.cardinalplace.co.uk).

Clifton Nurseries 5A Clifton Villas, W9 2PH (7289 6851/www.clifton.co.uk).

Coco de Mer 23 Monmouth Street, WC2H 9DD (7836 8882/www.coco-de-mer.co.uk).

Conran Shop 55 Marylebone High Street, W1U 5HS (7723 2223/www.conran.com).

COS 222 Regent Street, W1B 5BD (7478 0400/ www.costores.com).

Cox & Power 35C Marylebone High Street, W1U 4QA (7935 3530/www.coxandpower.com).

Crimson 7 Porchester Place, W2 2BS (7706 4146/www.crimsonclothes.com).

Daunt Books 83-84 Marylebone High Street, W1U 4QW (7224 2295/www.daunt books.co.uk).

Daylesford Organic 44B Pimlico Road, SW1W 8LP (7881 8060/www.daylesford organic.com).

Do 47 Beak Street, W1F 9SE (7494 9090/ www.do-shop.com).

Dover Street Market 17-18 Dover Street, W1S 4LT (7518 0680/www.doverstreet market.com).

DR Harris 29 St James's Street, SW1A 1HB (7930 3915/www.drharris.co.uk).

Fenwick 63 New Bond Street, W1A 3BS (7629 9161/www.fenwick.co.uk).

Fortnum & Mason 181 Piccadilly, W1A 1ER (7734 8040/www.fortnumandmason.co.uk).

Foyles 113-119 Charing Cross Road, WC2H 0EB (7437 5660/www.foyles.co.uk).

Fresh 92 Marylebone High Street, W1U 4RD (7486 4100/www.fresh.com).

La Fromagerie 2-4 Moxon Street, W1U 4EW (7935 0341/www.lafromagerie.co.uk).

Georgina Goodman 12-14 Shepherd Street, W1J 7JF (7499 8599/www.georgina goodman.com).

Ginger Pig 8-10 Moxon Street, W1U 4EW (7935 7788/www.thegingerpig.co.uk).

Jeffery-West 16 Piccadilly Arcade, SW1Y 6NH (7499 3360/www.jeffery-west.co.uk).

John Lewis 300 Oxford Street, W1A 1EX (7629 7711/www.johnlewis.co.uk).

Kabiri 37 Marylebone High Street, W1U 4QE (7224 1808/www.kabiri.co.uk).

Kent & Sons 59 St John's Wood High Street, NW8 7NL (7722 2258).

Kiehl's 29 Monmouth Street, WC2H 9DD (7240 2411/www.kiehls.com).

Kingly Court Carnaby Street, opposite Broadwick Street, W1B 5PW (7333 8118/ www.carnaby.co.uk).

KJ's Laundry 74 Marylebone Lane, W1U 2PW (7486 7855/www.kjslaundry.com).

Koh Samui 65-67 Monmouth Street, WC2H 9DG (7240 4280/www.kohsamui.co.uk).

Liberty Regent Street, W1B 5AH (7734 1234/ www.liberty.co.uk).

Luella 25 Brook Street, W1K 4HB (7518 1830/ www.luella.com).

Marylebone Farmers' Market Cramer Street car park, behind Marylebone High Street, W1U 4EA (7833 0338/www.lfm.org.uk).

Mint 70 Wigmore Street, W1U 2SF (7224 4406/www.mintshop.co.uk).

Mungo & Maud 79 Elizabeth Street, SW1W 9PJ (7952 4570/www.mungoandmaud.com).

Neal's Yard Dairy 17 Shorts Gardens, WC2H 9UP (7240 5700/www.nealsyard dairy.co.uk).

Neal's Yard Remedies 15 Neal's Yard, WC2H 9DP (7379 7222/ www.nealsyardremedies.com).

Orla Kiely 31-33 Monmouth Street, WC2H 9DD (7240 4022/www.orlakiely.com).

Ormonde Jayne 12 The Royal Arcade, 28 Old Bond Street, W1S 4SL (7499 1100/ www.ormondejayne.co.uk).

Paul Rothe & Son 35 Marylebone Lane, W1U 2NN (7935 6783).

Philip Treacy 69 Elizabeth Street, SW1W 9PJ (7730 3992/www.philiptreacy.co.uk).

PPQ 47 Conduit Street, W1S 2YP (7494 9789/ www.ppqclothing.com).

Poilâne 46 Elizabeth Street, SW1W 9PA (7808 4910/www.poilane.fr).

Press 134 St John's Wood High Street, NW8 7SE (7483 4441).

Raoul's Deli 8-10 Clifton Road, W9 1SS (7289 6649/www.raoulsgormet.com).

Rococo 45 Marylebone High Street, W1U 5HG (7935 7780/www.rococochocolates.com).

Rupert Sanderson 33 Bruton Place, W1J 6NP (0870 750 9181/www.rupertsanderson.co.uk).

Saltwater 98 Marylebone Lane, W1U 2QB (7935 3336/www.saltwater.net).

Selfridges 400 Oxford Street, W1A 1AB (0800 123 400/www.selfridges.com).

Les Senteurs 71 Elizabeth Street, SW1W 9PJ (7730 2322/www.lessenteurs.com).

Sheepdrove Organic Farm Family Butcher 5 Clifton Road, W9 1SZ (7266 3838/ www.sheepdrove.com).

Tube stations, rail stations and main bus routes dozens of tube, rail and bus services run through the City of Westminster; for maps and service information, visit www.tfl.gov.uk
River commuter and leisure boat services run east and west through London, with piers at the Savoy, Embankment, Westminster and Millbank

Shop at Maison Bertaux *27 Greek Street, W1D 5DF (05601 151584/www.shopat maisonb.com).*
Sixty 6 *66 Marylebone High Street, W1U 5JF (7224 6066).*
Skandium *86 Marylebone High Street, W1U 4QS (7935 2077/www.skandium.com).*
Souvenir *53 Brewer Street, W1F 9UY (7287 9877/www.souvenirboutique.co.uk).*
Stella McCartney *30 Bruton Street, W1J 6LG (7518 3100/www.stellamccartney.co.uk).*
Swaine Adeney Brigg *54 St James's Street, SW1A 1JT (7409 7277/www.swaineadeney. co.uk).*
Tracey Neuls *29 Marylebone Lane, W1U 2NQ (7935 0039/www.tn29.com).*
Weardowney Get-Up Boutique *9 Ashbridge Street, NW8 8DH (7725 9694/www.wear downey.com).*
Whiteleys *151 Queensway, W2 4YN (7229 8844/www.whiteleys.com).*
Winery *4 Clifton Road, W9 1SS (7286 6475/ www.thewineryuk.com).*

Arts & attractions

Cinemas & theatres

There's an incredible number of cinemas and theatres in the City of Westminster, most clustered in the district around Shaftesbury Avenue. We give just an overview below; for more – plus the latest developments, reviews and practical information – consult the 'Film' and 'Theatre' sections of the weekly *Time Out* magazine, or visit www.timeout.com.

Adelphi Theatre *Strand, WC2R 0NS (0870 403 0303/www.adelphitheatre.co.uk).*
Curzon *0870 756 4620/www.curzoncinemas. com; Mayfair, 38 Curzon Street, W1J 7TY; Soho, 93-107 Shaftesbury Avenue, W1D 5DY.*
Dominion Theatre *Tottenham Court Road, W1T 0AG (0870 169 0116/www.dominion theatre.co.uk).*
Empire *Leicester Square, WC2H 7JY (0871 224 4007/www.uidegon.co.uk).*
Lyceum Theatre *Wellington Street, WC2E 7RQ (0870 243 9000/www.lyceum-theatre.co.uk).*

Novello Theatre *Aldwych, WC2B 4LD (0870 950 0940/www.delfontmackintosh. co.uk).* The Royal Shakespeare Company's London home.
Open Air Theatre *Regent's Park, NW1 4NR (7935 5756/box office 0870 060 1811/ www.openairtheatre.org).* Alfresco theatre, perfect for summery Shakespeare romps.
Piccadilly Theatre *Denman Street, W1D 7DY (0870 060 0123/www.theambassadors. com/piccadilly).*
Prince Charles Cinema *7 Leicester Place, WC2H 7BP (7437 7003/www.princecharles cinema.com).* The best value in town for releases ending their first run elsewhere.
Prince of Wales Theatre *Coventry Street, W1D 6AS (0870 850 0393/www.delfont mackintosh.co.uk).*
Puppet Theatre Barge *Little Venice, opposite 35 Blomfield Road, W9 2PF (7249 6876/ www.puppetbarge.com).*
Queen's Theatre *Shaftesbury Avenue, W1D 6BA (0870 950 0930/www.delfontmackintosh. co.uk).*
St Martin's Theatre *West Street, WC2H 9NZ (7836 1443/www.stmartins-theatre.co.uk).*
Screen on Baker Street *Baker Street, W1U 6TJ (7935 2772/www.screencinemas.co.uk).*
Shaftesbury Theatre *210 Shaftesbury Avenue, WC2H 8DP (7379 5399/ www.shaftesbury-theatre.co.uk).*
Theatre Royal Drury Lane *Catherine Street, WC2B 5JF (0870 890 1109/www.theatreroyal drurylane.co.uk).*
Victoria Palace Theatre *Victoria Street, SWIE 5EA (0870 895 5577/www.victoria-palace-theatre.co.uk).*

Galleries & museums

This borough is the site of most of London's principal museums, galleries and tourist attractions. Below is a selection; for a more complete guide, see the *Time Out London Guide*, consult the 'Art' and 'Around Town' sections of *Time Out* magazine or visit www.timeout.com.

Benjamin Franklin House *36 Craven Street London, WC2N 5NF (7839 2006/www.benjamin franklinhouse.org).* Dramatic re-enactment tours at the home of the future Founding Father.
Lisson Gallery *www.lissongallery.com; 29 Bell Street, NW1 5BY (7535 7350); 52-54 Bell Street, NW1 5DA (7724 2739).* Contemporary art gallery with two spaces on Bell Street.
London Transport Museum *Covent Garden Piazza, WC2E 7BB (7379 6344/www.ltmuseum. co.uk.*
National Gallery *Trafalgar Square, WC2N 5DN (information line 7747 2885/ www.nationalgallery.org.uk).* A national treasure, founded in 1824, now with more than 2,000 pieces spanning virtually every school of art – and one of our favourite restaurants.

National Portrait Gallery *St Martin's Place, WC2H 0HE (7306 0055/www.npg.org.uk).* This attractive, manageable museum has fine views from the top-floor restaurant and bar.

Royal Academy of Arts *Burlington House, Piccadilly, W1J 0BD (7300 8000/www.royal academy.org.uk).* Britain's first art school, better known these days for its galleries.

Serpentine Gallery *Kensington Gardens, W2 3XA (7402 6075/www.serpentinegallery. org).* Fine exhibitions of contemporary art.

Somerset House *Strand, WC2R 0RN (Courtauld 7848 2526/www.courtauld.ac.uk/ Gilbert 7420 9400/www.gilbert-collection.org.uk/ Hermitage 7845 4630/www.hermitagerooms. co.uk).* Incorporates the Courtauld Institute of Art Gallery, the Gilbert Collection and the Hermitage Rooms; the grand courtyard is also used for open-air concerts in summer and ice skating in winter.

Tate Britain *Millbank, SW1P 4RG (7887 8888/ www.tate.org.uk).* The sexier Tate Modern gets all the attention, but don't forget this old stalwart: it contains London's second great collection of art, after the National Gallery.

Wallace Collection *Hertford House, Manchester Square, W1U 3BN (7563 9500/ www.wallacecollection.org).* Fine private art collection, bequeathed to the nation in 1897. Lovely covered courtyard restaurant too.

Music & comedy venues

See the weekly *Time Out* magazine or website (www.timeout.com) for full music and comedy listings in the borough.

Astoria *157 Charing Cross Road, WC2H 0EN (7434 9592/www.festivalrepublic.com).* This 2,000-capacity sweat box attracts big alt-rock names.

Coliseum *St Martin's Lane, WC2N 4ES (7632 8300/www.eno.org).* Home of the English National Opera.

Ronnie Scott's *47 Frith Street, W1D 4HT (7439 0747/www.ronniescotts.co.uk).* Famous jazz venue.

Royal Opera House *Bow Street, WC2E 9DA (7304 4000/www.royaloperahouse.org).* A new sound system allows passers-by to hear the music outside.

Wigmore Hall *36 Wigmore Street, W1U 3BN (7935 2141/www.wigmore-hall.org.uk).* Top concert venue for chamber music and song.

Other attractions

Buckingham Palace & Royal Mews *SW1A 1AA (7766 7300/www.royal.gov.uk).*

Houses of Parliament *Parliament Square, SW1A 0AA (Commons information 7219 4272/ Lords information 7219 3107/tours 0870 906 3773/www.parliament.uk).*

Institute of Contemporary Arts (ICA) *The Mall, SW1Y 5AH (7930 3647/www.ica. org.uk).* Its cinema shows art-house films, its theatre stages performance art and quality

leftfield gigs, and its art exhibitions are always talking points.

London Zoo *Outer Circle, Regent's Park, NW1 4RY (7722 3333/www.zsl.org).*

Royal Courts of Justice *Strand, WC2A 2LL (7947 6000/www.hmcourts-service.gov.uk).* Members of the public are allowed to attend certain trials.

St Martin-in-the-Fields *Trafalgar Square, WC2N 4JJ (7766 1100/www.stmartin-in-the-fields.org).* Recently refurbished 18th-century church, known for its classical concerts.

Westminster Abbey *20 Dean's Yard, SW1P 3PA (7222 5152/tours 7654 4900/ www.westminster-abbey.org).*

Westminster Cathedral *Victoria Street, SW1P 1QW (7798 9055/www.westminster cathedral.org.uk).*

Sport & fitness

The prices in council-run centres in Westminster are high, matching those found in private clubs in most other boroughs, but the facilities tend to be well maintained and of high quality. The independents are correspondingly pricey, but if you want personal attention and celeb-spotting opportunities, this borough's exclusive clubs should deliver.

Gyms & leisure centres

agua at Sanderson *50 Berners Street, W1T 3NG (7300 1414/www.sandersonlondon. com).* Private.

Bannatyne's *4 Millbank, SW1P 3JA (7233 3579/www.bannatyne.co.uk/fitness).* Private.

Berkeley Health Club & Spa *The Berkeley, Wilton Place, SW1X 7RL (7201 1699/www. theberkeleyhotellondon.com).* Private.

Cannons *www.cannons.co.uk; Endell Street, WC2H 9SA (7240 2446); 27-28 Kingly Street, W1B 5QE (7734 5002); 2 Sheldon Square, W2 6EZ (7289 4686).* Private.

Dorchester Spa *The Dorchester, 53 Park Lane, W1A 2HJ (7495 7335/www.dorchester hotel.com).* Private.

Fitness First *www.fitnessfirst.co.uk; 6 Bedford Street, WC2E 9HD (7240 8411); Berkeley Square House, Berkeley Square, W1J 6BR (7493 2311); Concourse Level, 1 Embankment Place, WC2N 6NM (7839 5411); 15 Great Marlborough Street, W1V 7HR (7287 8911); 59 Kingly Street, W1B 5QJ (7734 6226); Roebuck House, Stag Place, Palace Street, SW1E 5BA (7931 8011); 136-150 Victoria Street, SW1E 5LD (7828 8221).* Private.

Health Club at St James's Court *Crowne Plaza Hotel, 51 Buckingham Gate, SW1E 6AF (7963 8307).* Private.

Hilton Fitness by Precor *London Hilton, 22 Park Lane, W1K 1BE (7208 4080).* Private.

Jubilee Hall *30 The Piazza, WC2E 8BE (7836 4007/www.jubileehallclubs.co.uk).* Private.

City of Westminster

Jubilee Sports Centre *Caird Street, W10 4RR (8960 9629/www.westminster.gov.uk).*
LA Fitness *www.lafitness.co.uk; 7 Balcombe Street, NW1 6NA (7723 5757); Bayswater House, 6 Moscow Place, W2 4AP (0870 429 6385); 49 Hallam Street, W1W 6JW (7436 2881); Portland House, Stag Place, SW1E 5BH (7233 8444); Rex House, 4-12 Lower Regent Street, SW1Y 4PE (7839 8448); the Waldorf Hilton, Aldwych, WC2B 4DD (7379 5606).* Private.
LivingWell *Hilton London Metropole, 225 Edgware Road, W2 1JU (7616 6486/ www.livingwell.com).* Private.
Porchester Centre *Queensway, W2 5HS (7792 2919).*
Queen Mother Sports Centre *223 Vauxhall Bridge Road, SW1V 1EL (7630 5522).*
Seymour Leisure Centre *Seymour Place, W1H 5TJ (7723 8019).*
Virgin Active *www.virginactive.co.uk; Clifton Ford Hotel, Bulstrode Place, Marylebone Lane, W1U 2HU (7299 9595); Hereford House, 64 North Row, W1K 6DA (7659 4350); 120 Oxford Street, W1N 9DP (7436 0500); Shell Mex House, 80 The Strand, WC2R 0DT (7395 9595).* Private.
Zest! Health & Fitness Spa *Dolphin Square Hotel, Dolphin Square, SW1V 3LX (7798 8686).* Private.

Other facilities

Paddington Recreation Ground *Randolph Avenue, W9 1PD (7641 3642/www.westminster. gov.uk).* Facilities for tennis, cricket, football and athletics, plus a gym.
Queens Ice Rink & Bowling *17 Queensway, W2 4QP (7229 0172/www.queensiceandbowl. co.uk).*
Westminster Boating Base *136 Grosvenor Road, SW1V 3JY (7821 7389/www.westminster boatingbase.co.uk).* Boats, canoes and kayaks.

Spectator sports

Lord's Cricket Ground *St John's Wood Road, NW8 8QN (Marylebone Cricket Club 7289 1611/ tickets 7432 1000/www.lords.org).*

Schools

WHAT THE PARENTS SAY:

❝I chose Portland Place for my daughter after a previous bad experience with the state secondary system. State secondary choices are quite limited in Westminster, but there are good independent schools. Many parents – if they can afford it – choose this option. Westminster's independent schools are also popular with parents living outside the borough.

Portland Place has an inspiring headmaster, and I can honestly say that he is the main reason I chose the school for my daughter. Children have to pass entrance exams to attend the school,

but it's not all about top marks. The school believes that children should be taught together, but as individuals. Pupils with a wide range of backgrounds and natural ability are accepted and taught in small classes set by ability.

I've also heard good things about Queen's College – where Lily Allen and the Geldof girls went – and the Westminster School. I was previously very committed to educating my children in the state sector, but it didn't live up to my expectations. As a result, I didn't consider a state secondary when looking for a school for my daughter here.❞
Nichola Coulthard, mother of two

Primary

There are 38 state primary schools in the City of Westminster, 26 of which are church schools. There are also 16 independent primaries in the borough, including one American, one French, one International and one Jewish school; King Solomon Academy Infant School (Penfold Street, NW1 6RX, 3051 1650, www.arkschools. net) opened as an infant school in 2007, but plans eventually to have classes all the way to sixth form. See www.westminster.gov.uk, www.edubase.gov.uk and www.ofsted.gov.uk for more information.

Secondary

Grey Coat Hospital Girls' School *St Andrew's Building, Grey Coat Place, SW1P 2DY (7969 1998/www.gch.org.uk).* Girls only.
Paddington Academy *50 Marylands Road, W9 2DR (7479 3900/www.paddington-academy.org.uk).*
Pimlico School *Lupus Street, SW1V 3AT (7828 0881/www.pimlicoschool.org.uk).* There are plans for Pimlico to reopen as an academy in September 2008.
Portland Place *56-58 Portland Place, W1B 1NJ (7307 8700/www.portland-place.co.uk).* Private.
Queen's College *43-49 Harley Street, W1G 8BT (7291 7000/www.qcl.org.uk).* Girls only; private.
Quintin Kynaston School *Marlborough Hill, NW8 0NL (7722 8141/www.qkschool. org.uk).*
St Augustine's CE School *Oxford Road, NW6 5SN (7328 3434/www.staugustines high.org).*
St George's Catholic School *Lanark Road, W9 1RB (7328 0904/www.stgeorgesrc.org).*
St Marylebone CE School *64 Marylebone High Street, W1U 5BA (7935 4704/www. stmaryleboneschool.com).* Girls only; mixed sixth form.
Sylvia Young Theatre School *Rossmore Road, NW1 6NJ (7402 0673/www.sylviayoung theatreschool.co.uk).* The alma mater of a Spice Girl, two All Saints and most of the cast of *EastEnders.* Private.

Westminster Academy *255 Harrow Road, W2 5EZ (7121 0600/www.westminster academy.biz).*
Westminster City Boys' School *55 Palace Street, SW1E 5HJ (7641 8760/www.wcsch.com).* Boys only; private.
Westminster School *Little Dean's Yard, SW1P 3PF (7963 1000/www.westminster. org.uk).* Boys only; mixed sixth form. Private.

Property

WHAT THE AGENTS SAY:

❝Mayfair is very popular with Russians and international business people, while Marylebone is up and coming: it has the fastest growing high street in the country, with some wonderful bars, boutiques and restaurants. It's getting to be like Chelsea in terms of fashion – really raising its status.

Westminster and Victoria are slightly poorer relatives, which makes them better value. Maida Vale is a younger area, popular for families: if you look in an *A-Z*, there aren't actually very many streets because of the massive gardens and hidden parks.

There are some very grand white stucco houses in Little Venice, then – further along the canal into Paddington Basin – it's like a mini Docklands. Substantial developments are going on and it's only 15 minutes from Heathrow. I'm biased, though – I've just got a flat there.❞
David Cohen, Richard James & Company, Marble Arch

Average property prices
Detached £3,526,416
Semi-detached £1,299,850
Terraced £1,389,692
Flat £598,166

Local estate agents
Clevelands *98 Cleveland Street, W1T 6NR (7554 5300/www.clevelands.co.uk).*
Fox Gregory *102-104 Allitsen Road, NW8 7AY (7586 1500/www.foxgregory.co.uk).*
Manors *1A Baker Street, W1U 8ED (7486 5982/www.londonapartment.co.uk).*
Marsh & Parsons *53 Warwick Way, SW1 1QS (7828 8100/www.marshandparsons. co.uk).*
Richard James & Company *7 New Quebec Street, W1H 7RH (7723 7500/www.richard jamesandco.com).*
Robert Irving & Burns *23-24 Margaret Street, W1W 8LF (7637 0821/www.rib.co.uk).*
Wallsway *22 Devonshire Street, W1G 6PF (7224 0959/www.wallsway.co.uk).*
York Estates *81-82 Crawford Street, W1H 4AT (7724 0335/www.yorkestates.co.uk).*

RECYCLING
No. of bring sites 127 (for nearest, visit www.recycleforlondon.com)
Household waste recycled 17.79%
Main recycling centre there are three small sites in Marylebone (the biggest is on Paddington Street), but residents in the rest of the borough are encouraged to use the council's kerbside collection scheme
Other recycling services green waste collection; home composting; collection of white goods and furniture; computer recycling scheme
Council contact Environment & Leisure Department (Environmental Services), City Hall, 64 Victoria Street, SW1E 6QP (7641 2000)

COUNCIL TAX
A	up to £40,000	**£454.54**
B	£40,001-£52,000	**£530.20**
C	£52,001-£68,000	**£605.94**
D	£68,001-£88,000	**£681.68**
E	£88,001-£120,000	**£833.16**
F	£120,001-£160,000	**£984.65**
G	£160,001-£320,000	**£1,136.13**
H	over £320,000	**£1,363.36**

Other information

Council
Westminster City Council *PO Box 240, Westminster City Hall, 64 Victoria Street, SW1E 6QP (7641 6000/www.westminster.gov.uk).*

Legal services
Central London Law Centre *19 Whitcomb Street, WC2H 7HA (7839 2998/www.london lawcentre.org.uk).*
Westminster CAB *0870 126 4040/ www.adviceguide.org.uk.* Phone advice only.

Local newspapers
Westminster Independent *8961 3345/ www.londonlocals.uk.*
Westminster Reporter *7641 3041/ www.westminster.gov.uk.* Distributed free by the council six times a year. Also available online.
Westminster Times/Wood & Vale *7433 0000/www.westminstertimes.co.uk.*

Allotments & open spaces
There are no allotments in Westminster. For details of open spaces, visit www.westminster. gov.uk/leisureandculture. For its Royal Parks (Green Park, Hyde Park, St James's Park and Regent's Park), go to www.royalparks.org.uk.

> *'Boudicca took the City by storm down the street I can see when I do the ironing. I never get over it: great history and housework side by side.'*

Rev Katharine Rumens, rector, St Giles Cripplegate

City of London

There's no sign of a downturn in the Square Mile: cranes dominate the skyline and builders work overtime on new developments. Despite pockets of deprivation around the fringes, this really is a place apart. History, restaurants, architecture, location, location, location – the City of London has got it all.

Neighbourhoods

The City

One of the joys of the City is the population ebb and flow that ensures it never stays the same. By day, it's mobbed by nearly half a million office workers, plus a veritable army of tourists, white van drivers, cycle couriers and City of London police officers. By night (and at weekends), the streets are quiet – sometimes spookily so – and after-office drinkers take sanctuary in the islands of noise and light near the stations at Liverpool Street, Fenchurch Street, Cannon Street, Moorgate and Blackfriars. In fact,

fewer than one in 300 of the workers who clock in for duty on Monday morning are still here when the last train leaves Liverpool Street on Monday night.

At weekends, though, things are beginning to change – more City hotels are offering weekend breaks, and both the redevelopment of Paternoster Square and the knock-on effect of the crowds surging over the Millennium Bridge mean that the area around St Paul's has a definite buzz on the weekend.

The boundaries of the City are roughly delineated by the Roman city walls, but the 8,000 full-time residents of the district are squeezed into a much smaller area.

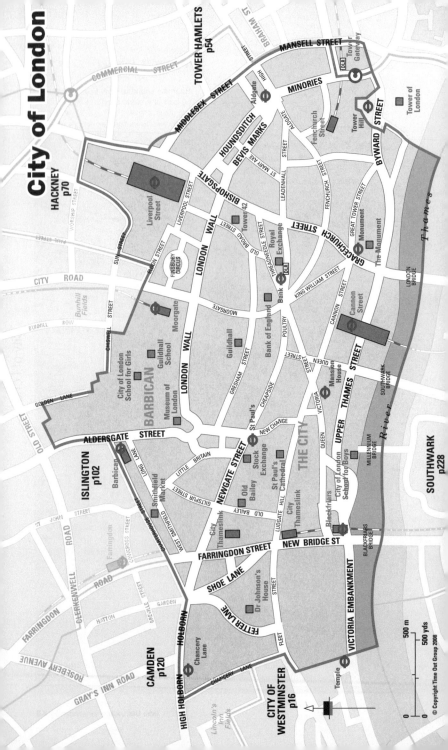

Most of the elegant townhouses built after the Great Fire of London were destroyed by German bombing in World War II, or transformed into offices by generations of town planners, leaving residents to make the best of small pockets of residential housing tucked away between the tower blocks, Wren churches and national monuments. With the massive focus on office space, amenities such as parks and children's play areas are in short supply, though the City is home to over 150 small 'city gardens' (see www.cityoflondon. gov.uk/corporation/living_environment/ open_spaces), and there's always the river to gaze at. What's more, the architecture is the most fascinating in London, with the showily modern (the Gherkin, Lloyd's of London) sitting alongside the beautifully ancient (St Bartholomew-the-Great is London's oldest parish church), and statues and public artworks are plentiful.

Most desirable residences are the handful of Georgian townhouses that escaped the fire-storm of the Blitz, found in clusters around Fleet Street, Fenchurch Street and Liverpool Street Station. If one of these properties comes on the market, snap it up; the chance to live in a genuine piece of London history doesn't come along very often. Most of the townhouses are broken up into luxury apartments, attracting young high-flyers who enjoy the proximity of the bars and restaurants in Islington and Tower Hamlets.

Inflated property prices tend to restrict the City to the wealthier sections of society. Gardens and parking spaces are almost unheard of, but most residents are happy to trade the luxury of space for the convenience of living five minutes from the office. The soaring Congestion Charge isn't really an issue; few bother with cars when the only available parking is in private car parks (besides, residents are eligible for a 90 per cent discount). With 1,200 police officers patrolling the streets, crime of the kind that affects home-owners is well below the London average. However, after-work binge drinking is one black mark on this otherwise enviable record.

Another inconvenience is that, thanks to the tidal nature of the daytime population, many shops, pubs and restaurants close over the weekend, and buying essentials after hours can involve an expedition to

the nearest train station with a Tesco Express. On the other hand, this is one of the easiest places in London to flag down a black cab, and with plentiful buses, and train and tube stations every few hundred yards, it's transport heaven.

Smithfield and Barbican

In recent years, renovation of the area around Smithfield Market has provided new loft apartments in converted warehouses and office buildings. The plan to demolish a set of Victorian buildings on the west side of Smithfield Market (running along Farringdon Road) and replace them with shops and offices is currently the subject of much debate, but looks set to go ahead. Many of the buildings are by Horace Jones, the architect who designed the rest of the market, but they have been allowed to lie derelict for many years.

The atmosphere in this area most resembles next-door Clerkenwell (in the borough of Islington); there are still local shops and small businesses, as well as destination restaurants and bars. Aside from the handsome meat market, the main landmark is historic St Bartholomew's Hospital. The pretty streets between

City of London

St Barts and Aldersgate contain some very covetable houses – the area oozes character.

The Barbican is easily the City's most famous residential address. The Barbican Estate was built on space largely created by wartime bomb damage; the government wanted to repopulate the City (down to around 5,000 residents in the 1950s), even though far more money could have been made by using the land for commercial purposes. Designed by architects Chamberlain, Powell & Bon, the Barbican terraces and towers were built between 1964 and 1975 (though the complex was officially opened in 1969 and the Barbican arts centre not finished until 1982).

The Estate covers around 40 acres and has just over 2,000 apartments (of well over 100 different types, ranging from studio flats to penthouses). It also contains the City of London School for Girls, the Museum of London and the Guildhall School of Music & Drama (though the latter is set to build controversial new premises on the site of Milton Court, next to the Barbican, due for completion in 2011). Opinion about the landmark concrete complex (now Grade II listed) has always been divided, and the layout can be confusing to visitors, but its stark charms are currently in fashion and the flats are much sought after. As they grow more and more expensive, the Golden Lane Estate (just north, on Fann Street) is becoming increasingly popular. Designed by the same architects (and also Grade II listed), Golden Lane was completed in the mid 1960s and holds 557 flats.

Restaurants & cafés

Most City eateries are open Monday to Friday; residents have to look to the fringes for weekend dining options. Smithfield is the most fruitful location: both hotel restaurant Brasserie de Malmaison and the four-storey Smiths of Smithfield (the complex holds two bars and two restaurants, which run from casual dining to high-end British) are open daily, for lunch and dinner. Other Smithfield restaurants tend to be open on Saturday nights at least: try the Smithfield Bar & Grill (steak-based American dishes), Café du Marché (traditional French), Club Gascon (deluxe French) and its more casual offshoot Comptoir Gascon.

Historic **Smithfield**. *See p45.*

The handsome Fox & Anchor is once again open, reborn as a gastropub. The Barbican complex offers several unalluring dining options, all of them very obviously run by catering companies; the poshest is Searcy's, a low-key venue offering Modern British cuisine. Looking like it's part of the estate, but independent, is modern pub-restaurant Wood Street.

The area around St Paul's and Paternoster Square has also become lively at weekends. The smartest options here are bar-restaurants Paternoster Chop House (British, and actually on the Square) and Northbank (also British, and just before the Millennium Bridge).

Inevitably, the City is not a cheap place to eat. Expense account dining at its most obvious is represented by the likes of Addendum, Bonds, Caravaggio, Chamberlain's, Le Coq d'Argent, 1 Lombard Street, Prism and Sauterelle – all serve top-notch food in impressive spaces. Gary Rhodes's place Rhodes Twenty Four has the added attraction of amazing views from the 24th floor of Tower 42. Slightly less imposing (and just a little cheaper) are the likes of Lanes, 1 Blossom Street, Refettorio, and the Grand Café & Bar in the Royal Exchange. Sir Terence Conran, once a major player in City dining, has sold all his properties, including the Great Eastern Hotel; renamed Andaz, it's now owned by Hyatt but still houses four restaurants and three bars, including a champagne bar.

An antidote to all this monied dining can be found at the Place Below, where breakfasts and vegetarian lunches are served in the Norman crypt of St Mary-le-Bow church, and at Austrian café-deli Kipferl (*see p51*). Ethnic restaurants also tend to be more affordable: try Haz (Turkish), K-10 and Moshi Moshi Sushi (Japanese), and Kenza (Middle Eastern). Slightly pricier are Nakhon Thai and Singapura (both oriental). The gastropub part of the White Swan also qualifies as a budget option, though its lovely first-floor Dining Room does not. Grazing is part-caff, part sandwich shop, and takes meat very seriously, while Hilliard is a self-styled 'gastro-café'. In addition, the City has more than enough chains – there are Pizza Expresses, Wagamamas, sandwich bars and coffeeshops all over (the branch of Paul next to St Paul's Cathedral is particularly well located). Newcomers include healthy lunch-hotspot Leon and the must-see branch of Konditor & Cook at 30 St Mary Axe.

Interesting one-offs include: Vivat Bacchus, where a serious wine list is balanced by an easygoing attitude and South African-influenced food; Missouri Grill, for quality meat; Rosemary Lane, an intimate French place at the eastern edge of the City; Terra Nostra for Sardinian dishes; and Bevis Marks Restaurant, a stylish kosher venue, next to the 18th-century synagogue of the same name. Sandeman's port, sherry and wine company was housed in what is now the appealing Don Bistro & Restaurant. And there's nowhere more characterful than our favourite City haunt – trad fish restaurant Sweetings. Only open for lunch on weekdays, it's unpretentious and charming, and merits a special trip, even if you don't live here.

Addendum *Apex City of London Hotel, 1 Seething Lane, EC3N 4AX (7977 9500/ www.addendumrestaurant.co.uk).*
Andaz *40 Liverpool Street, EC2M 7QN (7961 1234/www.london.liverpoolstreet.andaz.com).*
Bevis Marks Restaurant *Bevis Marks, EC3A 5DQ (7283 2220/www.bevismarksthe restaurant.com).*

Bonds *Threadneedle Hotel, 5 Threadneedle Street, EC2R 8AY (7657 8090/www.theeton collection.com).*
Brasserie de Malmaison *Malmaison, 18-21 Charterhouse Square, EC1M 6AH (7012 3700/ www.malmaison.com).*
Café du Marché *22 Charterhouse Square, Charterhouse Mews, EC1M 6AH (7608 1609/ www.cafedumarche.co.uk).*
Caravaggio *107 Leadenhall Street, EC3A 4AA (7626 6206/www.etruscagroup.co.uk).*
Chamberlain's *23-25 Leadenhall Market, EC3V 1LR (7648 8690/www.chamberlains.org).*
Club Gascon *57 West Smithfield, EC1A 9DS (7796 0600/www.clubgascon.com).*
Comptoir Gascon *63 Charterhouse Street, EC1M 6HJ (7608 0851/www.clubgascon.com).*
Coq d'Argent *No.1 Poultry, EC2R 8EJ (7395 5000/www.coqdargent.co.uk).*
Don Bistro & Restaurant *The Courtyard, 20 St Swithin's Lane, EC4N 8AD (7626 2606/ www.thedonrestaurant.com).*

STATISTICS

BOROUGH MAKE-UP
Population 7,800
Average weekly pay £1,021.40
Ethnic origins
White 83.12%
Mixed 2.59%
Asian or Asian British 9.09%
Black or Black British 3.89%
Chinese or other 2.59%
Students 7.93%
Retirees 9%

HOUSING STOCK
Borough size 3.2 km²
No. of households 5,370
Detached 0.3%
Semi-detached 0.3%
Terraced 1.5%
Flats (purpose-built) 89.3%
Flats (converted) 8%
Flats (both) 97.3%

CRIME PER 1,000 OF POPULATION
(average for England and Wales in brackets)
Burglary 4 (5)
Robbery 4 (2)
Theft of vehicle 8 (4)
Theft from vehicle 17 (9)
Violence against the person 105 (19)
Sexual offences 5 (1)

MP & COUNCIL
MP *Cities of London & Westminster*
Mark Field (Conservative)
CPA 4 stars; improving strongly

Glamour Grandeur
Sleaze Disease

Discover a great city in the making

FREE ENTRY

150 London Wall, EC2Y 5HN
St Paul's, Barbican
www.museumoflondon.org.uk

MUSEUM OF LONDON

SPICES SLAVERY
SKYSCRAPERS

MUSEUM IN DOCKLANDS

How the world came to the East End

KIDS GO FREE

West India Quay, London E14 4AL

Canary Wharf   West India Quay   www.museumindocklands.org.uk

Registered charity number: 1060415

Fox & Anchor *115 Charterhouse Street, EC1M 6AA (7250 1300/www.foxandanchor.com).*
Grand Café & Bar *The Royal Exchange, EC3V 3LR (7618 2480/www.royalexchange grandcafeandbar.com).*
Grazing *19-21 Great Tower Street, EC3R 5AR (7283 2932/www.grazingfood.com).*
Haz *9 Cutler Street, E1 7DJ (7929 7923/www.hazrestaurant.co.uk).*
Hilliard *26A Tudor Street, EC4Y 0AY (7353 8150).*
Kenza *10 Devonshire Square, EC2M 4YP (7929 5533/www.kenza-restaurant.com).*
K-10 City *20 Copthall Avenue, EC2R 7DN (7562 8510/www.k10.net).*
K-10 Moorgate *Northern Line Arcade, Moorgate Underground Station, EC2M 6TX (7614 9910/www.k10.net).*
Konditor & Cook *30 St Mary Axe, EC3A 8BF (0845 262 3030/www.konditorandcook.com).*
Lanes *East India House, 109-117 Middlesex Street, E1 7JF (7247 5050/www.lanes restaurant.co.uk).*
Leon *www.leonrestaurants.co.uk; 86 Cannon Street, EC4N 6HT (7623 9699); 12 Ludgate Circus, EC4M 7LQ (7489 1580).*
Missouri Grill *76 Aldgate High Street, EC3N 1BD (7481 4010/www.missourigrill.com).*
Moshi Moshi Sushi *Upper Level, Liverpool Street Station, EC2M 7QH (7247 3227/ www.moshimoshi.co.uk).*
Nakhon Thai *10 Copthall Avenue, EC2R 7DE (7628 1555/www.nakhonthai.co.uk).*
Northbank *1 Paul's Walk, EC4V 3QH (7329 9299/www.northbank.com).*
1 Blossom Street *1 Blossom Street, E1 6BX (7247 6530/www.1blossomstreet.com).*
1 Lombard Street *1 Lombard Street, EC3V 9AA (7929 6611/www.1lombardstreet.com).*
Paternoster Chop House *Warwick Court, Paternoster Square, EC4M 7DX (7029 9400/ www.paternosterchophouse.co.uk).*
The Place Below *St Mary-le-Bow Church, Cheapside, EC2V 6AU (7329 0789/ www.theplacebelow.co.uk).*
Prism *147 Leadenhall Street, EC3V 4QT (7256 3875/www.harveynichols.com).*
Refettorio *Crowne Plaza Hotel, 19 New Bridge Street, EC4V 6DB (7438 8052/www. refettorio.com).*
Rhodes Twenty Four *24th floor, Tower 42, Old Broad Street, EC2N 1HQ (7877 7703/ www.rhodes24.co.uk).*
Rosemary Lane *61 Royal Mint Street, E1 8LG (7481 2602/www.rosemarylane.btinternet.com).*
Sauterelle *The Royal Exchange, EC3V 3LR (7618 2483/www.restaurantsauterelle.com).*
Searcy's *Level 2, Barbican Centre, Silk Street, EC2Y 8DS (7588 3008/www.searcys.co.uk).*
Singapura *www.singapuras.co.uk; 1-2 Limeburner Lane, EC4M 7HY (7329 1133); 78-79 Leadenhall Street, EC3A 3DH (7929 0089).*
Smithfield Bar & Grill *2-3 West Smithfield, EC1A 9JX (0870 442 2541/www.barandgrill. co.uk).*

Smiths of Smithfield *67-77 Charterhouse Street, EC1M 6HJ (7251 7950/www.smithsof smithfield.co.uk).*
Sweetings *39 Queen Victoria Street, EC4N 4SA (7248 3062).*
Terra Nostra *27 Old Bailey, EC4M 7HS (3201 0077/www.terranostrafood.co.uk).*
Vivat Bacchus *47 Farringdon Street, EC4A 4LL (7353 2648/www.vivatbacchus.co.uk).*
White Swan Pub & Dining Room *108 Fetter Lane, EC4A 1ES (7242 9696/www.thewhite swanlondon.com).*
Wood Street *Wood Street, EC2Y 5EJ (7256 6990/www.woodstreetbar.com).*

Bars & pubs

Bar and pub chains have an incredibly strong presence in the City, but there are some wonderfully historic boozers and wine bars, and one or two excellent cocktail bars too. On and around Fleet Street, try the Viaduct Tavern (whose cellars are believed to be the last surviving cells of Newgate Prison), the Old Bell Tavern (which reputedly stands on the site of London's first print shop), the Black Friar (with its original 1905 interior) and labyrinth-like Ye Olde Cheshire Cheese.

Impressive buildings include champagne specialist La Grande Marque and the Old Bank of England, now a Fuller's pub. For great views, the Samuel Pepys has a sweeping view of the Thames towards the South Bank. El Vino is a family-run wine bar that specialises in claret; fans of Guinness might like Tipperary, London's first Irish pub and the first to sell the black stuff.

On Chancery Lane (the border between the Cities of London and Westminster), the prevailing sight is lawyers getting sloshed. Focus on the architecture instead: standouts include two ancient pubs: Ye Olde Mitre (dating from 1546) and the Cittie of Yorke (1430). Rather different is new Volupté, a neo-burlesque bar serving cocktails.

Around Mansion House, Monument and Bank, wine and champagne top the menu at Bar Bourse and Bow Wine Vaults. Leadenhall Market boasts the fine Lamb Tavern (a Young's pub); for more historic venues, try the rambling Williamson's Tavern, legend-heavy Ye Olde Watling, unpretentious Hatchet, and the atmospheric, half-timbered Bell – thought to be the City's oldest pub (the Swan Tavern has a different claim to fame, as the City's smallest).

TRANSPORT

Tube stations *Central* Chancery Lane, St Paul's, Bank, Liverpool Street; *Circle* Temple, Blackfriars, Mansion House, Cannon Street, Monument, Tower Hill, Aldgate, Liverpool Street, Moorgate, Barbican; *District* Temple, Blackfriars, Mansion House, Cannon Street, Monument, Tower Hill; *DLR* Bank, Tower Gateway; *Hammersmith & City* Liverpool Street, Moorgate, Barbican; *Metropolitan* Aldgate, Liverpool Street, Moorgate, Barbican; *Northern* Bank, Moorgate; *Waterloo & City* Bank

Rail stations *c2c* Fenchurch Street; *one* Liverpool Street; *Southeastern Trains* Cannon Street; *First Capital Connect Thameslink* Blackfriars, City Thameslink, Barbican, Moorgate

Main bus routes dozens of buses run through the City of London – for a full list, visit www.tfl.gov.uk/buses; *night buses* N8, N11, N15, N21, N26, N35, N47, N50, N55, N63, N76, N133; *24-hour buses* 23, 25, 43, 149, 214, 242, 243, 271, 344

River commuter and leisure boat services running east and west, with a pier at Blackfriars

The area around Liverpool Street heaves with City workers on Thursday and Friday nights, all with annihilation on their minds. A safer bet might be adjacent Spitalfields in Tower Hamlets, though the George (part of the Andaz hotel) and Hamilton Hall (a former ballroom restored to some kind of glory by JD Wetherspoon) are worth trying.

For a little more glamour, head towards Vertigo 42 – situated on the 42nd floor of the tallest edifice in the City – or the bars at Prism or 1 Lombard Street (for both, *see p49*) or lounge/party bar Mary Jane's. Or opt for Smithfield: thanks to Fabric (the destination club that draws enormous weekend queues), the bars on Charterhouse Street pull in a vibrant crowd – wedge-shaped Charterhouse, kookily designed Fluid and the multifaceted Smiths of Smithfield (*see p49*) are all popular pre-club pit-stops. There are some decent, underused pubs on the south side of the market too, such as the Bishops Finger and Hand & Shears, plus stellar wine bar Cellar Gascon.

Bar Bourse 67 *Queen Street, EC4R 1EE (7248 2200/www.barbourse.co.uk).*
Bell 29 *Bush Lane, EC4R 0AN (7929 7772).*

Bishops Finger 9-10 *West Smithfield, EC1A 9JR (7248 2341).*
Black Friar 174 *Queen Victoria Street, EC4V 4EG (7236 5474).*
Bow Wine Vaults 10 *Bow Churchyard, EC4M 9DQ (7248 1121/www.motcombs.co.uk).*
Cellar Gascon 59 *West Smithfield, EC1A 9DS (7600 7561/www.cellargascon.com).*
Charterhouse 38 *Charterhouse Street, EC1M 6JH (7608 0858/www.charterhousebar.co.uk).*
Cittie of Yorke 22 *High Holborn, WC1V 6BN (7242 7670).*
Fabric 77A *Charterhouse Street, EC1M 3HN (7336 8898/www.fabriclondon.com).*
Fluid 40 *Charterhouse Street, EC1M 6JN (7253 3444/www.fluidbar.com).*
George *Andaz Hotel, 40 Liverpool Street, EC2M 7QN (7618 7310/www.andaz.co.uk).*
La Grande Marque 47 *Ludgate Hill, EC4M 7JU (7329 6709/www.lagrandemarque.com).*
Hamilton Hall *The Concourse, Liverpool Street Station, EC2M 7PY (7247 3579/ www.jdwetherspoon.co.uk).*
Hand & Shears 1 *Middle Street, EC1A 7JA (7600 0257).*
Hatchet 28 *Garlick Hill, EC4V 2BA (7236 0720).*
Lamb Tavern 10-12 *Leadenhall Market, EC3V 1LR (7626 2454).*
Mary Jane's 124-127 *Minories, EC3N 1NT (7481 8195).*
Old Bank of England 194 *Fleet Street, EC4A 2LT (7430 2255).*
Old Bell Tavern 95 *Fleet Street, EC4Y 1DH (7583 0216).*
Samuel Pepys *Stew Lane, High Timber Street, EC4V 3PT (7489 1871/www.the samuelpepys.co.uk).*
Swan Tavern *Ship Tavern Passage, 77-80 Gracechurch Street, EC3V 1LY (7283 7712).*
Tipperary 66 *Fleet Street, EC4Y 1HT (7583 6470).*
Vertigo 42 *Tower 42, 25 Old Broad Street, EC2N 1HQ (7877 7842/www.vertigo42.co.uk).*
Viaduct Tavern 126 *Newgate Street, EC1A 7AA (7600 1863).*
El Vino 47 *Fleet Street, EC4Y 1BJ (7353 6786).*
Volupté 7-9 *Norwich Street, EC4A 1EJ (7831 1622/www.volupte-lounge.com).*
Williamson's Tavern 1 *Groveland Court, off Bow Lane, EC4M 9EH (7248 5750).*
Ye Olde Cheshire Cheese 145 *Fleet Street, EC4A 2BU (7353 6170).*
Ye Olde Mitre 1 *Ely Court, Ely Place (beside 8 Hatton Gardens), EC1N 6SJ (7405 4751).*
Ye Olde Watling 29 *Watling Street, EC4M 9BR (7653 9971).*

Shops

A huge shake-up is under way in City retailing: Cheapside and the surrounding streets will be almost unrecognisable once 12 new building schemes (creating 167 new retail units) are finished. Some, such as the One Wood Street complex, are nearing completion – it already contains branches of Jaeger and River Island. The biggest of them all, though, is One New Change. Scheduled to be ready by autumn 2010, it's currently an enormous building site next to St Paul's; to get an idea of the ambition involved, take a look at www.one newchange.com.

As with bars and pubs, chains predominate, even at the top end of the market. Swankiest of the lot is the Royal Exchange complex. Here there's a raft of jewellers (Tiffany, Tateossian, De Beers, Royal Exchange Jewellers, Watches of Switzerland, Searle & Co, Wint & Kidd, Theo Fennell), perfumers (Penhaligon's, Jo Malone, L'Artisan Parfumeur), deluxe brands (Hermès, Gucci, Cartier, Montblanc) and more quirky – though by no means budget – names such as Agent Provocateur, Lulu Guinness and Paul Smith.

Moving slightly downmarket, there's a useful mini version of House of Fraser just north of London Bridge. Otherwise, high-street chains abound: on Moorgate you'll find a big Marks & Spencer; on the corner of Moorfields and London Wall there's a huge New Look; in and around Liverpool Street and the Broadgate Centre there are branches of Hobbs, Reiss, Molton Brown, Space NK and REN, plus a big Tesco and independent wine retailer Uncorked.

Cheapside has yet more chains, and a another big Tesco; for a little more charm, wander down Dickensian Bow Lane for Jones the Bootmaker and a branch of Jigsaw with more accessories than most. Round the corner, on Queen Street, there's a Hugo Boss. Near St Paul's, Paternoster Square looks a treat, but the shops are run of the mill. Along Holborn Viaduct and Fleet Street, it's chain stores all the way, enlivened only by shops for the legal profession. More scenic is Leadenhall Market, over to the east, which is packed with shops and has a food market every Friday (10am-4pm).

But it's not all identikit retailers. For more interesting shops, look to the fringes of the City; around Smithfield Market there are deli/cafés such as Carluccio's (Italian) and Kipferl (Austrian), plus classy gift shop Ian Logan Design Company. Around Moorgate there's appealing independent gentlemen's outfitters T Fox & Co, the stylish frontage of which is only matched by F Flittner barbers (est. 1904).

Carluccio's *12 West Smithfield, EC1A 9JR (7329 5904/www.carluccios.com).*
F Flittner *86 Moorgate, EC2M 6SE (7606 4750/www.fflittner.com).*
House of Fraser *68 King William Street, EC4N 7HR (0870 160 7274/www.houseof fraser.co.uk).*
Ian Logan Design Company *42 Charterhouse Square, EC1M 6EA (7600 9888/www.ian-logan. co.uk).*
Kipferl *70 Long Lane, EC1A 9EJ (7796 2229/ www.kipferl.co.uk).*
Leadenhall Market *Whittington Avenue, off Gracechurch Street, EC3 (7929 0929/ www.leadenhallmarket.co.uk).*

City of London

Royal Exchange *EC3V 3LR (www.theroyal exchange.com).*
T Fox & Co *118 London Wall, EC2Y 5JA (7628 1868/www.tfox.co.uk).*
Uncorked *Exchange Arcade, Broadgate Centre, EC2M 3WA (7638 5998/www.uncorked.co.uk).*

Arts & attractions

Cinemas & theatres
Barbican Centre *Silk Street, EC2Y 8DS (7638 8891/www.barbican.org.uk).* A major arts centre, with theatres, cinemas and an art gallery. Also the home of the London Symphony Orchestra.

Galleries & museums
Bank of England Museum *Entrance on Bartholomew Lane, EC2R 8AH (7601 5491/ www.bankofengland.co.uk/museum).*
Barbican Art Gallery *Level 3, Barbican Centre, Silk Street, EC2Y 8DS (7638 8891/ www.barbican.org.uk).* Contemporary art and photography exhibitions.
Clockmakers' Museum *Guildhall Library, Aldermanbury, EC2V 7HH (7332 1868/ www.clockmakers.org).* Well-presented horological exhibition.
Dr Johnson's House *17 Gough Square, EC4A 3DE (7353 3745/www.drjohnsonshouse.org).* Wonderfully atmospheric museum celebrating the life and works of Samuel Johnson.
Guildhall Art Gallery *Guildhall Yard, off Gresham Street, EC2V 5AE (7332 3700/ www.guildhall-art-gallery.org.uk).* Work by Constable, Reynolds and Rossetti.
Museum of London *London Wall, EC2Y 5HN (0870 444 3852/www.museumoflondon.org.uk).* The history of the capital, now open late on the first Thursday of every month.
Museum of Methodism & John Wesley's House *Wesley's Chapel, 49 City Road, EC1Y 1AU (7253 2262/www.wesleyschapel.org.uk).*
Tower Bridge Exhibition *Tower Bridge, SE1 2UP (7403 3761/www.towerbridge.org.uk).* The history of the bridge. Stunning views from the high-level walkways.
Tower of London *Tower Hill, EC3N 4AB (0870 756 6060/www.hrp.org.uk).* The Crown Jewels, ravens, Beefeaters, tourists… and nearly 1,000 years of British royal history in this fortress on the Thames (actually within the borough of Tower Hamlets).

Other attractions
Old Bailey *Central Criminal Court, corner of Newgate Street & Old Bailey, EC4M 7EH (7248 3277/www.hmcourts-service.gov.uk).* The public galleries allow viewing of trials in session.
College of Arms *Queen Victoria Street, EC4V 4BT (7248 2762/www.college-of-arms.gov.uk).* Heraldic and genealogical history.
Guildhall *Gresham Street, EC2P 2EJ (7606 3030/www.corpoflondon.gov.uk).* Home of the Corporation of London. The cathedral-like Great Hall is mainly used for ceremonial events.

Monument *Monument Street, EC3R 8AH (7626 2717/www.themonument.info).* Built in 1677 to commemorate the Great Fire of London. Spectacular views from the top – but closed until December 2008 for a £4.5 million restoration.
St Bartholomew-the-Great *West Smithfield, EC1A 9DS (7606 5171/www.greatstbarts.com).* The City's finest medieval church.
St Paul's Cathedral *Ludgate Hill, EC4M 8AD (7236 4128/www.stpauls.co.uk).* Wren's masterpiece. Renovation continues in preparation for its 300th anniversary in 2008.

Sport & fitness

The City is dominated by big-name private chains. The one public centre is a charmer, though: Golden Lane Leisure Centre offers an oasis of unpretentious calm amid high salaries and high towers.

Gyms & leisure centres
Barbican YMCA *2 Fann Street, EC2Y 8BR (7628 0697/www.cityymca.org).* Private.
Cannons *Cousin Lane, EC4R 3XJ (7283 0101/ www.cannons.co.uk).* Private.
Citypoint Club *Citypoint, 1 Ropemaker Street, EC2Y 9AW (7920 6200/www.thecitypoint club.co.uk).* Private.

Fitness First *www.fitnessfirst.co.uk; Unit 12, Liverpool Street Station, EC2M 7PY (7247 5511); 55 Gracechurch Street, EC3V 6NN (7621 0911); 5-11 Fetter Lane, EC4A 1QX (7353 2311); 1 Thavie's Inn, EC4A 1AN (7822 0990); 1 America Square, EC3N 2LB (7488 9311).* Private.
Golden Lane Leisure Centre *Golden Lane Estate, Fann Street, EC1Y 0SH (7250 1464/ www.cityoflondon.gov.uk).*
LA Fitness *www.lafitness.co.uk; 20 Little Britain, EC1A 7DH (7600 0900); 48 Leadenhall Street, EC3A 2BE (7488 2934); 48 London Wall, EC2M 5QB (7628 9876); Cutlers Gardens, 9 Devonshire Square, EC2M 4WY (7626 3161); 1 Broadgate, EC2M 7HA (7920 0192); 106 Fenchurch Street, EC3M 5JE (7369 0700).* Private.
Slim Jim's Health Club *1 Finsbury Avenue, EC2M 2PF (7247 9982/www.slim-jims.co.uk).* Private.
Vie *122 Clerkenwell Road, EC1R 5DL (7278 8070/www.viehealthclubs.co.uk).* Private.
Virgin Active *www.virginactive.co.uk; 97 Aldersgate, EC1A 4JP (7374 0091); 1 Exchange Place, Appold Street, EC2M 2QT (7422 6400); Ibex House, 1 Haydon Street, EC3N 7HP (7680 5000).* Private.

Other facilities
Broadgate Ice Rink *Broadgate Circle, EC2M 2QS (7505 4068/www.broadgateice.co.uk).*

Schools

WHAT THE PARENTS SAY:

‘We feel lucky to have our boys at the City of London school as it has an excellent pass rate at GCSE and an overall good reputation. The boys' school is well known – not just in central London, but in the UK. It's been voted one of the top 15. It has a good international mix and often has speakers coming in from the political and financial worlds. Sports here are great, with around 20 football teams and there's a new theatre coming soon.’
Father of two, the City

Primary
There is only one state primary school within the City of London, the Sir John Cass's Foundation Primary School, and two independent schools, St Paul's Cathedral School and the Charterhouse Square School. See www.cityoflondon.gov.uk and www.edubase.gov.uk for more information.

Secondary
There are no state secondary schools in the City of London, but the borough has an arrangement with Tower Hamlets to provide places. Local children also gain priority admission to the City of London Academy in Southwark.

City of London School for Girls *St Giles' Terrace, Barbican, EC2Y 8BB (7847 5500/ www.clsg.org.uk).* Girls only; private.
City of London School for Boys *Queen Victoria Street, EC4V 3AL (7489 0291/ www.clsb.org.uk).* Boys only; private.

Property

WHAT THE AGENTS SAY:

‘The City is vibrant and always busy; as a place to live and go out it attracts a young crowd. It is close to everything, and the transport links out of London from Liverpool Street are brilliant. It is very expensive to buy here, so a lot of people rent – the cost of buying rose by about 25 per cent in the last year, although things have quietened down recently.

But it's not family-friendly. There are few schools and green spaces, and it's noisy and grimy. If you're just working and partying that doesn't matter much, but people tend to move west when they start a family. Much of the property we take on comes from couples who've just had their first child or have one on the way.’
Ben Garrett, Capital Dwellings

Average property prices
Detached, Semi-detached, Terraced n/a
Flat £449,314

Local estate agents
Bridge Estates *98A Curtain Road, EC2A 3AA (7749 1400/www.bridge.co.uk).*
Capital Dwellings *47 Fashion Street, E1 6PX (7375 1515/www.capitaldwellings.com).*
Frank Harris & Company *87 Long Lane, EC1A 9ET (7600 7000/www.frankharris.co.uk).*
Hamilton Brooks *73 Long Lane, EC1A 9ET (7606 8000/www.hamiltonbrooks.co.uk).*
Scott City *122 Newgate Street, EC1A 7AA (7600 0026/www.scottcity.co.uk).*
Square Mile Property Management *Global House, 5A Sandys Row, E1 7HW (7392 9111/www.m2pm.com).*

Other information

Council
Corporation of London *PO Box 270, Guildhall, EC2P 2EJ (7606 3030/www.cityof london.gov.uk).*

Legal services
City of London CAB *32 Ludgate Hill, EC4M 7DR (7236 1156/www.adviceguide.org.uk).*

Local newspapers
City of London & Dockland Independent *01840 779225/www.londonlocals.co.uk.*

City of London

'Poke around the Dickensian backstreets of Bethnal Green, Whitechapel or Mile End and you'll discover some of the most exciting art spaces in the world. Forget Montmartre, forget Chelsea, you have to come to Tower Hamlets.'

Iwona Blazwick, director, Whitechapel Gallery

Tower Hamlets

This is a borough of extremes, with the City pushing its way further and further into Spitalfields and Docklands skyscrapers looming over the Isle of Dogs. Elsewhere, grim tower blocks rub shoulders with some of London's most fashionable neighbourhoods, while pie and mash shops vie for trade with the swankiest of gastro boozers.

Neighbourhoods

Spitalfields and Brick Lane

You know a neighbourhood has lost its edge when groups of clipboard-wielding schoolchildren filling out local-history worksheets can be seen trailing the streets. Indeed, the seedier side of Spitalfields has become something of a distant memory. The City has crept ever closer over the last few years, bringing with it new public spaces, a market refurb and an enormous Foster-designed office building. But it'll take more than a few swanky new buildings to stamp out the spirit of Spitalfields. The area's strong sense of community remains intact despite the influx of shiny new shops and restaurants aimed at City workers.

Historically, Spitalfields has long been a first place of refuge for communities new to London. Over the years it has housed groups such as French Huguenots evading persecution by Catholics, and Ashkenazi Jews escaping Russian pogroms. Today the neighbourhood's most prominent immigrant community is the Bangladeshi one on and around Brick Lane (the Bengali New Year Festival, Baishakhi Mela, is a must-visit; see www.baishakhimela.com). Central to life here is the Brick Lane Mosque (opened 1976), previously a French Protestant church (1743), Methodist chapel (1819) and the Spitalfields Great Synagogue (1889).

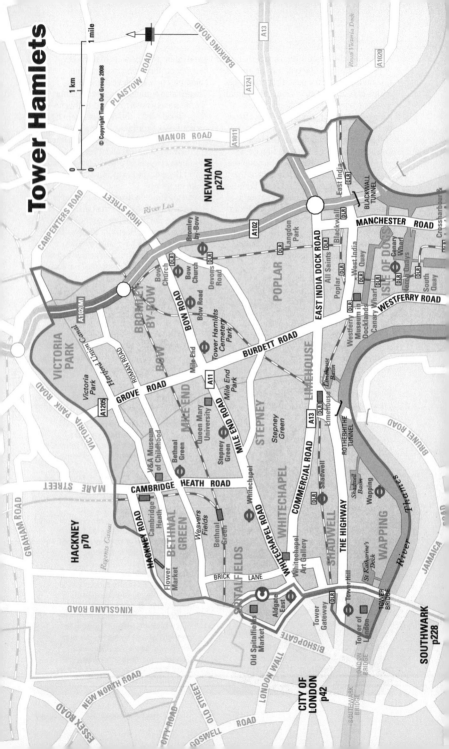

Meanwhile, the cheap studio space that once drew arty and creative types to the area has become a thing of the past. Property prices in this part of town have risen exponentially in recent years, and Spitalfields' role as a home for transient populations has almost certainly come to an end.

It's easy to see why house prices are so high – if you can get past the film crews shooting period dramas, peep through the windows at the exquisite interiors of the houses on Hanbury, Princelet and Fournier Streets (in the shadow of Hawksmoor's masterpiece Christ Church). Tracey Emin and writer Jeanette Winterson are among those who followed early pioneers Gilbert and George in restoring these Huguenot houses to Georgian splendour. They sell for well over £2 million today.

Evidence of the more gruesome elements of Spitalfields' history has all but vanished – though regular Jack the Ripper walking tours in the area offer locals the occasional overheard reminder of its murky past.

Sunday is when the neighbourhood's markets come to life. As well as Spitalfields Market itself, there's the newer Sunday (Up)Market and, of course, the cheap tat and banter of Brick Lane Market. To the west, Dray Walk, by the Old Truman Brewery (a handy short cut between Brick Lane and Hanbury Street) has embraced café society; on Sunday afternoons the street overflows with young hipsters getting over their hangovers.

Whitechapel and Stepney

The lower end of Brick Lane turns into Osborn Street, which merges into the traffic-clogged Whitechapel Road (A11). Tune out the horn-tooting chaos and you'll find there's more to this hectic thoroughfare than first meets the eye. For starters, there's the excellent Whitechapel Art Gallery, currently undergoing a £10.5 million expansion into the old library next door, which will almost double its size (due for completion 2009). Also serving the needs of the local community are the East London Mosque and London Muslim Centre, Whitechapel Road's street market and the glass-walled Idea Store, which brings the concept of the public library bang up to date for the 21st century. It's still a pretty run-down road, but a spot of Queen Anne architecture jollys things up, along with some interesting pockets of terraced housing off the main street and the obligatory new flat developments. There's also a huge branch of Sainsbury's.

Café society hasn't made it to this neck of the woods yet – you're more likely to encounter local drunks slurring their way into the Royal London's A&E department – but there are some excellent restaurants (Kolopata, Tayyab's) and old-school boozers (Blind Beggar, the Good Samaritan) to make up for it.

The gigantic flat-fronted Victorian red-bricks around Ashfield Street and Sidney Square are worth looking out for behind the Royal London Hospital. Meanwhile, in Stepney, things have improved since Dr Barnardo set up his first refuge in 1870 – Albert Gardens and Arbour Square are well-hidden green spots. Stepney Green is also pleasant.

Bethnal Green

In common with much of east London, World War II bomb damage has left an architectural patchwork in Bethnal Green, with no single style or period monopolising. The result is a neighbourhood that operates

Highs & Lows

▲ **Market mayhem** The borough has three of London's best markets – Spitalfields, Brick Lane and Columbia Road – not to mention numerous local street markets
Nightlife Tower Hamlets is home to some of the capital's quirkiest and coolest bars, pubs, clubs and restaurants
Cultural mix Successive waves of immigration over centuries have made this one of the most vibrant and varied areas in London

House price doom Locals wanting to clamber on to the property ladder have a struggle ahead, especially in Spitalfields and Docklands
Bomb damage The Blitz destroyed much of the East End, leading to a plethora of ugly tower blocks and windswept council estates
Schools Fine at primary level, but good state secondaries are few ▼ and far between

on a human scale and streets that each seem to have their own character. Newcomers are often pleasantly surprised when they realise how central Bethnal Green is – much of the area is in Zone 1, and it's a quick Central line journey from Bethnal Green tube station into the middle of town. The social attractions of Brick Lane and Shoreditch are within walking distance too. The area has its own green space, Weavers Fields, and the vast expanse of Victoria Park is not far away, at the end of Old Ford Road.

On Sundays, Columbia Road Flower Market is a multicoloured frenzy, and the terraced cottages around neighbouring Jesus Green are the most highly prized in the area, selling for the best part of half a million pounds, despite being on the poky side. As rising housing costs push creative types out of areas like Spitalfields, Bethnal Green's art scene has flourished. Property here is decidedly more affordable and, on the edge of Hackney, Vyner Street has its own mini-scene of galleries and musing artists.

It's not all bleeding-edge cool, though. On the main thoroughfare, Bethnal Green Road, you can also still sit down for a meal of pie, mash and jellied eels at a time-weathered local caff. There's also a strong community feel, even where the neighbourhood's murkier ex-residents are concerned – thousands lined the streets for Ronnie Kray's funeral in 1995, and his twin Reggie's in 2000, and many locals still won't hear a bad word said against the brothers.

Mile End

The City may only be a mile away, but its glittering towers on the horizon seem to come from a different world. Mile End still feels considerably down-at-heel, with few of the pockets of cool found in neighbouring Bethnal Green. The legacy of wartime bomb damage and slum clearances means property here is a hotch-potch of 18th-century terraces and expansive – often grim – estates (one of which was immortalised in the Pulp song 'Mile End'). Social housing and rentals make up a large proportion of the area's housing stock, but for those who do choose to buy here, prices remain lower than many other parts of Tower Hamlets.

And it's not all bad. Mile End may lack gastropubs and glamour, but it offers excellent access to other parts of the borough (the amenities of Victoria Park and Bow Wharf are within walking distance); transport links are excellent (with the Hammersmith & City, District and Central tube lines, as well as numerous bus routes) and it has its very own green space in the shape of Mile End Park.

An ambitious grass bridge (aka the Green Bridge) allows the park to stretch across Mile End Road, while, under the bridge, there's a handy hub of newish shops, restaurants and coffeeshops, including a branch of Budgens. Residents also make good use of the pleasant canal path, the Mile End Climbing Wall, the new leisure centre (opened 2006) and the outdoor karting track.

Opposite the park, Queen Mary, University of London, gives a studenty feel to this stretch of Mile End Road, with majestic older buildings sitting alongside the award-winning modern architecture of the university's Student Village.

Victoria Park

No longer the well-kept secret it once was, Victoria Park has gone the way of much of Tower Hamlets and become a serious property hotspot. If you're looking for a bargain Victorian flat conversion, that ship has sailed, but there's still much to love about the place of which Dickens said: 'No student of London life should miss seeing.'

Victoria Park is London's third largest cultivated green space, rivalled only by the parks Hyde and Regent's to the west, yet the East End location keeps it well off the tourist trail. Shaped like a wellington boot, the park was built in the mid 19th century in an attempt to bring health and vigour to the working classes. Sadly, its lido is no longer in use, but the lakes, deer enclosure and café compensate, as do annual events such as music festivals, outdoor film screenings and firework displays.

Grove Road slices the park in two. If you follow it north as it turns into Lauriston Road, a wonderful hidden village appears (across the borough boundary in Hackney). There's a cluster of shops around the very pleasant junction with Victoria Park Road – not to mention a bevy of estate agents, cashing in on the area's family-friendly layout. The spacious Victorian houses and villagey feel have made this one of the most sought-after pockets of east London, despite the nearest tube station (Bethnal Green) being a long walk down the Roman Road.

On the south side of the park runs the Hertford Union Canal, bordered by a variety of new-build flats and houses taking advantage of the waterside location. Follow the canal path along the park east to Cadogan Terrace and you'll find some fine four-storey houses. Unfathomable council clearances in the 1960s robbed these houses of some of their neighbours, and those that remain have their backs to another unpleasant 1960s phenomenon – the A12 flyover, beyond which the canal connects to the River Lee Navigation.

Bow, Bromley-by-Bow and Poplar

Poplar, once a crucial suburb of docks and dockers, is now riven by major thoroughfares – the approach to the Blackwall Tunnel, Aspen Way and the nascent A13, the East India Dock Road. Fast-food debris flutters along the last – testament to the predominant style of restaurant – and while the occasional Georgian terrace exists, much of the housing is of the Brutalist post-war variety. One notable landmark is Ernö Goldfinger's modernist Balfron Tower, a block of flats with a chimney-like lift shaft stuck on one side; the building mirrors Goldfinger's more famous Trellick Tower in west London.

Poplar's High Street itself has little to recommend it, good (and busy) though its greasy spoon is. North of here is Chrisp Street Market, site of Britain's first pedestrian shopping centre (built for the 1951 Festival of Britain), and one of the borough's Idea Stores.

Bow itself, named as long ago as 1110 for the bridge over the River Lee, has, in keeping with Mile End, some excellent Victorian housing, particularly in the Tredegar conservation area, up and across Roman Road to Zealand and Chisenhale Roads – where the Chisenhale building comprises artists' studios, a dance space and an art gallery.

Roman Road offers pie and mash shops and a vibrant street market that's been in operation since 1843. Just to the north-west, Bow Wharf sits astride the junction of Regent's and Grand Union Canals, and has restaurants, bars, a well-equipped gym and a branch of the Jongleurs comedy club. The defining testament to the area's development, however, is Bow Quarter –

A bit of posh in Bow: **Tredegar Square**.

a complex of luxury apartments in the vast former Bryant & May match factory, where in 1888 a strike by female workers signalled the beginning of the suffragette movement. Other new-build developments have sprung up in the area in anticipation of the arrival of the Olympics.

East of Bow sits Bromley-by-Bow, an unlovely corner of London. Historically just called Bromley, the 'by-Bow' suffix was dreamed up by London Underground to avoid confusion with the borough of Bromley, eight miles to the south. This is almost its only distinguishing feature. The area is dominated by ugly urban sprawl: industry, supermarkets, two- and three-lane highways and council estates. One nearby architectural highlight is Container City – live/work studios made out of shipping containers – on the border with Newham.

Wapping, Shadwell and Limehouse

The glass-fronted apartments of Wapping and Limehouse sit at odds with much of the world around them. Affluent incomers who buy flats off-plan might be shocked to see what exists outside the picture frame: endless estates and a brutal highway sucking traffic into the Rotherhithe Tunnel.

At least one half of Wapping has retained a villagey feel; the waterside area, with its atmospheric old pubs, is probably

Traffic Light Tree sculpture, **Docklands**.

the loveliest example of restoration in the whole of east London. The other half of the district is another matter: the prison-like enclosure of the News International office complex and its all-night-chugging printing press dominates.

Westwards, on the edge of the City, lie the iconic pinnacles of Tower Bridge and the Tower of London. Next door, in glossy St Katharine's Dock the sense of history all but disappears – this modern yacht-filled marina is overlooked by pricey penthouses, coffee chains, pubs and restaurants.

Further east, Limehouse Basin marina has a similar feel, with some impressive new (and old) architecture. Gordon Ramsay's gastropub the Narrow is here – take a post-prandial walk along the beautifully scenic (though annoyingly interrupted) riverside path and you can't help but breathe the seeping history, despite all the new glass and concrete.

Nearby Shadwell is an incongruous mix of smart new housing and pockets of social deprivation, though there has recently been some welcome regeneration around the DLR station and Watney Street Market. In addition, Shadwell Basin is now an excellent watersports and adventure centre.

Docklands and the Isle of Dogs

Very few peaceful cities ever have the chance to regenerate an area the size of the Docklands. And very few people gave such a project a chance of working in London. And yet, 20 years after building began on the site of the disused West India Quay, Canary Wharf is a successful, busy, bustling part of the city – a hub for business, a destination for shopping and an increasingly popular place to live.

For much of the 19th century these were the busiest docks in the world, employing up to 50,000 people. The project that Margaret Thatcher's government started in 1981 is now the workplace for over 90,000 and is predicted to employ 100,000 by 2009, with phase three in full flow, and cranes abounding once more.

The Wharf is featured in just about every film about London. Want a shot that sums up London as a business centre? Go to Canary Wharf (it has the UK's three tallest buildings). Want a cool-looking underground station? Look no further than the cathedral-like, Norman Foster-designed version here. There is, however, an undeniable sterility to the place – a feeling of not really being in London – particularly when the wind blows down the skyscraper-lined streets.

Local residents benefit from plentiful amenities – supermarkets, gyms, shops galore, a cinema and a good museum – and weekends are no longer the lonely experience they were in the 1990s. But it does all feel very corporate: there is a lack of good independent eateries, cool boutiques and a complete absence of corner shops. But then Canary Wharf was never going to be the next edgy, up-and-coming area: it doesn't pretend to be, either.

The rest of the Isle of Dogs is gradually experiencing the ripple effect. New housing developments are being constructed all over the peninsula, in particular around Millwall Dock, and while not everyone will be able to afford a piece of the waterfront dream, the effect is generally positive – more shops, more places to go out, better transport links. For the moment, though, this area remains somewhat in the shadow (literally and metaphorically) of its high-rise neighbours. The pubs are far from gastro (with the exception of the Gun on Coldharbour) and the estates are grim. But 'the Island' has a wonderful green space at its heart in Mudchute Park, and Mudchute City Farm within – a fabulous resource for both residents and visitors.

Restaurants & cafés

Barely an inch of space remains near Spitalfields Market that hasn't been redeveloped or earmarked for development, resulting in serious smartening-up of the neighbourhood's restaurants and cafés. For locals, the increased choice – branches of Pâtissere Valerie, Giraffe and British food specialist Canteen – is a definite plus, as is the fact that most places are now open on Saturdays, but the loss of two much-loved independent venues in 2007, Spitz and the Arkansas Café, left a bitter taste in the mouths of many. However, gems like St John Bread & Wine (British) and Hawksmoor (steak and great cocktails) are still going strong, as are the likes of S&M Café and the lovely Market Coffee House.

Up Brick Lane towards Shoreditch is a restaurant scene that's fast evolving. The Brick Lane Beigel Bake (a 24-hour, non-kosher Jewish bakery) is one of the best places to grab a quick (and cheap) bite. For something more upmarket, try the new Brickhouse supper club. Few of the Lane's Bangladeshi restaurants offer much more than formulaic curries, though there's a revival brewing with increasing numbers of diners seeking out basic home-style caffs like Sabuj Bangla. For real-deal Bangladeshi dishes (and English menus), Whitechapel's Kolapata is a worthy ambassador. Also worth a look in Whitechapel is busy locals' favourite Tayyab's (Pakistani).

On Bethnal Green Road, Mexican bar-restaurant Green & Red has made its mark. Nearby, the Rochelle Canteen – co-owned by Margot Henderson, wife of St John's Fergus – serves excellent British food for lunch to a mix of arty creatives (from the studios next door) and fashion-y local workers. Off the Circus on Calvert Avenue is chameleon-like Lennie's (breakfasts by day, Thai food by night), while on Club Row there's fabulously OTT Les Trois Garçons (French). This area will also play host to a new Conran restaurant (and hotel) in spring 2008 called the Boundary (www.theboundary.co.uk) – a sure sign that E2 really has up-and-come.

Along and around Columbia Road there's Jones Dairy Café, gastropub the Royal Oak, café-bar the Fleapit, tapas bar Laxeiro and StringRay Globe Café, Bar & Pizzeria. Moving east, Bistrotheque provides a delightful cocktail of Anglo-French food, great attitude and a groovy bar in a converted warehouse.

There are several old-fashioned pie and mash shops in the borough: G Kelly and S&R Kelly on Bethnal Green Road (also the home of ace greasy spoon E Pellicci), plus G Kelly in Bow. The Morgan Arms gastropub is also in Bow, while two vegetarian restaurants, Gallery Café and Wild Cherry, are near-neighbours in E2. Mile End has the Orange Room (Lebanese

Whitechapel's **Kolapata**: East End eating, Bangladeshi style.

and breakfasts), but otherwise notable eateries in the area are rare. Heading towards Victoria Park proves a better bet. The Empress of India on Lauriston Road (officially just over the border in Hackney) is an excellent gastropub; the Royal Inn on the Park also serves good food.

Towards the river, Wapping has its fair share of chains (Pizza Express, Pizza Paradiso and Smollensky's), but also boasts Wapping Food, a fascinating arts space and Modern European restaurant in a huge industrial building (formerly a hydraulic power station). Popular local restaurants include pizza and pasta joint Il Bordello, and barbecue outlet Rhodes B-B-Q Shack. Almost in the City (on the Whitechapel/ Wapping borders), Rosemary Lane offers excellent French cuisine in a relaxed setting. Limehouse boasts one of the newer additions to the Gordon Ramsay empire in the form of the Narrow gastropub.

Docklands is packed with smart chains (Carluccio's Caffè, Itsu, Moshi Moshi Sushi, Smollensky's, Tootsies Grill, Wagamama and Zizzi) and slick venues designed with suits and their credit cards in mind. Many have fabulous waterfront settings, including the laudable Royal China (Chinese), Curve (North American) and the Gaucho Grill (Argentinian steaks). The Gun gastropub also overlooks the Thames, though not from the dining room. Views are another USP: Ubon (the Docklands outpost of Nobu) has wonderful ones from its eyrie; Plateau (restaurant, grill and bar) has a slightly

less impressive outlook, but the space-age interior more than compensates.

Those prepared to venture further into the Isle of Dogs are rewarded with the likes of low-key bistro Hubbub, El Faro (Spanish), Mez (Turkish) and Elephant Royale (Thai) – this last restaurant is at the very tip of the Isle of Dogs, looking out over the Thames.

Bistrotheque *23-27 Wadeson Street, E2 9DR (8983 7900/www.bistrotheque.com).*
Il Bordello *81 Wapping High Street, E1W 2YN (7481 9950).*
Brickhouse *Old Truman Brewery, Brick Lane, E1 6RU (7247 0005/www.thebrick house.co.uk).*
Brick Lane Beigel Bake *159 Brick Lane, E1 6SB (7729 0616).*
Canteen *2 Crispin Place, off Brushfield Street, E1 6DW (0845 686 1122/www.canteen.co.uk).*
Curve *London Marriott Hotel, West India Quay, 22 Hertsmere Road, E14 4ED (7517 2808).*
Elephant Royale *Locke's Wharf, Westferry Road, E14 3AN (7987 7999/www.elephant royale.com).*
E Pellicci *332 Bethnal Green Road, E2 0AG (7739 4873).*
Empress of India *130 Lauriston Road, E9 7LH (8533 5123/www.theempressofindia.com).*
El Faro *3 Turnberry Quay, Pepper Street, E14 9RD (7987 5511/www.el-faro.co.uk).*
Fleapit *49 Columbia Road, E2 7RG (7033 9986/www.thefleapit.com).*
G Kelly *600 Roman Road, E3 2RW (8983 3552/www.gkellypieandmash.co.uk).*
G Kelly *414 Bethnal Green Road, E2 0DJ (7739 3603).*
Gallery Café *21 Old Ford Road, E2 9PL (8983 3624).*

Gaucho Grill 29 Westferry Circus, E14 8RR (7987 9494/www.gauchorestaurants.co.uk).

Green & Red 51 Bethnal Green Road, E1 6LA (7749 9670/www.greenred.co.uk).

Gun 27 Coldharbour, E14 9NS (7515 5222/ www.thegundocklands.com).

Hawksmoor 157 Commercial Street, E1 6BJ (7247 7392/www.thehawksmoor.com).

Hubbub 269 Westferry Road, E14 3RS (7515 5577/www.hubbubcafebar.com).

Jones Dairy Café 23 Ezra Street, E2 7RH (7739 5372/www.jonesdairy.co.uk).

Kolapata 222 Whitechapel Road, E1 1BJ (7377 1200).

Laxeiro 95 Columbia Road, E2 7RG (7729 1147).

Lennie's 6 Calvert Avenue, E2 7JP (7739 3628).

Market Coffee House 52 Brushfield Street, E1 6AG (7247 4110).

Mez 571 Manchester Road, E14 3NX (7005 0421/www.mezrestaurant.com).

Morgan Arms 43 Morgan Street, E3 5AA (8980 6389/www.geronimo-inns.co.uk).

Narrow 44 Narrow Street, E14 8DQP (7592 7950/www.gordonramsay.com).

Orange Room 63 Burdett Road, E3 4TN (8980 7336).

Plateau Canada Place, Canada Square, E14 5ER (7715 7100/www.danddlondon.com).

Rochelle Canteen The Canteen, Old School Building, Arnold Circus, E2 7ES (7729 5677/www.arnoldandhenderson.com).

Rosemary Lane 61 Royal Mint Street, E1 8LG (7481 2602/www.rosemarylane.btinternet.co.uk).

Rhodes B-B-Q Shack 61 Wapping Wall, E1W 3SJ (7474 4289/www.rhodesbbq.com).

Royal China 30 Westferry Circus, E14 8RR (7719 0888/www.royalchinagroup.co.uk).

Royal Inn on the Park 111 Lauriston Road, E9 7HJ (8985 3321).

Royal Oak 73 Columbia Road, E2 7RG (7729 2220).

Sabuj Bangla 102 Brick Lane, E1 6RL (7247 6222).

S&M Café 48 Brushfield Street, E1 6AG (7247 2252/www.sandmcafe.co.uk).

S&R Kelly 284 Bethnal Green Road, E2 0AG (7739 8676).

St John Bread & Wine 94-96 Commercial Street, E1 6LZ (7251 0848/www.stjohnbread andwine.com).

StringRay Globe Café, Bar & Pizzeria 109 Columbia Road, E2 7RL (7613 1141/ www.stringraycafe.co.uk).

Tayyab's 83-89 Fieldgate Street, E1 1JU (7247 6400/www.tayyabs.co.uk).

Les Trois Garçons 1 Club Row, E1 6JX (7613 1924/www.lestroisgarcons.com).

Ubon 34 Westferry Circus, E14 8RR (7719 7800/www.noburestaurants.com).

Wapping Food Wapping Hydraulic Power Station, Wapping Wall, E1W 3ST (7680 2080/ www.thewappingproject.com).

Wild Cherry 241 Globe Road, E2 0JD (8980 6678).

Bars & pubs

It's all about great music and outdoor drinking on Brick Lane. Vibe Bar packs a serious crowd into its courtyard at the first sign of summer. Bar, club and live music venue 93 Feet East (*see p67*) also has a great outside space, as does the Big Chill Bar off the Lane at Dray Walk. At weekends (particularly on Sunday when the markets are on) the whole area is a throng with hip young things drinking bottled lagers.

The closure of the Spitz in 2007 has had a negative impact on the area's music scene, but there's still plenty of creative action to be found if you know where to look. On Commercial Street, Public Life and Gramaphone offer a haphazard roster of club nights and events, while just off Hanbury Street, Corbet Place has serious Sunday sessions and creative goings-on. Pub fans should head for the unpretentious Pride of Spitalfields, the fabulous Golden Heart or the quirky Commercial Tavern. Or head up Brick Lane to Cheshire Street

LOCALS' TIPS

Forget cash machines after 11am on a Sunday in Spitalfields – market crowds mean hellish (and often fruitless) queues. Locals always recharge their wallets on Saturday night.

Indulge on the cheap at Bethnal Green's Spa London. Tower Hamlets residents get great discounts on entry – all you have to do is buy a £3 Spa London card.

For cool jewellery, vintage clothes and unusual interior design ideas, check out Story on Wilkes Street. It's open only on Sunday afternoons, but is packed with one-off gift ideas.

Take a trip to Greenwich from the Isle of Dogs via the Foot Tunnel. It's much easier than taking the DLR – it's amazing more people don't use it. You need to book these days for lunch at Rochelle Canteen in Bethnal Green – the secret is very much out.

Don't let rising property prices force you out of Tower Hamlets. Go bohemian and rent/buy a houseboat. There are loads of moorings in the borough. Call British Waterways (7985 7200) for details.

and the newly renovated Carpenter's Arms (once owned by the Krays).

At the top of Brick Lane on Bethnal Green Road, the Redchurch is a fine place to while away an evening (good music, late opening, minimal attitude); tequila fans should head for Green & Red (*see p63*) across the road. Elsewhere on Bethnal Green Road, a slick new branch of west London stalwart Beach Blanket Babylon (opened late 2007) is garnering mixed reviews from local barflies.

Away from Brick Lane, in Whitechapel and Stepney, the pub scene isn't quite so savoury (although the Blind Beggar does have three open fires – complete with two cats). Low-key gastropub L'Oasis is a better bet, with its mishmash crowd of old-timer locals, students and middle-class professionals drawn to the proper beer and quality food. The Good Samaritan (tucked away behind the Royal London Hospital) is a decent boozer that's popular with medical types. Bar and club life is hidden but promising: Indo offers a laid-back vibe, while the Rhythm Factory puts on a varied roster of quality nights and once played host to early Libertines/'Shambles gigs.

Bethnal Green also has its share of rough, no-frills hostelries – sprinkled with tastier bars. Trendies who can't be bothered to journey to Hoxton frequent the bare-bricked Napoleon Bar, attached to hip restaurant

Bistrotheque (*see p62*), or head to one of the roster of unusual nights and gigs at the Bethnal Green Working Men's Club (*see p67*). Also good are the Approach Tavern (with its upstairs art gallery) and done-up old boozer the Camel. Vyner Street's the Victory is the site of many an arty local gathering.

South to Limehouse and Wapping reveals a smattering of riverside pubs, many that have existed in some form or another for centuries: the Grapes in Limehouse (built 1720) and the Prospect of Whitby in Wapping (built 1520) are prime examples. Gordon Ramsay's gastropub the Narrow (*see p63*) offers more fine drinking. Further east towards Poplar, the Greenwich Pensioner attracts a youthful (if not entirely fashionable) crowd.

No longer considered the netherland between the fashionable East End and the wilder expanses of east london, Mile End and Bow have some excellent boozers to offer the discerning drinker. Highlights include stylish gastropub the Morgan Arms (*see p63*) and the time-warped Palm Tree (with 1950s cash register, piano and old-school regulars). Residents also head up to Victoria Park to the Royal Inn on the Park (*see p63*).

Eccentric touches are missing from the Docklands scene, though there are enough pubs and chain wine bars to get

Tracey Emin's local: the **Golden Heart** in all its retro glory.

the local office workers so drunk they won't notice. Highlights are the Ferry House and classy gastropub Gun (*see p63*), with its spectacular Thames views.

Approach Tavern *47 Approach Road, E2 9LY (8980 2321).*
Beach Blanket Babylon *19-23 Bethnal Green Road, E1 6LA (7749 3540).*
Big Chill Bar *Dray Walk, Old Truman Brewery, Brick Lane, E1 6QL (7392 9180/ www.bigchill.net).*
Blind Beggar *337 Whitechapel Road, E1 1BU (7247 6195/www.theblindbeggar.com).*
Camel *277 Globe Road, E2 0JD (8983 9888).*
Carpenter's Arms *73 Cheshire Street, E2 6EG (7739 6342).*
Commercial Tavern *142 Commercial Street, E1 6NU (7247 1888).*
Corbet Place *The Old Truman Brewery, 15 Hanbury Street, E1 6QR (7770 6028).*
Ferry House *26 Ferry Street, E14 3DT (7537 9587).*
Golden Heart *110 Commercial Street, E1 6LZ (7247 2158).*
Good Samaritan *87 Turner Street, E1 2AE (7247 9146).*
Gramaphone *60-62 Commercial Street, E1 6LT (7377 5332/www.thegramaphone.co.uk).*
Grapes *76 Narrow Street, E14 8BP (7987 4396).*
Greenwich Pensioner *2 Bazely Street, E14 0ES (7987 4414).*
Indo *133 Whitechapel Road, E1 1DT (7247 4926).*
Napoleon Bar *Bistrotheque, 23-27 Wadeson Street, E2 9DR (8983 7900/www.bistrotheque. com).*
L'Oasis *237 Mile End Road, E1 4AA (7702 7051/www.loasisstepney.co.uk).*
Palm Tree *127 Grove Road, E3 5BH (8980 2918).*
Pride of Spitalfields *3 Heneage Street, E1 5LJ (7247 8933).*
Prospect of Whitby *57 Wapping Wall, E1W 3SH (7481 1095).*
Public Life *82A Commercial Street, E1 6LY (7375 1631/www.publiclife.org.uk).*
Redchurch *107 Redchurch Street, E2 7DL (7729 8333).*
Rhythm Factory *16-18 Whitechapel Road, E1 1EW (7375 3774/www.rhythmfactory.co.uk).*
Vibe Bar *Old Truman Brewery, 91-95 Brick Lane, E1 6QL (7377 2899/www.vibe-bar.co.uk).*
Victory *27 Vyner Street, E2 2DQ (8980 5305).*

Shops

In Tower Hamlets, Sunday is a day of retail not rest. It's the day that stallholders at Spitalfields (firmly back in business after summer 2007 saw its main building close for refurbishment; also open weekdays) Sunday (Up)Market, Brick Lane and Columbia Road set up shop. Columbia Road is pick of the bunch for all things horticultural and starts early (the 8am crowd gets the choice blooms). It's testimony to the market's success that trading on Sunday mornings alone is enough to sustain many of the shopkeepers that line the streets either side of the stalls. These include hat specialist Fred Bare, children's shop Bob & Blossom, perfumier Angela Flanders and numerous homewares shops.

Development has seen the streets around Spitalfields evolve dramatically over the last five years, with names like Whistles, All Saints, Dower & Hall, Benefit and Sniff moving in. The real stars of the area, though, remain the likes of toy and fancy-dress shop Wood 'n' Things, quirky homewares shop Caravan, gifts and vintage treasure trove Story (tucked away behind a curtain of ivy on Wilkes Street) and Artillery Passage's Precious. On Hanbury Street, ukulele specialist Duke of Uke, bespoke jeweller Ben Day and vintage shop Absolute Vintage are the standouts; delis A Gold and Verde & Co on Brushfield Street and Commercial Street's Blondie (vintage) and Wine Bargains of Spitalfields are also local favourites. Between Brick Lane and Spitalfields is Dray Walk, home to record shop Rough Trade East, trainer specialist Gloria's and creative fashion store Junky Styling.

Brick Lane itself and side street Cheshire Street come up trumps for directional fashion. Rummage for vintage clobber in Rokit and everything from 1950s to '80s wares at Beyond Retro, or treat yourself to a self-designed, one-off tee at Luna & Curious's T-Shirt Patisserie. You'll find many-hued leather bags at Mimi, clothes and jewellery from Serbian designer Dragana Perisic, quirky homeware accessories at Shelf, and posh gardening and kitchen gear at Labour & Wait.

Brick Lane and Petticoat Lane Markets, meanwhile, are a throwback to a different era, with geezers selling cheap pants and fruit and veg by the bowlful. Towards the top of Brick Lane and its junction with Bethnal Green Road, makeshift stalls set up on blankets on the pavement (selling chipped teapots, '80s videos and other odds and ends) are another quirk of the East End. North of Bethnal Green Road, head for hip jeweller Tatty Devine and affordable,

TRANSPORT

Tube stations *Central* Bethnal Green, Mile End; *District* Tower Hill; *District/ Hammersmith & City* Aldgate East, Whitechapel, Stepney Green, Mile End, Bow Road, Bromley-by-Bow; *East London* (replacement bus service until 2010) Whitechapel, Shadwell, Wapping; *DLR* Tower Gateway, Shadwell, Limehouse, Westferry, Poplar; All Saints, Langdon Park, Devons Road, Bow Church; Blackwall, East India; West India Quay, Canary Wharf, Heron Quays, South Quay, Crossharbour, Mudchute, Island Gardens; *Jubilee* Canary Wharf
Rail stations *c2c* Limehouse; *one* Bethnal Green, Cambridge Heath
Main bus routes *into central London* 8, 15, 25, 26, 48, 55, 100, 188, 205, 381, 388; *night buses* N8, N15, N26, N55, N106, N108, N277, N381; *24-hour buses* 8, 25, 108, 277
River commuter and leisure boat services to/from central London, with piers at St Katharine's Dock, Masthouse Terrace and Canary Wharf
Developments East London line closed for extension work in December 2007; due to reopen as overland service in 2010 with a new station at Shoreditch High Street

innovative furniture maker Unto This Last. Alternatively, take a walk east along Bethnal Green Road. Here a string of nondescript discount stores and cheap supermarkets is brightened up by Asian clothes shops, wedding shops and jewellers. Bethnal Green Road and Roman Road street markets are lively places to buy the usual mix of household goods and food.

Tatty shops are the norm as Bethnal Green Road gives way to Roman Road, but there are a few above-average clothes shops: Blush sells women's streetwear, while its brother store Rockafella caters for men. Further east there are some designer options: swish boutique Pure, which sells shoes and bags by the likes of D&G, plus men's and women's branches of mini-chain Zee & Co. Roman Road is also home to record shop Rhythm Division.

The nicest shopping enclave near Victoria Park is just over the borough line in Hackney. Here, along and off Lauriston Road, small, independent shops such as friendly boutique Sublime and sweet toyshop Play, plus a handful of gift and antiques shops, provide succour to well-heeled locals. On Victoria Park Road you'll find excellent children's bookshop Victoria Park Books.

Stepney and Whitechapel offer more Asian clothes stores and grocers, plus the stalls of Whitechapel Market and a huge Sainsbury's. On Mile End Road in Stepney Green you'll find a very different shopping experience: a giant retail park, with branches of PC World, Halfords and Currys. Over in St Katharine's Docks sits a large Waitrose.

East into the Isle of Dogs, the best shopping can be found in the complex of subterranean malls around Canary Wharf, where pretty much every chain you can think of (Boots, Topshop, Reiss, the White Company, mobile-phone shops galore) has set up to cater to the legions of suited drones that flood the place on their lunch breaks. There's also a big branch of Waitrose (with eat-in food stalls).

Just north of Canary Wharf is a shopping centre from a different age – the giant Billingsgate fish market (you'll see its great plastic sign from Trafalgar Way at the east end of the Canary Wharf complex). Catering mainly to wholesale customers, there are nevertheless great stalls here for the individual: seafood, snacks, accessories and cooking utensils.

After the sheen of Canary Wharf, the street market on Chrisp Street in Poplar is a desolate place: it offers the usual cheap clothes and fruit and veg. On nearby Market Way, Polish grocery Polvital sells tinned food, Polish confectionery and excellent sourdough bread.

A Gold *42 Brushfield Street, E1 6AG (7247 2487/www.agold.co.uk).*
Absolute Vintage *15 Hanbury Street, E1 6QR (7247 3883/www.absolutevintage.co.uk).*
Angela Flanders *96 Columbia Road, E2 7QB (7739 7555/www.angelaflanders-perfumer.com).*
Ben Day *18 Hanbury Street, E1 6QR (7247 9977/www.benday.co.uk).*
Beyond Retro *110-112 Cheshire Street, E2 6EJ (7613 3636/www.beyondretro.com).*
Billingsgate Market *Trafalgar Way, E14 5ST (7987 1118).*
Blondie *Unit 2, 114-118 Commercial Street, E1 6NF (7247 0050).*
Blush *79 Roman Road, E2 0QN (8981 0011).*
Bob & Blossom *140 Columbia Road, E2 7RG (7739 4737/www.bobandblossom.com).*

Brick Lane Market *Brick Lane (north of railway bridge), Cygnet Street, Sclater Street, E1; Bacon Street, Cheshire Street, E2 (7364 1717).*
Caravan *11 Lamb Street, E1 6EA (7247 6467/ www.caravanstyle.com).*
Columbia Road Flower Market *Columbia Road, between Gosset Street & Royal Oak pub, E2 (www.columbia-flower-market.freeweb space.com).*
Dragana Perisic *30 Cheshire Street, E2 6EH (7739 4484/www.draganaperisic.com).*
Duke of Uke *22 Hanbury Street, E1 6QR (7247 7924/www.dukeofuke.co.uk).*
Fred Bare *118 Columbia Road, E2 7RG (7729 6962/www.fredbare.co.uk).*
Gloria's *6 Dray Walk, E1 6QL (7770 6222).*
Junky Styling *12 Dray Walk, Old Truman Brewery, 91-95 Brick Lane, E1 6RF (7247 1883/www.junkystyling.co.uk).*
Labour & Wait *18 Cheshire Street, E2 6EH (7729 6253/www.labourandwait.co.uk).*
Luna & Curious *198 Brick Lane, E1 6SA (7033 4411/www.lunaandcurious.com).*
Mimi *40 Cheshire Street, E2 6EH (7729 6699).*
Old Spitalfields Market *Commercial Street between Lamb Street & Brushfield Street, E1 (7247 8556/www.visitspitalfields.com).*
Petticoat Lane Market *Middlesex Street, Goulston Street, New Goulston Street, Toynbee Street, Wentworth Street, Bell Lane, Cobb Street, Leyden Street, Strype Street, E1 (7364 1717/ www.towerhamlets.gov.uk).*
Play *89 Lauriston Road, E9 7HJ (8510 9960/ www.playtoyshops.com).*
Polvital *11 Market Way, E14 3TB (7093 4091).*
Precious *16 Artillery Passage, E1 7LJ (7377 6668).*
Pure *430 Roman Road, E3 5LU (8983 2004/ www.puree3.com).*
Rhythm Division *391 Roman Road, E3 5QS (8981 2203/www.rhythmdivision.co.uk).*
Rockafella *81 Roman Road, E2 0QN (8981 5934).*
Rokit *101 & 107 Brick Lane, E1 6SE (7375 3864/www.rokit.co.uk).*
Roman Road Market *Roman Road, between Parnell Road & St Stephen's Road, E3 (7364 1717).*
Rough Trade East *Dray Walk, Old Truman Brewery, 91 Brick Lane, E1 6QL (7392 7788/ www.roughtrade.com).*
Shelf *40 Cheshire Street, E2 6EH (7739 9444/ www.helpyourshelf.co.uk).*
Story *4 Wilkes Street, E1 6QF (7377 0313).*
Sublime *225 Victoria Park Road, E9 7HJ (8986 7243).*
Sunday (Up)Market *Old Truman Brewery (entrances on Brick Lane & Hanbury Street), E1 (7770 6100/www.sundayupmarket.co.uk).*
Tatty Devine *236 Brick Lane, E2 7EB (7739 9191/www.tattydevine.com).*
Unto This Last *230 Brick Lane, E2 7EB (7613 0882/www.untothislast.co.uk).*
Verde & Co *40 Brushfield Street, E1 6AG (7247 1924).*

Victoria Park Books *175 Victoria Park Road, E9 7HD (8986 1124/www.victoriaparkbooks. co.uk).*
Wood 'n' Things *57 Brushfield Street, Old Spitalfields Market, E1 6AA (7247 6275/ www.woodnthings.uk.com).*
Wine Bargains of Spitalfields *139 Commercial Street, E1 6BJ (7375 2628).*
Zee & Co *www.zeeandco.co.uk; women 416 Roman Road, E3 5LU (8980 2122); men 454 Roman Road, E3 5LU (8983 3383).*

Arts & attractions

Cinemas & theatres

Mile End Genesis Cinema *93-95 Mile End Road, E1 4UJ (7780 2000/www.genesis-cinema.co.uk).*
Cineworld West India Quay *Hertsmere Road, E14 4AL (0871 200 2000/www.cineworld.co.uk).*

Galleries & museums

Chisenhale Gallery *64-84 Chisenhale Road, E3 5QZ (8981 4518/www.chisenhale.org.uk).*
Denis Severs' House *18 Folgate Street, E1 6BX (7247 4013/www.dennissevershouse.co.uk).* Curious but fascinating period museum: a 'still life drama' in a splendid Huguenot house.
Museum in Docklands *No.1 Warehouse, West India Quay, Hertsmere Road, E14 4AL (0870 444 3857/www.museumindocklands. org.uk).* Huge local museum covering everything from the Blitz to the area's modern development.
V&A Museum of Childhood *Cambridge Heath Road, E2 9PA (8983 5200/www. museumofchildhood.org.uk).* The V&A's East End offshoot.
Ragged School Museum *46-50 Copperfield Road, E3 4RR (8980 6405/www.raggedschool museum.org.uk).* Examining Dr Barnardo's Victorian education of the East End's urchins.
Royal London Hospital Archives & Museum *St Phillip's Church, Newark Street, E1 1BB (7377 7608/www.medicalmuseums.org).*
Whitechapel Art Gallery *80-82 Whitechapel High Street, E1 7QX (7522 7888/www. whitechapel.org).* One of the capital's leading contemporary galleries.

Music & comedy venues

Bethnal Green Working Men's Club *42-44 Pollard Row, E2 6NB (7739 2727/ www.workersplaytime.net).*
Jongleurs Bow *Bow Wharf, 221 Grove Road, E3 5SN (0870 787 0707/www.jongleurs.com).*
93 Feet East *150 Brick Lane, E1 6QL (7247 3293/www.93feeteast.co.uk).*

Other attractions

Chisenhale Dance Space *64-84 Chisenhale Road, E3 5QZ (8981 6617/www.chisenhale dancespace.co.uk).* Dance classes and workshops.
East London Mosque & London Muslim Centre *46-92 Whitechapel Road, E1 1JQ (7650 3000/www.eastlondonmosque.org.uk).*

Mudchute Park & Farm *Pier Street, E14 3HP (7515 5901/www.mudchute.org).*
Spitalfields City Farm *Buxton Street, E1 5AR (7247 8762/www.spitalfieldscityfarm.org).*

Sport & fitness

Tower Hamlet's leisure facilities have improved in the last couple of years. York Hall's face-lift is now complete, including a makeover of its Turkish baths – now budget spa facility Spa London (opened 2007). There's also a new centre in Mile End Park, opened in 2006. Mile End Climbing Wall draws climbers from across the capital, while the Docklands Sailing & Watersports Centre on Millwall Dock offers everything from dragon boat racing to Royal Yachting Association courses.

Gyms & leisure centres
Bodylines *461 Bethnal Green Road, E2 9QH (7613 1631/www.bodylinesfitness.co.uk).* Private.
Fitness First *www.fitnessfirst.com: Bow Wharf, Grove Road, E3 5SN (8980 2442); Spitalfields Health & Fitness, Fruit Exchange Building, Brushfield Street, E1 6EP (7655 4316); 15 Thomas More Square, E1 9YZ (7702 2777).* Private.
Island Sports Trust *100 Manchester Road, E14 3DW (7537 4762/www.islandsports trust.co.uk).*
John Orwell Sports Centre *Tench Street, E1 9QD (7488 9421/www.gll.org).*
Langdon Park Leisure Centre *35 Byron Street, E14 0RZ (7987 3575/www.gll.org).*
LA Fitness *www.lafitness.co.uk; 90 Mansell Street, E1 8AL (7265 1544); West India Quay, 5 Hertsmere Road, E14 4AN (7531 0191).* Private.
Mile End Park Leisure Centre *190 Burdett Road, E3 4HL (8709 4420/www.gll.co.uk).*
Mile End Park Stadium *Rhodeswell Road, E14 7TW (8709 4420/www.gll.co.uk).*
Muscle Works *2 Hague Street, E2 6HN (7256 0916/www.muscleworksgym.co.uk).*

RECYCLING
No. of bring sites 55 (for nearest, visit www.recycleforlondon.com)
Household waste recycled 8.85%
Main recycling centre Northumberland Wharf, Yabsley Street, Isle of Dogs, E14 9RG (7538 4526)
Other recycling services furniture collection; home composting; pink sack kerbside collection
Council contact London Borough of Tower Hamlets, Town Hall, Mulberry Place, Clove Crescent, E14 2BG (7364 6666)

Reebok Sports Club *16-19 Canada Square, E14 5ER (7970 0900/www.reeboksportsclub london.com).* Private.
St George's Swimming Pool *221 The Highway, E1W 9BP (7709 9714/www.gll.org).*
Tiller Centre *Tiller Road, E14 8PX (7987 5211/www.gll.org).*
Titan Fitness Centre *164-170 Mare Street, E8 3RD (8985 1287).* Private.
Virgin Active *West Ferry Circus, E14 8RR (7513 2999/www.virginactive.co.uk).* Private.
Whitechapel Sports Centre *Durwood Street, E1 5BA (7247 7538/www.gll.org).*
York Hall Leisure Centre *Old Ford Road, E2 9PJ (8980 2243/www.gll.org).* Also includes Spa London (8709 5845/www.spa-london.org).

Other facilities
Docklands Sailing & Watersports Centre *235A Westferry Road, Millwall Dock, E14 3QS (7537 2626/www.dswc.org).*
Mile End Climbing Wall *Haverfield Road, E3 5BE (8980 0289/www.mileendwall.org.uk).*
Mile End Karting Track *422-424 Burdett Road, Mile End Park, E3 4AA (7005 0318/ www.gokartinglondon.co.uk).*

Schools

WHAT THE PARENTS SAY:
❛Even though we recently moved out of the borough, we wanted to keep our children at school in Tower Hamlets so that we could maintain links with the area. We chose the Bethnal Green Technology College, and it's great for our kids. It has a whole new set of teachers who have really boosted things. The school was on special measures, but has been taken off now. Maths is one of the big subjects; there's been loads of improvement in that area since the new teachers came in. The school is also well known in the community because of its state-of-the-art sports hall. Loads of different groups use it for matches and other activities outside school hours. I really like the cultural mix you get in Tower Hamlets too.❜
Father of two, Newham

Primary
There are 65 state primary schools in Tower Hamlets, 16 of which are church schools. There are also three independent primaries: one Muslim school and two Montessori schools. See www. towerhamlets.gov.uk, www.edubase.gov.uk and www.ofsted.gov.uk for more information.

Secondary
Bethnal Green Technology College *Gosset Street, E2 6NW (7920 7900/www.bgtc.org.uk).*
Bishop Challoner Catholic Collegiate School *Hardinge Street, E1 0EB (7790 3634/*

www.bishop.towerhamlets.sch.uk). Boys and girls taught separately; mixed sixth form.

Bow School *Paton Close, Fairfield Road, E3 2QD (8980 0118).* Boys only.

Central Foundation Girls' School *College Terrace, E3 5AY (8983 1015).* Girls only.

George Green's School *100 Manchester Road, E14 3DW (7987 6032/www.lgfl.net/ lgfl/leas/tower-hamlets/schools/george-greens).*

Langdon Park School *Byron Street, E14 0RZ (7987 4811).*

Morpeth School *Portman Place, E2 0PX (8981 0921).*

Mulberry School for Girls *Richard Street, Commercial Road, E1 2JP (7790 6327/ www.mulberry.towerhamlets.sch.uk).* Girls only.

Oaklands School *Old Bethnal Green Road, E2 6PR (7613 1014/www.oaklands.tower hamlets.sch.uk).*

Raines Foundation School *Approach Road, E2 9LY (8981 1231/www.rainesfoundation. org.uk).*

St Paul's Way Community School *Shelmerdine Close, E3 4AN (7987 1883/ www.st-paulsway.towerhamlets.sch.uk).*

Sir John Cass Foundation & Redcoat School *Stepney Way, E1 0RH (7790 6712/ www.sjcr.net).*

Stepney Green Maths & Computing College *Ben Jonson Road, E1 4SD (7790 6361).* Boys only.

Swanlea School *31 Brady Street, E1 5DJ (7375 3267/www.swanlea.towerhamlets.sch.uk).*

Property

WHAT THE AGENTS SAY:

'The prices are catching up with Notting Hill – you've got a lot more bars and restaurants here now too. The multiples are also moving in: Strada, Nando's and Tesco have all opened on Commercial Street in the last year. As the area gets more gentrified, the rents go up and the independents can't afford it any more. Even if you go further out into Bow in search of a bargain, you'll find the Olympics is coming so everyone's jumping on that bandwagon. The demand is high because you've got a lot of City boys buying, who either live here during the week or buy-to-let. Price per square foot has gone from £400 to £500 capital value, to £700, even up to £1,000.'

Jeremy Tarn, Tarn & Tarn, Spitalfields

Average property prices

Detached n/a
Semi-detached £416,771
Terraced £409,660
Flat £323,444

Local estate agents

Alex Neil Property Agents *www.alexneil. co.uk; 2 offices in the borough (Bow 8980 7431/ Docklands 7537 9859).*

Atkinson Mcleod *www.atkinsonmcleod.com; 2 offices in the borough (Canary Wharf 7001 9670/Aldgate 7488 5555).*

Black Katz *68 Commercial Street, E1 6LT (7247 0066/www.black-katz.com).*

Capital Dwellings *47 Fashion Street, E1 6PX (7375 1515/www.capitaldwellings.com).*

LND Residential *107 Burdett Road, E3 4JN (8983 9333/www.lndresidential.co.uk).*

Hurford Salvi Carr *9 Branch Road, Limehouse Basin, E14 7JU (7791 7000/www.hurford-salvi-carr.co.uk).*

Peach Properties *53 Bethnal Green Road, E1 6LA (7739 6969/www.peachproperties.com).*

Tarn & Tarn *35 Artillery Lane, E1 7LS (7377 8989/www.tarn-tarn.co.uk).*

Other information

Council

Tower Hamlets Borough Council *The Town Hall, Mulberry Place, 5 Clove Crescent, E14 2BG (7364 5020/www.towerhamlets.gov.uk).*

Legal services

Tower Hamlets Advice Providers Directory *www.towerhamlets.gov.uk/data/ community/databases/regeneration/index.asp.*

Whitechapel CAB *Greatorex Street, E1 5NP (0870 126 4014/www.adviceguide.org.uk).*

Local newspapers

East End Life *7364 3179/www.towerhamlets. gov.uk.* Free weekly newspaper from the council.

East London Advertiser *7790 8822/www.eastlondonadvertiser.co.uk.*

Tower Hamlets Recorder *8472 1421/www.threcorder.co.uk.*

Allotments & open spaces

Reeves Road Allotment Society *1 Tibbetts Road, E3 (Mr T Fletcher 7515 7833).*

Stepping Stones Farm Allotments *Stepping Stones Farm, Stepney Way, E1 3DG (Lynne Bennett 7790 8204).*

Open spaces *www.towerhamlets.gov.uk/ data/discover/data/parks/index.cfm.*

COUNCIL TAX		
A	up to £40,000	**£760.17**
B	£40,001-£52,000	**£886.86**
C	£52,001-£68,000	**£1,013.56**
D	£68,001-£88,000	**£1,140.25**
E	£88,001-£120,000	**£1,393.64**
F	£120,001-£160,000	**£1,647.03**
G	£160,001-£320,000	**£1,900.42**
H	over £320,000	**£2,280.50**

'Hackney has many faces. Young professionals, West Indian grandmas, boisterous schoolchildren, Ridley Road Market, Clissold Park. Hackney embodies the variety that London is all about.'

Diane Abbott, MP for Hackney North & Stoke Newington

Hackney

One of the capital's most exciting boroughs, Hackney may suffer its share of inner-city problems (unemployment, crime and urban decay), but it's a district on the way up. It has a cutting-edge creative scene, fantastic Vietnamese and Turkish food, animated bars and clubs, and countless devoted locals who wouldn't dream of living anywhere else.

Neighbourhoods

Shoreditch and Hoxton

Edging into the City at the southern end of Hackney, Shoreditch and Hoxton straddle the boundary between loft-living and life on the estate. Some of the most expensive warehouse apartments in north-east London look out over tracts of community housing and boarded-up pubs and shops. Residents on both sides of the economic divide put up with the slightly decrepit surroundings for the location – just minutes from the City – and the urban vibe of the bars, clubs,

galleries and restaurants around Shoreditch High Street, Hoxton Square and Old Street.

The area has experienced highs and lows in its long and chequered history. In the 16th century, this was a bustling theatre district, attracting artists whose work was considered too avant-garde for the City (including one W Shakespeare). This sense of being outside the mainstream survived the post-industrial decline of the Victorian era and the double body blows of World War II bombing and 1960s urban planning.

Hoxton's renaissance began in the early 1990s, when artists, designers and creatives bought cheap units in the fading

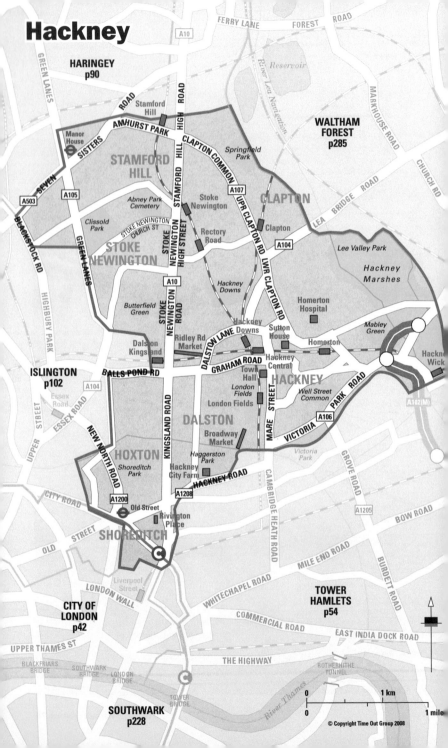

Victorian warehouses around Hoxton Square to use as studios and live-work spaces. The scene lured in YBAs like Damien Hirst and Gary Hume, fashion designer Alexander McQueen and counter-culture icons such as Jarvis Cocker before falling victim to its own success. With rising fame came soaring house prices, driving the impoverished artists north to London Fields. Alexander McQueen summed up the decline of Hoxton in a *Guardian* interview in 2003 – 'One day we looked out of the window and saw lots of people with mullets. The next day the landlord came round and doubled the rent.'

Nevertheless, this is still a desirable neighbourhood, particularly if you rate being close to the City. There are still some solid gold places to eat and drink, and transport links will improve significantly with the opening of the Shoreditch High Street and Hoxton stations on the East London Railway in 2010. The art scene has also received a boost with the opening of Rivington Place, a new space for 'artists from culturally diverse backgrounds', joining more established galleries like the White Cube on Hoxton Square.

North of Hoxton Square, high-rise council estates stretch to the fringes of De Beauvoir. It's not the most salubrious place to live, but the location counts for something and Hoxton Street has a modest street market and one of London's last pie and mash shops. Although neglected and run-down, the area benefits from the blisteringly authentic Vietnamese canteens on Kingsland Road and the elegant Geffrye Museum, which showcases changing domestic design through the centuries.

Despite the spread of affluence much of this area maintains its original gritty, urban edge. There are still pound-in-a-pint-pot strip clubs on Hackney Road and Shoreditch High Street and many walls and shopfronts are plastered with graffiti (including numerous works by Banksy and A-Z letters by local graffiti artist Eine). Of course, for many the grime is all part of the appeal – if you want a big garden and posh schools, move to Muswell Hill.

Hackney

The original working-class London suburb, Hackney was founded in Roman times near a ford across the River Lea. Once a rural idyll, it grew into a busy industrial centre in the Victorian era before sliding into decline after World War II. Over the next few decades, Hackney became the heartland of social disintegration in the capital; stark housing estates mushroomed, unemployment soared and Hackney Council picked up the European record for most demolitions by a local authority.

These days, pockets of gentrification are drawing young, wealthy professionals to the area, but Hackney still attracts superlatives. In recent years, newspapers have lambasted the borough for having the worst car crime in London, the worst-performing local council in England, the worst schools in Britain and one of the highest rates of dognapping in Europe. And if you were hoping to beat the house price inflation that has blighted Stoke Newington, Victoria Park and De Beauvoir, you've already missed the boat. Don't believe everything you read in the papers, though. Hackney has its problems, but most people who live here wouldn't want to live anywhere else.

Highs & Lows

▲ **Location** Handy for the City (for work) and Islington (for play)
The world on a plate The best Vietnamese, Turkish and Kurdish restaurants in London
Village vibrations Locals love the village vibe of gentrified Stoke Newington Church Street, Broadway Market and Victoria Park
East London Railway After decades of relying on buses, Hackney is set to get four new stations by 2010

Seediness Urban grit is a lure for some, but swathes of Hackney are grim and intimidating
Education Hackney is home to some of the worst-performing schools in Britain. Parents who can afford it look to private schools; higher-performing state students venture out of the borough
The Olympics Along with positives like urban regeneration and improved transport links, the 2012 Games spell soaring house prices and ▼ potentially massive disruption

East London foodies congregate at **Broadway Market** on Saturdays.

The bustling heart of Hackney is Mare Street, which runs south past the stately art deco Hackney Town Hall to Bethnal Green and Whitechapel. The area is known locally as Hackney Central, after the nearby train station. Following years of deprivation, the centre got a boost from the creation of the 'Hackney Cultural Quarter' in 2001. The modernist Technology & Learning Centre (housing a library and Hackney Museum) and the impressively restored Hackney Empire theatre (one of the best community theatres in London) are still going strong. Unfortunately, the third cultural enterprise near the Town Hall – the Ocean music venue – went bankrupt after just two years, followed by several new bars that had opened on the same wave of civic optimism.

Artistic endeavour in Hackney is focused on London Fields, just west of Mare Street. Driven from Old Street by soaring rents, painters and sculptors have colonised the warehouses and factories around the park, creating their own mini-Hoxton, complete with cutting-edge art spaces like Flowers East and the Hothouse 'creative cluster' on Richmond Road (home to the Free Form Arts Trust). Further evidence of regeneration can be found at the London Fields Lido, which reopened with great aplomb in 2006 after 20 years of neglect.

Out of hours, artists hang out in the Pub on the Park on the edge of London Fields – a much-needed and very popular green space – or the pubs and cafés on über-trendy Broadway Market. The Saturday market is one of the liveliest in London, attracting many of the gourmet food stalls that set up at Spitalfields. Wealthier market regulars might live in the grand Victorian townhouses to the west of London Fields, or the warehouse apartments that line the Regent's Canal (which provides a handy back route to Islington and Victoria Park).

On the other (east) side of Mare Street, Hackney Wick and Homerton have never quite recovered from the collapse of their Victorian industries. Both areas offer an unappealing mix of factories and council estates. However, with Stratford practically on the doorstep, residents are expecting great things from the Olympic regeneration programme – though a lot will depend on how Hackney Council decides to spend its share of the money.

In the far south-east of Hackney, Well Street Common nudges up against Victoria Park, just over the borough border in Tower Hamlets. Houses here are grand and expensive and residents take full advantage of the park, pubs, cafés and restaurants along villagey, family-friendly Lauriston Road.

Like most of the borough, Hackney is tube-less, so options are the bus (often crowded) or train (there are stations at Hackney Central, Hackney Downs, Homerton and London Fields).

Dalston

Long considered the poor cousin of Stoke Newington, Dalston will receive a major boost when the Dalston Junction rail station

Hackney

wagamama

delicious noodles | rice dishes

freshly squeezed juices | salads

wine | sake | japanese beers

for locations visit wagamama.com

positive eating + positive living

wagamama.com

opens in 2010. Like much of north-east London, this area has its share of run-down council estates and problems with crime, poor schools and unemployment. Despite this, Dalston has plenty worth shouting about – and isn't half as tough as some residents like to pretend.

Food is the undisputed highlight of Dalston living. Kingsland High Street and the southern end of Stoke Newington Road are home to some fantastic Turkish ocakbaşi restaurants, while the area's Vietnamese canteens serve dangerously addictive soups and noodle dishes. The African and Caribbean community is represented by an array of specialist hair and beauty shops, numerous restaurants, takeaways and bars. Then there's the excellent Ridley Road Market, one of the best places in London to buy African and Caribbean ingredients.

Though many of the shops and buildings on Dalston's main thoroughfares look like they could do with a spruce up, the area also offers roomy Victorian houses, a few interesting new-builds and, despite the increasing gentrification of the area, a properly useful high street (no chichi scented candles and cashmere babygros here, thank you).

In recent years, these down-to-earth amenities have been joined by jazz bars, theatres and politically minded cafés. The most striking new development is Gillett Square, a futuristic precinct flanked by the new Dalston Culture House art space and Vortex jazz bar (formerly located on Stoke Newington Church Street). Around the corner is another highlight, the Rio Cinema, a gorgeous art deco movie-house screening everything from European arthouse to Hollywood schmaltz.

Away from the hustle of the high street, Dalston is surprisingly quiet and residential, particularly south of Balls Pond Road. To the west is De Beauvoir, a leafy area with grand Dutch-gabled houses, marking the former country estate of the aristocratic de Beauvoir family. The air of grandeur extends to parts of somewhat less des-res Haggerston on the east side of Kingsland Road, in particular peaceful and lovely Albion Square.

Dalston sits at the intersection of several transport lines. Overland trains run east to Stratford (and the new Olympic Park) and west to Hampstead, Camden and Richmond, to be joined by the trains of the East London Railway from summer 2010 (a new station will also open at Haggerston). Regular buses serve Clapton, Stoke Newington and the City, and the faithful no.38 runs day and night between Dalston, Islington and the West End.

Stoke Newington

Before it was gobbled up by the expanding suburbs, Stoke Newington was a peaceful country village. A little of that village vibe still survives today, aided by enviable open spaces left over from the vast country estates that once sprawled across this part of town. Of course, not all the greenery survived (much of it vanished under bricks and mortar in the late 1860s) and by the turn of the 19th-century Stokey had evolved into a bustling suburb, home to hordes of commuters riding the trolleybuses down to Liverpool Street station each morning.

Today, Stoke Newington is a tale of two suburbs. The affluent middle classes congregate around Stoke Newington Church Street, a bijou strip of boutiques, second-hand bookshops, cafés, restaurants and

Abney Park Cemetery. *See p79.*

Sông Quê Café

Authentic Vietnamese Food

Open 7 days a week
Lunch: 12:00 – 3:00 Dinner: 5:30 – 11:00 (last orders) Sun: 12:00 – 11:00

Eat-in or Takeaway Available

134 Kingsland Road, London E2 8DY
Tel: 020 7613 3222

*"At this moment, it has to be the best Vietnamese
food in London....
Our meals at this new Vietnamese Restaurant have been
thrilling & memorable"*
Guy Dimond, Time Out

Winner of the Best Cheap Eats category
Time Out Eating & Drinking Awards 2003

Time Outs Top 50 places you must eat before
you leave London.
January 2008

New Jazz Late

Presented by
Charlie Wright's International Bar

Charlie Wright's International
45 Pitfield St, Hoxton, N1
Old Street Tube
Tel 0207 490 8345

For more info visit
www.myspace.com/charliewrights

Open all day 'til late
7 days a week

Thursday 10pm - 4am Entrance Fee £4 2 bands a night	**Saturday Disco Night 70's, 80's, 90's** **Soul and Funk 9pm till late** Entrance Fee £4

Mon - Weds 12-1

Friday Live Jazz and Dj 10pm - 4am Entrance Fee £5	**Sunday Fusion and Funk 9pm - 1am** Entrance Fee £3

estate agents shamelessly pushing up prices on account of the neighbourhood's family-friendly vibe. A disproportionate number of Church Street residents seem to be employed in the media, and almost everyone has a baby – sitting in front of Spence Bakery with a cappuccino and an all-terrain pushchair is positively de rigueur. However, families tend to move on when confronted by the poor standards of local secondary schools.

In contrast, Stoke Newington High Street is rougher and edgier, with a string of excellent Anatolian ocakbaşi restaurants and all-night Turkish grocers, and a decent selection of high-street shops and amenities. This split personality is partly a consequence of location: Church Street leans towards Islington while the High Street looks to Dalston and Hackney Central. The change in atmosphere at the intersection is quite striking.

Regardless of where they live, residents are united by their love of Clissold Park, a vast tree-lined expanse with tennis courts, an enclosure for deer, duck ponds, a kids' paddling pool and a pavilion café. Another popular spot for a promenade is the atmospheric and overgrown Abney Park Cemetery, final resting place of the founder of the Salvation Army and the perfect setting for a George A Romero zombie movie. The Clissold Leisure Centre – a £34 million swimming and sports complex that closed within months of opening because of serious design flaws – finally reopened at the end of 2007.

Stoke Newington residents are also known for their environmentally conscious leanings – hence the weekly organic market and thriving Fresh & Wild superstore – and community spirit. This was the home of the Angry Brigade in the 1970s and bus shelters are still routinely plastered with fliers for demos, protests and fringe causes. One recent cause of controversy was the closure in 2005 of the Vortex jazz club (now relocated to Dalston), which was briefly occupied by protesters before being torn down.

Most of the housing stock in Stokey is made up of Victorian terraces, though cheap houses in need of modernisation (which have drawn countless first-time buyers to the area in recent years) are few and far between these days. Stoke Newington

also loses points for limited parking, car crime and poor transport links. Reaching the City or the West End involves a 40-minute bus journey or a 20-minute train ride. The nearest tube stations are Finsbury Park and Manor House on the border with Haringey. On the other hand, buses pass through every few minutes, day and night, and you can cycle to Islington in ten minutes and the City in 20.

LOCALS' TIPS

At weekends, get your cash early: half the cash machines in the borough are out of notes by 8pm.
Public transport is Hackney's Achilles' heel – beat the traffic by taking backstreet cycle paths (20 minutes to the City, door to door). Transport for London publishes a free cycle guide to the area.
Housing estates in Hackney have hidden secrets – take the Wenlock Arms near Old Street, regularly voted pub of the year by the Campaign for Real Ale.
Broadway Market is bicycle gridlock every Saturday, so come on foot: London Fields station is just across the park, or you can take a scenic back route via the Regent's Canal. Tired of the urban crush? Pop over the borough boundary for peaceful riverbank strolls through the Hackney and Walthamstow Marshes.
Hackney has a bohemian vibe, and you can't get more bohemian than life on a narrowboat – there are berths for hire all along the Regent's Canal and the River Lee. Contact British Waterways (7985 7200, london@britishwaterways.co.uk) for more information.
Throwing a dinner party? Grab some houmous, taramasalata, olives and Mediterranean bread from a local Turkish grocer for instant mezedes.
Sports facilities in Clapton are limited, but you can exercise your heart out on the River Lee with the Lea Rowing Club (www.learc.co.uk), one of the oldest rowing clubs in London.
Save money while you shop with the Wedge card (www.wedgecard.co.uk), accepted by shops and restaurants thoughout Hackney.

Hackney

Stamford Hill

Few districts are as strongly associated with one community as Stamford Hill. The streets between Clapton Common and Seven Sisters Road are home to most of London's 25,000 Hasidic Jews.

Driven from continental Europe by pogroms and fascism, the Hasidim follow a strict form of Judaism, adhering to specific codes of dress and behaviour. On Saturdays neatly turned-out local families on their way to synagogue are a familiar neighbourhood sight. This is a culturally fascinating part of the capital, though there's little mixing between the Hasidic community and the rest of the local population.

On Stamford Hill, the area's main traffic-clogged thoroughfare, kosher food shops and bakeries join a typical London high-street melange of laundrettes, dodgy-looking outlets selling mobile phone accessories and fast-food joints. The road is hemmed in by menacing council blocks, but the surrounding terraces are bright and inviting, with numerous Hasidic schools, synagogues and community centres.

The prettiest area is north of Manor Road and Lordship Park; houses are positively palatial and the adjacent reservoir has the popular Castle Climbing Centre and the West Reservoir, a centre for watersports and environmental education.

Most of the shops and services are clustered around the intersection of Stamford Hill and Clapton Common; Seven Sisters tube station is a short hop north, and Stamford Hill rail station is just west of the main junction.

Clapton

Squeezed between Hackney Central and Walthamstow Marshes, Clapton has an unenviable reputation for inner-city violence. Until recently, the district held the British record for the highest number of bullets shot per head of population. The good news is that the closure of the notorious Chimes and Palace Pavilion nightclubs seems to have helped reduce the number of shootings in the area. The bad news is that yellow police signs appealing for witnesses to violent crimes are still depressingly common, particularly along unappealing, kebab shop-lined Upper and Lower Clapton Road – known locally as 'the Murder Mile'.

Recently, Hackney Council has spent some money on Clapton, tidying up the roundabout area and beautifying the grubby park at the top of Lower Clapton Road. There are even signs of creeping gentrification: new bars and trendy cafés are springing up among the jerk chicken joints at the Hackney Central end of Lower Clapton Road. Housing stock in Clapton is dominated by council estates and Victorian terraces, but there are a few historic gems – most notably, the gorgeous Georgian terraces around Sutton House (on the edge of Homerton).

Flanked by the well-funded but academically middling BSix Brooke House Sixth Form College, the massive Lea Bridge roundabout splits Clapton in two. Lower Clapton has the best of the shops and amenities, while Upper Clapton has the main train station (on the overland line to Hackney Central and Liverpool Street). Parking is in short supply, and the telltale piles of glass next to recently vacated bays provide a compelling case for using public transport. Frequent day and night buses connect Clapton with the City and surrounding districts.

Perks of living in Clapton include comparatively low property prices, the proximity of the revitalised Hackney town centre and the green open spaces of Springfield Park, Hackney Downs, Hackney Marshes and, across the River Lee in Waltham Forest, Walthamstow Marshes. And with the new Olympic Park just a discus throw away, Clapton could easily be another Victoria Park by 2012.

Restaurants & cafés

Hackney's restaurant scene (the affordable side of it at least) owes a massive debt to the borough's Turkish, Kurdish and Vietnamese communities. The borough has an impressive selection of Vietnamese canteens and Anatolian ocakbaşı grills serving superior food at bargain prices.

For a filling bowl of pho (Vietnamese noodle soup), make a beeline for Kingsland Road and Mare Street where the lion's share of Vietnamese restaurants and cafés are located. Recommendations include Green Papaya and Tre Viet (on Mare Street) and Hanoi Café, Loong Kee, Tay Do Café, Viet Hoa, Sông Quê and new northern

Tube stations Northern Old Street;
Piccadilly Manor House
Rail stations one London Fields,
Hackney Downs, Clapton, Rectory Road,
Stoke Newington, Stamford Hill; London
Overground Dalston Kingsland, Hackney
Central, Homerton, Hackney Wick
Main bus routes into central London
4, 8, 19, 21 26, 29, 30, 35, 38, 43,
48, 55, 56, 73, 76, 106, 141, 149,
153, 205, 214, 242, 243, 253, 259,
271, 341, 388, 394, 476; night buses
N8, N19, N26, N29, N35, N38, N41,
N55, N73, N76, N106, N253, N279;
24-hour buses 43, 149, 214, 242,
243, 271, 341
Developments The East London line
closed at the end of 2007. It will
reopen – as the East London Railway
– in 2010, with new stations at Dalston
Junction, Haggerston, Shoreditch and
Hoxton

Vietnamese specialist Thang Loi (on Kingsland Road). Also worth hunting down are Cây Tre on Old Street and Huong-Viet on Englefield Road.

The Turkish food on offer in Hackney is mainly Anatolian, which means lots of kebabs served straight from the ocakbaşi (charcoal grill). The best of the Turkish and Kurdish restaurants are strung out along Kingsland Road and Stoke Newington High Street. For no-nonsense kebabs, pide and lunchtime stews, try Sölen, Tava and Testi in Stoke Newington or Sömine in Dalston. Also in Dalston is old trouper Istanbul Iskembecisi, which stays open until 5am daily. Mangal II is a step upmarket from the rather spartan (and now legendary) original Mangal Ocakbaşi round the corner and the Mangal Turkish Pizza sister across the way. Another successful local chain is grill expert 19 Numara Bos Cirrik, with branches in Dalston, Stoke Newington and Hackney Central.

These sit-down restaurants have been joined by a string of casual Turkish café-bars, many offering live music and cultural events; try Bodrum Café, Dervish Bistro and Café Z Bar in Stoke Newington and Evin Café Bar in Dalston. Other good Turkish choices include Beyti and Sariyer Balik on Green Lanes, and Anatolia Ocakbaşi and Tad Restaurant in Hackney Central.

Indian restaurants are less well represented, but you'll find superior South Indian vegetarian cuisine at Rasa and sister outfit Rasa Travancore (which also serves meat and fish dishes) on Stoke Newington Church Street, and reliable favourites at nearby Anglo-Asian Tandoori. Thai cooking is available at the stylish but variable Yum Yum on Stoke Newington High Street, and at numerous pub kitchens throughout the borough. For decent Chinese fare, try Shanghai (a refurbished Dalston pie and mash shop) or Fang Cheng of China (on Mare Street). Nigerian cuisine is offered by loud, hearty and decidedly low-key Suya Obalende.

Stoke Newington also has a selection of Mediterranean cafés – Il Bacio (Italian), Clicia (mixed Mediterranean) and Blue Legume (sandwiches, salads and bakes) are neighbourhood favourites. Welcome new arrivals in Clapton include upbeat Italian café Parioli E5 and coffee shop Venetia.

Fans of gastropubs should make a beeline for the Fox and the Princess (both on Paul Street in Shoreditch), the Cat & Mutton on Broadway Market or newcomer the Prince Arthur, on the other side of London Fields. Also on Broadway Market, Buen Ayre specialises in carnivorous Argentinean grills. Eccentric local restaurants include the quirky, Egyptian-styled LMNT, fish and chips specialist Faulkner's, family-friendly Frizzante at Hackney City Farm, old-fashioned pie and mash shop F Cooke (with branches on Hoxton Street and Broadway Market), and east European specialist Little Georgia (much missed for a year while it looked for new premises).

Shoreditch has a scattering of more high-end restaurants. Best-known is Jamie Oliver's Fifteen, but Hoxton Apprentice also trains unemployed young people to prepare fine Modern European food. Other contenders for a serious gastronomic experience include Eyre Brothers (Iberian) and Will Ricker's Great Eastern Dining Room (oriental). Though the Real Greek, once the purveyor of standout Hellenic cuisine, has now amalgamated with the rest of its Real Greek Souvlaki & Bar chain (all of which are now known as the Real Greek), its – somewhat dumbed-down – mezédes make for a satisfying pick and mix meal. New arrivals include Water House – a

Hackney

sibling of eco-friendly King's Cross restaurant Acorn House – which opened next to the Regent's Canal in early 2008.

Anatolia Ocakbaşi *253 Mare Street, E8 3NS (8986 2223).*
Anglo-Asian Tandoori *60-62 Stoke Newington Church Street, N16 0NB (7254 3633).*
Il Bacio *61 Stoke Newington Church Street, N16 0AR (7249 3833).*
Beyti *113 Green Lanes, N16 9DA (7704 3165).*
Blue Legume *101 Stoke Newington Church Street, N16 0UD (7923 1303).*
Bodrum Café *61 Stoke Newington High Street, N16 8EL (7254 6464).*
Buen Ayre *50 Broadway Market, E8 4QJ (7275 9900/www.buenayre.co.uk).*
Café Z Bar *58 Stoke Newington High Street, N16 7PB (7275 7523).*
Cat & Mutton *76 Broadway Market, E8 4QJ (7254 5599).*
Cây Tre *301 Old Street, EC1V 9LA (7729 8662).*
Clicia *97 Stoke Newington Church Street, N16 0UD (7254 1025).*
F Cooke *9 Broadway Market, E8 4PH (7254 6458).*
F Cooke *150 Hoxton Street, N1 6SH (7729 7718).*
Dervish Bistro *15 Stoke Newington Church Street, N16 0NX (7923 9999).*
Evin Café Bar *115 Kingsland High Street, E8 2PB (7254 5634).*
Eyre Brothers *70 Leonard Street, EC2A 4QX (7613 5346/www.eyrebrothers.co.uk).*

Fang Cheng of China *239-241 Mare Street E8 3NS (8986 0072).*
Faulkner's *424-426 Kingsland Road, E8 4AA (7254 6152).*
Fifteen *15 Westland Place, N1 7LP (0871 330 1515/www.fifteenrestaurant.com).*
Fox *28-30 Paul Street, EC2A 4LB (7729 5708/ www.thefoxpublichouse.co.uk).*
Frizzante@City Farm *Hackney City Farm, 1A Goldsmith's Row, E2 8QA (7739 2266/ www.frizzanteltd.co.uk).*
Great Eastern Dining Room *54-56 Great Eastern Street, EC2A 3QR (7613 4545/ www.greateasterndining.co.uk).*
Green Papaya *191 Mare Street, E8 3QE (8985 5486/www.greenpapaya.co.uk).*
Hanoi Café *98 Kingsland Road, E2 8DP (7729 5610/www.hanoicafe.co.uk).*
Hoxton Apprentice *16 Hoxton Square, N1 6NT (7739 6022/www.hoxtonapprentice.com).*
Huong-Viet *An Viet House, 12-14 Englefield Road, N1 4LS (7249 0877/www.huongviet.co.uk).*
Istanbul Iskembecisi *9 Stoke Newington Road, N16 8BH (7254 7291).*
Little Georgia *87 Goldsmiths Row, E2 8QR (7739 8154).*
LMNT *316 Queensbridge Road, E8 3NH (7249 6727/www.lmnt.co.uk).*
Loong Kee *134G Kingsland Road, E2 8DY (7729 8344).*
Mangal II *4 Stoke Newington Road, N16 8BH (7254 7888/www.mangal2.com).*
Mangal Ocakbaşi *10 Arcola Street, E8 2DJ (7275 8981/www.mangal1.com).*
Mangal Turkish Pizza *27 Stoke Newington Road, N16 8BJ (7254 6999).*

19 Numara Bos Cirrik *34 Stoke Newington Road, N16 7XJ (7249 0400).*
19 Numara Bos Cirrik II *194 Stoke Newington High Street, N16 7JD (7249 9111).*
19 Numara Bos Cirrik III *1-3 Amhurst Road, E8 1LL (8985 2879).*
Parioli E5 *90 Lower Clapton Road, E5 0QR (7502 3288).*
Prince Arthur *95 Forest Road, E8 3BH (7249 9996/www.theprincearthurlondonfields.com).*
Princess *76-78 Paul Street, EC2A 4NE (7729 9270).*
Rasa *55 Stoke Newington Church Street, N16 0AR (7249 0344/www.rasarestaurants.com).*
Rasa Travancore *56 Stoke Newington Church Street, N16 0NB (7249 1340/www.rasa restaurants.com).*
Real Greek *14-15 Hoxton Market, N1 6HG (7739 8212/www.therealgreek.com).*
Sariyer Balik *56 Green Lanes, N16 9NH (7275 7681).*
Shanghai *41 Kingsland High Street, E8 2JS (7254 2878).*
Sölen *84 Stoke Newington High Street, N16 7PA (7923 3822).*
Sömine *131 Kingsland High Street, E8 2PB (7254 7384).*
Sông Quê *134 Kingsland Road, E2 8DY (7613 3222).*
Suya Obalende *523 Kingsland Road, E8 4AR (7275 0171/www.obalendesuya.com).*
Tad Restaurant *261 Mare Street, E8 3NS (8986 2612).*
Tava *17 Stoke Newington Road, N16 8BH (7249 3666).*

Tay Do Café *65 Kingsland Road, E2 8AG (7729 7223).*
Testi *38 Stoke Newington High Street, N16 7XJ (7249 7151).*
Thang Loi *122 Kingsland Road, E2 8DP (7729 3074).*
Tre Viet *251 Mare Street, E8 3NS (8533 7390).*
Venetia *55 Chatsworth Road, E5 0LH (8986 1642).*
Viet Hoa *70-72 Kingsland Road, E2 8DP (7729 8293).*
Water House Restaurant *10 Orsman Road, N1 5QJ (7003 0123).*
Yum Yum *187 Stoke Newington High Street, N16 0LH (7254 6751/www.yumyum.co.uk).*

Bars & pubs

Some say Shoreditch has had its day; that London's trendy brigade have moved on. It doesn't look that way to us: the weird and wonderfully dressed hordes keep coming to the rough triangle made up by Old Street, Great Eastern Street and Shoreditch High Street, packing into ramshackle bars such as Prague and Catch or party dens like Favela Chic, T Bar and club/live music venue Cargo (*see p88*). There really isn't a want of choice here: whether it be for classy cocktails (Loungelover), local legends (Mother; the reopened Electricity Showrooms), decent real ale (Wenlock Arms), an ultra-hidden location (Three Blind Mice) or even lederhosen-clad waitresses (Bavarian Beerhouse). Bar-rammed Hoxton Square is a great focal point in summer and there are even a few decent gastropubs: try the Princess or the Fox (for both, *see above*), or William IV on Shepherdess Walk.

Shoreditch is definitely Hackney's jewel in terms of nightlife, but other reaches of the borough have much to offer. Stoke Newington is well stocked with fine pubs: Church Street boasts the best, appealing to everyone from wine-lovers (Fox Reformed) to Guinness-lovers (Auld Shillelagh), the child-laden (Prince) to the child-avoiding (Rose & Crown). New arrival Mercado adds a boisterous Latin vibe. Round the corner on Stoke Newington High Street, quality dips. The best here is probably the White Hart despite the sometimes obnoxious crowd at weekends – its large beer garden is gorgeously green in summer.

To the south, Stoke Newington High Road becomes sporadically bar-dotted

Viet newcomer **Thang Loi**. *See p81.*

Kingsland Road. Past terrific underground music venue Barden's Boudoir there's Dalston Jazz Bar (for both see p88): an effortlessly hip, glass-walled den that almost feels as if it were put up overnight. At weekends, you can sample what must be some of the cheapest cocktails in London (£4.50 before midnight, £5 after).

Towards De Beauvoir, the Spurstowe is one of a clutch of the borough's old boozers, bought out and renovated by the group behind sister pubs the Birdcage (Stamford Hill), the Three Crowns, the Shakespeare and the Londesborough (all Stoke Newington) – it's popular with a buzzy crowd of youngsters and professionals, thanks to decent-enough pub grub, funky, inoffensive music and chummy staff. In complete contrast, the Prince George on Parkholme Road stands firm against gentrification; it hasn't even got a kitchen, so slip into the period Victorian interior and order a packet of crisps with your pint.

A few years back, Hackney Central was quite a lively spot for a night out. Then Ocean closed down, followed by several of the area's brightest bars. One place that still pulls a crowd is the Marie Lloyd Bar at the Hackney Empire. Over in London Fields, reliable watering holes include the Pub on the Park, and the Dove and Cat & Mutton (see p82) on Broadway Market.

Clapton isn't as blessed when it comes to drinking options, but don't write it off. Biddle Bros is a curious new bar in the shell of a former builders' merchants, popular with a mixed, egalitarian crowd; local pub the Eclipse, meanwhile, is embroiled in a long-running battle over its name, but the beautiful 1930s interior is still a joy to all who enter.

Auld Shillelagh 105 Stoke Newington Church Street, N16 0UD (7249 5951).
Bavarian Beerhouse 190 City Road, EC1V 2QH (7608 0925/www.bavarian-beerhouse.co.uk).
Biddle Bros Builders 88 Lower Clapton Road, E5 0QR (no phone).
Birdcage 58 Stamford Hill, N16 6XS (8806 6740).
Catch 22 Kingsland Road, E2 8DA (7729 6097/www.thecatchbar.com).
Dove Freehouse & Kitchen 24-28 Broadway Market, E8 4QJ (7275 7617/ www.belgianbars.com).
Eclipse 57 Elderfield Road, E5 0LF (8986 1591).
Electricity Showrooms 39A Hoxton Square, N1 6NN (7739 3939/www.electricityshowrooms.co.uk).
Favela Chic 91-93 Great Eastern Street, EC2A 3HZ (7613 5228/www.favelachic.com).
Fox Reformed 176 Stoke Newington Church Street, N16 0JL (7254 5975/www.fox-reformed.co.uk).
Londesborough 36 Barbauld Road, N16 0SS (7254 5865).
Loungelover 1 Whitby Street, E1 6JU (7012 1234/www.loungelover.co.uk).
Marie Lloyd Bar 289 Mare Street, E8 1EJ (8510 4500/www.hackneyempire.co.uk).
Mercado 26-30 Stoke Newington Church Street, N16 0LU (7923 0555).
Mother Bar 333 Old Street, EC1V 9LE (7739 5949/www.333mother.com).
Prague Bar 6 Kingsland Road, E2 8DA (7739 9110).
Prince 59 Kynaston Road, N16 0EB (7923 4766/www.theprincepub.com).
Prince George 40 Parkholme Road, E8 3AG (7254 6060).
Pub on the Park 19 Martello Street, E8 3PE.
Rose & Crown 199 Stoke Newington Church Street, N16 9ES (7254 7497).
Shakespeare 57 Allen Road, N16 8RY (7254 4190).
Spurstowe Arms 68 Greenwood Road, E8 1AB (7254 4316).
T Bar The Tea Building, 56 Shoreditch High Street, E1 6JJ (7729 2973).
Three Blind Mice 5 Ravey Street, EC2A 4QW (7739 7746).
Three Crowns 175 Stoke Newington High Street, N16 0LH (7241 5511).
Wenlock Arms 26 Wenlock Road, N1 7TA (7608 3406/www.wenlock-arms.co.uk).
White Hart 69 Stoke Newington High Street, N16 8EL (7254 6626).
William IV 7 Shepherdess Walk, N1 7QE (3119 3012/www.williamthefourth.co.uk).

RECYCLING

No. of bring sites 82 (for nearest, visit www.recycleforlondon.com)
Household waste recycled 11.84%
Main recycling centre Hackney doesn't have a site within the borough, so residents are directed to: Hornsey Street Waste & Recycling Centre, 40 Hornsey Street, N7 8HU (8884 5645/www.londonwaste.co.uk)
Other recycling services home composting; green waste collection; kitchen waste collection; collection of white goods and furniture
Council contact Recycling Department, 263 Mare Street, E8 3HT (8356 6688/ www.hackney.gov.uk/recycling)

Shops

Satisfying shopping around Hackney is all about knowing where to look. Hoxton and Shoreditch are the most dynamic shopping areas, packed with arty, creative endeavours. For brands you won't find on the high street – or even recognise if you don't move in the right circles – head to Hoxton Boutique, Relax Garden, no-one or Start. And to accessorise your new garms to perfection, check out the cutting-edge hats at Japanese CA4LA (pronounced 'cashila'). Men's grooming products and traditional wet shaves are order of the day at Murdock, while over on Curtain Road there's a much-used branch of American Apparel.

Hoxton design sensibilities inform the stock of nearby contemporary designer furniture and interior accessories store SCP. Also worth a peek is Sh!, an innovative sex shop set up for women (men can only enter with a female companion). High-quality groceries (predominantly of the organic variety) are on offer at Kingsland Road's excellent Grocery (open till 10pm daily, it usefully stocks magazines, booze and household items as well as fancy cheeses) and Food Hall on Old Street.

Broadway Market in London Fields is another food-fanatic must. The street's phenomenally popular Saturday market – where wealthier Hackney-ites stock up on artisan olive oil, fancy bread and freshly made gourmet lunches – is joined by the kind of appealing oddball boutiques that have already colonised Bethnal Green's Columbia Road Market. Standouts include French deli L'Eau à la Bouche, shoe and accessory outlet Black Truffle, kids' shop Buggies & Bikes, chic florist Rebel Rebel and Fabrications, which deals in 'eco-friendly' textiles and cool gifts.

Foodies looking for a break from all things artisan will find a wealth of Turkish/Kurdish ingredients in the shops along Stoke Newington High Street, Kingsland Road and Green Lanes. Dalston's Ridley Road Market offers a cornucopia of African and Caribbean ingredients, with particularly good fish stalls and fruit and veg the highlights. The Turkish Food Centre here is another must. Mare Street, meanwhile, is home to numerous Vietnamese supermarkets: Huong Nam, Vietnam Supermarket and the beautifully presented London Star Night Supermarket & Video make for excellent browsing. New French deli L'Epicerie@56 is a positive sign on Homerton's grimy Chatsworth Road.

Back to bijou, Stoke Newington's Church Street has a big branch of Fresh & Wild, along with several Italian delis and a popular farmers' market (open 10am-2.30pm Sat). And with this being kiddie-central, there are also numerous shops targeting parents and children; Route 73 Kids is an excellent toy shop, and several outlets specialise in trendy kids' clothes (Born, Olive Loves Alfie, Bored on Board). Hamiltons is good for home ornaments, Ribbons & Taylor and Casino carry an excellent stock of vintage clothes, and there are several good spots for second-hand books, including Church Street Bookshop, as well as the independent Stoke Newington Bookshop on the High Street. Nearby Rouge sells eye-catching imported Chinese furniture and ornaments.

Finally, randomly dotted about the borough, but useful in their different ways, are North One Garden Centre, the Burberry Factory Shop and London Fields Cycles.

Words worth: **Church Street Bookshop**.

American Apparel 123-125 Curtain Road, EC2A 3BX (7012 1112/www.american apparel.net).
Black Truffle 74 Broadway Market, E8 4QJ (7923 9450/www.blacktruffle.com).
Bored on Board 111 Stoke Newington Church Street, N16 0UD (7254 9740).
Born 168 Stoke Newington Church Street, N16 0JL (7249 5069/www.borndirect.com).
Broadway Market Broadway Market, E8 (www.broadwaymarket.co.uk).
Buggies & Bikes 23 Broadway Market, E8 4PH (7241 5382).
Burberry Factory Shop 29-53 Chatham Place, E9 6LP (8328 4287).
CA4LA 23 Pitfield Street, N1 6HB (7490 0055/www.weavetoshi.co.jp).
Casino 136 Stoke Newington Church Street, N16 0JU (7923 2225/www.casinovintage.com).
Church Street Bookshop 142 Stoke Newington Church Street, N16 0JU (7241 5411).
L'Eau à la Bouche 49 Broadway Market, E8 4PH (7923 0600/www.labouche.co.uk).
L'Epicerie@56 56 Chatsworth Road, E5 0LS (7503 8172).
Fabrications 7 Broadway Market, E8 4PH (7275 8043/www.fabrications1.co.uk).
Food Hall 374-378 Old Street, EC1V 9LT (7729 6005).
Fresh & Wild 32-40 Stoke Newington Church Street, N16 0LU (7254 2332/www.freshand wild.com).
Grocery 54-56 Kingsland Road, E2 8DP (7729 6855/www.thegroceryshop.co.uk).
Hamiltons 96 Stoke Newington Church Street, N16 0AP (7254 1703).
Hoxton Boutique 2 Hoxton Street, N1 6NG (7684 2083/www.hoxtonboutique.co.uk).
Huong-Nam Supermarket 185-187 Mare Street, E8 3RD (8985 8050).
London Fields Cycles 281 Mare Street, E8 1PJ (8525 0077/www.londonfieldscycles.co.uk).
London Star Night Supermarket & Video 213 Mare Street, E8 3QE (8985 2949).
Murdock 340 Old Street, EC1V 9DS (7729 2288/www.murdocklondon.com).
no-one 1 Kingsland Road, E2 8AA (7613 5314/www.no-one.co.uk).
North One Garden Centre The Old Button Factory, 25A Englefield Road, N1 4EU (7923 3553/www.n1gc.co.uk).
Olive Loves Alfie 84 Stoke Newington Church Street, N16 0AP (7241 4212/www.olivelovesalfie.co.uk).
Rebel Rebel 5 Broadway Market, E8 4PH (7254 4487/www.rebelrebel.co.uk).
Relax Garden 40 Kingsland Road, E2 8DA (7033 1881/www.relaxgarden.com).
Ribbons & Taylor 157 Stoke Newington Church Street, N16 0UD (7254 4735/www.ribbonsandtaylor.co.uk).
Ridley Road Market Ridley Road, off Kingsland High Street, E8.
Route 73 Kids 92 Stoke Newington Church Street, N16 0AP (7923 7873).

Rouge 158 Stoke Newington High Street, N16 7JL (7275 0887/www.rouge-shop.co.uk).
SCP 135-139 Curtain Road, EC2A 3BX (7739 1869/www.scp.co.uk).
Sh! 57 Hoxton Square, N1 6HD (7613 5458/www.sh-womenstore.com).
Start 42-44 Rivington Street, EC2A 3BN (7729 3334/www.start-london.com).
Stoke Newington Bookshop 159 Stoke Newington High Street, N16 0NY (7249 2808).
Stoke Newington Farmers' Market William Patten School, Stoke Newington Church Street, N16 0NX (7502 7588/www.growing communities.org).
Turkish Food Centre 89 Ridley Road, E8 2NH (7254 6754).
Vietnam Supermarket 193A Mare Street, E8 3QE (8525 1655).

Arts & attractions

Cinemas & theatres

Arcola Theatre 27 Arcola Street, E8 2DJ (7503 1646/www.arcolatheatre.com). Enterprising fringe theatre.
Courtyard Theatre Bowling Green Walk, 40 Pitfield Street, N1 6EU (7251 6018/ www.thecourtyard.org.uk).
Hackney Empire 291 Mare Street, E8 1EJ (8985 2424/www.hackneyempire.co.uk). Restored Edwardian music hall; shows run from stand-up comedy to Shakespeare.
Rio Cinema 107 Kingsland High Street, E8 2PB (7241 9410/www.riocinema.org.uk).

Galleries & museums

Drawing Room Tannery Arts, Brunswick Wharf, 55 Laburnum Street, E2 8BD (7729 5333/www.drawingroom.org.uk). Gallery with a focus on contemporary drawing.
Flowers East 82 Kingsland Road, E2 8DP (7920 7777/www.flowerseast.com). Contemporary art gallery.
Geffrye Museum 136 Kingsland Road, E2 8EA (7739 9893/www.geffrye-museum.org.uk). Domestic interiors from the 1600s to the present, housed in Georgian almshouses. The annual Christmas exhibition is a must-see.
Hackney Museum Technology & Learning Centre, 1 Reading Lane, off Mare Street, E8 1GQ (8356 3500/www.hackney.gov.uk). Celebrates the cultural diversity of the area.
Hothouse/Free Form Arts Trust 274 Richmond Road, E8 3QW (7249 3394/ www.freeform.org.uk).
Rivington Place Rivington Place, EC2A 3BA (7749 1240/www.rivingtonplace.org). This £8 million public gallery and library dedicated to visual arts and photography opened in October 2007. It's the first new-build public gallery in London since the Hayward opened in 1968.
Sutton House 2 & 4 Homerton High Street, E9 6JQ (8986 2264/www.nationaltrust.org.uk). This atmospheric red-brick Tudor mansion is the oldest home in east London.

Victoria Miro Gallery *16 Wharf Road, N1 7RW (7336 8109/www.victoria-miro.com).* Contemporary art gallery.
White Cube *48 Hoxton Square, N1 6PB (7930 5373/www.whitecube.com).* Contemporary art gallery.

Music & comedy venues

Barden's Boudoir *38-44 Stoke Newington Road, N16 7XJ (7249 9557/www.bardens bar.co.uk).* Cool bar, club and music venue.
Cargo *83 Rivington Street, EC2A 3AY (7739 3440/www.cargo-london.com).*
Comedy Café *66-68 Rivington Street, EC2A 3AY (7739 5706/www.comedycafe.co.uk).*
Dalston Jazz Bar *4 Bradbury Street, N16 8JN (7254 9728).*
Vortex Jazz Club *11 Gillett Street, N16 8JH (7254 4097/www.vortexjazz.co.uk).* One-time Stoke Newington stalwart, now in Dalston.

Sport & fitness

Management of most of Hackney's council-owned centres – including the renovated London Fields Lido and long-awaited Clissold Leisure Centre – was taken over by Greenwich Leisure in 2005. Hackney also has a smattering of private clubs; standout options include Sunstone and renowned martial arts studio Bob Breen Academy. Canoeing and sailing take place at the West Reservoir Sports Centre, while the old waterworks next door houses the Castle Climbing Centre. More watersports are possible at Clapton's Lea Rowing Club.

Gyms & leisure centres

Britannia Health & Fitness Centre *40 Hyde Road, N1 5JU (7729 4485/www.gll.org).*
Clissold Leisure Centre *63 Clissold Road, N16 9EX (www.gll.org).* Finally reopened at the end of 2007.
Kings Hall Leisure Centre *39 Lower Clapton Road, E5 0NU (8985 2158/www.gll.org).*
Queensbridge Sports & Community Centre *30 Holly Street, E8 3XW (7923 7773/www.gll.org).*
Space Centre *31 Falkirk Street, N1 6HQ (7613 9525).* Private.
Sunstone Health & Leisure Club for Women *16 Northwold Road, N16 7HR (7923 1991/www.sunstonewomen.com).* Private.

Other facilities

Bob Breen Academy *16 Hoxton Square, N1 6NT (7729 5789/www.bobbreen.co.uk).*
Castle Climbing Centre *Green Lanes, N4 2HA (8211 7000/www.castle-climbing.co.uk).*
Lea Rowing Club *The Boathouse, Spring Hill, E5 9BL (8806 8282/www.learc.co.uk).*

London Fields Lido *London Fields Westside, E8 3EU (7254 9038/www.hackney.gov.uk).* Dating to 1936, this art deco lido reopened in autumn 2006 after lying derelict for 20 years.
West Reservoir Sports Centre *Green Lanes, N4 2HA (8442 8116/www.gll.org).*

Schools

WHAT THE PARENTS SAY:

'We sent our eldest to the Betty Layward Primary School in Stoke Newington and found it excellent. The schools in Hackney are very diverse, so he's gained a broad understanding of different cultures. Based on this experience, we've decided to go with the local secondary school (we also didn't want him to have a taxing journey across London every day at such a young age).

One problem with the local state schools is the lack of good sporting facilities, though many have found creative solutions – like taking kids ice-skating or sailing on the reservoir.

I went to a girls' private school and my husband went to a Jesuit school, so entering an inner-city state-school system has been a bit of a leap of faith for us. But we really have been pleasantly surprised. The big advantage of going to school locally is that the kids can be part of the community and have local friends. Plus the teachers are dealing with such diverse issues they have to be incredibly innovative. They're much less stuffy and traditional than the teachers we had at school.'
Fiona Shields, mother of three, Stoke Newington

Primary

There are 53 state primary schools in Hackney, 11 of which are church schools and two of which are Jewish schools. There are also 21 independent primaries, including eight Jewish schools and two Muslim schools. See learningtrust.co.uk, www.edubase.co.uk and www.ofsted.gov.uk for more information.

Secondary

Bridge Academy *Audrey Street, E2 8QH; moving to Laburnum Street, E2, in September 2008 (7729 4623/www.bridgeacademy.hackney. sch.uk).* Opened September 2007.
BSix Brooke House Sixth Form College *Brooke House, Kenninghall Road, E5 8BP (8525 7150/www.bsix.ac.uk).*
Cardinal Pole RC School *Kenworthy Road, E9 5RB (8985 5150/www.cardinalpole.co.uk).*
Clapton Girls' Technology College *Laura Place, Lower Clapton Road, E5 0RB (8985 6641/www.clapton.hackney.sch.uk).* Girls only.
Hackney Free & Parochial *Paragon Road, E9 6NR (8985 2430/www.hackneyfree. hackney.sch.uk).*

Haggerston School *Weymouth Terrace, E2 8LR (7739 7324/www.haggerston.hackney. sch.uk).* Girls only.
Mossbourne Community Academy *100 Downs Park Road, E5 8JY (8525 5200/ www.mossbourne.hackney.sch.uk).*
Our Lady's Convent High School *6-16 Amhurst Park, N16 5AF (8800 2158/ www.ourladys.hackney.sch.uk).* Girls only; mixed sixth form.
Petchey Academy *Shacklewell Lane, E8 2EY (7254 8722/www.petcheyacademy.org.uk).* Opened September 2006.
Skinners' Company's School for Girls *117 Stamford Hill, N16 5RS (8800 7411).* Girls only.
Stoke Newington School *Clissold Road, N16 9EY (7254 0548/www.sns.hackney.sch.uk).*
Yesodey Hatorah Jewish School *2-4 Amhurst Park, N16 5AE (8800 8612).* Jewish; boys only. Private.
Yesodey Hatorah Senior for Girls *Egerton Road, N16 6UB (8826 5500).* Jewish; girls only.

Property

WHAT THE AGENTS SAY:

❝Stoke Newington has changed dramatically over the last ten years. Church Street now has loads of great restaurants, specialist shops and a real village atmosphere. Primary schools have improved and secondary schools are improving. And you've got three-bedroom houses going for over £600,000 that four years ago would have cost more like £300,000.

We've noticed an increase in single women aged between 24 and 35 moving into the area. And Hackney as a whole is more popular than it used to be. The council is targeting Dalston as a growth area – unfortunately, there is a lot of crime, but it's really no different from any other inner London borough. You find very expensive houses just round the corner from council estates, but that's basically what London is.❞
Ian Aarons, Phillips Estates, Stoke Newington

❝Hackney is becoming a very happening area. There's a lot of good Victorian housing stock, new apartments and flats being built, and lots of open space. People moving in tend to be professionals, City workers, artists and solicitors. A lot of the original East Enders just aren't here any more, which is unfortunate. Transport links are improving: there are loads of bus routes and the 277 goes all the way to Canary Wharf.❞
Philip Castle, Sovereign House, Hackney

Average property prices

Detached n/a
Semi-detached £613,666
Terraced £459,925
Flat £255,425

Local estate agents

City & Urban *www.cityandurbaninternational. com; 2 offices in the borough (Hackney 7275 7878/Shoreditch 7729 3344).*
Courtneys *544 Kingsland Road, E8 4AH (7275 8000/www.courtneys-estates.com).*
Excel Properties *140 Albion Road, N16 9PA (7923 2211/www.xlproperties.com).*
Hamilton Fox Estate Agents *326 Mare Street, E8 1HA (8985 5522/www.hamilton fox.co.uk).*
Homefinders *86 Amhurst Road, E8 1JH (8533 6461/www.homefinders-uk.com).*
Phillips Estates *7 Stoke Newington Church Street, N16 0NX (7241 0292/www.phillips estates.co.uk).*
Shaw & Co *29 Lower Clapton Road, E5 0NS (8986 7327/www.shawco.com).*
Sovereign House *www.sovereign-house.com; 2 offices in the borough (Hackney 8533 9500/ Victoria Park 8985 5800).*

Other information

Council

London Borough of Hackney Council *Town Hall, Mare Street, E8 1EA (8356 3000/ www.hackney.gov.uk).*

Legal services

Dalston CAB *491-493 Kingsland Road, E8 4AU (0870 126 4013/www.eastendcab.org.uk).*
Hackney Community Law Centre *8 Lower Clapton Road, E5 0PD (8985 8364).*
Mare Street CAB *236-238 Mare Street, E8 1HE (0870 126 4013/www.eastendcab.org.uk).*

Local newspapers

Hackney Gazette *7790 8822/ www.hackneygazette.co.uk.*
Hackney Today *8356 3275/www.hackney.gov.uk.* Distributed free by the council; available online.
N16 The Mag *7249 9943/www.n16mag.com.*

Allotments & open spaces

Hackney Allotment Society *Secretary, c/o 41 Dynevor Road, N16 0DL (www.hackneyallotments.org.uk).*
Open spaces *www.hackney.gov.uk/parks.*

COUNCIL TAX		
A	up to £40,000	£8,68.22
B	£40,001-£52,000	£1,012.91
C	£52,001-£68,000	£1,157.63
D	£68,001-£88,000	£1,302.33
E	£88,001-£120,000	£1,591.74
F	£120,001-£160,000	£1,881.15
G	£160,001-£320,000	£2,171.55

'A palace, a park, a New River, Green Lanes; a utopian mix of inner and outer London and one of the most proudly diverse communities in the capital – there's only one Haringey.'

Matt Cooke, councillor for Bounds Green, Haringey Council

Haringey

Leafy suburban splendour meets grim deprivation in what is one of the capital's most multicultural boroughs. The grubbier parts of Green Lanes and Bruce Grove may well lower the tone set by villagey Muswell Hill and Crouch End, but this is a borough with much to recommend it – the international shops of Finsbury Park, Grade II-listed 'Ally Pally' and pockets of affordable property for starters.

Neighbourhoods

Finsbury Park and Stroud Green

In common with much of the southerly end of the borough, Finsbury Park, an area that straddles the Haringey/Islington border, is not the most beautiful of environs. That's not to say that efforts aren't being made to improve things. The 112-acre Grade II-listed park that gives the area its name has undergone a major restoration project in an attempt to return it to the glories of its 1869 opening. The stunning Alexander flower gardens have been remodelled on their original design, there's a new café and Victorian-style seating shelters. In July 2007, the park was given a Green Flag award for being one of the nation's best green spaces. The four-mile Parkland Walk, which runs along a disused railway line from the park via Highgate to Alexandra Palace, is lovely.

The area's other major feature is the train station (confusingly, this offically falls into the borough of Islington) upon which local bus, rail and tube services focus. However, despite a string of improvements in 2006 – cycle parking and so on – it retains a shabby, down-at-heel feel.

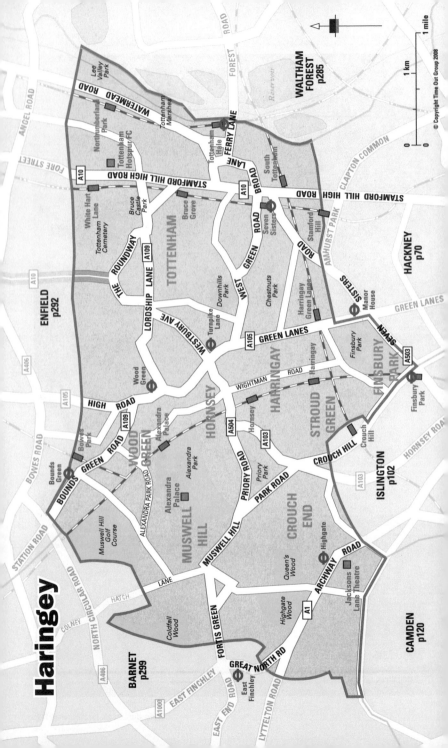

Other amenities include a slew of grotty late-opening grocery shops and takeaways, but towards Stroud Green Road (which lies on the Islington border), shopping improves, with traditional boozers flanking late-opening Turkish and Caribbean grocers, Italian delis, and Latin American and Thai restaurants. Such is the international demographic of this popular residential area, whose location on the borders of Crouch End sees Victorian and Edwardian buildings mixed with council blocks. The terraced houses of Woodstock, Perth and Ennis Roads, near popular backstreet local the Faltering Fullback, sell for upwards of £425,000. Further up towards Crouch End prices get higher still.

Another key feature of the district is the North London Central Mosque. Previously called Finsbury Park Mosque (which it continues to be known as locally), the mosque's rebranding began in 2005 following a media link with terrorism created by Abu Hamzah's extremist preaching and attendance of shoe bomber Richard Reid. It was later reclaimed by the Muslim Association of Britain in the name of the mainstream Muslim community in north London. If only they'd also do something about the horrible modern building it's housed in, then they'd really be on to something.

Crouch End

Initially developed as a settlement due to its location at the junction of four locally important roads, Crouch End's farmsteads made it an early centre of cultivation for the borough. Nowadays, it's still one of Haringey's leafier areas (residents benefit from easy access to Highgate and Queen's Woods). And, in common with much of London, leafy means wealthy.

Today Crouch End's money comes largely from the crop of young middle-class families, media and arty types who inhabit the neighbourhood's pricey townhouses (most of spoof horror film *Shaun of the Dead* was shot here, and in previous years the Eurythmics' Dave Stewart had his studio in the area – now rumoured to be owned by David Gray). They're drawn to the neighbourhood's proper local shops (bakers, grocers and the like), family-friendly ethos and villagey feel. Gathered on the streets surrounding the landmark

clock tower (built in 1895 as a monument to a local councillor) are cosy multicultural restaurants, cafés, pubs and gyms. As the gaggles of pram-toting yummie mummies that throng the streets might suggest, a night on the tiles isn't at the forefront of most residents' priority lists, so nightlife isn't a major feature.

Residents are far more likely to spend their free time musing the area's confusing parking system (between 9.30am and 5pm you need to pay to park in parking bays, between 5pm and 6.30pm there's no parking at all, and then after 6.30pm it's free. Simple, no?). There's also no tube here: locals who work in central London have to join the throng at Finsbury Park station to catch the W3 or W7 bus up Stroud Green Road.

Where Tottenham Lane runs up to Turnpike Lane tube, things become less gentrified, with the appearance of the area's estates. A large plot on the east side of Crouch End Hill is taken up by the staunchly pro-common man Trades Union Congress's National Education Centre, providing training and development services for professional trade unionists. All in all, though, it's probably telling that despite a lack of a proper local supermarket

Haringey

(Tesco Express and Budgens are the two closest options), there's still a Marks & Spencer food store here.

Muswell Hill

Haringey may be the tenth most deprived district in England, but you wouldn't know it in Muswell Hill. Sitting atop a steep hill leading up from Crouch End, this is the borough's own Hampstead. One of Haringey's two MPs, Lynne Featherstone (Lib Dem representative for Hornsey and Wood Green, and member of the wealthy family behind the Ryness electrical chain) lives in the area, and when polonium-210-poisoned ex-spy Alexander Litvinenko was installed in a residence by his billionaire Russian oligarch boss, it was Osier Crescent

STATISTICS
BOROUGH MAKE-UP
Population 225,700
Average weekly pay £461.50
Ethnic origins
 White 65.19%
 Mixed 4.73%
 Asian or Asian British 7.63%
 Black or Black British 18.74%
 Chinese or other 3.75%
Students 11.74%
Retirees 8.07%

HOUSING STOCK
Borough size 30.3km²
No. of households 96,000
Detached 3.1%
Semi-detached 9.5%
Terraced 31.8%
Flats (purpose-built) 27.4%
Flats (converted) 26.4%
Flats (both) 53.8%

CRIME PER 1,000 OF POPULATION
(average for England and Wales in brackets)
Burglary 12 (5)
Robbery 8 (2)
Theft of vehicle 6 (4)
Theft from vehicle 14 (9)
Violence against the person 25 (19)
Sexual offences 1 (1)

MPs & COUNCIL
MPs *Hornsey & Wood Green* Lynne Featherstone (Liberal Democrat); *Tottenham* David Lammy (Labour)
CPA 3 stars; improving well

that he picked (residents had to wait seven months for a £15,000 Haringey Council inquiry to conclude that there was no health risk to neighbours).

Among the area's leafy avenues and stately semi-detached residences (those without a spare million or so can forget about buying one) lies Alexandra Palace – the home of TV. Opened in 1873, it had to be rebuilt after burning to the ground just 16 days later. Reopened two years down the line, it went on to become the site of the first BBC television broadcast in 1936 (the BBC still uses the building for telecommunications). Nowadays, there are 196 acres of grounds, an ice rink at the building's north end and a bar with stunning views of north London. Events are what it does best: it's the site for what many consider London's best firework display, and has a tradition of mass-capacity gigs that includes a legendary 1967 Pink Floyd performance. The accompanying Alexandra Palace train station provides the area's only swift link to central London.

Muswell Hill's commercial hub is centred around the bustling, villagey Broadway, largely made up of independent shops and restaurants, although a humungous O'Neill's (replete with massive Guinness pelican hanging from the ceiling), a Tardis-like Sainsbury's and an Odeon cinema (housed in a striking Grade II-listed art deco building) do their bit for the chains.

Wood Green and Bounds Green

Very much the borough's nerve centre, Wood Green contains Haringey's main courthouse (the beautiful Georgian townhouse-style Wood Green Crown Court), Haringey Council's major administrative headquarters, and over 75 different bus routes. Once upon a time, higher rail fares compared with the rest of the borough made it home to Haringey's monied residents, but the fact that its current main purpose is as the borough's retail heart has been a great social leveller.

There are two multiscreen cinemas, a shopping centre with over 80 retailers and a high street crammed with major chain stores (although the recent death of Waterstone's has led to a vigorous campaign to launch an independent bookshop as an antidote to such

Middle-class **Crouch End** has plenty to satisfy parents and kids. *See p93.*

corporatisation). The streets are regularly thronged with a crowd that varies from well-heeled Muswell Hillites kitting out the kids to sportswear-clad B-boys. A collection of drunken tramps loiter outside Morrison's, seemingly revelling in the area's grotty greyness.

Indeed, diversity is the watchword nowadays: in a recent survey of the West Green neighbourhood, 51 per cent of residents described themselves as hailing from ethnic groups including Caribbean, African, Asian, Chinese, Albanian, Greek, Irish and Turkish Cypriot. It's estimated that over 200 languages are spoken in Haringey. Property here is a good deal more affordable than in the borough's swankier neighbourhoods – you might pick up a one-bed for around £220,000. In the desirable New River development to the south (between Wood Green and Harringay) prices are higher, around £300,000.

Bounds Green is a more residential area and a far quieter proposition. The grocery shops and takeaways punctuating the suburban roads (lots of decent-sized semis with gardens) are as exciting as things get around here – the area's very much a middle-class bolthole for when braving the Wooders' crush gets too much.

Harringay

Harringay (confusingly, spelled differently from the borough in which it sits) might have its low points – in 2003 Green Lanes was the site of Operation Narita, a police crackdown on the road's heavy involvement in the UK's heroin trade, only months after a 40-man turf war between two Kurdish and Turkish gangs that saw three men shot – but it has its highs too. With a mixed community of Turks, Kurds, Albanians, Italians, South Americans, Indians and Greeks, Green Lanes has an astonishingly cosmopolitan mix of food shops. The western side of the district is largely an extension of boho neighbour Crouch End, with some of the locale's only green streets and large £500,000 family homes.

Over the past few years, a mini-retail park has sprung up, encompassing a Homebase and a Sainsbury's that is open round the clock – as are most of the international grocers and kebab shops. A series of terraced Victorian streets runs horizontally between the two major north–south roads (Green Lanes and Wightman Road) and is known, inevitably, to locals as 'the Ladder'. Many of the period houses have been split into flats by canny investors.

There are good bus links to Camden, but Harringay's main transport link is Manor House tube station, whose grotty collection of chicken shops and newsagents is very much par for the course when it comes to the beauty of the neighbourhood.

Tottenham

Tottenham is not the borough's high-point. When it's not in the press for its football team's sporting achievements, you're more likely to hear its name in association with crime. Adel Yahya, one of the failed 21/7 bombers, was a resident; and, of late, the police have taken to mocking up a prison cell outside Seven Sisters station in an attempt to dissuade the local youth from engaging in gun crime (due in no small part to the fact that Haringey had the highest number of personal robberies out of seven neighbouring boroughs in 2006/7).

The glut of Spurs merchandise shops, tawdry takeaways and uninviting pubs makes the area look like it's been left to decay slowly for the best part of a century. The preponderance of densely packed terraced housing (the best surviving examples are largely on the west side of the High Road, particularly in Church Road and Cemetery Road) has led to a surfeit of low-income residents. But millions of pounds of regeneration money are now being poured into the neighbourhood – plans include the development of two new parks, more than 1,000 homes, a 100-bedroom hotel and a health centre, all expected to create 600 new jobs and an 18-storey building adjacent to Tottenham Hale station.

The area also has its fair share of history: 16th-century Bruce Castle manor house occupies the site of a castle once owned by Robert the Bruce (it now includes a small museum). This is something the Heritage Lottery Fund is recognising; the oldest stretch of the High Road is due a makeover, to install heritage lamp-posts and restore the shops to something of their former glory.

Restaurants & cafés

There's a stark east–west divide where Haringey dining is concerned. You'd be hard-pressed to find anything beyond standard takeaway fodder in down-at-heel Tottenham, while at the other end of the scale, affluent Crouch End's array of eating-out options, mainly clustered around Tottenham Lane and Park Road, seems almost excessive. Together with neighbouring Hornsey, it boasts a trio of good French restaurants – Les Associés, Bistro Aix and Le Bistro. The Pumphouse Dining Bar occupies a converted industrial building in Hornsey, while Crouch End brasserie Banners still draws crowds with its global menu and excellent weekend brunches. Also child-friendly is Californian diner Pick More Daisies. International options include Khoai Café (Vietnamese), Jerkmaica (Caribbean), La Bota (Spanish) and Wow Simply Japanese (obvious).

Muswell Hill is a bit chain-dominated, with branches of child-friendly Giraffe, Fine Burger Company, Pizza Express, Prezzo and ASK, as well as a Maison Blanc, but it also has famed fish and chip shop Toff's, gastropub Victoria Stakes (see p98), leisurely brasserie Café on the Hill and a superior Turkish restaurant, Bakko.

There's more Turkish fare in Harringay: amid the numerous cheap ocakbaşi joints on Green Lanes, we recommend Antepliler and Öz Sofra. In Finsbury Park, Turkish restaurants Yildiz and Petek are also worth seeking out, while Chez Liline serves terrific Mauritian seafood.

Stroud Green Road offers a variety of ethnic cuisines, including cracking

---

TRANSPORT

Tube stations *Piccadilly* Finsbury Park, Manor House, Turnpike Lane, Wood Green, Bounds Green; *Northern* Highgate, East Finchley; *Victoria* Finsbury Park, Seven Sisters, Tottenham Hale
Rail stations *one* Stamford Hill, Seven Sisters, Bruce Grove, White Hart Lane, Totteham Hale, Northumberland Park; *London Overground* Crouch Hill, Harringay Green Lanes, South Tottenham; *Capital First Connect Great Northern* Finsbury Park, Harringay, Hornsey, Alexandra Palace, Bowes Park
Main bus routes *into central London* 4, 19, 29, 43, 73, 76, 91, 134, 141, 149, 153, 214, 243, 253, 259, 271, 341, 476; *night buses* N19, N29, N41, N73, N76, N91, N253, N279; *24-hour buses* 43, 134, 149, 214, 243, 271, 341

Colombian Los Guaduales, South Indian (and vegetarian) Jai Krishna and a branch of lively mini-chain La Porchetta. There's also a constantly busy Nando's. Another highlight is the Triangle café, which serves everything from steak and chips to more exotic North African-influenced fare in a beguilingly intimate atmosphere.

Wood Green is blessed with cosy Greek restaurant Vrisaki, and Modern European bar-brasserie Mosaica @ the factory, but little else beyond cheap chain offerings. Pickings are even slimmer in Tottenham, although the Lock Dining Bar serves fine Modern European food. It's especially popular on a Sunday for its brunch and excellently priced roast.

Antepliler 46 Grand Parade, Green Lanes, N4 1AG (8802 5588/www.antepliler.co.uk).
Les Associés 172 Park Road, N8 8JT (8348 8944/www.lesassocies.co.uk).
Bakko 172-174 Muswell Hill Broadway, N10 3SA (8883 1111/www.bakko.co.uk).
Banners 21 Park Road, N8 8TE (8348 2930).
Le Bistro 36 High Street, N8 7NX (8340 2116).
Bistro Aix 54 Topsfield Parade, Tottenham Lane, N8 8PT (8340 6346/www.bistroaix.co.uk).
La Bota 31 Broadway Parade, Tottenham Lane, N8 9DB (8340 3082/www.labota.co.uk).
Café on the Hill 46 Fortis Green Road, N10 3HN (8444 4957).
Chez Liline 101 Stroud Green Road, N4 3PX (7263 6550).
Los Guaduales 53 Stroud Green Road, N4 3EF (7561 1929).
Jai Krishna 161 Stroud Green Road, N4 3PZ (7272 1680).
Jerkmaica 216 Middle Lane, N8 7LA (8348 2572/www.jerkmaica.co.uk).
Khoai Café 6 Topsfield Parade, Tottenham Lane, N8 8PR (8341 2120).
Lock Dining Bar Heron House, Hale Wharf, Ferry Lane, N17 9NF (8885 2829/www.thelockdiningbar.com).
Mosaica @ the factory The Chocolate Factory, Building C, Clarendon Road, N22 6XJ (8889 2400/www.mosaicarestaurants.com).
Öz Sofra 421 Green Lanes, N4 1EY (8347 7587).
Petek 96 Stroud Green Road, N4 3EN (7619 3933).
Pick More Daisies 12 Crouch End Hill, N8 8AA (8340 2288/www.pickmoredaisies.com).
La Porchetta 147 Stroud Green Road, N4 3PZ (7281 2892).
Pumphouse Dining Bar 1 New River Avenue, N8 7QD (8340 0400/www.phn8.co.uk).
Toff's 38 Muswell Hill Broadway, N10 3RT (8883 8656).
Triangle 1 Ferme Park Road, N4 4DS (8292 0516/www.thetrianglerestaurant.co.uk).

Vrisaki 73 Myddleton Road, N22 8LZ (8889 8760).
Wow Simply Japanese 18 Crouch End Hill, N8 8AA (8340 4539).
Yildiz 163 Blackstock Road, N4 2JS (7354 3899).

Bars & pubs

There isn't a massive choice of good boozers in Haringey, but that's not to say there are none. A short skip from Finsbury Park tube, the stately Victorian Salisbury Hotel offers a strong list of real ales, live jazz and poetry, and roasts by the fireside. Also in Harringay, the Oakdale Arms' darts, pool, air-hockey and table football distract from a tidy range of real ale.

Small and intimate (and the other side of Finsbury Park, along Stroud Green Road), Chapter One has a long list of cocktails; Stroud Green also has sleek gastro the Old Dairy and, on Perth Road, steady local pub the Faltering Fullback. The Triangle (see above) is wonderfully atmospheric for a Casablanca beer or glass of Moroccan merlot. The ever popular Harringay Arms attracts a blokey but friendly crowd with its 1950s decor, while the King's Head, best known for its stand-up (see p99), has a relaxed bar upstairs.

In Crouch End itself, the huge Queen's is a comfortable boozer serving tarted-up pub grub. Up in Hornsey, community-oriented Viva Viva bar-restaurant aims to bring café culture to the area, while the bar area of the Pumphouse (see above) serves proper cocktails. If you're after a boozer, the Three Compasses has pool, a Monday quiz and a good range of real ale; gay pub/club Catch 22 is near Turnpike Lane tube.

Then there are the steep slopes into Muswell Hill, offering beautiful views. The picnic tables outside the Phoenix, tucked into a corner of Alexandra Palace, have the best. Near the centre of Muswell Hill is gastropub Victoria Stakes. Chain bars are kept to a minimum here, although there is an All Bar One in Crouch End and an O'Neills in a converted church in Muswell Hill. To the east in Tottenham, drinking options are mostly confined to insalubrious or unremarkable, so try the cheap cocktails and inexpensive wines at Lock Dining Bar (see above).

Catch 22 Wellington Terrace, Turnpike Lane, N8 0PX (8881 1900).

Haringey

Chapter One *143 Stroud Green Road, N4 3PZ (7281 9630/www.chapteronebar.com).*
Faltering Fullback *19 Perth Road, N4 3HB (7272 5834/www.falteringfullback.com).*
Harringay Arms *153 Crouch Hill, N8 9QH (8340 4243).*
King's Head *2 Crouch End Hill, N8 8AA (8340 1028/www.downstairsatthekingshead.com).*
Oakdale Arms *283 Hermitage Road, N4 1NP (8800 2013/www.individualpubs.co.uk).*
Old Dairy *1-3 Crouch Hill, N4 4AP (7263 3337/www.realpubs.co.uk).*
Phoenix *Alexandra Palace Way, N22 7AY (8365 4356/www.alexandrapalace.com).*
Queen's *26 Broadway Parade, N8 9DE (8340 2031).*
Salisbury Hotel *1 Grand Parade, Green Lanes, N4 1JX (8800 9617).*
Three Compasses *62 High Street, N8 7NX (8340 2729).*
Victoria Stakes *1 Muswell Hill, N10 3TH (8815 1793/www.victoriastakes.co.uk).*
Viva Viva *18 High Street, N8 7PB (8341 0999/www.viva-viva.co.uk).*

Shops

Unsurprisingly, the bulk of the borough's more interesting shops are in well-heeled Muswell Hill and Crouch End. The former even has a branch of empire-building skincare emporium Space NK, plus the original outpost of expanding upmarket shoe chain Kate Kuba. Other shops cater to the family-oriented demographic: toys and kids' clothes, high-quality foodstuffs and homewares. Lovely Feast Deli and the self-explanatory Cheeses rub shoulders with toyshop Fagin's and the Children's Bookshop on Fortis Green Road, where you'll also find superior charity shop North London Hospice, proudly independent Muswell Hill Bookshop, Frocks Away mums-and-kids boutique and Les Aldrich's redoubtable classical music shop. The Broadway boasts superior fishmonger Walter Purkis & Sons (there's a branch in Crouch End, complete with century-old smokehouse), old-fashioned grocer W Martyn and the Scullery kitchen shop.

There's more kids' stuff in Crouch End: Soup Dragon, born out of a market stall, sells unusual clothes and toys for babies and children; Mini Kin has natural bath products and merino wool babygros as well as a kids' hairdressing salon; Red Shoes offers footwear from Birkenstock to Start-rite. Treehouse sells globally sourced treats for adults, such as embroidered cushions from India and Venetian glass jewellery,

and Indish is great for home accessories. Residents are well served by an organic butcher's, a friendly greengrocer's and the venerable Dunn's Bakery (established 1820). Right on the border with Islington, Floral Hall contains furniture sourced from France, as well as overmantel mirrors and even chandeliers, while, amid an otherwise unenticing array of shops, the Modern Flower Company is a very classy florist.

Among the wig shops and multicultural food stores of Stroud Green Road you'll find excellent fishmonger France Fresh Fish; just off it, you'll find long-established picture framer and art centre John Jones.

The Mall Shopping City dominates Wood Green; it's a useful local resource with branches of Argos, TK Maxx and HMV alongside high-street names (Topshop, New Look, Next), as well as numerous smaller shops. Result of a local crusade that followed the closure of the Wood Green Waterstone's, the Big Green Bookshop was due to open on Brampton Park Road as this guide went to press; keep up with its progress at www.wood greenbookshop.blogspot.com. There's also a farmers' market on selected Sunday mornings at Alexandra Palace.

To the north in Harringay, Green Lanes is known for its Turkish and Middle Eastern food shops – try Turkish Food Market and Yasar Halim. Nearby, the unpromising-looking Andreas Michli & Son stocks brilliant Greek, Cypriot and Turkish specialities such as figs flown in from Cyprus. Dandies without Gieves & Hawkes budgets can get outfitted by Savile Row-trained tailor George Christodoulou.

Given the low income of most of Tottenham's denizens, it's hardly surprising that it isn't exactly a shoppers' paradise – although fans of its football team may be tempted by the abundance of replica kit, leisurewear and accessories at the Spurs Megastore. There's also an excellent reggae shop, Body Music, in south Tottenham. If you do decide to buy and renovate a bargain property, the B&Q and other home-related superstores of Tottenham Hale Retail Park will no doubt become a regular weekend fixture.

Alexandra Palace Farmers' Market
Hornsey Gate Entrance, Alexandra Palace Way, Wood Green, N22 7AY (8365 2121/ www.alexandrapalace.com).

Andreas Michli & Son *405-411 St Ann's Road, N15 3JL (8802 0188).*
Body Music *261 High Road, N15 4RR (8802 0146).*
Cheeses *13 Fortis Green Road, N10 3HP (8444 9141).*
Children's Bookshop *29 Fortis Green Road, N10 3HP (8444 5500).*
Dunn's Bakery *6 The Broadway, N8 9SN (8340 1614/www.dunns-bakery.co.uk).*
Fagin's Toys *84 Fortis Green Road, N10 3HN (8444 0282).*
Feast Deli *56 Fortis Green Road, N10 3HN (8883 0117).*
Floral Hall *Corner of Crouch Hill & Haringey Park, N8 9DX (8348 7309).*
France Fresh Fish *99 Stroud Green Road, N4 3PX (7263 9767).*
Frocks Away *79-85 Fortis Green Road, N10 3HP (8444 9309).*
George's Tailors *50 Wightman Road, N4 1RU (8341 3614).*
Indish *16 Broadway Parade, N8 9DE (8342 9496/www.indish.co.uk).*
John Jones *4 Morris Place, off Stroud Green Road, N4 3JG (7281 5439/www.johnjones.co.uk).*
Kate Kuba *71 Muswell Hill Broadway, N10 3HA (8444 1227/www.katekuba.co.uk).*
Les Aldrich *98 Fortis Green Road, N10 3HN (8883 5631/www.lesaldrich.co.uk).*

Mall Shopping City *159 High Road, N22 6YQ (8888 6667/www.themall.co.uk).*
Mini Kin *22 Broadway Parade, N8 9DE (8341 6898).*
Modern Flower Company *282 Seven Sisters Road, N4 2HY (7561 9287/www.themodern flowercompany.co.uk).*
Muswell Hill Bookshop *70-72 Fortis Green Road, N10 3HN (8444 7588).*
North London Hospice *44 Fortis Green Road, N10 3HN (8444 8131).*
Red Shoes *30 Topsfield Parade, N8 8QB (8341 9555).*
Scullery *123 Muswell Hill Broadway, N10 3RS (8444 5236/www.scullery.co.uk).*
Soup Dragon *27 Topsfield Parade, Tottenham Lane, N8 8PT (8348 0224/www.soup-dragon. co.uk).*
Space NK *238 Muswell Hill Broadway, N10 3SH (8883 8568/www.spacenk.com).*
Spurs Megastore *1-3 Park Lane, N17 0HJ (8365 5042/www.tottenhamhotspur.com).*
Treehouse *7 Park Road, N8 8TE (8341 4326).*
Turkish Food Market *385-387 Green Lanes, N4 1EU (8340 4547).*
Walter Purkis & Sons *52 Muswell Hill Broadway, N10 3RT (8883 4355).*
W Martyn *135 Muswell Hill Broadway, N10 3RS (8883 5642/www.wmartyn.co.uk).*
Yasar Halim *493 Green Lanes, N4 1AL (8340 8090).*

LOCALS' TIPS

The Parkland Walk is underused by locals. The section just below Muswell Hill (accessible from Muswell Hill Road) offers stunning views of London that you can enjoy in peace and quiet.
Don't laugh at anyone wearing a kids' TV baseball cap. In March 2007, Lordship Lane saw a brawl between rival clans of youths whose gang affiliation is denoted by either a Thomas the Tank Engine or Bob the Builder baseball cap. Between 80 and 100 were involved, and it took eight policemen to keep them apart.
Appreciate the borough's musical heritage: over the years, Southern Studios (www.southern.net/southern) on Myddleton Road has played host to some of the world's best alt-rock bands. Fugazi, Jesus and Mary Chain and the Buzzcocks have all recorded here.
Pick up late-in-the-day bargains at the Mall Shopping City market in Wood Green. Towards the end of Saturday trading, you'll find the already cheap fruit and veg being offered for jaw-droppingly low prices.

Arts & attractions

Cinemas & theatres
Cineworld Wood Green *Wood Green Shopping City, off Noel Park Road, N22 6YA (0871 200 2000/www.cineworld.co.uk).*
Jacksons Lane Theatre *269A Archway Road, N6 5AA (8341 4421/www.jacksonslane. org.uk).* Arts centre housed in a converted Edwardian church, offering a wide range of activities and workshops.
Odeon Muswell Hill *Fortis Green Road, N10 3HP (0871 224 4007/www.odeon.co.uk).*
Showcase Wood Green *Hollywood Green, High Road, N22 6EJ (0870 162 8960/ www.showcasecinemas.co.uk).*

Galleries & museums
Bruce Castle Museum *Lordship Lane, N17 8NU (8808 8772/www.haringey.gov.uk).* Tottenham's local history museum.

Music & comedy venues
Alexandra Palace *Alexandra Palace Way, Wood Green, N22 7AY (8365 2121/ www.alexandrapalace.com).*
Downstairs at the King's Head *2 Crouch End Hill, N8 8AA (8340 1028/www.downstairs atthekingshead.com).*
Red Rose Comedy Club *129 Seven Sisters Road, N7 7QG (0871 332 4436/www.redrose comedy.co.uk).* Steeped in socialist history, this venue and pub also stages debates.

Sport & fitness

Haringey has four large and well-equipped leisure centres: Finsbury Park Track & Gym; Park Road Leisure Centre (formerly Park Road Swimming Pools); Tottenham Green Leisure Centre; and White Hart Lane Community Sports Centre. There are also some desirable private options, such as the luxurious (and pricey) Laboratory Spa & Health Club and down-to-earth women's gym Paradise Walk.

Gyms & leisure centres

Bodyworks Gym *Fountayne House, Fountayne Road, N15 4QL (8808 6580/www.bodyworksgym.co.uk).* Private.

Dragons (LA Fitness) *Hillfield Park, N10 3PJ (8444 8212/www.lafitness.co.uk).* Private.

Finsbury Park Track & Gym *Hornsey Gate, Endymion Road, N4 0XX (8802 9139/www.haringey.gov.uk/leisure).*

Fitness First *570-590 Tottenham High Road, N17 9TA (8808 7171/www.fitnessfirst.co.uk).* Private.

Flex Fitness *Cypress House, 2 Coburg Road, N22 6UJ (8881 8222/www.flexfitness.co.uk).* Private.

Hornsey YMCA Fitness Centre *184 Tottenham Lane, N8 8SG (8340 6088/www.ymcahornsey.org.uk).* Private.

Laboratory Spa & Health Club *The Avenue, N10 2QJ (8482 3000/www.labspa.co.uk).* Private.

Paradise Walk *17 Crouch Hill, N4 4AP (7272 6857/www.paradisewalk.com).* Private; women only.

Park Road Leisure Centre *Park Road, N8 8JN (8341 3567/www.haringey.gov.uk/leisure).*

Selby Centre *Selby Road, N17 8JL (8885 5499).* Private.

Tottenham Green Leisure Centre *1 Philip Lane, N15 4JA (8489 5322/www.haringey.gov.uk/leisure).*

Virgin Active *www.virginactive.co.uk; 98-100 High Street, N22 6YQ (8889 6161); 31 Topsfield Parade, Tottenham Lane, N8 8PT (8347 7763).* Private.

White Hart Lane Community Sports Centre *White Hart Lane, N22 5QW (8881 2323/www.haringey.gov.uk/leisure).*

Other facilities

Muswell Hill Golf Club *Rhodes Avenue, N22 7UT (8888 1764/www.muswellhillgolfclub.org.uk).* Private.

Rowans Tenpin Bowl *10 Stroud Green Road, N4 2DF (8800 1950/www.rowans.co.uk).*

Spectator sports

Tottenham Hotspur FC *Bill Nicholson Way, 748 High Road, N17 0AP (8365 5000/ticket office 0870 420 5000/www.spurs.co.uk).*

Schools

WHAT THE PARENTS SAY:

'There is a significant difference in the quality of schools between the east (Wood Green, Tottenham) and west of the borough (Crouch End, Muswell Hill), which no doubt reflects their social make-up – Muswell Hill and Crouch End are very middle class and full of aspirational parents. The secondary school that does best in the exam tables is Fortismere in Muswell Hill: it's probably one of the best-performing comprehensives in London. However, it's well known locally that the work of the school is supplemented by lots of the children having private tutors. People fight very hard to get into the school.

There are two other good schools: Alexandra Park and Highgate Wood. These don't do as well in the league tables as Fortismere, but more and more middle-class parents are sending their children there because they have no choice – Fortismere's catchment area is very small. There's some evidence that the exam performance of these schools is improving, but both seem to be around the national average – so it's nothing great.

As for the primary schools, most in the west of the borough have good reputations.'
Pauline, mother of two, Haringey

COUNCIL TAX

A	up to £40,000	£954.48
B	£40,001-£52,000	£1,113.55
C	£52,001-£68,000	£1,272.63
D	£68,001-£88,000	£1,431.71
E	£88,001-£120,000	£1,749.76
F	£120,001-£160,000	£2,068.04
G	£160,001-£320,000	£2,386.18
H	over £320,000	£2,863.42

RECYCLING

No. of bring sites 85 (for nearest, visit www.recycleforlondon.com)
Household waste recycled 16.08%
Main recycling centre Park View Road Reuse & Recycling Centre, Park View Road, N17 9AY
Other recycling services green waste collection; home composting; white goods and furniture collection
Council contact Haringey Accord Customer Care Team, Contract House, Park View Road, N17 9AY (8885 7700)

Primary

There are 54 state primary schools in Haringey, 17 of which are church schools. There are also ten independent primaries, including one Muslim school, one Montessori school and one Steiner school. See www.haringey.gov.uk, www.edubase.gov.uk and www.ofsted.gov.uk for more information.

Secondary

Alexandra Park School *Bidwell Gardens, N11 2AZ (8826 4880/www.alexandrapark. haringey.sch.uk).*
Channing School for Girls *Highgate, N6 5HF (8340 2328/www.channing.co.uk).* Private. Girls only.
Fortismere School *South Wing, Tetherdown, N10 1NE; North Wing, Creighton Avenue, N10 1NS (South Wing 8365 4400/North Wing 8365 4400/www.fortismere.haringey.sch.uk).*
Gladesmore Community School *Crowland Road, N15 6EB (8800 0884/www.gladesmore. haringey.sch.uk).*
Greig City Academy *High Street, N8 7NU (8609 0100/www.greigcityacademy.co.uk).*
Highgate School *North Road, N6 4AY (8340 1524/www.highgateschool.org.uk).* Previously boys only, but now has a mixed sixth form and is converting to be completely mixed. Private.
Highgate Wood School *Montenotte Road, N8 8RN (8342 7970/www.hws.uk.com).*
Hornsey School for Girls *Inderwick Road, N8 9JF (8348 6191/www.hornseyschool.com).* Girls only.
John Loughborough School *Holcombe Road, N17 9AD (8808 7837/www.john-loughborough. haringey.lgfl.net).*
Northumberland Park Community School *Trulock Road, N17 0PG (8801 0091/ www.northumberlandpark.haringey.sch.uk).*
Park View Academy *Langham Road, N15 3RB (8888 1722/www.parkview.haringey.sch.uk).*
St Thomas More RC School *Glendale Avenue, N22 5HN (8888 7122/www.stthomas moreschool.org.uk).*
Woodside High School *White Hart Lane, N22 5QJ (8889 6761/www.woodsidehigh school.co.uk).*

Property

WHAT THE AGENTS SAY:

'Harringay Village – or whatever you want to call it – is an interesting, vibrant urban area. We're surrounded by places like Crouch End, Muswell Hill and Islington, but you can still get a four-bedroom Victorian house for under £600,000. Transport links are good too. The trend seems to be that young families are moving out of the area, while first-time buyers and young professionals are moving in. They've rented elsewhere, Islington perhaps, but can't afford to buy there, so come here. It's ten minutes'

walk to Crouch End and all its restaurants and coffeeshops. We've been here 18 months and things are definitely evolving fast. There's a Tesco Metro, and talk of a Costa Coffee or Starbucks coming soon.'
Michael Persaud, Winkworth, Harringay

Average property prices

Detached £1,399,257
Semi-detached £559,213
Terraced £424,810
Flat £250,226

Local estate agents

Browne & Nathan *697 Seven Sisters Road, N15 5LA (8800 7677).*
Black Katz *1 Topsfield Parade, Middle Lane, N8 8PR (8347 3335/www.black-katz.co.uk).*
Castles *5 Turnpike Lane, N8 0EP (8341 6262/ www.castles.uk.com).*
Davies & Davies *85 Stroud Green Road, N4 3EG (7272 0986/www.daviesdavies.co.uk).*
Liberty *www.libertyproperty.co.uk; 2 offices in the borough (Crouch End 8348 6669/Finsbury Park 7281 3773).*
Tatlers *www.tatlers.co.uk; 2 offices in the borough (Muswell Hill 8444 1771/Crouch End 8341 4050).*
Thomas & Co *415 High Road, N17 6QN (8801 6068/www.thomasproperty.net).*
WJ Meade *1 Gladstone House, Gladstone Avenue, N22 6JS (8888 9595/www.wjmeade.co.uk).*

Other information

Council

London Borough of Haringey *Civic Centre, High Road, N22 8LE (8489 0000/ www.haringey.gov.uk).*

Legal services

Hornsey CAB *7 Hatherley Gardens, N8 9JJ (0870 126 4030/www.adviceguide.org.uk).*
Tottenham CAB *Town Hall Approach, N15 4RY (0870 126 4030/www.adviceguide. org.uk).*
Turnpike Lane CAB *14A Willoughby Road, N8 0JJ (0870 126 4030).*

Local newspapers

Haringey Independent *www.haringeyindependent.co.uk.*
Muswell Hill & Crouch End Times *www.crouchendtimes.co.uk.*
Tottenham & Wood Green Independent *www.tottenhamindependent.co.uk*

Allotments & open spaces

Council Allotments There are 25 sites in the borough, most with long waiting lists. Contact the council's parks services on 8489 5670.
Open spaces *www.haringey.gov.uk/greenspaces.*

'Tucked-away boozers with open fires, weekend food markets and canalside walks – Islington has got it all. I can't think of a finer place to while away a weekend.'

Sarah Ellison, sponsorship and events manager for the *Guardian*, and Islington resident for eight years

Islington

Once a resolutely working-class neighbourhood, Islington today is all swanky boutiques, trendy DJ pubs and increasingly inaccessible property prices. Spirited reminders of its roots remain – a Premiership football team and banter-filled street market – but its child-mobbed beer gardens and terraces of refurbished Victorian and Georgian houses show this is a borough that's definitely up and come.

Neighbourhoods

Angel and Pentonville

Angel's pretty name does little to ease the frustrations of drivers and commuters forced to chug through the interchange where Upper Street meets Pentonville Road and St John Street – it's one of the most congested in London. Still, it makes for a not-unpleasant hustle and bustle around Angel station, a buzzy area that's popular as an after-work meeting place due to all the local bars and restaurants. The name comes from a famous Victorian pub that's now a Co-op bank. Look out for the giant halo and wings that adorn the N1 Centre, a miniature shopping centre that's home to one of the area's two cinemas (the other, the Screen on the Green, further along Upper Street, shows more independent films and is a real looker when lit up at night).

The Angel end of Upper Street is probably best known as a night-out destination, and this creates mixed feelings for local residents. Though the number and variety of decent restaurants are a boon, the chain pubs that now dominate the area bring with them a brash, often intimidating crowd. A sober walk along the main road at closing time

Islington

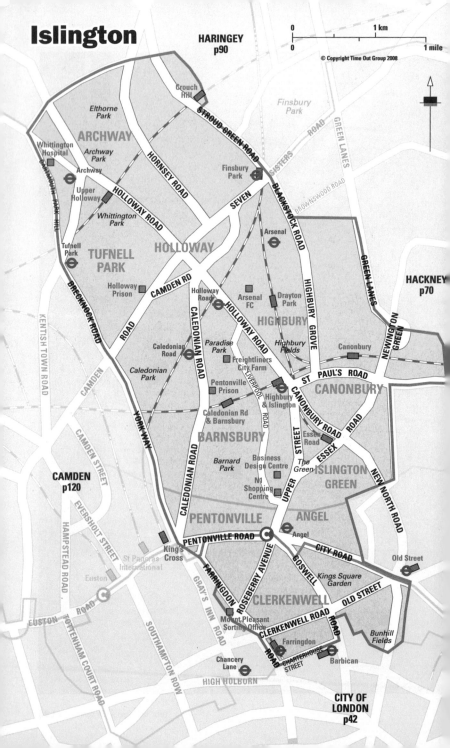

can be a grim experience, and fights are not uncommon. During the day, Angel is equally frenetic, though mostly with crowds rushing from the tube to work and to lunch and back.

As well as excellent eating options, Angel has other compensations for the crowds. Camden Passage is a gorgeous pedestrianised strip, home to a clutch of nice cafés, pubs and antiques shops as well as a flea market at weekends. Islington Green, at the junction between Upper Street and Essex Road, has recently been spruced up and now has more benches and (another) halo-themed sculpture. Chapel Market, meanwhile, is a gloriously downmarket run of stalls hawking everything from posh cheese to hair gel. The street also contains some busy late-opening bars at its far end. This, combined with the early-morning traders, makes it best suited to heavy sleepers as a residential location.

Pentonville Road itself is a rather soulless, sloping route towards King's Cross: the latter neighbourhood's process of gentrification has not spread this far yet. Dotted with numerous newsagents and cafés, plus an acting school, the road is almost entirely without character: the twin towers of Newton House, once the only buildings of note, are now a multicoloured eyesore following extensive renovation.

Islington Green and Canonbury

An area separate from the like-named green space mentioned above, Islington Green is one of many residential satellites surrounding Upper Street. In parts, it's beautiful (leafy Packington Square, for example). In others, it's hard-bitten and ugly (particularly the run-down roads around Islington Green School). Roving gangs of prank-pulling kids who never seem to be in school are a particular menace. In all, Islington Green is a prime example of the borough's dual personality: the swanky and the shit, side by side. One further oddity is the regularity of mounted police: the Met often use its wide, quiet roads to train horse-backed officers. For similar reasons, the area is also popular with local driving instructors.

Noisy, polluted, but with a certain charm, Essex Road is the bane of all those who crawl up and down it on a bus twice a day. On foot, there's a lot to see – better bars

than on Upper Street, old-fashioned traders like a butcher, a baker and a fishmonger, and quirky shops selling everything from vinyl to taxidermy. New North Road (half of which is in Islington), running south towards the City, has less to recommend it: it's a bleak, traffic-strewn route, notable only for trendy blocks of flats like the Gainsborough Studios next to the Regent's Canal (on the Islington/Hackney border) – formerly the site of film studios where Hitchcock worked. Accommodation on and around both these main roads – as well as offshoots Balls Pond Road and Southgate Road – is rarely peaceful. Living on principal bus arteries means residents must put up with chugging engines that run all through the night.

Running north from Essex Road rail station to Highbury Corner, residential Canonbury is markedly more peaceful.

Islington

Weekend strollers, picnickers and joggers abound in leafy **Highbury Fields**.

With a smattering of posh Georgian squares – Canonbury Square in particular, once home to George Orwell and Evelyn Waugh – it commands huge property prices (well over the £1.5 million mark) and is much hawked by estate agents.

Highbury and Newington Green

Arsenal FC's relocation in 2006 from Highbury Stadium to the Emirates Stadium in Ashburton Grove may have quietened this corner of Islington on match days, but it remains resolutely 'Gooner'. Near kick-off on a Saturday or Sunday, those in red and white shirts outnumber all others. Since the move, the stadium (bordered by the now distinctly more tranquil Aubert Park, Highbury Hill, Gillespie and Avenell Roads) has been transformed into luxury flats; the pitch is now a communal garden.

Roughly encompassing the postal district of N5, Highbury is often overlooked in favour of its gentrifying neighbours Canonbury and Stoke Newington, but the area has much to offer. Highbury Fields, Islington's largest green space, has tennis courts, football pitches, children's play areas and a well-equipped pool. Lesser-known is Gillespie Park, notable for its range of beautiful wildlife habitats and Ecology Centre (very popular with kids). Highbury Barn is a fashionable enclave boasting foodshops, restaurants and cafés.

On the eastern edge of Islington – a gateway of sorts to next-door Stoke Newington in Hackney – Newington Green is an area on the up, centred around its eponymous park. This thriving, community-driven green space is in the middle of a busy roundabout (traversed via a network of zebra crossings), but nevertheless draws families with its well-maintained play area and regular events. Surrounding the Green are a number of food shops and upmarket cafés, including a recently opened eaterie devoted to children, indicative of the area's popularity with young families.

Barnsbury

A residential refuge tucked to the north of Angel, Barnsbury is served by Liverpool Road, running parallel to Upper Street from the N1 Shopping Centre and the glass-fronted Business Design Centre, all the way up to Holloway Road. Packed with Edwardian terraces, it's generally much quieter than Upper Street – lacking the buzz as well as the sleaze – but can be noisy due to the regular presence of police cars using it as a short cut to trouble in Angel and beyond. The roads connecting the two parallel thoroughfares make for some of Islington's choicest places to live (fairly quiet with easy access to amenities) residences. Almeida Street is particularly appealing – home to both a theatre and a good French restaurant of the same name.

Caledonian Road is scruffier, but the skinny-jeaned Pete Doherty-alikes who live and drink in the area wouldn't have it any other way. Good travel options include both Piccadilly line and rail stations, making it a popular spot for lower-end renters and buyers. Many properties on the 'Cally Road' itself are above the likes of bookies and kebab shops; elsewhere, expect to find mostly ex-local authority conversions. The other principal residents of note are those serving at Her Majesty's pleasure in Pentonville Prison. No, this is not a part of town for the glamorous.

Archway, Tufnell Park and Holloway

The meat around an arterial traffic route, Holloway is a rather transient place, rarely stopped in by drivers chugging up and down the A1 (Holloway Road) to and from central London. Though far from pretty, the area benefits from the University of North London and an Odeon cinema built from a 1930s townhouse; it was once the site of Lord Tufnell's manor house, sited at the end of what is now Tufnell Park Road. Tufnell Park itself is pleasant enough, with reasonably priced property that, like Archway, is growing in popularity with London's up-and-comers, as well as parents looking to edge closer to desirable schools in north London. It is, after all, within sniffing distance of Hampstead and Highgate.

Scruffy Archway is seeing various improvements. Though unlovely around its Northern line station and throbbing traffic hub – not to mention the rather ugly Archway Tower – the area is being slowly dragged from the mire. Proximity to both classy, suburban Highgate and buzzy, urban Islington makes it an increasingly alluring premise for buyers and renters; council discussion regarding major redevelopment of the area seems endless.

Clerkenwell and Farringdon

South from Angel towards the City lies the mystery province of Finsbury (near Rosebery Avenue), an area designation that's been all but abandoned but occasionally crops up on maps and in the names of public buildings, causing confusion with Finsbury Park some way to the north. Some locals refer to it as Clerkenwell, a few as Mount Pleasant (after

the large Royal Mail sorting office, itself named after an old rubbish dump), while most stick to the safer 'Islington'.

Regardless, it's a lively, attractive area – kept young thanks to City University and its various sites around Northampton Square, and kept classy thanks to world-renowned dance theatre Sadler's Wells. In Exmouth Market, the area also has one of Islington's jewels: a thriving pedestrianised strip that boasts great bars, restaurants and shops.

To the south lies Clerkenwell proper, bordered by Farringdon Road to the west (a characterless road best known as the home of the *Guardian* newspaper – though not for much longer, as the paper is moving to new offices in King's Cross) and Smithfield meat market to the south. Running from

STATISTICS

BOROUGH MAKE-UP
Population 185,500
Average weekly pay £641.50
Ethnic origins
  White 75.14%
  Mixed 4.23%
  Asian or Asian British 6.24%
  Black or Black British 10.37%
  Chinese or other 4.07%
Students 11.08%
Retirees 7.84%

HOUSING STOCK
Borough size 14.9km²
No. of households 85,844
Detached 1%
Semi-detached 2.7%
Terraced 16%
Flats (purpose-built) 49.2%
Flats (converted) 29.8%
Flats (both) 79%

CRIME PER 1,000 OF POPULATION
(average for England and Wales in brackets)
Burglary 13 (5)
Robbery 8 (2)
Theft of vehicle 7 (4)
Theft from vehicle 20 (9)
Violence against the person 34 (19)
Sexual offences 2 (1)

MPs & COUNCIL
MPs *Islington North* Jeremy Corbyn (Labour); *Islington South & Finsbury* Emily Thornberry (Labour)
CPA 3 stars; improving well

Islington

LET'S FILL THIS TOWN WITH ARTISTS

EASELS

70% OFF

£12.95
WINSOR & NEWTON
DART SKETCHING EASEL
RRP £39.99

70% OFF

£64.20
DALER-ROWNEY
SALISBURY EASEL
RRP £214

PAINTS

DALER-ROWNEY
SYSTEM 3 250ML ACRYLIC
ALL HALF PRICE

WINSOR & NEWTON
14ML ARTISTS WATERCOLOUR

UP TO 40% OFF

HALF PRICE

BRUSHES

£12.95
CASS ART
HOG BRUSH PACK SET OF 6 RRP £18.95

UP TO 40% OFF

WINSOR & NEWTON
ARTIST OIL 37ML

CANVAS

WINSOR & NEWTON
ARTIST QUALITY CANVAS
OVER 60 SIZES

HALF PRICE

SETS AND GIFTS

LESS THAN HALF PRICE

A4 - £3.95
A5 - £2.95
DALER-ROWNEY EBONY
HARDBACK SKETCH PAD
RRP (A4) £8.95, (A5) £6.55

HALF PRICE

£13.50
LETRASET MANGA PACK
RRP £31.86

LESS THAN HALF PRICE

£9.95
WINSOR & NEWTON 8X14ML
DRAWING INKS SET RRP £19.95

HALF PRICE

£4.95
FABER-CASTELL 9000 12 ART
PENCILS 8B-2H IN TIN RRP £9.95

CASS PROMISE – CREATIVITY AT THE LOWEST PRICES. WE'RE CONFIDENT OUR PRICES CAN'T BE BEATEN

ISLINGTON - FLAGSHIP STORE
66-67 COLEBROOKE ROW, N1
020 7354 2999 OPEN 7 DAYS

CHARING CROSS
13 CHARING CROSS RD, WC2
020 7930 9940 OPEN 7 DAYS

KENSINGTON
220 KENSINGTON HIGH ST, W8
020 7937 6506 OPEN 7 DAYS

SOHO
24 BERWICK STREET, W1
020 7287 8504 OPEN 7 DAYS

CASS ART
WWW.CASSART.CO.UK
INFO@CASSART.CO.UK

ALL OFFERS SUBJECT TO AVAILABILITY & PRICES SUBJECT TO CHANGE. ALL PRICES VALID AT 01.01.08. CASS PROMISE, ASK IN STORES.

east to west is the area's main artery, Clerkenwell Road, once home to all sorts of craftsmen, but now filled with pricey furniture shops and expensively renovated flats. The developers haven't finished with this part of town, either – there are plans to redevelop the building that's currently home to famed nightclub Turnmills into offices. Close to the City and situated near some of London's best restaurants (Fergus Henderson's superlative St John, to name one), this is a hugely desirable place to live. Prices follow suit.

Clerkenwell Green is an attractive local focal point; good-natured pub crowds spill out on to the expansive paving during the summer. Indeed, the area is well known for its nightlife, with the enormously popular Fabric, among other nightclubs, just south on Charterhouse Street (in the City of London). This means a non-stop flow of people at weekends – hence 24-hour diner Tinseltown, one of few places in London to serve through the night.

The area east around Old Street is a bit of a hinterland between the bustling areas of Clerkenwell and Shoreditch. It is sometimes referred to as St Luke's (for the gorgeous Hawksmoor church of the same name, home of the London Symphony Orchestra) but most refer to it simply as Old Street, after the Northern line station that serves as a well-used meeting point. The busy roundabout above the station is a local landmark of sorts, with its arching advertising hoardings – no, this isn't an area big on architectural beauty. Travelling south towards Moorgate and the City along City Road, the view becomes more pleasant, taking in the likes of Bunhill Fields cemetery and Finsbury Circus, before arriving at historic London Wall.

Restaurants & cafés

The area of Islington around Angel has perhaps the best concentration of upper-end gastropubs in London. Barnsbury's Drapers Arms and Canonbury's House are both reliable, but it's a measure of the area's strength in depth that these worthy contenders are far from the best options. Organic specialist the Duke of Cambridge has gone from strength to strength since opening a decade ago, while the Marquess Tavern, winner of Best Gastropub in *Time Out*'s Eating & Drinking Awards 2006, consistently impresses with its simple English cooking. Last but not least, the lovely Charles Lamb in the winding backstreets of Islington Green is a corker: hearty, confidently prepared food, super-friendly staff and a cracking range of ales and bottled beers.

Islington doesn't lack for global cuisine, either. In Morgan M on Liverpool Road, it boasts one of the best French restaurants in north London; Almeida (formerly a Conran restaurant, now under the D&D London umbrella) offers excellent Gallic prix-fixe menus. Cosy, cellar-like Casale Franco and reliable Metrogusto (with an excellent pre-cinema set menu) provide Italian cuisine; newcomer Sa Sa Sushi serves up under-represented Japanese food; while the Gallipoli empire, with three outlets along Upper Street, serves well-priced Turkish food in party-friendly surroundings. In fact, there are plenty of Turkish restaurants in the vicinity, with Gem, Pasha and Sedir all good choices.

Afghan Kitchen (Afghan) and Sabor (Latin American) on Essex Road and Maghreb (Moroccan), Isarn (Thai), Upper Glas (Swedish), Rodizio Rico (Brazilian barbecue) and a branch of the Masala Zone chain (Indian) on Upper Street touch other corners of the globe. For a world of flavours on one plate, visit lovely café Ottolenghi, which combines British, Middle Eastern, Italian, French, Australian and Japanese influences; its breads and pastries are fantastic too.

Upper Street has no shortage of chain restaurants, of course, if you're in the mood for something familiar. You'll find branches of Strada, Pizza Express, Nando's, Fine Burger Company, Hamburger Union, Thai Square, FishWorks and Carluccio's Caffè, while the N1 Centre has a Yo! Sushi and a Wagamama. Bangers 'n' mash and other trad British dishes are on offer at the Essex Road branch of S&M Café, which occupies a beautiful art deco caff site.

North and east from Angel and Upper Street, options thin out a little. Highbury has branches of chirpy pizza mini-chains Il Bacio and StringRay Café, plus superb Turkish eaterie İznik; Newington Green has attractive French-accented café Belle Epoque. Holloway Road's budget Georgian venue Tbilisi (open evenings only) is worth seeking out too. In Archway, gastropubs the Landseer and St John's are fine places to dine, while Lalibela brings injera, wots and other Ethiopian delicacies to Tufnell Park locals. Holloway and Tufnell Park residents also benefit from the myriad dining options offered by neighbouring Camden.

Moving south to Clerkenwell and Farringdon reveals some absolute gems. Exmouth Market boasts an embarrassment of riches: the Modern European café-style Ambassador, Caribbean Cottons (which has a late-opening basement DJ bar), British restaurant Medcalf, and Spanish-North African dining room Moro, one of our favourite restaurants in the capital. Round the corner, the Quality Chop House serves classic British dishes in a charmingly old-fashioned setting. Nearby gastropubs the Easton, the Eagle and the Coach & Horses are yet more fine examples of the genre in the borough.

Budget options in the area include Tinseltown, which serves burgers and milkshakes 24 hours a day, chic little Vietnamese café Pho and a branch of cheap and cheerful pizzeria La Porchetta. For a touch of class, Farringdon Road's Flâneur combines a foodie heaven shopping experience with a great place to dine (the weekend breakfasts are fantastic), while Portal offers high-end Portuguese food. Vinoteca specialises in the pairing of reasonably priced wine with terrific Mod Euro dishes. Best of the bunch, though, is Fergus Henderson's seminal St John – a world-class, world-famous British restaurant that has managed to remain an extremely congenial venue. Order the bone marrow – you won't regret it.

Afghan Kitchen *35 Islington Green, N1 8DU (7359 8019).*
Almeida *30 Almeida Street, N1 1AD (7354 4777/www.almeida-restaurant.co.uk).*
Ambassador *55 Exmouth Market, EC1R 4QL (7837 0009/www.theambassador cafe.co.uk).*
Il Bacio Highbury *184 Blackstock Road, N5 1HA (7226 3339/www.ilbaciohighbury.co.uk).*
Belle Epoque Pâtisserie *37 Newington Green, N16 9PR (7249 2222/www.belle epoque.co.uk).*
Casale Franco *134-137 Upper Street, N1 1QP (7226 8994).*
Charles Lamb *16 Elia Street, N1 8DE (7837 5040/www.thecharleslambpub.com).*
Coach & Horses *26-28 Ray Street, EC1R 3DJ (7278 8990/www.thecoachandhorses.com).*

Cottons *70 Exmouth Market, EC1R 4QP (7833 3332/www.cottons-restaurant.co.uk).*
Drapers Arms *44 Barnsbury Street, N1 1ER (7619 0348/www.thedrapersarms.co.uk).*
Duke of Cambridge *30 St Peter's Street, N1 8JT (7359 3066/www.dukeorganic.co.uk).*
Eagle *159 Farringdon Road, EC1R 3AH (7837 1353).*
Easton *22 Easton Street, WC1X 0DS (7278 7608).*
Flâneur *41 Farringdon Road, EC1M 3JB (7404 4422/www.flaneur.com).*
Gallipoli *102 Upper Street, N1 1QN (7359 0630/www.cafegallipoli.com).*
Gallipoli Again *120 Upper Street, N1 1QP (7359 1578/www.cafegallipoli.com).*
Gallipoli Bazaar *107 Upper Street, N1 1QN (7226 5333/www.cafegallipoli.com).*
Gem *265 Upper Street, N1 2UQ (7359 0405).*
House *63-69 Canonbury Road, N1 2DG (7704 7410/www.themeredithgroup.co.uk).*
Isarn *119 Upper Street, N1 1QP (7424 5153/ www.isarn.co.uk).*
İznik *19 Highbury Park, N5 1QJ (7354 5697/ www.iznik.co.uk).*
Lalibela *137 Fortress Road, NW5 2HR (7284 0600).*
Landseer *37 Landseer Road, N19 4JU (7263 4658).*
Maghreb *189 Upper Street, N1 1RQ (7226 2305).*
Marquess Tavern *32 Canonbury Street, N1 2TB (7354 2975/www.marquesstavern.co.uk).*
Masala Zone *80 Upper Street, N1 0NU (7359 3399/www.masalazone.com).*
Medcalf *40 Exmouth Market, EC1R 4QE (7833 3533/www.medcalfbar.co.uk).*
Metrogusto *13 Theberton Street, N1 0QY (7226 9400/www.metrogusto.co.uk).*
Morgan M *489 Liverpool Road, N7 8NS (7609 3560/www.morganm.com).*
Moro *34-36 Exmouth Market, EC1R 4QE (7833 8336/www.moro.co.uk).*
Ottolenghi *287 Upper Street, N1 2TZ (7288 1454/www.ottolenghi.co.uk).*
Pasha *301 Upper Street, N1 2TU (7226 1454).*
Pho *86 St John Street, EC1M 4EH (7253 7624/www.phocafe.co.uk).*
La Porchetta *84-86 Rosebery Avenue, EC1R 4QY (7837 6060).*
Portal *88 St John Street, EC1M 4EH (7253 6950/www.portalrestaurant.com).*
Quality Chop House *92-94 Farringdon Road, EC1R 3EA (7837 5093/www.qualitychop house.co.uk).*
Rodizio Rico *77-78 Upper Street, N1 0NU (7354 1076/www.rodiziorico.com).*
S&M Café *4-6 Essex Road, N1 8LN (7359 5361/www.sandmcafe.co.uk).*
Sa Sa Sushi *422 St John Street, EC1V 4NJ (7837 1155/www.sasasushi.co.uk).*
Sabor *108 Essex Road, N1 8LX (7226 5551/www.sabor.co.uk).*
St John *26 St John Street, EC1M 4AY (7251 0848/www.stjohnrestaurant.com).*

Islington

St John's *91 Junction Road, N19 5QU (7272 1587).*
Sedir *4 Theberton Street, N1 0QX (7226 5489/www.sedirrestaurant.co.uk).*
StringRay Café *36 Highbury Park, N5 2AA (7354 9309/www.stringraycafe.co.uk).*
Tbilisi *91 Holloway Road, N7 8LT (7607 2536).*
Tinseltown *44-46 St John Street, EC1M 4DF (7689 2424/www.tinseltown.co.uk).*
Upper Glas *The Mall, 359 Upper Street, N1 0PD (7359 1932).*
Vinoteca *7 St John Street, EC1M 4AA (7253 8786/www.vinoteca.co.uk).*

Bars & pubs

When most punters think of drinking in Islington, they think of Upper Street – grubby, chain bar-filled and home to many a drunken fight after closing time. Actually, very few of the borough's best bars and pubs are found here. Sure, there's stalwart Medicine Bar, industrial-chic-style Keston Lodge, infamous rock den the Hope & Anchor and popular theatre pub the King's Head – but the best options are located on surrounding streets.

Essex Road is almost as obvious a destination as Upper Street, but already options improve with the likes of such newcomers as the New Rose (previously an old man's boozer) and Latino DJ bar Barrio North, as well as pub-of-the-moment the Old Queen's Head, which draws a queue of eager punters to its top-notch DJ nights every weekend. Venturing on to side roads reveals a clutch of leading gastropubs – the Duke of Cambridge and the Marquess Tavern (for both, *see p109*) – plus likeable cocktail bar 25 Canonbury Lane, quirky theatre pub the Rosemary Branch, and the gorgeous Island Queen, an oasis of a pub hidden in the roads around Islington Green. Equally secluded is the Charles Lamb (*see p109*), one of our favourite gastropubs in London, which caters equally well to drinkers as diners. And we were near-heartbroken when tiny wine bar Colebrooke's closed in 2007.

For a break from gastro shenanigans, try the fuss-free Camden Head, canalside Narrow Boat or the Hemingford Arms.

The roads to the north of Upper Street are equally well stocked with options. The Angelic is an attractive, two-floored bar, popular with a thirtysomething crowd; youngsters flock to music pub Filthy McNasty's, launch pad for a number

Great gastropub the **Charles Lamb**.

Triangle Restaurant

...oad, N4 4DS (8292 0516)
...ark tube. Open 6pm-12am Mon-Fri; 11am-12am Sat-Sun.
...thetrianglerestaurant.co.uk

Prepare to be transported to another world. Inside this palace of curiosities between Crouch End and Finsbury Park, with its rich fabrics, beaten metalwork, glowing candles and enchanting alcoves is a food-lover's heaven. Moroccan-inspired but with elements of Asian, European and even Australasian cuisine, the menu is as eclectic as the decor. We ate sardine salad with couscous - the fish moist with a perfectly crispy exterior, the couscous tender and spicy - then Thai green chicken curry, once again the ideal heat, texture and taste. My companion's sirloin steak had a garnish of ginger which had her squeaking with pleasure.

Owner Aziz Begdouri devised both the exotic interior (including a surreal bed with furniture stuck to the ceiling) and the funky fusion menu, having been a chef in both his native Morocco and in London. Triangle won Archant's Best Moroccan restaurant in London award in 2006 and chef of the year 2007.

Combined with the chilled music, the gracious and happy service, the small but idyllic garden, the low-level den where you sit cross-legged on cushions, the inventive wine list (try the Moroccan sauvignon blanc - it's knockout) and the plethora of intricate, lovingly worked details everywhere you look, this is a stunning triumph of a restaurant.

By David Nicholson

Don't be ■   *Go* ●   *To The* ▲

Photography by Emily Haley

of indie bands including the Libertines. Chapel Market has two reliable late-opening bars – Salmon & Compass and Anam – as well as the Elbow Room for pool-lovers.

Further north to Holloway, options get grubbier, but the Swimmer at the Grafton Arms is a cosy, worthy boozer and the Duchess of Kent – at the Holloway end of Liverpool Road – is a locals' favourite. Archway drinkers have quality options in gastropubs the Landseer and St John's (for both, see p110) – but little in terms of bars. Best to head to Tufnell Park, for Iberian joint Bar Lorca (on the border with the borough of Camden).

Business picks up as you head towards Clerkenwell. Just past the Angel there's another historic theatre pub, the Old Red Lion. Pedestrianised Exmouth Market goes from strength to strength, offering everything from table-football thrills (Café Kick) to fine wines (the bar at the Ambassador; see p110). Dollar Bar & Grill is good for a late-night cocktail, while Al's Café Bar has plenty of outdoor benches for summer boozing. Most bizarre is the Old China Hand, a fine pub that serves, er, dim sum.

Clerkenwell proper is littered with excellent pubs, from must-visit Jerusalem Tavern (the only London outpost of fine Suffolk brewery St Peter's) to the jocular Three Kings of Clerkenwell, tucked away in a secluded side street. Also of note are classily laid-back tapas bar the Green and after-work drinkers' magnet the Slaughtered Lamb. On Clerkenwell Road, Match EC1 is the standard bearer, with an excellent cocktail menu designed by mix-mogul Dale DeGroff. Or head to St John Street for a superior bottle of wine at St John(see p110) or Vinoteca (see p110).

Al's Café Bar *11-13 Exmouth Market, EC1R 4QD (7837 4821).*
Anam *3 Chapel Market, N1 9EZ (7278 1001/www.anambar.com).*
Angelic *57 Liverpool Road, N1 0RJ (7278 8433).*
Bar Lorca *156-158 Fortess Road, NW5 2HP (7485 1314).*
Barrio North *45 Essex Road, N1 2SF (7688 2882/www.barrionorth.com).*
Café Kick *43 Exmouth Market, EC1R 4QL (7837 8077/www.cafekick.co.uk).*
Camden Head *2 Camden Walk, N1 8DY (7359 0851).*
Dollar Bar & Grill *2 Exmouth Market, EC1R 4PX (7278 0077/www.dollargrills.com).*

Duchess of Kent *141 Liverpool Road, N7 8PR (7609 7104).*
Elbow Room *89-91 Chapel Market, N1 9EX (7278 3244/www.theelbowroom.co.uk).*
Filthy McNasty's *68 Amwell Street, EC1R 1UU (7837 6067/www.filthymacnastys.com).*
Green *29 Clerkenwell Green, EC1R 0DU (7490 8010/www.thegreenec1.co.uk).*
Hemingford Arms *158 Hemingford Road, N1 1DF (7607 3303).*
Hope & Anchor *207 Upper Street, N1 1RL (7354 1312/www.bugbearbookings.com).*
Island Queen *87 Noel Road, N1 8HD (7704 7631).*
Jerusalem Tavern *55 Britton Street, EC1M 5UQ (7490 4281/www.stpetersbrewery.co.uk).*
Keston Lodge *131 Upper Street, N1 1QP (7354 9535/www.kestonlodge.com).*
King's Head *115 Upper Street, N1 1QN (7226 4443/www.kingsheadtheatre.org).*

LOCALS' TIPS

Bus users, beware: though the intersection at Angel tube station is infamous for its volume of traffic, it's the slow crawl up and down Essex Road during rush hour that is the real commuter nightmare. Avoid if at all possible by using alternative routes along Upper Street or Southgate Road. **Arsenal match days cause havoc in the area. Parking is suspended for miles around and the Victoria, Northern and Piccadilly lines that run through Islington get rammed with home fans before and after the game. Whatever your feelings about football, get a fixture list.** A new housing development has opened at the eastern end of Pentonville Road, aimed squarely at students. Expect the average age of surrounding pubs to lower dramatically. **The grand streets that run off City Road towards New North Road are always worth exploring. As well as terrific hidden pubs like the Island Queen, there are oddities such as the house on Colebrooke Row that has a room filled with jukeboxes on its ground floor (the window is usually uncurtained so passers-by can have a look).** Tinderbox café (21 Upper Street, N1 0PQ, 7354 8929) is a great place for a late espresso, thanks to its US-style opening hours. Good coffee and cakes, and quirky interior design, have also helped build a strong local following

Islington

Match EC1 *45-47 Clerkenwell Road, EC1M 5RS (7250 4002/www.matchbar.com).*
Medicine Bar *181 Upper Street, N1 1RQ (7704 9536/www.medicinebar.net).*
Narrow Boat *119 St Peter's Street, N1 8PZ (7288 0572).*
New Rose *84-86 Essex Road, N1 8LU (7226 1082/www.newrose.co.uk).*
Old China Hand *8 Tysoe Street, EC1R 4RQ (7278 7678/www.oldchinahand.co.uk).*
Old Queen's Head *44 Essex Road, N1 8LN (7354 9993/www.theoldqueenshead.com).*
Old Red Lion *418 St John Street, EC1V 4PD (7837 7816/www.oldredliontheatre.co.uk).*
Rosemary Branch *2 Shepperton Road, N1 3DT (7704 2730/www.rosemarybranch.co.uk).*
Salmon & Compass *58 Penton Street, N1 9PZ (7837 3891/www.salmonandcompass.com).*
Slaughtered Lamb *34-35 Great Sutton Street, EC1V 0DX (7253 1516).*
Swimmer at the Grafton Arms *13 Eburne Road, N7 6AR (7281 4632).*
Three Kings of Clerkenwell *7 Clerkenwell Close, EC1R 0DY (7253 0483).*
25 Canonbury Lane *25 Canonbury Lane, N1 2AS (7226 0955).*

Shops

From the designer boutiques of Upper Street to the fetish shops of Holloway Road, there's plenty of scope in this neck of the woods for both the practical and pleasure-seeking shopper. At the very south of the borough, Clerkenwell Green is a crafts hub, boasting the Lesley Craze Gallery for jewellery and textiles, and a building occupied by Craft Central (formerly the Clerkenwell Green Association), which supports hundreds of designer-makers and holds regular open-studio events.

Pedestrianised Exmouth Market has a growing selection of independents. Highlights include compact but convivial CD shop-cum-café Brill, the equally welcoming Metropolitan Books, Family Tree (idiosyncratic gifts and clothes), EC One (modern jewellery) and Bagman & Robin for characterful, colourful bags of all sizes; foodwise, there's Brindisa (Spanish delicacies) and Sweet (baker and pâtisserie). Just to the north, a couple of gems are secreted on pretty Arlington Way – fab 1950s ceramics at Gary Grant Choice Pieces and Jacqueline Byrne's exquisite bridal gowns – while Amwell Street has an Emma Hope shoe store and second-hand book dealer Amwell Book Company.

The undoubted retail mecca of the borough, however, is shop-packed Upper Street. High-street chains (Borders, Gap, HMV, Next, Monsoon, M&S et al) are clustered in and around the shiny N1 Centre. Head out of the back of the mall to find the food, clothing and household goods stalls of old-fashioned Chapel Market.

Snaking behind Upper Street's east side is Camden Passage, a pedestrian alleyway once lined with antiques shops. Its character is evolving, though, with an influx of new independent shops, including gourmet confectioner Paul A Young Fine Chocolates, contemporary womenswear designer Susy Harper, Kirt Holmes jewellery, Dominic Crinson's tiles, eco boutique Equa and, at the northern end, the African Waistcoat Company (an utterly original fusion of Nigerian and British traditions). At the other end is chic shoe shop Lollipop London. Some antiques dealers remain, especially in the idiosyncratic Pierrepont Arcade, and the antiques market still operates on Wednesday and Saturday (plus a book market on Thursday and vintage clothes on Sunday). Annie's Vintage Clothing is a notable survivor.

On Upper Street proper, the more interesting shops tend to be towards Highbury, past Islington Green. Well-heeled locals furnish their refurbished Georgian terraces in contemporary style with purchases from Aria (recently relocated to larger premises just off Upper Street on Barnsbury Street), Atelier Abigail Ahern and Scandinavian specialist Twentytwentyone. Aficionados of 20th-century design also have plenty of choice at Castle Gibson, Fandango (on Cross Street) and Origin Modernism (in Camden Passage), while After Noah has some unusual vintage pieces (old-fashioned telephones, vintage signage) amid reproductions, gifts and kids' toys.

There are also some great boutiques: Diverse and Sefton for designer gear (for both women and men), Labour of Love for more avant-garde looks, jeweller Stephen Einhorn and, just off the main strip, Palette London, which mixes vintage and new fashion to hip effect. As you'd expect in a family-friendly area, there are some good kids' shops, including all-rounder Igloo. Cross Street has a cache of interesting shops, including Tallulah Lingerie and the wonderful Loop Knit Salon, a magnet for needle-clickers after unusual yarns.

Buying local made easy: **Islington Farmers' Market**.

Nip over to unlovely Essex Road for Handmade & Found, an affordable womenswear boutique that was recently given a makeover by TV retail guru Mary Portas, and a brace of great second-hand record stores, Flashback and Haggle Vinyl. Superior fishmonger Steve Hatt, which counts Nigel Slater among its customers, is also here.

Other notable food shops in the locale include the excellent Euphorium Bakery and, up on Highbury Park, deluxe deli/cheese shop La Fromagerie and prime butcher Frank Godfrey. Islington Farmers' Market is held behind the Town Hall (10am-2pm Sunday). Further north, Blackstock Road has plenty of shops with a Middle Eastern or Mediterranean flavour, many of them open late, while Clerkenwell's Flâneur (*see p110*) combines shelves of upmarket deli goods with tables for eating in.

To the west, an enclave of chic fetish shops (latex specialist House of Harlot is the best

known) on Holloway Road sits oddly with well-fed domesticity in the form of Waitrose a bit further up. Also look out for D&A Binder, a fascinating repository of reclaimed shop fittings. Although much of Archway Road's retail offerings are pretty grim, an indie music enclave is sprouting up on the border with Haringey, where Sound 323 shares premises with Second Layer. There aren't many browsing opportunities in Tufnell Park, but you can buy *MasterChef* winner Julie Friend's own-made dishes and fine foodstuffs at her deli, Flavours.

African Waistcoat Company *33 Islington Green, N1 8DU (7704 9698/www.african waistcoatcompany.com).*
After Noah *121 Upper Street, N1 1QP (7359 4281/www.afternoah.com).*
Amwell Book Company *53 Amwell Street, EC1R 1UR (7837 4891).*
Annie's Vintage Clothing *12 Camden Passage, N1 8ED (7359 0796/www.annies vintageclothing.co.uk).*

Aria *Barnsbury Hall, 2 Barnsbury Street, N1 1PN (7704 6222/www.aria-shop.co.uk).*
Atelier Abigail Ahern *137 Upper Street, N1 1QP (7354 8181/www.atelierabigailahern.com).*
Bagman & Robin *47 Exmouth Market, EC1R 4QL (7833 8780/www.bagmanand robin.com).*
Brill *27 Exmouth Market, EC1R 4QL (7833 9757).*
Brindisa *32 Exmouth Market, EC1R 4QE (7713 1666/www.brindisa.com).*
Castle Gibson *106A Upper Street, N1 1QN (7704 0927/www.castlegibson.com).*
Chapel Market *Off Liverpool Road, N1.*
Craft Central *33-35 St John's Square, EC1M 4DS (72510276/www.craftcentral.org.uk).*
D&A Binder *101 Holloway Road, N7 8LT (7609 6300/www.dandabinder.co.uk).*
Diverse *www.diverseclothing.com; women 294 Upper Street, N1 2TU (7359 8877); men 286 Upper Street, N1 2TZ (7359 0081).*
Dominic Crinson *27 Camden Passage, N1 8EA (7704 6538/www.crinson.com).*
EC One *41 Exmouth Market, EC1R 4QL (7713 6185/www.econe.co.uk).*
Emma Hope Shoes *33 Amwell Street, EC1R 1UR (7833 2367/www.emmahope.co.uk).*
Equa *28 Camden Passage, N1 8ED (7359 0955/www.equaclothing.com).*
Euphorium Bakery *202 Upper Street, N1 1RQ (7704 6905); 26A Chapel Market, N1 9EN (7837 7010).*

Coffee and CDs: **Brill**. *See p114.*

Family Tree *53 Exmouth Market, EC1R 4QL (7278 1084/www.familytreeshop.co.uk).*
Fandango *50 Cross Street, N1 2BA (7226 1777/www.fandango.uk.com).*
Flashback *50 Essex Road, N1 8LR (7354 9356/www.flashback.co.uk).*
Flavours *10 Campdale Road, N7 0EA (7281 6565/www.delibelly.com).*
Frank Godfrey *7 Highbury Park, N5 1QJ (7226 2425/www.fgodfrey.co.uk).*
La Fromagerie *30 Highbury Park, N5 2AA (7359 7440/www.lafromagerie.co.uk).*
Gary Grant Choice Pieces *18 Arlington Way, EC1R 1UY (7713 1122).*
Haggle Vinyl *114-116 Essex Road, N1 8LX (7704 3101/www.hagglevinyl.com).*
Handmade & Found *109 Essex Road, N1 2SL (7359 3898/www.handmadeandfound.co.uk).*
House of Harlot *90 Holloway Road, N7 8JG (7700 1441/www.house-of-harlot.com).*
Igloo *300 Upper Street, N1 2TU (7354 7300/www.iglookids.co.uk).*
Islington Farmers' Market *William Tyndale School, Upper Street, N1 2AQ (7833 0338/www.lfm.org.uk).*
Jacqueline Byrne *19 Arlington Way, EC1R 1UY (7833 0381/www.jacquelinebyrne.co.uk).*
Kirt Holmes *16 Camden Passage, N1 8ED (7226 1080/www.kirtholmes.com).*
Labour of Love *193 Upper Street, N1 1RQ (7354 9333/www.labour-of-love.co.uk).*
Lesley Craze Gallery *33-35A Clerkenwell Green, EC1R 0DU (7608 0393/www.lesleycraze gallery.co.uk).*
Lollipop London *114 Islington High Street, N1 8EG (7226 4005/www.lollipoplondon.com).*
Loop Knit Salon *41 Cross Street, N1 2BB (7288 1160/www.loop.gb.com).*
Metropolitan Books *49 Exmouth Market, EC1R 4QL (7278 6900/www.metropolitan books.co.uk).*
N1 Centre *21 Parkfield Street, N1 0PS (7359 2674/www.n1islington.com).*
Origin Modernism *25 Camden Passage, N1 8EA (7704 1326/www.origin101.co.uk).*
Palette London *21 Canonbury Lane, N1 2AS (7288 7428/www.palette-london.com).*
Paul A Young Fine Chocolates *33 Camden Passage, N1 8EA (7424 5750/ www.payoung.net).*
Second Layer *Basement, 323 Archway Road, N6 5AA (07855 140992/www.secondlayer.co.uk).*
Sefton *women 271 Upper Street, N1 2UQ (7226 9822); men 196 Upper Street, N1 1RQ (7226 7076).*
Sound 323 *323 Archway Road, N6 5AA (8348 9595/www.sound323.com).*
Stephen Einhorn *210 Upper Street, N1 1RL (7359 4977/www.stepheneinhorn.co.uk).*
Steve Hatt *88-90 Essex Road, N1 8LU (7226 3963).*
Susy Harper *35 Camden Passage, N1 8EA (7704 0688/www.susyharper.co.uk).*
Sweet *64 Exmouth Market, EC1R 4QP (7713 6777/www.sweetdesserts.co.uk).*

Islington

TRANSPORT

Tube stations *Hammersmith & City*
King's Cross, Farringdon, Barbican;
Circle King's Cross, Farringdon,
Barbican; *Metropolitan* King's Cross,
Farringdon, Barbican; *Piccadilly* King's
Cross, Caledonian Road, Holloway
Road, Arsenal, Finsbury Park; *Northern*
King's Cross, Old Street, Angel, Tufnell
Park, Archway; *Victoria* King's Cross,
Highbury & Islington, Finsbury Park
Rail stations *London Overground*
Caledonian Road & Barnsbury, Highbury
& Islington, Canonbury, Upper Holloway,
Crouch Hill; *First Capital Connect
Great Northern* Old Street, Essex
Road, Highbury & Islington, Drayton
Park, Finsbury Park, King's Cross
Main bus routes *into central London*
4, 17, 19, 29, 30, 38, 43, 55, 56,
73, 76, 91, 141, 153, 205, 214,
243, 271, 274, 341, 390; *night
buses* N19, N29, N38, N41, N55,
N73, N253; *24-hour buses* 43, 205,
214, 243, 271, 274, 341, 390

Tallulah Lingerie *65 Cross Street, N1 2BB
(7704 0066/www.tallulah-lingerie.co.uk).*
Twentytwentyone *274 Upper Street, N1 2UA
(7288 1996/www.twentytwentyone.com).*

Arts & attractions

Cinemas & theatres
Almeida Theatre *Almeida Street, N1 1TA
(7359 4404/www.almeida.co.uk).* A award-winning
theatre with a world-class reputation.
King's Head *115 Upper Street, N1 1QN
(7226 1916/www.kingsheadtheatre.org).*
A pioneer of the pub theatre scene.
Little Angel Theatre *14 Dagmar Passage,
off Cross Street, N1 2DN (7226 1787/
www.littleangeltheatre.com).* London's only
permanent puppet theatre.
Odeon Holloway *419-427 Holloway Road,
N7 6LJ (0871 224 4007/www.odeon.co.uk).*
Pleasance Theatre *Islington Carpenters
Mews, North Road, N7 9EF (7609 1800/
www.pleasance.co.uk).* Sister venue to the
Edinburgh Pleasance.
Rosemary Branch *2 Shepperton Road, N1
3DT (7704 2730/www.rosemarybranch.co.uk).*
Friendly, eccentrically decorated freehouse
with a 60-seat theatre upstairs.
Sadler's Wells *Rosebery Avenue, EC1R 4TN
(0870 737 7737/www.sadlerswells.com).* One of
the world's premier dance venues.
Screen on the Green *Islington Green,
Upper Street, N1 0NP (7226 3520/
www.screencinemas.co.uk).*

Vue Islington *Parkfield Street, N1 0PS
(0871 224 0240/www.myvue.com).*

Galleries & museums
Crafts Council *44A Pentonville Road, N1
9BY (7278 7700/www.craftscouncil.org.uk).*
Home to innovatively designed exhibitions
of contemporary crafts, with a new reference
library opening in 2008.
Cubitt *8 Angel Mews, N1 9HH (7278 8226/
www.cubittartists.org.uk).* Artist-run gallery
and studio space.
**Estorick Collection of Modern Italian
Art** *39A Canonbury Square, N1 2AN (7704
9522/www.estorickcollection.com).* Work by
Italian painters such as Balla, Boccioni and
Carra; also a museum, bookshop and café.
London Canal Museum *12-13 New
Wharf Road, N1 9RT (7713 0836/
www.canalmuseum.org.uk).* Housed in a
former 19th-century ice warehouse, built
for the ice-cream maker Carlo Gatti.
**Museum & Library of the Order of
St John** *St John's Gate, St John's Lane,
EC1M 4DA (7324 4005/www.sja.org.uk/
history).* Charts the evolution of the medieval
Order of Hospitaller Knights to its modern
incarnation as the world-renowned
ambulance service.
Parasol Unit *14 Wharf Road, N1 7RW
(7490 7373/www.parasol-unit.org).* Regular
exhibitions by contemporary artists.

Music & comedy venues
Carling Academy *Islington N1 Centre,
16 Parkfield Street, N1 0PS (7288 4400/
www.islington-academy.co.uk).* Slightly
soulless shopping mall venue; however,
the capital's lack of midsize spaces means
it's become a default haunt for international
cult acts.
Hen & Chickens *109 St Paul's Road, N1
2NA (7704 2001/www.henandchickens.com).*
Well-established comedy joint hosting a mix
of known names and newcomers.
LSO St Luke's *161 Old Street, EC1V 9NG
(7490 3939/www.lso.co.uk/lsostlukes).* Restored
Hawksmoor church now used for rehearsals
by the London Symphony Orchestra. Free
lunchtime and occasional evening concerts.

Other attractions
Bunhill Fields *City Road, EC1.* Famous
residents in this small, Nonconformist cemetery
include Daniel Defoe, John Bunyan and William
Blake and his wife.
Business Design Centre *52 Upper Street,
N1 0QH (7359 3535/www.businessdesign
centre.co.uk).* Trade fairs and conferences,
including some major art and design shows.
Candid Arts Trust *3 Torrens Street, EC1V
1NQ (7837 4237/www.candidarts.com).*
Two converted Victorian warehouses
behind Angel station, containing two
loft-style galleries, 20 art studios, rehearsal
space, a screening room and an excellent café.

Sport & fitness

Islington has a good range of public and private leisure facilities. Aquaterra Leisure, which runs seven of Islington's eight public centres, is a charity organisation that invests the money spent by the public back into the facilities. Saddlers Sports Centre is affiliated to the nearby City University and open to all.

Gyms & leisure centres

Archway Leisure Centre *McDonald Road, N19 5DD (7281 4105/www.aquaterra.org).*
Cally Pool *229 Caledonian Road, N1 0NH (7278 1890/www.aquaterra.org).*
Dowe Dynamics Gym *1-2 Central Hall Buildings, Archway Close, N19 3UB (7281 2267/www.onetoonetraining.net).* Private.
Esporta *Islington Green, 27 Essex Road, N1 3PS (7288 8200/www.esporta.com).* Private.
The Factory/Tango London *407 Hornsey Road, N19 4DX (7272 1122/www.tangolondon. com).* Private.
Finsbury Leisure Centre *Norman Street, EC1V 3PU (7253 2346/www.aquaterra.org).*
Fitness First *www.fitnessfirst.co.uk: 60-63 Bunhill Row, EC1Y 8NQ (7490 3555); 67-83 Seven Sisters Road, N7 6BU (7281 8585).* Private.
Highbury Pool *Highbury Crescent, N5 1RR (7704 2312/www.aquaterra.org).*
Inspirations *Holiday Inn Hotel, 1 King's Cross Road, WC1X 9HX (7837 0115).* Private.
Ironmonger Row Baths *1-11 Ironmonger Row, EC1V 3QF (7253 4011/www. aquaterra.org).*
Maximum Fitness *144 Fortess Road, NW5 2HP (7482 3941/www.maxfit. co.uk).* Private.
Saddlers Sports Centre *122 Goswell Road, EC1V 0HB (7040 5656/www.city. ac.uk/sportscentre).*
Sequin Park *240 Upper Street, N1 1RU (7704 9844/www.sequinpark.co.uk).* Private.
Sobell Leisure Centre & Ice Rink *Hornsey Road, N7 7NY (7609 2166/ www.aquaterra.org).*
Virgin Active *www.virginactive.co.uk: Colinwood Business Centre, Mercers Road, N19 4PJ (7561 5200); 333 Goswell Road, EC1V 7DG (0845 130 9222); 33 Bunhill Row, EC1Y 8LP (7448 5454).* Private.

Other facilities

Islington Tennis Centre *Market Road, N7 9PL (7700 1370/www.aquaterra.org).*

Spectator sports

Arsenal FC *Emirates Stadium, Highbury House, 75 Drayton Park, N5 1BU (7704 4000/box office 7704 4040/ tours 7704 4504/www.arsenal.com).*

Schools

WHAT THE PARENTS SAY:

'There are a few good primary schools in Islington that parents fight to get places at. One of these is Canonbury – made famous by the £40,000 raised at a parents' auction evening when Boris Johnson (a parent) bid to be shown around the House of Lords by Andrew Adonis (another parent). Also good are St John's (a church school), William Tyndale and Hanover.

The secondary schools, however, are terrible. Highbury Fields School is the best for girls. Boys' options are less impressive on the whole. St Mary Magdalene has just opened as an academy, though it's too early to know if it's any good. Islington's middle-class parents happily (or fairly happily) send their children to the primary schools, but tend to opt out at secondary level. Either they move out of the borough, or they send them to private schools – City of London, Channing, Highgate, Francis Holland, UCS, South Hampstead, Queens Westminster and so on. Or they get them into state selective schools (Latymer, for example). Islington also has an arrangement with Dame Alice Owen (a good comp in Potters Bar), which takes 20 bright children every year. Competition is fierce.'

Lucy Kellaway, mother of four, Islington

Primary

There are 45 state primary schools in Islington, 15 of which are church schools. There are also seven independent primaries, including one Montessori school and one Steiner school. See www.islington.gov.uk/education, www.edubase.gov.uk and www.ofsted.gov.uk for more information.

Secondary

Central Foundation Boys' School *City Road, EC2A 4SH (72533741/www.islingtonschools.net).* Boys only.
Elizabeth Garrett Anderson Language College *Risinghill Street, off Penton Street, N1 9QG (7837 0739/www.egas.islington. sch.uk).* Girls only.
Highbury Fields School *Highbury Hill, N5 1AR (7288 1888/www.highburyfields. islington.sch.uk).* Girls only.
Highbury Grove School *Highbury New Park, N5 2EG (7288 8900/www.highbury grove.islington.sch.uk).*
Holloway School *Hilldrop Road, N7 0JG (7607 5885/www.holloway.islington. sch.uk).*
Islington Arts & Media School *Turle Road, N4 3LS (7281 3302/www.iamschool.co.uk).*

Islington Green School *Prebend Street,
N1 8PQ (7226 8611/www.igschool.com).*
This will become City of London Academy
in September 2008.
Italia Conti Academy of Theatre Arts
*23 Goswell Road, EC1M 7AJ (7608 0047/
www.italiaconti.com).* Founded in 1911, former
pupils at this private theatre school include
Noël Coward and Patsy Kensit.
**Mount Carmel Technology College for
Girls** *Holland Walk, Duncombe Road, N19 3EU
(7281 3536/www.mountcarmel.islington.sch.uk).*
Girls only.
St Aloysius RC College *Hornsey Lane,
N6 5LY (7263 1391).* Boys only.
St Mary Magdalene Academy *Liverpool
Road, N7 8PG (7697 0123/www.smmacademy.
org).* Opened in September 2007.

Property

WHAT THE AGENTS SAY:

‘Islington is a fantastic place to live. You have
great restaurants on Upper Street, good bus
links, the gorgeous green space of Highbury
Fields, and it's walking distance from one of
the most important financial and legal districts
in the world. We mostly get professionals
moving here. There are also a lot of media
and creative types living in the area.

At the weekends, it's really buzzing. We also
get lots of students renting in the area as City
University is just down the road. Loads of people
want to live here. It is more expensive than some
other parts of London, but still better value than
parts of Clerkenwell or the City. We have a good
mix of property, from old Georgian and Victorian
houses to newer developments.’
James Neilson, Currell Residential

Average property prices
Detached n/a
Semi-detached £908,266
Terraced £799,294
Flat £346,117

Local estate agents
APS Estates *210-212 Caledonian Road, N1
0SQ (7837 0203/www.apsestates.com).*
Currell Residential *321 Upper Street, N1
2XQ (7226 4200/www.currell.com).*
Evans Baker *350 Upper Street, N1 0PD (7354
0066/www.evansbaker.co.uk).*
Jeffrey Nicholas *293 Upper Street, N1 2TU
(7354 0707/www.jeffreynicholas.co.uk).*
JTM Homes *695 Holloway Road, N19 5SE
(7272 1090/www.jtmhomes.co.uk).*
Moving On Property Services *79 Pitfield
Street, N1 6BT (7336 8882/www.movingon
london.com).*
myspace *328 Caledonian Road, N1 1BB (7609
3598/www.myspaceuk.com).*
Thomson Currie *313 Upper Street, N1 2XQ
(7354 5224/www.thomsoncurrie.co.uk).*
Urban Spaces *70 Clerkenwell Road, EC1M
5QA (7251 4000/www.urbanspaces.co.uk).*

RECYCLING
No. of bring sites 179 (for nearest,
visit www.recycleforlondon.com)
Household waste recycled 15.7%
Main recycling centre Household
Reuse & Recycling Centre, Hornsey
Street, N7 8HR (8884 5645)
Other recycling services green and
kitchen waste collection; home
composting; white goods collection;
real nappies scheme
Council contact Contact Islington, 222
Upper Street, London N1 1XR (7527
2000/www.islington.gov.uk/recycling)

COUNCIL TAX
A	up to £40,000	£812.94
B	£40,001-£52,000	£948.42
C	£52,001-£68,000	£1,083.92
D	£68,001-£88,000	£1,219.40
E	£88,001-£120,000	£1,490.38
F	£120,001-£160,000	£1,761.36
G	£160,001-£320,000	£2,032.34
H	over £320,000	£2,438.80

Other information

Council
Islington Council *222 Upper Street, N1 1XR
(7527 2000/www.islington.gov.uk).*

Legal services
Islington CAB *The Advice & Learning Centre,
86 Durham Road, N7 7DU (0870 751
0925/www.adviceguide.org.uk).*

Local newspapers
Islington Tribune *7419 9000/
www.thecnj.com.*
Islington Gazette *8342 5777/
www.islingtongazette.co.uk.*

Allotments & open spaces
Council Allotments The waiting list for
those hoping to secure an allotment in the
borough is now at least ten years. This list
has therefore been closed to new applicants
until further notice. For more information,
contact the Greenspace & Leisure Support
Services Team on 7527 4953.
Open spaces *www.islington.gov.uk/Leisure/
ParksAndRecreation.*

Islington

'Camden is very alternative.
To be revolutionary here
you need to wear a suit and
have a nine to five job.'

Marcus Davey, chief executive of the Roundhouse

Camden

It's all change in certain Camden quarters, with the Stables Market being scaled down to make way for developers, and King's Cross's grimy-to-glossy reinvention proceeding apace. All this seems a world away from the tranquillity of the borough's more exclusive enclaves: in the monied mews of Hampstead, tree-lined avenues of Belsize Park and Georgian squares of Bloomsbury, life proceeds at a more measured pace.

Neighbourhoods

Bloomsbury and Fitzrovia

After the rush of the West End, it's a relief to turn into the well-ordered streets and squares (Bedford and Tavistock Squares are much-admired) of Bloomsbury. The neighbourhood has long been a retreat for the literati and there's a blue plaque at every turn. Yeats, Eliot and Dickens are among its illustrious former residents – though it was Virginia Woolf's gatherings in the drawing room at 46 Gordon Square that assured its literary immortality.

It's still a proudly cultural area – celebrated in October's arty Bloomsbury Festival, now in its third year. Towering sculpture installations occasionally occupy the corner of Bedford Square, home to the Architectural Association, while in-the-know locals join budding thespians in RADA's pleasant café on Malet Street for lunch. Here too is the brooding, art deco Senate House (George Orwell's inspiration for the Ministry of Truth in *1984*) – the University of London's library.

Map-toting tourists also mingle with Bloomsbury's students and well-heeled residents. Hotels and upmarket B&Bs

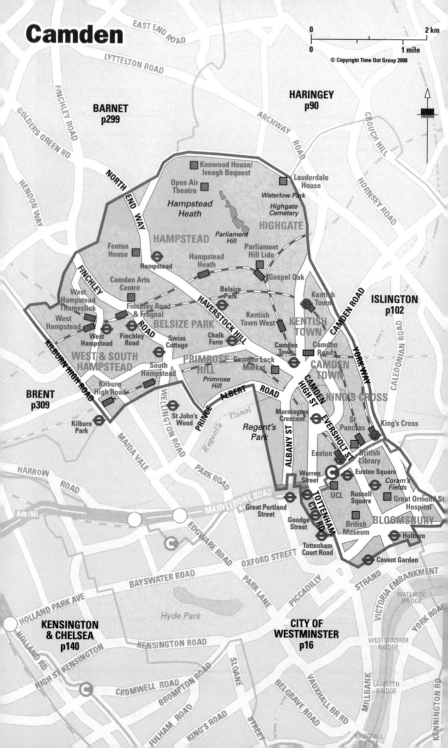

dot the area, while the domed British Museum on Great Russell Street is a visitor magnet, with Norman Foster's magnificent, light-filled Great Court at its heart. Most of Bloomsbury's charm, though, lies in quieter pleasures: browsing the specialist bookshops and art supply shops around the British Museum, or wandering along the elegant, colonnaded establishments on nearby Sicilian Avenue.

Another unassuming delight is boutique-lined Lamb's Conduit Street – also home to a small but superb bicycle repair shop and the much-loved Lamb pub. At the end of the road, Coram's Fields was the 18th-century site of philanthropist Thomas Coram's Foundling Hospital. Today it's a seven-acre child's paradise, with playgrounds and a pets' corner; adults are banned, unless accompanied by a child.

Just around the corner, the stark, 1960s Brunswick Centre houses flats and a shopping centre. A £24 million facelift, completed in 2006, brought in some upmarket names (Coast, Carluccio's) – though happily, delightful second-hand bookshop Skoob survived, as did the Renoir cinema, beloved of arthouse aficionados. Neighbouring Russell Square is one of Bloomsbury's loveliest gardens, with a café and fountains at the centre; once an infamous gay cruising ground, it's now locked at night.

To the west, busy Tottenham Court Road marks Bloomsbury's border with Fitzrovia. Cut-price electrical shops and charity collectors jostle for shoppers' attention at its southern end, while Heals and Habitat sit side by side near Warren Street tube. Running parallel to Tottenham Court Road, Charlotte Street is given over to an array of restaurants and bars.

Camden Town

Famed for its musical links and markets, Camden Town is a shameless clash of alternative culture and commercialism. Some things never change here: drug dealers around the station still murmur promises of good gear and nice prices, while on Chalk Farm Road, colourful shopfronts sport huge sculptures of their wares (Doc Marten boots, leather jackets and the like) and scowling 14-year-olds shop for stripy tights and vintage tees.

Highs & Lows

The Eurostar connection Step on the train in north London; two hours and 15 minutes later you could be quaffing coffee in Paris
Hampstead swimming ponds On a summer's day, a dip in the ponds is a bracingly chilly treat
Live music Camden is still a big player in the music scene, with venues such as the Forum, Barfly, Jazz Café and the Roundhouse at residents' disposal

Celebrity overkill We like spotting a celebrity as much as the next man, but not when they're blocking the way to the bar
The Stables demise Many locals fear development is set to ruin this local institution
Tourist hell Weekends are a roadblock in Camden Town. Locals tend to stick to backstreets and give the market a wide berth

The nightlife scene here has always been self-consciously cool. Britpop may be long gone and the Good Mixer's star has faded, but a new wave of scenesters have taken up residence in the likes of the Hawley Arms. Up-and-coming bands still take to the stage at the Barfly, the sticky-floored launch pad for acts including the Strokes and Coldplay, and the Camden Crawl remains a booze-fuelled annual institution – though at £48, tickets aren't the bargain they once were.

Nothing is sacred, though, as Camdenites recently discovered. Emanating incense fumes and an air of vague disrepute, the market has been an integral part of the local landscape since the 1970s. Locals may have moaned about the weekend crowds and chaos, but no one was celebrating when the council approved a £12 million redevelopment scheme for Stables Market, the biggest of the six markets around the area. The new plans involve a multistorey glass complex of boutiques and bars – a far cry from Camden's scruffy image of old.

There again, there's always been another side to the Camden of 'Tapas, fracas, alcohol, tobaccos/Bongs, bongo bingo, Portuguese maracas' that Suggs

Camden

sang about in 'Camden Town'. Local residents aged over 30 tend to give the market a wide berth: unless you live on Chalk Farm Road, it's easy to avoid getting entangled. Older, more discerning Camdenites prefer to stroll across the bridge to serene Primrose Hill, or meander along the canal to Regent's Park. At the northern end of Chalk Farm Road, the iconic, historic Roundhouse draws an arty crowd with its programme of music, dance and theatre. And there's always the Lock Tavern for a quick pint afterwards – because, deep down, every Camden resident still prides themselves on being a little bit hip.

Kentish Town

Often overshadowed by its raucous neighbour Camden, Kentish Town has an appeal all of its own. Gentrification has crept in as property prices have risen, but it's still endearingly tatty in places and has a genuinely diverse community. Take the high street, whose line-up includes down-at-heel greasy spoons, an upscale Sardinian eaterie, Rio's naturist spa and a tasteful organic food emporium. Polished-up gastropubs are present and correct, but so too are unreconstructed boozers with the football on the telly, frequented by men with dogs on bits of string. By the station, a fruit and veg stall sells everything from globe artichokes and fresh figs to bowls of apples for a pound; towards Chalk Farm, the chaotic Queen's Crescent street market opens on Thursday and Saturday.

Off the main drag there's some big-scale beauty in Kentish Town's buildings, with crescents of attractive Victorian terraces and the Grade II-listed St Pancras Public Baths on Prince of Wales Road – currently in the midst of massive refurbishment plans. Meanwhile, side streets lined with diminutive, pastel-painted terraced houses have a sweetly seaside feel – and not so sweet price tags.

Green spaces include Cantelowes Gardens, with its skate park and children's play area, and the spacious City Farm, founded in 1972. For those craving more greenery, Hampstead Heath is a mere 15 minutes' walk away.

King's Cross

Despite its regal moniker, King's Cross has had a less than salubrious reputation for years. Notorious for its drug deals and prostitution, and crowded with tacky takeaways and massage parlours, it wasn't a place to linger – unless you were heading to one of its bars, or the cluster of clubs that occupied York Way Goods Depot.

But times are changing (the clubs have gone for a start), with an immense regeneration project under way. The centrepiece is the renovated St Pancras Station – Eurostar's new London terminal. The glass-and-iron Victorian train shed has been painstakingly restored to its former glory, while sculptures, boutiques and a swish new champagne bar have been installed. The unlovely industrial wasteland to the north of the station is also in line for transformation, while on York Way, King's Place is to house a concert hall, art galleries and restaurants behind its rippling glass façade – along with the *Guardian* newspaper's new offices.

Other cultural establishments, looking for spacious but central premises, were quicker off the mark in spotting the area's potential. Back in 1998, the British Library cannily moved to Euston Road – now also home to the Wellcome Trust's new headquarters. Little-known outside the locality, it houses medical exhibits and modern art in an upstairs gallery, and has a splendid café run by Peyton & Byrne. Meanwhile, the old municipal garages on Britannia Street are now the Gagosian Gallery; a vast, starkly impressive showcase for contemporary art.

For its inhabitants, King's Cross's charm lies in its convenience. Islington, Bloomsbury and Camden are a mere stroll away, and transport connections are superb. The constant stream of foot traffic passing through means it rarely feels threatening, even late at night – though it does have a slightly anonymous feel. That said, a close-knit Italian community has spread across from Clerkenwell; an unofficial social hub is KC Continental Stores, where parmesan and salumi prices, like the decor, seem frozen in time. There are also some unexpectedly quiet streets tucked off the main thoroughfares; walking along quaintly cobbled Keystone Crescent, you could be in Islington. And if it all gets too much, there's always Camley Street Natural Park, a two-acre oasis of water and woodland.

Child's play: **Coram's Fields**. *See p123.*

Belsize Park

Halfway up the hill to Hampstead from Camden Town, Belsize Park was a Victorian development of the notorious 18th-century pleasure gardens that once surrounded Belsize House (now demolished). Much of the estate had been owned by Eton College since the Middle Ages. Grand white stuccoed terraces and red-brick mansions, most now converted into expensive one- or two-bed flats, were designed to compete with Kensington. The area acquired a rather seedy reputation, but is now more staid and salubrious than Camden Town and more bohemian than Hampstead. Typical recent celebrity residents include Sadie Frost, Jude Law, Gwyneth Paltrow and Anton 'Control' Corbijn. The tube emerges on the area's high street, the top end of Haverstock Hill, with banks, Budgens, chain restaurants, an organic grocer (Pomona) and the Screen on the Hill cinema (especially good for Jewish films). England's Lane, at the lower end of

Haverstock Hill, is more quirky and rarefied, with a slew of fine local pubs. Most delightful of all is Belsize Village, a pedestrianised oasis off Belsize Lane, with a good vet, excellent pharmacy and a deli among other attractions.

Hampstead

First fashionable for its spa waters in the 18th century, Hampstead has long been London's most gorgeous hilltop hideaway. It resisted the Victorian expansion of the city by conserving Hampstead Heath, a wonderful high tract of open countryside, and by preserving its own rural character.

Now many of the houses here cost as much as a farm. Though these may only be within reach of professional footballers and investment bankers, the area's artistic, literary and bohemian reputation is safe in the hands of a critical mass of genteel paupers. The likes of John Constable, John Keats and Robert Louis Stevenson started it; less genteel, Sid Vicious and John Lydon continued it (at a squat on Lutton Terrace, off Heath Street); and much less poor, Jonathan Ross, Helena Bonham-Carter and Jamie Oliver carry it on.

A relatively large area, Hampstead has several different districts. South End Green

King's Cross's alternative wild side – **Camley Street Natural Park**. *See p125.*

is the most affordable, close to Hampstead Heath station, and given a rougher edge by the Royal Free Hospital, Gospel Oak and Kentish Town. Fitzjohn's, on the other side of Rosslyn Hill, has avenues of fine red-brick Victorian villas and lots of private schools. Freud settled in Maresfield Gardens after fleeing Vienna, and his home is now a museum. Christchurch, east of Heath Street, is particularly delightful, close to the Heath, a warren of steep, winding lanes with raised pavements, old houses and fabulous views. Burgh House is the headquarters of the influential residents' association, the Heath & Hampstead Society. Hampstead tube emerges in Hampstead Village, where the High Street and Heath Street provide most of the area's shops and nightlife, including the luxurious Everyman Cinema. Just above is Holly Hill, another charming enclave.

The Heath is, of course, one of the area's biggest assets; at its north end lies the elegant neo-classical Kenwood House. It also contains three open-air swimming ponds: one for men, one for women and the third mixed. Local swimmers have won their battle to keep them open. There's a surfeit of schools in the area, many of them private, so congestion is hellish during the school run, the streets clogged with SUVs.

West and South Hampstead

Separated from Hampstead by the busy Finchley Road, West Hampstead is very much a district in its own right. Since West End Lane became a restaurant magnet, the area has emerged as a firm favourite with middle-class, pre-marriage-and-kids couples who aren't rich… yet. Slightly shabby in parts, surprisingly grand in others, much of West Hampstead is still on the up. If you want to move to north-west London and live this side of Kilburn and Willesden, you might still get lucky here.

Few Londoners know of the existence of South Hampstead as an area, unless they're familiar with the London Overground station (which takes you one stop to Euston in eight minutes). Closer to St John's Wood, at the top end of Abbey Road, the place should be famous for the Maryon Wilson Estate, which was built in the late 19th century and contains some of the area's most expensive housing. Property in South Hampstead consists mainly of stately red-brick mansion blocks or large detached villas such as those around Priory Road and Compayne Gardens. Several houses here remain gloriously spacious family homes, but many were converted into flats in the 1970s. Some of these are now quite scruffy and are one of the cheapest ways to buy into the area. Further north, around Fortune Green, the smaller Victorian terraces prove popular with young families.

Primrose Hill and Swiss Cottage

The quickest way to make enemies with Primrose Hill dwellers is to accuse them of living in Camden. This district is a genteel and well-heeled world away from its more raucous, easterly neighbour – and residents don't like you to forget it.

The eponymous mound provides lovely hilltop views of the city, within a smallish park, an extension of Regent's Park beyond London Zoo and the canal. Regent's Park Road and Gloucester Avenue are the local focal points, containing a pretty sprinkling of boutiques, cafés and some constantly busy gastropubs. Most of the diminutive area that constitutes Primrose Hill, however, is residential and this remains the chief draw for the beautiful people who set up home here. Rather like Hampstead, the neighbourhood has a reputation as a sanctuary for bohemian types. In reality it's too pricey for most such folk, but they still just about outnumber the banking whizzes who fancy a change from Kensington.

The large, three-storey stuccoed houses close to the park – not only Primrose Hill but the much larger Regent's Park to the south-east – fetch over £2 million if they haven't been converted into flats. Two-bed apartments in the same coveted streets, such as Regent's Park Road and the Chaltons (Crescent, Road and Street), go for more than £500,000; one-beds leave you little change from the same amount. An alternative is to bag a flat in one of the area's few post-war blocks; it might not look as grand, but it's the cheapest way of getting your foot in a Primrose Hill door.

Up the hill from here is Swiss Cottage (named after a 19th-century inn fashioned after a chalet), a bit of a non-area that's wedged north of St John's Wood, south-east of West Hampstead and west of Belsize Park. Housing prices are pretty similar to West Hampstead; public transport is excellent (Swiss Cottage and Finchley Road tubes, plus several bus routes). The Cottage apart, the most notable building is the modernist landmark of Swiss Cottage Library (designed by Sir Basil Spence and restored in 2003), recently joined by a state-of-the-art leisure centre, with a fine swimming pool and popular café.

Highgate and Dartmouth Park

Spilling out from the borough of Camden into Haringey, Highgate is known for its wild and wonderful cemetery (the West Cemetery) and the more ordered, municipal one (the East Cemetery) wherein lies Karl Marx. The area is far from dead, though, with a buoyant property market and one of the capital's most active community groups, the Highgate Society. The locality isn't quite as expensive to live in as Hampstead, but it's not far behind. Highgate also shares many of

Camden

Hampstead's advantages, such as its elevation and, of course, the lovely Heath (lying to the south-west).

Dartmouth Park is east of Highgate, just south of the cemetery – but isn't a park at all. The land bought by and named after the 18th-century Earl of Dartmouth is a residential area on the slopes up to Highgate, characterised by late 19th-century terraced and semi-detached houses. Both Dartmouth Park and Highgate are close to Parliament Hill, with its protected view over London. Once called Traitor's Hill, this elevation is now affectionately known as Kite's Hill, for obvious reasons.

Highgate Village is the prime place to reside in this neck of the woods – and talking of woods, Highgate Wood and Queen's Wood (both across borough boundaries in Haringey, but close) are very lovely. The Village's gated roads housing wealthy families are virtually free of the background hum of traffic. Such semi-rural serenity comes at a price, as does living anywhere very close to the Village, with its pretty shops and famous pub, the Flask. Around Pond Square, most houses are Victorian or Georgian, while some even older properties, built around the time of Charles II, can be glimpsed on the Grove. Five-bedroom, 18th-century piles command almost £3 million in this select enclave. High-end estates, such as the Holly Lodge Estate, are also popular, while Berthold Lubetkin's Highpoint flats, intended for workers in the 1930s, now house the chattering classes.

Public transport is a downside. The Northern line station is a hike from the Village on congested Archway Road. Still, you can't argue with the locals: you're doing all right if you've made it to N6.

Restaurants & cafés

Camden Town's cosmopolitan feel extends to the array of restaurants and cafés, cuisines and specialities on offer in the neighbourhood. Check out the classic Lebanese cooking at Le Mignon, reliable tapas at El Parador (or the rowdier Bar Gansa), homely Greek at Andy's Taverna or superior Caribbean at Mango Room. This is also the home of Haché, for top-notch burgers; if comfort food is your thing, also try Castle's on Royal College Street for trad pie and mash. Gilgamesh in Stables Market could hardly be more different: an opulent Babylonian temple to excess, with an estimable oriental restaurant. Pratt Street's Café Corfu offers decent Greek food and an upbeat vibe. Also worth a try are Cambodian Lemongrass and an outpost of the Belgian chain restaurant, Belgo Noord. A short stroll up the hill finds Chalk Farm institution Marine Ices, known for its own-made ice-cream. It also supplies the Coffee Cup Café on Hampstead High Street.

In classy Primrose Hill things take a price hike and pubs swing towards gastro. Most of the dining options are to be found along the villagey Regent's Park Road. Lemonia and older sister Limani continue to serve a bustling crowd with their excellent Greek-Cypriot cuisine; Polish staple Trojka is close by, as is Odette's, recently revamped by live music mogul Vince Power, opposite a branch of FishWorks. Vegetarians, vegans and even meat-eaters love the tasty raw delights at Little Earth Café within the Triyoga centre; charming Manna is also a good herbivorous option. All this is before you get to Primrose Hill's trio of top-notch gastropubs: Queens, the

Tuck in at **Retsina** in Belsize Village.

Landsdowne and the Engineer (for all, *see p131*). The Primrose Bakery (*see p134*), on Gloucester Avenue, does the most desirable cupcakes in London.

Belsize Park's the Hill (*see p131*) is also a good gastropub; the rest of the area's culinary scene is dominated by chains (among them the ever-excellent Gourmet Burger Kitchen), though Retsina, a new Greek restaurant in Belsize Village, is effortlessly authentic, hugely popular and very good value.

Things aren't great further up the hill in Hampstead: the feeble choice of eateries is always a surprise considering the money locals have to spend. Base meets its Mediterranean criteria well, though, while long-time favourites Jin Kichi (Japanese) and Safir (North African) please with their traditional cuisine. Off Haverstock Hill to the east, you'll find unpretentious and efficient Turkish Zara and family-friendly Fratelli la Bufala. Away from the busy streets, enjoy tea and cake at the charming Brew House café in Kenwood House.

Westwards in the busy thoroughfare of Swiss Cottage, Eriki impresses with its Indian fare, and kids love Japanese mini-chain Benihana, featuring performing chefs at each table. Singapore Garden is long-established local favourite. Tobia serves fine Ethiopian food on the first floor of a slightly drab community centre.

In West Hampstead, West End Lane keeps the resident middle classes well fed with Italian La Brocca and Modern European Walnut. A little further afield, on Fortune Green Road, is Nautilus, a proper chippie (eat-in or takeaway). Over in Highgate and its surrounds, gastropubs rule: the Bull (*see p132*) in Highgate (in a stunning listed building), spacious Junction Tavern in Dartmouth Park, and the Oxford (*see p131*) on Kentish Town Road.

In the vanguard of the transformation of King's Cross are Camino, a hip Spanish bar-restaurant run by the owners of Cargo in Shoreditch, and two eco-friendly restaurants: Konstam at the Prince Albert is brave enough only to source food from within reach of the tube network; Acorn House is a charming environmentally aware training restaurant (look out for a café spin-off called the Water House due to open in Canalside Works, De Beauvoir town). At the opposite end of the Euston Road, near

Eco-friendly **Acorn House**.

Camden

Warren Street, is the gastropub Queen's Head & Artichoke and the intimate African Kitchen Gallery. Fish Bone and North Sea Fish Restaurant are two of the best fish and chip shops in town.

Directly south of Euston, Bloomsbury houses a concentration of restaurants between Guilford Street and Theobald's Road: try superior pizza at La Porchetta or great Spanish at Cigala; the Perseverance is a worthy gastropub too. On Goodge Street, Ooze does quick and colourful risottos, while often-packed Salt Yard serves up superior tapas. Also west of Tottenham Court Road and just within Camden borders is restaurant hotspot Charlotte Street; best are Tex-Mex shack La Perla, Indian Rasa Samudra, Italian Bertorelli, superior tapas joint Fino, classy Japanese Roka and

southern Italian Passione. The Crazy Bear (see p133) restaurant and bar in Whitfield Street is stylish, decadent and supremely comfortable. Mini-chains Busaba Eathai (on Store Street) and Dim T café are also good, while Hakkasan, nestled in the borough's south-west corner on Hanway Street, serves up arguably the best Chinese food in town.

Acorn House 69 Swinton Street, WC1X 9NT (7812 1842/www.acornhouserestaurant.com).
African Kitchen Gallery 102 Drummond Street, NW1 2HN (7383 0918).
Andy's Taverna 81-81A Bayham Street, NW1 0AG (7485 9718/www.andystaverna.com).
Bar Gansa 2 Inverness Street, NW1 7HJ (7267 8909).
Base 71 Hampstead High Street, NW3 1QP (7431 2224/www.basefoods.com).
Belgo Noord 72 Chalk Farm Road, NW1 8AN (7267 0718/www.belgo-restaurants.com).
Benihana 100 Avenue Road, NW3 3HF (7586 9508/www.benihana.co.uk).
Bertorelli 19 Charlotte Street, W1T 1RL (7636 4174/www.santeonline.co.uk).
Brew House Kenwood House, Hampstead Lane, NW3 7JR (8341 5384/ www.company ofcooks.com).
La Brocca 273 West End Lane, NW6 1QS (7433 1989).
Busaba Eathai 22 Store Street, WC1E 7DS (7299 7900).
Café Corfu 7 Pratt Street, NW1 0AE (7267 8088/www.cafecorfu.com).
Camino 3 Varnisher's Yard, Regent's Quarter, N1 9FD (7841 7331/www.barcamino.com).
Castle's 229 Royal College Street, NW1 9LT (7485 2196).
Cigala 54 Lamb's Conduit Street, WC1N 3LW (7405 1717/www.cigala.co.uk).
Coffee Cup Café 74 Hampstead High Street, NW3 1QX (7435 7565).
Dim T 32 Charlotte Street, W1T 2NQ (7637 1122/www.dimt.co.uk).
Eriki 4-6 Northways Parade, Finchley Road, NW3 5EN (7722 0606/www.eriki.co.uk).
Fino 33 Charlotte Street, entrance on Rathbone Street, W1T 1RR (7813 8010/ www.finorestaurant.com).
Fish Bone 82 Cleveland Street, W1T 6NF (7580 2672).
FishWorks 57 Regent's Park Road, NW1 8XD (7586 9760/www.fishworks.co.uk).
Fratelli la Bufala 45A South End Road, NW3 2QB (7435 7814/www.fratellilabufala.com).
Gilgamesh Camden Stables Market, Chalk Farm Road, NW1 8AH (7482 5757/ www.gilgameshbar.com).
Gourmet Burger Kitchen 200 Haverstock Hill, NW3 2AG (7443 5335/www.gbkinfo.co.uk).
Haché 24 Inverness Street, NW1 7HJ (7485 9100/www.hacheburgers.com).
Hakkasan 8 Hanway Place, W1T 1HD (7907 1888).

TRANSPORT

Tube stations Central Chancery Lane, Holborn, Tottenham Court Road; Circle King's Cross St Pancras, Euston Square, Great Portland Street; Hammersmith & City King's Cross St Pancras, Euston Square, Great Portland Street; Jubilee Swiss Cottage, Finchley Road, West Hampstead; Metropolitan King's Cross St Pancras, Euston Square, Great Portland Street, Finchley Road; Northern Tottenham Court Road, Goodge Street, Warren Street, Euston, King's Cross St Pancras, Mornington Crescent, Camden Town, Chalk Farm, Belsize Park, Hampstead, Kentish Town; Piccadilly Holborn, Russell Square, King's Cross St Pancras; Victoria Warren Street, Euston, King's Cross St Pancras

Rail stations London Overground Camden Road, Kentish Town West, Gospel Oak, Hampstead Heath, Finchley Road & Frognal, West Hampstead; Euston, South Hampstead, Kilburn High Road; Capital First Connect Thameslink St Pancras International, Kentish Town, West Hampstead

Main bus routes dozens of buses run through Camden and into central London – for a full list, visit www.tfl. gov.uk/buses; night buses N1, N5, N7, N8, N10, N19, N20, N29, N38, N41, N55, N63, N68, N73, N91, N98, N171, N253, N279; 24-hour buses C2, 14, 24, 25, 27, 88, 134, 139, 176, 189, 205, 214, 242, 243, 274, 390

Jin Kichi *73 Heath Street, NW3 6UG (7794 6158/www.jinkichi.com).*

Junction Tavern *101 Fortess Road, NW5 1AG (7485 9400/www.junctiontavern.co.uk).*

Konstam at the Prince Albert *2 Acton Street, WC1X 9NA (7833 5040/www. konstam.co.uk).*

Lemongrass *243 Royal College Street, NW1 9LT (7284 1116).*

Lemonia *89 Regent's Park Road, NW1 8UY (7586 7454).*

Limani *154 Regent's Park Road, NW1 8XN (7483 4492).*

Little Earth Café *6 Erskine Road, NW3 3AJ (7483 3344/www.triyoga.co.uk).*

Mango Room *10-12 Kentish Town Road, NW1 8NH (7482 5065/www.mangoroom.co.uk).*

Manna *4 Erskine Road, NW3 3AJ (7722 8028/www.manna-veg.com).*

Marine Ices *8 Haverstock Hill, NW3 2BL (7482 9003/www.marineices.co.uk).*

Le Mignon *98 Arlington Road, NW1 7HD (7387 0600).*

Nautilus *27-29 Fortune Green Road, NW6 1DU (7435 2532).*

North Sea Fish Restaurant *7-8 Leigh Street, WC1H 9EW (7387 5892/www.northseafish restaurant.co.uk).*

Odette's *130 Regent's Park Road, NW1 8XL (7586 8569).*

Ooze *62 Goodge Street, W1T 4NE (7436 9444/www.ooze.biz).*

El Parador *245 Eversholt Street, NW1 1BA (7387 2789/www.elparadorlondon.com).*

Passione *10 Charlotte Street, W1T 2LT (7636 2833/www.passione.co.uk).*

La Perla *11 Charlotte Street, W1T 1RQ (7436 1744/www.cafepacifico-laperla.com).*

Perseverance *63 Lamb's Conduit Street, WC1N 3NB (7405 8278/www.theperseverance pub.com).*

La Porchetta *33 Boswell Street, WC1N 3BP (7242 2434/www.laporchetta.co.uk).*

Queen's Head & Artichoke *30-32 Albany Street, NW1 4EA (7916 6206/www.the artichoke.net).*

Rasa Samudra *5 Charlotte Street, W1T 1RE (7637 0222/www.rasarestaurants.com).*

Retsina *48-50 Belsize Lane, NW3 5AN (7431 5855).*

Roka *37 Charlotte Street, W1T 1RR (7580 6464/www.rokarestaurant.com).*

Safir *116 Heath Street, NW3 1DR (7431 9888/www.safir-restaurant.co.uk).*

Salt Yard *54 Goodge Street, W1T 4NA (7637 0657/www.saltyard.co.uk).*

Singapore Garden *83 Fairfax Road, NW6 4DY (7624 8233/www.singaporegarden.co.uk).*

Tobia *1st floor, 2A Lithos Road, NW3 6EF (7431 4213/www.tobiarestaurant.co.uk).*

Trojka *101 Regent's Park Road, NW1 8UR (7483 3765/www.trojka.co.uk).*

Walnut *280 West End Lane, NW6 1LJ (7794 7772/www.walnutwalnut.com).*

Zara *11 South End Road, NW3 2PT (7794 5498).*

Bars & pubs

In Camden Town, the Hawley Arms is famed for its excellent jukebox and fashionable following: packed in like sardines, Camdenites studiously feign indifference as Amy Winehouse necks a beer, or Rhys Ifans squeezes past to the bar. Drinking dens line nearby Inverness Street, from record-peddling Bar Vinyl to Britpop hangout of yesteryear the Good Mixer, but some of Camden's best bars are in its backstreets. Just off the high street, the dimly lit Crown & Goose serves unexpectedly accomplished food from its tiny kitchen; further off the beaten track, the ramshackle Monkey Chews is a cosy hideaway. Another unassuming gem is the Lord Stanley just off Camden Road.

Changes at Stables Market mean At Proud has moved – though only 20 yards, to the Horse Hospital, where a bigger space for gigs and smoker-friendly terrace are promised (due to open as this guide went to press). Gilgamesh (*see p128*), meanwhile, is staying put, with its theatrical decor and expensive cocktails. Further up towards Chalk Farm tube, the Lock Tavern hosts an eclectic line-up of DJs.

If the Camden scene is all about seeing and being seen, Kentish Town offers welcome respite. On the high street, Quinn's and O'Reilly's are battered, no-nonsense boozers of the old school. For those that like their floorboards a touch more polished, lively local gastropubs include the Oxford, Vine and Abbey – the latter famed for its Sunday evening acoustic sets. The grande dame of the neighbourhood, though, is the Pineapple. A local institution since 1868, it's a vision of Victorian splendour, although a recent refurbishment has done away with its red velvet banquettes and moth-eaten curtains. A short stagger away, the Bull & Gate is another great old-timer.

Despite their proximity to Camden Town, Belsize Park and Primrose Hill are more geared towards a quiet drink and a meal than riotous nights out, with stately gastropubs such as the Lansdowne, Engineer, Queens and the Hill catering for a well-heeled clientele. Standing firm against the tide of gentrification is the down-to-earth Princess of Wales, known for its Sunday jazz sessions. On Haverstock

Camden

Settle in for the evening at cosy Highgate boozer the **Flask**.

Hill, the Sir Richard Steele is another pleasingly old-fashioned drinking den with a cosily cluttered interior and regular quiz night.

Up the hill, historic pubs dot the tangled backstreets and leafy lanes of Hampstead. The oldest is the wonderfully atmospheric 16th-century Spaniard's Inn; equally snug is the warren of wood-panelled rooms at the Holly Bush – also a good spot for a sustaining roast after a hike over the Heath. The Wells offers good gastro fare, while at the Horseshoe you can wash down lunch with one of its microbrewery beers.

North-west in hilly West Hampstead, the nightlife is concentrated around West End Lane. Bars predominate over traditional pubs, though the Railway remains a handy spot for a pint, close to the tube. Local favourites include the Gallery and the laid-back, sofa-filled Sirous. Sophisticates sip cocktails on the terrace outside Eclipse Bar or lounge on the leather banquettes inside: it's open until 1am at weekends.

Over in Highgate, upmarket boozers filled with cliquey locals are the norm. The Wrestlers, Bull and Angel Inn are all pleasant spots for a pint, although the pick of the bunch is the low-ceilinged, intimate Flask, set by Highgate Village's tiny green. Along Archway Road, the late-licensed Boogaloo marks a total change of pace with its superb jukebox, eclectic

DJ nights and occasional celebrity clientele (the likes of Pete Doherty and Shane McGowan drop in from time to time).

Until recently, King's Cross was better known for its clubs than its pubs, with a trio of venues at the top of eerie York Way (Canvas, the Key and the Cross). All three have now closed down, victims of the area's sweeping regeneration project; EGG, tucked away on York Way, is the sole survivor. But it's not all doom and gloom. Opened in 2006, the Big Chill House offers relaxed daytime drinking on the roof terrace and late-night DJ sets, while 06 St Chad's Place, housed in a stripped-out warehouse space, epitomises self-conscious urban cool. On Caledonian Road, Ruby Lounge has lost its titular hue but retained its alluringly inexpensive cocktail menu. Cosier options include the King Charles I, with its open fire and rotating guest bitters, and the out-of-the-way Harrison.

In Camden's most southern reaches, Bloomsbury boasts a clutch of dignified old-timers, where the local literati once supped; the Museum Tavern, opposite the British Museum, counts Orwell and Marx among its former customers. Further off the tourist trail on Lamb's Conduit Street, the 18th-century Lamb serves well-kept Young's beers; the Perseverance (*see p130*) is just down the road. If you're feeling energetic, boozing and bowling are on offer at Bloomsbury Bowling Lanes and the swankier All-Star Lanes. West of New Oxford Street, hip DJ bar AKA caters to a clubby, youthful throng, while tucked-away Grape Street Wine Bar has well-priced wines and snug surrounds. Towards bar-studded Covent Garden, atmospheric and intimate basement bar Freud mixes a mean cocktail (great if you can get a seat – it's rammed most evenings).

West of Tottenham Court Road sees the beginning of Fitzrovia (half of which falls within Camden's bounds). The area's namesake, the Fitzroy Tavern, was infamous for the bohemian crowd of writers and poets who drank here in the 1930s; these days, their modern equivalents head for the endearingly scruffy Bradley's Spanish Bar. Sleek bars are increasingly par for the course round these parts, though, with modish Oscar, subterranean Crazy Bear and slick Shochu Lounge vying for affections.

Abbey *124 Kentish Town Road, NW1 9QR (7267 9449/www.abbey-tavern.com).*

AKA *18 West Central Street, WC1A 1JJ (7836 0110/www.akalondon.com).*

All Star Lanes *Victoria House, Bloomsbury Place, WC1B 4DA (7025 2676/www.allstarlanes. co.uk).*

Angel Inn, *37 Highgate High Street, N6 5JT (8347 2921).*

At Proud *Horse Hospital, Stables Market, Chalk Farm Road, NW1 8AH (7482 3867/ www.atproud.net).*

Bar Vinyl *6 Inverness Street, NW1 7HJ (7482 5545/www.barvinyl.com).*

Big Chill House *257-259 Pentonville Road, N1 9NL (7427 2540/www.bigchill.net/house.html).*

Bloomsbury Bowling Lanes *Basement, Tavistock Hotel, Bedford Way, WC1H 9EU (7691 2610/www.bloomsburylive.com).*

Boogaloo *312 Archway Road, N6 5AT (8340 2928/www.theboogaloo.co.uk).*

Bradley's Spanish Bar *42-44 Hanway Street, W1T 1UT (7636 0359).*

Bull *13 North Hill, N6 4AB (0845 456 5033/ www.inthebull.biz).*

Bull & Gate *389 Kentish Town Road, NW5 2TJ (8826 5000/www.bullandgate.co.uk).*

Crazy Bear *26-28 Whitfield Street, W1T 2RG (7631 0088/www.crazybeargroup.co.uk).*

Crown & Goose *100 Arlington Road, NW1 7HP (7485 8008).*

Eclipse *283-285 West End Lane, NW6 1RD (7431 1118).*

Engineer *65 Gloucester Avenue, NW1 8JH (7722 0950/www.the-engineer.com).*

Fitzroy Tavern *16 Charlotte Street, W1T 2LY (7580 3714).*

Flask *77 Highgate West Hill, N6 6BU (8348 7346).*

Freud *198 Shaftesbury Avenue, WC2H 8JL (7240 9933/www.freudliving.com).*

Gallery *190 Broadhurst Gardens, NW6 3AY (7625 9184).*

Good Mixer *30 Inverness Street, NW1 7HJ (7916 6176).*

Grape Street Wine Bar *222-224A Shaftesbury Avenue, WC2H 8EB (7240 0686).*

Harrison *28 Harrison Street, WC1H 8JF (7278 3966).*

Hawley Arms *2 Castlehaven Road, NW1 8QU (7428 5979).*

Hill *94 Haverstock Hill, NW3 2BD (7267 0033).*

Holly Bush *22 Holly Mount, NW3 6SG (7435 2892/www.hollybushpub.com).*

Horseshoe *28 Heath Street, NW3 6TE (7431 7206).*

King Charles I *55-57 Northdown Street, N1 9BL (7837 7758).*

Lamb *94 Lamb's Conduit Street, WC1N 3LZ (7405 0713).*

Lansdowne *90 Gloucester Avenue, NW1 8HX (7483 0409/www.thelansdownepub.co.uk).*

Lock Tavern *35 Chalk Farm Road, NW1 8AJ (7482 7163).*

Lord Stanley *51 Camden Park Road, NW1 9BH (7428 9488).*

Monkey Chews *2 Queen's Crescent, NW5 4EP (7267 6406/www.monkeychews.com).*

Museum Tavern *49 Great Russell Street, WC1B 3BA (7242 8987).*

O'Reilly's *289-291 Kentish Town Road, NW5 2JS (7267 4002).*

Oscar *Charlotte Street Hotel, 15 Charlotte Street, W1T 1RJ (7806 2000/www.charlotte streethotel.com).*

06 St Chad's Place *6 St Chad's Place, WC1X 9HH (7278 3355/www.6stchadsplace.com).*

Oxford *256 Kentish Town Road, NW5 2AA (7485 3521/www.realpubs.co.uk).*

Pineapple *51 Leverton Street, NW5 2NX (7284 4631).*

Princess of Wales *22 Chalcot Road, NW1 8LL (7722 0354).*

Queens *49 Regent's Park Road, NW1 8XD (7586 0408).*

Quinn's *65 Kentish Town Road, NW1 8NY (7267 8240).*

Railway *100 West End Lane, NW6 2LU (7624 7611).*

Ruby Lounge *33 Caledonian Road, N1 9BU (7837 9558/www.ruby.uk.com).*

Shochu Lounge *37 Charlotte Street, W1T 1RR (7580 9666/www.shochulounge.com).*

Sirous *268 West End Lane, NW6 1LJ (7435 8164/www.sirous.com).*

Sir Richard Steele *97 Haverstock Hill, NW3 4RL (7483 1261).*

Spaniards Inn *Spaniards Road, NW3 7JJ (8731 6571).*

Vine *86 Highgate Road, NW5 1PB (7209 0038/www.thevinelondon.co.uk).*

Wells *30 Well Walk, NW3 1BX (7794 3785/www.thewellshampstead.com).*

Wrestlers *98 North Road, N6 4AA (8340 4297).*

Shops

Although the borough's retail hotspots are Hampstead, Primrose Hill and the fringes of the West End, for most people, the words 'Camden' and 'shopping' evoke the sprawling, eponymous market – which is, in fact, made up of several distinct entities. Camden Lock Market, with its artisan shops, retains its boho character, but part of the adjacent Stables Market is undergoing redevelopment, which many locals fear will ruin its ramshackle charm. The markets are also open during the week, when they're considerably quieter, but be prepared for a tourist scrum at weekends. Nearby is vintage clothes shop Rokit and Rough Sleepers, a boutique with a conscience that invests profits in homeless charity Novas. Chinalife, the well-being arm of long-standing Chinese medicine clinic AcuMedic, is also worth checking out. The iconic Camden Coffee Shop, where George Constantinou has been roasting beans for 30 years, and – north in Kentish Town – new health food store Earth Natural Foods are local assets. Another gem on workaday Kentish Town Road is the Owl Bookshop.

In Primrose Hill, Regent's Park Road is a contender for London's most perfect high street, with a mix of practical traditional shops (hardware store, greengrocer, pet shop and the excellent Primrose Hill Books), plus delis, cafés, a smattering of fashionable boutiques, including Anna, Press (just off the main drag) and yummy-mummy heaven Elias & Grace. Residents don't have to travel far to furnish their coveted properties; there's a clutch of home-related shops, including Graham & Green. Studio Perfumery sells unusual European scents, and Spice fashion-led footwear. Gloucester Avenue is sprinkled with gems: Miss Lala's Boudoir for cheeky lingerie; Shikasuki for well-preserved vintage clothing and accessories; delicate jewellery at Sweet Pea; the Primrose Bakery, which has tables for eating in; and superior deli Melrose & Morgan. Around the corner is a new outpost of much-loved Herne Hill children's bookshop Tales on Moon Lane.

On Haverstock Hill, which links Belsize Park to Hampstead, is a branch of Daunt Books; there's also one in the charming enclave of South End Green. This part of London has no shortage of delis, including

Belsize Village and, in Hampstead itself, stalwart Rosslyn Delicatessen. Beetroot, a Polish food shop, makes for a welcome change. Also of eastern European extraction (but of over 40 years' standing), Louis' Pâtisserie provides Hungarian-style cakes. Hampstead has plenty of fashion too; as well as branches of upmarket brands like Jigsaw, there are less ubiquitous labels at boutique Cochinechine. Little girls love Mystical Fairies, while kids in general can be indulged at traditional toyshop Happy Returns.

Further east in (otherwise barren) Gospel Oak is Kristin Baybars's fascinating shop, full of exquisite miniaturist scenes and dolls' house kits. On the border with Haringey, Highgate High Street is home to second-hand bookshop Fisher & Sperr.

Back in the centre of town, Tottenham Court Road has too many electrical goods shops to mention, plus a line-up of homeware stores, including stalwarts Heal's and Habitat. For more unusual interior goods by independent designers, take a detour down Warren Street for Thorsten van Elten's contemporary showroom. Across the road is an outpost of shoe shop Black Truffle, which also runs footwear- and accessory-making classes downstairs. Further south-east lie the joys of Bloomsbury: here are James Smith & Son, venerable vendor of umbrellas, and in the streets around the British Museum, small shops selling everything from books to antiquarian maps and rubber stamps. It's also home to the recently revamped Brutalist residential/retail centre the Brunswick, which now contains a Waitrose, high-street fashion stores, various eateries and the Skoob second-hand bookshop. Lamb's Conduit Street has blossomed into a well-rounded shopping destination, offering everything from contemporary made-to-measure suits at Pokit and hip menswear at Folk to forgotten women's fiction at niche publisher Persephone Books. Tucked away on Rugby Street you'll find unusual jewellery at French's Dairy and Susannah Hunter's handmade bags.

Anna *126 Regent's Park Road, NW1 8XL (7483 0411/www.shopatanna.co.uk).*
Beetroot *92 Fleet Road, NW3 2QX (7424 8544/www.beetrootdeli.co.uk).*
Belsize Village Deli *39 Belsize Lane, NW3 5AS (7794 4258).*
Black Truffle *52 Warren Street, W1T 5NJ (7388 4547/www.blacktruffle.com).*

Take the weight off in Bloomsbury's **Tavistock Square**. *See p120.*

Camden Coffee Shop *11 Delancey Street, NW1 7NL (7387 4080).*
Camden Markets *(7267 3417/ www.camdenmarkets.org).*
Chinalife *99-105 Camden High Street, NW1 7JN (7388 5783/www.acumedic.com).*
Cochinechine *74 Heath Street, NW3 1DN (7435 9377/www.cochinechine.com).*
Daunt Books *www.dauntbooks.co.uk: 193 Haverstock Hill, NW3 4QL (7794 4006); 51 South End Road, NW3 2QB (7794 8206).*
Earth Natural Foods *200 Kentish Town Road, NW5 2AE (7482 2211/www.earthnatural foods.co.uk).*
Elias & Grace *158 Regent's Park Road, NW1 8XN (7449 0574/www.eliasandgrace.com).*
Fisher & Sperr *46 Highgate High Street, N6 5JB (8340 7244).*
French's Dairy *13 Rugby Street, WC1N 3QT (7404 7070/www.frenchsdairy.com).*
Folk *49 Lamb's Conduit Street, WC1N 3NG (7404 6458/www.folkclothing.com).*
Graham & Green *164 Regent's Park Road, NW1 8XN (7586 2960/www.grahamand green.co.uk).*
Happy Returns *36 Rosslyn Hill, NW3 1NH (7435 2431).*
James Smith & Son *53 New Oxford Street, WC1A 1BL (7836 4731/www.james-smith.co.uk).*
Kristin Baybars *7 Mansfield Road, NW3 2JD (7267 0934).*

Louis' Pâtisserie *32 Heath Street, NW3 6DU (7435 9908).*
Melrose & Morgan *42 Gloucester Avenue, NW1 8JD (7722 0011/www.melroseand morgan.com).*
Miss Lala's Boudoir *148 Gloucester Avenue, NW1 8JA (7483 1888/www.misslalas boudoir.co.uk).*
Mystical Fairies *12 Flask Walk, NW3 1HE (7431 1888/www.mysticalfairies. co.uk).*
Owl Bookshop *209 Kentish Town Road, NW5 2JU (7485 7793).*
Persephone Books *59 Lamb's Conduit Street, WC1N 3NB (7242 9292/www.persephone books.co.uk).*
Pokit *53 Lamb's Conduit Street, WC1N 3NB (7430 9782/www.pokit.co.uk).*
Press *3 Erskine Road, NW3 3AJ (7449 0081).*
Primrose Bakery *69 Gloucester Avenue, NW1 8LD (7483 4222/www.primrose bakery.org.uk).*
Primrose Hill Books *134 Regent's Park Road, NW1 8XL (7586 2022/www.primrose hillbooks.com).*
Rokit *225 Camden High Street, NW1 7BU (7267 3046/www.rokit.co.uk).*
Rough Sleepers *43 Chalk Farm Road, NW1 8AJ (7485 4848/www.novas.org).*
Rosslyn Delicatessen *56 Rosslyn Hill, NW3 1ND (7794 9210/www.delirosslyn.co.uk).*

The revamped **Brunswick Centre**. *See p134.*

Shikasuki 67 *Gloucester Avenue, NW1 8LD*
(7722 4442/www.shikasuki.com).
Skoob *Unit 66, The Brunswick, WC1N 1AE*
(7278 8760/www.skoob.com).
Spice Shoes 162 *Regent's Park Road, NW1*
8XN (7722 2478/www.spiceshu.co.uk).
Studio Perfumery 170 *Regent's Park Road,*
NW1 8XN (7722 1478).
Susannah Hunter 7 *Rugby Street, WC1N 3QT*
(7692 3798/www.susannahhunter.com).
Sweet Pea 77 *Gloucester Avenue, NW1 8LD*
(7449 9393/www.sweetpeajewellery.com).
Tales on Moon Lane 9 *Princess Road, NW1*
8JN (7722 1800/www.talesonmoonlane.co.uk).
Thorsten van Elten 22 *Warren Street, W1T*
5LU (7388 8008/www.thorstenvanelten.com).

Arts & attractions

Cinemas & theatres

Camden People's Theatre 58-60 *Hampstead*
Road, NW1 2PY (7419 4841/bookings 0870
060 0100/www.cptheatre.co.uk).
Diorama Arts Centres 3-7 *Euston Centre,*
NW1 3JG (7916 5467/www.diorama-arts.
org.uk). Community arts centre with a gallery
and rehearsal space; a theatre is due to open
in 2009.
Drill Hall 16 *Chenies Street, WC1E 7EX*
(7307 5060/www.drillhall.co.uk). Lesbian- and
gay-centred performance art and activities.
Etcetera Theatre 265 *Camden High Street,*
NW1 7BU (7482 4857/www.etceteratheatre.
com). Mini theatre above the Oxford Arms pub.
Everyman Cinema 5 *Holly Bush Vale,*
NW3 6TX (0870 066 4777/www.everyman
cinema.com).
Hampstead Theatre *Eton Avenue, NW3 3EU*
(7722 9301/www.hampsteadtheatre.com).
Horse Hospital *Colonnade, WC1N 1HX*
(7713 7370/www.thehorsehospital.com). Offbeat
arts venue and new home of At Proud.
Odeon *0871 224 4007/www.odeon.co.uk;*
Camden Town: 14 Parkway, NW1 7AA;
Swiss Cottage: 96 Finchley Road, NW3 5EL.
The Place 17 *Duke's Road, WC1H 9PY*
(7121 1100/www.theplace.org.uk). Leading
contemporary dance centre.
Renoir Cinema *Brunswick Square, WC1N*
1AW (7837 8402/www.artificial-eye.com).
Shaw Theatre 100-110 *Euston Road, NW1*
2AJ (0870 033 2600/www.theshawtheatre.com).
Screen on the Hill 203 *Haverstock Hill, NW3*
4QG (7435 3366/www.screencinemas.co.uk).
Cinema.
Theatro Technis 26 *Crowndale Road, NW1*
1TT (7387 6617/www.theatrotechnis.com).
Fringe theatre established in 1957.
Upstairs at the Gatehouse *Corner of*
Hampstead Lane & North Road, Highgate
Village, N6 4BD (8340 3488/www.upstairs
atthegatehouse.com). Theatre pub.
Vue Finchley Road *O2 Centre, 255 Finchley*
Road, NW3 6LU (0871 224 0240/
www.myvue.com).

Galleries & museums

British Museum *Great Russell Street, WC1B*
3DG (7323 8000/www.thebritishmuseum.ac.uk).
Camden Arts Centre *Arkwright Road, NW3*
6DG (7472 5500/www.camdenartscentre.org).
Galleries, studios, a café and landscaped gardens.
Cartoon Museum *Old Dairy, 35 Little Russell*
Street, WC1A 2HH (7631 0793/www.cartoon
centre.com).
Fenton House *Windmill Hill, NW3 6RT*
(7435 3471/information 01494 755563/
www.nationaltrust.org). Collection of
antique musical instruments and porcelain;
the sunken gardens and orchard are a delight.
Freud Museum 20 *Maresfield Gardens, NW3*
5SX (7435 2002/www.freud.org.uk). Former
home of Sigmund and his daughter Anna.
Keats House *Keats Grove, NW3 2RR (7435*
2062/www.cityoflondon.gov.uk/keats). Closed for
refurbishment until Oct 2008.
Kenwood House *Hampstead Lane, NW3 7JR*
(8348 1286/www.english-heritage.org.uk).
Impressive neo-classical house on Hampstead
Heath; houses the Iveagh Bequest art collection.
176 Gallery 176 *Prince of Wales Road, NW5*
3PT (7428 8940/www.projectspace176.com).
Impressive new home of the Zabludowicz
Collection of contemporary art.
Sir John Soane's Museum 13 *Lincoln's Inn*
Fields, WC2A 3BP (7405 2107/www.soane.org).
Atmospheric home of 18th-century architect
showcasing his collection of art and artefacts.

Music & comedy venues

Barfly 49 *Chalk Farm Road, NW1 8AN*
(7691 4243/www.barflyclub.com). Music venue.
Dublin Castle 94 *Parkway, NW1 7AN*
(7485 1773/www.bugbearbookings.com).
Music venue and pub.
Electric Ballroom 184 *Camden High Street,*
NW1 8QP (7485 9006/www.electricballroom.
co.uk). Music venue and club.
Forum 9-17 *Highgate Road, NW5 1JY (7284*
1001/www.meanfiddler.com). Music venue.
Jazz Café 5 *Parkway, NW1 7PG (7534*
6955/www.meanfiddler.com). Jazz venue.
Jongleurs Camden *Middle Yard, Chalk Farm*
Road, Camden Lock, NW1 8AB (0870 787
0707/www.jongleurs.com). Comedy club.
KOKO 1A *Camden High Street, NW1 7JE*
(0870 432 5527/www.koko.uk.com). Music
venue and club.
Monkey Business Chalk Farm
97 *Haverstock Hill, NW3 4RL (07932 338203/*
www.monkeybusinesscomedyclub.co.uk). Comedy
club. Also at O'Reilly's pub in Kentish Town on
Thur, Fri and Sat.
Roundhouse *Chalk Farm Road, NW1 8EH*
(0870 389 1846/www.roundhouse.org.uk).
Pioneering music venue, reopened in 2006
after extensive refurbishment.
Scala 275 *Pentonville Road, N1 9NL*
(7833 2022/www.scala-london.co.uk).
Music venue and club.
Water Rats 328 *Gray's Inn Road, WC1X 8BZ*
(7837 7269). Music venue.

Other attractions

British Library 96 Euston Road, NW1 2DB
(0870 444 1500/www.bl.uk). One of the greatest
libraries in the world. Access to the reading
rooms requires a reader's pass (free, but subject
to a rigorous interrogation by library staff).
Kentish Town City Farm 1 Cressfield Close,
NW5 4BN (7916 5421/www.aapi.co.uk/cityfarm).
Pirate's Castle Oval Road, NW1 7EA (7267
6605/www.thepiratecastle.org). Canalside activity
centre for young people.
St Pancras International Euston Road, NW1
9QP (7843 4250/www.stpancras.com). Reopened
at the end of 2007, the new terminus for Eurostar
promises to be a 'destination station', with a
shopping arcade, daily market and the longest
champagne bar in Europe. Or you could just
marvel at the Victorian Gothic architecture.

Sport & fitness

Camden has a good selection of public
facilities, including the Talacre Community
Sports Centre, the open-air swimming
ponds of Hampstead Heath and the Oasis
centre with its heated outdoor pool. In the
private sector, the borough is blessed with
the Central YMCA, one of the top sports
centres in London.

Gyms & leisure centres

Armoury 25 Pond Street, NW3 2PN
(7431 2263/www.jubileehallclubs.co.uk). Private.
Central YMCA 112 Great Russell Street,
WC1B 3NQ (7343 1700/www.centralymca.
org.uk). Private.
Esporta Unit 2, Level 1, O2 Centre, 255
Finchley Road, NW3 6LU (7644 2400/
www.esporta.com). Private.
Fitness First www.fitnessfirst.co.uk; 128 Albert
Street, NW1 7NE (7284 2244); 81-84 Chalk
Farm Road, NW1 8AR (7284 0004); Coram
Street, WC1N 1HB (7833 1887). Private.
Gymbox 100 High Holborn, WC1V 6RD
(7400 1919/www.gymbox.co.uk). Private.
Kieser Training Greater London House,
Hampstead Road, NW1 7DF (0800 037 0370/
www.kieser-training.com). Back specialists;
private.
LA Fitness www.lafitness.co.uk; 53-79
Highgate Road, NW5 1TL (0870 607 2142);
Lacon House, 84 Theobald's Road, WC1X
8RW (0870 607 2143). Private.
Mallinson Sports Centre Bishopswood Road,
N6 4NY (8342 7272/www.highgateschool.
org.uk/Activities/Sports_Centre.htm). Private.
Mornington Sports & Fitness Centre
142-150 Arlington Road, NW1 7HP
(7267 3600/www.camden.gov.uk/sport).
Oasis Sports Centre 32 Endell Street, WC2H
9AG (7831 1804/www.camden.gov.uk/sport).
Soho Gym www.sohogyms.com; 193 Camden
High Street, NW1 7JY (7482 4524); 12 Macklin
Street, WC2B 5NF (7242 1290). Private.

Spring Health Leisure Club 81 Belsize
Park Gardens, NW3 4NJ (7483 6800/
www.springhealth.net). Private.
Swiss Cottage Leisure Centre Adelaide
Road, NW3 (7974 2012/www.camden.
gov.uk/sport).
Talacre Community Sports Centre Dalby
Street, off Prince of Wales Road, NW5 3AF
(7974 8765/www.camden.gov.uk/sport).
Virgin Active 50 Triton Square, NW1 3XB
(7388 5511/www.virginactive.co.uk). Private.

Other facilities

Hampstead Heath Swimming Ponds
Hampstead Heath, NW5 1QR (7485 4491).
Parliament Hill Lido Parliament Hill Fields,
Gordon House Road, NW5 2LT (7485 5757/
www.cityoflondon.gov.uk/openspaces).
Triyoga 6 Erskine Road, NW3 3AJ (7483 3344/
www.triyoga.co.uk).

Schools

WHAT THE PARENTS SAY:

'In my opinion, the two best primary schools
in Hampstead are the Hampstead Parochial CofE
and Christchurch CofE. Hampstead Parochial
is probably a neck or two ahead, largely because
of the influences of Rebecca Harris, the new
headteacher, and the vicar of Hampstead,

COUNCIL TAX

A	up to £40,000	**£867.02**
B	£40,001-£52,000	**£1,011.51**
C	£52,001-£68,000	**£1,156.02**
D	£68,001-£88,000	**£1,300.52**
E	£88,001-£120,000	**£1,589.53**
F	£120,001-£160,000	**£1,878.53**
G	£160,001-£320,000	**£2,167.54**
H	over £320,000	**£2,601.04**

RECYCLING

No. of bring sites 98 (for nearest,
visit www.recycleforlondon.com)
Household waste recycled 22.24%
Main recycling centre Regis Road
Recycling Centre, Regis Road, NW5
3EW (7974 6914)
Other recycling services home
composting bins; collection of furniture
(8493 0900/www.restorecommunity
projects.org); multi-curbside recycling;
recycling of IT equipment
Council contact Street Environment
Services, 2nd floor, Cockpit Yard, WC1N
2NP (7974 6914/www.camden.gov.uk/
recycling)

Stephen Tucker. Close third would be the non-church Fitzjohn's. Fleet School, on the borders of Kentish Town and Hampstead, is another good state primary, with a mixed constituency. Some of the primary schools are in extremely deprived areas, particularly in the south of the borough. St Michael's is one example of a school on the up.

At secondary level, girls are dramatically better served in both the private and state sectors than boys. Parents with boys tend to migrate into the depths of Hertfordshire in search of private education. **'**
Robin Saikia, father of three, Hampstead

Primary

There are 39 state primary schools in Camden, 20 of which are church schools. There are also 22 independent primaries, including one French school, one international school and two Montessori schools. See www.camden.gov.uk, www.edubase.gov.uk and www.ofsted.gov.uk for more information.

Secondary

Acland Burghley School *Burghley Road, NW5 1UJ (7485 8515/www.aclandburghley. camden.sch.uk).*
Camden School for Girls *Sandall Road, NW5 2DB (7485 3414/www.csfg.org.uk).* Girls only.
Hampstead School *Westbere Road, NW2 3RT (7794 8133/www.hampsteadschool.org.uk).*
Haverstock School *24 Haverstock Hill, NW3 2BQ (7267 0975/www.haverstock. camden.sch.uk).*
La Sainte Union Catholic Secondary School *Highgate Road, NW5 1RP (7428 4600/ www.lsu.camden.sch.uk).* Girls only.
Maria Fidelis Convent School *34 Phoenix Road, NW1 1TA (7387 3856/www.maria fidelis.camden.sch.uk).* Girls only.
Parliament Hill School *Highgate Road, NW5 1RL (7485 7077/www.parliamenthill. camden.sch.uk).* Girls only.
South Camden Community School *Charrington Street, NW1 1RG (7387 0126/ www.sccs.camden.sch.uk).*
William Ellis School *Highgate Road, NW5 1RN (7267 9346/www.williamellis.camden. sch.uk).* Boys only.

Property

WHAT THE AGENTS SAY:

'People love the nightlife in Camden Town – it's buzzy, you've got a lot of bars and clubs, and there's always somewhere to go till 6am. Hampstead Heath, Regent's Park and Primrose Hill are all nearby. The amount of people who want to live here is amazing – and rents are crazy. I was brought up in Camden and it has got worse in terms of gangs and drugs. The street market is

so packed you can't lift your arm to scratch your nose. Ten years ago, King's Cross was a dump, but it's being transformed. There's not so much of the prostitution or crime that used to be there, but, sadly, some of it has moved up here.**'**
Anthony Coulouras, London Residential, Camden

Average property prices

Detached £2,555,993
Semi-detached £2,030,063
Terraced £784,866
Flat £437,072

Local estate agents

Alexanders *337 West End Lane, NW6 1RS (7431 0666/www.alexanders-uk.com).*
Black Katz *www.black-katz.com; 2 offices in the borough (Camden 7284 3111/West Hampstead 7624 8131).*
Christo & Co *148 Kentish Town Road, NW1 9QB (7424 9474/www.christo.co.uk).*
Day Morris Associates *www.daymorris.co.uk; 2 offices in the borough (Hampstead 7482 4282/ Highgate 8348 8131).*
Jeremy Bass *50 Chalcot Road, NW1 8LS (7722 8686/www.jeremybass.co.uk).*
London Residential *172 Royal College Street, NW1 0SP (7267 0909/www.ldn-res.com).*
Olivers *189 Kentish Town Road, NW5 2JU (7284 1222/www.nw5.com).*
Ringley *Ringley House, 349 Royal College Street, NW1 9QS (7267 2900/www.ringley.co.uk).*

Other information

Council

Camden Council *Camden Town Hall, Judd Street, WC1H 9JE (7278 4444/ www.camden.gov.uk).*
Camden Direct Information Service *7974 5974.*

Legal services

Camden Community Law Centre *2 Prince of Wales Road, NW5 3LQ (7284 6510/ www.lawcentres.org.uk).*
Holborn CAB *3rd floor, Holborn Library, 32-38 Theobald's Road, WC1X 8PA (0845 120 2965/ www.adviceguide.org.uk).*

Local newspapers

Camden Gazette *8342 5777/ www.camdengazette.co.uk.*
Camden New Journal, Islington Tribune & West End Extra *7419 9000/ www.camdennewjournal.co.uk.*

Allotments & open spaces

Council Allotments *Allotments Officer, c/o Parks & Open Spaces Section, Crowndale Centre, 218 Eversholt Street, NW1 1BD (7974 8819).*
Open spaces *www.camden.gov.uk/parks.*

Camden

'I love the way the old ladies dress in Kensington and Chelsea – you see them shopping in Waitrose in their 1970s YSL turban and kaftan ensemble.'

Katie Walker, fashion designer and resident

Kensington & Chelsea

The Royal Borough certainly lives up to its illustrious name, with palatial properties, world-class museums, sumptuous shopping, green space galore and the highest life expectancy in the country. Unfortunately, it will cost you a king's ransom to buy a piece of the action, and away from the posh postcodes there are still large areas of economic deprivation.

Neighbourhoods

Kensington and Holland Park

The biggest thing to hit Kensington High Street in recent years was the US food giant Whole Foods Market, which took over the old Barkers building in 2007 and turned it into a temple of organica, a deli of department-store dimensions. That High Street Ken's latest corporate invader is a chain should come as no surprise – it has been many years since this west London artery was lined with anything other than a chain of, well, chains (the famously offbeat indoor Kensington Market was long ago replaced by the famously off-putting PC World), and Barkers had been dead on its feet for several years. For a taste of more traditional Kensington, Kensington Church Street houses a selection of pricier boutiques and antiques parlours, more suited to the grand stucco-fronted houses that line the backstreets.

Kensington & Chelsea

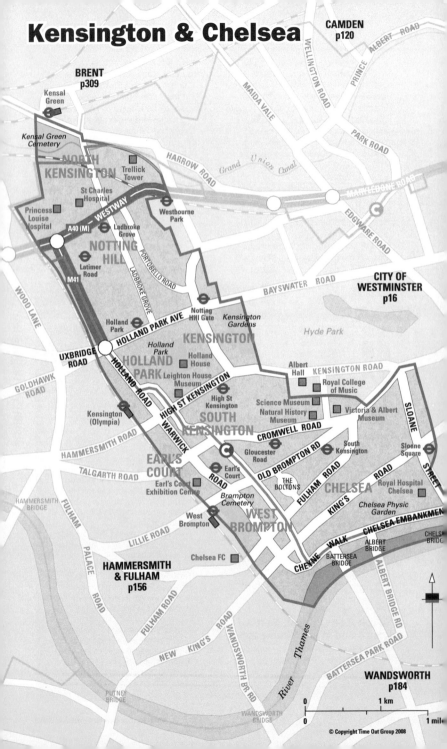

The other end of Kensington High Street is marked by another behemoth: the Commonwealth Institute, which introduced many a young child to the Empire's furthest outposts, abuts Holland Park. For the time being, the building lies sadly dormant, although its Grade II* status should protect it from the vagaries of property developers eager to get their mitts on one of London's most prized pieces of real estate.

Outdoor types, especially in-line skaters and cyclists, gravitate towards Kensington Gardens (which merges with Hyde Park). There, families head for the brilliant Diana Princess of Wales Playground, replete with near life-size pirate ship and urban beach, while a stroll round the Round Pond is a traditional Sunday afternoon jaunt for well-heeled locals. It's easy to forget the dense traffic of Kensington Road – Ken Livingstone's western extension to the Congestion Charge zone seems to have done little to alleviate W8's rush-hour gridlock problems.

Kensington also incorporates Holland Park, which, tellingly, is where Edina and Patsy lived the high life in the TV sitcom *Absolutely Fabulous*. In real life, this area's extravagant Georgian and Victorian terraces are relatively tranquil, although myriad posh delis, beauty salons and vintage clothing boutiques (most of them on Holland Park Avenue or Portland Road) are signs of an undeniably ab-fab locale. Holland Park itself is an impressively planned and surprisingly untouristy public space, with a Japanese garden, an art gallery, a summer open-air opera season and one of the city's most handsomely situated youth hostels. It's also one of London's wildest parks, with squirrels and peacocks roaming about. Located just a short stroll away, Leighton House Museum was once the residence of the Victorian artist Frederic, Lord Leighton. Visit for the lavish marble and tiled interior and collection of paintings.

South Kensington, Earl's Court and West Brompton

Between Kensington High Street and Cromwell Road rests South Kensington, a distinctly elegant part of the capital. The sprucing up of South Ken tube station is still provoking political wrangles, but the

surrounding cluster of shops, cafés and restaurants manages to make this area welcoming, with just the hint of a French accent (the Lycée Français and Institut Français are both nearby). This is also museum mile. A triumvirate of world-famous (and free) museums stand cheek by jowl: the V&A, the Science Museum and the Natural History Museum, replete with outdoor ice-rink between November and January and, from December 2007, the Vault, a permanent display of precious stones. The NHM's Darwin Centre is home to the 'scientists and bottled specimens'. Free tours can be booked for a poke around the specimens, which include 8.6 metres of giant squid caught in 2004.

There's architectural splendour at nearly every turn in this neighbourhood, from the florid Italianate Brompton Oratory Catholic church to the iconic Royal Albert Hall (technically, just outside the borough – but this whole neighbourhood is sometimes referred to as 'Albertopolis' due to its Victorian heritage). Exhibition Road, named after the 1851 Great Exhibition and a direct route to Hyde Park, is lined with grand 19th- and 20th-century

Highs & Lows

▲ **Holland Park** The actual park. It's a real urban adventure, just two minutes from Notting Hill, with peacocks, rabbits and well-heeled nippers all running wild

Capital museums It's education, education, education all the way, with the Science Museum, Natural History Museum and V&A all lined up for learning

Notting Hill Carnival Still the best party in town, despite Ken's party-pooper instincts

Notting Hill Carnival …but it can be a headache for home-owners, not to mention those local businesses that board up their shopfronts against the mob

Property prices Want something bigger than a broom cupboard? Then it's time to move to W12

Traffic chaos Despite the arrival of the C-Charge, jams continue unabated. Must be all those 4x4s

buildings – and has an excessive amount of north–south traffic. During the summer, don't miss the chance to eat or drink on the Goethe-Institut's bijou terrace, which opens on to a lovely private garden. Besides tourists and wealthy residents, South Kensington is home to a sizeable student population (the Royal College of Art, Royal College of Music, Imperial College and numerous language schools are all here) and lots of embassies.

Directly north from the Royal Albert Hall is the Albert Memorial, opened in 1872. Commissioned by Queen Victoria in memory of her late husband, it is now sparkling thanks to a lengthy restoration project by English Heritage. On the corner of Exhibition Road and Kensington Gore sits the venerable Royal Geographical Society, which was formed in 1892 to advance geographical science and along the way absorbed such groups as the 'Association for Promoting the Discovery of the Interior Parts of Africa'.

It's a safe bet that almost every Londoner has taken a journey through the capital that involved passing through Earl's Court, with its busy District and Piccadilly line interchange. Above ground, Earl's Court connects with South Kensington via the very busy Cromwell Road (A4). Further local amenities can be found dotted around Gloucester Road, but the area otherwise remains a sprawl of side streets, hotels, private garden squares, youth hostels and bedsits; the latter often have sadly crumbling interiors behind their imposing stuccoed façades. There's a transient spirit to the district, which does at least make for an appealing cultural mix. Earl's Court has long been a base for Antipodean communities, while Hogarth Road has some interesting Filipino groceries and cafés. The Earl's Court Exhibition Centre – which has hosted concerts by the likes of Madonna, Kylie and Oasis, as well as annual events such as the Daily Mail Ideal Home Show – is very centrally located for a venue that covers 12 acres.

In contrast to Earl's Court, neighbouring West Brompton is a classy residential area, incorporating plenty of high-value property, including the facing crescents of the Boltons (which swarmed with paparazzi when Hugh Grant and Liz Hurley lived here). The district's most memorable landmark is Brompton Cemetery on Fulham Road, worth a visit for its 19th-century design; the many famous graves include that of the suffragette pioneer Emmeline Pankhurst. From here, it's a short walk to Stamford Bridge, home of Chelsea FC – just over the border in Hammersmith & Fulham.

Chelsea

This fancy neighbourhood is bisected by the King's Road. Originally Charles II's private route from St James's Palace, this traffic-clogged artery has subsequently been the epicentre of 1960s swinging London and home to the punk explosion, but now acts as a catwalk for Chelsea's smartest men and machines, the perfect place for an upmarket passeggiata.

STATISTICS

BOROUGH MAKE-UP
Population 178,000
Average weekly pay £501.30
Ethnic origins
  White 77.19%
  Mixed 3.98%
  Asian or Asian British 6.37%
  Black or Black British 6.37%
  Chinese or other 6.26%
Students 10.21%
Retirees 8.29%

HOUSING STOCK
Borough size 12.4km^2
No. of households 83,880
Detached 1.3%
Semi-detached 2.9%
Terraced 12.8%
Flats (purpose-built) 44.8%
Flats (converted) 35.4%
Flats (both) 80.2%

CRIME PER 1,000 OF POPULATION
(average for England and Wales in brackets)
Burglary 7 (5)
Robbery 4 (2)
Theft of vehicle 4 (4)
Theft from vehicle 12 (9)
Violence against the person 18 (19)
Sexual offences 1 (1)

MPs & COUNCIL
MPs *Kensington & Chelsea* Sir Malcolm Rifkind (Conservative); *Regent's Park & Kensington North* Karen Buck (Labour)
CPA 4 stars; improving strongly

Hidden oasis: **Chelsea Physic Garden**.

High-end designers and private galleries are concentrated towards the Sloane Square end of the King's Road and on luxurious Sloane Street, which connects Chelsea to Knightsbridge. Sloane Square, named after its 18th-century owner Sir Hans Sloane, features a central fountain depicting Venus. Dominating the square is Peter Jones, newly refurbished and still the spiritual home of upper middle-class life in SW3. John Betjeman once said that, when the end of the world came, he wanted to be in the haberdashery department 'because nothing unpleasant could ever happen there'. A recent plan to drive a four-lane road through the middle of the square and create two pedestrianised spaces – a large one outside Sloane Square underground station and a smaller one outside Peter Jones – seems unlikely to happen.

The Royal Court Theatre, next to Sloane Square tube station, sent shockwaves round the world with its première of John Osborne's *Look Back in Anger* in 1956, and productions continue to err on the side of edgy. Just off the opposite corner of the square, Duke of York Square is a pricey but pretty place to meet and pose; a dinky ice-rink operates in winter.

At the other end of the King's Road is the once-notorious World's End estate, a large council development of tower blocks and a shopping complex, built in the 1970s. The estate is slowly but surely shaking off its reputation for drug-related crime – and estate agents are certainly keen to tout the area – but it's still very evidently the poorest pocket of Chelsea.

There's a wealth of English Heritage blue plaques in this area. The composer Thomas Arne is believed to have conceived 'Rule Britannia' at his home, 215 King's Road. For truly famous neighbours, check out the quaint riverside Cheyne Walk, which dates back to the 18th century; residents have ranged from George Eliot, JMW Turner and Dante Gabriel Rossetti to the Rolling Stones' Keith Richards and Mick Jagger (at nos.3 and 48 respectively). Nearby Cadogan Pier provides boat services up and down the Thames.

If you're not spotting names, look out for the Chelsea Pensioners in their dapper scarlet uniforms and tricorne hats. These retired servicemen live at the Royal Hospital Chelsea, which was designed by Sir Christopher Wren and Sir John Soane, among others; the grounds host the lavish Chelsea Flower Show every May, as well as hiding some of the most peaceful public tennis courts in London. Another great secret haven is the Chelsea Physic Garden. Founded in 1673, it has acres of plants dedicated to the science of healing.

Knightsbridge

While much of Knightsbridge technically falls under the aegis of the City of Westminster, it seamlessly continues on from Sloane Street as a ritzy, label-saturated enclave. The main drag is dominated by two temples to conspicuous consumption: Harrods, whose traditional opulence has become comically OTT under Al-Fayed's reign (a case in point is the £20 million Egyptian Escalator), and the more restrained, slickly fashionable Harvey Nicks. However, even these two mammoth shops are likely to be overshadowed by the completion of One Hyde Park. Former home of grim 1950s office block Bowater House, this space next to the Mandarin Oriental hotel is set to break records for the most expensive property in London, with the four penthouses in blocks designed by Richard Rogers rumoured to be on the market at £84 million each. Ken Livingstone's affordable housing programme hasn't quite reached SW7, although some manage to rent tiddly bedsits in the area's tucked-away streets.

Notting Hill

Emerging for the first time at Notting Hill Gate tube, you might wander what all the fuss is about. Traffic-clogged Notting Hill Gate isn't a particularly attractive high street, lined as it is with unexceptional chain stores and eateries. But get off the main drag and the appeal of the area is plain to see, with rows of imposing stuccoed houses and myriad garden squares – although any attempt to re-enact Hugh Grant's jumping over the fence from the film *Notting Hill* will be met by stern faces, since the gardens are only accessible to resident key holders who can muster an annual fee of up to £1,500. Money is no object for many of Notting Hill's present incumbents, who are satirised in Rachel Johnson's (Boris's younger sister) book *Notting Hell*.

The district is otherwise best known for hosting Europe's largest street party, the Notting Hill Carnival, a raucous celebration of the neighbourhood's Afro-Caribbean heritage. The Carnival emerged as a positive stand against the race riots of the 1960s. Four decades later, it draws around a million revellers to these streets and neighbouring North Kensington every August Bank Holiday weekend.

There are, however, enough fashionable shops and hangouts to keep the crowds flocking here throughout the year. Film buffs head to Notting Hill's atmospheric arty cinemas, the Gate, the Coronet and the Electric. Fashionistas head to label-heavy Ledbury Road, while Westbourne Grove is awash with seriously smart antiques shops and more couture creations – even the public toilet is designer.

Hilly Ladbroke Grove, named after its affluent 19th-century landowners, branches into curved parades of Victorian townhouses. The top of the hill was once home to a racecourse, but waterlogging meant the venture only lasted from 1837 to 1841, when the owners decided to build houses instead. Some of the borough's hippest streets are to its east: Westbourne Grove, Portobello Road and self-consciously upmarket All Saints Road. Powis Square was the setting for the cult 1960s film *Performance*, starring Mick Jagger and James Fox.

Portobello Road Market is still a good place to find antiques and emerging designers, although there's a fair amount of tat and a huge amount of tourist of the antiques stalls are at the Notting Hill Gate end; the most interesting clothing stalls are crammed beneath the Westway flyover, which carries travellers in and out of central London on the A40(M). The Westway now has its own development trust (www.westway.org), which runs the well-equipped Westway Sports Centre.

North Kensington

On the northern side of the Westway, North Kensington has the edgiest feel of any neighbourhood in the borough. Ladbroke Grove, so gentrified at the Holland Park end, is here lined with late-night shops and fast-food joints, though there are also some handsome houses, long since converted into flats and grimy from decades of traffic congestion.

The district was built around the local St Charles and Princess Louise hospitals, giant Victorian edifices that have been softened slightly with recent revamps. Buildings in the area certainly contrast with each other; take Barlby Road, which has snug-looking terraced houses as well as the imposing 1911 Pall Mall Depository, which now contains office units and a café. North Kensington is also spiritual home to the 'Notting Hill Set', a phrase that refers to a powerful clique of young Conservatives that includes David Cameron and George Osborne.

Kensington & Chelsea

Swanky fish and chips at **Geales**.

At the area's northernmost boundary, you'll find the green oasis of Kensal Green Cemetery, the first of London's grand Victorian burial grounds and last resting place of Trollope, Thackeray and Isambard Kingdom Brunel. Also here are the striking canalside studios of Kensal Town and the borough-run Canalside Activity Centre, which focuses on youth recreation.

Finally, mention should be made of what is surely North Kensington's most famous building: Hungarian Ernö Goldfinger's 31-storey Trellick Tower, originally designed as cheap social housing in 1972. It has shrugged off a troubled reputation in recent years to become one of the most sought-after addresses in the area – now Grade II* listed, it is a modernist icon.

Restaurants & cafés

There's no shortage of restaurants in the Royal Borough. What follows is a taste; for a full menu of options, consult the *Time Out London Eating & Drinking Guide*.

Chelsea brims with quality. Tom Aikens has two restaurants in the area: haute cuisine Tom Aikens and the simpler, cheaper Tom's Kitchen. Both are excellent. Gordon Ramsay too has a superlative, eponymous restaurant – his first and still one of his best. Aubergine is another pricey, haute cuisine gem; Bluebird on the King's Road offers more affordable Modern European fare. Pig's Ear and Lots Road Pub & Dining Help Chelsea rival Islington for gastropub excellence, while Chutney Mary, Rasoi Vineet Bhatia and Painted Heron are all Modern Indian heavyweights – though none could be described as cheap. Try excellent brasserie Napket for more budget-conscious cooking.

The restaurant scene in Knightsbridge is similar: high quality, high prices. The Capital serves haute cuisine in the exclusive environs of the Capital hotel; the Mandarin Oriental's Foliage likewise. There's also first-rate French restaurant Racine, sleek Japanese bar-restaurant Zuma, sleekly appointed Indian and Pakistani restaurant Amaya, and Chinese destination Mr Chow, which still draws a pedigree crowd despite being a little passé. Ramsay-affiliated Pétrus and Boxwood Café consistently impress for haute cuisine; at the other end of the scale entirely is O Fado, a homely

basement restaurant that's London's oldest (and best) Portuguese. Located inside Harvey Nichols and Harrods respectively, the stylish Fifth Floor (for Modern European) and Ladurée (for superb cakes) prove that dining in department stores needn't be dreary.

The range of high-end options doesn't diminish in South Ken. Bibendum (Modern European) has an excellent location in the Michelin Building; sister operation Bibendum Oyster Bar is in the lovely tiled foyer. Elsewhere, Papillon serves a cracking French vegetarian menu, Lundum's offers Scandinavian cuisine, and Cambio de Tercio serves some of the city's best new-wave (or *nueva cocina*) Spanish cooking. On Gloucester Road, L'Etranger (Modern European) and Pasha (North African) offer wonderful food, at a price.

Minimalist Mod Euro gem 11 Abingdon Road and Spanish oddball L Restaurant & Bar are the best bets in Kensington; the Kensington Palace Orangery (for coffee and cake) and Sticky Fingers (for ribs and the like) are great places to take the family. In Holland Park – actually in the park – is lovely French brasserie the Belvedere; otherwise pop into Notting Grill for a steak. Notting Hill is crammed with options: try damn-near-perfect French restaurant the Ledbury, Tex-Mex diner Taqueria, family-run Malaysian café Nyonya or rural-England-themed gastropub Bumpkin.

If all you want is a plate of fish and chips, there's cheap and cheerful Costas or posher, refurbed Geales.

A string of terrific cafés mark out Ladbroke Grove: Spanish-run Café Garcia, Portuguese pair Café Oporto and Lisboa Pâtisserie, cupcake specialist Hummingbird Bakery and the café within cookbook haven Books for Cooks (*see p152*). For a proper meal, try Fat Badger (gastropub), celebrity magnet E&O (oriental) or Moroccan Tagine (North African). North to Westbourne Grove, there's kid-friendly pizzeria Mulberry Street, first-rate Lebanese restaurant Al Waha and charming tea shop/café Tea Palace. Tom Conran is the brains behind three operations: gastropub the Cow, one of London's best; laid-back US-style diner Lucky 7; and bohemian brunch favourite Tom's Deli.

Al Waha *75 Westbourne Grove, W2 4UL (7229 0806/www.alwaharestaurant.com).*
Amaya *15 Motcomb Street, Halkin Arcade, SW1X 8JT (7823 1166/www.amaya.biz).*
Aubergine *11 Park Walk, SW10 0AJ (7352 3449/www.auberginerestaurant.co.uk).*
Belvedere *Holland House, off Abbotsbury Road, in Holland Park, W8 6LU (7602 1238/ www.whitestarline.org.uk).*
Bibendum *Michelin House, 81 Fulham Road, SW3 6RD (7581 5817/www.bibendum.co.uk).*
Bibendum Oyster Bar *Michelin House, 81 Fulham Road, SW3 6RD (7589 1480/ www.bibendum.co.uk).*
Bluebird *350 King's Road, SW3 5UU (7559 1000/www.danddlondon.com).*
Boxwood Café *The Berkeley, Wilton Place, SW1X 7RL (7235 1010/www. gordonramsay.com).*
Bumpkin *209 Westbourne Park Road, W11 1EA (7243 9818/www.bumpkinuk.com).*
Café Garcia *246 Portobello Road, W11 1LL (7221 6119/www.cafegarcia.co.uk).*
Café Oporto *62A Golborne Road, W10 5PS (8968 8839).*
Cambio de Tercio *163 Old Brompton Road, SW5 0LJ (7244 8970/www.cambiodetercio.co.uk).*
The Capital *22-24 Basil Street, SW3 1AT (7589 5171/7591 1200/www.capitalhotel.co.uk).*
Chutney Mary *535 King's Road, SW10 0SZ (7351 3113/www.chutneymary.com).*
Costas Fish Restaurant *18 Hillgate Street, W8 7SR (7727 4310).*
Cow *89 Westbourne Park Road, W2 5QH (7221 0021/www.thecowlondon.co.uk).*
E&O *14 Blenheim Crescent, W11 1NN (7229 5454/www.rickerrestaurants.com).*
11 Abingdon Road *11 Abingdon Road, W8 6AH (7937 0120/www.abingdonroad.co.uk).*
L'Etranger *36 Gloucester Road, SW7 4QT (7584 1118/www.etranger.co.uk).*

Fat Badger *310 Portobello Road, W10 5TA (8969 4500/www.thefatbadger.com).*
Fifth Floor *Harvey Nichols, Knightsbridge, SW1X 7RJ (7235 5250/www.harveynichols.com).*
Foliage *Mandarin Oriental Hyde Park, 66 Knightsbridge, SW1X 7LA (7201 3723/ www.mandarinoriental.com).*
Geales *2 Farmer Street, W8 7SN (7727 7528/www.geales.com).*
Gordon Ramsay *68 Royal Hospital Road, SW3 4HP (7352 4441/www.gordonramsay.com).*
Hummingbird Bakery *133 Portobello Road, W11 2DY (7229 6446/www.humming birdbakery.com).*
Kensington Palace Orangery *The Orangery, Kensington Palace, Kensington Gardens, W8 4PX (7376 0239/www.digbytrout.co.uk).*
Ladurée *Harrods, entrance on Hans Road, SW1X 7XL (7893 8293/www.laduree.com).*
Ledbury *127 Ledbury Road, W11 2AQ (7792 9090/www.theledbury.com).*
Lisboa Pâtisserie *57 Golborne Road, W10 5NR (8968 5242).*
Lots Road Pub & Dining Room *114 Lots Road, SW10 0RJ (7352 6645/ www.thespiritgroup.com).*
L Restaurant & Bar *2 Abingdon Road, W8 6AF (7795 6969/www.l-restaurant.co.uk).*
Lucky 7 *127 Westbourne Park Road, W2 5QL (7727 6771/www.lucky7london.co.uk).*
Lundum's *117-119 Old Brompton Road, SW7 3RN (7373 7774/www.lundums.com).*
Moroccan Tagine *95 Golborne Road, W10 5NL (8968 8055).*
Mr Chow *151 Knightsbridge, SW1X 7PA (7589 7347/www.mrchow.com).*
Mulberry Street *84 Westbourne Grove, W2 5RT (7313 6789/www.mulberrystreet.co.uk).*
Napket *342 King's Road, SW3 5UR (7352 9832/www.napket.com).*
Notting Grill *123A Clarendon Road, W11 4JG (7229 1500/www.awtrestaurants.com).*
Nyonya *2A Kensington Park Road, W11 3BU (7243 1800/www.nyonya.co.uk).*
O Fado *50 Beauchamp Place, SW3 1NY (7589 3002/www.restauranteofado.co.uk).*
Painted Heron *112 Cheyne Walk, SW10 0DJ (7351 5232/www.thepaintedheron.com).*
Papillon *96 Draycott Avenue, SW3 3AD (7225 2555/www.papillonchelsea.co.uk).*
Pasha *1 Gloucester Road, SW7 4PP (7589 7969/www.pasha-restaurant.co.uk).*
Pétrus *The Berkeley, Wilton Place, SW1X 7RL (7235 1200/www.petrus-restaurant.com).*
Pig's Ear *35 Old Church Street, SW3 5BS (7352 2908/www.thepigsear.co.uk).*
Racine *239 Brompton Road, SW3 2EP (7584 4477).*
Rasoi Vineet Bhatia *10 Lincoln Street, SW3 2TS (7225 1881/www.vineetbhatia.com).*
Sticky Fingers *1A Phillimore Gardens, W8 7EG (7938 5338/www.stickyfingers.co.uk).*
Taqueria *139-143 Westbourne Grove, W11 2RS (7229 4734/www.coolchiletaqueria.co.uk).*
Tea Palace *175 Westbourne Grove, W11 2SB (7727 2600/www.teapalace.co.uk).*

Kensington & Chelsea

Tom Aikens *43 Elystan Street, SW3 3NT (7584 2003/www.tomaikens.co.uk).*
Tom's Deli *226 Westbourne Grove, W11 2RH (7221 8818).*
Tom's Kitchen *27 Cale Street, SW3 3QP (7349 0202/www.tomskitchen.co.uk).*
Zuma *5 Raphael Street, SW7 1DL (7584 1010/www.zumarestaurant.com).*

Bars & pubs

Kensington is relatively short of decent drinking venues – recently refurbed pub the Kensington Arms, with its fine Cornish beer Sharp's Doom Bar, and the Tenth Bar (due to reopen in spring 2008 after refurbishments) with its magnificent views, are probably our favourites – but South Kensington is spoilt for choice. Catering to the area's curious mix of Sloanes, rootless cosmopolitans and crims are options ranging from hotel bar 190 Queensgate to historic boozer the Anglesea Arms, once a favourite of DH Lawrence and Dickens.

Hopping over to the King's Road, options in Chelsea are almost as good. The two star performers, gastropubs Lots Road Pub & Dining Room and the Pig's Ear (for both, *see p148*), are offset by glamorous cocktail bars such as Apartment 195, which is so discreet you need to press a buzzer to get in.

To the north-east, on Old Brompton Road, ancient boho den the Troubadour delights locals in its various roles as a deli, café, wine bar and performance venue. Though close geographically, bars in Knightsbridge are a million miles away in terms of clientele and ethos. Expect to find London's elite, ordering only the best in the cracking Mandarin Bar and super-chic Japanese bar-restaurant Zuma (*see p148*).

Newcomer cocktail bar Montgomery Place joins a spate of quality bars in Notting Hill, Dick Bradsell's Lonsdale, subterranean hotspot Trailer Happiness and cinema-affiliated Electric Brasserie chief among them; boho boozers Portobello Gold and Sun in Splendour round out the choice. East to Holland Park, we like the gorgeous Ladbroke Arms, a pub with a front garden that's gorgeous in summer.

North towards Westbourne Grove and the Westway, the Fat Badger is an impressively dressed pub, though we prefer gastropub the Cow (*see p149*). Also run by Tom Conran is vampish, Mexican-themed venue

Crazy Homies; if you really want crazy, however, look no further than Tiroler Hut, a bonkers bar that celebrates everything Tyrolean (including lederhosen and cowbells). In Westbourne Park, converted pub Grand Union has a fine view over Regent's Canal. To the east of Chepstow Road, there's a clutch of fine bars and pubs that fall into the borough of City of Westminster.

Anglesea Arms *15 Selwood Terrace, SW7 3QG (7373 7960/www.capitalpubcompany. com/anglesea/).*
Apartment 195 *195 King's Road, SW3 5ED (7351 5195/www.apartment195.co.uk).*
Crazy Homies *125 Westbourne Park Road, W2 5QL (7727 6771).*
Electric Brasserie *191 Portobello Road, W11 2ED (7908 9696/www.the-electric.co.uk).*
Fat Badger *310 Portobello Road, W10 5TA (8969 4500/www.thefatbadger.com).*
Grand Union *45 Woodfield Road, W9 2BA (7286 1886).*
Kensington Arms *41 Abingdon Road, W8 6AH (7938 3841/www.kensingtonarms.com).*
Ladbroke Arms *54 Ladbroke Road, W11 3NW (7727 6648/www.capitalpubcompany.com).*
Lonsdale *48 Lonsdale Road, W11 2DE (7727 4080/www.thelonsdale.co.uk).*
Mandarin Bar *Mandarin Oriental Hyde Park, 66 Knightsbridge, SW1X 7LA (7235 2000/www.mandarinoriental.com).*
Montgomery Place *31 Kensington Park Road, W11 2EU (7792 3921/ www.montgomeryplace.co.uk).*
190 Queensgate *The Gore, 190 Queensgate, SW7 5EX (7584 6601/www.gorehotel.co.uk).*
Portobello Gold *95-97 Portobello Road, W11 2QB (7460 4910/www.portobellogold.com).*
Sun in Splendour *7 Portobello Road, W11 3DA (7313 9331).*
Tenth Bar *Royal Garden Hotel, 2-24 Kensington High Street, W8 4PT (7361 1910/ www.royalgardenhotel.co.uk).*
Tiroler Hut *27 Westbourne Grove, W2 4UA (7727 3981/www.tirolerhut.co.uk).*
Trailer Happiness *177 Portobello Road, W11 2DY (7727 2700/www.trailerhappiness.com).*
Troubadour *265 Old Brompton Road, SW5 9JA (7370 1434/www.troubadour.co.uk).*

Shops

Kensington & Chelsea has some of the capital's prime consumer destinations: Knightsbridge, the King's Road, Notting Hill. Knightsbridge may be a tourist-clogged nightmare on a Saturday afternoon, but weekday mornings are quiet enough for you to appreciate the extravagantly tiled Edwardian food halls at Harrods.

Kensington & Chelsea

For the latest designer fashion, though, head for coolly sophisticated Harvey Nichols, then stroll down Sloane Street for more international superbrands. Presiding over Sloane Square in an impressive former bank, Bamford & Sons offers luxurious, understated clothes for men, women and boys; nearby is Peter Jones department store, John Lewis's posh western sibling. Continue on to Lower Sloane Street for L'Artisan du Chocolat's 'couture' confections.

After its 1960s and '70s heyday, the King's Road had become a bland, chain-dominated strip, but it was given a boost a few years back when the old Duke of York barracks were reborn as an attractive shopping square. Notable retailers within its confines include cult favourite Liz Earle Naturally Active Skincare, denim boutique Trilogy and Italian food specialist Manicomio. Don't miss wonderful indie bookshop John Sandoe, tucked away on a side street. Further along the King's Road, kids' all-rounder Daisy & Tom, with its carousel and puppet shows, is a life-saver

TRANSPORT

Tube stations *Bakerloo* Kensal Green; *Central* Notting Hill Gate, Holland Park; *Circle* Sloane Square, South Kensington, Gloucester Road, High Street Kensington, Notting Hill Gate; *District* Sloane Square, South Kensington, Gloucester Road, High Street Kensington, Notting Hill Gate, Earl's Court, Kensington (Olympia), West Brompton; *Hammersmith & City* Westbourne Park, Ladbroke Grove, Latimer Road; *Piccadilly* Knightsbridge, South Kensington, Gloucester Road, Earl's Court

Rail stations *London Overground* Kensal Green, West Brompton, Kensington (Olympia); *Southern* West Brompton, Kensington (Olympia)

Main bus routes *into central London* 7, 9, 10, 11, 14, 18, 19, 22, 23, 27, 74, 94, 137, 148, 390; *night buses* N7, N9, N10, N11, N18, N19, N22, N52, N74, N97, N137, N207; *24-hour buses* 14, 23, 27, 94, 148, 390

River Commuter and leisure boat services running to/from central London, with stops at Cadogan Pier (under Albert Bridge) and Chelsea Harbour Pier

for harassed parents. The restaurant/retail complex in the landmark Bluebird garage contains the Shop at Bluebird, which sells a combination of designer clobber, furniture, books and gadgets, and posh deli Bluebird Epicerie. Austique has a lovely collection of stylish clothes, lingerie and accessories for women. King's Road fixture Antiquarius is an arcade that sells everything from old Louis Vuitton trunks to original film art. You have to walk further (it may really feel like World's End by the time you get there) for Vivienne Westwood's original shop, which she opened with Malcolm McLaren in 1970 as Let It Rock. On the way, take a detour down quiet Old Church Street for shoe king Manolo Blahnik's discreet salon.

In South Kensington, designer boutiques and glossy contemporary furniture stores cluster around Brompton Cross. The Conran Shop flagship is located in the spectacular art nouveau Michelin Building, and there's a spacious new Skandium nearby. A mix of upmarket children's stores and interior designers' showrooms line pretty Walton Street, where you'll also find Farmacia Santa Maria Novella for old-world herbal products. Interiors shops cluster on nearby Elystan Street.

Chain-choked Kensington High Street is another former fashion star that has lost its sparkle, although the iconic Barkers department store is now occupied by swanky US organic superstore Whole Foods Market. From the high street, Kensington Church Street – lined with rarefied antiques shops – leads up to Notting Hill. The area around the intersection of Westbourne Grove and Ledbury Road (on the border with the City of Westminster) is boutique central: Aimé, Feathers, JW Beeton, Matches… the list goes on. Also worth a look are J&M Davidson for beautifully crafted bags, Alice & Astrid's adorable lingerie, One's unique, customised vintage pieces, British perfumery Miller Harris, and interior designer Madame Sera's fashion boutique, Sera of London. The stunning post-war and contemporary furniture and decorative art at Themes & Variations would make striking additions to the area's expansive 19th-century properties. No doubt catering to the area's jet-set demographic, there's not one but three shops in the locale dedicated to year-round swimwear: Heidi Klein, Odabash and (technically in Westminster) Pistol Panties.

Clarendon Cross in Holland Park is a lovely shopping spot: browse in well-loved boutique the Cross, stock up on fine kitchenware at Summerill & Bishop or have lunch and a pedicure at the London outpost of Babington House's Cowshed spa, which doubles as a café.

Around Portobello Road, there's a funky mix of vintage clothes shops, hip boutiques (Coco Ribbon, Nancy Pop), Paul Smith's stucco-mansion flagship, specialist stores (Spice Shop, Books for Cooks) and record shops, notable among them Rough Trade, Honest Jon's and, for rare vinyl, Intoxica!. Even children are immaculately turned out in this well-heeled patch: Their Nibs provides mini retro-vibe fashions, while Honeyjam, co-owned by former-model mum Jasmine Guinness, sells toys that won't jar with stylish interiors. In addition to numerous delis, picturesque butcher Kingsland and fishmonger Golborne Fisheries are in the area.

On Saturdays, popular – and tourist-mobbed – Portobello Road Market comprises three parts: the antiques stalls and arcades at the Notting Hill end, food stalls further north and, under the Westway flyover, up-and-coming designers and vintage clothes sellers (also on Fridays). Here, the Portobello Green Arcade contains an interesting selection of units (many only open at weekends). Those who keep walking are rewarded by designer Duro Olowu's shop, showcasing his vibrant print dresses (open only Fridays and Saturdays) and, on Golborne Road, celebrated vintage emporium Rellik.

Aimé 32 Ledbury Road, W11 2AB (7221 7070/www.aimelondon.com).
Alice & Astrid 30 Artesian Road, W2 5DD (7985 0888/www.aliceandastrid.com).
Antiquarius 131-141 King's Road, SW3 5PH(7823 3900/www.antiquarius.co.uk).
L'Artisan du Chocolat 89 Lower Sloane Street, SW1W 8DA (7824 8365/www.artisanduchocolat.com).
Austique 330 King's Road, SW3 5UR (7376 4555/www.austique.co.uk).
Bamford & Sons The Old Bank, 31 Sloane Square, SW1W 8GA (7881 8010/www.bamfordandsons.com).
Bluebird Epicerie 350 King's Road, SW3 5UU (7559 1140/www.conran.com).
Books for Cooks 4 Blenheim Crescent, W11 1NN (7221 1992/www.booksforcooks.com).

Coco Ribbon 21 Kensington Park Road, W11 2EU (7229 4904).
Conran Shop Michelin House, 81 Fulham Road, SW3 6RD (7589 7401/www.conran.com).
Cowshed 119 Portland Road, W11 4LN (7078 1944/www.cowshedclarendoncross.com).
The Cross 141 Portland Road, W11 4LR (7727 6760/www.thecrossshop.co.uk).
Daisy & Tom 181-183 King's Road, SW3 5EB (7352 5000/www.daisyandtom.com).
Duro Olowu 365 Portobello Road, W10 5SG (8960 7570/www.duroolowu.com).
Farmacia Santa Maria Novella 117 Walton Street, SW3 2HP (7460 6600).
Feathers 176 Westbourne Grove, W11 2RW (7243 8800).
Golborne Fisheries 75-77 Golborne Road, W10 5NP (8960 3100).
Harrods 87-135 Brompton Road, SW1X 7XL (7730 1234/www.harrods.com).
Harvey Nichols 109-125 Knightsbridge, SW1X 7RJ (7235 5000/www.harveynichols.com).
Heidi Klein 174 Westbourne Grove, W11 2RW (7243 5665/www.heidiklein.com).
Honest Jon's 278 Portobello Road, W10 5TE (8969 9822/www.honestjons.com).
Honeyjam 267 Portobello Road, W11 1LR (7243 0449/www.honeyjam.co.uk).
Intoxica! 231 Portobello Road, W11 1LT (7229 8010/www.intoxica.co.uk).
J&M Davidson 42 Ledbury Road, W11 2AB (7313 9532/www.jandmdavidson.com).
John Sandoe 10 Blacklands Terrace, SW3 2SR (7589 9473/www.johnsandoe.com).
JW Beeton 48-50 Ledbury Road, W11 2AJ (7229 8874).
Kingsland, the Edwardian Butcher 140 Portobello Road, W11 2DZ (7727 6067).
Liz Earle Naturally Active Skincare 53 Duke of York Square, King's Road, SW3 4LY (7730 9191/www.lizearle.com).
Manicomio 85 Duke of York Square, King's Road, SW3 4LY (7730 3366/www.manicomio.co.uk).
Manolo Blahnik 49-51 Old Church Street, SW3 5BS (7352 3863).
Matches 60-64 & 85 Ledbury Road, W11 2AJ (7221 0255/www.matchesfashion.com).
Miller Harris 14 Needham Road, W11 2RP (7221 1545/www.millerharris.com).
Nancy Pop 19 Kensington Park Road, W11 2EU (7221 9797/www.nancypop.com).
Odabash 48B Ledbury Road, W11 2AJ (7229 4299/www.odabash.com).
One 30 Ledbury Road, W11 2AB (7221 5300).
Paul Smith Westbourne House, 120 & 122 Kensington Park Road, W11 2EP (7727 3553/www.paulsmith.co.uk).
Peter Jones Sloane Square, SW1W 8EL (7730 3434/www.peterjones.co.uk).
Pistol Panties 75 Westbourne Park Road, W2 5QH (7229 5286/www.pistolpanties.com).
Portobello Green Arcade 281 Portobello Road, W10 5TZ (www.portobellodesigners.com).
Portobello Road Market Portobello Road, W10, W11; Golborne Road, W10.

Organic rules at Kensington's **Whole Foods Market**. *See p151.*

Rellik *8 Golborne Road, W10 5NW (8962 0089/www.relliklondon.co.uk).*
Rough Trade *130 Talbot Road, W11 1JA (7229 8541/www.roughtrade.com).*
Sera of London *3 Lonsdale Road, W11 2BY (7467 0799/www.seraoflondon.com).*
Shop at Bluebird *350 King's Road, SW3 5UU (7351 3873/www.theshopatbluebird.com).*
Skandium *247 Brompton Road, SW3 2EP (7584 2066/www.skandium.com).*
Spice Shop *1 Blenheim Crescent, W11 2EE (7221 4448/www.thespiceshop.co.uk).*
Summerill & Bishop *100 Portland Road, W11 4LN (7221 4566/www.summerilland bishop.com).*
Their Nibs *214 Kensington Park Road, W11 1NR (7221 4263/www.theirnibs.com).*
Themes & Variations *231 Westbourne Grove, W11 2SE (7727 5531/www.themes andvariations.com).*
Trilogy *33 Duke of York Square, King's Road, SW3 4LY (7730 6515/www.trilogystores.co.uk).*
Whole Foods Market *The Barkers Building, 63-97 Kensington High Street, W8 5SE (7368 4500/www.wholefoodsmarket.com).*
World's End (Vivienne Westwood) *430 King's Road, SW10 0LJ (7352 6551/ www.viviennewestwoodonline.co.uk).*

Arts & attractions

Cinemas & theatres

Chelsea Cinema *206 King's Road, SW3 5XP (7351 3742/www.artificial-eye.com).*
Ciné Lumière *Institut Français, 17 Queensbury Place, SW7 2DT (7073 1350/www.institut-francais.org.uk).* Mostly screens films in French, with English subtitles.
Cineworld *0871 200 2000/www.cineworld. co.uk; 279 King's Road, SW3 5EW; 142 Fulham Road, SW10 9QR.*
Coronet Cinema *103 Notting Hill Gate, W11 2LB (7727 6705/www.coronet.org).*

Electric Cinema *191 Portobello Road, W11 2ED (7908 9696/www.electriccinema.co.uk).*
Gate Cinema *87 Notting Hill Gate, W11 3JZ (7792 8939/www.picturehouses.co.uk).*
Gate Theatre *11 Pembridge Road, W11 3HQ (7229 5387/www.gatetheatre.co.uk).*
Odeon Kensington *263 Kensington High Street, W8 6NA (0871 224 4007/ www.odeon.co.uk).*
Royal Court Theatre *Sloane Square, SW1 8AS (7565 5000/www.royalcourttheatre.com).*
Science Museum IMAX *Science Museum, Exhibition Road, SW7 2DD (0870 870 4771/www.sciencemuseum.org.uk).*

Galleries & museums

Carlyle's House *24 Cheyne Row, SW3 5HL (7352 7087/www.nationaltrust.org.uk).* The home of writer Thomas Carlyle offers an intriguing snapshot of Victorian life.
Leighton House Museum & Art Gallery *12 Holland Park Road, W14 8LZ (7602 3316/ www.rbkc.gov.uk/leightonhousemuseum).*
National Army Museum *Royal Hospital Road, SW3 4HT (7730 0717/www.national-army-museum.ac.uk).* Exhibits run from 15th-century Agincourt to present-day peace-keeping.
Natural History Museum *Cromwell Road, SW7 5BD (information 7942 5725/switchboard 7942 5000/www.nhm.ac.uk).*
Science Museum *Exhibition Road, SW7 2DD (7942 4454/booking & information 0870 870 4868/www.sciencemuseum.org.uk).*
Victoria & Albert Museum *Cromwell Road, SW7 2RL (7942 2000/www.vam.ac.uk).*

Music & comedy venues

Cadogan Hall *5 Sloane Terrace, SW1X 9DQ (7730 4500/www.cadoganhall.com).* This fine classical concert hall is home to the Royal Philharmonic.
Notting Hill Arts Club *21 Notting Hill Gate, W11 3JQ (7460 4459/www.nottinghillartsclub. com).* Specialist music and arts venue.

Kensington & Chelsea

Royal Albert Hall *Kensington Gore, SW7 2AP (7589 8212/www.royalalberthall.com).* World-famous concert hall known for classical performances, including the Proms; also hosts pop and rock concerts.
Royal College of Music *Prince Consort Road, SW7 2BS (7589 3643/www.rcm.ac.uk).*

Other attractions

Brompton Oratory *Thurloe Place, Brompton Road, SW7 2RP (7808 0900).* England's second largest Catholic church (after Westminster Cathedral).
Chelsea Physic Garden *66 Royal Hospital Road, SW3 4HS (7352 5646/www.chelsea physicgarden.co.uk).*
Earl's Court Exhibition Centre *Warwick Road, SW5 9TA (7385 1200/www.eco.co.uk).*
Goethe-Institut *50 Princes Gate, Exhibition Road, SW7 2PH (7596 4000/www.goethe.de/london).* German cultural institute.
Institut Français *17 Queensberry Place, SW7 2DT (7073 1350/www.institut-francais. org.uk).* French cultural institute, which includes Ciné Lumière (see p153).
Kensington Palace *W8 4PX (0844 482 7777/bookings 0870 751 5180/www.hrp.org.uk).* Though still a royal residence, some rooms and apartments are open to the public.
Royal Hospital Chelsea *Royal Hospital Road, SW3 4FR (7881 5200/www.chelsea-pensioners.co.uk).*

Sport & fitness

Leisure centres here tend towards private, highly polished and pricey. Exceptions include the no-nonsense Club Kensington, while Portobello Green Fitness Club defies expectations (and its somewhat seedy location) with a good range of community-driven, family-friendly activities at affordable prices. The borough also has two of the capital's premier public facilities: Kensington Leisure Centre (excellent design and a wide scope of activities) and the Westway Sports Centre (everything from all-weather football pitches to a large indoor climbing wall).

Gyms & leisure centres

Aquilla Health Club *11 Thurloe Place, SW7 2RS (7225 0225/www.aquillahealthclub.com).* Private.
Chelsea Club *Chelsea Village, Fulham Road, SW6 1HS (7915 2200/www.thechelseaclub.com).* Private.
Chelsea Sports Centre *Chelsea Manor Street, SW3 5PL (7352 6985/ www.cannons.co.uk).*
Club Kensington *201-207 Kensington High Street, W8 6BA (7937 5386/www. clubkensington.com).* Private.

David Lloyd *116 Cromwell Road, SW7 4XR (7341 6401/www.davidlloydleisure.co.uk).* Private.
Earl's Court Gym *254 Earl's Court Road, SW5 9AD (7370 1402/www.sohogyms.com).* Private.
Fitness First *Petersham House, 29-37 Harrington Road, SW7 3HD (7590 5000/ www.fitnessfirst.co.uk).* Private.
The Harbour Club *Watermeadow Lane, SW6 2RR (7371 7700/www.harbourclub.co.uk).* Private.
Kensington Leisure Centre *Walmer Road, W11 4PQ (7727 9747).*
LA Fitness *63-81 Pelham Street, SW7 2NJ (7838 0500/www.lafitness.co.uk).* Private.
Lambton Place Health Club *Lambton Place, W11 2SH (7229 2291/www.lambton.co.uk).* Private.
Portobello Green Fitness Club *3-5 Thorpe Close, W10 5XL (8960 2221/www.westway. org.uk).* Private.
Virgin Active *www.virginactive.co.uk; 3rd floor, 17A Old Court Place, W8 4HP (7761 0000); 119-131 Lancaster Road, W11 1QT (7243 4141).* Private.

Other facilities

Canalside Activity Centre *Canal Close, W10 5AY (8968 4500).*
Westway Sports Centre & Climbing Wall *1 Crowthorne Road, W10 5XL (8969 0992/ www.westway.org).*

COUNCIL TAX

A	up to £40,000	£687.44
B	£40,001-£52,000	£802.00
C	£52,001-£68,000	£916.58
D	£68,001-£88,000	£1,031.15
E	£88,001-£120,000	£1,260.30
F	£120,001-£160,000	£1,489.44
G	£160,001-£320,000	£1,718.59
H	over £320,000	£2,062.30

RECYCLING

No. of bring sites 25 (for nearest, visit www.recycleforlondon.com)
Household waste recycled 19.29%
Main recycling centre Kensington & Chelsea's main recycling centre has closed, so residents are directed to: Western Riverside Civic Amenity Site, Smugglers Way, SW18 1JS (8871 2788, www.wrwa.gov.uk)
Other recycling services orange bag recycling service; green waste collection; collection of furniture and white goods; green waste recycling; real nappies campaign
Council contact Waste Management, the Council Offices, 37 Pembroke Road, W8 6PW (Streetline 7361 3001)

Schools

WHAT THE PARENTS SAY:

'This is an area where an awful lot of parents choose to send their kids to private schools from an early age. State schools, especially secondary, suffer as a result. Notable state primaries include St Mary Abbott's on Kensington High Street and Fox just off Notting Hill Gate, but entry to both of these is incredibly difficult. In North Kensington, Oxford Gardens is a decent option with an excellent head. Secondary schools include Holland Park, London's first purpose-built comprehensive, but a much better option is Catholic Cardinal Vaughan, which gets excellent results. Again, it's very hard to get into.'

Father of one, Kensington

Primary

There are 26 state primary schools in Kensington & Chelsea, 15 of which are church schools. There are also 25 independent primaries, including one Spanish school and one French school. See www.rbkc.gov.uk, www.edubase.gov.uk and www.ofsted.gov.uk for more information.

Secondary

Cardinal Vaughan Memorial School
89 Addison Road, W14 8BZ (7603 8478/ www.cvms.co.uk). Boys only.
Holland Park School *Airlie Gardens, Campden Hill Road, W8 7AF (7908 1000/ www.hollandparkschool.co.uk).*
Sion Manning RC School for Girls
St Charles Square, W10 6EL (8969 7111/ www.sion-manning.com). Girls only.
St Thomas More School *Cadogan Street, SW3 2QS (7589 9734/www.stm.rbkc.sch.uk).*

Property

WHAT THE AGENTS SAY:

' Property prices increased hugely in 2007 in Notting Hill, Portobello and North Kensington, probably by about 25 per cent. More City bankers are moving in, fuelled by their bonuses, but also more families. Previously, this was 'flat land', with Victorian buildings converted into flats, but now they're being converted back into houses, especially in the garden squares. North Ken is where Chelsea was in the 1980s now: new Sloane Rangers and a lot of City workers.

The introduction of the Congestion Charge hasn't put people off – it's like it never happened – but then we have tube connections throughout the borough, and Paddington is nearby. Crossrail, if it ever happens, will also be a massive improvement.

It is getting extremely expensive; many buyers are priced out. However, the area manages to retain a mix of people, probably because there are quite a few council buildings, preventing it from becoming a "rich man's ghetto".'

Gordon Blausten, Bruten & Co

Average property prices

Detached n/a
Semi-detached £2,674,943
Terraced £2,296,852
Flat £752,619

Local estate agents

Bruten & Co *4A Wellington Terrace, W2 4LW (7229 9262/www.brutens.com).*
Carter Jonas *8 Addison Avenue, W11 4QR (7371 1111/www.carterjonas.co.uk).*
Chelsea International *15 Radnor Walk, SW3 4BP (7349 9495/www.chelseainternational.co.uk).*
Coutts de Lisle *66 Pembroke Road, W8 6NX (7603 4444/www.cdlestates.co.uk).*
Executive Lettings *329 Chelsea Cloisters, Sloane Avenue, SW3 3EE (07957 170 697/ www.executivelettings.com).*
Marsh & Parsons *www.marshandparsons.co.uk; 6 offices (Bayswater 7243 5390/Chelsea 7591 5570/Holland Park 7605 6890/Kensington 7368 4450/North Kensington 7313 8350/Notting Hill 7313 2890).*
Westways *20 Great Western Road, W9 3NN (7286 5757/www.westwaysuk.com).*

Other information

Council

The Royal Borough of Kensington & Chelsea *Town Hall, Hornton Street, W8 7NX (7361 3000/www.rbkc.gov.uk).*

Legal services

Chelsea CAB *Old Town Hall, King's Road, SW3 5EE (0870 122 2313/ www.adviceguide.org.uk).*
Kensington CAB *140 Ladbroke Grove, W10 5ND (0870 122 2313/www.adviceguide.org.uk).*
North Kensington Law Centre *74 Golborne Road, W10 5PS (8969 7473/www.nklc.co.uk).*
Nucleus Legal Advice Centre *298 Old Brompton Road, SW5 9JF (7373 6262/4005).*

Local newspapers

Kensington & Chelsea Independent *8961 3345/www.londonlocals.co.uk.*

Allotments & open spaces

Allotments There are no allotments in Kensington & Chelsea.
Open spaces *www.rbkc.gov.uk/parksand gardens; www.kensalgreen.co.uk (Kensal Green Cemetery); www.royalparks.org.uk (Kensington Gardens).*

'The large Polish community gives the area a really nice buzz, and you can always get great borscht on King Street.'

Lucien Clayton, film editor and resident

Hammersmith & Fulham

While Fulham continues to attract a stream of double buggies, Shepherd's Bush and Hammersmith have been experiencing an upturn in fortunes as Notting Hillbillies flee the ferocious property prices of W11. To satisfy these well-heeled arrivistes, the borough's wastelands are hastily being transformed into middle-class malls. Rumour has it they might even clean up Shepherd's Bush Green.

Neighbourhoods

Shepherd's Bush

It's all change at Shepherd's Bush, the skyline a sea of cranes as the finishing touches are laid to Europe's largest urban shopping centre, Westfield London, due to open in October 2008. The statistics are impressive, or shocking if you live in the immediate vicinity, with a planned 270 stores, some 40 restaurants and two new stations, Wood Lane underground station on the Hammersmith & City line and the overground Shepherd's Bush station on the West London line. Construction of the latter has been an embarrassment to developer Westfield – the platform is 18 inches too narrow and is being rebuilt at a cost of £7 million.

All this development will inevitably impact on down-at-heel Shepherd's Bush, with plans also in place to tart up Shepherd's Bush Green and build a new '21st-century' library. As for the ugly West 12 mall on the north side, its days must be numbered.

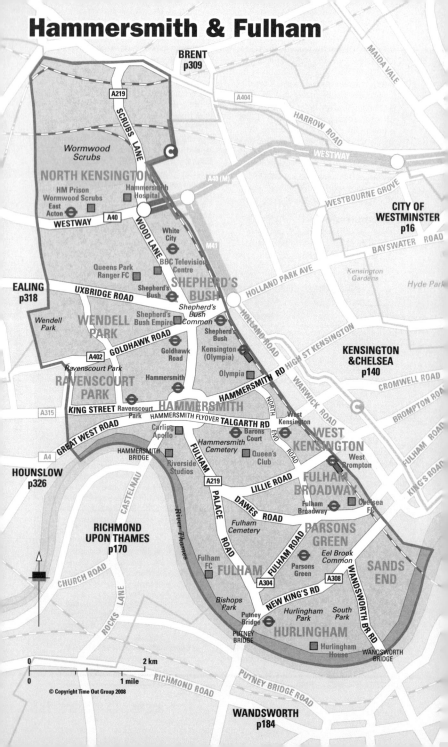

Within walking distance of the vast BBC Media Village complex in White City, Shepherd's Bush has other links with the entertainment world, having spawned members of the Who, the Sex Pistols and current tabloid bête noire Pete Doherty. It's also famous for the Shepherd's Bush Empire. Other defining features of the area include football ground Loftus Road, home to the 'Super Hoops' (Queen's Park Rangers). North of the Westway is Wormwood Scrubs common land, the largest open space in the borough, and adjoining it the infamous prison.

Hammersmith

The heart of Hammersmith may have been torn in two by the thundering A4 and Hammersmith flyover, but things are slowly changing for the better in this windswept corner of west London. The main new development is the approval of a controversial new office block, nicknamed the 'Strawberry', which will occupy an NCP car park earmarked for development since 1981. More interestingly, the building will also house a four-screen branch of Hampstead's Everyman cinema, restaurant and bar.

Not that this area is lacking in places of entertainment, both high- and low-brow. Cultural offerings include the Hammersmith Apollo, Lyric Hammersmith and Riverside Studios. The slightly shabby Hammersmith Palais, though, which brought in hordes of twentysomethings for the regular School Disco nights, is closed awaiting reinvention as an office block – a sad end for a legendary gig venue.

Shopping is centred on busy King Street, which leads west to Chiswick. It's a grubby thoroughfare, providing the usual raft of Dixons, Boots and charity shops, plus an unappealing shopping centre, Kings Mall. Further on lies Lowiczanka Polish Cultural Centre. Home to a theatre, restaurant and the largest Polish library outside Poland, it is a meeting place for Hammersmith's expansive Polish community. Noisy chain pubs dominate the area around the tube station; far better are the lovely riverside pubs west of green-and-gold Hammersmith Bridge, the city's oldest suspension bridge.

Property here is dominated by conversion flats – this is one of the largest private rented sectors in London – and you'll need

to venture up Shepherd's Bush Road to leafy Brook Green and Blythe Village for converted family homes, along with medium-sized Victorian houses and modern luxury apartment blocks.

Olympia Exhibition Centre on the border with Kensington & Chelsea hosts a variety of trade shows; locals tend to resent it for the traffic it creates. The area's transport is generally a plus, though, especially the fast links (by road and tube) to Heathrow airport – hence the presence of such multinational companies as Coca-Cola, L'Oréal, Sony Ericsson and Disney.

Brackenbury Village and Ravenscourt Park

This area – bounded by Goldhawk Road to the west and north, King Street to the south and Hammersmith Grove to the east – is an island of middle-class calm in a sea of urban through-traffic. It feels quite distinct from surrounding Hammersmith and Shepherd's Bush. Appealing Ravenscourt Park, a much-needed open space in a very built-up part of the capital, adds to the community feel. Come Guy

Highs & Lows

▲ **Westfield London** An upmarket mega-mall in the middle of the Bush: what more could W12's ex-Notting Hillbillies want?
Ravenscourt Park Playgrounds, paddling pools, sports pitches and urban peace and quiet – a rare treat in this corner of west London
Culture club The Palais may have shut, but that still leaves the Apollo, Empire, Lyric, Bush Theatre, Bush Hall and Riverside Studios for a cultural fix

Westfield London With thousands of parking spaces, nearly 300 shops and no C-charge, traffic here can only get worse
King Street Hammersmith & Fulham's 'Smarter Borough' tagline seems wholly inappropriate after a few minutes' walk down this grotty main shopping drag
Shepherd's Bush Green There are ▼ few less appealing expanses of green in the capital. Time for a clean-up

Fawkes Night, it offers the best fireworks display in west London, and the brilliant Carter's Steam Fair is an annual visitor.

Minimal traffic and one of London's best state primary schools (John Betts) make the area enormously popular with young families, as do the rows of pretty terraced cottages that dominate the area, although prices are pushing many prospective villagers further west to Acton in search of familial space. Wingate Road is probably the area's most desirable address, with its pastel-coloured houses going for up to £1.5 million. Such assets, combined with clever estate agent marketing (the 'Village' is a relatively recent addition to Brackenbury), also draw BBC staff eager for a quick commute to White City – local celebs include Jeremy Vine and John Humphrys.

Cathnor Park and Wendell Park

This wedge-shaped area west of Shepherd's Bush is hemmed in by two major arteries – Goldhawk Road to the south and Uxbridge Road to the north. It leans towards ethnic diversity of Shepherd's Bush, with a thriving Muslim community, although Brackenbury exiles move across the Goldhawk Road divide in search of extra bedrooms when their bijou cottages fill up.

Uxbridge Road is a wonderfully spicy mix, boasting everything from 24-hour grocers (including former resident Nigella Lawson's favourite supermarket) to ethnic restaurants, internet cafés and pound shops, plus quirky music venue Bush Hall, which has spent the last 100 years variously as a dance hall, a soup kitchen, a bingo hall and a snooker den. Goldhawk Road, meanwhile, is torn between two worlds, simultaneously hosting smart bar-restaurants like BBC fave the Bush Bar & Grill and old-style greasy caffs and Subway franchises.

During the day, smallish Wendell Park can make an adequate setting for a sit or a stroll, but it is beset by its reputation as a hangout for the area's troublemaker teens.

West Kensington and Barons Court

West Ken is the part of Kensington that fashionistas ignore; the name might sound posh to outsiders, but most residents know this is the wrong side of the tracks. The area sits awkwardly between the sprawling concrete of Hammersmith to the west and well-heeled Kensington & Chelsea to the east, with the thundering Talgarth Road (aka the A4) slicing through its centre, notable solely for a row of stunning Grade II-listed artists' studios built in the 1890s. The long spine of the North End Road – pebble-dashed with kebab shops, mini-marts and a lively street market – cuts through from Olympia Exhibition Centre in the north to Fulham Broadway in the south.

The district is primarily residential, consisting mainly of Victorian terraces, plus newer apartment blocks. Properties become larger and smarter the nearer you get to Barons Court, which is also home to the Queen's Club, one of the capital's most

Tunes for all at **Shepherd's Bush Empire**. *See p158.*

exclusive tennis clubs. Transport is a strong point, with easy access to the A4 and three tube stations: Barons Court to the west, West Kensington in the centre, and Kensington (Olympia) to the north.

Fulham

Leafy Fulham has changed radically since the 1960s. The former Labour stronghold's tightly packed terraces, once home to working-class families employed in the heavy industry that dominated the riverside, are now full of young, monied professionals. The population is much less diverse than in Hammersmith next door: there's truth to the clichéd image of private-school-educated, Porsche-driving young men who work in the City and their blonde-bobbed spouses. Yet the area is just as popular with families, thanks to relatively crime-free streets and an abundance of private nurseries and prep schools.

Originally a market garden area, the architecture is largely Victorian, offering row upon row of neat terraced houses and converted flats. Gardens tend to be tiny (a drawback for families), except for the 'alphabet' streets between Fulham Palace Road and the river. Middle-class needs are met by a range of exclusive boutiques, antiques shops, gyms, upmarket bars and restaurants – many clustered along Fulham Road, the main retail street. Two major

bugbears are a lack of parking spaces (mainly controlled by resident parking permits) and traffic congestion. Public transport can also be a problem. There is no overground rail service and the nearest tubes (Putney Bridge, Parsons Green and Fulham Broadway) are all a bit of a hike.

The only green area of any size is hugely popular Bishops Park. Bordering the river, and with views across to Putney, it includes no fewer than 15 tennis courts, an ornamental park and Grade I-listed Fulham Palace museum (it was the summer home of the Bishops of London from around 700 until 1973). The café here has just been taken over by upmarket caterer Oliver Peyton, and visiting on a Sunday morning feels like gatecrashing some fancy country house party, with French doors leading out to the ornamental gardens. The only disappointment is the rather drab playground and paddling pool in the park, but these are set for a makeover soon. Next door is Craven Cottage, home of Fulham Football Club since 1896 and still a charmingly old-fashioned ground.

Parsons Green and Fulham Broadway

Avenues lined with stately plane trees give Parsons Green a villagey air. Complete with its own (eponymous) green, a church and the perennially popular White Horse

pub, it is slightly more affordable than neighbouring Chelsea. Eel Brook Common, offering children's play areas, tennis courts, football-cum-netball pitches and dog-free grass sections, is a big draw for families.

The streets north-east of Parsons Green are noticeably busier but also highly desirable. Fulham Broadway itself is a thriving shopping area, with all the standard high-street names, supermarkets, pubs, restaurants and the shiny new Fulham Broadway Centre atop the (revamped) tube station. An upper-class version of Shepherd's Bush's ugly West 12 centre, this US-style mall boasts assorted chain shops and eateries, plus a nine-screen cinema complex and a David Lloyd fitness club. Next door is Stamford Bridge, Chelsea FC's ground: congestion on match days is a major downer.

Peterborough Estate and Hurlingham

Lying south of the New Kings Road, this area is a tale of two estates. One is the exclusive Peterborough Estate, built in the 19th century for local workers. Conversions, extensions and increasing gentrification due to the Chelsea overspill have combined to make these elaborately detailed red-brick houses highly sought after. The original 500 'Lion' houses – so-named because of the miniature rooftop stone lions – now regularly go for over £1 million (when, that is, they make a rare appearance on the market). Nearby, meanwhile, sits the Sullivan Estate – an area known for 'hoodie' street gang kids and petty crime. The clash can be an uncomfortable one.

Catering to the richest residents is the exclusive Hurlingham Club, located at 18th-century Hurlingham House. Best described as a country mansion (site of many a glittering party), it sits in 42 acres of grounds, which cater for tennis, croquet, cricket, bowls, golf, squash and swimming. Arrivistes beware – there is currently a 15-year waiting list for membership. Nearby is a smaller green space, South Park (open to all), while the proximity of both the New Kings Road and more affordable Wandsworth Bridge Road cover the retail side of life. As for transport, Putney Bridge tube and slow buses service the area.

Sand's End

In the south-east corner of the borough and previously seen as Fulham's poor relation, Sand's End is in a state of flux. The fortress-like Imperial Wharf – a dramatic residential complex featuring soaring glass towers, a ten-acre park and stunning riverside views – has given the area an aura of glamour that has local estate agents drooling, no matter that transport links remain pretty poor. As part of the development, a new overground station is still in the pipeline. First mooted back in 2000, with an estimated layout of £1.5 million, seven years later the wrangling continues and the cost has risen to nearly £8 million.

Moving inland from the river sees a mix of more affordable public and private housing, with facilities for those on lower incomes, such as the Sand's End Community Centre. Wandsworth Bridge Road is the main shopping street, containing upmarket pine and antiques shops, cosy cafés and one of the best butcher's in town (Randalls). Plus, naturally, a slew of estate agents touting for business.

LOCALS' TIPS

Spend a sophisticated Sunday morning over brunch and the papers at Oliver Peyton's delightful new café at Fulham Palace (www.fulhampalace.org).

Enjoy free theatre at the Lyric, which celebrates the first night of many of its shows with free tickets for borough residents. Go to the ticket office in person, with proof of address, from 9.30am the Saturday before.

Hop on the Duck Bus (no.283) and head over Hammersmith Bridge for a day at the WWT Wetland Centre (www.wwt.org.uk), a huge slice of rural P&Q just a flutter away from the chaos of King Street.

Mind where you drive – much of the borough borders the C-charge's new western extension. One wrong turn and you could be £8 poorer.

Switch off the television set and take a tour round the studios instead. The BBC (www.bbc.co.uk/tours/tvc.shtml) organises 90-minute tours of Television Centre, during which you can visit BBC News and loosen up in the interactive studio. Lights, camera...

Restaurants & cafés

The excellent spread of places to eat around Shepherd's Bush owes much to its racially mixed population and increasing number of upwardly mobile residents. Long-standing Modern European bar-restaurant Bush Bar & Grill still attracts a cool crowd to its sleek venue on grimy Goldhawk Road. Goldhawk Road's other offerings include veggie haven Blah Blah Blah, the Tardis-like Bush Garden Café and, at the Stamford Brook end, quality North American restaurant Pacific Bar & Grill. Gastropub the Havelock Tavern (see *p166*) is another much-loved local venue.

Elsewhere, Shepherd's Bush boasts some excellent world cuisine, ranging from Syrian (low-budget, high-quality Abu Zaad) to South-east Asian (unassuming Thai Esarn Kheaw), via East European (Polish old-timer Patio) and Greek-Cypriot (Vine Leaves). Askew Road typifies the district's forte in modest ethnic eateries: Adam's Café (Tunisian) is worth a look.

Travelling south on Shepherd's Bush Road towards Hammersmith, Snows on the Green is a smart neighbourhood eaterie with Italian leanings. Opposite sits the charming Los Molinos tapas restaurant. In Hammersmith itself, Ruth Rogers and Rose Gray's River Café makes good use of a curvaceous stretch of the Thames; close behind in the fame stakes is the excellent vegetarian Gate.

At a less exalted level, King Street has long been known for its Polish and Indian restaurants. You'll get the whole east European experience within the concrete block of the Lowiczanka Polish Cultural Centre, while homely Polish cooking at low prices is the remit of deli-restaurant Polanka. As for the South Asian contenders, the best choices are low-priced Sagar (South Indian vegetarian) and Agni (pan-Indian). King Street also houses Saigon Saigon (Vietnamese), Tosa (Japanese), Green Chilli (pan-Indian) and fabulously authentic Iranian restaurant Mahdi.

Away from the major thoroughfares, the pocket of gentility that is Brackenbury Village has the Brackenbury, a cherished, long-standing Modern European venue; you'll find similarly monied clientele at the Anglesea Arms gastropub. On Hammersmith Grove, smart Chez Kristof

Famous local the **River Café**.

serves marvellous regional French cuisine, and there's a sister deli-café next door.

West Kensington is a good place to look for a cheap eat, the market street North End Road being well served with takeaways (best is Turkish Best Mangal). Further down the same street is 222 Veggie Vegan, with its (you guessed it) vegan menu. At West Ken's northern boundary is Olympia, boasting some great curries at Karma and recently opened Mirch Masala, plus the Popeseye Steak House, strictly for meat-lovers. As for gastropubs, the genial Cumberland Arms has a good-value Mediterranean and North African menu.

Fulham's restaurants mainly cater to the area's young professionals. Off towards Fulham Broadway, the Farm is a cosy, relaxed bar-restaurant serving Modern European cuisine. Around Fulham Broadway, Blue Elephant (Thai) and pizzeria Napulé are both recommended. Fulham's fish-lovers head for the river, where Deep serves a fascinating, Scandinavian-influenced menu. Nearby Parsons Green offers quality chains and fabulous Thai restaurant Sukho.

Abu Zaad *29 Uxbridge Road, W12 8LH (8749 5107/www.abuzaad.co.uk).*
Adam's Café *77 Askew Road, W12 9AH (8743 0572).*
Agni *160 King Street, W6 0QU (8846 9191/ www.agnirestaurant.com).*

Anglesea Arms *35 Wingate Road, W6 0UR (8749 1291).*
Best Mangal *104 North End Road, W14 9EX (7610 1050).*
Blah Blah Blah *78 Goldhawk Road, W12 8HA (8746 1337).*
Blue Elephant *4-6 Fulham Broadway, SW6 1AA (7385 6595/www.blueelephant.com).*
Brackenbury *129-131 Brackenbury Road, W6 0BQ (8748 0107).*
Bush Bar & Grill *45A Goldhawk Road, W12 8QP (8746 2111/www.bushbar.co.uk).*
Bush Garden Café *59 Goldhawk Road, W12 8EG (8811 1795).*
Chez Kristof *111 Hammersmith Grove, W6 0NQ (8741 1177/www.chezkristof.co.uk).*
Cumberland Arms *29 North End Road, W14 8SZ (7371 6806/www.thecumberland armspub.co.uk).*
Deep *The Boulevard, Imperial Wharf, SW6 2UB (7736 3337/www.deeplondon.co.uk).*
Esarn Kheaw *314 Uxbridge Road, W12 7LJ (8743 8930/www.esarnkheaw.com).*
The Farm *18 Farm Lane, SW6 1PP (7381 3331/www.thefarmfulham.co.uk).*
The Gate *51 Queen Caroline Street, W6 9QL (8748 6932/www.thegate.tv).*
Green Chilli *220 King Street, W6 0RA (8748 0111/www.greenchillirestaurant.co.uk).*
Karma *44 Blythe Road, W14 0HA (7602 9333/ www.k-a-r-m-a.co.uk).*
Lowiczanka Polish Cultural Centre *1st floor, 238-246 King Street, W6 0RF (8741 3225/www.lowiczankarestaurant.co.uk).*
Mahdi *217 King Street, W6 9JT (8563 7007).*
Mirch Masala *3 Hammersmith Road, W14 8XJ (7602 4555).*
Los Molinos *127 Shepherd's Bush Road, W6 7LP (7603 2229/www.losmolinosuk.com).*
Napulé *585 Fulham Road, SW6 5UA (7381 1122).*
Pacific Bar & Grill *320 Goldhawk Road, W6 0XF (8741 1994).*
Patio *5 Goldhawk Road, W12 8QQ (8743 5194).*
Polanka *258 King Street, W6 0SP (8741 8268/www.polanka-rest.com).*
Popeseye Steak House *108 Blythe Road, W14 0HD (7610 4578).*
River Café *Thames Wharf, Rainville Road, W6 9HA (7386 4200/www.rivercafe.co.uk).*
Sagar *157 King Street, W6 9JT (8741 8563).*
Saigon Saigon *313-317 King Street, W6 9NH (0870 220 1398).*
Snows on the Green *166 Shepherd's Bush Road, W6 7PB (7603 2142/www.snowsonthe green.co.uk).*
Sukho Thai Cuisine *855 Fulham Road, SW6 5HJ (7371 7600).*
Tosa *332 King Street, W6 0RR (8748 0002).*
222 Veggie Vegan *222 North End Road, W14 9NU (7381 2322/www.222veggie vegan.com).*
Vine Leaves Taverna *71 Uxbridge Road, W12 8NR (8749 0325/www.vineleaves taverna.co.uk).*

Bars & pubs

Shepherd's Bush's inexorable push upmarket is not yet reflected in the area's pubs, which remain a fairly insalubrious collection. Venues such as the Defector's Weld, with its smart pub, 'snug' cocktail bar and unobtrusive DJ sounds, are hopefully a sign of things to come. On the other side of Goldhawk Road is a fine gastropub, the Anglesea Arms (*see above*). The nearby Thatched House is a relaxed local that serves decent pub food. Heading towards Kensington, nestled on a quiet residential road, is the Havelock Tavern, which has risen from the ashes of a fire a couple of years back to serve the decent real ales and top-notch gastro grub that originally made its name. Close to Shepherd's Bush tube, a string of chain pubs is unlikely to pique your interest.

The cluster of pubs on the western side of Hammersmith Bridge includes the Old Ship, with its happy marriage of Thames views and outside space, and the 17th-century Dove. Both serve Fuller's beers, and are prime spots for watching the Boat

TRANSPORT

Tube stations *Central* Shepherd's Bush, White City, East Acton; *District* Kensington (Olympia), West Kensington, Baron's Court, Hammersmith, Ravenscourt Park, West Brompton, Fulham Broadway, Parsons Green, Putney Bridge; *Hammersmith & City* Shepherd's Bush, Goldhawk Road, Hammersmith; *Piccadilly* Barons Court, Hammersmith

Rail stations *London Overground* Willesden Junction, Kensington (Olympia), West Brompton; *Southern* Kensington (Olympia), West Brompton

Main bus routes *into central London* 7, 9, 10, 11, 14, 22, 27, 74, 94, 148, 211, 414; *night buses* N7, N9, N10, N11, N22, N28, N74, N97, N207; *24-hour buses* 14, 27, 94, 148

Development plans Shepherd's Bush Central line station to connect to London Overground; Shepherd's Bush Hammersmith & City line station to be renamed Shepherd's Bush Market; a new station on Wood Lane to open in 2008 with arrival of the Westfield shopping centre

Race in spring. Just north from the river is the beautifully ornate Salutation; further north still you can enjoy Young's beers and live jazz, blues or comedy at the handsome, newly refurbished Brook Green Hotel. Just behind King Street and its chain pubs is the Stonemasons Arms, one of the original gastro brigade, and the newly refurbished Dartmouth Castle, with a great front patio.

Even though Fulham covers such a large area, from the riverside to the busy lower stretches of the King's and Fulham Roads, there's not a great deal to shout about before you reach the pastoral pleasures of Parsons Green, where well-heeled locals hang out at the White Horse, one of London's finest ale pubs.

Aragon House on New Kings Road is a fine neo-Georgian boozer with an ivy-clad exterior and a lovely garden. Just east of the borough, on the far side of Fulham Broadway tube and in close proximity to Chelsea's football ground, are the grand King's Arms (previously Finch's) and the charming, unpretentious Fox & Pheasant.

Aragon House *247 New Kings Road, SW6 4XG (7731 7313/www.aragonhouse.net).*
Brook Green Hotel *170 Shepherd's Bush Road, W6 7PB (7603 2516/www.brookgreen hotel.co.uk).*
Dartmouth Castle *26 Glenthorne Road, W6 0LS (8748 3614/www.thedartmouth castlepub.co.uk).*
Defector's Weld *170 Uxbridge Road, W12 8AA (8749 0008).*
Dove *19 Upper Mall, W6 9TA (8748 9474).*
Fox & Pheasant *1 Billing Road, SW10 9UJ (7352 2943).*
Havelock Tavern *57 Masbro Road, W14 0LS (7603 5374/www.thehavelocktavern.co.uk).*
King's Arms *190 Fulham Road, SW10 9PN (7351 5043/www.kingsarmschelsea.co.uk).*
Old Ship *25 Upper Mall, W6 9TD (8748 2593/www.oldshipw6.co.uk).*
Salutation *154 King Street, W6 0QU (8748 3668).*
Stonemasons Arms *54 Cambridge Grove, W6 0LA (8748 1397).*
Thatched House *115 Dalling Road, W6 0ET (8748 6174/www.thatchedhouse.com).*
White Horse *1-3 Parsons Green, SW6 4UL (7736 2115/www.whitehorsesw6.com).*

Shops

At the time of writing, the borough's best-known retail attractions were colourful, cut-price Shepherd's Bush Market and the classy interiors and antiques shops of

Fulham. That's all set to change at the end of 2008, however, when the biggest urban shopping centre in Europe, Westfield London (www.westfield.com/london), opens in White City, offering luxury brands of the calibre of Louis Vuitton alongside upmarket eateries and a spa. It will be a far cry from the area's celebrated sell-'em-cheap bazaar. Running between Uxbridge and Goldhawk Roads, Shepherd's Bush Market offers an intriguing mix of just about everything you can think of, from produce and fabrics to reggae music and wedding gowns. There is also an impressive array of food shops on Uxbridge Road, including global supermarket Al-Abbas. The nearby West 12 mall contains basic chains such as Boots and Books etc, as well as a Vue Cinema.

Hammersmith's Kings Mall shopping precinct houses a branch of Habitat, and there are more chains at the Broadway mall in the centre of the tube/bus station complex. Healthy ingredients can be found at Soil Association-registered Bushwacker Wholefoods and superior fishmonger Cape Clear Fish Shop, in

COUNCIL TAX

A	up to £40,000	£795.56
B	£40,001-£52,000	£928.14
C	£52,001-£68,000	£1,060.74
D	£68,001-£88,000	£1,193.33
E	£88,001-£120,000	£1,458.52
F	£120,001-£160,000	£1,723.70
G	£160,001-£320,000	£1,988.89
H	over £320,000	£2,386.66

RECYCLING

No. of bring sites 48 (for nearest, visit www.recycleforlondon.com)
Household waste recycled 21%
Main recycling centre Western Riverside Civic Amenity Site, Smugglers Way, Wandsworth, SW18 1JS (8871 2788/www.wrwa.gov.uk)
Other recycling services green waste collection; home composting; fridge and freezer collection; collection of furniture, by either the council, Furnish (8969 3332) or the Notting Hill Housing Group Furniture Store (8960 3005)
Council contact Environmental Services Department, Hammersmith Town Hall, King Street, W6 9JU (8753 3279)

Riverside fave the **Old Ship**. See p165.

nearby Brook Green, which counts über-chef Heston Blumenthal among its customers.

Residents of Hammersmith, West Kensington and Fulham converge to stock up on comestibles at the North End Road street market; it's also worth seeking out the Polish deli Prima a few streets north.

Unsurprisingly, affluent Fulham has the lion's share of browse-worthy shops, in addition to the Sainsbury's and workaday chains of the Fulham Broadway Centre. Near the tube, excellent specialist Pure Massage is a serene minimalist sanctuary.

The stretch of the Fulham Road near Parsons Green has enough upmarket chains (Cologne & Cotton, Cath Kidston) and interesting one-offs (Cine Art Gallery) to occupy the locals on a Saturday afternoon. Men can get fitted out in relaxed, Italian tailoring at Palmer, and yummy mummies rely on good-value Blooming Marvellous for maternity wear, kids' clobber and toys. Towards the river on Fulham High Street is a brace of fine vintage shops: Circa, which specialises in glamorous dresses, and Old Hat, where cash-strapped dandies can pick up a (previously worn) Savile Row suit. On the food front, there's a trio of upmarket delis in the general locale – Elizabeth King, Megan's and Moroccan/Middle Eastern Del'Aziz (next to Aziz restaurant) – plus excellent butcher Randalls.

Catering to the numerous nesters, this end of the King's Road and Wandsworth Bridge Road is known for smart furniture and interiors shops and, increasingly,

20th-century design – Talisman opened in a beautifully restored art deco building in 2006, while Core One, a varied group of dealers, has colonised the old gas works in Sand's End. Another resident, Carpenters Workshop Gallery, showcases interesting contemporary pieces. Leigh Harmer is strong on new British design, as well as European modern classics.

Lillie Road isn't quite the antiques enclave it used to be, but some unusual shops remain, including Andrew Bewick and Stephen Sprake.

Al-Abbas *258-262 Uxbridge Road, W12 7JA (8740 1932).*
Andrew Bewick *287 Lillie Road, SW6 7LL (7385 9025).*
Blooming Marvellous *725 Fulham Road, SW6 5UL (7371 0500/www.blooming marvellous.co.uk).*
Broadway Shopping Centre *The Broadway, W6 9YE (8563 0131/www.hammersmith broadway.co.uk).*
Bushwacker Wholefoods *132 King Street, W6 0QU (8748 2061).*
Cape Clear Fish Shop *119 Shepherds Bush Road, W6 7LP (7751 1609/www.capeclear fishshop.co.uk).*
Carpenters Workshop Gallery *The Gas Works, 2 Michael Road, SW6 2AD (7384 2211/www.cwgdesign.com).*
Cath Kidston *668 Fulham Road, SW6 5RX (7731 6531/www.cathkidston.co.uk).*
Cine Art Gallery *759 Fulham Road, SW6 5UU (7384 0728/www.cineartgallery.com).*
Circa Vintage Clothes *64 Fulham High Street, SW6 3LQ (7736 5038/www.circa vintage.com).*
Cologne & Cotton *791 Fulham Road, SW6 5HD (7736 9261/www.cologneandcotton.com).*
Core One *The Gas Works, 2 Michael Road, SW6 2AD.*
Del'Aziz *24-32 Vanston Place, SW6 1AX (7386 0086).*
Elizabeth King *32-34 New Kings Road, SW6 4ST (7736 2826/www.elizabethking.com).*
Fulham Broadway Centre *Fulham Road, SW6 1BW (7385 6965/www.fulham broadway.com).*
Kings Mall Shopping Centre *King Street, W6 0PZ (8741 2121).*
Leigh Harmer *253 New King's Road, SW6 4RB (7736 5111/www.leighharmer.co.uk).*
Megan's Delicatessen *571 King's Road, SW6 2EB (7371 7837/www.megansdeli.com).*
Old Hat *66 Fulham High Street, SW6 3LQ (7610 6558).*
Palmer *771 Fulham Road, SW6 5HA (7384 2044).*
Prima Delicatessen *192 North End Road, W14 9NX (7385 2070).*
Pure Massage *3-5 Vanston Place, SW6 1AY (7381 8100/www.puremassage.com).*

...tchers *113 Wandsworth Bridge ?TE (7736 3426).*
... Bush Market *east side of the railway viaduct, off Goldhawk Road, W12.*
Stephen Sprake *283 Lillie Road, SW6 7LL (7381 3209).*
Talisman *79-91 New Kings Road, SW6 4SQ (7731 4686/www.talismanlondon.com).*
West 12 Centre *The Broadway, W12 8PP (8746 0038/www.west12online.com).*

Arts & attractions

Cinemas & theatres
Bush Theatre *Shepherd's Bush Green, W12 8QD (7610 4224/www.bushtheatre.co.uk).*
Cineworld Hammersmith *207 King Street, W6 9JT (0871 200 2000/www.cineworld.co.uk).*
Lyric Hammersmith *Lyric Square, King Street, W6 0QL (0870 050 0511/www.lyric. co.uk).* Excellent local theatre.
Riverside Studios *Crisp Road, W6 9RL (8237 1111/www.riversidestudios.co.uk).* Performance arts and repertory cinema.
Vue *0871 224 0240/www.myvue.com;* Fulham Broadway *Fulham Broadway Centre, Fulham Road, SW6 1BW;* Shepherd's Bush *West 12 Centre, Shepherd's Bush Green, W12 8PP.*

Galleries & museums
Fulham Palace *Bishop's Avenue, SW6 6EA (7736 8140/www.fulhampalace.org).* Museum, gallery, gardens – and fine café.
Kelmscott House *26 Upper Mall, W6 9TA (8741 3735/www.morrissociety.org).* William Morris's 1878-96 home is a private house, but the basement and coach house are open to the public on Thursday and Saturday afternoons.

Music & comedy venues
Bush Hall *310 Uxbridge Road, W12 7LJ (8222 6955/www.bushhallmusic.co.uk).* Stages chamber concerts and low-key rock shows.
Hammersmith Apollo *Queen Caroline Street, W6 9QH (8748 8660/www.getlive.co.uk).* Powerhouse music venue with a 5,000 capacity.
Shepherd's Bush Empire *Shepherd's Bush Green, W12 8TT (8354 3300/www.shepherds-bush-empire.co.uk).* Great mid-sized music venue.

Sport & fitness

The last few years have seen serious improvements in Hammersmith & Fulham's sports facilities. The £4 million Phoenix Fitness Centre & Janet Adegoke Swimming Pool opened in early 2006, adding a much-needed public facility to the borough (the only other public swimming option is the pool at the Normand Park Virgin Active). A swanky new private

facility, Thirtysevendegrees, opened in late 2007 in Olympia.

The borough is home to three football clubs too – Chelsea, Fulham and QPR – as well as the prestigious Queen's tennis club, which hosts the Artois Championship (an annual, men-only precursor to Wimbledon).

Gyms & leisure centres
Charing Cross Sports Club *Aspenlea Road, W6 8LH (8741 3654/www.ccsclub.co.uk).* Private.
David Lloyd *Unit 24, Fulham Broadway Retail Centre, Fulham Road, SW6 1BW (7386 2200/ www.davidlloydleisure.co.uk).* Private.
Fitness First *West 12 Centre, W12 8PP (8743 4444/www.fitnessfirst.co.uk).* Private.
Hammersmith Fitness & Squash Centre *Chalk Hill Road, W6 8DW (8741 4640/ www.gll.org).*
Lillie Road Fitness Centre *Lillie Road, SW6 7PH (7381 2183/www.gll.org).*
Phoenix Fitness Centre & Janet Adegoke Swimming Pool *Bloemfontein Road, W12 0RQ (8735 4900/www.gll.org).*
Thirtysevendegrees *10 Beaconsfield Terrace Road, W14 0PP (7610 4090/www.www.thirty sevendegrees.co.uk).* Private.
Virgin Active *www.virginactive.co.uk; Normand Park, Lillie Road, SW6 7ST (7471 0450); 181 Hammersmith Road, W6 8BS (8741 0487); 188A Fulham Road, SW10 9PN (7352 9452).* Private.

Other facilities
Hurlingham Club *Ranelagh Gardens, SW6 3PR (7471 8240/www.hurlinghamclub.org.uk).* Private members' club with a long history, and even longer waiting list for new members.
Linford Christie Outdoor Sports Centre *Artillery Way, off Du Cane Road, W12 0DF (7736 1504/www.lbhf.gov.uk).*
Queen's Club *Palliser Road, W14 9EQ (7385 3421/www.queensclub.co.uk).* Upmarket tennis club; private.

Spectator sports
Chelsea FC *Stamford Bridge, Fulham Road, SW6 1HS (0870 300 2322/www.chelseafc.com).*
Fulham FC *Craven Cottage, Stevenage Road, SW6 6HH (0870 442 1222/www.fulhamfc.com).*
Queen's Park Rangers FC *Loftus Road Stadium, South Africa Road, W12 7PA (8743 0262/www.qpr.co.uk).*

Schools

WHAT THE PARENTS SAY:
‘There are a lot of famous private schools in the area, such as St Paul's Girls, Godolphin & Latymer and Latymer Upper, and this has a negative impact on secondary state schools. The primaries fare better, especially Catholic

Hammersmith & Fulham

church schools such as St Mary's and Larmenier, and John Betts is one of inner London's best state primaries. As far as secondary schools go, Lady Margaret and Sacred Heart, both girls only, are the ones to try for. For boys, the London Oratory School also gets good results, or you need to cross just over the borough border to Kensington & Chelsea's Cardinal Vaughan. There's no point in applying unless you are a Catholic, though. **9**
Mother of three, Hammersmith

Primary

There are 35 state primary schools in Hammersmith & Fulham, including 12 church schools. There are also 12 independent primaries, including one Muslim school, one French school, one theatre school and one Montessori school. See www.lbhf.gov.uk, www.edubase.gov.uk and www.ofsted.gov.uk for more information.

Secondary

Burlington Danes Academy *Wood Lane, W12 0HR (8735 4950/www.arkschools.org).*
Fulham Cross *Munster Road, SW6 6BP (7381 0861/www.fulhamcross lbhf.sch.uk).* Girls only.
Godolphin & Latymer School *Iffley Road, W6 0PG (8741 1936/www.godolphinand latymer.com).* Private; girls only.
Henry Compton School *Kingwood Road, SW6 6SN (7381 3606/www.henrycompton school.ik.org).* Boys only.
Hurlingham & Chelsea School *Peterborough Road, SW6 3ED (7731 2581).*
Lady Margaret School *Parsons Green, SW6 4UN (7736 7138/www.ladymargaret. lbhf.sch.uk).* Girls only.
London Oratory School *Seagrave Road, SW6 1RX (7385 0102/www.london-oratory.org).* Boys only; mixed sixth form.
Phoenix High School *The Curve, W12 0RQ (8749 1141/www.phoenixhighschool.org).*
Sacred Heart High School *212 Hammersmith Road, W6 7DG (8748 7600/ www.sacredhearthighschool.org.uk).* Girls only.
St Paul's Girls' School *Brook Green, W6 7BS (7603 2288/www.spgs.org).* Private; girls only.
William Morris Sixth Form *St Dunstan's Road, W6 8RB (8748 6969/www.wma.ac.uk).*

Property

WHAT THE AGENTS SAY:

6Fulham has always been a hotspot for property and this has now spread to Hammersmith and Shepherd's Bush, where prices have shot up. With Fulham, you're right on the river, but with access to the A4, which takes you on to the M4. Bishops Park is awesome, with great tennis courts, and there are a lot of gyms in the area. Because of Imperial College, there's a large

student population and, with so much demand, a lot of investors are buying to let.**9**
Brian Corson, Lawsons & Daughters, Fulham

Average property prices

Detached n/a
Semi-detached £836,812
Terraced £846,893
Flat £385,089

Local estate agents

Black Katz *24 Shepherd's Bush Road, W6 7PJ (7371 2333).*
Chard *www.chard.co.uk; 2 offices in the borough (Brook Green 7603 1415/Fulham 7731 5115).*
Faron Sutaria *www.faronsutaria.co.uk; 3 offices in the borough (Brook Green 7348 0016/Fulham 7610 2080/Shepherd's Bush 8740 7766).*
John Hollingsworth *www.johnhollingsworth. co.uk; 2 offices in the borough (Fulham 7731 3888/West Kensington 7602 8511).*
Lawsons & Daughters *68 Fulham Palace Road, W6 9PL (8563 0202/www.lawsonsand daughters.com).*
Marsh & Parsons *www.marshandparsons. co.uk; 2 offices (Brook Green 7605 7760/ Fulham 7736 9822).*
Ravenscourt Residential *3 Seven Stars Corner, Paddenswick Road, W12 8ET (8740 5678/www.ravenscourtresidential.co.uk).*
Sebastian Estates *www.sebastianestates. co.uk; 2 offices in the borough (Fulham 7610 6716/Hammersmith 7381 4998).*

Other information

Council

London Borough of Hammersmith & Fulham Council *Hammersmith Town Hall, King Street, W6 9JU; Fulham Town Hall, Fulham Broadway, SW6 1ET (8748 3020/ www.lbhf.gov.uk).*

Legal services

Hammersmith & Fulham CAB *The Pavilion, 1 Mund Street, W14 9LY (0845 458 2515/ www.fulhamcab.org.uk).*
Shepherd's Bush Advice Centre *338 Uxbridge Road, W12 7LL (8753 5913).*

Local newspapers

Hammersmith & Fulham Independent *8961 3345/www.londonlocals.co.uk.*

Allotments & open spaces

Fulham Palace Meadow Allotments Association *c/o Fulham Palace, Bishop's Avenue, SW6 6EA (7731 6055).*
Open spaces *www.lbhf.gov.uk/Directory/ Environment_and_Planning/Parks_and_open_ spaces/; www.scrubs-online.org.uk.*

'Richmond has everything you need on tap, but the river and tons of green space mean you can easily escape the throng – and have a picnic almost on your doorstep.'

Sally Stratton, resident for 17 years

Richmond upon Thames

Richmond is the only London borough that straddles both sides of the Thames, and its gorgeous riverside location, spacious parks and commons – it's also the capital's greenest borough – abundance of private schools and attractive housing make it a magnet for the affluent. Only the relentless air traffic spoils this sylvan scene.

Neighbourhoods

Barnes, Mortlake and Sheen

Barnes lives up to its semi-rural, villagey reputation. At its centre is a large duck pond and adjoining green (site of a popular annual midsummer fair), surrounded by a mix of independent shops, pubs and restaurants. To the south is the buffer zone of wild and wooded Barnes Common, while the London Wetland Centre (an expansive bird reserve converted from defunct reservoirs) sits to the east of Castelnau, the long spine that leads to Hammersmith Bridge. And enclosing it all is a sharp loop of the Thames, offering riverside walks and rowers aplenty – the Oxford and Cambridge boat crews race this stretch each year, finishing at Mortlake.

Combine such attractions with some of London's best private schools, the proximity of Hammersmith (and its tube station) just over the bridge, a regular

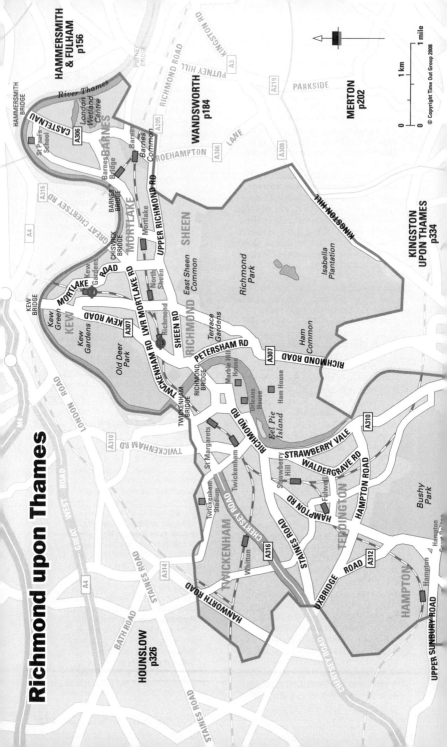

Richmond upon Thames

service to Waterloo from Barnes and Barnes Bridge stations and it's clear why affluent families and retirees love the area so much. Consequently, property prices – there are plenty of attractive Edwardian and Victorian houses, and a few grand mansions, including a house near the pond once lived in by writer Henry Fielding – are very high: seven figures is common.

Barnes has an oddly musical heritage: Gustav Holst lived in a bow-fronted riverside property; the Rolling Stones, Jimi Hendrix and Led Zeppelin recorded at the Olympic studios; the Bull's Head pub has been a leading jazz venue since 1959; and Marc Bolan, er, died on Queen's Ride in 1977 (a bronze bust and well-kept shrine mark the spot).

West from Barnes, sandwiched between the Upper Richmond Road and the Thames, is Mortlake, presided over by the mammoth Budweiser brewery (the air is often thick with beery odours). The river is hidden from view here, and the area is split in two by the railway line (hanging around at level crossings is a local pastime). Any village atmosphere disappeared long ago and it feels a bit of a no-man's-land, but property prices are significantly lower than in Barnes; there are some handsome Edwardian terraces, and cute cottages and allotments around the railway tracks.

Despite local protests, a new residential/ supermarket development at the river end of White Hart Lane (the main shopping street, lined with independent boutiques and restaurants) is going ahead – though residents feel it will 'rip the heart' out of this low-key, low-rise area.

The residential area of East Sheen sits between the Upper Richmond Road – the main commercial artery, aka the South Circular – and East Sheen Common and the northern fringe of Richmond Park. House prices are as astronomical as in many other parts of the borough, with some grand Victorian and Edwardian villas near the park (the Parkside and Palewell Park areas are sought after). North Sheen is a relatively small pocket abutting Kew, hemmed in by the Lower Richmond Road and Mortlake Road.

There's no tube (as is the case in most of the borough), but the overground from North Sheen and Mortlake stations can get commuters to work in a jiffy.

Kew

Everyone knows Kew Gardens (officially the Royal Botanic Gardens, Kew); this exquisitely planned extravaganza of botanical biodiversity, stretching south along the Thames from Kew Bridge, attracts almost two million visitors a year. But it's not the only chunk of green in this greenest of London boroughs: adjoining the Gardens to the south is the Old Deer Park and the exclusive Royal Mid-Surrey Golf Course, while Kew Green abuts the northern end.

Across Kew Road is the main residential area, with assorted restaurants and shops on Sandycombe Road. Property is relatively varied – Queen Anne to Victorian houses, converted flats and modern purpose-built apartments – and exceedingly popular with prosperous middle-class families who appreciate the highly rated primary schools and good transport connections (tube and train to get into central London, easy access to the A4 and M4 to get out). A villagey vibe remains, especially in the characterful cluster of local shops and restaurants around Kew Gardens station.

The riverside stretch from Kew to Teddington is currently in the final phase of Arcadia, a £3.3 million project designed to regenerate and improve the local landscape.

Highs & Lows

▲ **Greenery** Richmond has more open space than any other London borough, and Richmond Park is the capital's largest
Education Some of the best schools in London are in Richmond and Barnes; most of these, though, are private
A river runs through it The stretch of the Thames Path from Barnes to Hampton Court is the loveliest riverside walk in London

Plane pain The noise caused by flights to and from Heathrow is non-stop, a persistent local complaint
Property costs The houses in Richmond, Kew and Barnes are well beyond the reach of all but the wealthiest Londoners
Cultural diversity Or lack of it. Richmond has the most limited
▼ ethnic spread of any London borough

Richmond

After Henry VIII built his palace here in the late 15th century he decided to rename the area, then called Shene, after one of his favourite rural retreats: Richmond, Yorkshire. It was a prescient gesture. Today Richmond is just what it says in the name: a very, very rich mound (on a hill rising up from the Thames). After Kensington & Chelsea, this is the most affluent borough in England. The pretty riverside setting, huge green spaces and stunning period houses have proved an irresistible lure for monied professionals, especially since the City is scarcely half an hour away by train or tube. Yet Richmond avoids the haughtiness of K&C, retaining a villagey air and a harmonious sense of community. It is clean, safe, peaceful (except for the relentless Heathrow air traffic) and has excellent schools.

West of the park is Richmond Hill, where Mick Jagger and Pete Townshend's palatial mansions enjoy an unrivalled, idyllic view over the Thames and the pastures of Surrey. Gracing the hill, on the steeper side, are the Terrace Gardens, another pristine enclosure of parterres and winding stone pathways that is currently under restoration, due for completion in 2009. Near the top sits a dainty cluster (shops, restaurants, a pub) known as Richmond Village.

The road down the hill takes you into the confusingly planned town centre, a hive of shopping, eating and drinking establishments. The riverside by Richmond Bridge is a buzzing spot, with ducks, swans, fishermen, boats for hire and popular pubs and restaurants perfect for an alfresco meal in good weather.

Tucked away behind George Street (essentially the high street) is Richmond Green, one of the borough's proudest assets. Remnants of Henry VIII's palace still stand in one corner, now converted into lodgings. When the sun's out, the grass is invariably strewn with lounging locals – except when cricket is being played on it, in an authentically casual, village-green fashion. The Green has a diminutive adjunct, the Little Green; opposite this is Richmond's most famous cultural venue, its Victorian theatre – the annual Christmas panto is always a sell-out.

West of the town centre is the borough's biggest open space, Richmond Park. In fact, it's London's largest park: 2,500 acres of rolling woodland, grassland, ponds and gardens where the Queen's deer graze. The park was first enclosed for hunting by Charles I and not much has changed since then (though fewer bloodsports take place nowadays). Here you'll find runners, cyclists, kite fliers, birdwatchers, dog walkers, horse riders, picnickers, families out for a stroll – and drivers on the roads that criss-cross it – but there's always a bit of empty space somewhere. The Isabella Plantation, a carefully tended enclosure of azaleas and rhododendrons, is at its best in May (it also has good disabled access). There are also two golf courses adjoining the park's western edge.

Ham & Petersham

The famous view from Richmond Hill of cows grazing on Petersham meadows is preserved by an Act of Parliament no less (in 1902, the culmination of a public campaign to prevent a housing estate being built here). The meadows once formed part of the estate of Ham House, a spectacular Stuart mansion set further along the river (and also visible from the hill), which is now owned by the National Trust.

Ham and Petersham villages have maintained their rural character thanks to their secluded location, hemmed in by the Thames on one side, and Ham Common and Richmond Park on the other. Petersham has some particularly fine 17th- and 18th-century mansions (including Rutland Lodge, Montrose House and Petersham House) alongside Victorian cottages and more modern dwellings. Regular polo matches (Ham Polo Club is the only club of its kind left in London) and events such as the Richmond Regatta in June add to the countrified vibe – as does the absence of a train station.

Twickenham

Oval-ball fans around the world revere Twickenham for its connection with rugby, but there's no shortage of local rugger buggers too – as evident from the thronged pubs, packed railway station and traffic jams around Twickenham Stadium on match days. South from the stadium lies the town centre, around Heath Road, London Road and King Street. It has none of the grandeur of Richmond across the river, and too many pound shops, but proud residents would assert that they have Church Street instead – a cobbled lane off the main road flanked by restaurants, pubs and independent shops.

Well-kept late Victorian and Edwardian terraces dominate Twickenham's residential districts, and property prices are more palatable, certainly compared to Richmond. But it's the riverside that is (and has always been) the area's main attraction.

Eminently fashionable in the 17th and 18th centuries, this bank of the Thames was lined by posh countryside retreats built by the likes of Horace Walpole and Alexander Pope. Most of these mansions are long gone, though Marble Hill House, Strawberry Hill House and York House (now council offices) remain. Of the once-numerous ferries, only Hammertons Ferry still operates (February to October) – it's the best way to get between Marble Hill House and Ham House.

Watery activities have always been big business: Ferry Road retains old watermen's cottages and boatsheds, while Eel Pie Island (connected by a footbridge to the mainland)

Richmond upon Thames

One of the borough's many green spaces: **Richmond Green**.

Will you dine with a
Blonde or Brune tonight?

At last, Speciality Beers such as Leffe are finding their rightful place at the dinner table

A beer with dinner?

It's not such a strange question. The parallels between Speciality Beers and wine are plenty. Both have a rich tradition stretching back through generations and can be favourably paired with many culinary delights. But with such a tempting array of beers to choose from, how can you recognise a brew that's really special?

The clue is in the name. Speciality Beers really are special. Brewed in their country of origin, these authentic beers are made from age-old recipes. Each has its own unique taste and style, enhanced by the flavours of natural ingredients such as coriander, curaçao, roasted barley or morello cherries. They are brewed rather differently to your average lager, too. Abbots, at the Abbey de Leffe in Belgium, have been brewing Leffe for almost 800 years.

The beer is fermented at a higher temperature, producing the aromatic qualities. Any beer brewed with such care and attention deserves to be savoured and enjoyed. Drinking it is a ritual, never to be rushed. The perfect Leffe should be served in the unique Leffe Chalice glass, crafted to heighten the drinking experience. Master Beer Sommelier and Belgian Beer Ambassador, Marc Stroobandt says, "Speciality Beers such as Leffe are full of tantalising flavours and stimulating aromas. They are great with food and enjoyed by wine and beer drinkers alike." Similar to wine pairing, Speciality Beers can add a whole new depth to the gastronomic experience.

Leffe Blonde and Leffe Brune each have their own distinct character. Blonde has a well-balanced, fruity flavour, while Brune is a darker and maltier brew. Whichever brew you choose, Leffe is an ideal introduction to the world of Speciality Beers. So why not discover Leffe with your dinner tonight?

For more information on Leffe and other Speciality Beers visit:
www.specialitybeerselection.com

Discover Life. Discover Leffe

is home to Twickenham Rowing Club and Richmond Yacht Club – and about 50 much-prized houses. The island was also the centre of a a thriving music scene in the 1950s and '60s, with the likes of George Melly, the Rolling Stones, the Who, Eric Clapton and Rod Stewart all performing here. Local band the Mystery Jets continue the island's musical heritage.

Twickenham lacks the tube unfortunately, but there are three train stations at St Margarets, Twickenham and Strawberry Hill, and easy access to the M3 via the busy Chertsey Road (A316).

Restaurants & cafés

Eating options aren't as splendid as you might expect, given the amount of money sloshing around this part of town. Family-friendly chain restaurants are plentiful – you'll find branches of all the leading pizza outlets, as well as Giraffe, Nando's and Wagamama – plus more adult-oriented chains, such as Carluccio's Caffè and Maison Blanc. Otherwise, expect reliable neighbourhood joints that have built up their reputation and clientele over decades, rather than the latest culinary trends.

The uncrowned king of local eating must be chef John McClements, who's steadily building a mini-empire across the borough (although we wish he'd control his habit of frequently changing the names of his restaurants). As well as his flagship French restaurant La Brasserie McClements, next to Twickenham station, he can boast three branches of homely bistro Ma Cuisine (in Twickenham, Kew and now Barnes), two branches of Mediterranean tapas bar Tapas y Vino (in Twickenham and Kew) and Kew Fish, a fishmonger with attached oyster bar. TV chef Antony Worrall Thompson has also made his mark, with Barnes Grill and Kew Grill – visit for quality steaks and burgers and a relaxed, unstuffy vibe.

In Richmond itself, independents include Don Fernando's for classic Spanish tapas, galettes and cider at Breton specialist Chez Lindsay, and Korean and Japanese dishes at Matsuba. Fragrant infusions and floral aromas are the order of the day at cosy new café Tea Box. Popular Argentine grill chain Gaucho has taken over the lovely riverside premises formerly occupied by Canyon. More meat's on offer (Bavarian sausages,

this time) a short walk along the towpath at Stein's beer garden (open Easter to Christmas only). Just over Richmond Bridge, in Twickenham, A Cena provides muscular Italian cuisine. For a tip-top alfresco meal, have lunch amid the boho-chic greenhouses of Skye Gyngell's Petersham Nurseries Café – though such bucolic beauty doesn't come cheap.

Barnes has a trio of excellent, long-running spots: Sonny's (Modern European), Riva (Italian) and the less formal riverside brasserie the Depot – the perfect spot for sunset-viewing. Newcomer Orange Pekoe is a gem of a café, with a sterling selection of loose teas. Nearby East Sheen has smart Mod Euro restaurant/hotel the Victoria and top-notch new gastropub the Brown Dog (though locals are lamenting the loss of neighbourhood stalwart Redmond's, which closed at the end of 2007).

Elsewhere, the Glasshouse next to Kew Gardens station is an extremely polished

LOCALS' TIPS

Don't miss the Friday morning sale of home-made cakes and savouries at Rose House on Barnes High Street. There's often a queue waiting for the doors to open at 10am. **Twickenham & Thames Valley Bee-Keepers' Association (8568 2869, www.twickenham-bees.org.uk), founded 1919, runs courses from March to September for budding bee-keepers, plus free lectures in winter.** Old-fashioned fairs and fêtes abound in this countrified part of town. There's the Twickenham Festival in June, Barnes Fair and St Margarets Fair in July, and Kew Fayre in September. **The annual Christmas panto at Richmond Theatre is one of the best in town, with quality thesps such as Simon Callow, Nigel Havers and Robert Powell appearing in recent years. It's very popular, though, so book well ahead.** The child-friendly café in Marble Hill's Coach House is handy for breakfast, lunch and tea. You can also bribe youngsters with the promise of three decent playgrounds (each with refreshments) on the walk from Richmond Bridge to Twickenham.

Mod Euro restaurant, while homely French brasserie Brula, long popular with locals of St Margarets, has produced a couple of clones in recent years: La Buvette (Richmond) and La Saveur (East Sheen).

The borough's overwhelmingly white demographic – nearly 90 per cent, the highest in London – means that ethnic restaurants are generally noticeable by their absence. Exceptions include Pallavi (Keralan), Tangawizi (North Indian), a branch of mini-chain Sagar (South Indian vegetarian) – all in Twickenham – and a new Iranian restaurant, Faanoos, in East Sheen.

A Cena *418 Richmond Road, TW1 2EB (8288 0108).*
Barnes Grill *2-3 Rocks Lane, SW13 0DB (8878 4488/www.awtrestaurants.com).*
La Brasserie McClements *2 Whitton Road, TW1 1BJ (8744 9598).*
Brown Dog *28 Cross Street, SW13 0AP (8392 2200).*
Brula *43 Crown Road, TW1 3EJ (8892 0602/www.brula.co.uk).*
La Buvette *6 Church Walk, TW9 1SN (8940 6264/www.brula.co.uk).*
Chez Lindsay *11 Hill Rise, TW10 6UQ (8948 7473/www.chez-lindsay.co.uk).*
Depot *Tideway Yard, 125 Mortlake High Street, SW14 8SN (8878 9462/ www.depotbrasserie.co.uk).*

Don Fernando's *27F The Quadrant, TW9 1DN (8948 6447/www.donfernando.co.uk).*
Faanoos *481 Upper Richmond Road West, SW14 7PU (8878 5738/8876 8938).*
Gaucho Richmond *Richmond Towpath, west of Richmond Bridge, TW10 6UJ (8948 4030/www.gauchorestaurants.co.uk).*
Glasshouse *14 Station Parade, TW9 3PZ (8940 6777/www.glasshouserestaurant.co.uk).*
Kew Fish *8 Station Approach, TW9 3QB (8940 6617/www.macuisinegroup.co.uk).*
Kew Grill *10B Kew Green, TW9 3BH (8948 4433/www.awtrestaurants.com).*
Ma Cuisine Le Petit Bistrot *www.macuisinegroup.co.uk: 6 Whitton Road, TW1 1BJ (8607 9849); The Old Post Office, 9 Station Approach, TW9 3QB (8332 1923); 7 White Hart Lane, SW13 0PX (8878 4092).*
Matsuba *10 Red Lion Street, TW9 1RW (8605 3513).*
Orange Pekoe *3 White Hart Lane, SW13 0PX (8876 6070/www.orangepekoeteas.com).*
Pallavi *Cross Deep Court, Heath Road, TW1 4QJ (8892 2345).*
Petersham Nurseries Café *Church Lane, off Petersham Road, TW10 7AG (8605 3627/ www.petershamnurseries.com).*
Riva *169 Church Road, SW13 9HR (8748 0434).*
Sagar *27 York Street, TW1 3JZ (8744 3868).*
La Saveur *201 Upper Richmond Road West, SW14 8QT (8876 0644/www.brula.co.uk).*
Sonny's *94 Church Road, SW13 0DQ (8748 0393/www.sonnys.co.uk).*
Stein's *Richmond Towpath (rear of 55 Petersham Road), TW10 6UX (8948 8189/ www.stein-s.com).*

Charmingly cosy East Sheen gastropub the **Brown Dog**. *See p177.*

Tangawizi *406 Richmond Road, Richmond Bridge, TW1 2EB (8891 3737).*
Tapas y Vino *www.macuisinegroup.co.uk: 111 London Road, TW1 1EE (8892 5417); 306 Sandycombe Road, TW9 3NG (8940 3504).*
Tea Box *7 Paradise Road, TW9 1RX (8940 3521).*
Victoria *10 West Temple Sheen, SW14 7RT (8876 4238/www.thevictoria.net).*

Bars & pubs

Real ales, rugby and riverside settings are the three Rs of Richmond's drinking scene. If you want a well-kept Young's or Fuller's pint in an old-fashioned inn that could be in the countryside, you're in the right part of town; if you're after a sophisticated cocktail bar or a late-night urban dive, tough.

Typical is the White Cross on the riverside near Richmond Bridge: Young's beers on tap, pies and sausages on the menu, real fires inside, tables outside overlooking the water. Sometimes too much water, in fact: the towpath here gets flooded regularly, and there's a special entrance for high tide. Away from the river, on the edge of spacious Richmond Green, are two handsome hostelries: the Cricketers (a Greene King establishment) and the Prince's Head (Fuller's). Cricket matches are a common occurrence in summer – get your pint in a plastic glass and stretch out by the boundary for a few wickets.

Barnes and Mortlake also have pubs overlooking the Thames. The former's Ye White Hart offers a perfect view of the Varsity boat race once a year; the latter's Ship, dwarfed by the Budweiser brewery next door, is a pleasant enough place, made special by its sun-drenched patio. Also in Barnes is the Bull's Head; a legendary jazz venue since the late 1950s, it still has gigs every night, alongside Young's ales and a well-priced Thai restaurant in the former stables at the back. More modern – in looks, food and drink (a global selection of bottled beers and a good wine list) – is the Sun Inn, idyllically positioned opposite the duck pond. The outdoor tables at the front get packed in good weather.

Drinking (and eating) options in Kew have improved with the arrival of two stylish new gastropubs: the Inn at Kew Gardens, just next to Kew Gardens station, and the Botanist, on the edge of Kew Green. Also adjoining the Green is the Coach &

Horses, an airy and congenial Young's pub offering traditional Sunday roasts.

Towpath flooding is a factor too at the White Swan in Twickenham – hence the steep steps up to the entrance, which leads into a simple, homely interior decorated with rugby memorabilia. Opposite lies the counter-cultural bastion of Eel Pie Island and nearby, on pretty Church Street, is the low-key and very popular Eel Pie, serving fine Hall & Woodhouse beers.

Botanist *3-5 Kew Green, TW9 3AA (8948 4838/www.thebotanistkew.com).*
Bull's Head *373 Lonsdale Road, SW13 9PY (8876 5241/www.thebullshead.com).*
Coach & Horses *8 Kew Green, TW9 3BH (8940 1208/www.coachhotelkew.co.uk).*
Cricketers *The Green, TW9 1LX (8940 4372).*
Eel Pie *9-11 Church Street, TW1 3NJ (8891 1717).*
Inn at Kew Gardens *292 Sandycombe Road, TW9 3NG (8940 2220/www.theinnat kewgardens.com.*
Prince's Head *28 The Green, TW9 1LX (8940 1572).*
Ship *10 Thames Bank, SW14 7QR (8876 1439).*
Sun Inn *7 Church Road, SW13 9HE (8876 5256).*
White Cross *Water Lane, TW9 1TH (8940 6844).*
White Swan *Riverside, TW1 3DN (8892 2166).*
Ye White Hart *The Terrace, SW13 0NR (8876 5177).*

Shops

Richmond residents don't need to head into the West End to do their shopping: they've got pretty much every high-street chain on their doorstep (or they can pop to the smart Bentall Centre in neighbouring Kingston). From Richmond station, a confusing tangle of streets around the main drag of the Quadrant/George Street houses numerous familiar names (Boots, French Connection, Gap, HMV, Jigsaw, Monsoon, Reiss and many more) plus a Habitat, Waterstone's, M&S and Topshop. Anchoring it all is department store House of Fraser.

Head up Hill Street and its extension Hill Rise to drop some serious dosh on antiques or top-end fashion from the likes of Kate Kuba, Caroline Charles, Joseph, Matches, MaxMara and Whistles. Elsewhere, more posh frocks can be found at Fenn Wright Manson and Margaret Howell. Chocoholics can splurge at much-praised chocolatier

William Curley; fans of organic food should head to Source. Placate the kids with a visit to toyshop Toy Station or fabulous children's bookshop the Lion & Unicorn.

Further along the Thames is Petersham Nurseries, a supremely picturesque and upmarket outlet for all things horticultural, with a lovely café (see p177). Over on the Twickenham side of the river, the Real Ale Shop specialises in real ales, ciders, perries and beers from British microbreweries.

There's no candlestick-maker in villagey Barnes, but it's still got a butcher and a baker – plus a fishmonger, a greengrocer, a great local bookshop and the lovely Real Cheese Shop – all can be found on Barnes High Street/Church Street. Other independent shops on offer include the Farmyard for toys, a smattering of upmarket fashion boutiques such as Question Air, and Blue Door for tasteful Swedish furniture and knick-knacks. The main shopping street in adjoining Mortlake is White Hart Lane, home to posh deli Gusto & Relish and a couple of swanky interiors shops: Tobias & the Angel and the Dining Room Shop.

East Sheen offers a less attractive retail experience, with shoppers having to negotiate the constant traffic on the busy Upper Richmond Road. But there are plenty of useful chains (Woolworths, Superdrug, Boots, WH Smith, a small Waitrose, Kew for womenswear, Oliver Bonas for gifts) alongside charity shops and furniture and kitchen suppliers.

In Kew, there's a cluster of independent outlets around Kew Gardens station. For high-street brands, visit user-friendly Kew Retail Park, off the A205, which has a huge M&S, Gap, Boots, Mothercare, Next and lots of parking.

Middle-class sensibilities and incomes mean there are no fewer than three farmers' markets in the borough, in Barnes (opposite the pond), Richmond (Heron Square) and Twickenham (Holly Street car park). All are held on Saturday.

Barnes Bookshop 60 Church Road, SW13 0DQ (8741 0786).
Blue Door 77 Church Road, SW13 9HH (8748 9785/www.bluedoorbarnes.co.uk).
Caroline Charles 18 Hill Rise, TW10 6UA (8948 7777/www.carolinecharles.co.uk).
Dining Room Shop 62-64 White Hart Lane, SW13 0PZ (8878 1020/www.thediningroom shop.co.uk).

Farmyard 63 Barnes High Street, SW13 9LF (8878 7338/www.thefarmyard.co.uk).
Fenn Wright Manson 1 The Quadrant, TW9 1BP (8940 6852/www.fennwrightmanson.com).
Gusto & Relish 56 White Hart Lane, SW13 0PZ (8878 2005).
Joseph 28 Hill Street, TW9 1TV (8940 7045).
Kate Kuba 22 Hill Street, TW9 1TW (8940 1004/www.katekuba.co.uk).
Lion & Unicorn Bookshop 19 King Street, TW9 1ND (8940 0483/www.lionunicorn books.co.uk).
Margaret Howell 1 The Green, TW9 1HP (8948 5005/www.margarethowell.co.uk).
Matches 13 Hill Street, TW9 1FX (8332 9733/www.matchesfashion.com).
MaxMara 32 Hill Street, TW9 1TW (8332 2811).
Petersham Nurseries Church Lane, off Petersham Road, TW10 7AG (8940 5230/ www.petershamnurseries.com).
Question Air 129 Church Road, SW13 9HR (8741 0816/www.question-air.co.uk). Sale shop at No.86.
Real Ale Shop 371 Richmond Road, TW1 2EF (8892 3710/www.realale.com).
Real Cheese Shop 62 Barnes High Street, SW13 9LF (8878 6676).
Source 27D The Quadrant, TW9 1DN (8439 9866/www.sourcefood.com).
Tobias & the Angel 68 White Hart Lane, SW13 0PZ (8878 8902/www.tobiasandthe angel.com).
Toy Station 6 Eton Street, TW9 1EE (8940 4896).
Whistles 19 Hill Street, TW9 1SX (8332 1646/www.whistles.co.uk).
William Curley 10 Paved Court, TW9 1LZ (8332 3002/www.williamcurley.co.uk).

Arts & attractions

Cinemas & theatres
Odeon Richmond 72 Hill Street, TW9 1TW; 6 Red Lion Street, TW9 1RW (0871 224 4007/ www.odeon.co.uk).
Orange Tree Theatre 1 Clarence Street, TW9 2SA (8940 3633/www.orangetreetheatre.co.uk).
Richmond Film House 3 Water Lane, TW9 1TJ (0870 850 6928/www.richmondfilm house.co.uk).
Richmond Theatre The Green, TW9 1QJ (8939 9277/box office 0870 060 6651/ www.theambassadors.com/richmond).
Vue Staines Two Rivers, Mustard Mill Road, TW18 4BL (0871 224 0240/www.myvue.com).

Galleries & museums
Museum of Richmond Old Town Hall, Whittaker Avenue, TW9 1TP (8332 1141/ www.museumofrichmond.com). A loyal parade of Richmond's regal history.
Orleans House Gallery Riverside, TW1 3DJ (8831 6000/www.richmond.gov.uk/arts).

The borough's principal art gallery, fabulously located right on the river in Twickenham. **Twickenham Museum** *25 The Embankment, TW1 3DU (8408 0070/www.twickenham-museum.org.uk).* Local history museum.

Music & comedy venues

Bull's Head *373 Lonsdale Road, SW13 9PY (8876 5241/www.thebullshead.com).*
Cabbage Patch *67 London Road, TW1 3SZ (8892 3874/www.cabbagepatch.co.uk).* Family-run pub with regular music nights hosted by the Eel Pie Club (www.eelpieclub.com).

Other attractions

Ham House *Ham Street, TW10 7RS (8940 1950/www.nationaltrust.org.uk).* Lavish riverside mansion built in 1610, with an Orangery and a terrace café.
Hampton Court Palace *East Molesey, KT8 9AU (0870 751 5175/information 0870 752 7777/www.hrp.org.uk).* Dazzling Tudor palace with a famous maze, changing interior exhibitions, and an ice rink in winter.
London Wetland Centre *Queen Elizabeth Walk, SW13 9WT (8409 4400/www.wwt.org.uk).*
Marble Hill House *Richmond Road, TW1 2NL (8892 5115/www.english-heritage.org.uk).* Elegant Palladian house built in 1724 by George II for his mistress, Henrietta Howard.
National Archives *Ruskin Avenue, TW9 4DU (8876 3444/www.nationalarchives.gov.uk).* Accessible archives office in Kew, housing 1,000 years of official government and law records.
Royal Botanic Gardens, Kew *TW9 3AB (8332 5655/www.rbgkew.org.uk).*
Strawberry Hill House *St Mary's College, Waldegrave Road, TW1 4SX (0870 626 0402).* Horace Walpole's 'little Gothic castle' is under restoration, but occasional tours are still held.

Sport & fitness

Surprisingly, Richmond is not the best equipped borough for leisure facilities. The council-run centres are decent, but not state of the art. However, as you'd expect, no one gets short-changed on quality at Richmond's private health clubs.

Gyms & leisure centres

Cannons *www.cannons.co.uk; Stoop Memorial Ground, Langhorn Drive, TW2 7SX (8892 2251); Richmond Athletic Ground, Kew Foot Road, TW9 2SS (8948 3743).* Private.
Cedars Health & Leisure Club *144-150 Richmond Hill, TW10 6RW (8332 1010/ www.foliohotels.com/cedars).* Private.
Fitness First *1st floor, 20-28 Broad Street, TW11 8QZ (8614 6650/www.fitnessfirst.com).* Private.
Hampton Sport, Arts & Fitness Centre *Hanworth Road, TW12 3HB (8941 4334/ www.richmond.gov.uk).*

Pools on the Park/Springhealth Leisure Club *Old Deer Park, Twickenham Road, TW9 2SF (8940 0561/www.springhealth.net).*
Richmond Hill Health Club *Lewis Road, TW10 6SA (8948 5523/www.fit4ever.co.uk).* Private.
Shene Sports & Fitness Centre *Park Avenue, SW14 8RG (8878 7578/ www.richmond.gov.uk).*

Island idyll: **Eel Pie**. *See p175.*

Teddington Pools & Fitness Centre
*Vicarage Road, TW11 8EZ (8977 9911/
www.richmond.gov.uk).*
Teddington Sports Centre *Teddington
School, Broom Road, TW11 9PJ (8977 0598/
www.richmond.gov.uk).*
Whitton Sports & Fitness Centre
*Percy Road, TW2 6JW (8898 7795/
www.richmond.gov.uk).*

Other facilities
Ham Polo Club *The Polo Office, Petersham
Road, TW10 7AH (8334 0000/www.hampolo
club.org.uk).*
Hampton Heated Open Air Pool
*High Street, TW12 2ST (8255 1116/
www.hamptonpool.co.uk).*

Spectator sports
Rugby rules in Richmond; clubs in the borough
include Harlequins (www.quins.co.uk), London
Welsh (www.london-welsh.co.uk), London
Scottish (www.londonscottish.com) and
Rosslyn Park (www.rosslynpark.co.uk).

Twickenham Stadium *Rugby Road, TW1
1DZ (0870 405 2001/www.rfu.com).* Home of the
England rugby team and the Museum of Rugby;
stadium tours are held on non-match days.

Schools

WHAT THE PARENTS SAY:

'The state primary schools in Richmond upon
Thames are fantastic. Our children go to Queen's
in Kew and are thriving. Kew Riverside and both
St Elizabeth's RC and Marshgate in Richmond
have excellent reputations too. When it comes
to secondary schools, however, the situation
couldn't be more different. Richmond upon
Thames is an affluent borough and many parents
send their children to private schools once they
reach secondary age. It's hard to blame them
when the state secondary schools on offer are so
dismal in comparison to the primaries. Christ's in

TRANSPORT
Tube stations *District* Kew Gardens,
Richmond
Rail stations *South West Trains* Barnes,
Barnes Bridge, Mortlake, North Sheen,
Richmond, St Margarets, Twickenham,
Whitton, Strawberry Hill, Hampton Wick,
Teddington, Fulwell, Hampton; *London
Overground* Kew Gardens, Richmond
Bus routes *night buses* N10, N22,
N74; *24-hour buses* 65, 72, 281, 285
River leisure boat services (Apr-Oct),
with piers at Kew Gardens, Richmond
and Hampton Court Palace

Richmond has improved significantly in recent
months and if it continues to do so we would
consider it for our eldest. On the whole, though,
the standards gap between the borough's
secondary and primary provision is just too
large. We believe strongly in state education
but our options in Richmond upon Thames
are just too limited. We may well reluctantly
end up – like many other parents – moving,
remortgaging or hoping our children can
get private scholarships. It's such a waste
of an excellent primary education system.'
Kate Street, mother of two, Kew

Primary
There are 41 state primary schools in Richmond,
including 15 church schools. There are also 18
independent primaries, including one German
and one Swedish school. See www.richmond.
gov.uk, www.edubase.gov.uk and www.
ofsted.gov.uk for more information.

Secondary
Christ's School *Queen's Road, TW10 6HW
(8940 6982/www.christs.richmond.sch.uk).*
Grey Court School *Ham Street, TW10 7HN
(8948 1173/www.greycourt.richmond.sch.uk).*
Hampton Community College *Hanworth
Road, TW12 3HB (8979 3399/www.hcc.
richmond.sch.uk).*
Hampton School *Hanworth Road, TW12
3HD (8979 5526/www.hamptonschool.org.uk).*
Boys only; private.
The Harrodian School *Lonsdale Road, SW13
9QN (8748 6117/www.harrodian.com).* Private.
Lady Eleanor Holles School *Hanworth
Road, TW12 3HF (8979 1601/www.lehs.org.uk).*
Girls only; private.
Orleans Park School *Richmond Road,
TW1 3BB (8891 0187/www.orleanspark.
richmond.sch.uk).*
St Paul's *Lonsdale Road, SW13 9JT
(8748 9162/www.stpaulsschool.org.uk).*
Boys only; private.
Shene School *Park Avenue, SW14 8RG
(8876 8891/www.shene.richmond.sch.uk).*
Teddington School *Broom Road, TW11 9PJ
(8943 0033/www.teddington.richmond.sch.uk).*
Waldegrave School *Fifth Cross Road,
TW2 5LH (8894 3244/www.waldegrave.
richmond.sch.uk).* Girls only.
Whitton School *Percy Road, TW2 6JW
(8894 4503/www.whitton.richmond.sch.uk).*

Property

WHAT THE AGENTS SAY:
'Barnes still has a definite country village
atmosphere – it even has a pond and a proper
village green. It's away from the bustle of the
city, but just 22 minutes to Waterloo from

Barnes Bridge station. And there are regular buses to Hammersmith, where you can get on various tube lines.

Barnes is well developed and needs little improvement. There is plenty of green space, but it's owned by the council and so can't be built on, which locals are very glad about. Residents are often upwardly mobile professionals in their thirties and forties. And families are drawn here by the excellent schools – some of the best in the country.

Property prices are quite steep, and they went up by about 25 per cent last year. We sell houses mostly; there aren't many flats and certainly no new high-rise developments. ⁷
Peter Rixon, Boileaus, Barnes

❛Richmond is always popular: it's near the Thames and Richmond Park, and only 15 minutes by train from central London. People here are fairly well heeled, and when they move to the area, they tend to stay. The town centre isn't big, but Kingston is nearby, so there's no need to go into town to shop. There are good schools, private and state.

What's bad about Richmond? I suppose it is very pricey – one of the most expensive areas in London. And you have to get used to the planes, but that's the same for the rest of west London.❜
Andrew Barnett, Major Son & Phipps, Richmond

Average property prices
Detached £1,111,560
Semi-detached £682,143
Terraced £479,545
Flat £323,582

Local estate agents
Antony Roberts *www.antonyroberts.co.uk; 2 offices in the borough (Kew 8940 9401/ Richmond 8940 9403).*
Boileaus *135 Church Road, SW13 9HR (8741 7400/www.boileaus.com).*
Major Son & Phipps *5A The Square, TW9 1DX (8940 2233/www.major-estateagents.com).*
Marquis & Co *Marquis House, 54 Richmond Road, TW1 3BE (8891 0222/www.marquis andco.uk).*
Marsh & Parsons *73-75 Church Road, SW13 9HH (8563 8333/www.marshandparsons.co.uk).*
Philip Hodges *www.philip-hodges.co.uk; 3 offices in the borough (Hampton Hill 8783 1007/Richmond Bridge 8891 2121/St Margarets 8891 6391).*
Stuart MacKenzie Residential *212B Upper Richmond Road West, SW14 8AH (8876 4445/ www.pemberstone.co.uk).*
W Hallet & Co *6 Royal Parade, Station Approach, TW9 3QD (8940 1034).*

Other information

Council
London Borough of Richmond upon Thames Council *Civic Centre, 44 York Street, Twickenham, Middx TW1 3BZ (8891 1411/out of office hours 8744 2442/ www.richmond.gov.uk).*

Legal services
Civic Centre *44 York Street, TW1 3BZ (8487 5005/www.richmond.gov.uk).*
Richmond upon Thames CAB *Linfield House, 26 Kew Road, TW9 2NA (8940 2501/ www.rcabs.org).*

Local newspapers
Richmond & Twickenham Times *8744 4200/www.rttimes.co.uk.*

Allotments & open spaces
Council Allotments *The Allotments Officer, Civic Centre, 44 York Street, TW1 3BZ (mornings only 8831 6110).*
Royal Paddocks Allotments *www.paddocks-allotments.org.uk.*
Open spaces *www.richmond.gov.uk/parks; www.royalparks.org.uk; www.wwt.org.uk (London Wetland Centre).*

RECYCLING
No. of bring sites 123 (for nearest, visit www.recycleforlondon.com)
Household waste recycled 21.06%
Main recycling centre Townmead Road Reuse & Recycling Centre, Kew, Surrey TW9 4EL (8876 3281)
Other recycling services Richmond Scrapstore (8891 7063) for scrap materials to be used in art projects; reusable paint collection; kitchen waste collection; home composting; collection of white goods and furniture; adopt-a-recycling-site scheme
Council contact Recycling Office, Central Depot, Langhorn Drive, Twickenham, Middx TW2 7SG (8891 7329/www.ecoaction.richmond.gov.uk)

COUNCIL TAX
A	up to £40,000	**£993.74**
B	£40,001-£52,000	**£1,159.35**
C	£52,001-£68,000	**£1,324.98**
D	£68,001-£88,000	**£1,490.60**
E	£88,001-£120,000	**£1,821.85**
F	£120,001-£160,000	**£2,153.09**
G	£160,001-£320,000	**£2,484.34**
H	over £320,000	**£2,981.20**

Richmond upon Thames

'With its broad boulevards and pulsating nightlife, Balham is like a cross between Paris and Rio de Janeiro. Also very handy for East Croydon.'

Arthur Smith, broadcaster, comedian, writer and self-styled Mayor of Balham

Wandsworth

After Westminster and RBK&C, Wandsworth has the largest number of million-pound residential properties in London. It's not just the mellow Victorian villas of Putney and Clapham fetching these prices, either. Frenetic gentrification of Wandsworth Town and the reinventing of its Thames-side area as the Riverside Quarter has attracted new money. It's the Chelsea overspill, apparently, although we'd say there's more than a river separating the old money from the new.

Neighbourhoods

Battersea

Battersea is attractive to all-comers, be they young families, speculators or monied pied-à-terre hunters. There's no tube station, but connections to central London are fast thanks to Battersea Park and Queenstown Road overground stations, and Chelsea is a short walk away over the Battersea, Albert and Chelsea Bridges. The district's name is renowned around the world for two sights: Battersea Dogs & Cats Home (proof, if any

were needed, that the British are pet-obsessed) and Battersea Power Station, one of the capital's most iconic buildings. Sprawling Battersea Park, with its fountain-filled lake, peace pagoda, children's zoo, sports pitches and Thames vistas is the area's most valuable asset (and gives blessed relief from all the new riverside apartment developments).

At the eastern edge of the park, on the other side of Queenstown Road, looms the roofless hulk of the power station. Designed in 1930 by Sir Giles Gilbert Scott and occupying a sprawling chunk of prime

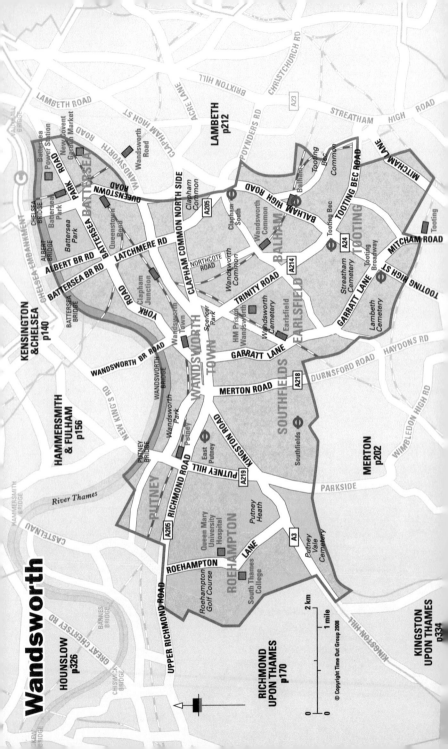

Wandsworth

HOUNSLOW p326

KENSINGTON & CHELSEA p140

HAMMERSMITH & FULHAM p156

LAMBETH p212

BATTERSEA

WANDSWORTH TOWN

PUTNEY

ROEHAMPTON

EARLSFIELD

SOUTHFIELDS

BALHAM

TOOTING

MERTON p202

RICHMOND UPON THAMES p170

KINGSTON UPON THAMES p334

River Thames

© Copyright Time Out Group 2006

riverside territory, it has been slowly falling apart for years. Since the station ceased functioning in 1983, various developers have proposed assorted schemes, from theme parks to hotels, circuses to cinemas – all to no avail. The crumbling, weather-beaten shell is currently in the hands of Real Estate Opportunities (REO), which bought the site from previous owner Parkview for £400 million in 2006. Parkview wanted to destroy and rebuild the corroding 330-foot-high chimneys (a move approved by Wandsworth Council), but REO has yet to announce a new masterplan for the site. The building's listed status was upgraded to Grade II* in October 2007, though it's unclear what effect that will have on its future.

To the south, across Battersea Park Road, the area's marshy beginnings as a fertile spot for market gardens are remembered in the ultimate garden market, Nine Elms, where fruit, veg and flower wholesalers were moved from Covent Garden in 1974.

The triangle formed by Queenstown and Silverthorne Roads, known as the Parktown Estate conservation area – 'the Diamond', for short – is much in demand, with townhouses and Victorian terraced cottages that sell for upwards of half a million. Away from the Diamond, the Park and chichi little desirables such as Battersea Square there are some less appealing prospects. Ex-council high-rises and estates around the Clapham Junction side of Battersea remind you that Wandsworth has its fair share of rough too.

Walk west along the Thames (where you can) and there's a seemingly endless ribbon of high-tech luxury flats all the way to Wandsworth Bridge. Victorian warehouses that were once hives of industry, such as Price's Candles on York Road, have also been converted into top-end apartments, attracting the kind of lunatic prices that would get on the wick of anyone trying to get on Wandsworth's property ladder.

Clapham Junction and Clapham Common

An area defined by its famously frenetic railway station, Clapham Junction is, in fact, nearer to Battersea than Clapham proper, but when it was developed in the 1860s the powers-that-be decided that Clapham's salubrious connotations were better suited

Highs & Lows

Council tax My, it's cheap, isn't it? You'll pay less here than anywhere else in central London
Eating and drinking Old boozers and smart gastros, top-notch Mod Euro restaurants and characterful curry houses – this is a great borough for food-lovers
The great outdoors Battersea Park, Clapham, Wandsworth and Tooting Bec Commons, Putney Heath: Wandsworth is full of green spaces. And it's not bad on cycle paths either, thanks to the likes of the Wandsworth Cycling Campaign (www.wandsworthcyclists.org.uk)

Transport congestion Too many 4WDs, traffic jams everywhere, nowhere to park, crowded tubes and trains – the list goes on
House prices Up, up and away. First-time buyers haven't a hope in most of the borough, and even Tooting and Balham are getting beyond the pale
Post problems Mailing a parcel is a challenge; 13 of the borough's post offices have closed in recent years, and another five were facing the chop as we went to press

to such a major transport interchange. After years of driving commuters potty with its run-down subways and fiendishly confusing platform information system, Clapham Junction station is having an overhaul. It's starting small (new lifts, better signage and lighting, more CCTV) but plans include a connection to the under-construction East London Railway at Surrey Quays. Other irritations, such as the Gatwick Express failing to stop at the Junction (locals have to go to Victoria to pick it up), should be remedied too. There's also the more contentious plan to get Clapham Junction in on the Crossrail act.

North of the station, around Grant Road, the neighbourhood looks unpromising. The Winstanley is every inch the tough council estate, always in the local news for drug raids and Asbos. Its main claim to fame is that the founding members of the south London garage blingers So Solid Crew were brought up here. In huge contrast is

Wandsworth Park, one of the few riverside areas not built on.

the Shaftesbury Park Estate, south-east of the Junction, containing about 1,200 homes, mostly two-storey cottages plus a few larger houses, all with Gothic Revival flourishes, built by the Artisans', Labourers' & General Dwellings Company in 1873-77. Many are owned by the Peabody Trust, which has limited the changes residents can make to properties in this delightful conservation zone.

Elsewhere, there's evidence of the council's much-vaunted efforts to improve the lack of affordable homes in the borough. The Hidden Homes initiative, involving collaborations with housing associations, is intended to create cost-effective homes from vacant and disused areas on council estates; Wynter Street, towards Wandsworth Bridge, is one of the areas set for improvement.

Just outside Clapham Junction there are plenty of shops along St John's Hill and Lavender Hill, as well as performing arts powerhouse Battersea Arts Centre, which is currently in negotiations with the council to secure its artistic future while undertaking costly repairs of its Grade II-listed building.

The most sought-after housing is not up the Junction, but south of Battersea Rise (A3), 'between the commons', as the estate agents say. Here are big houses, green spaces, access to the tube, and the numerous shops, bars and restaurants of Northcote and Bellevue Roads. Wealthy thirtysomethings who have made a mint in law or finance come here to breed, a fact that has earned Clapham the overused moniker Nappy Valley. Clapham's prep schools, which feed the capital's public schools, do good business here. Those who prefer to send children to a state primary (Honeywell is considered pretty good) tend to invest in private tutors to get their children through the entrance exams. Just to the west is Lambeth: the borough cuts through the middle of Clapham Common, from Wix's Lane to Clapham South station.

Wandsworth Town

For years the borough's flagship town centre was a bit of an embarrassment: a traffic-clogged mess of roads, without a proper centre that forever harked back to past glories. The smell of hops from the famous Young's Brewery ceased to blow across Ram Street in 2006, when Young's sent its brewing operations up to Bedford. Now the biggest business in Wandsworth Town is property development. The Brewery will be a new residential quarter, part of a multi-million-pound regeneration of the area that includes the re-creation of a library – Wandsworth is the only town centre in the borough without one – in the premises formerly occupied by sweet little Wandsworth Museum (which will move to a new home in the old West Hill Library site).

Wandsworth Town has some upsides, including Southside, the regenerated shopping centre that used to be a ghastly Arndale. More attractive is the residential area known as the Tonsleys, near the river and town centre, with picturesque shops and cafés along largely traffic-free Old York Road. The gorgeous Victorian houses around here attract high prices.

Sky-high premiums are, of course, paid for river views in Wandsworth's ever-developing Thames-side quarter. New mega-developments include Battersea Reach, at the south end of Wandsworth Bridge, and Point Pleasant, next to Wandsworth Park and once a rather unpleasant industrial area, dominated by a waste transfer station. Little Victorian terraces and the antique Cat's Back pub add charm, but, mostly, Wandsworth Riverside is like a whole new town, daunting in its shininess.

The council pledges affordable housing will be developed alongside the swanky penthouses, and developers are having to improve play areas in local parks and contribute to the upkeep of the promised riverside walkway. But locals are worried that the current level of transport and leisure provision will not be enough for all the new residents.

Putney

A reputation for wholesomeness – more than 20 rowing clubs are based on the Thames at Putney Embankment and there's plenty of open space – sells Putney to the middle classes. The riverside area has pubs and a path rather than apartment blocks; there's also a heath, a busy high street and shopping centre, and some fantastic houses with mature gardens. What's not to like? Easy. Planes, trains and automobiles.

Namely, the incessant noise of the Heathrow flight path, the oversubscribed rush-hour train services into Waterloo, the lack of tube in the westerly reaches, and the clogged South Circular (A205) and Roehampton Lane (A306). Other turn-offs are the stupidly high house prices (for some really quite boring terraced three-beds) and a sense of being lost in the suburbs.

The rest of London turns its gaze on Putney every spring, when the Boat Race attracts huge crowds – though the Great River Race (in autumn) is much more fun to watch. The riverside path provides glorious walking to Barnes and beyond. Away from the Thames, Putney Heath, together with nearby Wimbledon Common, accounts for half of all London's heathland.

Putney remains aloof from too much new housing development because about 50 per cent of its current stock is in a designated conservation area. The streets between Upper Richmond Road (aka the South Circular) and Chartfield Avenue contain the most spacious and expensive abodes. Coalecroft Road and Parkfields, with their terraced Victorian cottages, original lamp-posts and herringbone brick roads, rank among the most attractive. Of more interest, however, is the area near the river, including idiosyncratic Lower Common

STATISTICS

BOROUGH MAKE-UP
Population 279,000
Average weekly pay £532.30
Ethnic origins
  White 79.31%
  Mixed 3.18%
  Asian or Asian British 7.16%
  Black or Black British 7.92%
  Chinese or other 2.46%
Students 8.62%
Retirees 7.40%

HOUSING STOCK
Borough size 34.3km²
No. of households 124,719
Detached 2.3%
Semi-detached 7.1%
Terraced 26.3%
Flats (purpose-built) 40.2%
Flats (converted) 23.1%
Flats (both) 63.3%

CRIME PER 1,000 OF POPULATION
(average for England and Wales in brackets)
Burglary 9 (5)
Robbery 6 (2)
Theft of vehicle 4 (4)
Theft from vehicle 11 (9)
Violence against the person 20 (19)
Sexual offences 1 (1)

MPs & COUNCIL
MPs *Battersea* Martin Linton (Labour); *Putney* Justine Greening (Conservative); *Tooting* Sadiq Khan (Labour)
CPA 4 stars; improving strongly

South on the edge of Putney Lower Common, and the quaint, cosy streets around Cardinal Place.

Popular new developments include the Sir Giles Gilbert Scott building, a handsome Grade II-listed red-brick construction in Whitelands Park, just off Sutherland Grove from West Hill. It now contains some fancy new flats, plus a communal gym, grounds and parking. Also in the park, the new-build Hannay House is part of the council's shared ownership scheme for key workers.

Roehampton

Wandsworth's most westerly outpost is Roehampton, which in parts is more like down-at-heel Surrey suburbia, what with its traffic issues and troublesome housing estates. The latter problem is the most pressing one for the council's crime unit.

Alton Estate, one of the largest council estates in the country – a vast swathe of concrete, mixing low- and high-rise modernist architecture – lies in the south-east corner of Richmond Park. West Alton, inspired by French architect Le Corbusier, is now Grade II listed, and many of the flats fetch reasonably good prices (about £250,000 for a two-bed with a park view), but people still feel threatened as they walk between blocks. Much is being done to improve its image, however, and council residents say they love it and are unwilling to let the council regenerate them out of what they know is a smart part of town, even if there are no train or tube links (though the A3 is very nearby).

Elsewhere are smaller spatterings of council housing (currently being developed as part of the council's Hidden Homes scheme) and some attractive tree-lined roads. One of London's tallest plane trees can be seen in Minstead Gardens.

There are students galore here – studying at Roehampton University, South Thames College and Queen Mary's Hospital, the main structure of which was built in 1712 and later enlarged by Sir Edwin Lutyens. Both the Grade I-listed Roehampton House and other parcels of ex-hospital land are being turned into smart housing schemes, designed to be in keeping with the gracious buildings hereabouts.

The Putney Heath district is the poshest neighbourhood, with huge elaborate Edwardian houses that seem to belong

TRANSPORT

Tube stations *District* East Putney, Southfields; *Northern* Clapham South, Balham, Tooting Bec, Tooting Broadway
Rail stations *London Overground* Clapham Junction; *Southern* Battersea Park, Wandsworth Road, Clapham Junction, Wandsworth Common, Balham, Tooting; *South West Trains* Queenstown Road, Clapham Junction, Wandsworth Town, Putney, Earlsfield
Main bus routes *into central London* 14, 19, 22, 35, 74, 77, 77A, 87, 137, 344, 414; *night buses* N10, N19, N22, N35, N44, N74, N77, N87, N133, N137, N155; *24-hour buses* 14, 344

more in the stockbroker belt. Off the north-west edge of the heath, Roehampton Village is also a desirable quarter, with families living in picturesque terraced buildings, near a high street that has a good mix of independent shops, a pub and a parish church. Famous names buried in Putney Vale Cemetery, on the other side of the A3, include Howard Carter, discoverer of Tutankhamen's tomb, writer Enid Blyton, footballer Bobby Moore and racing driver James Hunt.

Earlsfield and Southfields

Earlsfield, once considered a rather nondescript residential area, has become a far more attractive prospect – mainly because it contains spacious homes with gardens that hit the spot for well-paid Londoners who don't want to sever their links with the Smoke. Such people aren't likely to be too fazed by the crime horror stories coming from the area's three rather challenging council estates: the Aboyne, the Burtop and the Henry Prince (the latter isn't as bad as it's often painted, with ongoing refurbishments and increased police foot patrols).

Garratt Lane, which parallels the flow of the River Wandle from Summerstown, is Earlsfield's main road. This is where you'll find most of the restaurants, bars and pubs, as well as a few old-fashioned businesses that time (and rates hikes) forgot. Magdalen Road, behind the rail station, is a cheerily middle-class area. Gorgeous King George's Park, along which the Wandle flows, separates Earlsfield from the well-established

Wandsworth

LOST SOCIETY

INTELLIGENT DRINKING WITHIN THE LIBRARY BAR

DELECTABLE DINING IN THE MEZZANINE

LOUNGING IN THE BLACK AND WHITE BAR

SUMPTUOUS COCKTAILS IN THE SECRET GARDEN

BENDY BEATS PLAYING IN THE CRYSTAL BALLROOM

CHINESE WHISPERS IN THE ORIENTAL LOUNGE

ALL HOUSED WITHIN A TWO STOREY 16TH CENTURY BARN

LOST SOCIETY
697 WANDSWORTH ROAD
CLAPHAM , LONDON
SW8, 3JF

ALL ENQUIRIES CALL 0207 652 6526 OR EMAIL: INFO@LOSTSOCIETY.CO.UK

WWW.LOSTSOCIETY.CO.UK

WINNER OF TIME OUT 'BEST BAR' 2006

pocket of posh that is Southfields. There's also much excitement on the wildlife front here, as water voles are to be returned to the riverbanks.

Southfields has plenty of handsome Victorian terraces and semis with large mature gardens; the neatly appointed properties in 'the Grid' (south-east of the station) are most sought after. Similar houses around Wimbledon Park Road are also popular. The agreeable cafés and shops on low-key Replingham Road give the place the peaceful air of a Home Counties town. Southfields has a tube, but it's on the slow District line – it's quicker to use Earlsfield's excellent overground station. Nonetheless, Southfields trumps Earlsfield on the grounds that it has no unsightly council estates and the houses are bigger and grander; consequentially, the whole atmosphere is rather smug.

Balham

If the presence of a Waitrose, an organic butcher and a weekend farmers' market signals gentrification, Balham long ago reached the sunny uplands of desirability – certainly as far as estate agents are concerned. High house prices are a given, but it still has issues with its level of cool. The Balham Kitchen & Bar cruelly divested the area of its trendy Soho House associations when it closed (it's been reborn as Harrison's). Bars and restaurants open apace, but Balham's workaday town centre and High Road (Iceland, Nando's, Woolies), despite various council initiatives to sex it up, evoke a sense of grinding tedium rather than metropolitan cool.

Balham can boast a huge stock of Victorian houses of good proportions (even if the gardens are a bit tiddly), many on the hallowed Heaver Estate conservation area near Tooting. It also has a train and tube station (albeit on the Northern line), and a close relationship with Wandsworth and Tooting Bec Commons. Young professionals untroubled by plans for procreation invest in serviced flats in Du Cane Court, a distinctive 1937 art deco apartment block on Balham High Road.

Tooting

House prices are pushing the well-to-do further and further south and west, but Tooting will never really be highfalutin. This agreeably diverse area, familiar to telly addicts of all ages (from *Citizen Smith* to *Little Britain*) is defined by the stretch of Upper Tooting Road between the Bec and Broadway tube stations – the curry corridor. Tooting is the only area in London where you can find good East African Asian, Gujarati, South Indian, Pakistani and Sri Lankan restaurants within a ten-minute walk of one another. There are plenty of Asian greengrocers too for exotic fruit, veg, snacks, spices and sweets.

St George's Hospital is one of the biggest employers in Wandsworth, and dominates the ebb and flow of people around Tooting Broadway. The preponderance of low-paid health workers with nowhere to live has led to frantic demands for the council to create more affordable housing for key workers. This it is doing, and proudly trumpeting the fact, but plenty of property speculators have focused on Tooting too – numerous tiny expensive flats are being squeezed into defunct commercial buildings all over the district. House hunters favour Furzedown (near Tooting Bec) and the more affordable Edwardian terraces of Tooting Broadway. The residential roads around the two local commons (Wandsworth and Tooting Bec) are very smart, with plenty of million-pound houses.

The other reason for living in Tooting is the easy access to large green spaces and sports facilities. Tooting Bec Common has football pitches, tennis courts and the lovely Tooting Bec Lido. Built in 1906, it's London's most beautiful open-air pool, and its biggest: an exhausting 100 yards by 33 yards.

Restaurants & cafés

You're in the right borough for sociable grazing. Wandsworth has dining options galore, from upmarket French restaurants to budget Indian caffs, family-oriented chains to riverside gastropubs. Fashionable eating streets, such as Northcote Road and Bellevue Road, fill up quickly at weekends, but there's plenty of choice elsewhere.

A focal point for good food for families, Northcote Road has plenty of chain restaurants (Gourmet Burger Kitchen, Nando's, FishWorks) and a couple of famously child-friendly cafés: Boiled Egg & Soldiers and Crumpet. Young couples gaze romantically over classic Bolognese

Modern-style Turkish bar-restaurant **Kazans** in Earlsfield.

specialities in Osteria Antica Bologna or innovative tapas at modern Spanish newcomer Lola Rojo. Niksons is a lively bar-restaurant offering good Modern European cuisine.

Round the corner, Battersea Rise has thriving French bistro Le Bouchon Bordelais, jolly Pizza Metro, Argentinian La Pampa Grill, Japanese Tokiya and budget orientalist Banana Leaf Canteen, as well as branches of Strada and Giraffe. A couple of options are found on St John's Hill – smart Caribbean at Brown Sugar, top-notch fish and chips at the Fish Club – while Donna Margherita on Lavender Hill draws a loyal local crowd for its classic pasta dishes.

Further north, the beautifully restored Greyhound offers an excellent (and well-priced) wine list and superior gastro grub. Near Battersea Park, Ransome's Dock is the epitome of a relaxed neighbourhood restaurant, with a varied Modern European menu and a stellar wine list. Next door is newcomer Butcher & Grill, combining shop, bar and brasserie. Queenstown Road also has a couple of standouts, namely Tom Ilic' – the first go-it-alone venture for a talented young chef acclaimed for his adventurous Modern European cooking – and cheerful Argentine grill Santa Maria del Sur.

On the Balham edge of Wandsworth Common, well-regarded French veteran Chez Bruce is king of all it surveys on Bellevue Road. Amici is a more relaxed, Italian alternative, while kids love the over-the-top puddings at family-friendly burger joint Dexter's. Also ideal for parents is café Munchkin Lane: it's got a basement playroom. On the northern tip of the common is a textbook gastropub, the Freemasons.

Wandsworth Town's new riverside developments are blessed with the Waterfront, a splendid modern gastropub run by Young's, and Marco Polo, a lively Italian restaurant that appeals to all age groups. For fish and chips, try posher than average Brady's near the train station.

Restaurants in Putney tend to cluster on Upper Richmond Road and Putney High Street. The former contains Ma Goa, which showcases Portuguese-influenced Goan specialities; family-run French bistro L'Auberge; Spanish tapas bar Olé; long-running Japanese Chosan; and zebra-striped Chakalaka, a haven for expat South Africans. The High Street tends towards chain restaurants (Maison Blanc, the Real Greek, Wagamama), but also has family-oriented Eddie Catz, Spanish outpost La Mancha, and Enoteca Turi, a classy

Italian with a superb wine list. Just off the High Street, Royal China is reliable for dim sum and daily specials. Head towards the river and on Lower Richmond Road you'll find the flagship branch of the Thai Square chain, housed in a striking modern building next to Putney Bridge. Further along, the Phoenix Bar & Grill (Italian-accented Mod Euro) sets the standard for a great local restaurant.

Earlsfield's eateries are found mainly along Garratt Lane. Kazans is a fine Turkish, while wine bar Willie Gunn (see p197) has a posh restaurant attached. Across St George's Park to Southfields the very splendid Earl Spencer gastropub still hits all the right buttons, with its wide-ranging menu, big portions and fine ales.

Eating in Balham is getting better. The area's finest restaurant is still Lamberts, a Modern European stalwart, though newcomer Harrison's, with its zinc bar, metropolitan vibe and smart brasserie food, is hot on its heels. Family-friendly Italian options are ever-popular Ciullo's, on the High Road, and new arrival Raviolo, by the station. Trinity Stores café-deli is a safe bet for a fancy takeaway supper. Bedford Hill has branches of Pizza Express and the Fine Burger Co.

Tooting has long been famed for Indian cuisine, with many different regions represented. Two favourites are Kastoori (East African Gujarati vegetarian) and Radha Krishna Bhavan (South Indian). Good, cheap and fiery-hot food is the speciality of two local Sri Lankan cafés, Apollo Banana Leaf and Jaffna House. European alternatives are provided by Rick's Café (Mod Euro with a Spanish edge) and Harrington's (pie and mash).

Amici Bar & Italian Kitchen *35 Bellevue Road, SW17 7EF (0871 971 4196/www.amici italian.co.uk).*
Apollo Banana Leaf *190 Tooting High Street, SW17 0SF (8696 1423).*
L'Auberge *22 Upper Richmond Road, SW15 2RX (8874 3593/www.ardillys.com).*
Banana Leaf Canteen *75-79 Battersea Rise, SW11 1HN (7228 2828).*
Boiled Egg & Soldiers *63 Northcote Road, SW11 1NP (7223 4894).*
Le Bouchon Bordelais *5-9 Battersea Rise, SW11 1HG (7738 0307/www.lebouchon.co.uk).*
Brady's *513 Old York Road, SW18 1TF (8877 9599/www.bradysfish.co.uk).*
Brown Sugar *165-167 St John's Hill, SW11 1TQ (7228 7713/www.brownsugarlondon.com).*

Butcher & Grill *39-41 Parkgate Road, SW11 4NP (7924 3999/www.thebutcherandgrill.com).*
Chakalaka *136 Upper Richmond Road, SW15 2SP (8789 5696/www.chakalaka restaurant.co.uk).*
Chez Bruce *2 Bellevue Road, SW17 7EG (8672 0114/www.chezbruce.co.uk).*
Chosan *292 Upper Richmond Road, SW15 6TH (8788 9626).*
Ciullo's *31 Balham High Road, SW12 9AL (8675 3072).*
Crumpet *66 Northcote Road, SW11 6QL (7924 1117/www.crumpet.biz).*
Dexter's Grill & Bar *20 Bellevue Road, SW17 7EB (8767 1858).*
Donna Margherita *183 Lavender Hill, SW11 5TE (7228 2660/www.donna-margherita.com).*
Earl Spencer *260-262 Merton Road, SW18 5JU (8870 9244/www.theearlspencer.co.uk).*
Eddie Catz *68-70 Putney High Street, SW15 1SF (0845 201 1268/www.eddiecatz.com).*
Enoteca Turi *28 Putney High Street, SW15 1SQ (8785 4449/www.enotecaturi.com).*
Fish Club *189 St John's Hill, SW11 1TH (7978 7115/www.thefishclub.com).*
Freemasons *2 Wandsworth Common Northside, SW18 2SS (7326 8580/ www.freemasonspub.com).*
Greyhound *136 Battersea High Street, SW11 3JR (7978 7021/www.thegreyhound atbattersea.co.uk).*
Harrington's *3 Selkirk Road, SW17 0ER (8672 1877).*
Harrison's *15-19 Bedford Hill, SW12 9EX (8675 6900/www.harrisonsbalham.co.uk).*
Jaffna House *90 Tooting High Street, SW17 0RN (8672 7786/www.jaffnahouse.co.uk).*
Kastoori *188 Upper Tooting Road, SW17 7EJ (8767 7027).*
Kazans *607-609 Garratt Lane, SW18 4SU (8739 0055/www.kazans.com).*
Lamberts *2 Station Parade, Balham High Road, SW12 9AZ (8675 2233/www.lamberts restaurant.com).*
Lola Rojo *78 Northcote Road, SW11 6QL (7350 2262/www.lolarojo.net).*
Ma Goa *242-244 Upper Richmond Road, SW15 6TG (8780 1767/www.ma-goa.com).*
La Mancha *32 Putney High Street, SW15 1SQ (8780 1022/www.lamancha.co.uk).*
Marco Polo *6-7 Riverside Quarter, Eastfields Avenue, SW18 1LP (8874 6800/www.marco poloriverside.co.uk).*
Munchkin Lane *83 Nightingale Lane, SW12 8NX (8772 6800).*
Niksons *172-174 Northcote Road, SW11 6RE (7228 2285/4040/www.niksons.co.uk).*
Olé *240 Upper Richmond Road, SW15 6TG (8788 8009/www.olerestaurants.com).*
Osteria Antica Bologna *23 Northcote Road, SW11 1NG (7978 4771/www.osteria.co.uk).*
La Pampa Grill *60 Battersea Rise, SW11 1EG (7924 4774).*
Phoenix Bar & Grill *162-164 Lower Richmond Road, SW15 1LY (8780 3131/ www.sonnys.co.uk).*

Pizza Metro *64 Battersea Rise, SW11 1EQ (7228 3812/www.pizzametropizza.com).*
Radha Krishna Bhavan *86 Tooting High Street, SW17 0RN (8682 0969/ www.mcdosa.co.uk).*
Ransome's Dock *35-37 Parkgate Road, SW11 4NP (7223 1611/www.ransomes dock.co.uk).*
Raviolo *1 Balham Station Road, SW12 9SG (8772 0433/www.raviolo.co.uk).*
Rick's Café *122 Mitcham Road, SW17 9NH (8767 5219).*
Royal China *3 Chelverton Road, SW15 1RN (8788 0907).*
Santa Maria del Sur *129 Queenstown Road, SW8 3RH (7622 2088/www.santa mariadelsur.co.uk).*
Thai Square *2-4 Lower Richmond Road, SW15 1LB (8780 1811/www.thaisq.com).*
Tokiya *74 Battersea Rise, SW11 1EH (7223 5989/www.tokiya.co.uk).*
Tom Ilic' *123 Queenstown Road, SW8 3RH (7622 0555/www.tomilic.com).*
Trinity Stores *5 & 6 Balham Station Road, SW12 9SG (8673 3773/www.trinitystores.co.uk).*
Waterfront *Baltimore House, Juniper Drive, SW18 1TZ (7228 4297/www.waterfront london.co.uk).*

Bars & pubs

Old and new money sloshes around Wandsworth, making this a great district for drinking, whatever your tipple. In the established honeypots of Battersea and Clapham – especially Northcote Road – young, loud professionals quaff cocktails in style bars such as Iniquity. The casual Holy Drinker has a soundtrack of laid-back funk and an impressive line-up of beer. Raffish Frieda B offers a tiny front bar for canoodling in and a downstairs space filled with brown leather. Nearer to Battersea Park, Dusk is a cosmopolitan cocktail/DJ bar. There's also established pub theatre the Latchmere, new cocktail bar Alchemist and, opposite Wandsworth Common, popular gastropub the Freemasons (*see p195*).

Wandsworth Town's most famous watering hole is the beautiful, green-tiled Alma, now a Young's pub with a dining room that peddles gargantuan portions of gastro favourites. The Ship, also part of the Young's empire, has a riverside setting (but not overly inspiring views), a garden and barbecue. Pubs away from the river include the East Hill and the cramped former lighterman's pub Cat's Back.

In Putney, the cavernous Duke's Head (another handsome Young's hostelry) insists

Radha Krishna Bhavan. *See p195.*

it offers views of the Thames, although these are hard to achieve given the numbers of drinkers outside on a summer evening. The nearby Half Moon, also a Young's pub, is a prime venue for bands of all musical persuasions (*see p199*). There's also the Coat & Badge, the unpretentious Whistle & Flute (a rare Fuller's outpost in these parts) and Putney Station, a bright, modern wine bar with good food to boot.

Many of Balham's pubs lead a double life, catering for both sides of the gentrification divide. The Bedford hosts top comedy nights and low-key acoustic sets while maintaining a noisy bar. The Duke of Devonshire has older local customers at the front and younger hipsters in the back. Exhibit offsets its unappealing location (adjoining a supermarket car park) with a trendy cinema space, comfort food and a relaxed, cocktail bar vibe. Newcomer the Balham Bowls Club was indeed a bowls club; now it's an eccentric bar with original fixtures and fittings intact.

Tooting offers the cheap and cheerful Trafalgar Arms: its gloriously mixed clientele includes medics from nearby St George's Hospital, as well as waifs and strays drawn in by the promise of quiz nights, burgers, beers and board games. Garden House appeals to arty types with its mismatched furniture, exhibitions and eclectic soundtrack. The Selkirk feels like a proper local pub, with amiable staff, not overly poncey food and great beers. Further south, in Earlsfield, is popular wine bar Willie Gunn.

Alchemist *225 St John's Hill, SW11 1TH (7326 7456/www.alchemistbar.co.uk).*
Alma *499 Old York Road, SW18 1TF (8870 2537/www.almawandsworth.com).*
Balham Bowls Club *7-9 Ramsden Road, SW12 8QX (8673 4700/www.antic-ltd.com).*
Bedford *77 Bedford Hill, SW12 9HD (8682 8940/www.thebedford.co.uk).*
Cat's Back *86-88 Point Pleasant, SW18 1NN (8877 0818/www.thecatsback.com).*
Coat & Badge *8 Lacy Road, SW15 1NL (8788 4900/www.geronimo-inns.co.uk).*
Duke of Devonshire *39 Balham High Road, SW12 9AN (8673 1363).*
Duke's Head *8 Lower Richmond Road, SW15 1JN (8788 2552/www.dukesheadputney.co.uk).*
Dusk *339 Battersea Park Road, SW11 4LS (7622 2112/www.duskbar.co.uk).*
East Hill *21 Alma Road, SW18 1AA (8874 1833/www.geronimo-inns.co.uk).*
Exhibit *12 Balham Station Road, SW12 9SG (8772 6556/www.theexhibit.uk.com).*

Frieda B *46 Battersea Rise, SW11 1EE (7228 7676/www.frieda-b.co.uk).*
Garden House *196 Tooting High Street, SW17 0SF (8767 6582).*
Holy Drinker *59 Northcote Road, SW11 1NP (7801 0544/www.holydrinker.co.uk).*
Iniquity *8-10 Northcote Road, SW11 1NT (7924 6699).*
King's Head *84 Upper Tooting Road, SW17 7PB (0871 332 5739).*
Latchmere *503 Battersea Park Road, SW11 3BW (7223 3549).*
Putney Station *94-98 Upper Richmond Road, SW15 2SP (8780 0242/www.brinkleys.com).*
Selkirk *60 Selkirk Road, SW17 0ES (8672 6235/www.theselkirk.co.uk).*
Ship *41 Jew's Row, SW18 1TB (8870 9667/ www.theship.co.uk).*
Trafalgar Arms *148 Tooting High Street, SW17 0RT (8767 6059).*
Whistle & Flute *46-48 Putney High Street, SW15 1SQ (8780 5437).*
Willie Gunn *422 Garratt Lane, SW18 4HW (8946 7773).*

Shops

The most picturesque (if not the most useful or economical) way to shop for food has to be basket over arm, down Northcote Road. Select local honey from the Hive, traceable steak from butcher A Dove & Sons and cheese from Hamish Johnston, to be washed down with wine from Philglas & Swiggot or Vingt. Pick up some flowers from the Stem & Petal Company, and you're the ultimate Wandsworth statement shopper. On parallel Webb's Road, there's romantic florist La Maison des Roses and hi-fi and home cinema equipment at Oranges & Lemons. With a small antiques market for collectable china and restored furniture, along with a traditional street market, Northcote Road is all about living the dream, family style.

You won't find much in the way of adult grooming apart from surfy clothes at White Stuff, shoes and bags at Opus and high-quality toiletries at Verde, but once the children come along there's plenty of choice. For the early days there's JoJo Maman Bébé, then mini-fashions from Quackers, shoes from One Small Step One Giant Leap, toys from QT and the wherewithal for a musical education from Northcote Music. Bolingbroke Bookshop has a large kids' section and is also the lifeline for local reading groups.

Elsewhere, Battersea does all right for independents, and benefits from vicarious Sloaniness thanks to its proximity

LOCALS' TIPS

Newcomers to Battersea/Clapham should visit the Bolingbroke Bookshop. It's as much a community centre as a literary retailer – you'll find details of local groups, clubs and societies, where your Wandsworth soulmate may be waiting.

Putney Bridge is a beautiful starting point for the loveliest bike ride in the capital – along the Thames, through Richmond Park and Hampton Court all the way to Weybridge – if you have the energy for 18 miles of pedalling. Find the route on the Sustrans website (www.sustrans.org.uk).

Get your mind off the house prices by singing your heart out with the friendly South West London Choral Society (01252 726001, www.swlcs.org.uk), established in 1886. Members meet at Balham Baptist Church, 21 Ramsden Road, SW12 at 7.30pm on Mondays. No auditions, all they ask is that you sing in tune.

The King's Head pub on Tooting High Road (see p197) – a Victorian pile with etched windows and real ales – is a great place for watching a big footie match. Afterwards, you can walk to any of the best Indian and Pakistani restaurants in London.

Northcote Road is the only place for breakfast. Come early for a fry-up at Boiled Egg & Soldiers or see if you can spot Nitin Sawhney, who likes to take his porridge at Café Brew (No.45, 7801 9300). Crumpet is the spot for afternoon tea.

14-screen Cineworld and 65 high-street stores, from H&M to HMV. There's a food market near the train station on Saturdays.

Balham and Tooting run the gamut of shopping experiences. Both are loath to let go of their scruffy high streets and local markets. Tooting, in particular, still specialises in Afro-Caribbean and Asian produce, available in the covered 1930s arcades of Broadway Market and Tooting Market. Deepak Cash & Carry is the place for Asian staples and spices. Balham tries harder to appease the incomers, with affordable modern furniture at Dwell, organic meat at Chadwick's and a popular Sunday farmers' market on Hildreth Street. Amid the Bedford Hill cafés and bars sits Lucas Bond, a kookily elegant gift shop.

Putney High Street is traffic-clogged and lined with unenticing chains, though the Exchange Shopping Centre is a pleasant, well-appointed mall with a Waitrose. Independents include lovely knitting shop Stash Yarns; Pop UK, which deals in high-end furniture by the likes of Ron Arad and Philippe Starck; and a branch of Shula Starkey's pristine mini-chain Ark Health & Beauty. At Will's Art Warehouse – which has been dubbed the 'Oddbins of the art world' – you can pick up affordable artworks to decorate your home.

A Dove & Sons *71 Northcote Road, SW11 6PJ (7223 5191).*
Anita's Vintage Fashion Fairs *Battersea Arts Centre, Lavender Hill, SW11 5TN (8325 5789/www.vintagefashionfairs.com).*
Ark Health & Beauty *339 Putney Bridge Road, SW15 2PG (8788 8888/www.arkhealth andbeauty.com).*
Bolingbroke Bookshop *147 Northcote Road, SW11 6QB (7223 9344/www.bolingbroke bookshop.tbpcontrol.co.uk).*
Chadwick's Organic Butchers *208 Balham High Road, SW12 9BS (8772 1895).*
Deepak Cash & Carry *953-959 Garratt Lane, SW17 0LR (8767 7819).*
Designer Alterations *220A Queenstown Road, SW8 4LP (7498 4360/www.designer alterations.com).*
Dwell *264 Balham High Road, SW17 7AN (0870 060 0182/www.dwell.co.uk).*
Edwina Ibbotson *45 Queenstown Road, SW8 3RG (7498 5390).*
Exchange Shopping Centre *High Street, SW15 1TW (8780 1056/www.theexchange sw15.com).*
Hamish Johnston *48 Northcote Road, SW11 1PA (7738 0741).*
Hive Honey Shop *93 Northcote Road, SW11 6PL (7924 6233/www.thehivehoneyshop.co.uk).*

to Chelsea. Designer Alterations specialises in alterations and repairs and offers a wardrobe 'detox' service, while milliner Edwina Ibbotson will do you a titfer for Ascot. Anita's Vintage Fashion Fairs, held six times a year at Battersea Arts Centre, offer vintage clothing from Biba, Ossie Clark, Dior and more. Interiors specialists include the London Door Company, Kitchen Clinic and Tablemakers – all on St John's Hill.

Apart from unlovely retail parks at either end of Wandsworth Bridge, Wandsworth Town's retail resources are boosted by the Southside Shopping Centre, which has a Waitrose, a Virgin Active health club, a

JoJo Maman Bébé *68 Northcote Road,
SW11 6DS (7228 0322/www.jojomaman
bebe.co.uk).*
Kitchen Clinic *149 St John's Hill, SW11 1TQ
(7924 7877/www.kitchenclinic.co.uk).*
London Door Company *155 St John's Hill,
SW11 1TQ (7801 0877/www.londondoor.co.uk).*
Lucas Bond *45 Bedford Hill, SW12 9EY
(8675 9300/www.lucasbond.com).*
La Maison des Roses *48 Webb's Road,
SW11 6SF (7228 5700/www.maison-des-
roses.com).*
Northcote Music *155C Northcote Road,
SW11 6QB (7228 0074).*
Northcote Road Antiques Market *155A
Northcote Road, SW11 6QB (7228 6850).*
One Small Step One Giant Leap *49
Northcote Road, SW11 1NJ (7223 9314/
www.onesmallsteponegiantleap.com).*
Opus *57 Northcote Road, SW11 1NP
(7978 4240/www.opusshoes.co.uk).*
Oranges & Lemons *61 Webb's Road, SW11
6RX (7924 2040/www.oandlhifi.co.uk).*
Philglas & Swiggot *21 Northcote Road,
SW11 1NG (7924 4494/www.philglas-
swiggot.com).*
Pop UK *278 Upper Richmond Road, SW15
6TQ (8788 8811/www.popuk.com).*
Quackers *155D Northcote Road, SW11 6QB
(7978 4235).*
QT Toys *90 Northcote Road, SW11 6QN
(7223 8637/www.qttoys.co.uk).*
Southside Shopping Centre *SW18 4TF
(8870 2141/www.southsidewandsworth.com).*
Stash Yarns *213 Upper Richmond Road,
SW15 6SQ (8246 6666/www.stashyarns.co.uk).*
Stem & Petal Company *132 Northcote
Road, SW11 6QZ (7924 3238).*
Tablemakers *153 St John's Hill, SW11 1TQ
(7223 2075/www.tablemakers.co.uk).*
Verde *133A Northcote Road, SW11 6PX
(7223 2095).*
Vingt *20 Northcote Road, SW11 1NX
(7924 6924/www.vingt.co.uk).*
White Stuff *39 Northcote Road, SW11 1NJ
(7228 7129/www.whitestuff.com).*
Will's Art Warehouse *180 Lower
Richmond Road, SW15 1LY (8246
4840/www.wills-art.com).*

Arts & attractions

Cinemas & theatres
Battersea Arts Centre (BAC) *Lavender
Hill, SW11 5TN (7223 6557/www.bac.org.uk).*
Forward-thinking theatre specialising in new
writers and companies.
Cineworld Wandsworth *Southside Shopping
Centre, Wandsworth High Street, SW18 4TF
(0871 200 2000/www.cineworld.co.uk).*
Odeon Putney *26 Putney High Street, SW15
1SN (0871 224 4007/www.odeon.co.uk).*
Putney Arts Theatre *Ravenna Road,
SW15 6AW (8788 6943/www.putneyarts
theatre.org.uk).*

Galleries & museums
Albion *8 Hester Road, SW11 4AX (7801
2480/www.albion-gallery.com).* Stunning
riverside art gallery near Battersea Park.
De Morgan Centre *38 West Hill, SW18 1RZ
(8871 1144/www.demorgan.org.uk).* Work
by William De Morgan, the Victorian ceramic
artist and his wife Evelyn, the painter.
London Sewing Machine Museum
*312 Balham High Road, SW17 7AA (8682
7916/www.sewantique.com).*
Pump House Gallery *Battersea Park,
SW11 4NJ (7350 0523).* Tiny art gallery
in a 19th-century building.

Music & comedy venues
Half Moon *93 Lower Richmond Road, SW15
1EU (8780 9383/www.halfmoon.co.uk).* One of
London's longest-running music venues, this
jovial Young's pub has hosted almost everyone
(the Stones, Elvis Costello, the Who, U2…).

Other attractions
Battersea Dogs & Cats Home *4 Battersea
Park Road, SW8 4AA (7622 3626/www.dogs
home.org).* Casual visitors are welcome at this
world-famous animal sanctuary.
Battersea Park Children's Zoo *Entrance
at Chelsea Gate, Queenstown Road, SW11 4NJ
(7924 5826/www.batterseaparkzoo.co.uk).*

Sport & fitness

The council's sports centres (run by DC
Leisure) are excellent: a government survey
in autumn 2007 voted Wandsworth's leisure
services the best in London. A £15 million
overhaul of all the centres in the borough
was completed with the reopening of
Roehampton Sport & Fitness Centre in
early 2008. The private sector is dominated
by the big-name chains.

Gyms & leisure centres
Balham Leisure Centre *Elmfield Road, SW17
8AN (8772 9577/www.dcleisurecentres.co.uk).*
Cannons *www.cannons.co.uk; King George's
Park, Burr Road, SW18 4SQ (8874 1155);
Sheepcote Lane, Burns Road, SW11 5BT
(7228 4400).* Private.
Esporta *Smugglers Way, SW18 1DG
(8875 2222/www.esporta.com).* Private.
Fitness First *www.fitnessfirst.co.uk;
34 St John's Hill, SW11 1SA (7738 0067);
279-291 Balham High Road, SW17 7BA
(8672 2904); 276-288 Lavender Hill, SW11
1LJ (7924 5252).* Private.
Latchmere Leisure Centre *Burns
Road, SW11 2DY (7207 8004/www.dc
leisurecentres.co.uk).*
Physical Culture Studios *21-22 The
Arches, Winthorpe Road, SW15 2LW
(8780 2172).* Private.

RECYCLING

No. of bring sites 35 (for nearest, visit www.recycleforlondon.com)
Household waste recycled 20.63%
Main recycling centres www.wrwa. gov.uk: Western Riverside Civic Amenity Site, Smugglers Way, SW18 1JS (8871 2788); Cringle Dock Civic Amenity Site, Cringle Street, SW8 5BX
Other recycling services green waste collection; home composting; collection of white goods
Council contact Waste Services, Room 57A, Town Hall, Wandsworth High Street, SW18 2PU (8871 8558/ www.wandsworth.gov.uk/waste management)

Putney Leisure Centre *Dryburgh Road, SW15 1BL (8785 0388/www.dcleisurecentres. co.uk).*
Roehampton Sport & Fitness Centre *Laverstoke Gardens, SW15 4JB (8785 0535/ www.dcleisurecentres.co.uk).*
Tooting Leisure Centre *Greaves Place, off Garratt Lane, SW17 0NE (8333 7555/ www.dcleisurecentres.co.uk).*
Virgin Active *154-160 Upper Richmond Road, SW15 2SW (8246 6676/www.virginactive.co.uk).* Private.
Wandle Recreation Centre *Mapleton Road, SW18 4DN (8871 1149/www.dcleisure centres.co.uk).*
Yorky's *24-28 York Road, SW11 3QA (7228 6266).* Private.

Other facilities

There are plenty of sports pitches in Battersea Park, and numerous rowing clubs along the Thames in Putney.

Sivananda Yoga Vedanta Centre *51 Felsham Road, SW15 1AZ (8780 0160/ www.sivananda.co.uk).* Long-established yoga centre offering numerous classes.
Tooting Bec Lido *Tooting Bec Road, SW16 1RU (8871 7198/www.dcleisurecentres.co.uk).* The second-largest open-air pool in Europe, open from May to September. Home of the South London Swimming Club (www.slsc.org.uk).

Schools

WHAT THE PARENTS SAY:

❛It's the same old London story: none of the schools is really bad, but the middle classes all want to stick together. If all the lovely boys that were in my daughter's primary had gone to Ernest Bevin (full of hoodies, though it has a wonderful sports block), it would change. Same

goes for Burntwood Girls. The teachers are inspirational, it has a fab art department and dance studio, and they get good results. Graveney School (my daughter's school) has a real mix of kids. But they prize the clever ones, so the benchmark is raised; the bright pull the rest up, not the other way around. Plus, they are strict. Bad behaviour and you are out. They are tough on uniform too.

The two highly regarded primaries are Fircroft and Honeywell, although the latter is often emptied after Year 2 when all the rich kids go off to private school. You can get into Graveney by taking the Wandsworth Year 6 Test. The catchment area is tiny, and we're miles out – fortunately, my daughter scored well. ❜
Annie Millar, mother of one, Tooting

Primary

There are 55 state primary schools in the borough, including 17 church schools and one Muslim school. There are also 22 independent primaries, including one French school, one Montessori school and one Steiner school. See www.wandsworth.gov.uk, www.edu base.gov.uk and www.ofsted.gov.uk for more information.

Secondary

Ashcroft Technology Academy *100 West Hill, SW15 2UT (8877 0357/www.ashcroft academy.org.uk).*
Battersea Technology College *401 Battersea Park Road, SW11 5AP (7622 0026/www.battersea-tech.wandsworth.sch.uk).*
Burntwood School *Burntwood Lane, SW17 0AQ (8946 6201/www.burntwoodschool.com).* Girls only; mixed sixth form.
Chestnut Grove School *45 Chestnut Grove, SW12 8JZ (8673 8737).*
Elliot School *Pullman Gardens, SW15 3DG (8788 3421/www.elliott-school.org.uk).*
Emanuel School *Battersea Rise, SW11 1HS (8870 4171/www.emanuel.org.uk).* Private.
Ernest Bevin College *Beechcroft Road, SW17 7DF (8672 8582/www.ernestbevin. org.uk).* Boys only; mixed sixth form.
Graveney School *Welham Road, SW17 9BU (8682 7000/www.graveney.org).*
John Paul II RC School *Princes Way, SW19 6QE (8788 8142).*
Putney High School *35 Putney Hill, SW15 6BH (8788 4886/www.gdst.net/putneyhigh).* Private; girls only.
St Cecilia's, Wandsworth School *Sutherland Grove, SW18 5JR (8780 1244/ www.saintcecilias.wandsworth.sch.uk).*
Salesian College *Surrey Lane, SW11 3PB (7228 2857/www.salesiancollege.co.uk).* Boys only.
Southfields Community College *333 Merton Road, SW18 5JU (8875 2600/ www.southfields.wandsworth.sch.uk).*

COUNCIL TAX

		Main borough area	Commons area
A	up to £40,000	£450.78	£465.71
B	£40,001-£52,000	£525.90	£543.32
C	£52,001-£68,000	£601.03	£620.95
D	£68,001-£88,000	£676.16	£898.56
E	£88,001-£120,000	£826.42	£853.80
F	£120,001-£160,000	£976.68	£1,009.03
G	£160,001-£320,000	£1,126.93	£1,164.27
H	over £320,000	£1,352.32	£1,397.12

Property

WHAT THE AGENTS SAY:

'Earlsfield has been up and coming for years, but more so recently. We're the longest-serving estate agent here and we've seen great improvements in the area. People used to come because they couldn't afford Putney or Battersea, but now they're here by choice. There are lots of young families, good schools, and you're not far from Wimbledon Park. Wimbledon Village is a five-minute drive away. Earlsfield station has good links to the city, and the area around it is being regenerated, with lots of shops and restaurants, and there's going to be a Marks & Spencer.'

Nick Craigie, Craigie & Co, Earlsfield

'The key to Clapham is the transport. Clapham Junction is the biggest station in London, and there are excellent bus routes. The council tax is one of the lowest in the UK, and the council does what it is supposed to do, for not exorbitant sums. Northcote Road is mainly bars and restaurants, but there are also boutiques and baby shops too; at the weekend, with the market, it's not unlike Notting Hill. Battersea Park is more exclusive and north Battersea is popular as you're getting close to Chelsea and the King's Road. There's a huge amount of activity in the property market – it never seems to slow down.'

David Huggett, Cochrane & Wilson, Battersea

Average property prices

Detached £2,259,850
Semi-detached £817,896
Terraced £609,735
Flat £344,823

Local estate agents

Andrews www.andrewsonline.co.uk; 5 offices in the borough (Battersea 7326 8171/Balham 8675 2244/Earlsfield 8944 9044/Southfields 8874 6686/Putney 8780 2233).

Cochrane & Wilson www.cochraneandwilson. com; 2 offices (Battersea Park 7062 1062/ Lavender Hill 7924 5444).
Craigie & Co 309 Garratt Lane, SW18 4DX (8874 7475/www.craigie-co.co.uk).
First Union www.first-union.co.uk; 2 offices (Battersea 7771 7100/Wandsworth 8480 4444).
John Thorogood 140 Northcote Road, SW11 6QZ (7228 7474/www.john-thorogood.co.uk).
Penmans 260 Balham High Road, SW17 7AN (8672 4422/www.penmansestateagents.co.uk).
Rolfe East 168 Putney High Street, SW15 1RS (8780 3355/www.rolfe-east.com).
Time2move 28 London Road, SW17 9HW (8640 0146/www.time2move.com).

Other information

Council

Wandsworth Borough Council The Town Hall, Wandsworth High Street, SW18 2PU (8871 6000/www.wandsworth.gov.uk).

Legal services

Battersea CAB 14 York Road, SW11 3QA (8333 6960/www.wandsworthcabx.org.uk).
Battersea Law Centre 14 York Road, SW11 3QA (7585 0716).
Roehampton CAB 166 Roehampton Lane, SW15 4HR (8333 6960/www.wandsworth cabx.org.uk).
Tooting & Balham CAB 4th floor, Bedford House, 215 Balham High Road, SW17 7BQ (8333 6960/www.wandsworthcabx.org.uk).

Local newspapers

South London Press 8769 4444/ www.southlondonpress.co.uk.
Wandsworth Borough News/ Wandsworth Guardian 8329 9244/ www.wandsworthguardian.co.uk.

Allotments & open spaces

Council Allotments 8871 6441/ www.wandsworth.gov.uk.
Roehampton Garden Society Paula Alderson 8789 5836/www.roehampton allotments.co.uk.
Open spaces www.wandsworth.gov.uk/parks; www.parkexplorer.org.uk.

Wandsworth

'There's a sense of being on the edge of London and the home counties here – Merton has a bit of everything. And few summer pleasures beat a picnic on Wimbledon Common on a balmy day.'

Sophia Lyde, lifelong Merton resident

Merton

The name Merton – meaning 'farmstead by the pool' – dates from the tenth century, and while this is a fairly modern London borough (it was formed in 1965), it hasn't completely relinquished its prettily bucolic, old-fashioned feel. Despite its reserved spirit, Merton is a borough of bustling amenities and burgeoning town centres, handy transport links and intriguing contrasts.

Neighbourhoods

Wimbledon, Wimbledon Village and Wimbledon Park

Every year in late June, Wimbledon becomes the focus of international attention as its All England Lawn Tennis Club hosts the championship fortnight. The area blossoms during the tournament, but at any time of year Wimbledon town centre is the buzzing hub of Merton, with excellent transport links (train, tube and lots of buses).

The main thoroughfare, the Broadway, is a shopping hotspot by day – you'll find most chain retailers here, concentrated in the Centre Court shopping centre, formerly the town hall, adjoining Wimbledon station. The dwindling number of independent outlets is partly down to the glut of new-build property developments in the area. The latest, Broadway House, is due for completion in 2009; like the flats on the site of the former Wimbledon football ground, this has drawn controversy, over the demolition of a parade of local shops.

Property has never been cheap in Wimbledon and, if money isn't an issue, there are plenty of razzle-dazzle houses located around Wimbledon Village and the

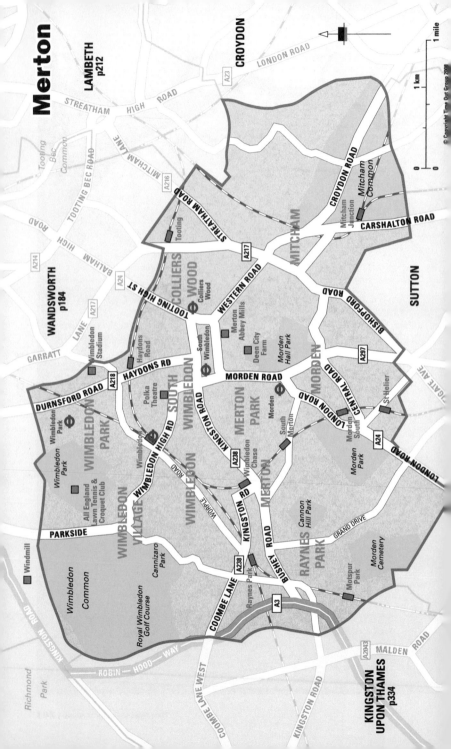

Merton

LAMBETH p212

WANDSWORTH p184

CROYDON

SUTTON

KINGSTON UPON THAMES p334

MALDEN

STREATHAM HIGH ROAD

Tooting Bec Common

TOOTING BEC ROAD

MITCHAM LANE

A216

A214

BALHAM HIGH ROAD

A24

A217

GARRATT LANE

Tooting

STREATHAM ROAD

Wimbledon Stadium

TOOTING HIGH ST

COLLIERS WOOD

Colliers Wood

Haydons Road

South Wimbledon

WESTERN ROAD

A217

MITCHAM

CROYDON ROAD

Mitcham Junction

Mitcham Common

CARSHALTON ROAD

LONDON ROAD

A23

DURNSFORD ROAD

A218

Wimbledon Park

HAYDONS RD

Polka Theatre

Wimbledon Park

WIMBLEDON PARK

SOUTH WIMBLEDON

Merton Abbey Mills

Deen City Farm

Morden Hall Park

MORDEN ROAD

MERTON PARK

Morden

MORDEN

BISHOPSFORD ROAD

St Helier

A297

CENTRAL ROAD

A24

LONDON ROAD

GATE AVE

PARKSIDE

All England Lawn Tennis & Croquet Club

WIMBLEDON VILLAGE

Cannizaro Park

Royal Wimbledon Golf Course

WIMBLEDON HIGH RD

Wimbledon

WORPLE ROAD

KINGSTON ROAD

WIMBLEDON

A238

Wimbledon Chase

MERTON

KINGSTON RD

Raynes Park

RAYNES PARK

Cannon Hill Park

GRAND DRIVE

Morden South

Morden Park

Morden Cemetery

Motspur Park

Windmill

Wimbledon Common

Richmond Park

KINGSTON ROAD

ROBIN HOOD WAY

COOMBE LANE WEST

COOMBE LANE

A238

BUSHEY ROAD

A3

A2043

KINGSTON ROAD

MALDEN ROAD

© Copyright Time Out Group 2008

1 mile

1 km

Common, where prices easily soar into multi-millions. You'll find interesting architectural variety on the upper climes of hilly Arthur Road, adjacent Vineyard Hill Road and the parkside stretch of Wimbledon Park Road (which overlooks a golf club) – but it will cost you.

Residents are also well provided with cultural amenities. Theatregoers have the pick of three venues on the Broadway: the plushly restored New Wimbledon Theatre, its intimate Studio space and the child-friendly jewel that is the Polka Theatre. The area has also spawned an array of acclaimed musicians – current hipsters Jamie T and MIA grew up around here – so it's a shame the nightlife, including a cinema and numerous bars and restaurants, mostly comprises identikit chains.

Wimbledon Village, up the hill from the town centre, is the smartest and most desirable district, with the boutique-lined High Street running through it to Wimbledon Common. A strangely rustic sight for London are the horses that regularly stop the traffic: there's been a riding stables here for over 100 years.

Of Merton's many green spaces, Wimbledon Common (the stamping ground of Elisabeth Beresford's loveable eco-warriors *The Wombles*) offers 1,140 acres of woodland, including its own windmill and golf club. It has also proved popular with fungi foragers, although there has recently been a clampdown on wild mushroom picking. Less famous, but equally unmissable, are the romantic landscaped gardens of Cannizaro House hotel (West Side Common); it's a quaint place to take afternoon tea, while Cannizaro Park features an aviary, sculptures and hosts an annual outdoor theatre festival. One tube stop along the District line, the compact satellite of Wimbledon Park provides another local green haven, including kids' playgrounds, tennis courts, bowling greens, football pitches and a boating lake.

South Wimbledon and Colliers Wood

History hasn't been as well preserved in these neighbourhoods – a shame, as they conceal some of the most interesting local stories. You'd never guess that, in 1963, the Beatles played at the Wimbledon Palais on

Merton High Street – a site that now consists of fairly bland residences.

Merton's new-build phenomenon is most pronounced in South Wimbledon, traditionally the more rough and ready end of the Broadway, but increasingly home to young professionals who've taken advantage of the cheaper property prices. The side streets off Haydons Road are worth checking out for Victorian and Edwardian terraces, while in the so-called 'Poet's Corner' (a quiet enclave from Tennyson Road to Wilfred Owen Close) houses tend to be newer.

Moving towards Colliers Wood, you'll find evidence of the area's cultural mix, from Asian grocers to Irish pubs, plus a few late-night bars and soulless but convenient retail parks. One dubious landmark is the Tower, a 19-storey 1960s concrete office block, which featured in a Channel 4 programme about Britain's worst buildings.

The 12th-century Merton Abbey once educated the likes of Thomas Becket; its ruins can be seen behind the Savacentre supermarket car park. The new apartments

Highs & Lows

▲ **Wimbledon Common** Nature trails, horse tracks, cycle paths, sports grounds – and Wombles, of course
Tennis For two weeks a year, the nation's attention turns to SW19 for the Wimbledon tournament; more enterprising residents set up stalls on their driveways
Global tastes Merton is more cosmopolitan than you might think: foodies can feast on treats from eastern Europe, the Middle East, South Africa and more

Grim patches There's a reason Colliers Wood is so often used as the location for episodes of *The Bill*...
Morden and Mitcham Morden Hall Park is nice, but the streets of these two districts are not massively welcoming at night
New-builds Yes, it's 'progress', but many locals feel new-build developments are sapping the character from the borough. And ▼ who exactly is supposed to afford all these 'luxury apartments'?

here have brought a chain gym and more fast-food outlets to the area – give these a miss, and instead head to the former Liberty silk works at Abbey Mills, which hosts a weekend craft and book market. On summer evenings, this is a convivial spot to drink and catch jazz and folk acts, alongside the River Wandle.

Morden, Mitcham and Raynes Park

Acclaimed young indie rockers the Good Shoes promoted a 2007 song about their home town with the slogan: 'Morden Life Is Rubbish'. Morden might date back further than the Domesday Book (just 14 occupants were recorded here in 1086), but it's seen little improvement since the 1980s.

Located at the southernmost end of the Northern line, this is where Merton Council is based, in the grim Crown House tower block on traffic-clogged London Road. There's no specific town centre, and time was called on its best-known pub, the Crown Inn (apparently for 'additional office space'), in summer 2007; you're better off heading into Wimbledon for nightlife.

Morden Hall Park is a welcome retreat, with meadows, wetlands, waterways and the Old Snuff Mill environmental education centre. There's also a well-stocked garden centre. Head to the park's northern side for Deen City Farm, a big hit with kids.

Like Morden, Mitcham's streets don't seem particularly welcoming after dark – perhaps unsurprisingly, ITV's police drama *The Bill* has been filmed around here (and in neighbouring South Wimbledon) for years. Still, its local shops offer a few treats, including lots of south Asian groceries.

It might be hard to believe that this sprawling suburb was once full of lavender fields (expansive Mitcham Common is now the main local green space), or that remains of a Roman settlement were unearthed near the gasworks. But Mitcham still lays claim to the world's oldest cricket green (dating back to 1730); these days, players have to cross the busy Cricket Green Road to reach the pavilion. It was also home to the pioneering Surrey Iron Railway, between 1803 and 1846; the modern transport links aren't nearly as grand.

Another commuter thoroughfare with rural roots is Raynes Park. Taking its name from 19th-century landowners, it's clearly the most affluent district, with the biggest family residences outside of Wimbledon Village (particularly on Grand Drive), and the lowest crime rates. Developed as a garden suburb (like nearby Merton Park), Raynes Park is sometimes referred to as 'West Wimbledon' by estate agents.

Restaurants & cafés

Merton offers pretty much every kind of chain restaurant on a plate – including such staples as Wagamama and Pizza Express (two branches – on Wimbledon Broadway and Wimbledon Village) and family-friendly Giraffe. In fact, it's even the launch pad for prototype chains – an appealing arrival in 2007 was French brasserie Côte, from the team who conceived the Strada pizza chain (naturally, there's a Strada here too, on Wimbledon High Street). Mini-chain Jo Shmo's (there are branches in Kingston and Guildford) is another decent choice with its buzzy vibe, Americana menu and family-oriented ethos.

A few places with a more personal touch are worth checking out too, such as old-school chippie Broadway Place Fish Bar (locals tend to take away, but you can also eat in the low-key restaurant). La Nonna and Al Forno, meanwhile, are both popular Italian pit-stops. Opposite Wimbledon Park tube, Dalchini – launched by the owners of the sadly defunct Sarkhels in nearby Southfields – specialises in Hakka Indo-Chinese cuisine. Further north, Café 377 (opened 2007) serves up full English breakfasts and fresh smoothies to a mix of builders and local yummy mummies. Bright and informal 'shish and mezze' joint Limon makes an appealing break from the chains, as does kushiyaki (skewer grilling) specialist Kushi-Tei.

Other finds include Watch Me – a cosy and reasonably priced Sri Lankan restaurant on busy Morden Road (the restaurant's name refers to its open kitchen) – and Cah Chi, a convivial Korean canteen in Raynes Park (close to the established Korean community of New Malden; for more, see the Kingston chapter). Cocum offers decent South Indian cuisine.

Al Forno *2A Kings Road, SW19 8QN (8540 5710).*
Broadway Place Fish Bar *8-10 Hartfield Road, SW19 3TA (8947 5333).*
Café 377 *377 Durnsford Road, SW19 8EF (8946 7733).*
Cah Chi *34 Durham Road, SW20 0TW (8947 1081).*
Cocum *9 Approach Road, SW20 8BA (8540 3250/www.cocumrestaurant.co.uk).*
Côte *8 High Street, SW19 5DX (8947 7100/www.cote-restaurants.co.uk).*

Dalchini *147 Arthur Road, SW19 8AB (8947 5966/www.dalchini.co.uk).*
Jo Shmo's *33 High Street, SW19 5BY (8879 3845/www.joshmos.com).*
Kushi-Tei *264 The Broadway, SW19 1SB (8543 1188/www.kushi-tei.com).*
Limon *62 Wimbledon Hill Road, SW19 7PA (8944 5675/www.limonrestaurant.co.uk).*
La Nonna *213-217 The Broadway, SW19 1NL (8542 3060/www.lanonna.co.uk).*
Watch Me *108 Morden Road, SW19 3BP (8286 7900).*

Bars & pubs

Chain bars and pubs dominate the main haul of Wimbledon town centre. Standouts include quirky cocktail bar Sia, and the youthful Suburban Bar & Lounge (though, again, this is part of a burgeoning chain, and occupies the former – independent – Hartfield's Wine Bar). The Alexandra occupies a grand 19th-century building; it has a bijou 'roof garden', but the interior is pretty unexceptional.

For drinks with real character, head further into Wimbledon Village – beyond the chains, you'll find charmingly rustic establishments such as the Fox & Grapes, located on the edge of Wimbledon Common; the supposedly haunted Hand in Hand, which serves old-fashioned fruit wines and draws crowds to the lawn outside in the summer; and the Rose & Crown – a spruced-up Young's hotel that dates from 1659. Also on the High Street is the Eclipse (a popular evening venue, where well-heeled punters splash out on cocktails).

For real ale fans, the Sultan pub in South Wimbledon remains a homely hotspot. Much lauded by CAMRA, it hosts 'beer evenings' every Wednesday. The William Morris, near the Merton Abbey Mills crafts enclave, has a beer garden next to the River Wandle.

Alexandra & Smart Alex *33 Wimbledon Hill Road, SW19 7NE (8947 7691).*
Bar Sia *105-109 The Broadway, SW19 1QG (8540 8339/www.barsia.com).*
Eclipse *57 High Street, SW19 5EE (8944 7722/www.eclipse-ventures.com).*
Fox & Grapes *9 Camp Road, SW19 4UN (8946 5599/www.massivepub.com).*
Hand in Hand *7 Crooked Billet, SW19 4RQ (8946 5720).*
Rose & Crown *55 High Street, SW19 5BA (8947 4713/www.roseandcrownwimbledon.co.uk).*
Suburban Bar & Lounge *27 Hartfield Road, SW19 3SG (8543 9788/www.suburbanbar.com).*

Merton

Sultan *78 Norman Road, SW19 1BT (8542 4532).*
William Morris *20 Watermill Way, SW19 2RD (8540 0216).*

Shops

Merton offers a mixed bag for shopaholics. Wimbledon town centre is the main retail area, with a wide range of high-street chain stores (plus a handful of independent retailers and charity shops) located on the Broadway. Centre Court shopping mall has plenty of familiar names, including a branch of Debenhams. Local department store Elys was revamped in 2007, but retains an old-fashioned atmosphere. There are bigger branches of chains in the Priory Retail Park on Merton High Street.

Even Wimbledon Village, once a bastion of high-end boutiques, is now becoming increasingly chain-led (although these are still of the exclusive mini-chain variety, such as Question Air and the long-established Matches boutique). Also worth a browse on the High Street are Bayley & Sage (speciality foods), Cath Kidston (colourful retro homewares), Diane von Furstenberg (one of just two stand-alone DVF shops in London) and MaxMara. On Church Street, Luella's Boudoir offers shoes, accessories, bridesmaids' dresses and planning advice for brides-to-be.

The borough's compact farmers' market, held every Saturday (9am-1pm) in the playground of Wimbledon Park First School, is popular. The pedestrianised area outside Morrison's supermarket (so-called 'Wimbledon Piazza') also hosts regular continental food markets. And for a more down-to-earth street market experience, Wimbledon Stadium's vast car park features weekend stalls – fruit and veg, clothing and groceries on Sunday, plus a popular car boot sale on Saturday, with second-hand furniture, clothes and music.

DJs and record collectors should also check out Marks Classics, a surprising haven for rare and deleted dance vinyl in otherwise unremarkable Morden. The tunes don't come cheap, but service is friendly.

The industrial estates off busy Durnsford Road conceal the marvellous Vallebona Sardinian Gourmet, open for public tastings most Saturdays between 9.30am and 4pm. It's worth a visit for the climate-controlled cheese room alone.

On the High Street in Colliers Wood, Burge & Gunson is a bathroom centre with strikingly designed furniture and fittings, as well as high-tech toys for those who want to take bathing to a new level. Nearby, the Boat Harbour is a well-stocked nautical shop – and the only place you can get your jet-skis fixed in this neck of the Wood. Near South Wimbledon tube, Architectural Salvage is a good place for unusual interior fittings, including fireplaces and doors.

For gifts and collectibles, stroll around the Merton Abbey Mills market at the weekend; it's a hotchpotch of antiques and crafts (scented candles, jewellery, second-hand books and so on), plus food stalls selling everything from noodle dishes to Belgian waffles. Indulge your

Canine competitors at **Wimbledon Stadium**. *See p210.*

inner hippie at Charlie's Rock Shop, purveyor of healing crystals, windchimes and the like.

Architectural Salvage *83 Haydons Road, SW19 1HH (8543 4450).*
Bayley & Sage *60 High Street, SW19 5EE (8946 9904/www.bayley-sage.co.uk).*
Boat Harbour *40 High Street, SW19 2AB (8542 5857).*
Burge & Gunson *13-27 High Street, SW19 2JE (8543 5166/www.burgeandgunson.co.uk).*
Cath Kidston *3 High Street, SW19 5DX (8944 1001/www.cathkidston.co.uk).*
Centre Court *4 Queens Road, SW19 8YA (8944 8323/www.centrecourtshopping.co.uk).*
Charlie's Rock Shop *The 1929 Shop, Merton Abbey Mills, 18 Watermill Way, SW19 2RD (8544 1207/www.charliesrockshop.com).*
Diane von Furstenberg *56 High Street, SW19 5EE (8944 5995/www.dvf.com).*
Elys of Wimbledon *16 St Georges Road, SW19 4DP (8946 9191/www.elysofwimbledon. co.uk).*
Luella's Boudoir *33 Church Road, SW19 5DQ (8879 7744/www.luellasboudoir.co.uk).*
Marks Classics *25 Abbotsbury Road, SM4 5LJ (8646 4605/www.marksclassics.co.uk).*
Matches *34 High Street, SW19 5BY (8947 8707/www.matchesfashion.com).*
MaxMara *37 High Street, SW19 5BY (8944 1494).*
Merton Abbey Mills *Watermill Way, SW19 2RD (7287 1766/www.mertonabbeymills.com).*
Question Air *77-78 High Street, SW19 5DX (8946 6288/www.question-air.com).*
Vallebona Sardinian Gourmet *Unit 14, 59 Weir Road, SW19 8UG (8944 5665/ www.vallebona.co.uk).*
Wimbledon Farmers' Market *Wimbledon Park First School, Havana Road, SW19 8EJ (7833 0338/www.lfm.org.uk).*
Wimbledon Stadium Market *Wimbledon Stadium Car Park, Plough Lane, SW17 0BL (7240 7405).*

Arts & attractions

Cinemas & theatres

Colour House Theatre *Merton Abbey Mills, Watermill Way, SW19 2RD (8542 5511/ www.wheelhouse.org.uk).*
New Wimbledon Theatre & Studio Theatre *The Broadway, SW19 1QG (0870 060 6646/www.theambassadors.com/newwimbledon).*
Odeon Wimbledon *39 The Broadway, SW19 1QB (0871 224 4007/www.odeon.co.uk).*
Polka Theatre for Children *240 The Broadway, SW19 1SB (8543 4888/www.polka theatre.com).*

Galleries & museums

Wimbledon Lawn Tennis Museum *Centre Court, All England Lawn Tennis & Croquet Club, Church Road, SW19 5AE (8946 6131/www.wimbledon.org/museum).* Reopened in 2006, with new interactive displays enhancing its collection of costumes, memorabilia and film footage.
Wimbledon Society Museum of Local History *22 Ridgway, SW19 4QN (8296 9914/ www.wimbledonmuseum.org.uk).* Charts the 3,000-year history of the area.
Wimbledon Windmill Museum *Windmill Road, Wimbledon Common, SW19 5NR (8947 2825/www.wimbledonwindmillmuseum.org.uk).* This old dear, built in 1817, is still working, but only on high days and holidays.

Other attractions

Buddhapadipa Temple *14 Calonne Road, Wimbledon Parkside, SW19 5HJ (8946 1357/ www.buddhapadipa.org).* London's first Buddhist temple.
Cannizaro House *West Side, Wimbledon Common, SW19 4UE (8879 1464/www. cannizarohouse.com).* Huge Queen Anne mansion, now a hotel; the fabulous gardens are open to the public.

Merton

COUNCIL TAX

		Main borough	Wimbledon Common area
A	up to £40,000	**£902.94**	**£917.87**
B	£40,001-£52,000	**£1,053.42**	**£1,070.84**
C	£52,001-£68,000	**£1,203.92**	**£1,223.83**
D	£68,001-£88,000	**£1,354.40**	**£1,376.80**
E	£88,001-£120,000	**£1,655.38**	**£1,682.76**
F	£120,001-£160,000	**£1,956.36**	**£1,988.71**
G	£160,001-£320,000	**£2,257.34**	**£2,294.67**
H	over £320,000	**£2,708.80**	**£2,753.60**

Deen City Farm *39 Windsor Avenue, SW19 2RR (8543 5300/www.deencityfarm.co.uk).* Tidy-sized community farm on the edge of the beautiful Morden Hall Park Estate.
Merton Priory *Off Merantun Way, Merton Abbey, SW19 2RD (8543 9608/www.merton priory.org).* 12th-century Augustinian priory.
Southside House *3-4 Woodhayes Road, Wimbledon Common, SW19 4RJ (8946 7643/ www.southsidehouse.com).* Grand house, open to visitors (April-Sept) and the site of occasional concerts and lectures.

Sport & fitness

Greenwich Leisure manages Merton's public fitness centres. Merton's private health clubs have to battle for business with the popular chains, but there's enough elitism among the racket-loving Wimbledon Village locals for a continued reign by the independent clubs.

Gyms & leisure centres

Cannons *The Broadway, SW19 1QB (8947 9627/www.cannons.co.uk).* Private.
Canons Leisure Centre *Madeira Road, CR4 4HD (8640 8543/www.gll.org.uk).*
Christopher's Squash & Fitness Club *Wimbledon Stadium, Plough Lane, SW17 0BL (8946 4636/www.christopherssportsclub.co.uk).* Private.
David Lloyd *Bushey Road, SW20 8TE (8543 8020/www.davidlloydleisure.co.uk).* Private.
Esporta *21-33 Worple Road, SW19 4JS (8545 1700/www.esporta.com).* Private.
Fitness First *1-3 Upper Green East, CR4 2PE (8640 9944/www.fitnessfirst.co.uk).* Private.
King's Club *Woodhayes Road, SW19 4TT (8255 5401/www.kcs.org.uk).* Private.
Morden Park Pool *Morden Park, London Road, SM4 5HE (8640 6727/www.gll.org.uk).*
Wimbledon Club *Church Road, SW19 5AG (8971 8090).* Private.
Wimbledon Leisure Centre *Latimer Road, SW19 1EW (8542 1330/www.gll.org.uk).*
Wimbledon Racquets & Fitness Club *Cranbrook Road, SW19 4HD (8947 5806/ www.wimbledonclub.co.uk).* Private.

YMCA *200 The Broadway, SW19 1RY (8542 9055/www.kwymca.org.uk).* Private.
Virgin Active *Battle Close, North Road, SW19 1AQ (8544 9111/www.virginactive.co.uk).* Private.

Other facilities
Wimbledon Village Stables *24A/B High Street, SW19 5DX (8946 8579/www.wvstables.com).*

Spectator sports
All England Lawn Tennis Club *Church Road, SW19 5AE (8946 2244/www.wimbledon.org).* Site of the annual Wimbledon tournament.
Wimbledon Stadium *Plough Lane, SW17 0BL (0870 840 8905/www.lovethedogs.co.uk).* Greyhound and speedway racing.

Schools

WHAT THE PARENTS SAY:

'The primary schools in Merton have always been of a very good standard – all my children had a happy start at Wimbledon Park First School. However, I've found there are fewer options generally as they approach sixth form, unless you're considering going private. There's also more of a focus on single-sex schooling here, although Raynes Park High School is a mixed comprehensive. Some of the schools do have rowdy reputations, and Wimbledon town centre is often packed with noisy schoolgirls in the afternoons. My daughter has just finished her GCSEs at Ricards Lodge High School; she worked really hard and did very well. But, like the rest of my kids, she's leaving the borough to do her A levels.'
Mother of four, Wimbledon

Primary
There are 43 state primary schools in Merton, including 12 church schools. There are also eight independent primaries, including one Norwegian school. See www.merton.gov.uk/ learning, www.edubase.gov.uk and www.ofsted. gov.uk for more information.

Time Out London for Londoners

Secondary

Bishopsford Community School *Lilleshall Road, SM4 6DU (8687 1157/www.bishopsford. org).*
Harris Academy Merton *Wide Way, CR4 1BP (8623 1000/www.harrismerton.org.uk).*
King's College School *Southside, Wimbledon Common, SW19 4TT (8255 5300/www.kcs. org.uk).* Private; boys only.
St Mark's Academy *Acacia Road, CR4 1SF (8648 6627/www.stmarksacademy.com).*
Raynes Park High School *Bushey Road, SW20 0JL (8946 4112/www.raynespark. merton.sch.uk).*
Ricards Lodge High School *Lake Road, SW19 7HB (8946 2208/www.ricardslodge. merton.sch.uk).* Girls only.
Rutlish School *Watery Lane, SW20 9AD (8542 1212/www.rutlish.merton.sch.uk).* Boys only.
Ursuline High School *Crescent Road, SW20 8HA (8255 2688/www.ursulinehigh.merton. sch.uk).* Girls only; mixed sixth form with Wimbledon College.
Wimbledon College *Edge Hill, SW19 4NS (8946 2533/www.wimbledoncollege.org.uk).* Boys only; mixed sixth form with Ursuline High School.

Property

WHAT THE AGENTS SAY:

'Wimbledon is well known for the obvious, but there is a lot more to it than tennis. The travel links are good, as are the local shops, restaurants, the Common – it's got a little bit of everything. The Village is where the money is, we've had properties there going for four or five million. The town is more built-up, with more grid-like streets, but you frequently see properties for two to three million. South Wimbledon is not as nice, but is changing all the time. If you go past the theatre, there's a huge residential and commercial development that will change the face of the area.'
Marcus Short, Hawes & Co, Wimbledon Broadway

Average property prices

Detached £1,821,561
Semi-detached £485,524
Terraced £347,413
Flat £250,094

Local estate agents

Christopher St James *61 High Street, SW19 2JF (8296 1270/www.christopher-st-james.plc.uk).*
Cross & Prior *85 The Broadway, SW19 1QE (8540 2299/www.crossprior.com).*
Dicksons *194 Merton High Street, SW19 1AX (8542 8595/www.dicksons-estate.com).*
Eddison White *34 Christchurch Road, SW19 2NX (8540 9828/www.eddisonwhite. co.uk).*
Ellisons *www.ellisons.uk.com; 3 offices in the borough (Wimbledon 8944 9494/Raynes Park 8944 9595/Morden 8543 1166).*
Hawes & Co *www.hawesandco.co.uk; 4 offices in the borough (Wimbledon Village 8946 1000/Wimbledon Broadway 8542 6600/ Wimbledon Park 8947 1000/Raynes Park 8946 3000).*
Reynolds *44 Coombe Lane, SW20 0LD (8946 6511/www.reynolds-estates.co.uk).*

Other information

Council

London Borough of Merton Council *Civic Centre, London Road, Morden, Surrey SM4 5DX (8274 4901/www.merton.gov.uk).*
Out-of-hours Social Services *Sutton Civic Offices (8770 5000).*

Legal services

Merton Law Centre *112 London Road, SM4 5AX (8543 4069/www.lawcentres.org.uk).*

Local newspapers

My Merton *www.merton.gov.uk/mymerton.* Council magazine distributed across the borough every two months; also available online.
Wimbledon Guardian *www.wimbledonguardian.co.uk.*
Wimbledon News *www.wimbledonnews.co.uk.*

Allotments & open spaces

Council Allotments *8545 3665/www.merton.gov.uk/allotments.*
Open spaces *www.merton.gov.uk/parks.*

Merton

'Lambeth is a potent mix of sights and sounds, colours and cultures – with a heart that no amount of bad press or faceless gentrification will stop from beating'

Jay Halliday, Brixton Walking Tours

Lambeth

A multicultural microcosm of everything London has to offer, Lambeth mixes some of the capital's most exciting nightlife with sprawling open spaces, gastropubs with greasy spoons, luxurious Victorian refurbs with crime-crippled estates and a spectacular riverside retreat that's as popular with locals as it is with tourists. When a man is tired of Lambeth, he is truly tired of life.

Neighbourhoods

South Bank, Waterloo and Lambeth North

Though it has Lambeth's lowest population, the South Bank remains one of the best bets in town for weekend unwinding or entertaining out-of-towners. Stunning Thames views make it a place that even the hardest of hearts would have to struggle not to enjoy. The stretch between Westminster Bridge and Blackfriars Bridge is where most of the tourist money gets spent – there's the London Aquarium, the London Eye, Royal Festival Hall, the Hayward Gallery, the IMAX Cinema, BFI Southbank and the National Theatre. (The Saatchi Gallery in County Hall closed in 2005, but is due to reopen in Chelsea in 2008.) There's also a huge range of places to eat and drink, with some of the most popular clustered outside the refurbished Royal Festival Hall and around terraced Gabriel's Wharf, while nearby Oxo Tower (which falls into the borough of Southwark) offers alternatives with views to die for.

Lambeth locals also benefit from the array of free entertainment on offer in the area. Assorted festivals and open-air

Lambeth

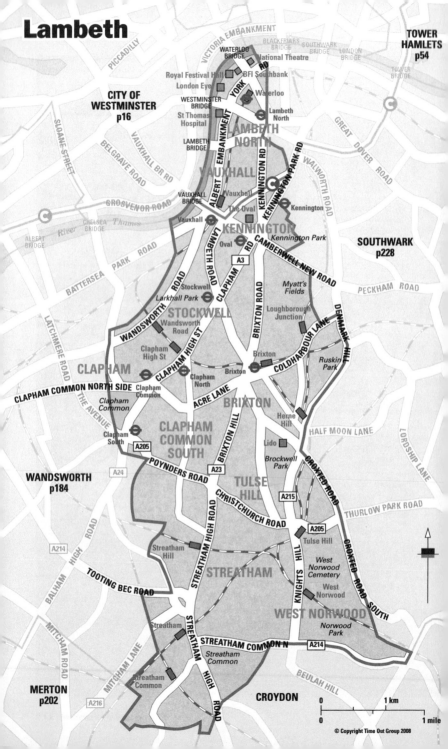

Lambeth

TOWER HAMLETS p54

CITY OF WESTMINSTER p16

VICTORIA EMBANKMENT

BLACKFRIARS BRIDGE

SOUTHWARK BRIDGE

LONDON BRIDGE

TOWER BRIDGE

National Theatre

WATERLOO BRIDGE

RD

Royal Festival Hall

BFI Southbank

London Eye

YORK

Waterloo

WESTMINSTER BRIDGE

St Thomas' Hospital

Lambeth North

LAMBETH NORTH

GREAT DOVER ROAD

LAMBETH BRIDGE

VAUXHALL

KENNINGTON RD

KENNINGTON PARK RD

WALWORTH ROAD

ALBERT EMBANKMENT

VAUXHALL BRIDGE

Vauxhall

Kennington

The Oval

SOUTHWARK p228

Vauxhall

ALBERT BRIDGE

CHELSEA BRIDGE

GROSVENOR ROAD

River Thames

KENNINGTON

LAMBETH RD

Oval

CAMBERWELL NEW ROAD

Kennington Park

PECKHAM ROAD

A3

BATTERSEA PARK ROAD

SLOANE STREET

BELGRAVE ROAD

VAUXHALL BR RD

WANDSWORTH ROAD

Stockwell

Myatt's Fields

LATCHMERE ROAD

Larkhall Park

STOCKWELL

Loughborough Junction

DENMARK HILL

Wandsworth Road

BRIXTON ROAD

COLDHARBOUR LANE

Clapham High St

Brixton

Ruskin Park

CLAPHAM

CLAPHAM HIGH ST

Brixton

Clapham North

Clapham Common

ACRE LANE

BRIXTON

CLAPHAM COMMON NORTH SIDE

Clapham Common

Clapham Common

Herne Hill

HALF MOON LANE

THE AVENUE

BRIXTON HILL

Clapham South

Lido

LORDSHIP LANE

A205

CLAPHAM COMMON SOUTH

Brockwell Park

WANDSWORTH p184

A24

POYNDERS ROAD

A23

TULSE HILL

CROXTED ROAD

A215

THURLOW PARK ROAD

CHRISTCHURCH ROAD

A205

Tulse Hill

A214

STREATHAM HIGH ROAD

KNIGHTS HILL

West Norwood Cemetery

CROXTED ROAD SOUTH

Streatham Hill

STREATHAM

West Norwood

BALHAM HIGH ROAD

TOOTING BEC ROAD

WEST NORWOOD

Norwood Park

MITCHAM ROAD

Streatham

STREATHAM HIGH ROAD

Streatham Common N

A214

BEULAH HILL

MITCHAM LANE

Streatham Common

MERTON p202

A216

Streatham Common

HIGH ROAD

CROYDON

0 — 1 km

0 — 1 mile

© Copyright Time Out Group 2008

summer events take place, as well as occasional raves on the banks of the Thames, while beneath Queen Elizabeth Hall, you'll find the spiritual home of London skateboarding. Living here, however, remains prohibitively expensive, and not just on the river itself. The priciest penthouse flats in the Perspective building at 100 Westminster Bridge Road, just beside Lambeth North tube station, head ever closer to the £5 million mark – proof, if proof were needed, that the 'South Bank Effect' is slowly creeping south and eradicating the character of what was once one of London's seediest but most soulful areas. Baylis Road retains some less upmarket local authority housing, but gone are the legendary market stalls of Lambeth Walk, now home to modern flat developments that make it hard to believe the famous promenade ever existed at all.

Between Lambeth North and the South Bank sits Waterloo, best known to tourists for Terry and Julie's legendary sunset encounter and for its train station, although the latter's importance suffered a major blow in 2007 when the international Eurostar service moved to refurbished St Pancras station. At least the terminal ugliness of the Westminster Bridge Road end has been eased by the long overdue demolition of the former County Hall Island Block – voted Britain's 11th ugliest building in a Channel 4 programme – and the construction of the Park Plaza aparthotel, due for completion in 2010. Until then, Waterloo boasts everything from the community market stalls of Lower Marsh Street to the gastropubs of the Cut – the latter popular with those anticipating or reflecting on a night of theatrical entertainment at either the Old or Young Vics – while the bridge continues to offer one of the capital's best views, at sunset or any other time.

Vauxhall

All that is left of the sprawling Vauxhall Pleasure Gardens, which drew visitors from all over the world between the 17th and 19th centuries, is a miniature park called Spring Gardens, the area having traded green for grey following the completion of Vauxhall Bridge in 1816 and the subsequent establishment of heavy industrial centres for the likes of Royal

Doulton, Marmite and Vauxhall Iron Works, which later became the car manufacturer.

The Vauxhall of today is a smog-shrouded criss-cross of major roads and underpasses, a hectic interchange with a strangely forlorn air despite its central location and riverside views of Tate Britain and Millbank Tower. Heavy industry gave way to offices long ago – most noticeably the bizarre structure housing the MI6 headquarters – and the local demographic includes a large number of MPs and civil servants thanks to the proximity of Parliament.

Not that it's all po-faced and political: Vauxhall is also home to one of the most thriving gay communities in London, with clubs like Fire and pubs like the legendary Royal Vauxhall Tavern at its core. The resulting carnival of madness regularly stretches weekends into Mondays and even Tuesdays, giving sedated suits and ties something to ogle in disbelief as they shuffle into work.

And while Vauxhall isn't the most aesthetically inspired corner of the capital, the new bus station by engineering giants Arup – with its enigmatic ramped roof and solar-powered lighting – may well be a sign of things to come. The area is also home to various charming corners, including lovely pubs and cafés, wonderful Vauxhall City Farm (on Tyers Street) and some well tended allotments.

Kennington

Traditionally a working-class area, Kennington was once blighted by the fumes of countless factories (the Hayward's pickle factory's acrid smell plagued a young Charlie Chaplin) and largely bereft of entertainment save the Lambeth Walk, an evening promenade immortalised in Noel Gay's song of the same name from the 1937 musical *Me and My Girl*.

These days, Kennington is increasingly popular with first-time buyers thanks to its tube station and the wide variety of housing (from LCC estates of various vintages to the Duchy of Cornwall cottages west of Kennington Cross). It's also a political hangout of sorts – the faces of Charles Kennedy and John Prescott feature prominently in the windows of the Kennington Tandoori. Nor is the place's relationship with politics limited to the

Lambeth

mainstream, with incidents of political dissent dating from the Chartist rally of 1848 all the way up to the final eviction in 2005 of squatters who had occupied the entirety of St Agnes Place for over 30 years.

That said, and despite its location on a major crossroads at the edge of the congestion charge zone, Kennington remains a peaceful place to live thanks to Kennington Park (home to an excellent concrete skate bowl dating back to the late 1970s) and a range of local amenities including the White Bear pub theatre and Cleaver Square, a secluded space lined with gorgeous Georgian houses. For many, however, Kennington is all about cricket, with the nearby Brit Oval sending the place into a beer-fuelled hysteria that can often be felt (and heard) for miles around.

Stockwell and South Lambeth

For many people, the horrific shooting of Brazilian plumber Jean Charles de Menezes was the first event that brought the name 'Stockwell' to their attention – hardly a favourable first impression for a place already blighted by higher than average crime levels and an overabundance of unattractive concrete blocks.

Yet it's not all bad news. Stockwell remains a popular location for first-time buyers unable to afford Clapham but keen to avoid the bustle of Brixton. There are various amenities beyond that notorious tube station (now home to a semi-permanent memorial), most of them – including charming Larkhall Park, assorted sweeping, tree-lined Victorian streets and a real-life Albert Square – lying west of Clapham Road. There's also the local air-raid-shelter-turned-war-memorial complete with colourful murals, 19th-century St Michael's Church with its stained-glass windows by John Trinick, and looming Stockwell Bus Garage, built in 1952 and surely the only listed bus depot in London. And while Stockwell may have remained largely in the margins of London's history books since its days as a 17th-century village green, it was once home to Vincent Van Gogh, whose former house on Hackford Road is marked by a blue plaque. It's a short walk from the Type Museum, a favourite with font fanatics the world over.

Stockwell is also home to one of London's best skateparks, a rare example of 1980s concrete wave construction that draws skaters from across the country and provides an excellent resource for kids from the surrounding estates. Local boozers vary from sweat-box meat markets like the Swan to more genteel establishments; restaurants from tatty takeaways to the numerous bars,

Lively, multicultural, unmissable **Brixton Market** – a London icon.

restaurants and bakeries of South Lambeth Road, known as Little Portugal thanks to its sizeable Portuguese contingent.

Property-wise, Stockwell is a mix of Victorian terraces jostling for space with council and ex-council blocks – not the most visually attractive place, perhaps, but somewhere with a strong sense of community that causes many to stick around longer than they'd intended.

Brixton

Few places embody the potential harmony of London's multicultural make-up like Brixton, yet its name retains a certain notoriety (usually among those who have never set foot in the place) thanks to decades of social unrest that ghettoised its large Caribbean contingent and led to widespread rioting in the 1980s. Nor has the area emerged entirely unscathed: drug-peddling remains rife on certain streets, and the blaring of police sirens is a constant reminder of the gun and knife crime between gangs on less salubrious estates.

Not that this is something that overly bothers the influx of (mostly) white, middle-class professionals staking a claim on the place thanks to its affordable housing, ease of access and seemingly limitless capacity to entertain.

Gentrification continues apace, especially in the charming Victorian housing forking off Acre Lane and Effra Road, but seems destined never to completely uproot the Caribbean character: sure, there are occasional stabs at exclusivity – the unmarked Modern European restaurant Upstairs on Acre Lane, for example – but for the most part it's a case of community in action, from the West Indian foods and wares of the market stalls behind the railway station (including those on Electric Avenue, the first shopping street in London to boast electric lighting) to the wealth of cross-cultural bars and restaurants.

Nor does the area's creative fire (a few of those to namecheck Brixton in their songs include Pink Floyd, Eddy Grant and the Clash, who cut their teeth in the back room of the Telegraph pub) seem in any danger of sputtering out soon, thanks to a range of artistic amenities including the awesome Ritzy cinema, the upstairs café of which has a wonderfully international music programme of its own.

There's also a rash of small, eclectic venues such as the Windmill (near Brixton's actual windmill, in use until the construction of a nearby building blocked out the wind in 1860) and the Effra, which has excellent jazz acts. A stone's throw way, Brixton Academy hosts international superstars and souped-up club nights alike, while a rash of more conventional nightlife venues (Plan B, the Fridge, Mass) ensure that the High Street is often as busy at 6am as it is at 6pm.

One thing Brixton does lack, however, is a decent open space of its own, although Max Roach Park (named after the late jazz drummer) does have a nature trail and a children's play area, and it's only a ten-minute walk to Brockwell Park, with its programme of festivals (from seasonal fairs to cannabis legalisation rallies) and refurbished lido. Brixton Recreation Centre is also undergoing a rolling renovation programme that aims to bring its facilities bang up to date.

Clapham and Clapham North

Everyone has an opinion on Clapham, from embittered locals raging at the braying rugger buggers cluttering up their High Street on weekends, to aspiring near-neighbours who see it as an idyllic mix of the sleepily suburban and the fiercely forward-thinking.

Whatever the angle, there's no denying the increasingly lurid diplays of wealth – the fleets of bankers in their soft-top Porsches, some of them barely out of university; their WAGish girlfriends weighed down with bags from the local boutiques – but there's a real community feel to Clapham that no amount of money can erase. Its Picturehouse is one of the best cinemas in London, and the Landor one of the best pub theatres.

The cream of Clapham's society types tend to settle around Old Town, a genteel quadrangle of posh shops, tarted-up pubs and premium-value Victorian property – there are even three Queen Anne-style houses (nos.39, 41 and 43) – that also doubles as a bus depot. Not that it's all swank and celebrity-spotting. Clapham can also be seen as something of a cultural melting pot, with million-pound dream houses sited a stone's throw from council estates harking back to the area's less upwardly mobile era.

For the most part, however, Clapham is more up-and-come than up-and-coming, its High Street crammed with faceless bars pumping lobotomised house music and packed on weekends with obnoxiously

inebriated young professionals on the pull. That said, there are plenty more enigmatic establishments off the beaten track, from bohemian local pubs like Bread & Roses to quirky clubs such as Lost Society and a plethora of decent restaurants.

Clapham Common South and Clapham Park

Clapham Common South actually straddles the border of Lambeth and Wandsworth – the line runs through the Common, although Lambeth technically controls the area – and enjoys an aesthetic that manages to be neither entirely Balham nor Clapham proper, but a strange mix of mundane and magnificent. Clapham's regenerative tendrils have taken hold along the South Side itself, host to increasingly swanky eating and drinking options, while Abbeville Road, with its flower-shrouded Victorian houses, shops and restaurants, was a destination for society types long before the fancy franchises of the High Street started turning a trade. However, not all locals live a charmed life: the nearby Clapham Park Estate was notorious enough for journalist Polly Toynbee to

Highs & Lows

▲ **Arts attack** Music, theatre, film, art: culture vultures are spoilt for choice at the numerous world-class venues around the South Bank
Room to breathe Clapham Common, Streatham Common, Kennington Park, West Norwood Cemetery – Lambeth has more than its fair share of sprawling open spaces
No sleep till Brixton Jazz at the Effra, breaking bands at the Windmill, global superstars at the Academy, plus DJs at Plan B and the Telegraph

Crime Lambeth has a disturbing level of everything from muggings and drug dealing to gang-related murders
Clapham High Street at night The bars filled with pukey boys, the barely dressed girls passed out in doorways, the grown men in suits relieving themselves by the cashpoint
Stone cold ugliness Lambeth still has too many grim intersections blighted by concrete monstrosities

settle here in 2003 while researching her book *Hard Work: Life in Low-Pay Britain*.

Regardless of income, however, Clapham Common itself remains a democratic place to rest, recharge or run riot – reason enough to want to live here. Sure, summer months see informal public school reunions determined to turn the entire common into one big beer garden, but it's not all moronic chanting and yummy mummies – you're just as likely to see a full cross-section of south London living, from Jamaican barbecue parties and children flying kites to bell-ringing weed dealers, sunbathing kids from the surrounding estates and, later in the evening, gay cruisers straying momentarily from the bijou wooded stretch to the west.

Streatham

Streatham's reputation is inextricably bound up with its High Street, voted the worst street in Britain in a controversial 2002 BBC poll due to its mix of damaged paving, downtrodden (and occasionally downright empty) shopfronts and less discerning nightlife options, including Caesars, a rite of passage for button-down boys and their criminally under-clothed girlfriends since the year dot. Then there are the albums of negative press cuttings: most notably the prostitutes loitering around St Leonard's (the area has been tied with the sex trade since Cynthia Payne set up her notorious brothel on Ambleside Avenue) and the woefully regular incidents of gun and knife crime.

Not that it puts off first-time buyers: Streatham has been an initial rung on the property ladder for decades, something attributable to its relative ease of access (estate agents often refer to it as 'Brixton Hill' to make the Victoria line sound closer than it is) and affordable house prices. That said, there is a growing diversity among both the types of properties (from Victorian terraces to spacious 20th-century housing estates) and their prices – those around the Telford Park conservation area tend to go for a third more than those in Streatham Vale, for example. And while crime may make the headlines, there remains a widespread community spirit (seen in pubs like the recently reopened Earl Ferrers, meetings of the popular Streatham Society and occasional residents' street parties,

bunting and all), not to mention a range of amenities, including the Streatham Ice Arena (threatened with rebuilding to Olympic standard as part of a Tesco-centred 'Streatham Hub', although spiralling costs have left plans looking less than certain) and sprawling Streatham Common.

Tulse Hill and West Norwood

Tulse Hill is the embodiment of south London suburbia: it feels peaceful and settled, even in the less picturesque estates. Housing tends to cluster in identikit rows of net-curtained semis, although the whole spectrum is represented, from affordable flats on the site of the former Tulse Hill School (erstwhile educator of Ken Livingstone) to the Regency-style

Lambeth

parkside houses and apartments where the Dick Shepherd School used to be.

That is not to say that all the local schools in this area have been turned into residences: West Norwood has plenty, both private and state, encouraging an influx of young families. There's a real sense of community here, with active local churches, the L'Arche centre for disabled residents, a mix of local pubs and restaurants and the excellent South London Theatre. There are also various fascinating buildings in the neighbourhood – from the South London Botanical Institute to the Old Library (designed by Sidney Smith of Tate Britain fame) – not to mention a wealth of open spaces including child-friendly Norwood Park and sprawling West Norwood Cemetery, the latter an overgrown testament to Victorian grandeur rivalling any in the city.

And while there's no tube line, West Norwood is very well served by trains and buses to the West End and beyond. Only in the eating, drinking and retail stakes does the area suffer: decent pubs and restaurants are few and far between, and Norwood High Street is no upmarket shopping mecca, although the recent installation of a CCTV system has at least made it a safer place to stroll after the night bus drops you off.

Restaurants & cafés

Once a dining desert, the South Bank's restaurant scene has improved massively following the Royal Festival Hall revamp. For classy Modern European fare and fantastic Thames views, try Skylon, or, for cheaper British dishes, Canteen – both attached to the RFH. There's a host of chain options just outside, next to the river, including Giraffe, Strada and Wagamama, as well as dim sum at Ping Pong and Latin American at Las Iguanas. Diners here tend to be either tourists or theatregoers, with a resulting tendency for large crowds and above-average prices – especially within the clutter of terraced bars and restaurants in Gabriel's Wharf. Old-timer wine bar-restaurant the Archduke has decent pre-theatre options, while Japanese Ozu is the best of the various eateries inside County Hall (although locals tend to prefer the less showy Inshoku, on Lower Marsh).

Waterloo has various eating options: the Cut alone boasts long-standing gastropub the Anchor & Hope and branches of Pizza Paradiso, Livebait and Tas, while Troia is a decent Turkish on the blind side of the London Eye. Budget options include standout chippie Masters Super Fish (on the Lambeth/Southwark border) and any of the unpretentious cafés closer to Lambeth North – Perdoni's, with its all-day breakfasts and Italian standards, is pick of the crop.

Vauxhall is a less assured dining destination, although there is a decent Portuguese port of call in the form of the Madeira Pâtisserie and a popular BYO vegetarian diner, the Bonnington Centre Café. Nearby Kennington is better served, from the nautical but nice French fish restaurant Lobster Pot and Eritrean outpost Adulis, to the cheap and cheerful Windmill Fish Bar and a newly opened branch of the Dulwich-born gastro bastion Franklins. The Kennington Tandoori is favoured by high-profile political types (as testified by various politico snaps greying behind the glass).

Further south, Stockwell boasts an excellent Spanish restaurant, Rebato's, and quality Indian and West African curries at Hot Stuff. The neighbourhood is also predictably heavy on Portuguese cuisine,

Lambeth

with Bar Estrela (*see p223*) the best for flawless puddings and a party vibe, especially during Portuguese football games, and nearby Grelha d'Ouro nipping closely at its heels. Brixton is similarly big on international flavours, with places such as Eritrean restaurant Asmara and Caribbean hotspots Bamboula and Negril keeping the area's large African and West Indian communities smiling. Recent years have seen Brixton's culinary remit grow relentlessly, with Thai food on a budget at Baan Thai, 'world tapas' at the upmarket Brixton Bar & Grill and artful Modern European cuisine at the unmarked Upstairs.

It's Clapham, however, that retains the prize for the most diverse list of restaurants in Lambeth. Sure, those on the High Street tend to be branches of upmarket chains (there are a few exceptions, including Polish paradise Café Wanda and upbeat Tex-Mex cantina Café Sol), but dive off the beaten track and you'll find yourself spoilt for choice. Clapham North is well served by excellent Japanese restaurant Tsunami and sophisticated Modern European newcomer Fouronine. Old Town has also had a boost with two recent arrivals: expect French flair at award-winning Trinity and upmarket Italian dishes at Mooli. Clapham Common tube overlooks adventurous internationals Rapscallion and the Sequel, and Gallic stalwart Gastro. Over in Clapham Park, meanwhile, long-standing brasserie Newtons continues to serve the bohemian baby boomers of Abbeville Road.

Streatham is less well developed when it comes to eating out, although there are a few alternatives to the High Street's faceless takeaways, including party-hearty Tex-Mex favourite El Chicos, vegetarian café Wholemeal (which does an excellent homity pie) and Perfect Blend, café by day, bar-restaurant by night and easily the best turned-out eaterie on the High Street. There are also a couple of good Asian options, Slurp and Oishii, with staff at the latter notorious for drawing out games of Chinese poker long after they've drawn the blinds.

Adulis 44-46 Brixton Road, SW9 6BT (7587 0055/www.adulis.co.uk).
Anchor & Hope 36 The Cut, SE1 8LP (7928 9898).
Archduke Concert Hall Approach, SE1 8XU (7928 9370/www.thearchduke.co.uk).
Asmara 386 Coldharbour Lane, SW9 8LF (7737 4144).

Baan Thai 401 Coldharbour Lane, SW9 8LQ (7737 5888/www.baanthairestaurant.co.uk).
Bamboula 12 Acre Lane, SW2 5SG (7737 6633/www.walkerswood.com).
Bonnington Centre Café 11 Vauxhall Grove, SW8 1TD (7820 7466).
Brixton Bar & Grill 15 Atlantic Road, SW9 8HX (7737 6777).
Café Sol 56 Clapham High Street, SW4 7UL (7498 9319/www.cafesol.net).
Café Wanda 153 Clapham High Street, SW4 7SS (7738 8760).
Canteen Royal Festival Hall, Belvedere Road, SE1 8XX (0845 686 1122/www.canteen.co.uk).
El Chicos 62 Streatham High Road, SW16 1DA (8677 5100).
Fouronine 409 Clapham Road, SW9 9BT (7737 0722/www.fouronine.co.uk).
Franklins 205-209 Kennington Lane, SE11 5QS (7793 8313/www.franklins restaurant.com).
Gastro 67 Venn Street, SW4 0BD (7627 0222).
Giraffe Riverside Level, Belvedere Road, SE1 8XX (7928 2004/www.giraffe.net).
Grelha d'Ouro 151 South Lambeth Road, SW8 1XN (7735 9764/www.grelhadouro.com).
Hot Stuff 19 Wilcox Road, SW8 2XA (7720 1480).
Las Iguanas Festival Terrace, Belvedere Road, SE1 8XX (7620 1328/www.iguanas.co.uk).
Inshoku 23-24 Lower Marsh, SE1 7RJ (7928 2311).
Kennington Tandoori 313 Kennington Road, SE11 4QE (7735 9247).
Livebait 41-45 The Cut, SE1 8LF (7928 7211).
Lobster Pot 3 Kennington Lane, SE11 4RG (7582 5556/www.lobsterpotrestaurant.co.uk).
Madeira Pâtisserie 46A-C Albert Embankment, SE1 7TL (7820 1117).
Masters Super Fish 191 Waterloo Road, SE1 8UX (7928 6924).
Mooli 36A Old Town, SW4 0LB (7627 1166/ www.moolirestaurant.com).
Negril 132 Brixton Hill, SW2 1RS (8674 8798).
Newtons 33-35 Abbeville Road, SW4 9LA (8673 0977/www.newtonsrestaurants.co.uk).
Oishii 70 Streatham Hill, SW2 4RD (8674 6888).
Ozu County Hall, Westminster Bridge Road, SE1 7BH (7928 7766/www.ozulondon.com).
Perdoni's 18-20 Kennington Road, SE1 7BL (7928 6846).
Perfect Blend 8-9 Streatleigh Parade, Streatham High Road, SW16 1EQ (8769 4646/ www.perfect-blend.co.uk).
Ping Pong Festival Terrace, Belvedere Road, SE1 8XX (7960 4160/www. pingpongdimsum.com).
Pizza Paradiso 61 The Cut, SE1 8LL (7261 1221/www.pizzaparadiso.co.uk).
Rapscallion 75 Venn Street, SW4 0BD (7787 6555/www.therapscallion.co.uk).
Rebato's 169 South Lambeth Road, SW8 1XW (7735 6388/www.rebatos.com).
Sequel 75 Venn Street, SW4 0BD (7622 4222/ www.thesequelclapham.com).

Skylon *Southbank Centre, Belvedere Road, SE1 8XX (7654 7800/www.danddlondon.com).*
Slurp *104-106 Streatham High Road, SW16 1BW (8677 7786).*
Strada *Riverside Level, Belvedere Road, SE1 8XX (7401 9126/www.strada.co.uk).*
Tas *33 The Cut, SE1 8LF (7928 2111/ www.tasrestaurant.com).*
Trinity *4 The Polygon, Clapham Old Town, SW4 0JG (7622 1199/www.trinityrestaurant. co.uk).*
Troia *3F Belvedere Road, SE1 7GQ (7633 9309).*
Tsunami *5-7 Voltaire Road, SW4 6DQ (7978 1610/www.tsunamirestaurant.co.uk).*
Upstairs Bar & Restaurant *89B Acre Lane, SW2 5TN (7733 8855).*
Wagamama *Riverside Level, Belvedere Road, SE1 8XX (7021 0877/www.wagamama.com).*
Wholemeal *1 Shrubbery Road, SW16 2AS (8769 2423/www.wholemealcafe.com).*
Windmill Fish Bar *211 Kennington Lane, SE11 5QS (7582 5754).*

Bars & pubs

There are few places more fertile for nightlife venues to prosper than Brixton, a result of its blend of street cred and increasingly monied young professionals on the prowl for a good time. The list of clubs seems never-ending, from legendary trance and techno behemoth the Fridge and nearby Mass, set in converted St Matthew's Church,

TRANSPORT

Tube stations *Bakerloo* Waterloo, Lambeth North; *Northern* Waterloo, Kennington, Oval, Stockwell, Clapham North, Clapham Common, Clapham South; *Victoria* Vauxhall, Stockwell, Brixton
Rail stations *South Eastern Trains* Brixton, Herne Hill; *Southern* Waterloo East; Wandsworth Road, Clapham High Street; Streatham Common, Streatham, Tulse Hill, West Norwood, Streatham Hill; *South West Trains* Waterloo, Vauxhall; *First Capital Connect Thameslink* Loughborough Junction, Herne Hill, Tulse Hill, Streatham
Main bus routes *into central London* 1, 2, 3, 4, 12, 26, 35, 42, 45, 59, 68, 76, 77, 77A, 87, 88, 133, 137, 139, 159, 168, 171, 172, 176, 188, 243, 341, 344, 436, 521, RV1, X68; *night buses* N1, N2, N3, N35, N44, N68, N76, N77, N133, N137, N155, N159, N171, N381, N343; *24-hour buses* 12, 88, 139, 176, 188, 243, 341, 344

to the more upmarket Plan B and spanking new members' club Dex. Then there's the seemingly endless list of DJ bars and pubs – the always heaving White Horse, Acres, the Dogstar, Caribbean Mango Landin' and the recently refurbed Telegraph, with its throbbing dance and live music venue – plus enigmatic institutions such as jazz dive the Effra and the Windmill, an achingly out-there pub stage that has hosted everyone from Hard Fi to Hot Chip. Not that it's all swinging, swaying and records playing: those seeking a quiet pint are equally well served by a range of characterful pubs including the Trinity Arms and the Duke of Edinburgh, which has a superb beer garden.

Options become more limited towards Stockwell, although the Far Side does a good job of pandering to residents who like to pretend they live in Clapham, the Priory Arms and Surprise are good local pubs, and there are several places catering to the Portuguese contingent – the best is Bar Estrela, which heaves during Portuguese football games. The Swan, meanwhile, is a cavernous meat market hosting tribute bands and is popular with Antipodeans.

Streathamites are best off trekking down Brixton Hill, although local alternatives include the Railway (which also does decent food), aspiring cocktail bar Mint and a handful of locals' locals including the recently reopened Earl Ferrers. Nor are Tulse Hill or West Norwood exactly drinking destinations, although Kennington is developing nicely as a self-contained nightspot, with community boozers such as the Beehive and the Prince of Wales on charming Cleaver Square, upbeat melting pots like the Dog House, the White Hart and the Three Stags (now unrecognisable as the pub in which Charlie Chaplin's father drank himself to death) and even a courageously camp Hawaiian theme bar, South London Pacific.

Vauxhall's gay scene tends to wet its whistle at the Royal Vauxhall Tavern, while the Fentiman Arms fills the gastro gap and the new Riverside boasts floor-to-ceiling windows and a contemporary piazza setting. Then, of course, there's Clapham, where come weekends it's hard to take a step without tripping over a casualty from one of the various joyless vodka and cocktail bars along the High Street. That said, there are more personable places to

Award-winning bar **Lost Society**.

drink locally, including lefties' favourite
Bread & Roses, the Windmill on the
Common and the Abbeville, plus a handful
of quirky venues such as Lost Society that
have far more to offer than rugger-bugger
dens like Revolution and Inferno's.

Waterloo has more than its fair share
of fine drinking establishments, from
gastropub the Anchor & Hope (*see p221*)
and real ale favourite the King's Arms to
Cubana and theatre bars at the Old and
Young Vics (Pit Bar and the Cut Bar).
Finally, poor weather notwithstanding,
drinking on the South Bank is its own
reward: there may be an absence of
characterful bars, but few people-watching
experiences beat a pint in a plastic glass
on the wooden benches outside the Film
Café, beneath Waterloo Bridge.

Abbeville *67-69 Abbeville Road, SW4 9JW*
(8675 2201).
Acres *40 Acre Lane, SW2 5SP (7978 9796/*
www.acresbar.co.uk).
Bar Estrela *111-115 South Lambeth Road,*
SW8 1UZ (7793 1051).
Beehive *51 Durham Street, SE11 5JA*
(7582 7608).
Bread & Roses *68 Clapham Manor Street,*
SW4 6DZ (7498 1779/www.breadandroses
pub.com).

Cubana *48 Lower Marsh, SE1 7RG*
(7928 8778/www.cubana.co.uk).
Cut Bar *The Young Vic, 66 The Cut, SE1 8LZ*
(7928 4400/www.thecutbar.com).
Dex *467 Brixton Road, SW9 8HH (7326 4455/*
www.dexclub.co.uk).
Dog House *293 Kennington Road, SE11 6BY*
(7820 9310).
Dogstar *389 Coldharbour Lane, SW9 8LQ*
(7733 7515/www.thedogstar.co.uk).
Duke of Edinburgh *204 Ferndale Road,*
SW9 8AG (7326 0301).
Earl Ferrers *22 Ellora Road, SW16 6JF*
(8835 0354).
Effra *38A Kellet Road, SW2 1EB (7274 4180).*
Far Side *144 Stockwell Road, SW9 9TQ*
(7095 1401).
Fentiman Arms *64 Fentiman Road, SW8 1LA*
(7793 9796).
Film Café *BFI Southbank, Belvedere Road,*
SE1 8XT (7633 0274/www.bfi.org.uk).
Fridge *1 Town Hall Parade, Brixton Hill,*
SW2 1RJ (7326 5100).
Inferno's *146 Clapham High Street, SW4 7UH*
(7720 7633/www.infernos.co.uk).
King's Arms *25 Roupell Street, SE1 8TB*
(7207 0784).
Lost Society *697 Wandsworth Road,*
SW8 3JF (7652 6526/www.lostsociety.co.uk).
Mango Landin' *40 St Matthew's Road,*
SW2 1NL (7737 3044/www.mangolandin.com).
Mass *St Matthew's Church, Brixton Hill,*
SW2 1JF (7738 7875/www.mass-club.com).
Mint *5 Streatham High Road, SW16 1EF*
(8677 0007/www.mintsteatham.co.uk).
Pit Bar *The Old Vic, The Cut, SE1 8NB*
(7928 2975/www.oldvictheatre.com).
Plan B *418 Brixton Road, SW9 7AY*
(7924 0480/www.plan-brixton.co.uk).
Priory Arms *83 Lansdowne Way, SW8 2PB*
(7622 1884).
Prince of Wales *48 Cleaver Square, SE11*
4EA (7735 9916).
Railway *2 Greyhound Lane, SW16 5SD*
(8835 0307).
Revolution *95-97 Clapham High Street, SW4*
7TB (7720 6642/www.revolution-bars.co.uk).
Riverside *5 St George's Wharf, SW8 2LE*
(7735 8129/www.riversidelondon.com).
Royal Vauxhall Tavern *372 Kennington*
Lane, SE11 5HY (7820 1222/www.theroyal
vauxhalltavern.co.uk).
South London Pacific *340 Kennington*
Road, SE11 4LD (7820 9189/www.south
londonpacific.com).
Surprise *16 Southville, SW8 2PP (7622 4623).*
Swan *215 Clapham Road, SW9 9BE (7978*
9778/www.theswanstockwell.co.uk).
Telegraph *228 Brixton Hill, SW2 1HE*
(8678 0777).
Three Stags *67-69 Kennington Road, SE1 7PZ*
(7928 5974).
Trinity Arms *45 Trinity Gardens, SW9 8DR*
(7274 4544).
White Hart *185 Kennington Lane, SE11 4EZ*
(7735 1061).

Lambeth

White Horse *94 Brixton Hill, SW2 1QN (8678 6666/www.whitehorsebrixton.com).*
Windmill *Clapham Common South Side, SW4 9DE (8673 4578/www.windmillclapham.co.uk).*
Windmill *22 Blenheim Gardens, SW2 5BZ (8671 0700/www.windmillbrixton.co.uk).*

Shops

Lambeth is not the most obvious of retail destinations, though its culturally diverse food shops are well worth seeking out.

Vauxhall's Portuguese contingent is well served by Madeira Pâtisserie (*see p221*), which turns out the finest custard tarts in town, while the Luis Deli next door offers cold cooked meats and sandwiches. Interesting non-food-related stores in Vauxhall include LASSCO, an intriguing clutter of architectural antiques and relics, and I Knit, a gay-friendly knitting shop offering classes and clubs.

Stockwell is similarly well served for Portuguese food, with Funchal Bakery doing a nice line in soups and pastries. Further afield, Wandsworth Road has the Ryad Halal Way Butchers & Deli, which sells halal meats; South Lambeth has Di Lieto Bakery & Deli; and Brixton Road has Delicatessen Alberobello. Down in Streatham, Korona is a one-stop shop for French, Italian, eastern European and South African deli goods.

The Old Post Office Bakery (the oldest in south London) in Clapham North stocks a huge selection of breads, while Breads Etcetera, on the High Street, supplies various upmarket restaurants around the capital. Closer to Clapham Common, Macaron is an authentic French pâtisserie and M Moen & Sons a well-respected organic butcher, and the North Street Deli offers top-quality charcuterie, breads and cakes. Brixton, meanwhile, continues its climb upmarket with Spoon, a deli from the former pastry chef at L'Escargot, while Brixton Market remains an enormously enjoyable (if strikingly unorganised) food shopping experience: the stalls along Electric Avenue are piled high with yams, plantains, mangoes and other exotic items.

Not that food is the sum total of Brixton Market's charms: move on to Atlantic Road for clothes, towels and wallets, then to Brixton Station Road for second-hand clobber (Saturday only). In Brixton Village (once Granville Arcade) there are African and Caribbean food stores, household goods and crafts. One of the market's strongest suits is music, with three of the best specialist record shops in the capital: stock up on reggae, gospel and soca at Supertone, jazz and hip hop at Reds, and soul and roots at Selectors. Coldharbour Lane has African and West Indian record stores as well as new-age bookstore Book Mongers.

For literature elsewhere, Soma Books in Kennington imports a wide range of texts from India. There's also the fantastic Riverside Walk Book Market under the arches of Waterloo Bridge and a branch of Foyle's beneath the Royal Festival Hall, while Crockatt & Powell, on nearby Lower Marsh, is a decent independent organising monthly book groups and poetry readings. Also upping the ante on this otherwise rather tawdry market strip is the wonderfully cluttered second-hand classical music shop Gramex.

In Clapham, tiny Places & Spaces has one of the most interesting selections of furniture, lighting and accessories in London, while textiles designer Lisa Stickley has just opened her first shop here too. On Abbeville Road, Josephine Ryan

Antiques & Interiors is an essential stop for chic furniture and trinkets. Nearby, Tessa Fantoni's photo albums, desk accessories and toiletries make excellent gifts, and the Common Sense clinic stocks a host of alternative remedies.

South in Streatham, the High Road has all the usual amenities (and a great many charity shops). More interesting is Cenci, in West Norwood: once based in Covent Garden, this vintage clothes store has a fantastic collection from the 1960s.

Book Mongers *439 Coldharbour Lane, SW9 8LN (7738 4225).*
Breads Etcetera *127 Clapham High Street, SW4 7SS (7720 3601/www.breadsetcetera.com).*
Brixton Market *Electric Avenue, Pope's Road, Brixton Station Road, Atlantic Road, SW9.*
Cenci *4 Nettlefold Place, SE27 0JW (8766 8564/www.cenci.co.uk).*
Common Sense *7-7A Clapham Common Southside, SW4 7AA (7720 8817/www.south londonnaturalhealthcentre.com).*
Crockatt & Powell *119-120 Lower Marsh, SE1 7AE (7928 0234).*
Delicatessen Alberobello *2 Brixton Road, SW9 6BU (7735 2121).*
Di Lieto Bakery & Deli *175 South Lambeth Road, SW8 1XW (7735 1997).*
Foyle's *Festival Riverside, South Bank Centre, SE1 8XX (7440 3213/www.foyles.co.uk).*
Funchal Bakery *141 Stockwell Road, SW9 9TN (7733 3134).*
Gramex *25 Lower Marsh, SE1 7RJ (7401 3830/www.gramexlondon.com).*
I Knit *13 Bonnington Square, SW6 1TE (7582 5213/www.iknit.org.uk).*
Josephine Ryan Antiques & Interiors *63 Abbeville Road, SW4 9JW (8675 3900/ www.josephineryanantiques.co.uk).*
Korona *30 Streatham High Road, SW16 1DB (8769 6647).*
LASSCO *Brunswick House, 30 Wandsworth Road, SW8 2LG (7394 2100/www.lassco.co.uk).*
Lisa Stickley *74 Landor Road, SW9 9PH (7737 8067/www.lisastickleylondon.co.uk).*
Luis Deli *46 Albert Embankment, SE1 7TL (7820 0314).*
Macaron *22 The Pavement, SW4 0HY (7498 2636).*
M Moen & Sons *24 The Pavement, SW4 0JA (7622 1624/www.moen.co.uk).*
North Street Deli *26 North Street, SW4 0HB (7978 1555).*
Old Post Office Bakery *76 Landor Road, SW9 9PH (7326 4408/www.oldpostoffice bakery.co.uk).*
Places & Spaces *30 Old Town, SW4 0LB (7498 0998/www.placesandspaces.com).*
Reds *500 Brixton Road, SW9 8EQ (7274 4476).*
Riverside Walk Book Market *Outside BFI Southbank, under Waterloo Bridge, SE1 9PX.*

Ryad Halal Way Butchers & Deli *248 Wandsworth Road, SW8 2JS (7738 8811).*
Selectors Music Emporium *100B Brixton Hill, SW2 1AH (7771 2011).*
Soma Books *38 Kennington Lane, SE11 4LS (7735 2101/www.somabooks.co.uk).*
Spoon *48 New Park Road, SW2 4UN (8674 6572).*
Supertone Records, Videos & CDs *110 Acre Lane, SW2 5RA (7737 7761/ www.supertonerecords.co.uk).*
Tessa Fantoni *73 Abbeville Road, SW4 9JN (8673 1253/www.tessafantoni.com).*

Arts & attractions

Cinemas & theatres

BFI London IMAX *1 Charlie Chaplin Walk, SE1 8XR (0870 787 2525/www.bfi.org.uk/incinemas/imax).* 3-D spectaculars at the UK's biggest cinema screen.
BFI Southbank *Belvedere Road, South Bank, SE1 8XT (7928 3232/www.bfi.org.uk).* London's best cinema, with an unrivalled programme of retrospective seasons and previews.
Clapham Picture House *76 Venn Street, SW4 0AT (0870 755 0061/www.picturehouses. co.uk).* Arthouse and quality mainstream films.
Landor *70 Landor Road, SW9 9PH (7274 4386/www.landortheatre.co.u).*
National Theatre *South Bank, SE1 9PX (info 7452 3400/box office 7452 3000/ www.nationaltheatre.org.uk).* Under artistic director Nicholas Hytner, the National gets better and better. Three theatres (Olivier, Lyttleton, Cottesloe) present an eclectic mix of new plays and classics.
Odeon Streatham *44-47 Streatham High Road, SW16 1PW (08712 244 007/www. odeon.co.uk).*
Old Vic *The Cut, SE1 8NB (0870 060 6628/ www.oldvictheatre.com).* Kevin Spacey continues as artistic director at this historic theatre.
Ritzy *Brixton Oval, Coldharbour Lane, SW2 1JG (0870 755 0062/www.picturehouses.co.uk).* Much-loved local cinema, with café, jazz bar and Saturday art fairs.
South London Theatre *2A Norwood High Street, SE27 9NS (box office 8670 3474/ members' club 8670 4661/www.southlondon theatre.co.uk).*
Young Vic *66 The Cut, SE1 8LZ (7922 2922/ www.youngvic.org).*

Galleries & museums

Dalí Universe *County Hall, Riverside Building, Queen's Walk, SE1 7PB (7620 2720/www.dali universe.com).* More than 500 works by surrealist artist Salvador Dalí, displayed in suitably labyrinthine galleries.
Florence Nightingale Museum *St Thomas' Hospital, 2 Lambeth Palace Road, SE1 7EW (7620 0374/www.florence-nightingale.co.uk).* Honours the remarkable life and Crimean War work of 'the lady with the lamp'.

Hayward Gallery *South Bank Centre, SE1 8XX (0870 380 0400/www.hayward.org.uk).* One of London's leading art galleries, presenting a mix of contemporary and older work.
Museum of Garden History *Lambeth Palace Road, SE1 7LB (7401 8865/ www.cix.co.uk/~museumgh).* The world's first horticultural museum.
Type Museum *100 Hackford Road, SW9 0QU (7735 0055/www.typemuseum.org).* Printing and typographical exhibitions.

Music & comedy venues
Carling Academy Brixton *211 Stockwell Road, SW9 9SL (7771 3000/www.brixton-academy.co.uk).* Major concert venue.
Southbank Centre *Belvedere Road, SE1 8XX (0870 380 0400/www.southbankcentre. co.uk).* Three concert halls – the majestic Royal Festival Hall, smaller Queen Elizabeth Hall and tiny Purcell Room – cover classical and contemporary music and dance. The RFH reopened in 2007 following major renovations.

Other attractions
British Airways London Eye *Next to County Hall, Riverside Building, Westminster Bridge Road, SE1 7PB (0870 500 0600/www.ba-londoneye.com).* Superb views from the capital's favourite new icon.
London Aquarium *County Hall, Riverside Building, Westminster Bridge Road, SE1 7PB (7967 8000/www.londonaquarium.co.uk).* One of Europe's largest exhibitions of global aquatic life, displayed in giant tanks and touch pools.

Sport & fitness

Lambeth's residents have access to five council-owned sports centres. Private clubs range from small operations squeezed between big buildings and main roads to large facilities in quieter, more remote areas. Also on offer is Vauxhall's Paris Gym, previously a 'gay-only' facility but now also open to straight men who are comfortable in that environment.

Gyms & leisure centres
Brixton Recreation Centre *27 Brixton Station Road, SW9 8QQ (7926 9779/ www.gll.org).*
Clapham Leisure Centre *141 Clapham Manor Street, SW4 2AU (7926 0700/ www.gll.org).*
Ferndale Community Sports Centre *Nursery Road, SW9 8PB (0845 130 8998/ www.gll.org).*
Fitness First *www.fitnessfirst.co.uk; Blue Star House, 234-244 Stockwell Road, SW9 9FP (7733 5522); 7 Streatham High Road, SW16 1EH (0870 898 0609).* Private.
Flaxman Sports Centre *Carew Street, SE5 9DF (7926 1054/www.gll.org).*

Paris Gym *73 Goding Street, SE11 5AW (7735 8989/www.parisgym.com).* Men only; private.
Soho Gym *95-97 Clapham High Street, SW4 7TB (7720 0321/www.sohogyms.com).* Private.
South Bank Club *124-130 Wandsworth Road, SW8 2LD (7622 6866/www.southbankclub. co.uk).* Private.
Streatham Leisure Centre *384 Streatham High Road, SW16 6HX (7926 6744/www. gll.org).*
Virgin Active *www.virginactive.co.uk; 4-20 North Street, SW4 0HB (7819 2555); 20 Ockley Road, SW16 1UB (8769 8686).* Private.

Other facilities
Brockwell Lido *Lido Park Gardens, Brockwell Park, Dulwich Road, SE24 0PA (7274 3088/ www.thelido.co.uk).* This lovely 1930s lido reopened in 2005 after an impressive revamp.
Streatham Ice Arena *386 Streatham High Road, SW16 6HT (8769 7771/www.streatham icearena.co.uk).*

Spectator sports
The Oval *Surrey County Cricket Club, Kennington, SE11 5SS (7582 6660/ www.surreycricket.com).*

Schools

WHAT THE PARENTS SAY:

'Lambeth's primary schools are generally fine, but the growing population means parents can't always secure places at their local institutions. At secondary level, some brand-new schools are heavily oversubscribed: Lambeth Academy in Clapham, the Elmgreen School in Norwood, and highly popular Dunraven School in Streatham.

The borough is a nightmare at secondary level. Most of the places are at faith schools and girls' schools (60 per cent each); coupled with a general shortage of year seven places, this means that 70 per cent of 11-18s are educated outside the borough – many have very long journeys to school. Parents have been campaigning vigorously for years to get Lambeth to invest in new secondary schools; we've had some success with two new schools opening, plus a third due soon. There's also a heated political battle about the need for a school in the centre of the borough: parents have led the campaign for the Nelson Mandela School to open on Brixton Hill. '
Devon Allison, mother of two and chair of the Secondary Schools Campaign in Lambeth

Primary
There are 59 state primary schools in Lambeth, 21 of which are church schools, and one a Muslim school. There are also nine independent

primaries, including two Muslim schools. See
www.lambeth.gov.uk, www.edubase.gov.uk
and www.ofsted.gov.uk for more information.

Secondary

Archbishop Tenison's CE School
55 Kennington Oval, SE11 5SR (7735 3771).
Boys only.
Bishop Thomas Grant RC School *Belltrees
Grove, SW16 2HY (8769 3294/www.btg.ac).*
Charles Edward Brooke CE School
*Langton Road, SW9 6UL (7274 6311/www.
charlesedwardbrooke.lambeth.sch.uk).* Girls only.
Dunraven School *94-98 Leigham Court
Road, SW16 2QB (8677 2431/www.dunraven-
school.org.uk).*
Elmgreen School *Gipsy Road, SE27 9TG
(8766 5020/www.elmgreenschool.com).*
Moving to Elmcourt Road in 2009.
Evelyn Grace Academy *temporary site
2008-9: Somerleyton Road, SW9 8ND (7395
2080/www.evelyngrace.org.uk).* Opening in
autumn 2008, this new academy is expected to
move to its permanent site (designed by Zaha
Hadid Architects) on Shakespeare Road in 2009.
Lambeth Academy *Elms Road, SW4 9ET
(7498 5004/www.lambeth-academy.org).*
Lilian Baylis Technology School
323 Kennington Lane, SE11 5QY (7091 9500).
London Nautical School *61 Stamford
Street, SE1 9NA(7928 6801/www.lns.org.uk).*
Boys only.
Norwood School *Crown Dale, SE19 3NY
(8670 9382/www.norwood-secondary.lambeth.
sch.uk).*
La Retraite RC School *Atkins Road, SW12
0AB (8673 5644/www.laretraiteclapham
school.co.uk).* Girls only.
St Martin-in-the-Fields CE School
*155 Tulse Hill, SW2 3UP (8674 5594/
www.stmartins.lambeth.sch.uk).* Girls only.
Stockwell Park High School *Clapham
Road, SW9 0AL (7733 6156/www.stockpark.
lambeth.sch.uk).*

Property

WHAT THE AGENTS SAY:

❝We deal with young professionals rather than
families: media types who need good access to
town but also want a lively social life. Brixton's
got the Fridge, Mass… people used to leave here
for a night out, now they come in from outside
the area. Property ranges from flats for £200,000
up to half and even three-quarters of a million –
there are no million-pound properties – yet! It's
families that have got that much money, and they
go further out for space and better schools. If the
budget's tight, it's south-east: Norwood, Norbury,
Penge. If there's more money, then it's south-west.
Brixton's not really a family place.❞

Andy Blass, Murray Estates

Average property prices

Detached £886,272
Semi-detached £514,122
Terraced £528,465
Flat £277,807

Local estate agents

Aspire *www.aspire.co.uk; 2 offices in the
borough (Clapham South 8675 1222/North
Clapham 7840 3700).*
Daniel Cobb *191 Kennington Lane, SE11
5QS (7735 9510/www.danielcobb.co.uk).*
Harmens *www.harmens.co.uk; 2 offices in
the borough (Brixton 7737 6000/Streatham
8769 4777).*
Hooper & Jackson *76 Streatham High
Road, SW16 1BS (8769 8000/www.hooper
jackson.com).*
Keating Estates *25 Clapham Common
South Side, SW4 7AB (7720 2113/www.
keatingestates.com).*
Martin Barry *4 Acre Lane, SW2 5SG (7738
5866/www.martinbarrypartnership.co.uk).*
Murray Estates *92-96 Stockwell Road, SW9
9HR (7733 4203/www.murrayestates.com).*
Opendoors Estates *91 Acre Lane, SW2
5TU (7733 4000/www.opendoorsestates.com).*

Other information

Council

Lambeth Council *Town Hall, Brixton Hill,
SW2 1RW (7926 1000/www.lambeth.gov.uk).*

Legal services

Lambeth Law Centre *11 Mowll Street,
SW9 6BG (7840 2000/2030).*
Streatham Hill CAB *Ilex House, 1 Barrhill
Road, SW2 4RJ (8715 0707/www.adviceguide.
org.uk).*

Local newspapers

Lambeth Life *7926 2485/www.lambeth.gov.
uk.* Distributed free by the council and also
available online.
**South London Press & The Streatham
Post** *8769 4444/www.icsouthlondon.co.uk.*
Streatham Guardian *8329 9244/
www.streathamguardian.co.uk.*

Allotments & open spaces

Lorn Road Allotments *Lorn Road, SW9
(7926 6214/6209).*
Rosendale Allotments Association
*227 Rosendale Road, SE21 8LR (www.rosendale-
allotments.org.uk).*
Streatham Vale Allotments *SW16, c/o
Streatham Vale Property Occupiers Association
(www.svpoa.org.uk).*
Vauxhall Allotments *Tyers Street, SE11,
c/o Vauxhall City Farm, 165 Tyers Street,
SE11 5HS (7582 4204).*
Open spaces *www.lambeth.gov.uk/parks.*

'Southwark's history is rooted in trade, industry and entertainment, attracting settlers from around the world since Roman times. Today over 100 languages are spoken in the borough.'

Catherine Hamilton, heritage collections and operations manager, Cuming Museum

Southwark

Gentrification and widespread regeneration have turned this into a borough of layers: popular cultural attractions and riverside walks to the north; green spaces and smart food shops in the south; and down-on-their-luck housing estates and vibrant high streets across the middle. As reconstruction continues, this is a borough on the move – upwards.

Neighbourhoods

Borough and Bankside

Bankside has historically been a place of entertainment and fun, hedonism and artistic delight. Though associated with light industry until as recently as the 1980s, it is once again a vibrant cultural quarter. Shakespeare's Globe was rebuilt with painstaking historical accuracy in 1997, the Oxo cold store converted into small-scale design workshops and a rooftop restaurant with stunning views in 1996, and, most importantly, Tate Modern opened in 2000 in the former Bankside power station. The addition of Norman Foster's Millennium Bridge has changed the geography of this part of London, linking it directly with the City and St Paul's Cathedral.

By restyling itself as 'London's Larder' in the late 1990s, Borough Market has now become one of the city's top tourist attractions. It attracts gourmet food merchants, although wholesale fruit and veg are traded at night. The market is surrounded by characterful old pubs and the historic streets around it are often used in period films. Other landmarks include 13th-century Southwark Cathedral, a replica

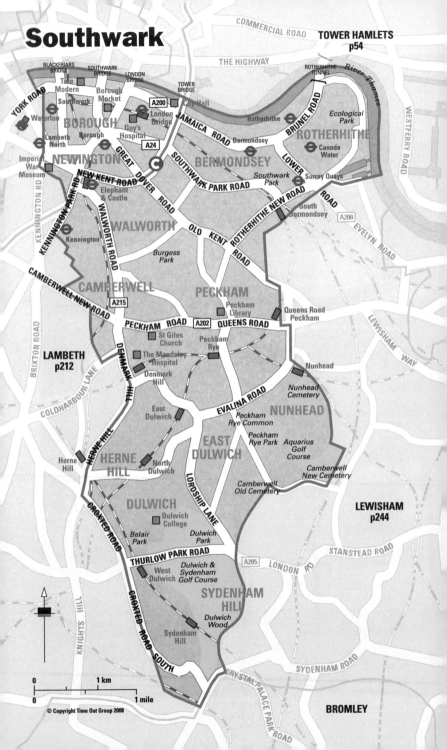

of Francis Drake's flagship the *Golden Hinde*, the Clink Prison, the Old Operating Theatre Museum and, in a courtyard off Borough High Street, the 17th-century George Inn, the last galleried coaching inn left in London.

The area to the east of London Bridge has been given new importance by shiny commercial development More London and the relocation of the Greater London Authority to purpose-built City Hall, a glass and steel ovoid in the shadow of Tower Bridge. Outdoor amphitheatre the Scoop often hosts free performances and film screenings, while new public spaces host specially commissioned artworks. Newly opened Potters Field Park has transformed the wasteland next to Tower Bridge into a versatile green space. In the past few years the area has also seen the opening of innovative theatres Menier Chocolate Factory and Unicorn Theatre, as well as Shunt Vaults, a multi-arts venue under the heavy arches under London Bridge Station.

The Dickensian wharfs beyond Tower Bridge were, in the 1980s, the site of some of the first forays into warehouse redevelopment. Here too is the Design Museum, opened in 1989 by Terence Conran as a declaration of optimism for the area.

Behind London Bridge Station is Bermondsey Street, spiritually more connected to the prosperity of Borough than down-at-heel Bermondsey on the other side of Tower Bridge Road. Technicolour designer and local resident Zandra Rhodes chose to open her pink and orange Fashion & Textiles Museum here in 2003, although it is currently closed for refurbishment. This has been followed by Wi-Fi cafés, upmarket restaurants, media companies, trendy boutiques, smart galleries, a fancy florist and some hip residents.

London Bridge Station is the key interchange for most Southwark residents, taking trains from all over Kent and south-east London and funnelling them into Charing Cross and up through the City, or swapping commuters on to the Jubilee and Northern lines. Though the station itself is terminally shoddy, it is about to be put on the map by the building above it – Renzo Piano's 310-metre glass 'Shard' (www.shardlondonbridge.com) will be the tallest building in London when it is completed in 2011.

Elephant & Castle and Walworth

Once known as the Piccadilly of south London, the busy Elephant & Castle double roundabout is effectively the gateway to south London. Radiating off the roundabout are the New Kent Road and historic Old Kent Road; perennially busy, bus-laden Walworth Road, which runs down to Camberwell, and Newington Butts, heading south-west to Kennington and thence to Clapham. Beneath it is a forbidding warren of foot tunnels.

Dominating everything is the bright red (once pink) Elephant & Castle shopping centre, the building most Londoners love to hate. It is scheduled for demolition in 2010 as part of massive redevelopment of the whole area, some of which has begun (for details, see www.elephantandcastle. org.uk). Despite its reputation, the area is

Highs & Lows

Green space Residents in the south of the borough are surrounded by the open spaces of Peckham Rye, Dulwich Park, Dulwich Woods and, just over the border, Crystal Palace Park and Brockwell Park. Residents in the north get fine riverside walks
Culture Southwark has more than ten theatres, 14 public art galleries (plus many small independents), and several important museums
Public architecture The council's planning department has given the public such inspiring buildings as Tate Modern, Peckham Library, City Hall and the Millennium Bridge

Secondary education There may be top-notch private schools, but many parents feel poorly served by the borough's state secondary options
No tube Beyond Elephant & Castle you're relying on trains and buses. Locals tend to see this as a plus, since it keeps uninitiated north Londoners out
Gangs Teenage shootings in Camberwell and Peckham have been widely reported, as have the activities of notorious gangs such as the Peckham Boys

Southwark

Surrey Docks Farm, Rotherhithe.

not without its charms. There's a vibrant Colombian community who come together at La Bodeguita café, a popular bowling alley (Superbowl) and a street market (every day except Sunday). Two big colleges – South Bank University and London College of Communication – and some large halls of residence bring lots of students into the mix.

Towards Lambeth North and the borough boundary, streets become prettier and return to a more human scale. Highlights include the new and architecturally exciting Siobhan Davies Dance Studios and the Imperial War Museum. There is also an attempt being made to woo an annexe of the Science Museum to the area, using the Faraday Memorial – a shiny steel box that currently sits stranded in the middle of one of the roundabouts – as an incentive.

The £1.5 billion Elephant & Castle regeneration will no doubt see a change in fortunes of this unloved area of London, with a ripple effect through Walworth encouraged by a tram route down to Burgess Park (the exact route is still subject to local wrangling – and it may all be called off as other transport projects siphon off transport funding). At present, the Walworth Road is a hit-and-miss affair, where down-at-heel sofa outlets and high-street chains rub shoulders with local gems such as the Cuming Museum (great for local history), the 24-hour Bagel King, Turkish grocer Oli's (which famously never closes),

Dragon Castle dim sum restaurant, one of London's first-ever health shops (G Baldwin & Co), and cheap and cheerful East Street Market. Behind the chaos, there are even pockets of gentility such as Liverpool Grove and Addington Square.

Bermondsey

Bermondsey is perhaps the bleakest stretch of Southwark. From medieval times, it was home to the leather industry (witness such addresses as Leathermarket Street), and further light industry developed during the 19th century, causing overcrowding and unsavoury smells. The area became known as 'London's larder' (a moniker now used by the far more salubrious Borough Market) because of the amount of food processing done in the area, with the industrial work continuing until the docks closed in the 1970s. Famous names that had factories here include Sarson's vinegar, Hartley's jam, Peek Freans biscuits and Crosse & Blackwell. The housing estates that were built after slum clearances in the 1920s and '30s and the Blitz now seem bleak and endless, with more than their share of flags of St George hung in windows.

Eschewing its rough reputation and industrial roots, this part of town has steadily emerged as a fashionable place in which to live. The central swathe of Bermondsey (along Spa Road, between Grange Road and Jamaica Road) is currently undergoing extensive regeneration. Spa Park has already been landscaped, and new buildings are to welcome new shops, key-worker housing, live-work units, business space and even penthouse flats. The opening back in 1999 of the Jubilee line's Bermondsey station doubtless encouraged this activity.

A little to the south-east, you'll find Southwark Park Road and occasional pretty terraces. By South Bermondsey rail station, 'The Den' – Millwall Football Club's ground – is still a focus of local pride (and occasional violence, although the club itself runs a commendable community programme). To the south, Old Kent Road creaks on, sustaining boxing gyms and Nigerian cafés, intimidating lounge bars and DIY superstores. To the north, families and amateur sports clubs enjoy the improved Southwark Park, which – post-regeneration – features an Italian coffee hut, a great playground and the artist-run Café Gallery (www.cafegalleryprojects.org). It is London's oldest municipal park.

At the west, Bermondsey Square remains a hub of activity. The long-term draw is Bermondsey Square Antiques Market (6am-2pm Friday), good for china and silver. Factory conversions to loft-style flats at Alaska and the Jam Factory (formerly Hartley's) have already brought more affluent residents to this end of Bermondsey, while the arrival of a boutique hotel and 60-seat cinema, perhaps in summer 2008, could push the area further upmarket. Redevelopment should leave space for 200 market traders.

Rotherhithe

On emerging from Rotherhithe tube station, an eerie silence greets you, a silence that is rarely broken anywhere across this isolated peninsula. The area is rich in maritime history: the Mayflower pub marks the departure point of the Pilgrim Fathers, while the Finnish Church and seaman's mission on Albion Street are reminders of more recent Scandinavian seafarers. The diminutive Brunel Museum is housed in the pumping house for the world's first underwater tunnel, which was dug under the Thames in 1843.

The fringes of the Rotherhithe peninsula are now marked by riverfront apartments and a Hilton hotel, but you'll rarely see a soul. The best chances of finding life are at the charming Surrey Docks Farm, home to cows, pigs, sheep, fowl and bees (their honey is available in the farm shop), or at Lavender Pond & Nature Park reserve, where the ponds, reed beds, meadow and marshland are complemented by the Pumphouse Educational Museum. There are also superb Docklands views from Stave Hill Ecological Park on Salter Road.

Most of the docks had been filled in by the 1980s, with the few that remain developed into luxury housing complexes. The swanky South Dock is the capital's largest working marina, with over 200 berths. In Greenland Dock you'll find late comedian Malcolm Hardee's Wibbley Wobbly barge, a popular restaurant and drinking den for locals in the know.

Major regeneration followed the linking of Canada Water to the West End by the arrival of the Jubilee line, and new housing, retail, business units and community facilities have already been planned with an eye to the East London line extension (connecting Canada Water and Surrey Quays north to Dalston – and eventually Highbury & Islington – and as far south as West Croydon). The bad news is that the entire East London line closed in 2007 while the work is completed. A replacement bus service will run until the line reopens as the East London Railway, apparently in 2010.

Camberwell

Once a small farming village, Camberwell predates the Domesday Book, which mentions it having a church (a sign of the

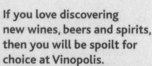

village's importance). Today's church of St Giles was built on the site of the original by architect Giles Gilbert Scott. It features stained-glass windows by one-time local resident John Ruskin. Rapid expansion in Victorian times bequeathed attractive terraces, but the street that really impresses is the Georgian Camberwell Grove.

Camberwell can probably claim to be the best connected area in Southwark, lying on the crossroads between central London to the north and southerly Dulwich, east of Vauxhall and west of Peckham. You can get anywhere from here, providing you're prepared to use the bus.

The other famous past resident, the Camberwell Beauty, is celebrated in a small shopping arcade, Butterfly Walk, but much of the high street is fairly down at heel. The most popular pubs, bars, restaurants and food shops are found up Peckham Road and around the bottom of Camberwell Grove. The presence of Camberwell College of Arts continues Ruskin's aesthetic legacy and many artists live in the area.

Other institutions that dominate the area are King's College Hospital (technically in Lambeth) and the Maudsley psychiatric hospital, which serve the wider south London community. William Booth College (headquarters of the Salvation Army) looms over the lot. Also designed by Giles Gilbert Scott in 1929, the college has an imposing tower that's 190 feet tall. Visible for miles around, it lords it over the poor lost souls of south London.

Dulwich Village, Herne Hill and Sydenham Hill

Dulwich Village is an anomaly – being here is more like being in rural Kent than in a near-neighbour like Brixton or Peckham. Elizabethan actor Edward Alleyn bought the land and set up Dulwich College here to help educate the poor; the trustees still guard against overdevelopment of the area. There are white picket fences, wooden signposts, an impressive coaching inn (the Crown & Greyhound) and, on College Road, a functioning toll gate – but nothing useful like a cashpoint. This is a posh area, where you'll find some of the capital's most expensive real estate (Georgian villas, Victorian cottages, 1930s suburban homes) and three top private schools (Dulwich College, Alleyn's and James Allen's Girls).

Attractions include England's first public art gallery, Dulwich Picture Gallery, which was designed by Sir John Soane. It contains an important collection of 17th- and 18th-century masters and has a great café. The area also has extensive green spaces that stretch from the heights of Sydenham Hill (where there are allotments, a golf course, a cricket pitch and ancient Dulwich Wood) all the way down to Herne Hill (with more sports pitches and a velodrome) and, crossing the border into Lambeth, the rolling slopes of Brockwell Park. Dulwich Park, in the heart of Dulwich Village, is popular and well maintained, with an excellent children's playground, bike hire, tennis courts and a lake.

Herne Hill is characterised by lively shops and cafés, which mainly cluster around the station and on Half Moon Lane. These serve a population of affluent, well-dressed foodies and plentiful young families. Property here is generally grander than in East Dulwich or Brixton, with some houses in the conservation area known as the Hamlets surpassing the million pound mark. The area is served by good rail links to Victoria and Blackfriars and plenty of buses, but traffic is often gridlocked at the main junction.

East Dulwich and Nunhead

In the past ten years East Dulwich has managed to reinvent itself. No longer Dulwich Village's rough neighbour, it is now a desirable bourgeois enclave with rocketing house prices. Almost entirely built in the late 19th century (as was much of this part of London), before which it was all farms and fields, East Dulwich is now made up of attractive Victorian terraces.

The area's busy spine is Lordship Lane, which has long been full of glam bars, good restaurants, chichi boutiques, organic food shops and eager estate agents. The opening of a brash, imposing branch of Foxtons and the steady appearance of chains such as Caffè Nero, however, foretells an erosion of the charm of a street proud of its independent shops. North Cross Road is taking up the slack with boutiques, art galleries and a lively market on Friday and Saturday. Goose Green is the old village centre and often hosts local fêtes.

East Dulwich's proximity to big open spaces such as Peckham Rye (where William Blake famously saw angels, hence a mural on the gable end of a house off Ady's Road) and Dulwich Park, and improvements to the local primary schools, have made the area very attractive to families. Sometimes you can't move for pushchairs. Heading south, the land rises. These first major hills to the south of London afford superb views back over London to the Houses of Parliament and the City.

As East Dulwich gets increasingly clichéd, Nunhead – the other side of Peckham Rye – is somewhere to watch. Reasonable Victorian housing stock has attracted young, middle-class families as well as a gastropub (the Old Nun's Head) and art gallery (the Surgery, www.the surgery.turnpiece.net). Nunhead is also famous for its Victorian cemetery.

Peckham

Peckham suffers from a poor reputation, reinforced by reports of teenage gun crime and the TV legacy of *Only Fools and Horses*. Although the area north of Peckham Road and Peckham High Street is still troubled, the notorious North Peckham estate is being flattened as part of an

ongoing £300 million regeneration that has already seen a change in the fortunes of much of the rest of the area. Will Alsop's unconventional, award-winning library and the well-equipped sports centre and swimming pool Peckham Pulse have indicated that planners are willing to embrace new ideas and marked the town centre as a dynamic place.

The most desirable area of Peckham is around Bellenden Road, given a smart but relaxed air by pavement cafés, an arts bookshop, good restaurants and Antony Gormley-designed bollards. There are also a few surprises: delightful Lyndhurst Square and Elm Grove, the Regency villas of Holly Grove. Plenty of artists have been attracted to the area by the proximity of Camberwell College of Arts and the excellent South London Gallery (www. southlondongallery.org), with funky art squats lending the area a frisson of cool.

There's constant hubbub along Rye Lane, where the wares are as varied and colourful as the patrons. You'll find plantains, yams, hair extensions, Chinese medicine, fish, goats, international phone cards, a Primark, Pentecostal churches, the Wing Tai Chinese supermarket and a very cheap cinema.

East of Rye Lane, things are still fairly desolate but the area is definitely on the up, with stylish new housing and even a deli popping up along Consort Road. At Queens Road Peckham, several new residential developments are adding more apartments for key workers and commuters, while down St Mary's Road there's a mix of architecture including a 1960s church and the 1930s Pioneer Centre, a gated community with its own swimming pool and tennis courts.

Restaurants & cafés

Southwark has no shortage of quality places to eat. For starters, there are many dining-with-a-view options along the riverfront. Among the predictable chains, there are exceptions such as the Oxo Tower (two Modern European restaurants and a bar, plus Japanese yakitoria Bincho and buzzing brasserie Tamesa@Oxo) and, at Bankside, the Tate Modern Café (the family-friendly one on the second floor is our favourite). Past Tower Bridge, near the Design Museum (home to the Blueprint Café), are Butlers Wharf Chop House and Le Pont de la Tour.

Away from the river, near Southwark tube, is stylish east European restaurant Baltic and quirky international bistro Laughing Gravy. Up on Southwark Street, budget canteen the Table (on the ground floor of the offices of architects Allies & Morrison) is a definite don't miss.

The area surrounding foodie magnet Borough Market holds real culinary gems. Try bustling, no-bookings-taken Tapas Brindisa, British restaurant Roast, Wright Brothers Oyster & Porter House or retro café Shipp's Tea Rooms. Nearer London Bridge, on Tooley Street, is new British restaurant Magdalen. Nearby Bermondsey Street has some great places: charming restaurant/gallery Delfina, Bermondsey Kitchen and the Garrison gastropub. Tower Bridge Road is home to M Manze – gloriously old-fashioned and probably

the oldest extant pie and mash shop in London, dating right back to 1902.

The Elephant & Castle complex is still mourning the loss of much-loved Pizzeria Castello (demolished at the end of 2006 in preparation for the redevelopment of Castle House), but do check out Colombian café La Bodeguita. There's also excellent dim sum and Cantonese cuisine at Walworth Road's Dragon Castle.

Over in Camberwell, local favourite Mozzarella e Pomodoro continues to serve top-notch pizza and pasta, while new gastropub the Dark Horse (*see p239*) does a good line in hearty meat and fish dishes. Peckham has slightly less of note, although pie-and-mash stalwart M Manze (run by the same family as the Tower Bridge Road branch), appealing café Petitou and low-key south Indian Ganapati all deserve their fans. Also of note is the Old Nun's Head (*see p239*) in Nunhead, which dishes up decent pub grub.

East Dulwich does rather better. Try Sea Cow's excellent fish and chips, the Gowlett (*see p239*), the Herne Tavern (*see p239*), the Palmerston gastropub or recently expanded wine-bar-cum-shop Green & Blue (*see p239*). Café culture is burgeoning in SE22: Jack's Tea & Coffee House and Blue Mountain Café are standouts. Dulwich Park's Pavilion Café makes a fine lunchtime escape. For something more upmarket, make a beeline for swanky Beauberry House, which serves Modern European food in an elegant setting, or ever-popular British restaurant Franklins. In West Dulwich, meanwhile, dead-end boozer the Rosendale has been utterly transformed into a first-rate gastropub – it won *Time Out*'s Best Gastropub award in 2007. Herne Hill's finest include Olley's for fish and chips and Spanish restaurant Number 22.

Baltic *74 Blackfriars Road, SE1 8HA (7928 1111).*
Beauberry House *Gallery Road, SE21 7AB (8299 9788/www.circagroupltd.co.uk).*
Bermondsey Kitchen *194 Bermondsey Street, SE1 3TQ (7407 5719/www.bermondsey kitchen.co.uk).*
Bincho *2nd floor, Oxo Tower Wharf, Barge House Street, SE1 9PH (7803 0858/ www.bincho.co.uk).*
Blue Mountain Café *18 North Cross Road, SE22 9EU (8299 6953/www.bluemo.co.uk).*
Blueprint Café *Design Museum, 28 Shad Thames, SE1 2YD (7378 7031/www.dandd london.com).*

A fishy business: **Wright Brothers**, next to Borough Market. *See p237.*

La Bodeguita *Unit 222, Elephant & Castle Shopping Centre, SE1 6TE (7701 9166/ www.labodeguita.co.uk).*

Butlers Wharf Chop House *Butlers Wharf Building, 36E Shad Thames, SE1 2YE (7403 3403/www.danddlondon.com).*

Delfina *50 Bermondsey Street, SE1 3UD (7357 0244/www.delfina.org.uk).*

Dragon Castle *114 Walworth Road, SE17 1JL (7277 3388/www.dragoncastle.co.uk).*

Franklins *157 Lordship Lane, SE22 8HX (8299 9598/www.franklinsrestaurant.com).*

Ganapati *38 Holly Grove, SE15 5DF (7277 2928).*

Garrison *99-101 Bermondsey Street, SE1 3XB (7089 9355/www.thegarrison.co.uk).*

Jack's Tea & Coffee House *85 Pellatt Road, SE22 9JD (8693 0011).*

Laughing Gravy *154 Blackfriars Road, SE1 8EN (7721 7055/www.thelaughinggravy.com).*

Magdalen *152 Tooley Street, SE1 2TU (7403 1342/www.magdalenrestaurant.co.uk).*

M Manze *87 Tower Bridge Road, SE1 4TW (7407 2985/www.manze.co.uk).*

M Manze *105 Peckham High Street, SE15 5RS (7277 6181/www.manze.co.uk).*

Mozzarella e Pomodoro *21-22 Camberwell Green, SE5 7AA (7277 2020).*

Number 22 *22 Half Moon Lane, SE24 9HU (7095 9922/www.number-22.com).*

Olley's *65-69 Norwood Road, SE24 9AA (8671 8259/www.olleys.info).*

Oxo Tower Restaurant, Bar & Brasserie *8th floor, Oxo Tower Wharf, Barge House Street, SE1 9PH (7803 3888/www.harvey nichols.com).*

Palmerston *91 Lordship Lane, SE22 8EP (8693 1629).*

Pavilion Café *Dulwich Park, SE21 7BQ (8299 1383/www.pavilioncafedulwich.co.uk).*

Petitou *63 Choumert Road, SE15 4AR (7639 2613).*

Le Pont de la Tour *36D Shad Thames, SE1 2YE (7403 8403/www.danddlondon.com).*

Roast *The Floral Hall, Borough Market, Stoney Street, SE1 1TL (7940 1300/www. roast-restaurant.com).*

Rosendale *65 Rosendale Road, SE21 8EZ (8670 0812/www.therosendale.co.uk).*

Sea Cow *37 Lordship Lane, SE22 8EW (8693 3111).*

Shipp's Tea Rooms *4 Park Street, SE1 9AB (7407 2692).*

Table *83 Southwark Street, SE1 0HX (7401 2760/www.thetablecafe.com).*

Tamesa@Oxo *2nd floor, Oxo Tower Wharf, Barge House Street, SE1 9PH (7633 0088/ www.oxotower.co.uk).*

Tapas Brindisa *18-20 Southwark Street, SE1 1TJ (7357 8880/www.brindisa.com).*

Tate Modern Café 2 *2nd floor, Tate Modern, Sumner Street, SE1 9TG (7401 5014/ www.tate.org.uk).*

Wright Brothers Oyster & Porter House *11 Stoney Street, SE1 9AD (7403 9554/ www.wrightbros.eu.com).*

Bars & pubs

Lucky Borough. The area is home to the best concentration of good pubs in London. The tiny Lord Clyde, the quintessential backstreet local, has been run immaculately by the Fitzpatrick family for more than 50 years, while on the edge of Borough Market are the Rake (run by the folks behind the Utobeer stall) and the Market Porter, with its peerless range of ale and 6am opening time. Best of the bunch, though, is the Royal Oak behind Borough tube, it's the only London outpost of Sussex brewery Harvey's.

Southwark

Boozing in Bermondsey was recently bolstered by Hide Bar, an ambitious cocktail bar with an encyclopaedia-like menu. Modern-chic Village East is fine for a less showy drink; boat pub the Wibbley Wobbly is as laid-back as they come, playing host to a regular comedy night and all manner of eccentric regulars.

Camberwell has also been improved by newcomers – gastro-leaning pubs the Dark Horse and the Bear – and East Dulwich offers the lovely Herne Tavern, with its large, kid-friendly garden. On nearby Lordship Lane, wine bar Green & Blue is hard to fault. Over in Nunhead, the appropriately named Old Nun's Head does its bit for real ale and decent pub grub.

Dulwich and the surrounding area is something of a hotspot for grand pubs. Dulwich Village stalwart the Crown & Greyhound is a wonderful old pub; Sydenham's Dulwich Wood House is even better; and the Rosendale (see p238) is a textbook example of a fine gastropub.

Though Elephant & Castle has a cast-iron nightlife rep, thanks to world-renowned Ministry of Sound, decent bars and pubs are thin on the ground. Peckham fares better, with cheery gastropub the Rye Hotel, trendy Bar Story and the relaxed Gowlett pub, server of locally adored pizza.

Bar Story *213 Blenheim Grove, SE15 4QL (7635 6643/www.barstory.co.uk).*
Bear *296A Camberwell New Road, SE5 0RP (7274 7037/www.thebear-freehouse.co.uk).*
Crown & Greyhound *73 Dulwich Village, SE21 7BJ (8299 4976).*
Dark Horse *16 Grove Lane, SE5 8SY (7703 9990).*
Dulwich Wood House *39 Sydenham Hill, SE26 6RS (8693 5666).*
Gowlett *62 Gowlett Road, SE15 4HY (7635 7048/www.thegowlett.com).*
Green & Blue *38 Lordship Lane, SE22 8HJ (8693 9250/www.greenandbluewines.com).*
Herne Tavern *2 Forest Hill Road, SE22 0RR (8299 9521).*
Hide Bar *39-45 Bermondsey Street, SE1 3XF (7403 6655).*
Lord Clyde *27 Clennam Street, SE1 1ER (7407 3397).*
Market Porter *9 Stoney Street, SE1 9AA (7407 2495).*
Ministry of Sound *103 Gaunt Street, SE1 6DP (0870 060 0010/http://club.ministryof sound.com/club).*
Old Nun's Head *15 Nunhead Green, SE15 3QQ (7639 4007).*
Rake *14A Winchester Walk, SE1 9AG (7407 0557).*

Royal Oak *44 Tabard Street, SE1 4JU (7357 7173).*
Rye Hotel *31 Peckham Rye, SE15 3NX (7639 5397).*
Village East *171-173 Bermondsey Street, SE1 3UW (7357 6082/www.villageeast.co.uk).*
Wibbley Wobbly *Greenland Dock, Rope Street, SE16 7SZ (7232 2320).*

Shops

Borough Market is probably the best, certainly the most famous, food market in London, selling everything from organic cakes and breads to Spanish ham from acorn-fed pigs. Fridays and Saturdays are always packed (it's become a major tourist attraction), so Thursdays can provide a good alternative. Permanent food shops in the area include branches of Spanish food importer Brindisa (see p238 Tapas Brindisa), cake shop Konditor & Cook and Neal's Yard Dairy. At the other end of the borough, both Dulwich and Peckham host regular farmers' markets.

Not food-oriented, but with a charm all its own, Bermondsey Square Antiques Market (sometimes called New Caledonian Market) specialises in ramshackle Victoriana. Busy and bustling East Street Market, off the Walworth Road, is a traditional London street market.

Beside the river, the Oxo Tower hosts a community of independent designer-makers: look out for Bodo Sperlein's delicate porcelain, quirky crockery and teatowels from W2, and stained-glass designs from Kate Maestri. The hippest shops in the area are on Bermondsey Street, including United Nude/Terra Plana ethical shoes, Cock & Magpie's cult casuals, men's fashion from the former head of Burberry's menswear division at Bermondsey 167, and Igloo florist/wine shop.

Surrey Quays shopping centre and Canada Water Retail Park are grim but functional, with a massive branch of French sports superstore Decathlon. The Old Kent Road, similarly uninspiring, nevertheless is home to big branches of superstores such as PC World and B&Q.

In Camberwell, seek out Caribbean bakery Mixed Blessings, Edwardes bikes and old-school purveyor Men's Traditional Shoes. In business since 1861, it still sells handmade leather brogues alongside Tricker's, Church's and Loakes.

It's cheap and cheerful down Rye Lane and Peckham High Street, where streetlife is dominated by the Afro-Caribbean population. This means exotic fish and vegetables, colourful market stalls and plenty of nail and hair shops. Persepolis sells Moroccan food and fancy goods, Review has a good stock of art and design books, and Wing Tai supermarket is a useful source of all things oriental.

In the south of the borough, pretty gift shops suit Dulwich and Herne Hill's genteel air. Dulwich Trader on Croxted Road (the border with Lambeth) has a well-edited array of furniture, clothing, ceramics and textiles, including pieces from Cath Kidston, Lulu Guinness and Lola Rose jewellery. In Herne Hill, delightful children's bookshop Tales on Moon Lane is a birthday present fail-safe, as is Just William's toyshop across the road. You'll find deli goods at Mimosa and baby and maternity wear at Merry Go Round. Stardust is a good choice for unusual gifts, while Blackbird Bakery is superb for bread, cakes, tarts and muffins.

Despite recent chain incursions, East Dulwich is still ruled by independent boutiques. Among the best of them are Grace & Favour, stella b shoes, Petals and Mrs Robinson. The area also draws foodies from miles around: they are only too happy to join the lengthy queues at Moxon's fishmonger, William Rose butcher, the Cheese Block, the East Dulwich Deli, Green & Blue wine shop and Hope & Greenwood's old-school sweet shop. A range of food stalls open on North Cross Road for the Friday and Saturday markets. The new Ed Warehouse brings together a collection of independent traders under one roof.

Bermondsey 167 *167 Bermondsey Street, SE1 3UW (7407 3137).*
Bermondsey Square Antiques Market *Corner of Bermondsey Street & Long Lane, SE1 4QB (7525 6000/www.southwark.gov.uk).*
Blackbird Bakery *208 Railton Road, SE24 0JT (7095 8800/www.4andtwenty.co.uk).*
Bodo Sperlein *Unit 1.05, Oxo Tower Wharf, Barge House Street, SE1 9PH (7633 9413/ www.bodosperlein.com).*
Borough Market *8 Southwark Street, SE1 1TL (7407 1002/www.boroughmarket.org.uk).*
Cheese Block *69 Lordship Lane, SE22 8EP (8299 3636).*
Cock & Magpie *96 Bermondsey Street, SE1 3UB (7357 6482/www.cockandmagpie.com).*
Decathlon *Canada Water Retail Park, Surrey Quays Road, SE16 2XU (7394 2000/ www.decathlon.co.uk).*
Dulwich Farmers' Market *South Gravel, Dulwich College, Dulwich Common, SE21.*
Dulwich Trader *9-11 Croxted Road, SE21 8SZ (8761 3457).*
East Dulwich Deli *15-17 Lordship Lane, SE22 8EW (8693 2525).*
East Street Market *East Street, SE17 1EL (Street Trading Office 7525 6000).*
Edwardes *221-225 Camberwell Road, SE5 0HG (7703 5720).*
Ed Warehouse *1 Zenoria Street, SE22 8HP (8693 3033).*
Grace & Favour *35 North Cross Road, SE22 9ET (8693 4400).*
Green & Blue *36-38 Lordship Lane, SE22 8HJ (8693 9250/www.greenandbluewines.com).*
Hope & Greenwood *20 North Cross Road, SE22 9EU (8613 1777/www.hopeand greenwood.co.uk).*
Igloo Flowers *88 Bermondsey Street, SE1 3UB (7403 7774/www.iglooflowers.com).*
Just William's *18 Half Moon Lane, SE24 9HU (7733 9995).*
Kate Maestri *Unit 2.11, Oxo Tower Wharf, Barge House Street, SE1 9PH (7620 0330/ www.katemaestri.com).*
Konditor & Cook *10 Stoney Street, SE1 9AD (7407 5100/www.konditorandcook.com).*
Men's Traditional Shoes *171 Camberwell Road, SE5 0HB (7703 4179).*
Merry Go Round *21 Half Moon Lane, SE24 9JU (7737 6452).*
Mimosa *16 Half Moon Lane, SE24 9HU (7733 8838/www.mimosafoods.com).*

Southwark

COUNCIL TAX

A	up to £40,000	£787.30
B	£40,001-£52,000	£981.51
C	£52,001-£68,000	£1,049.73
D	£68,001-£88,000	£1,180.94
E	£88,001-£120,000	£1,443.37
F	£120,001-£160,000	£1,705.80
G	£160,001-£320,000	£1,968.24
H	over £320,000	£2,361.88

RECYCLING

No. of bring sites 54 (for nearest, visit www.recycleforlondon.com)
Household waste recycled 11.55%
Main recycling centre Manor Place Depot, 30-34 Penrose Street, SE17 3DW (7252 7717)
Other recycling services green waste collection; home composting; white goods, home and office furniture collection
Council contact Recycling Unit, 30-34 Penrose Street, SE1 7 3DW (7525 2000)

Mixed Blessings *12-14 Camberwell Road, SE5 0EN (7703 9433).*
Moxon's *149 Lordship Lane, SE22 8HX (8299 1559).*
Mrs Robinson *128-130 Lordship Lane, SE22 8HD (8693 0693).*
Neal's Yard Dairy *6 Park Street, SE1 9AB (7645 3554/www.nealsyarddairy.co.uk).*
Peckham Farmers' Market *Peckham Square, Peckham High Street, SE15 5QN (7833 0338/ www.lfm.org.uk).*
Persepolis *30 Peckham High Street, SE15 5DT (7639 8007).*
Petals *16 Melbourne Grove, SE22 8OZ (8299 3939).*
Review *131 Bellenden Road, SE15 4QY (7639 7400/www.reviewbookshop.co.uk).*
Stardust *294 Milkwood Road, SE24 0EZ (7737 0199/www.stardustkids.co.uk).*
stella b *51 North Cross Road, SE22 9ET (8693 5052/www.stellabshoes.com).*
Tales on Moon Lane *25 Half Moon Lane, SE24 9JU (7274 5759/www.talesonmoonlane.co.uk).*
United Nude/Terra Plana *124 Bermondsey Street, SE1 3TX (7407 3758/www.unitednude. com/www.terraplana.com).*
W2 *Unit 1.22, Oxo Tower Wharf, Barge House Street, SE1 9PH (7922 1444/www. W2products.com).*
William Rose *26 Lordship Lane, SE22 8HD (8693 9191).*
Wing Tai *Unit 11A, Aylesham Centre, SE15 5EW (7635 0714).*

Arts & attractions

Cinemas & theatres

Menier Chocolate Factory *51-53 Southwark Street, SE1 1RU (7907 7060/www.menier chocolatefactory.com).* Gallery, restaurant, theatre and rehearsal space.
Odeon Surrey Quays *Surrey Quays Leisure Park, Redriff Road, SE16 7LL (0871 224 4007/ www.odeon.co.uk).*
Peckham Multiplex *95A Rye Lane, SE15 4ST (0870 042 9399/www.peckhamplex.com).*
Scoop *South Bank, between London Bridge & Tower Bridge, SE1 (www.morelondon.com).*
Shakespeare's Globe *21 New Globe Walk, SE1 9DT (7401 9919/tours 7902 1500/ www.shakespeares-globe.org).* Very popular re-creation of the original Elizabethan theatre, complete with thatched roof and standing room for the peasants.
Shunt Vaults *20 Stainer Street (entrance in Joiner Street), SE1 9RL (7378 7776/ www.shunt.co.uk).* Home to an experimental arts collective, who perform a variety of new plays, stage readings and also showcase unusual music installations.
Siobhan Davies Dance Studios *85 St George's Road, SE1 6ER (7091 9650/www. siobhandavies.com).* Completed in 2006, the building is as striking as the exhibitions and dance performances within.

Unicorn Theatre *147 Tooley Street, SE1 2HZ (7645 0560/www.unicorntheatre.com).* A purpose-built theatre for children.

Galleries & museums

Bramah Museum of Tea & Coffee *40 Southwark Street, SE1 1UN (7403 5650/ www.bramahmuseum.co.uk).* First museum dedicated to the nation's favourite warm drinks.
Brunel Museum *Railway Avenue, SE16 4LF (7231 3840/www.brunelenginehouse.org.uk).*
Clink Prison Museum *1 Clink Street, SE1 9DG (7403 0900/www.clink.co.uk).* Prison exhibition with re-creation of original cells.
Cuming Museum *Old Walworth Town Hall, 151 Walworth Road, SE17 1RY (7525 2332/ www.southwark.gov.uk/cumingmuseum).* Southwark's local history from Roman times.
Design Museum *28 Shad Thames, SE1 2YD (7403 6933/www.designmuseum.org).* Museum of modern and contemporary design.
Dulwich Picture Gallery *Gallery Road, SE21 7AD (8693 5254/www.dulwichpicturegallery. org.uk).* An exquisite collection of Old Masters, housed in England's first purpose-built art gallery, designed by Sir John Soane in 1811.
Fashion & Textiles Museum *83 Bermondsey Street, SE1 3XF (7407 8664/www.ftmlondon.org).* Shrine to the fashion industry, with the Zandra Rhodes Collection.
Imperial War Museum *Lambeth Road, SE1 6HZ (7416 5000/www.iwm.org.uk).*
Livesey Museum for Children *682 Old Kent Road, SE15 1JF (7635 5829/www.livesey museum.org.uk).* Interactive kids' museum, with temporary shows and a courtyard to play in.
London Dungeon *28-34 Tooley Street, SE1 2SZ (7403 7221/www.thedungeons.com).* Ever-popular re-creation of the unpleasant aspects of London's history.
Old Operating Theatre Museum & Herb Garret *9A St Thomas's Street, SE1 9RY (7188 2679/www.thegarret.org.uk).* A 16th-century herb loft and 17th-century operating theatre.
Tate Modern *Bankside, SE1 9TG (7887 8000/ www.tate.org.uk).* Iconic leader of London's modern art scene – its setting as impressive as its contents.
Winston Churchill's Britain at War Experience *64-66 Tooley Street, SE1 2TF (7403 3171/www.britainatwar.co.uk).* Re-creation of an Anderson shelter during a World War II air raid.

Other attractions

City Hall *The Queen's Walk, SE1 2AA (7983 4100/www.london.gov.uk).*
Dulwich Festival *8299 1011/www.dulwich festival.co.uk.* Annual shindig of music, theatre, poetry and art, held in May.
Golden Hinde *Unit 1 & 2, Pickfords Wharf, Clink Street, SE1 9DG (0870 011 8700/ www.goldenhinde.org).*
HMS Belfast *Morgan's Lane, Tooley Street, SE1 2JH (7940 6300/www.iwm.org.uk).* Retired World War II battlecruiser, open to view.

St Giles Camberwell *81 Camberwell Church Street, SE5 8RB (7703 4504/www.stgiles camberwell.org.uk).*
Southwark Cathedral *London Bridge, SE1 9DA (7367 6700/tours 7367 6734/www. southwark.anglican.org).* Small but handsome cathedral, the oldest of its kind in London.
Surrey Docks Farm *South Wharf, Rotherhithe Street, SE16 5EY (7231 1010/www.surrey docksfarm.org).*

Sport & fitness

Well-organised, grant-funded outfit Fusion maintains the borough's public leisure facilities. Its trademark, wipe-clean cardiovascular machines have replaced many antiquated sweat boxes, and Peckham Pulse has reopened. Dulwich Leisure Centre and the Colombo Centre are worth tracking down, as is the Surrey Docks Watersports Centre. The private Miami Health Club is a well-disguised gem, while the Dojo Physical Arts centre is a beacon for wannabe Karate Kids and kick-boxing champions. Unfortunately, many of the borough's Victorian swimming baths are currently under threat – Camberwell's looks especially vulnerable.

Gyms & leisure centres

Camberwell Leisure Centre *Artichoke Place, off Camberwell Church Street, SE5 8TS (7703 3024/www.fusion-lifestyle.com).*
Club & Spa at County Hall *County Hall, SE1 7BP (7928 4900/www.theclubatcountyhall. co.uk).* Private.
Colombo Centre *34-68 Colombo Street, SE1 8DP (7261 1658/www.colombo-centre.org).*
Dojo Physical Arts *10-11 Milroy Walk, Upper Ground, SE1 9LW (7928 3000/ www.physical-arts.com).* Private.
Dulwich Leisure Centre *45 East Dulwich Road, SE22 9AN (8693 1833/www.fusion-lifestyle.com).*
Elephant & Castle Leisure Centre *22 Elephant & Castle, SE1 6SQ (7582 5505/ www.fusion-lifestyle.com).*
Fitness First *www.fitnessfirst.co.uk; Cottons Building, Tooley Street, SE1 2QN (7403 1171); London Bridge Hotel, 8-81 London Bridge Street, SE1 9SG (0870 898 0687); 1st floor, 332-344 Walworth Road, SE17 2NA (7252 4555).* Private.
Hamlets Health Club *Edgar Kail Way, Dog Kennel Hill, SE22 8BD (7274 8707).* Private.
K4 Fitness *127 Stamford Street, SE1 9NQ (7633 2196/www.kclsu.org/k4).* Private.
LivingWell *265 Rotherhithe Street, SE16 5HW (7064 4421/www.livingwell.com).* Private.
Miami Health Club *208-210 Old Kent Road, SE1 5TY (7703 9811/www.miamihealthclub. co.uk).* Private.

Peckham Pulse Healthy Living Centre *10 Melon Road, SE15 5QN (7525 4999/ www.fusion-lifestyle.com).*
Seven Islands Leisure Centre *Lower Road, SE16 2TU (7237 3296/www.fusion-lifestyle.com).*
Surrey Docks Watersports Centre *Rope Street, off Plough Way, Greenland Dock, SE16 7SX (7237 4009/www.fusion-lifestyle.com).*
Thirtysevendegrees *2B More London, Riverside, SE1 2AP (7940 4937/www.thirty sevendegrees.co.uk).*
Tokei Martial Arts & Fitness Club *Lion Court, 28 Magdalen Street, SE1 2EN (7403 5979/www.tokeicentre.org).* Private.

Other facilities

Dulwich & Sydenham Hill Golf Club *Grange Lane, College Road, SE21 7LH (8693 3961/www.dulwichgolf.co.uk).* Private.
Dulwich Sports Club *Burbage Road, SE21 7JA (7274 1242/www.dulwichsportsclub.com).*
Herne Hill Velodrome *Burbage Road, SE24 9HE (www.vcl.org.uk).* This cycling track is claimed to be the last remaining venue from the 1948 Olympic Games still in use.

Schools

WHAT THE PARENTS SAY:

❝The situation in Southwark is like that in other inner London boroughs: the primary schools are good and improving, while high-achieving secondary schools are unacceptably scarce.

In East Dulwich, where a few years ago there was a single sought-after primary school, now three or four are close to being oversubscribed. That's partly an effect of huge demographic changes, but also the result of a deliberate attempt to transform previously failing schools. Four years ago my daughter's primary school was in special measures; now, it has outstripped its nearest competitors in the league tables.

Secondary schools are a different matter. There are new academies for boys and girls in Peckham, though these have a sporting or vocational ethos rather than an academic one. The catchment area of the one academically oriented state secondary is tiny. Friends with secondary-school-age children have either sent them out of the borough, to schools in Lewisham or Bromley, or gone private – there are several excellent independent schools. That's a choice parents across London will be familiar with.❞
Jonathan Derbyshire, father of two, East Dulwich

Primary

There are 68 state primary schools in the borough of Southwark, 20 of which are church schools. There are also six independent primaries.

See www.southwark.gov.uk, www.edubase.gov. uk and www.ofsted.gov.uk for more information.

Secondary

Academy at Peckham *112 Peckham Road, SE15 5DZ (7703 4417/www.peckhamacademy. southwark.sch.uk).*
Alleyn's *Townley Road, SE22 8SU (8557 1500/www.alleyns.org.uk).* Private.
Bacon's College *Timber Pond Road, SE16 6AT (7237 1928/www.baconsctc.co.uk).*
Charter School *Red Post Hill, SE24 9JH (7346 6600/www.charter.southwark.sch.uk).*
City of London Academy Southwark *240 Lynton Road, SE1 5LA (7394 5100/ www.cityacademy.co.uk).*
Dulwich College *SE21 7LD (8693 3601/ www.dulwich.org.uk).* Boys only; private.
Geoffrey Chaucer Technology College *Harper Road, SE1 6AG (7407 6877/ www.geoffreychaucer.southwark.sch.uk).*
Harris Academy Bermondsey *55 Southwark Park Road, SE16 3TZ (7237 9316).* Girls only.
Harris Girls' Academy East Dulwich *Homestall Road, SE22 0NR (7732 2276/www.hgaed.org.uk).* Girls only.
James Allen's Girls' School *144 East Dulwich Grove, SE22 8TE (8693 1181/ www.jags.org.uk).* Girls only; private.
Kingsdale School *Alleyn Park, Dulwich, SE21 8SQ (8670 7575/www.kingsdale. southwark.sch.uk).*
Notre Dame RC Girls' School *118 St George's Road, SE1 6EX (7261 1121).* Girls only.
Sacred Heart RC School *Camberwell New Road, SE5 0RP (7274 6844/www.sacredheart. southwark.sch.uk).*
St Michael & All Angels Academy *Farmers Road, Camberwell, SE5 0UB (7701 4166/www.stmichaelandallangelsacademy.org).*
St Michael's RC School *John Felton Road, SE16 4UN (7237 6432).*
St Saviour's & St Olave's CE School *New Kent Road, SE1 4AN (7407 1843/ www.ssso.southwark.sch.uk).* Girls only.
St Thomas the Apostle College *Hollydale Road, SE22 2EB (7639 0106/www.stac. southwark.sch.uk).* Boys only.
Walworth Academy *Shorncliffe Road, SE1 5UJ (7450 9570/www.walworthacademy.co.uk).*

Property

WHAT THE AGENTS SAY:

'People have got tired of walloping up and down the Northern line into the City, which is good news for Borough. Right on the City's doorstep, it's full of restaurants, shops, Borough Market, of course, and Bankside. It's changed and continues to change. Take all the local authority housing estates: the old tenants bought their place for tuppence, did their three or ten years, then off they go with a fistful of cash. It's

certainly not family-oriented. The schools are pretty rubbishy from what we can gather, and families are moving out.'
Jeremy Hewitt, Field & Sons, Borough

Average property prices

Detached £1,095,125
Semi-detached £592,180
Terraced £402,614
Flat £288,542

Local estate agents

Alex Neil *146 Lower Road, SE16 2UG (7394 9988/www.alexneil.co.uk).*
Bairstow Eves *www.bairstoweves.co.uk; 2 offices in the borough (Camberwell 7708 2002/ Peckham 7277 6644).*
Burnet Ware & Graves *www.b-w-g.co.uk; 3 offices in the borough (East Dulwich 8693 4201/Herne Hill 7733 1293/Surrey Quays 7232 0333).*
Dulwich & Village Residential *www.dulwichhomes.com; 2 offices in the borough (Dulwich 8693 4999/East Dulwich 8693 7999).*
Field & Sons *54 Borough High Street, SE1 1XL (7407 1375/www.fieldandsons.co.uk).*
Hastings International *www.hastingsinternational.com; 3 offices in the borough (Borough 7378 9000/Rotherhithe 7231 4973/Shad Thames 7407 1066).*
Osbourne Stewart *106 Grove Vale, SE22 8DR (8299 1444/www.osbourne-stewart.com).*
Roy Brooks *2 Barry Parade, Barry Road, SE22 0JA (8299 3021/www.roybrooks.co.uk).*

Other information

Council

Southwark Council *Town Hall, 31 Peckham Road, SE5 8UB (7525 5000/www.southwark. gov.uk).*

Legal services

Bermondsey CAB *8 Market Place, Southwark Park Road, SE16 3UQ (0844 499 4134/ www.adviceguide.org.uk).*
Cambridge House Law Centre *137 Camberwell Road, SE5 0HF (7358 7025).*
Peckham CAB *97 Peckham High Street, SE15 5RS (0844 499 4134/www.adviceguide.org.uk).*

Local newspapers

South London Press *8769 4444/ www.southlondonpress.co.uk.*
Southwark News/Southwark Weekender *7231 5258/www.southwarknews.co.uk.*

Allotments & open spaces

Allotments For details of allotments in the borough, visit Southwark Council's website (www.southwark.gov.uk).
Open spaces *www.southwark.gov.uk/parks.*

'Lewisham knocks the spots off those smug, poncey north London boroughs. We've got everything – leafy parks, the Horniman Museum and proper inner-city crime.'

Phil Nice, actor/writer/comedian and resident
of Telegraph Hill for 25 years

Lewisham

One of only three London boroughs to have a directly elected mayor, Lewisham's Kentish roots are evident in its southernmost suburbs, but its northern edge – riverside Deptford – couldn't be more urban. Access to all areas should be improved with Lewisham's designation as a 'Zone of Change' in the Thames Gateway London Project. This means large-scale regeneration, growth and social advancement.

Neighbourhoods

New Cross and Telegraph Hill

Excitable references to New Cross becoming the new Camden may be a tad optimistic, but there's no doubt this area's strategic position in the Deptford Triangle of cool has bestowed some glamour. New Cross (or New Crossfire as some rags would have it, following the tragic shooting of an innocent Polish woman in a gang gun battle) is the only part of Lewisham with a tube station, though this is currently closed

– as is the whole of the East London line – until 2010 (a bus replacement service is running). Moreover, Goldsmiths College (Malcolm Maclaren's alma mater) is here, which trendies things up a bit. The area also boasts enough pub-cum-club-cum-gig venues to keep local musos happy.

Also of note is Clifton Rise, the starting point of a proud moment in Lewisham's history when, in 1977, the biggest street battle against fascists since the Battle of Cable Street in 1936, took place here.

Goldsmiths College, part of the University of London, occupies various buildings. The Ben Pimlott Building,

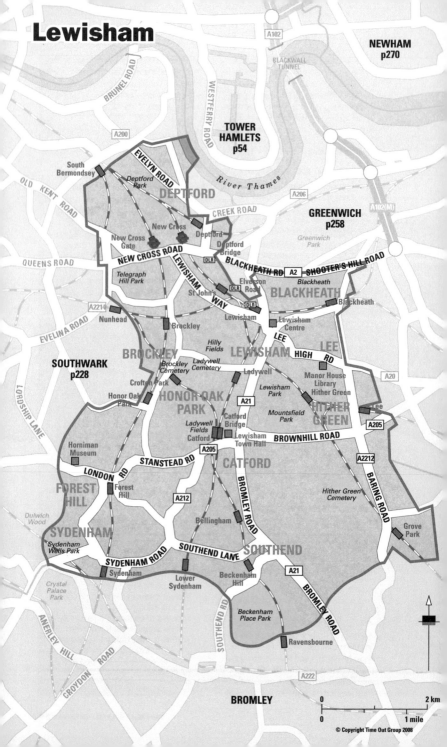

a dramatic glass and steel construction, is a Will Alsop creation. Up the steeply climbing wide roads, away from all the hullabaloo of the main drag, Telegraph Hill is a largely unspoilt residential area with some impressive-looking Edwardian bay-fronted houses. The park here affords inspiring views over the city and has great play facilities, as well as a rangers' HQ.

Deptford and St John's

The social problems arising from rapid gentrification on an area's bemused working-class population were crystallised, if simplified, in *The Tower*, Anthony Wonke's 2007 documentary for the BBC. Deptford's position as Lewisham's only piece of waterside real estate has made it a regeneration hotspot for ages. A tower block that was once part of the notorious Pepys Estate was sold to developers and turned into smart river-view apartments, yet the other Pepys towers, away from the water, remain council flats. Cue serious social tensions. It's the same story throughout this neighbourhood. The 13th-century Convoys Wharf, once part of Deptford Strand and Henry VIII's extensive dockyards, is now owned by News International, which plans to sell the site for a development of flats, leisure facilities and a school. Elsewhere, Silwood Estate, Deals Gateway and station redevelopment plans continue apace.

Deptford High Street, a mish-mash of pound shops and pie and mash caffs, with its lively market – stalls sell everything from fruit and veg to second-hand clothes and household junk – is a very old-school retail experience. There's not much sign of gentrification here yet. Veer off for beautiful Albury Street, built in the early 18th century and all the more elegant for its proximity to the chaotic High Street. Between here and Church Street stands the Roman Baroque church of St Paul's, where there's a plaque to Myididdee, a Tahitian who sailed with Captain Bligh and died in Deptford in 1793.

Follow Church Street riverward to find St Nicholas's Church, where Christopher Marlowe is rumoured to have been buried following his violent end in a Deptford pub, or go east to Creekside, Deptford's artists' quarter. This slightly spooky area, with its mudflats and rotting hulks of old boats, is lit up by sudden flashes of artistic licence. Creekside is home to Cockpit Arts (www.cockpitarts.com) – a charity that supports designer-makers – as well as the studios and workshops of the neighbourhood's many creative souls.

Laban, the contemporary dance centre, is housed in an iridescent, coloured-perspex building that looks like it's been marooned on the muddy creek when you look at it from the Ha'penny Hatch Bridge. Opposite, the prize-winning Ferranti Park has transformed a disused road salt depot. If you really want to get stuck in to this area's (natural) history, pull on your gumboots and get down to the Creekside Centre, which, along with jolly Twinkle Park, was one of many post-millennial prettification projects that have helped improve Deptford's profile over the years.

Away from the river, St John's sits between Deptford and Lewisham town

Highs & Lows

▲ **Value for money** You can forget Blackheath, Telegraph Hill and anywhere else picturesque but, on the whole, Lewisham is one of London's cheaper boroughs
Greenery Loads of parks mean this is a top place for dog-owners and child-rearers to roam
Connections Fleets of buses jostle their way into the West End and City. Trains take ten or 15 minutes to get to London Bridge and Charing Cross. There's also the DLR and the East London line developments

Stupid building ventures Enough with the shiny chrome and coloured glass developments. People don't want to live in tiny apartments with no room for a decent cooker, however seductive they look in the poster campaigns
Violent crime In the inner-city areas, it's still worrying. Witness the shooting of an innocent passer-by in New Cross in September 2007
Traffic, traffic, traffic Clogging up the South Circular and causing ructions on the A2, A21 and any ▼ other As worth taking in and out of town

centres. Developed in the the mid 19th century as New Deptford, it's a handsome conservation pocket, with lots of spacious Victorian and Edwardian houses clustered around its own station and church.

Blackheath

Every borough has a bit of posh. Lewisham's is bijou Blackheath Village, although, as with every desirable enclave in the smoke, the village tag is somewhat misplaced. One of London's oldest recorded settlements, the area is characterised by a huge open space – the heath itself – whose verdant airiness is somewhat compromised by the incessant traffic of the A2, once known as Watling Street, the Roman road to Canterbury. Wat Tyler assembled his revolting peasants on Blackheath in 1381, and Henry VIII and Anne of Cleves met for the first time for a right royal picnic here in 1540, after which the King escorted his new bride over to his pad in Greenwich (and not long after kicked her out again). These days, the heath is favoured by dogwalkers, kite-fliers, sporting clubs and travelling circuses. The Blackheath tea hut, located here since the 1950s, has resisted various attempts to have it closed down. Beloved by clubbers, bikers and long-distance lorry drivers, it continues a proud tradition of providing refreshments to pilgrims.

The houses overlooking the heath are grand (and very expensive), but the smartest address of all is the Paragon, near South Row, a semicircle of seven colonnaded houses designed around 1800 by Michael Searles. The southern end of the Village, on the road to Lee, is home to the Blackheath Conservatoire (an old-established music school) and Blackheath Halls (now part of Greenwich's Trinity College of Music).

Lewisham

Sitting at the centre of a major road junction (the A20, A21 and A2211 for the A2 all radiate from the roundabout), with its own bus terminus, busy railway station and DLR station, Lewisham is certainly well connected. With the expansion of the East London line, the town's links with the City, West End and north London are set to become stronger. Add the ongoing regeneration of the area, scheduled to be complete by 2014, and Lewisham looks

like a sensible proposition for those looking for housing bargains south of the river.

The long-awaited makeover has started on a positive note. As the new housing development Rivermill Park was built on the ruins of the nasty Sundermead Estate near the town centre, landscapers freed the Ravensbourne River from its concrete channel and planted the banks with shrubs and grasses. Paved walkways with sculpture and benches, grassy expanses and well-lit paths constitute Lewisham's newest park, Cornmill Gardens. Over on the High Street in the shopping centre, the atmosphere is rather less restful. The newest and largest building here is the police station (the biggest in Europe) – which is apt, given the frequency with which things kick off in town.

Incomers attracted by the good transport links should not judge Lewisham by its High Street and unappealing indoor mall, although the street market has a certain rowdy charm. Bruce Williams's Lewisham mural, commissioned to celebrate the shopping centre's 21st birthday in 1998, is also worth a look. Estate agents urge housebuyers to explore areas around Lewisham Park, Belmont Hill and the roads connecting the High Street to Ladywell. They're seduced by the size and relative cheapness of the houses, easily accessible from town via wide, tree-lined roads.

Ladywell, Brockley and Honor Oak

Ladywell sits as a genteel halfway house between uncouth Lewisham and Catford town centres. There's a baker, a post office, an art shop, a fine independent hardware store, a florist, a barber and, er, a tattoo and piercing parlour. Ladywell is surrounded by greenery: Ladywell Fields, Brockley Cemetery and Hilly Fields all conspire to make Ladywell feel villagey.

In 1977, Ladywell Fields was the first meeting point of the All Lewisham Campaign Against Racism and Fascism (ALCARAF) demonstration. Over 5,000 people heard speeches by the Mayor of Lewisham, the Bishop of Southwark and the exiled Bishop of Namibia. They did not predict a riot, but that's what happened. Thirty years later, in an EU and Lewisham

Borough-funded bid to improve the quality of life for residents, and design out trouble into the bargain, Ladywell Fields has been transformed. The Ravensbourne River, now rechannelled in an attractive, meandering fashion across the fields from Catford, has little ponds and bridges at intervals. And with its running track, tennis courts, skate and BMX park and café, Ladywell Fields is a major resource for a burgeoning community. It also attracts wildlife, but not as much as Brockley Cemetery – a nature reserve and final resting place in one.

Across wide and traffic-calmed Adelaide Avenue rises Hilly Fields: a lovely, airy park with Prendergast girls' school at its centre and grassy slopes that look out over Lewisham town centre. Hilly Fields also has a mini Stonehenge: a stone circle of 12 granite boulders with two tall shadow-casting stones, erected to mark the new millennium. Artistic types tend to settle around here, and have done much to improve Brockley's profile – the Brockley Road (stations Crofton Park and Brockley) is rich in meeting places for the area's creatives. As well as cafés and galleries, there's the famous Brockley Jack pub-theatre managed by Southside Arts.

Also of note is the grand old Rivoli Ballroom, which started life as the Crofton Park Picture Palace in 1913. The large sprung maple dancefloor dates from its conversion to a ballroom in 1957. The place's old-fashioned good looks have given it London-wide kudos and made it an apt venue for the International Gay Ballroom Dancing Championship. Although mostly used for tea dances and classes, it was chosen by the White Stripes for a homely gig in summer 2007.

The housing here is dominated by modest Victorian terraces built for local workers. Brockley Rise, meanwhile, takes you to Honor Oak, a hilly residential area just over the borough boundary in Southwark. The main road through the area is called Honor Oak Park, as is the local overground station. For great views climb One Tree Hill, where there's a beacon (last lit for the millennium).

Lee and Hither Green

Residents of Lee are keen for Lewisham Council to spare a bit of its regeneration budget for this rather put-upon section of the borough, whose centre is swamped by heavy traffic and ill-advised building developments. It is to be hoped that the ugly 1960s shopping centre will be for the chop if a refurb is in the offing.

Away from the centre, however, some of Lee's residential streets are beautiful, and houses here are more affordable than in nearby Blackheath. The community benefits from the gorgeous Manor House Gardens, a pretty park with duck pond and café, set around Manor House, a 1775 mansion built for Sir Francis Baring, the banker. The building houses the local library and is due to undergo refurbishment. Another valuable local resource is Stark Gallery, which has three exhibition spaces and holds yoga and Pilates classes.

STATISTICS

BOROUGH MAKE-UP
Population 255,700
Average weekly pay £478.80
Ethnic origins
  White 65.28%
  Mixed 4.19%
  Asian or Asian British 5.33%
  Black or Black British 22.35%
  Chinese or other 2.80%
Students 9.95%
Retirees 8.69%

HOUSING STOCK
Borough size 34.7km²
No. of households 110,800
Detached 2.9%
Semi-detached 12.9%
Terraced 31.5%
Flats (purpose-built) 32.5%
Flats (converted) 19.4%
Flats (both) 51.9%

CRIME PER 1,000 OF POPULATION
(average for England and Wales in brackets)
Burglary 10 (5)
Robbery 11 (2)
Theft of vehicle 7 (4)
Theft from vehicle 9 (9)
Violence against the person 33 (19)
Sexual offences 2 (1)

MPs & COUNCIL
MPs *Lewisham East* Bridget Prentice (Labour); *Lewisham, Deptford* Joan Ruddock (Labour); *Lewisham West* Jim Dowd (Labour)
CPA 4 stars; improving well

Lewisham

Old-school pie 'n' mash at **Manze's**.

From Manor House Gardens, a walk west brings you to Hither Green, where the terraced housing looks more mundane. Once a hamlet in the Great North Wood, this is a densely populated residential area with a major railway junction (London Bridge is 11 minutes away) – it's also a short walk from Lewisham town centre. The site of the grand neo-Gothic Hither Green Hospital, dating from 1878, has become an extensive housing development. A few preserved remnants of the old buildings remain, most obviously the water tower, a local landmark.

Catford

Once upon a time wild cats gambolled by a ford and a settlement grew up called Catford (there are other theories involving a cattle ford). Today it is characterised by the giant black and white fibreglass feline atop the shopping centre. This is, sadly, one of the more attractive features of Catford, although attempts have been made with various street sculptures to improve the town's ill-favoured looks.

Apart from the elegant art deco Broadway Theatre, Catford's dominant architectural theme is Brutalist. The town's once-beautiful Broadway market area now cowers behind a 1971 carbuncle containing Lewisham Town Hall and Civic Suite; another culprit, Laurence House (across the dreadful A205 gyratory), houses the local library. More tower blocks – Eros House, Rosenthal House and the

horrible council flats known as Milford Towers – complete a depressing picture.

Catford's disused greyhound track is earmarked for housing development, a fact that causes some perturbation among residents, who avow that there are already too few amenities for its population.

Away from the gyratory, green spaces and huge, reasonably priced Edwardian family houses are reasons enough for settling here. Towards Hither Green the well-built houses of the Corbett Estate (built by Archibald Cameron Corbett MP around 1900) are coveted for their generous proportions. There are no pubs near Corbett houses, though: the developer was a strict Presbyterian. Mountsfield Park, between Rushey Green and Hither Green, is the scene of Lewisham's People's Day every summer.

Forest Hill and Sydenham

Traditionally, young professionals hearing the pitter patter of little feet have traded in their priccy Camberwell and Clapham flats for large family houses in Forest Hill. With its accessible green spaces and most famous landmark, the Horniman Museum, it is one of the most rewarding parts of Lewisham in which to bring up children.

To the south, Upper Sydenham has broader streets, some big houses and wide open spaces, such as the gorgeous Sydenham Wells Park and the soon-to-be spectacular-again Crystal Palace Park. The area where Upper gives way to Lower Sydenham at Kirkdale's meeting with Westwood Hill is known as Cobbs Corner. Here a pub called the Greyhound has been much on the mind of the Sydenham Society, not because it was ever a particularly good boozer, but because it was threatened with demolition to create flats. The society thinks the building's architectural and historical significance, and its landmark status, give this little piece of Sydenham a centre. The developers want those flats built. Watch that boarded-up space.

The Bell Green end of Sydenham, curving round towards more downmarket Catford, is less than salubrious, but expects much from the proposed regeneration of the land around the ugly gas containers and the domineering Savacentre.

The transport future's bright for Forest Hill and Sydenham. Both areas will benefit from the development of the East London

Lewisham

Join the local muso crowd for gigs at the **New Cross Inn**. *See p253.*

line, poised to provide a metro-style (National Rail) train service north to Highbury & Islington, south to West Croydon and west to Clapham Junction. Phase one of the project, from New Cross Gate south to Crystal Palace and West Croydon, should be completed by June 2010.

Grove Park, Southend and Downham

Travelling south from Hither Green, down Baring Road past the cemetery, eventually brings you to Grove Park and Chinbrook Meadows, at the borough's most south-easterly edge. The meadows were quite unpleasant until the Quaggy Waterways Action Group rolled up its sleeves and remodelled the Quaggy River's flow to create a small floodplain. Indeed, it is the parks and open spaces around this part of Lewisham that make the rest of it more palatable.

Council housing is the norm. Downham is dominated by the unprepossessing Downham Estate. Grove Park is similarly characterised by the massive Grove Park Estate. Southend, historically the most rural and backward part of the borough, shares with the south Catford community of Bellingham a 'cottage estate' of red-brick, two-bedroom dwellings with gardens, which are more attractive.

Another green highlight is the Forster Memorial Park, though the biggest attraction in this neck of the woods is the extensive

Beckenham Place Park, whose Grade II-listed mansion house is home to the clubhouse for an excellent municipal pay-and-play golf course.

Restaurants & cafés

Doughnut, noodle and sausage vans dominate Lewisham Market, but if it's fuel food you're after, look no further than fish and chip perfection at Something Fishy. Up Lee High Road, Sri Lankan caff Arru Suval doles out decent high-street curries for indecently low prices (spend more than seven quid and you might explode).

The cheap and spicy theme continues in the other direction, on Loampit Hill, where Everest Curry King, another Sri Lankan specialist, has cramped surroundings and raging hot curries and snacks. More down-to-earth fodder (breakfasts, stews, roasts) is available from Maggie's Café, by the station, voted best in the world by the well-fed readers of the *Catford News Shopper*.

In New Cross, students tuck into fiery dishes from Esarn and Laos at tiny Thailand, or Turkish barbecued meats, meze and pide at Meze Mangal. North of New Cross Road, Deptford's budget eating places include AJ Goddard's and Manze's eel, pie and mash shops.

Blackheath is altogether a different story. In posh Chapter Two there's a Modern European menu replete with veloutés and remoulades. Blackheath is also home to

Lewisham

Laicram, a cosy neighbourhood Thai, and various organically inspired deli-cafés. El Pirata is a family-friendly Spanish tapas restaurant overlooking the heath.

The biggest noise in Brockley is the ineffably smart modern Indian Babur Brasserie. Also worth checking out are cafés Moonbow Jakes and Toads Mouth Too, which is also an art gallery.

Very few people would consider eating out in Catford unless they knew about the uncannily good Japanese restaurant Sapporo Ichiban, and its not-half-bad Rushey Green rival, Hello Tokyo. Catfordites also fill up on noodles at Tai Won Mein and handmade pizzas at La Pizzeria Italiana, which attractsincongruous numbers of middle-class diners to its premises under a block of flats. Catford's Rushey Green has plenty of refreshment stops, and there's a great little café in the Broadway Theatre. Good coffee is available at comfortable Appetito, which doesn't let the inconvenience of having Eros House sitting on top of it spoil the atmosphere. Blue Mountain, over at the Cobbs Corner conservation area in Sydenham, is a first-rate café-deli.

AJ Goddard 203 Deptford High Street, SE8 3NT (8692 3601).
Appetito 9 Eros House, Brownhill Road, SE6 2EF (8697 8333).
Arru Suval 19 Lee High Road, SE13 5LD (8297 6452).
Babur Brasserie 119 Brockley Rise, SE23 1JP (8291 4881/www.babur.info).
Blue Mountain Café 260 Kirkdale, SE26 1RS (8659 6016).
Chapter Two 43-45 Montpelier Vale, SE3 0TJ (8333 2666/www.chaptersrestaurants.co.uk).
Everest Curry King 24 Loampit Hill, SE13 7SW (8691 2233).
Hello Tokyo 81 Rushey Green, SE6 4AF (8285 1988/www.hellotokyo.co.uk).
Laicram 1 Blackheath Grove, SE3 0DD (8852 4710).
Maggie's Café & Restaurant 320-322 Lewisham Road, SE13 7PA (8244 0339).
Manze's 204 Deptford High Street, SE8 3PR (8692 2375).
Meze Mangal 245 Lewisham Way, SE4 1XF (8694 8099/www.meze-mangal.co.uk).
Moonbow Jakes 325 Brockley Road, SE4 2QZ (8694 9128/www.moonbowjakes.moonfruit.com).
El Pirata 15-16 Royal Parade, SE3 0TL (8297 1880).
La Pizzeria Italiana Eros House, Brownhill Road, SE6 2EF (8461 4606).
Sapporo Ichiban 13 Catford Broadway, SE6 4SP (8690 8487).

Something Fishy 117-119 Lewisham High Street, SE13 6AT (8852 7075).
Tai Won Mein 90-92 Rushey Green, SE6 4HW (8690 8238).
Thailand 15 Lewisham Way, SE14 6PP (8691 4040).
Toads Mouth Too 188 Brockley Road, SE4 2RN (8469 0043).

Bars & pubs

The only pubs worth visiting near Lewisham town are those at a decent remove from the centre, such as the homely Dacre Arms

LOCALS' TIPS

The Waterlink Way from Bell Green and Beckenham to Catford and Lewisham, alongside the Ravensbourne River, is a pedalling pleasure. The Brookmill Park route from Lewisham to Deptford is another joy for cyclists. **Deptford's famous Dog & Bell pub does the best Sunday lunch for miles, although the lunchers of New Cross would beg to differ. They say the only place to come for your roast is the quirky Montague Arms.** Lewisham has no cinema, but a night at the flicks is really cheap if you go to one of the film screenings at the Broadway Theatre in Catford. A fiver a ticket and no depressing merchandise or irritating ads. **Such is the preponderance of comedians, artists, musicians and writers in the Telegraph Hill Conservation Area that the annual festival (February/March, see www. thehill.org.uk/festival) provides quality stand-up and music gigs in an intimate setting for not very much money.** Feeling broody? Can't afford a family home? Catford beckons. We confidently wager that there is nowhere else in Zone 3 where you can buy a five-bedroom semi with a large garden, near parks, bus stops, shops and stations for about £280,000. **Top borough snapshot? Stand on the Ha'penny Hatch Bridge. Line up Laban, with Canary Wharf and Docklands behind it, and hulking old barges, swans and the muddy waters of the Creek in the foreground. It's even more atmospheric at night.**

Lewisham

(be prepared for a walk). The Jolly Farmers, near the hospital and mostly frequented by its employees, is a popular post-work boozer.

In Blackheath, the choice is wide. Of the many fine pubs, the centuries-old Hare & Billet and the Georgian Princess of Wales are the grandest. Livelier options include Zero Degrees, with its microbrewed beers and inventive bar food, the upbeat Railway, and Cave Austin, a slick wine bar with basement club and chill-out room.

Elsewhere in the borough, down-to-earth Deptford has the real ales, good Sunday lunches and unpretentious charm of the Dog & Bell, and the late-night revelry of the Bar Tudor to recommend it. In New Cross, former grunge house Goldsmiths Tavern has been transformed into an oasis of squishy sofas, fine wine and sea bass; in contrast, the Hobgoblin remains resolutely studenty. The New Cross Inn, not to be confused with the cheapo backpackers' hostel of the same name next door, is a modish music pub. For bands, indie-leaning Amersham Arms (run by the same people behind the Lock Tavern in Camden) and kitsch Montague Arms are popular; a third Arms, the Forresters Arms, south in Forest Hill, hosts popular jazz nights.

In Catford, Young's pub the Catford Ram may look unpromising, being stuck in the shopping centre, but its position near the Broadway Theatre means it attracts a more urbane crowd than you'd think, and the pleasing pub grub is another attraction. The Blythe Hill Tavern is a lively, Irish-run local exuding comfort and cheer. Further up Stanstead Road towards Brockley Rise is an old boozer reborn in 2007 as the Honor Oak, offering music, comedy and gastronomic nights.

Forest Hill has the Dartmouth Arms gastropub, while Sydenham offers the Dolphin (from the same stable). The most exciting addition to these parts, however, has to be the Perry Hill, an excellent gastropub with good beers and a top-notch beer garden for leisurely summer afternoon drinking.

Amersham Arms *388 New Cross Road, SE14 6TY (8469 1499/www.amersham-arms.co.uk).*
Bar Tudor *41-42 Deptford Broadway, SE8 4PH (8469 2121/www.tudorgroup.org).*
Blythe Hill Tavern *319 Stanstead Road, SE23 1JB (8690 5176).*
Catford Ram *9 Winslade Way, SE6 4JU (8690 6206).*

Cave Austin *7-9 Montpelier Vale, SE3 0TA (8852 0492/www.caveaustin.co.uk).*
Dacre Arms *11 Kingswood Place, SE13 5BU (8852 6779).*
Dartmouth Arms *7 Dartmouth Road, SE23 3HN (8488 3117/www.thedartmouth arms.com).*
Dog & Bell *116 Prince Street, SE8 3JD (8692 5664).*
Dolphin *121 Sydenham Road, SE26 5HB (8778 8101/www.thedolphinsydenham.com).*
Forresters Arms *53 Perry Vale, SE23 2NE (8699 3311).*
Goldsmiths Tavern *316 New Cross Road, SE14 6AF (8691 8875).*
Hare & Billet *1A Elliot Cottages, Hare & Billet Road, SE3 0QJ (8852 2352).*
Hobgoblin *272 New Cross Road, SE14 6AA (8692 3193).*
Honor Oak *1 St German's Road, SE23 1RH (8690 8606).*
Jolly Farmers *354 Lewisham High Street, SE13 6LE (8690 8402).*
Montague Arms *289 Queens Road, SE14 2PA (7639 4923).*
New Cross Inn *323 New Cross Road, SE14 6AS (8692 1866).*
Perry Hill *78-80 Perry Hill, SE6 4EY (8699 5076/www.theperryhill.co.uk).*
Princess of Wales *1A Montpelier Row, SE3 0RL (8297 5911).*
Railway *16 Blackheath Village, SE3 9LE (8852 2390).*
Zero Degrees *29-31 Montpelier Vale, SE3 0TJ (8852 5619/www.zerodegrees.co.uk).*

TRANSPORT

Tube stations *East London* (replacement bus service until 2010) New Cross Gate, New Cross; *DLR* Lewisham
Rail stations *South Eastern Trains* Deptford, Nunhead, Lewisham, Blackheath, Crofton Park, Catford, Bellingham, Beckenham Hill, Ravensbourne; New Cross, St John's, Ladywell, Catford Bridge, Lower Sydenham; Hither Green, Grove Park, Lee; *Southern* South Bermondsey, New Cross Gate, Brockley, Honor Oak Park, Forest Hill, Sydenham
Main bus routes *into central London* 21, 47, 53, 171, 172, 176, 185, 188, 436, 453; *night buses* N21, N36, N47, N89, N171, N343; *24-hour buses* 53, 176, 453
Development plans East London line closed for extension work in December 2007 (due to reopen as overland service in 2010), with extensions north and south to Brockley, Honor Oak Park, Forest Hill and Sydenham

Shops

The borough's retail heart, the Lewisham Centre, is long overdue its makeover, part of a general regeneration project expected to take up to eight years. In the short term the indoor shopping centre is a lot brighter for its improved lighting and flooring. The usual chains (Sainsbury's, Next, M&S, Woolies) are inside, while outside there's a loud market and an awful lot of pound shops. Little pockets of interest rise above the dross. There's Rolls & Rems textiles shop, fab for one-off bolts of unusual fabric, and the coffee- and cheese-scented Genarro Deli serves the borough's large Italian community.

For a proper old-fashioned street market, visit Deptford on Wednesday, Friday or Saturday. Numerous stalls – fruit and veg, clothes second-hand and new, household goods and more – cluster along Deptford High Street, Douglas Way and Giffin Street.

Ladywell has a villagey feel with its florists, bakers, barber and hardware shops. Creare should satisfy your paper-craft needs, and 21st Century Tattoos caters for the skin craft ones.

Lee High Road has Harlequin, a fancy-dress hire and sales shop with good budget accessories. Nearby Snapdragon contains an attractive jumble of pots, planters and vases for the garden, as well as gifts and homewares. Keep going to find the legendary Allodi Accordions (closed Monday morning, Wednesday and Sunday), which has several rooms of accordions and a repair workshop.

Outside Hither Green train station lie the Staplehurst Road shops, overseen by FUSS (Friends & Users of Staplehurst Road Shops). These doughty shopkeepers keep the community close. You Don't Bring Me Flowers, a florist that also encompasses a café, knitting group and writers' club, is central to this arty scene. The Education Interactive maths initiative has a shop full of number puzzles and the sort of toys bought by conscientious parents.

Blackheath Village provides the genteel antidote to Lewisham. Independent traders are the norm (discreet chains include Neal's Yard Remedies, Phase Eight, Fat Face and Ryman). Upmarket gourmet shops such as Hand Made Food, the Village Deli and Jade Boulangerie help shunt up the grocery bill.

Blackheath's **Laicram**. *See p252.*

Proper sweets, such as rosy apples and cola cubes, are the forte of the gift shop in the atmospheric Age Exchange centre (*see p256*). There are far too many gift shops, but 2nd Impressions is a joy, with many floors and an extensive toy department. Near the heath, Cookery Nook is a large kitchen equipment shop; at the Lee end, Hortus is a garden design and maintenance business. Blackheath's association with hockey and cricket is evident in specialist sports shop Furley & Baker.

In Forest Hill's Dartmouth Road, sassy boutique Bunka is separated from slick men's outfitter Mayo Maker by a dry-cleaners. Next door, Antoinette Costume Hire is open mostly by appointment, though there's usually someone around in the mornings. Just up the road is Provender, an excellent organic bakery that's great for cakes. A large ski, snowboarding and mountain-biking store, Finches Ski Emporium, hides behind the South Circular on Perry Vale. Sydenham and Kirkdale also have fine shopping areas, strong on arts and antiques. For gewgaws and trinkets, there's Koochie Bazaar. The Kirkdale Bookshop & Gallery provides art and literature, and the handsome art deco wares at Behind the Boxes include furniture, ceramics, jewellery and glass.

Allodi Accordions *143-145 Lee High Road, SE13 5PF (8244 3771/www.accordions.co.uk).*
Antoinette Costume Hire *10A Dartmouth Road, SE23 3XU (8699 1913).*
Behind the Boxes Art Deco *98 Kirkdale, SE26 4BG (8291 6116/www.behindtheboxes-artdeco.co.uk).*
Bunka *4 Dartmouth Road, SE23 3XU (8291 4499/www.bunka.co.uk).*
Cookery Nook *32 Montpelier Vale, SE3 0TA (8297 2422).*
Creare *89 Ladywell Road, SE13 7JA (8690 9514).*
Education Interactive *10 Staplehurst Road, SE13 5NB (8318 6380/www.education-interactive.co.uk).*
Finches Ski Emporium *25-29 Perry Vale, SE23 2NE (8699 6768/www.finches-ski.com).*
Furley & Baker *34 Montpelier Vale, SE3 0TA (8463 0752/www.furleyandbaker.com).*
Gennaro Delicatessen *23 Lewis Grove, SE13 6BG (8852 1370).*
Hand Made Food *40 Tranquil Vale, SE3 0BD (8297 9966/www.handmadefood.com).*
Harlequin *254 Lee High Road, SE13 5PR (8852 0193).*
Hortus *26 Blackheath Village, SE3 9SY (8297 9439/www.hortus-blackheath.co.uk).*

Jade Boulangerie *44 Tranquil Vale, SE3 0BD (8318 1916).*
Kirkdale Bookshop & Gallery *272 Kirkdale, SE26 4RS (8778 4701).*
Koochie Bazaar *140 Sydenham Road, SE26 5JZ (8659 8042).*
Lewisham Centre *33A Molesworth Street, SE13 7HB (8852 0094/www.lewishamcentre.co.uk).*
Mayo Maker *8 Dartmouth Road, SE23 3XU (8314 4050).*
Provender *103 Dartmouth Road, SE23 3HT (8699 4046/www.provender.org.uk).*
Rolls & Rems *111 High Street, SE13 6AT (8852 8686).*
2nd Impressions *10 Montpelier Vale, SE3 0TA (8852 6192).*
Snapdragon *266 Lee High Road, SE13 5PL (8463 0503/www.snapdragonpots.co.uk).*
21st Century Tattoos *224 Algernon Road, SE13 7AG (8690 7774).*
Village Deli *1-3 Tranquil Vale, SE3 0BU (8852 2015).*
You Don't Bring Me Flowers *15 Staplehurst Road, SE13 5ND (8297 2333/www.youdontbring meflowers.co.uk).*

Arts & attractions

Cinemas & theatres

Albany *Douglas Way, SE8 4AG (8692 4446/www.thealbany.org.uk).* Deptford's busy community arts centre.
Blackheath Halls *23 Lee Road, SE3 9RQ (8463 0100/www.blackheathhalls.com).* Concerts (classical and contemporary), community events and more.
Broadway Theatre *Rushey Green, SE6 4RU (8690 0002/www.broadwaytheatre.org.uk).* Handsome art deco theatre that is scruffy Catford's pride and joy.
Brockley Jack Theatre *410 Brockley Road, SE4 2DH (8291 6354/www.brockleyjack.co.uk).* Popular theatre (and pub) that hosts drama productions, plus regular music, comedy and live events.
Laban *Creekside, SE8 3DZ (8691 8600/www.laban.org).* Independent conservatoire for contemporary dance training, housed in stunning, award-winning premises designed by Tate Modern architects Herzog & de Meuron.

Galleries & museums

Horniman Museum *100 London Road, SE23 3PQ (8699 1872/www.horniman.ac.uk).* Eccentric art nouveau museum, with natural history and anthropological displays, a spacious café, lovely gardens and an animal enclosure.
Lewisham Arthouse *140 Lewisham Way, SE14 6PD (8244 3168/www.lewisham arthouse.co.uk).* Gallery in an impressive Edwardian hall.
Stark Gallery *384-386 Lee High Road, Lee Green, SE12 8RW (8318 4040).* Pleasant local gallery and community venue.

Other attractions

Age Exchange Reminiscence Centre
*11 Blackheath Village, SE3 9LA (8318 9105/
www.age-exchange.org.uk).* Nostalgic museum
experience that aims to improve quality of
life for elderly people by emphasising the
value of memories.
Creekside Centre *14 Creekside, SE8 4SA
(8692 9922/www.creeksidecentre.org.uk).*
Environmental education centre.
Goldsmiths College *University of London,
SE14 6NW (7919 7171/www.goldsmiths.ac.uk).*
Famous art college with various sites around
New Cross and Deptford; the fabulously ornate
building on Lewisham Way (once Deptford
Town Hall) is particularly attractive.
Manor House Library & Gardens *34 Old
Road, SE13 5SY (8852 0357/www.lewisham.
gov.uk).* One of the grandest local libraries in
London, built in 1772.
Rivoli Ballroom *346-350 Brockley Road, SE4
2BY (0871 971 4333).* Stylish old ballroom used
for tea dances and classes.

Sport & fitness

Ladywell Leisure Centre is facing the axe
in 2010, by which time a new centre in
Loampit Vale will be a thriving addition
to the borough's facilities. Forest Hill Pools,
meanwhile, is in the middle of an extensive
facelift. South of the borough is new
venture the Downham Leisure Centre,
with amenities like a GP and dentist
alongside a library, community hall
and sports facilities.

Gyms & leisure centres

Bridge Leisure Centre *Kangley Bridge Road,
SE26 5AQ (8778 7158/www.leisure-centre.com).*
Coliseum *15 Davids Road, SE23 3EP
(8699 3342).* Private.
Colfe's Leisure Centre *Horne Park Lane,
SE12 8AW (8297 9110/www.colfes.com/
leisurecentre).* Private.
Downham Health & Leisure Centre
*7-9 Moorside Road, BR1 5EP (8461 9200/
www.leisureconnection.co.uk).* A new Lewisham
venture, despite being in Bromley.
Fitness First *61-71A High Street, SE13 5JX
(8852 4444/www.fitnessfirst.co.uk).* Private.
Ladywell Arena *Silvermere Road, SE6 4QX
(8314 1986/www.leisure-centre.com).*
Ladywell Leisure Centre *261 Lewisham
High Street, SE13 6NJ (8690 2123/
www.leisure-centre.com).*
LA Fitness *291 Kirkdale, SE26 4QE
(8778 9818/www.lafitness.co.uk).* Private.
Lucky's Gym *19B Marischal Road, SE13
5LE (8318 5630/www.luckysgym.com).*
Private.
Skyline Gym *96-102 Rushey Green, SE6
4HW (8314 1167).* Private.

Wavelengths Leisure Centre *Giffin Street,
SE8 4RJ (8694 1134/www.leisure-centre.com).*
New pool opening summer 2008.

Other facilities

AMF Bowling *11-29 Belmont Hill, SE13 5AU
(0844 826 3021/www.amfbowling.co.uk).*
Beckenham Place Park *Beckenham Place
Park, Beckenham Hill Road, BR3 5BP (8650
2292/www.glendale-golf.com).* 18-hole public
golf course.

Spectator sports

Millwall FC *The New Den, Zampa Road,
SE16 3LN (7231 9999/www.millwallfc.co.uk).*

Schools

WHAT THE PARENTS SAY:

'There are some supposedly good schools in
Lewisham. Certainly, the primary schools
improve every year, according to the council
website. Some of the primary schools, such as
the Horniman School, look lovely, and All Saints
in Blackheath always scores well in league tables
– presumably because it's posh round there. Our
children went to Dulwich Prep until I lost my job.
After that they went to Haberdashers', which is
about as good as state schools can be, although
the sport is rubbish. It attracts some bright kids,
but it also trades off the reputation of the one in
Elstree where Sacha Baron Cohen went.

Forest Hill is a good school – it's specialist
arts. They're all specialist something these days.
Haberdashers' is specialist music. Prendergast
is good for girls.'
Richard Jones, father of three, Catford

Primary

There are now 6 state primary schools in Lewisham,
including 20 church schools. There are also six
independents, including one Muslim school. See
www.lewisham.gov.uk/educationandlearning,
www.edubase.gov.uk and www.ofsted.gov.uk
for more information.

Secondary

Addey & Stanhope School *472 New Cross
Road, SE14 6TJ (8305 6100/www.as.lewisham.
sch.uk).*
Bonus Pastor RC School *Winlaton Road,
Downham, BR1 5PZ (8695 2100/www.bp.
lewisham.sch.uk).*
Catford High School *Bellingham Road, SE6
2PS (8697 8911/www.chs.lewisham.sch.uk).*
Formerly girls only, now mixed.
Crofton School *Manwood Road, SE4 1SA
(8690 1114/www.crofton.lewisham.sch.uk).*
Crossways Academy *Sprules Road, SE4
2NL (7358 2400/www.crossways.ac.uk).* Sixth
form only.

Lewisham

Deptford Green School *Amersham Vale, SE14 6LQ (8691 3236/www.deptfordgreen. lewisham.sch.uk).*
Forest Hill School *Dacres Road, SE23 2XN (8699 9343/www.foresthill.lewisham.sch.uk).* Boys only; mixed sixth form.
Haberdashers' Aske's Hatcham College *Pepys Road, SE14 5SF (7652 9500/ www.hahc.org.uk).*
Haberdashers' Aske's Knights Academy *Launcelot Road, BR1 5EB (8698 1025/ www.hahc.org.uk).*
Northbrook CE School *Leehurst Road, SE13 5HZ (8852 3191/www.northbrook.lewisham. sch.uk).*
Prendergast School *Hilly Fields, Adelaide Avenue, SE4 1LE (8690 3710).* Girls only.
St Dunstan's College *Stanstead Road, SE6 4TY (8516 7200/www.stdunstans.org.uk).* Private.
St Matthew Academy *Lee Terrace, SE3 9TY (8852 5614/www.stmatthewacademy.co.uk).* New mixed school, opened 2007.
Sedgehill School *Sedgehill Road, SE6 3QW (8698 8911/www.sedgehill.lewisham.sch.uk).*
Sydenham School *Dartmouth Road, SE26 4RD (8699 6731/www.sydenham.lewisham. sch.uk).* Girls only.

Property

WHAT THE AGENTS SAY:

❛They're spending millions regenerating Lewisham town centre and that has a knock-on effect in the rest of the borough. A lot of the 1960s tower block estates are now gone, replaced by new-builds, with a mix of shared ownership and affordable housing. Transport links are great, so professionals are moving in – City workers, and people working in Canary Wharf.❜
Tony Ravenscroft, Acorn Estate Agents, Lewisham

Average property prices
Detached £469,902
Semi-detached £357,805
Terraced £282,453
Flat £195,847

Local estate agents
Acorn Estate Agents *153 High Street, SE13 6AA (8852 4455/www.acorn.ltd.uk).*
Beaumont Residential *111B Rushey Green, SE6 4AF (8695 0123/www.beaumont-residential.com).*
1st Avenue *343 Lee High Road, SE12 8RU (8852 9444/www.1stavenue.co.uk).*
James Johnston *www.jamesjohnston.com; 2 offices in the borough (Blackheath 8852 8383/ Brockley 8691 3311).*
Property World *4 Sydenham Road, SE26 5QW (8488 0011/www.propertyworlduk.net).*

Reeds Estate Agents *195 Deptford High Street, SE8 3NT (8691 9009).*
Sebastian Roche *www.sebastianroche.com; 2 offices in the borough (Forest Hill 8291 9441/Lewisham 8690 8888).*

Other information

Council
Lewisham Council *Lewisham Town Hall, Catford Road, SE6 4RU (8314 6000/ www.lewisham.gov.uk).*

Legal services
Catford CAB *120 Rushey Green, SE6 4HQ (0870 1264037/www.adviceguide.org.uk).*
Sydenham CAB *299 Kirkdale, SE26 4QD (0870 126 4037/www.adviceguide.org.uk).*

Local newspapers
Lewisham & Greenwich Mercury *8769 4444/www.icsouthlondon.co.uk.*

Allotments & open spaces
Council Allotments *Main Building Wearside Service Centre, Wearside Road, SE13 7EZ (8314 2277/www.lewisham.gov.uk).*
One Tree Hill Allotment Society *One Tree Hill, SE23 1NX (8699 6099/www.othas.org.uk).*
Open spaces *www.lewisham.gov.uk/leisure andculture/parksandrecreation.*

COUNCIL TAX
A	up to £40,000	**£863.85**
B	£40,001-£52,000	**£1,007.82**
C	£52,001-£68,000	**£1,151.80**
D	£68,001-£88,000	**£1,295.77**
E	£88,001-£120,000	**£1,583.72**
F	£120,001-£160,000	**£1,871.67**
G	£160,001-£320,000	**£2,159.62**
H	over £320,000	**£2,591.54**

RECYCLING
No. of bring sites 48 (for nearest, visit www.recycleforlondon.com)
Household waste recycled 11.96%
Main recycling centre Landmann Way Reuse & Recycling Centre, Landmann Way, off Surrey Canal Road, SE14 5RS (8314 7171)
Other recycling services green garden rubbish collection; home composting; white goods and furniture collection
Council contact Beth Sowden, Waste Education Officer, Wearside Service Centre, Wearside Road, SE13 7EZ (8314 2053/www.lewisham.gov.uk/ recycling)

Lewisham

'Greenwich is full of surprises – you come here for the Georgian architecture and find a sassy bar. It always seems to offer more than you expect: an hour's visit to Greenwich Park or Market always turns into a day.'

James Haddrell, director, Greenwich Theatre

Greenwich

These are exciting times for the borough of Greenwich. It's not just the Olympics, the Crossrail and the Thames Gateway Bridge, nor is it the recent arrival of the O2 Arena. Away from the tourist-oriented attractions of historic Greenwich itself, the once maligned districts of Thamesmead, Kidbrooke and Eltham are all getting a makeover. This is a borough with potential.

Neighbourhoods

Greenwich

Though its seaside town feel, sense of community and attractive Georgian and Victorian properties make Greenwich a very desirable residential area, the focus here always fall on the neighbourhood's historic side. Royal, horological and maritime history take precedence – except in 2012 when three venues in the borough will host six sports for the Olympics. Many of Greenwich's main attractions are set around the panoramic Greenwich Park or the Thames waterfront, now accessible by a regular Thames Clipper boat service from the West End. The superbly overhauled Royal Observatory is the spectacular don't miss; the Weller Astronomy Galleries and the Time Galleries both do justice to the Observatory's influential heritage and provide enough free entertainment for families and school groups to gawp at for a good couple of hours. Shows at the Peter Harrison Planetarium and stargazing in winter provide affordable alternatives. The nearby Queen's House and National Maritime Museum are also free.

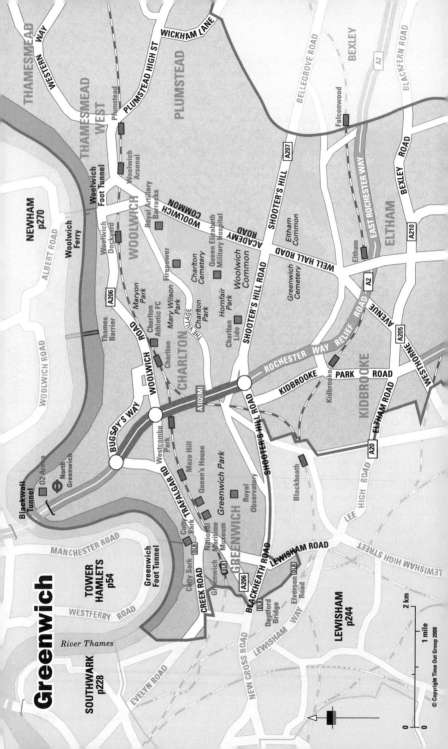

The fire that swept through the *Cutty Sark* in May 2007 damaged much of the skeleton, but the artefacts and half the timbers of the famous tea clipper have been stored away as part of a £25 million restoration project now set for completion a year behind schedule in 2010.

Equally newsworthy are the transport plans for the borough. Already the Thames Clipper has proved a great success for tourists and commuters, as well as rock fans heading for the O2 Arena at the previously vilified Dome and North Greenwich Peninsula – a string of sell-out dates by Prince in 2007 saw to that. Work has already begun on the DLR extension down to Woolwich, due to open in 2009. A year later there will be a rapid transit bus service in place between Abbey Wood, Thamesmead, Woolwich, the Peninsula and Greenwich, linking with the Abbey Wood/Woolwich branch of the east–west Crossrail project given the green light for funding in autumn 2007 – although trains are not expected to run for another ten years. Meanwhile, the four-lane Thames Gateway Bridge between Thamesmead and Beckton in east London awaits approval pending a second public enquiry.

Back in Greenwich, it's business as usual around the twisting streets on and off focal Greenwich Church Street and its second-hand bookshops, independent boutiques and covered market. At weekends both the indoor and outdoor markets, and many nearby restaurants, are mobbed.

For culture, Greenwich boasts the plush Greenwich Picture House, Greenwich Theatre (due to launch a children's festival in March 2008), Greenwich Playhouse and quality stand-up comedy at Up the Creek. Atmospheric recitals (and regular record fairs) take place at St Alfege's Church, built in 1714 by Nicholas Hawksmoor.

Residents also have the excellent green space of Greenwich Park at their disposal. This tranquil, undulating space includes a boating lake, a children's play area, flower gardens, a deer enclosure and one of the finest views in, and of, London from the top of One Tree Hill (where the Observatory stands). The attractions of the Old Royal Naval College, Queen's House and National Maritime Museum spread in historic splendour over the foot of the hill by the park entrance.

Less obvious attractions lie a short bus journey north. The much maligned North Greenwich Peninsula is no longer an industrial wasteland centrepieced by a white elephant Dome. Locals make the most of the Thames Path, which is dotted with lesser-known sculptures by Antony Gormley and Richard Wilson, and culminates in the Greenwich Peninsula Ecology Park, a four-acre wetland awash with birds, plants and insects. Around it stands the recently opened Millennium Village, an inventive residential development centred on a wildlife lake shared with the park. It's not just Greenwich residents who are taking advantage either – the O2 Arena, the David Beckham Football School and events such as the Tutankhamun exhibition brought thousands of Londoners here in 2007.

Greenwich centre is well served by overland rail, the DLR and the old Greenwich Foot Tunnel to the Isle of Dogs.

Highs & Lows

▲ **O2 Arena** If you have to see a big-name act in a large-scale venue, there are far worse places in London than this. It's brought the crowds back to the North Greenwich Peninsula for the first time since New Year's Eve 1999

Transport links By 2010 Woolwich will be connected to the City via the DLR extension – and by 2017 to the rest of London via Crossrail. And the Thames Clipper is the best thing to happen to Greenwich since late-night licensing

Annual Car Free Day A great, family-friendly event held every September. A real success – the kind of thing Greenwich does so well

Greenwich Park A marvellous resource – but why isn't there an affordable café?

Charlton Athletic FC The community club that had to make 25 of its own community redundant after relegation

▼ **Teenage gangs** Despite laudable regeneration projects, some streets in Woolwich, Plumstead, Kidbrooke and Eltham are not the kind of places you'd like your kids to walk down

STATISTICS

BOROUGH MAKE-UP
Population 218,856
Average weekly pay £514.10
Ethnic origins
White 74.28%
Mixed 3.02%
Asian or Asian British 7.49%
Black or Black British 12.45%
Chinese or other 2.75%
Students 9.47%
Retirees 10.34%

HOUSING STOCK
Borough size 50.9km²
No. of households 97,522
Detached 3.8%
Semi-detached 17.9%
Terraced 35.7%
Flats (purpose-built) 32.7%
Flats (converted) 9.2%
Flats (both) 41.9%

CRIME PER 1,000 OF POPULATION
(average for England and Wales in
brackets)
Burglary 8 (5)
Robbery 6 (2)
Theft of vehicle 6 (4)
Theft from vehicle 10 (9)
Violence against the person 33 (19)
Sexual offences 2 (1)

MPs & COUNCIL
MPs *Eltham* Clive Efford (Labour);
Greenwich & Woolwich Nick Raynsford
(Labour); *Erith & Thamesmead* John
Austin (Labour)
CPA 3 stars; improving well

Kidbrooke

The lofty and elegant houses at the north-western end of Kidbrooke, by the border with Blackheath, quickly make way for a bleak landscape of 1960s Brutalist architecture and run-down tower blocks south of Kidbrooke rail station. This is not the borough's most desirable area, but things are improving. A £750 million redevelopment programme is ongoing, including the demolition of 2,000 dwellings on the infamous Ferrier Estate – one of the largest in London – and the recent opening of the Kidbrooke Station Interchange and its network of well-lit footpaths was welcomed by locals. The David Lloyd Club is already a major leisure attraction.

Charlton, Woolwich and Eltham

Charlton offers tree-lined residential streets around Charlton Park and more shady havens of teenage gangland culture elsewhere. Move east towards Woolwich Dockyard and the less affluent part of town and you'll find hoodie culture and soulless surroundings abound. The main regeneration here concerns the new council offices in Wellington Street, with a rooftop gallery and library to open in 2008. New parks and public squares are also planned. In nearby Eltham, the council-run Eltham Centre opened at the end of 2007, with three swimming pools, a fitness centre, a dance studio and kids' play area.

Attractions for locals and visitors in these three neighbourhoods include the magnificent Jacobean Charlton House (set in beautiful grounds) and vestiges of Charlton's village roots, such as St Luke's parish church. The Firepower Royal Artillery Museum and Thames Barrier Learning Centre provide local diversions in Woolwich, to be joined for the 2012 Olympics by the London Aquatic Centre. Eltham Palace and its fabulous pre-war art deco interiors are another surprise. Open spaces include Charlton Park and Woolwich Common. The art deco Charlton Lido is popular in summer.

All will be more accessible once the DLR extension and other transport infrastructure are in place. In the meantime, overland rail and the Woolwich Ferry are the best links.

Thamesmead

Even Thamesmead, the 1960s' planners' nightmare known for its *Clockwork Orange* backdrops and intimidating high-rises, is currently undergoing regeneration. Admittedly, its redevelopment has suffered more than its fair share of bureaucratic delays, but a joint commitment by both Greenwich and Bexley councils (which Thamesmead straddles), supported by the only community development charity working in the area, Trust Thamesmead (www.trust-thamesmead.co.uk), bodes well for the future.

The annual Summer Festival in Birchmere Park is one of the biggest community events south of the river, while its parks, lakes and canals are home to an array of migratory birds.

Restaurants & cafés

Much of the borough's local restaurant trade is driven by tourism. Standard pub lunches are the norm, interspersed by uninspiring, catch-all Mexican and Asian eateries, and chain restaurants (Nando's, Pizza Express, Prezzo, Zizzi). Exceptions include contemporary European cuisine at Inside, upmarket British cooking at the Rivington Grill Bar and tasty nibbles at deli-cum-diner Buenos Aires, one of a handful of independent foodie boutiques branching out into trendy table service. Bar du Musée, with its diverse dining and drinking spaces, is also very popular. You won't get a bad meal at the SE10 Restaurant & Bar, slightly off the beaten track, nor at the Hill, the pick of the gastropubs.

Away from the main drag, in North Greenwich, Chinese restaurant Peninsula occupies the whole ground floor of a budget commuter hotel. It serves dim sum every afternoon, as well as evening meals.

Bar du Musée *17 Nelson Road, SE10 9JB* *(8858 4710/www.bardumusee.com).*
Buenos Aires Café & Deli *86 Royal Hill, SE10 8RT (8488 6764).*
The Hill *89 Royal Hill, SE10 8SE (8895 2984).*
Inside *19 Greenwich South Street, SE10 8NW (8265 5060/www.insiderestaurant.co.uk).*
Peninsula *Holiday Inn Express, Bugsby's Way, SE10 0GD (8858 2028/www. mychinesefood.co.uk).*
Rivington Grill Bar *178 Greenwich High Road, SE10 8NN (8293 9270/www.rivingtongrill.co.uk).*
SE10 Restaurant & Bar *62 Thames Street, SE10 9BX (8858 9764).*

Bars & pubs

Even in Nelson's day, Greenwich was a popular spot for a pint. These days a handful of attractive late-opening bars – in particular Inc Bar (decor courtesy of Laurence Llewelyn-Bowen, inspired by the 'slum and splendour' of Georgian Greenwich) and the Bar du Musée (*see p263*) – complement an atmospheric lunchtime and evening scene set around the river and the market. Most improved landmark boozer is the Gipsy Moth, right beside the *Cutty Sark*, with continental beers and a real buzz about it. Mention must also be made of the Greenwich Union, flagship outlet of Alistair Hook's lauded Meantime Brewing Company, where knowledgeable and friendly staff

Greenwich Foot Tunnel. *See p261.*

serve signature Union, Chocolate, Golden, Raspberry and Stout beers along with superior bar food. Bang next door is exemplary old-school Young's pub Richard I.

Other worthy boozers in the area include the stately Trafalgar Tavern, which has a superb location next to the lapping Thames; the Coach & Horses in Greenwich Market, a key local meeting place; and the Ashburnham Arms, an excellent locals' boozer with Shepherd Neame ales, decent wines, superior pub food and a garden that's popular in the summer.

For a more lively night, head to party zone Polar Bar, a late-opening DJ bar. The North Pole on Greenwich High Road still gets some action: it's a stylish three-floor club-bar-restaurant with DJs downstairs at weekends. Davy's Wine Vaults, part of the London-wide Davy's wine bar chain, is handy for thirsty commuters (it's next to Greenwich train station).

If you're looking further afield, then the Pilot Inn is the perfect place for a pre-show pint within walking distance of the O2 Arena. In Charlton, Eltham and Woolwich it's pretty much a case of finding a trusted local and sticking with it.

Ashburnham Arms *25 Ashburnham Grove,
SE10 8UH (8692 2007).*
Coach & Horses *13 Greenwich Market,
SE10 9HZ (8293 0880).*
Davy's Wine Vaults *161 Greenwich High
Road, SE10 8JA (8858 6011/www.davy.co.uk).*
Gipsy Moth *60 Greenwich Church Street,
SE10 9BL (8858 0786).*
Greenwich Union *56 Royal Hill, SE10 8RT
(8692 6258/www.greenwichunion.co.uk).*
Inc Bar *7 College Approach, SE10 9HY
(8858 6721/www.greenwich-inc.com).*
North Pole *131 Greenwich High Road, SE10
8JA (8853 3020/www.northpolegreenwich.com).*
Pilot Inn *68 River Way, SE10 0BE
(8858 5910).*
Polar Bar *13 Blackheath Road, SE10 8PE
(8691 1555).*
Richard I *52-54 Royal Hill, SE10 8RT
(8692 2996).*
Trafalgar Tavern *Park Row, SE10 9NW
(8858 2909/www.trafalgartavern.co.uk).*

Shops

Greenwich has bundles of shops, boutiques
and market stalls to browse – shopping is
one of the area's main attractions. A new
website (www.lovegreenwich.co.uk) details
all the latest openings, particularly where
independent stores are concerned, a
particular local strongpoint.

Greenwich Market is spread over three
sites. The smallest, the Weekend Market,
is mostly bric-a-brac with a handful of
traders dealing in second-hand books
and vinyl, with a few punk bootlegs
available. For second-hand clothes head
to the Village Market, where you'll find
Chinese silk dresses plus home furnishings
and ethnic ornaments. The Crafts Market
is jam-packed with handicrafts, jewellery,
home furnishing and clothes.

The shops on the fringes of the covered
market are worth investigating. Greenwich
Printmakers offers original, affordable
artworks; Music & Video Exchange
deals in CDs in all genres; and Compendia
specialises in games from around the
world like Mexican train dominoes and
the Japanese board game Go.

Nearby, the Emporium has a fine stock
of vintage clothes, at much better prices
than in central London. Worth crossing
town for, Pickwick Papers & Fabrics has
huge selection of wallpapers and fabric.
Local kitsch merchant Flying Duck
Enterprises sadly closed at the end of
January 2008 but continues to ply its

wares online (www.flying-duck.com). Pets
& the City has a witty selection of toys,
clothes and accessories for cats and dogs.

Greenwich is also known for its
antiquarian and second-hand bookshops;
Halcyon Books is a fine trove, while
Maritime Books covers naval and
mercantile history up to the end of World
War II, with contemporary and historical
naval magazines to boot. For more Nelson
memorabilia, elegant brass porthole mirrors
and vintage china from an 1822 shipwreck,
visit jaunty little marine shop Nauticalia;
Warwick Leadlay also specialises in
antique maps as well as Nelsonia.

For clothes and accessories, Hide All
has an excellent selection of bags; Bullfrogs
deals in urban footwear; Johnny Rocket,
purveyor of creative, contemporary
jewellery, has its main outlet in College
Approach; Red Door trades in ceramics
and handmade gifts; and Meet Bernard
offers Carhartt and other streetwear.
New arrival So Organic deals in beauty
treatments, cleaning products and bedding
and bathwear of every description.

A recent trend has been the rise of niche
food stores. The Nevada Street Deli offers
high-quality meats, cheeses and sausages;
the Creaky Shed specialises in herbs, jams
and organic products; and Cheeseboard
carries more than 100 varieties.

Bugsby's Way, which links North
Greenwich to Charlton, is lined with huge
supermarkets (Asda, Sainsbury's) and
shopping centres containing fashion stores
(including Matalan), B&Q, Comet and
so on. The heart of Charlton provides
an old-style high street experience, while
Woolwich has a bigger shopping precinct
with M&S, Mothercare and others.

Bullfrogs *22 Greenwich Church Street, SE10
9BJ (8305 2404/www.bullfrogs.co.uk).*
Cheeseboard *26 Royal Hill, SE10 8RT (8305
0401/www.cheese-board.co.uk).*
Compendia *10 Greenwich Market, SE10 9HZ
(8293 6616/www.compendia.co.uk).*
Creaky Shed *20 Royal Hill, SE10 8RT
(8269 0333).*
The Emporium *330-332 Creek Road, SE10
9SW (8305 1670).*
Greenwich Market *Greenwich Market, SE10
(enquiries 8293 3110/www.greenwichmarket.net).*
Greenwich Printmakers *1A Greenwich
Market, SE10 9HZ (8858 1569/www.greenwich-
printmakers.org).*
Halcyon Books *1 Greenwich South Street, SE10
8NW (8305 2675/www.halcyonbooks.co.uk).*

Soak up the Jacobean splendour of **Charlton House**. *See p262.*

Hide All *9 Greenwich Market, SE10 9HZ (8858 6104/www.hideall.co.uk).*
Johnny Rocket *10 College Approach, SE10 9HY (8269 1814/www.johnnyrocketltd.com).*
Maritime Books *66 Royal Hill, SE10 8RT (8692 1794).*
Meet Bernard *23 Nelson Road, SE10 9JB (8858 4047/www.meetbernard.com).*
Music & Video Exchange *23 Greenwich Church Street, SE10 9BJ (8858 8898/ www.mveshops.co.uk).*
Nauticalia *25 Nelson Road, SE10 9JB (8858 1066/www.nauticalia.com).*
Nevada Street Deli *8 Nevada Street, SE10 9JL (8293 9199/www.nevadastreetdeli.co.uk).*
Pets & the City *334 Creek Road, SE10 9SW (8858 3527/www.petsandthecityuk.com).*

Pickwick Papers & Fabrics *6 Nelson Road, SE10 9JB (8858 1205/www. pickwickpapers.co.uk).*
Red Door *10 Turnpin Lane, SE10 9JA (8858 2131/www.reddoorgallery.co.uk).*
So Organic *Eagle House, 7 Turnpin Lane, SE10 9JA (0800 169 2579/www.soorganic.com).*
Warwick Leadlay *5 Nelson Road, SE10 9JB (8858 0317/www.warwickleadlay.com).*

Arts & attractions

Cinemas & theatres

Greenwich Playhouse *189 Greenwich High Road, SE10 8JA (8858 9256/ www.galleontheatre.co.uk).*
Greenwich Picture House *180 Greenwich High Road, SE10 8NN (0870 755 0065/ www.picturehouses.co.uk).*
Greenwich Theatre *Crooms Hill, SE10 8ES (8858 4447/www.greenwichtheatre.org.uk).* Musical theatre productions.
Odeon Greenwich *Bugsby Way, SE10 0QJ (0871 224 4007/www.odeon.co.uk).*

Galleries & museums

Cutty Sark *King William Walk, SE10 9HT (8858 3445/www.cuttysark.org.uk).*
Fan Museum *12 Crooms Hill, SE10 8ER (8305 1441/www.fan-museum.org).* More than 3,000 fans from around the world.
Firepower *Royal Artillery Museum, Royal Arsenal, SE18 6ST (8855 7755/ www.firepower.org.uk).* Artillery through the ages, from catapults to nuclear warheads.
National Maritime Museum *Romney Road, SE10 9NF (8858 4422/information 8312 6565/tours 8312 6608/www.nmm.ac.uk).*
Old Royal Naval College *King William Walk, SE10 9LW (8269 4747/tours 8269 4791/ www.greenwichfoundation.org.uk).* Built by Sir Christopher Wren at the turn of the

TRANSPORT
Tube stations *DLR* Cutty Sark, Greenwich, Deptford Bridge, Elverson Road; *Jubilee* North Greenwich
Rail stations *South Eastern Trains* Greenwich, Maze Hill, Westcombe Park, Charlton, Woolwich Dockyard, Woolwich Arsenal, Plumstead; Blackheath, Kidbrooke, Eltham, Falconwood
Main bus routes *into central London* 53, 188; *night buses* N1, N21; *24-hour buses* 53, 188
River Woolwich Ferry; commuter and leisure boat services to/from central London, including the new Thames Clipper (www.thamesclippers.com), with piers at Greenwich, O2 Arena and Woolwich Arsenal
Development plans DLR extension to Woolwich Arsenal by 2010; Crossrail by 2017

17th-century; originally a hospital, then a naval college, it is set in landscaped grounds in the centre of the Maritime Greenwich World Heritage Site.

Royal Observatory & Planetarium
Greenwich Park, SE10 9NF (8312 6565/ www.rog.nmm.ac.uk). Also by Wren, built for Charles II in 1675, and the home of Greenwich Mean Time and the Prime Meridian Line. After a £15 million development, it now features new space galleries and a state of the art planetarium.

Thames Barrier Information & Learning Centre *1 Unity Way, SE18 5NJ (8305 4188/ www.environment-agency.gov.uk).* Learn about London's flood defence system: the world's largest adjustable dam, built in 1982 for £535 million. This small learning centre would be submerged if it stopped working.

Music & comedy venues

St Alfege's Church *Church Street, SE10 9BJ (www.st-alfege.org).*

Up the Creek *302 Creek Road, SE10 9SW (8858 4581/www.up-the-creek.com).* Comedy and cabaret club.

Other attractions

Age Exchange Reminiscence Centre
11 Blackheath Village, SE3 9LA (8318 9105/ www.age-exchange.org.uk). A charity that emphasises the value of memories through exhibitions, theatre and educational programmes.

Charlton House *Charlton Road, SE7 8RE (8856 3951/www.greenwich.gov.uk).* Grand Jacobean manor house, now used as a community centre and library.

Eltham Palace *Court Yard, SE9 5QE (8294 2548/www.english-heritage.org.uk).* Two sights in one: a medieval royal palace and an art deco home. Run by English Heritage.

Greenwich & Docklands Festivals
6 College Approach, SE10 9H (8305 1818/ www.festival.org) A festival and event producing organisation working across east London.

Greenwich Tourist Information Centre
Pepys House, 2 Cutty Sark Gardens, SE10 9LW (0870 608 2000). Includes an exhibition on the history of Greenwich.

The O2 *Peninsula Square, SE10 0DX (www.theo2.co.uk).* Includes the O2 Arena music venue, an 11-screen Vue cinema, various eateries and (until 31 August 2008) a Tutankhamun exhibition. It will host gymnastics, trampolining and basketball events at the 2012 Olympics.

Queen's House *Romney Road, SE10 9NF (8312 6565/www.nmm.ac.uk).* Palladian house designed by Inigo Jones in 1616 for James I's wife. It's now home to the National Maritime Museum's art collection (including paintings by Hogarth and Gainsborough) – and a ghost.

Ranger's House (Wernher Collection)
Chesterfield Walk, SE10 8QX (8853 0035/ www.english-heritage.org.uk). Medieval and Renaissance art, housed in an 18th-century villa right next to Greenwich Park. Run by English Heritage.

Sport & fitness

National Lottery money, and the investment of Greenwich Leisure (which manages sports facilities in a number of London boroughs), has meant an upturn in fortunes for the public leisure centres in Greenwich – they can certainly give the private clubs a run for their money. The Waterfront Leisure Centre, in particular, is outstanding, with excellent swimming facilities and ample provision for other sports. The new Eltham Centre is also very good. The private sector can offer PhysioActive, a gym that specialises in sports injuries; Gordon's is the place if you're into body-building.

Charlton Lido – one of just three lidos in south-east London still in operation – is a local gem.

Gyms & leisure centres

Arches Leisure Centre *80 Trafalgar Road, SE10 9UX (8317 5020/www.gll.org.uk).*

Charlton Health & Fitness Centre
Charlton Athletic Football Club, The Valley, West Stand, Floyd Road, SE7 8BL (8853 5454/www.gll.org.uk).

Coldharbour Leisure Centre *Chapel Farm Road, SE9 3LX (8851 8692/www.gll.org.uk).*

David Lloyd Kidbrooke *Kidbrooke Park Road, at Weigall Road, SE12 8HG (8331 3901/ www.davidlloydleisure.co.uk).* Private.

Eltham Centre *2 Archery Road, SE9 1HA (8921 4344/www.gll.org).*

Fitness First *Unit 1, Macbean Street, SE1 6LW (8312 7190/www.fitnessfirst. co.uk).* Private.

Gordon's Gym *29A Herbert Road, SE18 3SZ (8854 6273).* Private.

Meadowside Leisure Centre *Tudway Road, SE3 9XT (8856 0101/www.gll.org).*

PhysioActive *Old Bank House, Mottingham Road, SE9 4QZ (8857 6000/www.physioactive. com).* Private.

RECYCLING

No. of bring sites 29 (for nearest, visit www.recycleforlondon.com)
Household waste recycled 18.16%
Main recycling centre Nathan Way Waste Transfer Station, Nathan Way, SE28 0AN (8311 5229)
Other recycling services garden waste collection; home composting; furniture and white goods collection
Council contact Peter Dalley, Greenwich Council, Waste Services, Birchmere Business Park, Thamesmead, SE28 8BF (8921 4641)

LOCALS' TIPS

Take the Thames Clipper to work: it sure beats having to stand on the tube with your nose in someone's armpit. **Greenwich Park is an all-day winner for kids: it has a well-equipped play area, a boating lake, the Observatory and a bloody big hill to roll down. Do pack a picnic, though.** Bring plenty of cash if you're heading for the market on Sunday morning: the cashpoint queues are far too long. **Take out a membership for the Greenwich Picture House and treat yourself and a loved one to a private screening evening.** Spend an afternoon dandering along the Thames Path: you can walk east to the Thames Barrier or west to the City. Better yet, take a bike. **Try the cocktails at the fabulous Inc Bar, where high-end ingredients come at relatively rock-bottom prices. Free entry too.** Don't bother buying the papers before heading out for Saturday morning brunch: the wonderful Buenos Aires café stocks them all – and offers damn fine coffee too.

Plumstead Leisure Centre *Speranza Street, SE18 1JL (8855 8289).*
Royal Herbert Leisure Club *Royal Herbert Pavilions, Shooter's Hill Road, SE18 4PE (8319 0720).* Private.
Thamesmere Leisure Centre *Thamesmere Drive, SE28 8RE (8311 1119/www.gll.org.uk).*
Waterfront Leisure Centre *High Street, SE18 6DL (8317 5000/www.gll.org.uk).*

Other facilities
Charlton Lido *Hornfair Park, Shooter's Hill Road, at Charlton Park Lane, SE18 4LX (8856 7180/www.gll.org.uk).* Summer only.
David Beckham Academy *East Parkside, Greenwich Peninsula, SE10 0JF (8269 4620/ www.thedavidbeckhamacademy.com).* Open during school holidays, this football coaching centre aims to teach eight- to 15-year-olds how to bend it like the man himself.
Royal Blackheath Golf Club *Court Road, SE9 5AF (8850 1795/www.royalblackheath.com).* Reputedly the oldest golf club in England, established in 1608.
Shooters Hill Golf Club *Lowood, Eaglesfield Road, SE18 3DA (8854 1216).*

Spectator sports
Charlton Athletic FC *The Valley, Floyd Road, SE7 8BL (8333 4000/www.cafc.co.uk).*

Schools

WHAT THE PARENTS SAY:

'The primary schools I've visited have all been terrific. Eltham CE in a cul-de-sac off Eltham High Street is amazing for sport with pro coaches in seven sports (including dance) – they're particularly hot on basketball. Charlton Manor has a pupil-led 'Green Council', which does weird and wonderful things for the planet (they won a London education award for it) and badgers local businesses to be greener. Millennium Primary has started well and benefits from a state-of-the-art building.

Secondary schools, I'm afraid, are another story – apart from the ones disciplined by Catholicism. One ray of hope is Greenwich being chosen as one of half a dozen boroughs for the government's Building Schools for the Future programme, with millions earmarked for refurbishments or completely new buildings to provide an environment more conducive to study. Detailed plans are already available for five venues. Plumstead Manor (girls only) is an excellent all-rounder and grabs headlines for achievements in various fields including performing arts.'
Father of two and local sports coach, Greenwich

Primary
Greenwich has 65 state primary schools, 17 of which are church schools. There are also eight independents, including a Steiner school and a theatre academy. See www.greenwich.gov.uk, www.edubase.gov.uk and www.ofsted.gov.uk for more information.

Secondary
Abbey Wood School *Eynsham Drive, SE2 9AJ (8310 9175).* Closing 2009 when St Paul's Academy will move to the site.
Blackheath Bluecoat CE School *Old Dover Road, SE3 8SY (8269 4300/www.bbcs. greenwich.sch.uk).*
Colfe's School *Horn Park Lane, SE12 8AW (8852 2283/www.colfes.com).* Private.
Crown Woods School *Riefield Road, SE9 2QN (8850 7678).*
Eltham Green *Middle Park Avenue, SE9 5EQ (8859 0133/www.elthamgreen.co.uk).*
Eltham Hill Technology College for Girls *Eltham Hill, SE9 5EE (8859 2843/www. elthamhill.greenwich.sch.uk).* Girls only.
The John Roan School *Maze Hill, SE3 7UD (8516 7555/www.thejohnroanschool.co.uk).*
Kidbrooke School *Corelli Road, SE3 8EP (8516 7977/www.kidbrooke.greenwich.sch.uk).*
Plumstead Manor School *Old Mill Road, SE18 1QF (3260 3333/www. plumsteadmanor.com).* Girls only.

St Paul's Academy *Wickham Lane, SE2 0XX (8311 3868/www.stpaulsacademy.org.uk).*
Moving to Eynsham Drive – site of Abbey Wood School in 2009.
St Thomas More RC Comprehensive School *Footscray Road, SE9 2SU (8850 6700/ www.stmcomprehensive.org).*
St Ursula's Convent School *Croom's Hill, SE10 8HN (8858 4613/www.stursulas.com).*
Girls only.
Shooters Hill Post-16 Campus *Red Lion Lane, SE18 4LD (8319 9700/www.shootershill. ac.uk).* Sixth form only.
Thomas Tallis School *Kidbrooke Park Road, SE3 9PX (8856 0115/www.thomastallis.co.uk).*
Woolwich Polytechnic School *Hutchins Road, SE28 8AT (8310 7000/www.woolwich poly.greenwich.sch.uk).* Boys only.

Property

WHAT THE AGENTS SAY:

❝Beautiful and pretty – I live in Greenwich myself and it's a very, very safe area. There are great parks, it's next to the river, there are loads of historical buildings and a real village atmosphere. A lot of people come over from Canary Wharf, which is a bit of a soulless area – there's much more life here in Greenwich.

You've got good schools nearby in Blackheath, and Halstow in East Greenwich also is very popular. There are a lot of new builds, plenty of Victorian houses, flats, ex-council properties and lots of terraced housing towards the west.

Bad points? I can't really think of any… The traffic can be a bit busy in the centre. And there's no big supermarket, though that could also be a good point. The prices are high, but that could be a good point too.

Also worth noting is the Greenwich Reach development. It's huge, with around 500 luxury balconied apartments on Greenwich's last remaining riverside development site. The developers are looking to recreate a Butler's Wharf-type scenario with a mix of bars and restaurants. Alfresco dining is the main objective. This will really complete the package of recent developments in Greenwich. It's not due to be completed until 2012 but 75% of it has already been sold. Prices are in the region of £280,000 for a one-bed… and up. The larger four-beds could even top a million.❞

Peter Booth, Oliver Bond

Average property prices

Detached £595,687
Semi-detached £301,684
Terraced £267,986
Flat £209,147

Local estate agents

Alan Ives Estates *118 Plumstead High Street, SE18 1SJ (88540101/www.alanives.co.uk).*
Cockburn *352 Footscray Road, SE9 2EB (8859 8590/www.cockburn-online.co.uk).*
Greenwich Estates *115A Trafalgar Road, SE10 9TS (8858 8833/www.greenwich-estates.co.uk).*
Harrison Ingram *www.harrisoningram.co.uk; 4 offices in the borough (Charlton 8858 3434/ Eltham 8859 4419/Plumstead 8316 6616/ Thamesmead 8312 4111).*
James Johnston *22 College Approach, SE10 9HY (8858 9986/www.jamesjohnston.com).*
Oliver Bond *38 King William Walk, SE10 9HU (8858 9595/www.oliverbond.co.uk).*
Redwood Estates *13 Cumberland House, Erebus Drive, SE28 0GE (8316 8990/ www.redwoodestates.co.uk).*

Other information

Council

London Borough of Greenwich *Town Hall, Wellington Street, SE18 6PW (8854 8888/ www.greenwich.gov.uk).*

Legal services

Greenwich (Eltham) CAB *The Eltham Centre, Archery Road, SE9 1HA (08451 202931/www.adviceguide.org.uk).*
Greenwich (Woolwich) CAB *Old Town Hall, Polytechnic Street, SE18 6PN (08451 202931/www.adviceguide.org.uk).*
Greenwich Community Law Centre *187 Trafalgar Road, SE10 9EQ (8305 3350).*

Local newspapers

The Lewisham & Greenwich Mercury *8769 4444/www.southlondonpress.co.uk.*

Allotments & open spaces

Council Allotments *8856 2232/ www.greenwich.gov.uk.*
Kidbrooke Allotments *Kidbrooke Park Road, SE3 (John Morgan 8853 5803).*
Prior Street Allotments *www.priorstreetgardens.org.uk.*
Open spaces *www.greenwich.gov.uk/parks; www.urbanecology.org.uk (Greenwich Peninsula Ecology Park); www.royalparks.org.uk.*

COUNCIL TAX

A	up to £40,000	**£843.83**
B	£40,001-£52,000	**£984.46**
C	£52,001-£68,000	**£1125.11**
D	£68,001-£88,000	**£1265.74**
E	£88,001-£120,000	**£1547.02**
F	£120,001-£160,000	**£1828.29**
G	£160,001-£320,000	**£2109.57**
H	over £320,000	**£2531.48**

Greenwich

Newham

Dubbed the third worst place to live in Britain by a 2007 Channel 4 poll, Newham is a borough dogged by bad press. Yet there are diamonds to be found in the rough – if you know where to look. Newham boasts the most culturally diverse population in Britain and, as host borough for the 2012 Olympics, is set for significant regeneration.

Neighbourhoods

Stratford, Forest Gate and Manor Park

In terms of infrastructure at least, Stratford is Newham's most pleasant corner. There's a respectable amount of culture, shedloads of transport and (unfortunately) rather a lot of concrete. What matters, though, is that despite its aesthetic failings Stratford offers Newham residents amenities such as the Theatre Royal, the Picturehouse cinema and the recently relaunched Stratford Circus arts centre. Then there's the Stratford Centre shopping mall (with a bigger and better one – Stratford City – on the way after the Olympics), the main campus of the University of East London, and even a couple of decent pubs.

Still, E15 can feel somewhat soulless at times. Many of the people who bought into the Olympic property bubble never intended to live in the borough – they bought-to-let; what's left is a feeling of a population in transit: students, City workers and immigrant communities (a recent influx of eastern Europeans has added to the area's cultural mix), all renting in east London.

Some desirable areas exist – principally the self-proclaimed 'Village' of two-bed Victorian houses formed by the triangle of Romford Road, West Ham Lane and Vicarage Lane. Or, if a new-build appeals, there are 170 new 'units' in a Meccano-style building in the Theatre Square area. According to local estate agents, the Olympic property boom effect may have already been and gone, but could kick in again after Beijing as anticipation builds for our own fortnight jamboree.

Of course, Stratford's excellent transport links are one of the major reasons for this grandiose sporting arrival. Spectators will be able to choose from a panoply of options: the DLR; the Central and Jubilee tube lines; London Overground; the mainline from Liverpool Street and Essex; and soon the daddy of them all, Eurostar. Stansted airport is less than an hour by coach and then there's brilliant London City airport. Stratford is definitely easy to leave – Canary Wharf is five minutes away, the City ten, the West End no more than 20.

Get on a train towards Essex, however, and within minutes you're in Forest Gate, Manor Park and Little Ilford, on the outer edges of the borough. Get off here and you feel like you've left the busy city far behind

Highs & Lows

The Olympics Two weeks in 2012 will define the borough for years to come. The legacy of the Games should leave Newham with some of the best sports facilities in the world

Transport Stratford has the tube, trains, the DLR and buses. Then there's City airport and, eventually, a Channel Tunnel link too

The Olympics The Olympic flame does not burn brightly for all. Some of the borough's facilities have already had to make way, such as the Eastway cycle circuit, and there are concerns about the tax burden for residents

Beckton With a vast sewage works on one side, and the rather soulless world of Custom House and the ExCeL exhibition centre on the other, Beckton is not one of London's most desirable neighbourhoods

East End old and new at **Queen's Market**.

and arrived in the leafy suburbs. There's certainly less 'to do' in this part of Newham, but there are rows of pleasant enough Victorian semis on tree-lined streets to compensate. There are some wonderful green spaces too, such as heathy Manor Park, Wanstead Flats (just across the borough border in Redbridge) and even the colossal City of London Cemetery, last resting place of Newham's favourite son, Bobby Moore. In fact, the borough as a whole seems to have a disproportionately high acreage of cemeteries, which may explain why so much of it is quite so quiet.

Plaistow, Upton Park, East and West Ham

There is a hard-to-shake feeling that the further south you travel in the borough and the closer you get to the old docks, the worse everything gets. This isn't the most prosperous part of town and classic inner-city problems such as crime, pollution, unemployment and overcrowding abound. It's not all bad – far from it – you just have to look a bit harder than you would in some other London areas to find the good parts.

A strong sense of community, particularly in East and West Ham, is one obvious 'good'. Newham was formed in 1965 by the merging of the former Essex county boroughs of East Ham and West

Ham with Greater London. In both neighbourhoods you'll find plenty of community spirit and an ethnically diverse – Cockney meets subcontinental – population. According to the 2001 census, Newham has the highest proportion of non-whites in the country and on High Street North and, more famously, Green Street, shoppers from India, Sri Lanka, Pakistan, Bangladesh and beyond bustle in and out of sari shops, jewellers, grocers and the like. Meanwhile, despite – currently thwarted – redevelopment plans, Queen's Market (featured in the 2005 film *Wal-Mart: The High Cost of Low Price*) and its huge concrete umbrella echoes to the sort of trading banter you'd expect from a marketload of East Enders.

The leafy side streets of the north-east of the borough continue down High Street North into East Ham; the poet-named streets around Plashet Park and the area known as the Burges Estate, which extends towards the Barking Relief Road, are quiet and anonymous. Central Park, an oasis of greenery that ties together many of the quieter Victorian residential streets in the heart of East Ham, is another popular area. Further west, the area bordering West Ham Park, particularly Ham Park Road, has some excellent housing stock. West Ham Park itself is one of the borough's many

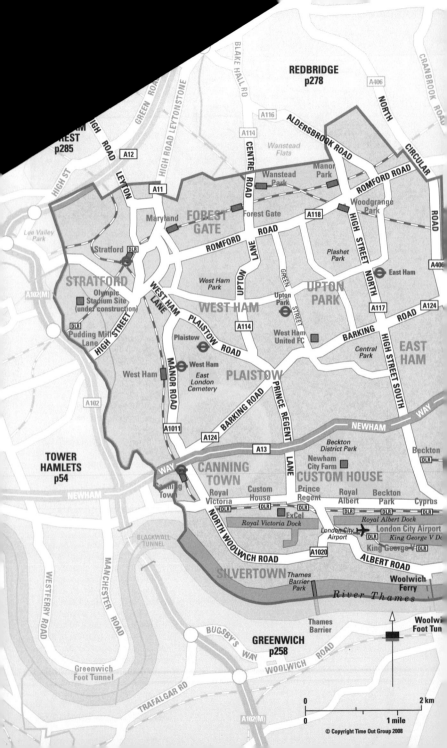

fine open spaces, with some good tennis courts, cricket nets and football pitches – both grass and all-weather.

The Hams even have some respectable architecture in the form of the attractive old Town Hall, East Ham's fabulous period Underground station and the ornate Boleyn cinema, but easily the borough's most famous building, and perhaps the focal point of the whole community, is the Boleyn Ground – home to the pride of the East End, West Ham United.

Match days see pubs such as the Duke of Edinburgh on Green Street heave with battalions of the claret and blue army. Yet these are still able to support events like Diwali with groups of Indian singers – further evidence of a relaxed, multiracial neighbourhood.

Further west, into Plaistow, and the rough definitely gets thicker, the diamonds smaller therein. Housing becomes less attractive, places of interest dwindle. But even here you've got the Greenway, a four-mile walking and cycling artery that follows the path of the Northern Outfall Sewer (no, really) linking Hackney and Beckton, as well as the green and pleasant Lee Valley Park, with Three Mills Island (containing film studios and a cluster of historical mill buildings) at the confluence of the area's rivers.

The area south of Plaistow tube station as far as Barking Road consists of cheerless houses and high-rise estates, though the main artery, Prince Regent Lane, broadens and lightens in atmosphere around Newham Sixth Form College and Newham General Hospital. The streets teem with schoolkids on weekdays, a reminder that Newham has one of London's youngest populations.

Canning Town, Custom House and the Royal Docks

The view from the Woolwich Ferry as it docks at North Woolwich pier rather sums up the southern third of Newham: brutal remnants of the docks; unloved and unassimilated modern architecture; and, precariously intermingled, some surprisingly nice green spaces – in this case the gorgeous little Royal Victoria Gardens with its superb tennis courts, pavilion and weeping willows. In fact, in an area dominated by ugliness – the sprawling, war-influenced estates, the vast,

STATISTICS

BOROUGH MAKE-UP
Population 248,400
Average weekly pay £482
Ethnic origins
  White 39.21%
  Mixed 3.60%
  Asian or Asian British 33%
  Black or Black British 20.46%
  Chinese or other 3.76%
Students 13.63%
Retirees 7.79%

HOUSING STOCK
Borough size 36.4km²
No. of households 97,000
Detached 4.3%
Semi-detached 8.6%
Terraced 45.5%
Flats (purpose-built) 31.1%
Flats (converted) 9.7%
Flats (both) 40.8%

CRIME PER 1,000 OF POPULATION
(average for England and Wales in brackets)
Burglary 9 (5)
Robbery 10 (2)
Theft of vehicle 8 (4)
Theft from vehicle 18 (9)
Violence against the person 31 (19)
Sexual offences 1 (1)

MPs & COUNCIL
MPs *East Ham* Stephen Timms (Labour); *Greenwich & Woolwich* Nick Raynsford (Labour); *Poplar & Canning Town* Jim Fitzpatrick (Labour); *West Ham* Lyn Brown (Labour)
CPA 3 stars; improving well

almost Stalinist ExCeL exhibition centre, the huge scar of the Beckton Reach Sewage Treatment Works, and the bleak, underused expanses of the Royal Docks themselves – it is parks and open spaces that provide the only real highlights – a delightful little railway museum at North Woolwich Old Station aside.

Thames Barrier Park (www.thames barrierpark.org.uk), in particular, with its good café, sculpted gardens, interesting industrial views and a great kids' play area, is a modern triumph. Just the other side of London City airport, Beckton District Park stretches as far as the A13 and beyond, and contains football pitches aplenty, space

Thames Barrier Park. *See p273*.

to run your dog ragged, and one of those wonderful hidden gems – a city farm, where pigs, sheep and exotic birds stand proudly educational in the greying cityscape. You might also see ponies and goats rather randomly tethered amid the joggers and amblers in the park proper.

Parks aside, Canning Town is really little more than a transport hub amid a maze of mediocre streets – a minor league Stratford. Silvertown, North Woolwich and Custom House form what is essentially a windblown desert of dockland with oases of 'luxury' flats, Premier Travel Inns and Novotels. On the positive side there's another campus of the University of East London, a good athletics track, a horse riding centre, and there might, if the developers can find the money, one day be a replacement for the Beckton Alps, formerly the UK's steepest dry ski slope.

South of the docks, the Victorian workers' township of Silvertown (named after the boss of a 19th-century rubber firm) is afflicted by the sickly rotten smell from the Tate & Lyle sugar refinery, and the roar of aeroplanes. And, if none of the above appeals, there are now two spurs of the DLR on which to leave this corner of Newham, one of which leads directly to the brilliantly bijou City airport.

Restaurants & cafés

Unsurprisingly, nowhere in Newham will be troubling the Gordon Ramsays of this world any time soon. There are very, very few good independent eateries, and the borough lacks even a reasonable selection of the sort of just-above-average chain restaurants that you would take for granted elsewhere, apart from a Pizza Express at the Stratford Picturehouse.

There is the odd place at ExCeL, such as Kombu (Japanese) and Super Star (Chinese, notably dim sum), but unless you're there for an exhibition, these represent a somewhat lonely option.

A smattering of curry houses exist on Green Street, such as Mobeen (a self-service Pakistani café) and Vijay's Chawalla (Gujarati vegetarian dishes), and while these aren't exactly world-beaters, they at least avoid the tourist circus and pavement hassle of Brick Lane. Other popular local choices include the India Gate (pan-Indian) on the Grove in Stratford and its oriental counterpart Chan's on High Street North.

Alternatively, if you're hankering after a taste of the old East End, try Robins Pie & Mash in East Ham, or Queen's Fish Bar on Green Street. Also worth a mention is Café Mondo at the Stratford library and family restaurant the Manus on West Ham Lane.

Café Mondo *Stratford Library, 5 The Grove, E15 1EL (8555 1319)*.
Chan's *321 High Street North, E12 6PQ (8472 3384)*.

Newham

India Gate *150 The Grove, E15 1NS
(8534 6565).*
Kombu *Warehouse K, 2 Western Gateway,
E16 1DR (7474 1459).*
Manus *45 West Ham Lane, E15 4PH
(8534 7856).*
Mobeen *224 Green Street, E7 8LE
(8470 2419).*
Queen's Fish Bar *406 Green Street, E13 9JJ
(8471 2457).*
Robins Pie & Mash *105 High Street, E6 1HZ
(8472 1956).*
Super Star *2 Western Gateway, Royal Victoria
Dock North, E16 1DR (7474 0808/www.super
starlondon.com).*
Vijay's Chawalla *268-270 Green Street,
E7 8LF (8470 3535).*

Bars & pubs

Good spots for drinking are barely more
numerous than those for eating – you
won't be coming to Newham on your stag
do. King Edward VII, known locally as
King Eddie's, in Stratford is a rare example
of a proper pub with decent beer and
passable food. The next best option is
probably the bar at the Theatre Royal (*see
p276*), which has free live entertainment
every night of the week.

If you want to watch sport, try the
Queen's Head on West Ham Lane; if you
want a late drink, the Railway Tavern in
Stratford has the borough's only 24-hour
licence. If you like to know exactly what
you're getting, head for the Fox chain bars
in Stratford and at ExCeL, or the Golden
Grove, part of the Wetherspoon's empire.

The choice thins even more as you go
further east. Head for the Blakesley Arms
for a quiet pint, or, if you're a heavy metal
fan, the Ruskin Arms.

Blakesley Arms *53 Station Road, E12 5BP
(8553 4321).*
Fox ExCeL *Warehouse K, 2 Western Gateway,
E16 1DR (7473 2288/www.foxbars.com).*
Fox Stratford *108-110 The Grove, E15 1NS
(8221 0563/www.foxbars.com).*
Golden Grove *146-148 The Grove, E15 1NS
(8519 0750).*
King Edward VII *47 Broadway, E15 4BQ
(8534 2313/www.kingeddie.co.uk).*
Queen's Head *5 West Ham Lane, E15 4PH
(8536 1066).*
Railway Tavern *131 Angel Lane, E15 1DB
(8534 3123/www.railwaytavernhotel.co.uk).*
Ruskin Arms *386 High Street North, E12 6PH
(8472 0377/www.ruskinarms.co.uk).*
Theatre Royal Bar *Theatre Royal Stratford
East, Gerry Raffles Square, E15 1BN (8279
1161/www.stratfordeast.com).*

TRANSPORT

Tube stations *Central* Stratford;
District/Hammersmith & City West
Ham, Plaistow, Upton Park, East Ham;
Jubilee Stratford, West Ham, Canning
Town; *DLR* Stratford, Pudding Mill Lane,
Canning Town, Royal Victoria, Custom
House, Prince Regent, Royal Albert,
Beckton Park, Cyprus, Gallions Reach,
Beckton, West Silvertown, Pontoon
Dock, London City Airport, King George V
Rail stations *c2c* West Ham; *one*
Stratford, Maryland, Forest Gate, Manor
Park; *London Overground* Stratford;
Wanstead Park, Woodgrange Park
Main bus routes *into central London*
25, 115; *night buses* N8, N15, N50;
24-hour buses 25
River Woolwich Ferry
Development plans DLR extension to
Woolwich Arsenal opening 2009, with
plans for a link between Stratford and
Royal Victoria by 2010

Shops

Newham has one shopping centre (just
about) worth the name – the Statford Centre
on Broadway in the heart of Stratford.
This is not a classic of the genre, however,
and residents will have to wait until after
the Olympics for the arrival of the mega
new Stratford City, with around 120 shops
including a John Lewis and an M&S.

Queen's Market at Upton Park tube
station is a hustle and bustle of cheap
clothes and fresh food. Green Street in
West Ham and the High Street running
south from Plashet to East Ham are
busy thoroughfares, fine for basics and
absolutely excellent if you're in the market
for jewellery or a sari. However, by far the
best options for a serious shopping trip lie
five minutes west on the tube at Canary
Wharf, or 20 minutes by car down the A13
at Lakeside Shopping Centre in Essex.

Arts & attractions

Cinemas & theatres
Boleyn Cinema *7-11 Barking Road, E6 1PN
(8471 4884).*
Brick Lane Music Hall *443 North Woolwich
Road, E16 2DA (7511 6655/www.bricklane
musichall.co.uk).*
Stratford Circus *Theatre Square, E15 1BX
(8279 1080/www.stratford-circus.com).*

Newham

Stratford East Picturehouse *Theatre Square, E15 1BN (8555 3366/bookings 0870 755 0064/www.picturehouses.co.uk).*
Theatre Royal Stratford East *Gerry Raffles Square, E15 1BN (8534 7374/www.stratford east.com).*

Other attractions
Discover *1 Bridge Terrace, E15 4BG (8536 5555/www.discover.org.uk).* Popular interactive play centre.
ExCeL Exhibition Centre *1 Western Gateway, Royal Victoria Dock, E16 1XL (7069 5000/www.excel-london.co.uk).* Trade fairs, conferences, sporting events and concerts.
Newham City Farm *Stansfield Road, E6 5LT (7474 4960).*
North Woolwich Old Station Museum *Pier Road, E16 2JJ (7474 7244).*

Sport & fitness

The private sector has hardly registered a presence in Newham. However, there's more than adequate compensation in the very varied shapes of its four public centres. East Ham Leisure Centre is justly the flagship facility, but usage is high at the other centres too. The private Peacock Gymnasium in Canning Town is an atmospheric and motivating place. Also popular are the various watersports centres in the old docks.

The Eastway cycle circuit on the edge of Lee Valley Park has been temporarily relocated to Redbridge during construction of the Olympic Park.

Gyms & leisure centres
Atherton Leisure Centre *189 Romford Road, E15 4JF (8536 5500/www.gll.org).*
Balaam Leisure Centre *Balaam Street, E13 8AQ (7476 5274/www.gll.org).*

RECYCLING
No. of bring sites 150 (for nearest, visit www.recycleforlondon.com)
Household waste recycled 8.63%
Nearest recycling centre Jenkins Lane Reuse & Recycling Centre, Jenkins Lane, Barking, Essex IG11 0AD (0800 389 9918)
Other recycling services green waste collection; home composting; collection of white goods, electrical goods, furniture and other household items
Council contact The Recycling Team, Central Depot, Folkestone Road, E6 6BX (8430 3960)

East Ham Leisure Centre *324 Barking Road, E6 2RT (8548 5850/www.gll.org).*
Fit for Life *2nd floor, Hawley House, 5-7 High Street, E13 0AD (8552 1776).* Private.
Newham Leisure Centre *281 Prince Regent Lane, E13 8SD (7511 4477/www.gll.org).*
Peacock Gymnasium *Peacock House, Caxton Street North, E16 1JL (7476 8427).* Private.

Other facilities
Docklands Equestrian Centre *2 Claps Gate Lane, E6 6JF (7511 3917).* Riding lessons for all ages.
Docklands Watersports Club *Gate 14, King George V Dock, Woolwich Manor Way, E16 2NJ (7511 5000).* Members of this jet-ski club need to provide their own equipment and personal water craft. Membership £350/yr.
London Regatta Centre *Dockside Road, E16 2QT (7511 2211/www.london-regatta-centre.org.uk).* Training facilities for rowing clubs, a fully equipped gym and boat hire.
Royal Victoria Dock Watersports Centre *Gate 5, Tidal Basin Road, off Silvertown Way, E16 1AF (7511 2326).* The RVDWC offers canoeing, bellboating and sailing lessons for both individuals and groups.

Spectator sports
West Ham United FC *Boleyn Ground, Green Street, E13 9AZ (8548 2748/www.whufc.com).*

Schools

WHAT THE PARENTS SAY:
❝I feel that the schools in Newham, at both primary and secondary level, are average. There are some good primaries, such as Godwin, which is sought after – as are the church schools like St Anthony's – but the secondary schools leave a lot to be desired. St Bonaventure's (a boys' school) is great, but I wouldn't be happy for my kids to go to the others.

My daughter is seven and goes to school in Redbridge, the neighbouring borough. The main reason is that Redbridge has a solid education reputation, better secondaries and I like the multicultural mix of pupils and parents. Her school also offers more social interaction than the Newham ones do. However, I'm aware that there is a programme of improvement in place in Newham and plenty of investment.❞
Father of one, Newham

Primary
There are 62 state primary schools in Newham, including ten church schools. There are also six independent primaries, and three Muslim schools. See www.newham.gov.uk, www.edubase.gov.uk and www.ofsted.gov.uk for more information.

Newham

Secondary

Brampton Manor School *Roman Road, E6 3SQ (7540 0500/www.bramptonmanor. newham.sch.uk).*
Cumberland School *Oban Close, E13 8SJ (7474 0231/www.cumberland.org.uk).*
Eastlea Community School *Exning Road, E16 4ND (7540 0400/www.eastlea.newham. sch.uk).*
Forest Gate Community School *Forest Street, E7 0HR (8534 8666/www.forestgate. newham.sch.uk).*
Kingsford Community School *Kingsford Way, E6 5JG (7476 4700/www.kingsford school.com).*
Langdon School *Sussex Road, E6 2PS (8471 2411/www.langdon.newham.sch.uk).*
Lister Community School *St Mary's Road, E13 9AE (8471 3311/www.lister.newham.sch.uk).*
Little Ilford School *Browning Road, E12 6ET (8478 8024/www.littleilford.newham.sch.uk).*
Newham College of Further Education *High Street South, E6 6ER (8257 4000/ www.newham.ac.uk).*
Newham Sixth Form College *Prince Regent Lane, E13 8SG (7473 4110/ www.newvic.ac.uk).*
Plashet School *Plashet Grove, E6 1DG (8471 2418/www.plashet.newham.sch.uk).* Girls only.
Rokeby School *Pitchford Street, E15 4RZ (8534 8946/www.rokebyschool.net).* Boys only.
Royal Docks Community School *Prince Regents Lane, E16 3HS (7540 2700).*
St Angela's Ursuline Convent School *St George's Road, E7 8HU (8472 6022/ www.stangelas-ursuline.co.uk).* Girls only; mixed sixth form.
St Bonaventure's RC School *Boleyn Road, E7 9QD (8472 3844).* Boys only; mixed sixth form.
Sarah Bonnell School *Deanery Road, E15 4LP (8534 6791/www.sarahbonnellonline.co.uk).* Girls only.
Stratford School *Upton Lane, E7 9PR (8471 2415/www.stratford.newham.sch.uk).*

Property

WHAT THE AGENTS SAY:

‘At the moment this is a very poor borough. A high percentage of people in Newham and Stratford are claiming benefit and Newham Council is always short of money. The place is horrible, it's dirty, the streets aren't clean, it's an eyesore, there isn't even a place to get a decent meal.

The Bow flyover is a major boundary. Further west it's more trendy – what I'm hoping is that the Olympics are going to extend that boundary out to Stratford. The rail links are brilliant, the landscape is getting a facelift, and we are seeing

COUNCIL TAX		
A	up to £40,000	**£813.16**
B	40,001-£52,000	**£948.69**
C	£52,001-£68,000	**£1,084.22**
D	£68,001-£88,000	**£1,219.74**
E	£88,001-£120,000	**£1,490.79**
F	£120,001-£160,000	**£1,761.85**
G	£160,001-£320,000	**£2,032.90**
H	over £320,000	**£2,439.48**

a more discerning tenant, but all they're doing is going home to sleep, they don't go out in the area. I just hope it's not up to the council to maintain all the new facilities after the circus has left town, because they can't afford it.’
Martin Tozer, Jonathan Webb & Co, Stratford

Average property prices

Detached £352,000
Semi-detached £288,340
Terraced £241,659
Flat £210,325

Local estate agents

Charles Living & Son *14-16 Romford Road, E15 4BZ (8534 1163/www.charlesliving.com).*
Jonathan Webb *196 The Grove, E15 1NS (8519 3210/www.jonathan-webb.co.uk).*
Marvel Estates *367 Katherine Road, E7 8LT (8471 0845/www.marvelestates.com).*
McDowalls *54-56 Barking Road, E6 3BP (8472 4422/www.mcdowalls.com).*
Samuel King *110A Barking Road, E16 1EN (7474 6000/www.samuelking.co.uk).*
Spencer's Property Services *70 Woodgrange Road, E7 0EN (8555 5666/www.spencers property.co.uk).*

Other information

Council

London Borough of Newham Council *Newham Town Hall, Barking Road, E6 2RP (8430 2000/www.newham.gov.uk).*

Legal services

Newham CAB *Stratford Advice Arcade, 107-109 The Grove, E15 1HP (0870 126 4097/ www.adviceguide.org.uk).*

Local newspapers

Newham Recorder
8472 1421/www.newhamrecorder.co.uk.

Allotments & open spaces

Council Allotments *The Allotment Officer, 292 Barking Road, E6 3BA (8430 2455/3606).*
Open spaces *www.newham.gov.uk/parks.*

Redbridge

Don't believe everything you read about E numbers. In this part of town people are healthy and wealthy. Redbridge boasts green acres, good schools and plenty of space for families to spread out.

Neighbourhoods

Wanstead

The Green Man roundabout separates Leytonstone (in Waltham Forest) from Wanstead. It also marks a distinct change in mentality. Where the former remains urban in appearance and attitude, the latter is more typically suburban. It's leafier, visibly prosperous and boasts a wealth of clubs and societies that reflect a life independent of the capital – even though a daily commute on the Central line is the reality for most residents.

The actual county boundary may be a couple of miles further out, but this stretch of E11 is where London fringes into Essex. The result is the occasional lairy mansion and 'East End made good' mentality more common in the so-called 'golden triangle' of Chigwell, Buckhurst Hill and Loughton. However, since Wanstead is popular with City execs, business folk and professional

families, it also means Saturday socialising in the stylish new delis and cafés springing up along the attractive High Street.

Central Wanstead and the Aldersbrook Estate, which is surrounded by historic Wanstead Park (buy a guidebook from the tea stall here for fascinating historical insights) and the vast playing fields of Wanstead Flats, consist predominantly of large, classic late Victorian terraced houses. Most are occupied by families keen to maintain Wanstead's strong community feel; there are active churches, residents' associations and societies. Elsewhere, 18th-century merchants' houses near Snaresbrook Crown Court and a plethora of stylish but pricey blocks of flats reflect the other extremes of the property market. After-hours aggravation from bored teenagers can sometimes be a problem, with Christchurch Green – pleasant by day – a particular hotspot.

When the M11-A12 link road was tunnelled through the area in the early 1990s, with protesters gaining national attention by creating the 'independent republic of Wanstonia', many feared that Wanstead's character would be destroyed. The road, always jammed at the Redbridge roundabout, still arouses fierce passion, but Wanstead has managed ro retain the feel of a small town within reach of, but at arm's length from, London.

South Woodford

The latest block of flats, squeezed into a tiny space between Sainsbury's and the cinema, reflects the currently confused reality of life in E18. Its appeal, particularly for well-heeled young City workers, is obvious: a vibrant bar and restaurant scene, a large branch of Waitrose, plus easy access both to London for work and the M11 to put the latest four-wheeled status symbol through its paces. For older

Highs & Lows

Seat of learning Redbridge's state primary and secondary schools are among the best in the country, making the borough popular with young families
Wide open spaces Wanstead Park has a fascinating history, Epping Forest is east London's traditional green lung and Woodford Green boasts some magnificent trees

South Woodford's new flats Some locals feel insensitive planning is damaging an otherwise understated residential neighbourhood
Suburban smugness A few folk round this way have done well for themselves – and want you to know it

Victorian terraces lining spacious **Wanstead Flats**.

and more established South Woodfordians, however, the preponderance of glass and chrome is damaging what has been a smart but understated residential area since the 19th century.

At one end of E18 is the Drive: the local millionaires' row of 1930s mansions. At the other, London becomes Essex at Woodford Green. In between are streets of large Victorian and Edwardian properties radiating out from the shopping centre in George Lane. The area is popular with families thanks to the good local schools, both state and private. The Odeon, the only mainstream picture house for miles around, keeps the local teenagers happy when they're not getting kicked out of the George pub next door.

The other downside of South Woodford is the inescapable presence of the North Circular Road. Its six lanes lie in a deep cutting, with the High Road crossing over on a bridge, and offer an unappealing vista for residents of the adjacent housing estate being constructed on the old Queen Mary College site. Unlike in neighbouring Wanstead, where the A12 goes underground through the central town area, the planners of an earlier generation paid less heed to the physical and psychological damage caused by constant heavy traffic.

Woodford Green

As the name implies, Epping Forest is all around you in Woodford Green. Surrounded by ponds and magnificent chestnut trees is the green itself, on which the local cricket club have played since 1735. Entrusted to the care of the City of London by an Act of Parliament in 1878, the forest's protected status has helped to limit development and retain the area's verdant feel. There are few modern blocks of flats, while the large, detached houses in the Woodford Wells neighbourhood, off Monkham's Lane, are extremely desirable.

Sir Winston Churchill was the local MP for 40 years and his presence is still felt, notably in the famous statue outside Hurst House, the area's grandest residence. Another prime minister, Clement Attlee, also lived here – as did suffragette campaigner Sylvia Pankhurst. Compared to the bustling building site that is South Woodford, Woodford Green is working hard to stay in touch with its history.

Restaurants & cafés

Top of the local restaurant league is Wanstead's Applebee's, the offshoot of an upmarket fish stall in Borough Market.

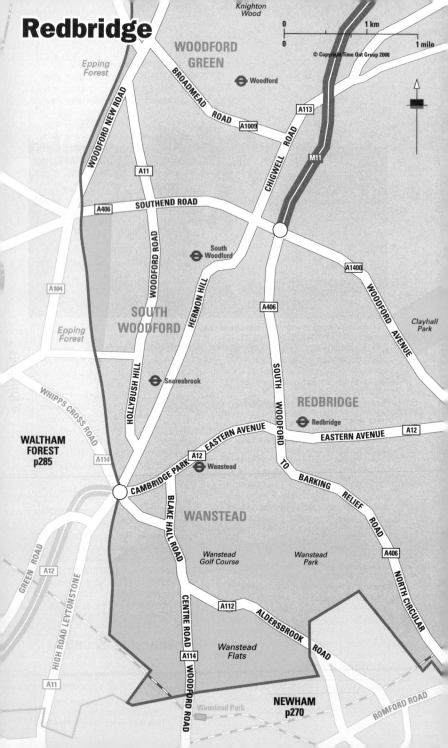

The impeccable provenance of its modern British menu has set a challenge to old favourite Hadley House, whose hefty meat dishes attract a regular, well-heeled clientele. Nam An is an oasis of oriental opulence serving high-quality Vietnamese food just yards from the A12 interchange, while Gastrodome is part of a small chain of diners specialising in grills and spit-roasted chicken.

Several upmarket food stores and cafés opened in 2007 to joust for custom with stalwart Nice Croissant. These include Italian deli Olive Branch, Kylie's Kitchen and, the pick of the lot, the Larder.

The South Woodford equivalent is the 1950s-styled Soul Stop Café, while good-value fish restaurant Ark offers more substantial fare. You'll need to travel further afield to find the best ethnic options: Curry Special (North Indian) in Newbury Park and Mandarin Palace (Chinese) by the Gants Hill roundabout.

If you've got kids to entertain, don't miss Pizzeria Bel-Sit in Woodford Green. Every inch of wall and ceiling is crammed with signed football shirts, balls and photos.

Applebee's 17 Cambridge Park, E11 2PU (8989 1977).
Ark 142 Hermon Hill, E18 1QH (8989 5345/ www.arkfishrestaurant.co.uk).
Curry Special 2 Greengate Parade, Horns Road, IG2 6BE (8518 3005).
Gastrodome 17 High Street, E11 2AA (8989 8943).
Hadley House 27 High Street, E11 2AA (8989 8855).
Kylie's Kitchen 14 High Street, E11 2AJ (8989 1988).
Larder 39 High Street, E11 2AA (8989 7181).
Mandarin Palace 559-561 Cranbrook Road, IG2 6JZ (8550 7661).
Nam An 157 High Street, E11 2RL (8532 2845).
Nice Croissant 119A High Street, E11 2RL (8530 1129).
Olive Branch 141 High Street, E11 2RL (8530 7089).
Pizzeria Bel-Sit 439 High Road, IG8 0XE (8504 1164).
Soul Stop Café 154 George Lane, E18 1AY (8989 1849).

Bars & pubs

The watering holes along Wanstead's High Street and South Woodford's George Lane attract a young and sometimes brash clientele, so don't turn up at the Cuckfield,

Bar Room Bar and Russells in E11, or Switch in E18, if you're after a quiet glass of pinot noir. More low-key drinking options are found away from the main drag. Fine local pubs with well-kept beer and an enthusiastic welcome are the Nightingale in Wanstead and the Cricketers and the Travellers Friend, both in Woodford Green. Faces nightclub in Gants Hill attracts minor celebs and wannabe hangers-on.

Bar Room Bar 33-34 High Street, E11 2AA (8989 0552/www.barroombar.com).
Cricketers 299-301 High Road, IG8 9HQ (8504 2734).
Cuckfield 31 High Street, E11 2AA (8532 2431).
Faces 458-462 Cranbrook Road IG2 6LE (8554 8899/www.facesnightclub.co.uk).

STATISTICS

BOROUGH MAKE-UP
Population 251,900
Average weekly pay £478.70
Ethnic origins
White 59.48%
Mixed 2.89%
Asian or Asian British 26.59%
Black or Black British 9.04%
Chinese or other 2.01%
Students 9.24%
Retirees 11.32%

HOUSING STOCK
Borough size 56.3km²
No. of households 94,174
Detached 5.6%
Semi-detached 26.8%
Terraced 40.3%
Flats (purpose-built) 19%
Flats (converted) 7.9%
Flats (both) 26.9%

CRIME PER 1,000 OF POPULATION
(average for England and Wales in brackets)
Burglary 8 (5)
Robbery 5 (2)
Theft of vehicle 6 (4)
Theft from vehicle 13 (9)
Violence against the person 17 (19)
Sexual offences 1 (1)

MPs & COUNCIL
MPs *Chingford & Woodford Green* Iain Duncan Smith (Conservative); *Leyton & Wanstead* Harry Cohen (Labour)
CPA 3 stars; improving well

Redbridge

Nightingale *51 Nightingale Lane, E11 2EY*
(8530 4540).
Russells *44 High Street, E11 2RJ (8518 8477).*
Switch *77-81 George Lane, E18 1JJ*
(www.switchbarlounge.com).
Travellers Friend *496-498 High Road,*
IG8 0PN (8504 2435).

Shops

Ilford is the main destination for Redbridge
residents, with the Exchange Mall offering
most major names and a medium-sized
branch of Marks & Spencer.

Wanstead offers a more low-key
experience, with the emphasis on high-end
goods. Its villagey ambience is enhanced
by an excellent butcher, AG Dennis, and
greengrocer, Harvey's (both of which have
won awards from residents' association
the Wanstead Society for high quality
and friendly service). Up the road, South
Woodford has branches of Sainsbury's
and Waitrose supermarkets.

Contemporary style comes in the form
of Wanstead's Devon House Interiors and
One Deko, the latter a super-slick lifestyle
store that also has a branch in Spitalfields.
There's also a home furnishings branch
of Laura Ashley in South Woodford, while
Provence in Woodford Green sells furniture,
frou-frou and flowers. You'll find stylish
men's clothes at Santa Fe in Wanstead,
though anyone getting ready for a night
out may prefer the clobber at brilliant
menswear store Jun-Qi in Woodford Green.
South Woodford's Source has fashion by
Noa Noa, ZPM make-up and vanity bags,
and great handbags from independent label
Tabitha. To complete the look, Zoology is
an award-winning hair salon.

If lugging everything home leaves more
than your wallet screaming for mercy, the
Back Pain Centre is run by Terry Chimes –
the Clash's original drummer who's been a
registered chiropractor since 1994.

AG Dennis *3 Clock House Parade, High Street,*
E11 2AG (8989 2691).
Back Pain Centre *50 Chigwell Road, E18 1LS*
(8989 3330/www.chimes-chiropractic.co.uk).
Devon House Interiors *3-5 Hermon Hill,*
E11 2AW (8518 8112/www.devonhouse
interiors.co.uk).
Exchange Mall *High Road, IG1 1RS*
(8553 3000/www.themall.co.uk).
Harvey's *6 Clock House Parade, High Street,*
E11 2AG (8989 6369).
Jun-Qi *172 High Road, IG8 9EF (8559 2122).*
Laura Ashley *12-14 Electric Parade, George*
Lane, E18 2LY (0871 223 1468/www.laura
ashley.com).
One Deko *151 High Street, E11 2RL*
(8989 3377/www.onedeko.co.uk).
Provence *212 High Road, IG8 9HH*
(8505 8988).
Santa Fe *119 High Street, E11 2RL*
(8518 8922).
Source *227 High Road, E18 2PB (8505 6697/*
www.sourcelifestyle.com).
Zoology *145 High Street, E11 2RL*
(8530 3005/www.zoology-hair.com).

Arts & attractions

Cinemas & theatres
Cineworld Ilford *Clements Road, IG1 1BP*
(0871 200 2000/www.cineworld.co.uk).
Kenneth More Theatre *Oakfield Road,*
IG1 1BT (8553 4464/www.kenneth-more-
theatre.co.uk).
Odeon South Woodford *58-66 High Street,*
E18 2QL (0871 224 4007/www.odeon.co.uk).

Galleries & museums
Redbridge Museum *Central Library,*
Clements Road, IG1 1EA (8708 2432/
www.redbridge.gov.uk). Local history museum.

Other attractions
Valentines Mansion *Emerson Road, IG1*
4XA (membership 8554 4063/www.valentines
mansion.org.uk). This 17th-century mansion in
Valentines Park is occasionally open to visitors.
You can stroll in the gardens at any time.

Sport & fitness

This middle-class segment of east London suburbia plays host to countless sports clubs amid its green acres. The trust-run Redbridge Sports & Leisure Centre is superb – among the very best fitness clubs in the capital. Physicals is the pick of the other private clubs, although the chains are establishing an ever-stronger presence. In contrast, public-sector provision is poor: just one sports centre (Wanstead) and two pools (Fullwell Cross and Ilford).

Gyms & leisure centres

David Lloyd *Roding Lane, IG9 6BJ (8559 8466/www.davidlloydleisure.co.uk).* Private.
Fitness First *261-275 High Road, IG1 1NJ (8514 7666/www.fitnessfirst.co.uk).* Private.
Fullwell Cross Leisure Centre *High Street, IG6 2EA (8550 2366/www.vision-rcl.org.uk).*
Ilford Pools Leisure Centre *468 High Road, IG1 1UE (8553 0639/www.vision-rcl. org.uk).*
Physicals *327 High Road, IG8 9HQ (8505 4914/www.physicalsfitness.co.uk).* Private.
Redbridge Sports & Leisure Centre *Forest Road, IG6 3HD (8498 1000/ www.rslonline.co.uk).* Private.
Wanstead Leisure Centre *Redbridge Lane West, E11 2JZ (8989 1172).*

Other facilities

Wanstead Golf Course *Overton Drive, E11 2LW (8989 3938/0604/www.wanstead golf.org.uk).* Private.

Schools

WHAT THE PARENTS SAY:

❝If you ask people why they've moved to Redbridge, those with children will invariably mention the schools. The borough is usually ranked in the top three or four in the UK and there are very few poor schools. Only one state secondary, Hainault Forest, has been in special measures recently, though this was removed in 2006 and its reputation is improving. Redbridge has kept its grammar schools and there is fierce competition to win places at Woodford County for girls and Ilford County for boys. For those who miss out and can afford to go private, Chigwell, Bancroft and Forest are all within easy reach.

We actually live a couple of hundred yards over the borough boundary in Waltham Forest, but we wanted our kids to have a Christian-based education so they all attended Wanstead Church School. They've had to move out of the borough again to attend a C of E secondary:

St Edward's in Havering. At primary level, the schools are in the top ten nationally. Our Lady of Lourdes is another denominational primary school with an excellent reputation, while Churchfields in South Woodford and Snaresbrook Primary are both popular.

If education is a factor in choosing where to live, then Redbridge should be among the top choices anywhere in London.❞
Andrew Shields, father of three, Leytonstone

Primary

There are 51 state primary schools in Redbridge, including seven church schools and two Jewish schools. There are also 16 independent primaries, including three faith schools. See www. redbridge.gov.uk/learning, www.ofsted.gov.uk and www.edubase.gov.uk for more information.

Secondary

Bancroft's School *High Road, Woodford Green, IG8 0RF (8505 4821/www.bancrofts. essex.sch.uk).*
Beal High School *Woodford Bridge Road, IG4 5LP (8551 4954/www.bealhighschool. org.uk).*
Canon Palmer Catholic School *Aldborough Road South, IG3 8EU (8590 3808/ www.canonpalmer.redbridge.sch.uk).*
Caterham High School *Caterham Avenue, IG5 0QW (8551 4321/www.caterham. redbridge.sch.uk).*
Chadwell Heath Foundation School *Christie Gardens, RM6 4RS (8252 5151/ www.chadwellheath.redbridge.sch.uk).*
Chigwell School *High Road, IG7 6QF (8501 5700/www.chigwell-school.org).*
Forest School *2 College Place, E17 3PY (boys 8520 1744; girls 8521 7477/www.forest. org.uk).*
Hainault Forest High School *Harbourer Road, IG6 3TN (8500 4266/www.hainaultforest. redbridge.sch.uk).*

Redbridge

Ilford County High School for Boys
Fremantle Road, IG6 2JB (8551 6496/
www.ichs.org.uk). Boys only.
Ilford Ursuline High School *Morland Road,*
IG1 4JU (8554 1995/www.ilfordursuline-high.
org.uk). Girls only.
King Solomon High School *Forest Road,*
IG6 3HB (8501 2083/www.kshsonline.com).
Loxford School of Science & Technology
Loxford Lane, IG1 2UT (8514 4666).
Mayfield School *Pedley Road, RM8 1XE*
(8590 5211).
Oaks Park High School *45-65 Oaks Lane,*
IG2 7PQ (8590 2245/www.oakspark.co.uk).
Opened in 2003.
Seven Kings High School *Ley Street, IG2*
7BT (8554 8935/www.skhs.net).
Trinity Catholic High School *Mornington*
Road, IG8 0TP (8504 3419/www.trinity.
redbridge.sch.uk).
Valentines High School *Cranbrook Road,*
IG2 6HX (8554 3608/www.valentines-sch.
org.uk).
Wanstead High School *Redbridge Lane*
West, E11 2JZ (8989 2791/www.wanstead
high.co.uk).
Woodbridge High School *St Barnabas Road,*
IG8 7DQ (8504 9618/www.woodbridgehigh
school.co.uk).
Woodford County High School for Girls
High Road, IG8 9LA (8504 0611/www.
woodford.redbridge.sch.uk). Girls only.

Property

WHAT THE AGENTS SAY:

❝Woodford Green is a leafy suburb with easy
access to central London. However, head just
five minutes up the road and you're in the middle
of the forest. Ten minutes the other way and
you're heading into central London and the City.
It's an area that's very popular with families.
It's safe and has good schools, both private
and public. Heading out of the East End and
Docklands it's the first family-oriented area you
come to really. South Woodford and Wanstead
are the main centres for nightlife.❞
Adrian Sinclair, Spencer's Property Services,
Woodford Green

Average property prices
Detached £598,575
Semi-detached £325,851
Terraced £285,044
Flat £190,826

Local estate agents
Churchill Estates *32 High Street, E11 2RJ*
(8989 0011/www.churchill-estates.co.uk)
Homes & Co *131 High Road, E18 2PA*
(8504 8844/www.homesandco.com).

Richard John Clarke *397 High Road, IG8*
0XG (8559 1555/www.richardjohnclarke.com).
Sandra Davidson *www.sandradavidson.com;*
2 offices in the borough (Redbridge 8551 0211/
Seven Kings 8597 7372).
Spencer's Property Services
www.spencersproperty.co.uk; 2 offices in the
borough (Woodford Green 8559 2110/Ilford
8518 5411).

Other information

Council
Redbridge Council Town Hall, *128-142*
High Road, IG1 1DD (8554 5000/
www.redbridge.gov.uk).

Legal services
Loughton CAB *St Mary's Parish Centre,*
High Road, IG10 1BB (8502 0031/
www.adviceguide.org.uk).
Redbridge CAB *2nd floor, Broadway*
Chambers, 1 Cranbrook Road, IG1 4DU
(0870 126 4140/www.adviceguide.org.uk).

Local newspapers
Wanstead & Woodford Guardian
www.guardian-series.co.uk.

Allotments & open spaces
Council Allotments *8th floor, Lynton House,*
255-259 High Road, IG1 1NY (8708 3091/
www.redbridge.gov.uk).
Open spaces *www.redbridge.gov.uk/*
cms/leisure__culture/parks__open_spaces.aspx.

TRANSPORT
Tube stations *Central* Wanstead,
Redbridge, Gants Hill, Newbury Park,
Barkingside, Hainault, Grange Hill,
Roding Valley, Woodford, South
Woodford, Snaresbrook
Rail stations *one* Ilford, Seven Kings,
Goodmayes, Chadwell Heath; *London*
Overground Wanstead Park
Main bus routes *into central London*
25; *night buses* N8, N55; *24-hour*
buses 25

COUNCIL TAX

A	up to £40,000	**£887.00**
B	£40,001-£52,000	**£1,034.83**
C	£52,001-£68,000	**£1,182.67**
D	£68,001-£88,000	**£1,330.50**
E	£88,001-£120,000	**£1,626.16**
F	£120,001-£160,000	**£1,921.83**
G	£160,001-£320,000	**£2,217.49**
H	over £320,000	**£2,660.99**

Waltham Forest

As one of the five 'Olympic boroughs', Waltham Forest is poised to capitalise on the investment and infrastructure that the 2012 Games will bring to this long-neglected part of east London. Though many areas are still scruffy and run-down, a dynamic council is starting to generate real change – with a community-focused football club to the fore.

Neighbourhoods

Walthamstow

Once famous only for a greyhound track and a boy band, Walthamstow's new weekly farmers' market is helping E17 to assert a more middle-class image. Although swathes of the area are blighted by grime and industrial eyesores, notably on the North Circular Road, Lea Bridge Road and Forest Road, there remains at Walthamstow's heart a genuine village. Around the attractively overgrown churchyard of St Mary's huddle a handful of quiet streets with cute cottages, there are decent restaurants and pubs on Orford Road, a rumbling train line and the excellent Vestry House Museum (though locals are enraged by the reduction in opening hours, both here and at the William Morris Gallery, caused by recent council cost-cutting).

Walthamstow was assessed in the Domesday Book at £28 in gold – not bad for a farming village of just 82 people. More recently, first-time buyers have recognised there's value to be had in these parts; while the days when you could buy a three-bedroom house in Walthamstow for the price of a one-bed flat in Stoke Newington have long gone, it remains one of London's more affordable neighbourhoods. Warnings that prices would rocket across the borough once Olympic regeneration work began in nearby Stratford have yet to be realised, though locals insist it's only a matter of time. There's another connection between E17 and E15: the fictional Walford of *EastEnders* is a combination of 'Wal' from Walthamstow and 'ford' from Stratford.

Away from the centre, dark-brick terraces and housing estates predominate, home to a mix of young professionals and families.

A particular feature are the terraces of purpose-built Warner maisonettes. More than 5,000 were built from the 1880s to the 1930s, a remarkable enterprise by a local family to provide housing for the masses. These one- and two-bedroom properties are popular with first-time buyers, though few are still painted in the original colours of green and cream.

Just off the North Circular, near the sports grounds of Wadham Lodge, is Walthamstow Stadium: Britain's most famous greyhound track, with an atmospheric art deco exterior. A few minutes' walk away is pleasant Lloyd Park. The park surrounds the childhood home of the late Victorian designer and socialist William Morris; the attractive gallery here has a collection of his Arts and Crafts fabrics and wallpaper

Walthamstow is rightly proud of its street market, which is reckoned to be the longest in Europe and sprawls along the mainly pedestrianised High Street. It's a bustling and characterful affair, run by

Highs & Lows

▲ **William Morris Gallery** A cultural gem in a borough with few famous locals to celebrate
Affordable housing Plenty of choice for first-timers in Leytonstone – who may find they like it enough to stay

▼ **Dismal shopping** The supermarkets and North Circular superstores have killed off most of the independents
Poverty Despite parts of Walthamstow and Leytonstone moving upmarket, some wards in Leyton and south Chingford are among the most deprived in Britain

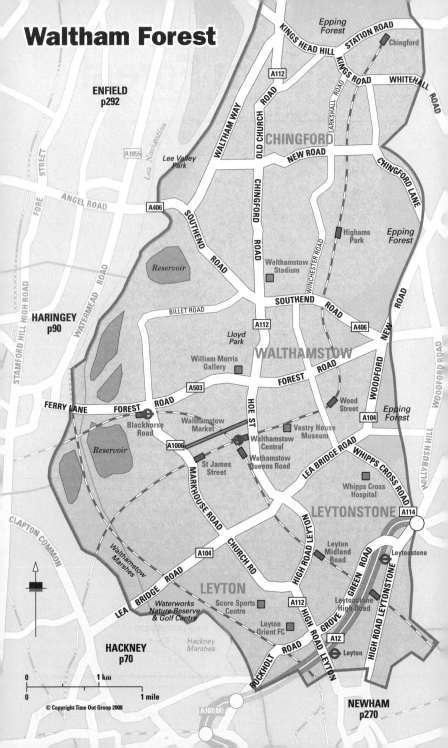

gor-blimey East Enders selling bowls of fruit and veg for a quid, along with every household item you can think of. On Sunday mornings, quality comes to the fore at the farmers' market in the Town Square.

Transport connections are excellent: Walthamstow is linked to central London by the Victoria line and no fewer than five rail stations, plus a plethora of buses. Nevertheless, the commute, on the tube in particular, can be a crowded affair.

Leyton

Leyton is also well served for transport, with the Central line whisking commuters to the heart of the City, the A12 running east to Essex and the A102 speeding traffic south across the Thames. However, these very visible rail and road links leave the area feeling less of a destination and more like somewhere people merely pass through. Despite the alluring proximity of E10 to the main Olympic site, development so far has been piecemeal and nondescript.

The much-publicised blocks of flats built on the four corners of Leyton Orient's football ground are the main evidence of a desire to attract greater youth and vitality to the neighbourhood. Across the road from the Matchroom Stadium is the jewel in Leyton's crown, the £10 million Score centre. This outstanding facility offers a huge indoor sports hall, high-quality outdoor pitch, a nursery, a Primary Care Centre and the local development trust O-Regen. It's also home to the award-winning Leyton Orient Community Sports Programme, which extends way beyond the provision of mere football coaching and does sterling work in schools, on problem estates, with refugees and with the ethnically diverse local population.

For now, Leyton remains more inner-city than suburban. There are some pleasant terraced rows and the restored Coronation Gardens on the High Road are a delight, but there are almost as many industrial zones and concrete estates. Shopping options are little better. Along the High Road you'll find a very limited selection (a run-of-the-mill Tesco at one end and Asda at the other) and a bizarre lack of banks – a persistent local complaint. At the south end is the Leyton Mills shopping mall, with familiar and resolutely downmarket brands.

Fringing Walthamstow is the Lee Valley Park, a very welcome green space that sprawls north and south along the River Lea (confusingly, both Lea and Lee are acceptable spellings for the waterway). In addition, there's a riding school, an ice rink and marina, and miles of meadows for walking on the Walthamstow Marshes. Also here is the Waterworks Nature Reserve and Golf Centre on what used to be the Essex Filter Beds.

Leytonstone

The 2007 Rugby World Cup Final showed Leytonstone at its best – or worst, depending on your point of view. Zulu's bar on the High Road is the adopted home for the estimated 20,000 South Africans who live and work in east London – and it seemed every single one of them was dancing in the street blocking the traffic following their home nation's win over England. Some locals insist their presence adds colour to the area, others (mainly those living within earshot of the bar) report only aggravation.

New blocks of flats on the High Road confirm Leytonstone's reputation as a target for teachers, nurses and local authority personnel, while the 20-minute Central line journey to Liverpool Street is a strong lure for City workers. Once settled, these newcomers often find they don't want to leave: Leytonstone is scruffy but generally safe, with a surprisingly strong sense of community that shows itself in an annual arts festival and car-free day. A bohemian edge is provided by 491 Gallery, which calls itself a Sustainable Community Regeneration Art Project (SCRAP), and the tiny Vertigo cinema next door.

Leytonstone is a product of mid 19th-century railway expansion and the terraces that sprang up as a result are now occupied by middle-class British and Asian families. Upper Leytonstone has a Hindu temple, Bushwood claims the mosque, while the vicar of St John's by the junction of Church Lane and the High Road is a popular figure for his efforts to bring together locals of all faiths and none.

Though first impressions on emerging from the tube station are not very appealing – a handful of independent retailers scratching a living alongside bottom-end chain stores – E11 greatly benefits from the greenery of Epping Forest and Wanstead Flats, which fringes the popular Bushwood area and straddles the boundary with Redbridge. A boat ride on Hollow Ponds off Whipps Cross Road is a popular Sunday afternoon outing. There's even a mooted return for the legendary Leytonstone cows, which until the early 1990s were free to roam and often caused havoc – and hilarity – at the busy Green Man roundabout.

Restaurants & cafés

Walthamstow Village is increasingly a destination for food-lovers. A recent neighbour to the pleasantly idiosyncratic trattoria La Ruga is laid-back tapas bar Orford Saloon, and a quality butcher, baker and deli are promised. Further afield on Forest Road is the quietly stylish La Cafeteria, while pie and mash shop L Manze on Walthamstow High Street offers a touch of authenticity. Opened in 1929, it's a welcome respite from otherwise ubiquitous fast-food outlets.

Leyton has a couple of passable Pakistani canteens, while culinary variation is offered by the growing Portuguese community who have opened a café (Delicatessen Palmiera) opposite the library – but the overall prevalence of uninspiring takeaways is a continuing disappointment.

Leytonstone High Road has a handful of places worth checking out, notably Petch Sayam and Singburi (both Thai) and Mudra (South Indian). The Eatery (North Indian) on Church Lane is also popular and has a chill-out bar downstairs.

La Cafeteria *841 Forest Road, E17 4AT (8527 1926).*
Delicatessen Palmiera *234 High Road, E10 5PS (8539 9520).*
The Eatery *7 Church Lane, E11 1HG (8518 7463).*
L Manze *76 Walthamstow High Street, E17 7LD (8520 2855).*
Mudra *715 Leytonstone High Road, E11 4RD (8539 1700).*
Orford Saloon *32 Orford Road, E17 9NJ (8503 6542).*
Petch Sayam *682 High Road, E11 3AA (8556 6821).*

LOCALS' TIPS

Get top-quality fish from Davies on Hoe Street, near the Bakers Arms – it's the best traditional fishmonger for miles.
Wood Street Market in Walthamstow is a quirky maze of small stalls, artists' workshops and units selling everything from James Bond memorabilia to cake decorations and baby-carrying slings.
Horizon pâtisserie on Leytonstone High Road is a treat for great coffee and cakes.
Don't stop by the cafés on Whipps Cross Road if you're planning a picnic at Hollow Ponds. Walk a few hundred yards and you'll feel like you're in the depths of the countryside.
Walthamstow's street market has posh veg if you know where to look. The stall on the corner of Cleveland Park Avenue often has Fairtrade and organic stuff going cheap.

Walthamstow Market. *See p285.*

La Ruga *59 Orford Road, E17 9NJ (8520 5008).*
Singburi *593 Leytonstone High Road, E11 4PA (8281 4801).*

Bars & pubs

Leyton and Leytonstone hide a few unexpected gems for the pub connoisseur. Leyton's Birkbeck Tavern is the favoured haunt of discerning Orient fans and was voted divisional pub of the year for 2006-7 by the *Football and Real Ale Guide*; the handsome William IV may no longer have its own microbrewery but it would be a credit to any neighbourhood.

In Leytonstone, the tiny North Star is the focal point of the Browning Road conservation area, while the Sir Alfred Hitchcock Hotel (Hitch was born in Leytonstone) recalls a grander age –

TRANSPORT
Tube stations *Central* Leyton, Leytonstone; *Victoria* Blackhorse Road, Walthamstow Central
Rail stations *one* St James Street, Walthamstow Central, Wood Street, Highams Park, Chingford; *London Overground* Blackhorse Road, Walthamstow Queens Road, Leyton Midland Road, Leytonstone High Road
Main bus routes *into central London* 48, 55, 56; *night buses* N8, N26, N38, N55, N73

though the hotel bar's interior is a little unkempt. Raucous Zulu's is popular with local South Africans and is rammed at weekends, and the Sheepwalk's terrific What's Cookin' club (www.whatscookin.co.uk) serves up regular blues, cajun, country and rock 'n' roll gigs.

Over in Walthamstow, the Flower Pot is a marvellously archaic den, with an interior apparently untouched since the war (possibly even the first one). The Nag's Head is a little more refined (as is Orford Road, where it's situated) and the Village, on the same strip, is one of the few pubs in E17 with a half-decent beer garden.

Birkbeck Tavern *45 Langthorne Road, E11 4HL (8539 2584).*
Flower Pot *128 Wood Street, E17 3HX (8520 3600).*
Nag's Head *9 Orford Road, E17 9LP (8520 9709).*
North Star *24 Browning Road, E11 3AR (8989 5777).*
Sheepwalk *692 Leytonstone High Road, E11 3AA (8556 1131).*
Sir Alfred Hitchcock Hotel *147 Whipps Cross Road, E11 1NP (8530 3724).*
The Village *31 Orford Road, E17 9NL (8521 9982).*
William IV *816 Leyton High Road, E10 6AE (8556 2460).*
Zulu's *640 Leytonstone High Road, E11 3AA (8558 6846/www.zulus.co.uk).*

Shops

Waltham Forest, sadly, is a shopping desert. Apart from Walthamstow Village and Station Road up in Chingford, specialist stores and attractive independent retailers are few and far between. Most residents head for villagey Wanstead (in Redbridge) instead. Proximity to the North Circular Road at least gives access to IKEA and the major electrical, DIY and home furnishing superstores, but for a decent-sized department store or even a Marks & Spencer it's a trip out of the borough to Stratford, Ilford, Romford or beyond.

Always worth a visit – if only to marvel at its scale – is Walthamstow's epic street market, a teeming strip of some 450 stalls and 300 shops stretching the entire length of the High Street (linking Hoe Street to St James's Street). It's open Tuesday to Saturday; on Sunday the farmers' market takes over in the Town Square. For conventional chain stores, the Selborne

Waltham Forest

Walk shopping centre at the High Street's east end suffices, while Hoe Street has a continuous chain of shops and takeaways running south to High Road Leyton.

Walthamstow Farmers' Market *Town Square, by Selborne Walk shopping centre, E17 (7833 0338/www.lfm.org.uk).*
Walthamstow Market *High Street, E17 (Street Trading Section 8496 3000).*

Arts & attractions

Galleries & museums
491 Gallery *491 Grove Green Road, E11 4AA (www.491gallery.com).* Art, performances and yoga classes.
Vestry House Museum *Vestry Road, E17 9NH (8509 1917/www.lbwf.gov.uk).* Local history museum.
William Morris Gallery *Lloyd Park, Forest Road, E17 4PP (8527 3782/www.lbwf.gov.uk).*

Sport & fitness
Waltham Forest's five public centres are managed by Greenwich Leisure and are pleasant and well maintained. Waltham Forest Pool & Track is the most recent to benefit from an upgrade. The Score complex in Leyton offers high-quality facilities for a wide range of sports and has become one of the major venues for handball as Britain strives to develop a squad capable of competing in 2012.

Gyms & leisure centres
Bannatyne's Health & Fitness Club Chingford *2 Morrison Avenue, E4 8SA (8503 2266/www.bannatyne.co.uk).* Private.
Cathall Leisure Centre *Cathall Road, E11 4LA (8539 8343/www.gll.org).*
E4 Fitness & Leisure *14A Hickman Avenue, E4 9JG (8523 5133).* Private.
Fitness First *Unit 6, Leyton Mills Retail Park, Marshall Road, E10 5NH (0870 898 0663).* Private.
Greens Health & Fitness *175 New Road, E4 9EY (8523 7474/www.greensonline.co.uk).* Private.
Kelmscott Leisure Centre *243 Markhouse Road, E17 8RN (8520 7464/www.gll.org).*
Larkswood Leisure Centre *Larkswood Leisure Park, New Road, E4 9EY (8523 8215/www.gll.org).*
Leyton Leisure Lagoon *763 High Road, E10 5AB (8558 8858/www.gll.org).*
Waltham Forest Pool & Track *170 Chingford Road, E17 5AA (8527 5431/www.gll.org).*

Other facilities
Lee Valley Ice Centre *Lea Bridge Road, E10 7QL (8533 3154/www.leevalleypark.org.uk).*

Lee Valley Riding Centre *Lea Bridge Road, E10 7QL (8556 2629/www.leevalleypark.org.uk).*
Score *100 Oliver Road, E10 5JY (8539 8474).*

Spectator sports
Walthamstow Stadium *Chingford Road, E4 8SJ (8498 3300/www.wsgreyhound.co.uk).* Greyhound racing.
Leyton Orient Football Club *Matchroom Stadium, Brisbane Road, E10 5NF (8926 1111/www.leytonorient.com).*

Schools

WHAT THE PARENTS SAY:
❝Although many of the brightest children try for schools in next-door Redbridge – at the fee-paying Forest School or the two grammar schools – Waltham Forest is moving into the middle bracket of London boroughs in both primary and secondary league tables, which shows how standards are improving. The council is investing heavily through the Building Schools for the Future programme, and Leytonstone School has got a great new sports centre.

Beaumont Primary in Leyton is the only school in the borough in special measures, but others turn in poor value-added scores, which means the catchment areas for the better schools are rigidly enforced. Davies Lane in Leytonstone was Jonathan Ross's old school, but has bumped along at the bottom of the primary league table for years. Yardley in Chingford is one of the top primaries, with Chingford Foundation and Highams Park heavily oversubscribed as follow-on secondaries. Walthamstow Girls' School was rated 'outstanding' in its last Ofsted report and Connaught School for Girls in Leytonstone is also very popular, despite being hemmed in by roads and lacking any green space. You probably need to live within half a mile to get a place.❞
Elaine Burgess, mother of three, Leytonstone

Primary
There are 52 state primary schools in Waltham Forest, seven of which are church schools. There are also seven independent primaries, including six faith schools and one Montessori school. See www.edubase.gov.uk and www.ofsted.gov.uk for more information.

Secondary
Aveling Park School *Aveling Park Road, E17 4NR (8527 5794/www.avelingparkschool.ik.org).*
Chingford Foundation School *Nevin Drive, E4 7LT (8529 1853/www.chingford-school.co.uk).*
Connaught School for Girls *Connaught Road, E11 4AB (8539 3029).* Girls only.
George Mitchell School *Farmer Road, E10 5DN (8539 6198/www.gmschool.org).*

Heathcote School *Normanton Park, E4 6ES*
(8498 5110).
Highams Park School *Handsworth Avenue,*
E4 9PJ (8527 4051/www.highamspark.
waltham.sch.uk).
Holy Family Technology College *Shernhall*
Street, E17 3EA (8520 0482/www.holyfamily.
waltham.sch.uk).
Kelmscott School *Markhouse Road, E17*
8DN (8521 2115).
Lammas School *150 Seymour Road,*
E10 7LX (8988 5860).
Leytonstone School *Colworth Road, E11 1JD*
(8988 7420/www.leytonstoneschool.org).
Norlington Boys' School *Norlington Road,*
E10 6JZ (8539 3055). Boys only.
Rushcroft School *Rushcroft Road, E4 8SG*
(8531 9231/www.rushcroft.waltham.sch.uk).
Tom Hood School *Terling Close, E11 3NT*
(8534 3425).
Walthamstow Academy *Billet Road, E17*
5DP (8527 3750/www.walthamstow-
academy.org).
Walthamstow Girls' School *Church Hill,*
E17 9RZ (8509 9446). Girls only.
Warwick Boys' School *www.warwick-*
waltham.co.uk; Lower School Brooke Road,
E17 9HJ; Upper School Barrett Road, E17
3ND (8520 4173). Boys only.
Willowfield School *Clifton Avenue, E17 6HL*
(8527 4065/www.willowfield.waltham.sch.uk).

RECYCLING
No. of bring sites 40 (for nearest,
visit www.recycleforlondon.com)
Household waste recycled 13.44%
Main recycling centres South Access
Road Household Waste & Recycling
Centre, South Access Road, Markhouse
Avenue, Walthamstow, E17 8AX; Leyton
Reuse & Recycling Centre, Gateway
Road, off Orient Way, Leyton, E10 7AS
Other recycling services garden and
kitchen waste collection; home
composting; white goods collection
Council contact Street Services,
London Borough of Waltham Forest,
Low Hall Depot, Argall Avenue, E10
7AS (8496 3000)

Property

WHAT THE AGENTS SAY:
❛Converted flats are always popular, probably
more so than the purpose-built blocks along
Leytonstone High Road: people like the original
features. Bushwood and Upper Leytonstone are
the most desirable areas – they're either side of
the tube station, and near to the Forest and local
amenities. First-time buyers may be able to
stretch to two bedrooms here when they'd only
get one elsewhere, and we find more and more
people discovering how much they like the area.❜
Sean Crisp, Prestige Property Services

Average property prices
Detached £477,999
Semi-detached £319,991
Terraced £267,345
Flat £188,468

Local estate agents
Alan Harvey *658 High Road, E11 3AA (8539*
4000/www.alanharvey.co.uk).
Allen Davies & Co *342 High Road, E10 5PW*
(8539 2121/www.allendavies.co.uk).
Clarke Hillyer *www.clarkehillyer.co.uk; 2 offices*
in the borough (Chingford 8529 7100/
Walthamstow 8521 8875).
Prestige Property Services *708 High Road,*
E11 3AL (8556 7700/www.prestigeproperty.biz).
Village Estates *54-56 Hoe Street, E17 4PG*
(8223 0784/www.villageestates.org.uk).

Other information

Council
Waltham Forest Council *Town Hall, Forest*
Road, E17 4JF (8496 3000/www.waltham
forest.gov.uk).

Legal services
Leytonstone CAB *547-551 High Road, E11*
4PB (8988 9620/www.walthamforestcab.org.uk).
Walthamstow CAB *167 Hoe Street, E17 3AL*
(0870 126 4026/www.walthamforestcab.org.uk).

Local newspapers
www.guardian-series.co.uk.
The Guardian series of newspapers publishes
the *Walthamstow Guardian, Chingford*
Guardian, Leyton & Leystonstone Guardian
and *Waltham Forest Independent.*

Allotments & open spaces
Council Allotments *Environmental Services,*
Greenspace Group, Low Hall Depot, Argall
Avenue, E10 7AS (8496 5529).
Open spaces *www.walthamforest.gov.*
uk/parks.

Waltham Forest

Enfield

The capital's northernmost borough encompasses the down-at-heel grit of urban Edmonton, popular suburb Palmers Green and the family-friendly affluence of Winchmore Hill and Hadley Wood. Generous amounts of open space and proximity to the green belt mean residents have access to their fair share of park life.

Neighbourhoods

Enfield Town and Edmonton

Church Street is Enfield Town's main thoroughfare, a narrow, down-to-earth shopping street with charity shops aplenty. Just off it, historic Enfield Market (established over 700 years ago) bursts into life four days a week, selling a cheap and cheerful mix of clothing, household goods and fresh fruit and veg. The other side of the road sees local trading in its 21st-century form – the Palace Gardens Centre and the Palace Exchange Centre (opened late 2006). Avert your eyes from the street-level bargains in Superdrug and New Look and you might notice the *Enfield Word Wall*, a public art installation that uses extracts from Enfield conversations past and present to create a snapshot of local life – 'You don't know names you just know the faces, but everyone says hello when you go past'; 'I was evacuated during the war but back in time for the doodlebugs and

our Anderson shelter.' Just a short stroll from here, Gentleman's Row, with its much sought-after large Georgian and Victorian houses, offers a reminder of the town's prosperous past.

Surrounded by huge arterial, traffic-clogged roads and light industrial estates, Edmonton struggles to achieve a distinct identity and suffers from many of the problems traditionally associated with deprived, inner-city areas. Cheap rented housing – much of it in the form of looming twin and triplet towers of council estate flats – is characteristic rather than owner-occupied houses. The 2005 opening of IKEA on Glover Drive remains lodged in the memories of many locals – and not because it signalled a new dawn in cheap home furnishings. Opening night saw scenes of farcical, near fatal, madness as a flat-pack crazed mob charged the doors.

Edmonton Green, with its railway station and bus terminal, is the public transport hub of the neighbourhood and home to a shopping centre in the throes of 'development'. The centre is currently a drab and unlovely place, home to budget chain stores (such as Bonmarché), numerous betting shops, a handful of food stalls and cut-price shops such as Megasave and Poundland. Developers St Modwen are planning to add a 65,000 sq ft ASDA, due for completion in summer 2008. Whether or not this will regenerate the neighbourhood has divided local opinion.

Palmers Green and Southgate

Found along the stretch of Green Lanes to the north of the North Circular, Palmers Green is a popular north London suburb, home to a substantial Greek Cypriot community. At the heart of the area is

Sports fields, landscaped gardens, ponds: **Broomfield Park** has got it all.

Broomfield Park, a much-loved and much-used public green space. With its playing fields, picturesque gardens, tennis court and bowling green, the park provides many amenities for local people, while its ponds attract waterfowl and model-boat enthusiasts alike.

Alongside the park is Alderman's Hill and the peaceful roads laddering off it are known as 'the Lakes' (they're named after British lakes). These streets are home to the area's most desirable residences. The stretch of Green Lanes from the Triangle (a junction at the foot of Alderman's Hill) up to St John's Church on Bourne Hill is lined with shops, cafés and restaurants. The usual chain suspects are well represented, but there is also a sprinkling of independents. In contrast to the low-key daytime bustle, evenings see the area become a rougher, tougher kind of place.

Traditionally a stepping stone to suburban life for those leaving Wood Green, Southgate's good transport connections – served by the Piccadilly line and several bus routes – make it a convenient place to live. The pivotal hub of the area is the circular art deco tube station, a classic designed by Charles Holden and opened in 1932.

Students from nearby Southgate College hang out in the assorted cafés and fast food joints around the station. Shops and eateries here are humdrum on the whole, with a 24-hour ASDA the dominant retail presence. Southgate's rough-and-ready feel takes on an edge at night as the streets fill up with boy racers showing off their mock-alloy wheels. Head away from the station, however, and you'll find peaceful residential streets, lined predominantly with mock-Tudor houses. Greenery is plentiful,

including Grovelands Park, with its boating lake and tennis courts, and Oakwood Park. Both are well used by local families. For wider green spaces, travel a little further to Trent Country Park for bracing walks through woods and grassland. Near the Bramley Sports Ground (home of Saracens rugby club), the dynamic Chicken Shed Theatre offers true community theatre, running a drama club for able-bodied and disabled children. Shows are often excellent and the annual panto is a regular sell-out.

Winchmore Hill and Hadley Wood

Keeping hold of its village credentials, peaceful Winchmore Hill has a pace of life that suits its family-focused residents down to the ground. The area's overground railway station, Winchmore Hill, is handily positioned by the picturesque old village green. Here, a cluster of independent shops and restaurants mean locals can stock up for Sunday lunch (at the butcher on Wades Hill), choose a new colour palette for their home (at interiors specialist the House) and stop off for drinks or coffee without venturing outside their neighbourhood. A short stroll down the hill to Green Lanes reveals yet more shops, cafés, pubs and eateries. Fresh air is also in ample supply, thanks to nearby Grovelands and Grange parks. Sports-lovers are well served by Winchmore Hill Cricket Club – a local institution that also offers tennis, football and hockey – and Enfield Golf Course.

As one might expect, prices here are notably higher than in other parts of Enfield. Properties are larger and more characterful, with some notably lavish houses along the Broadwalk.

Enfield

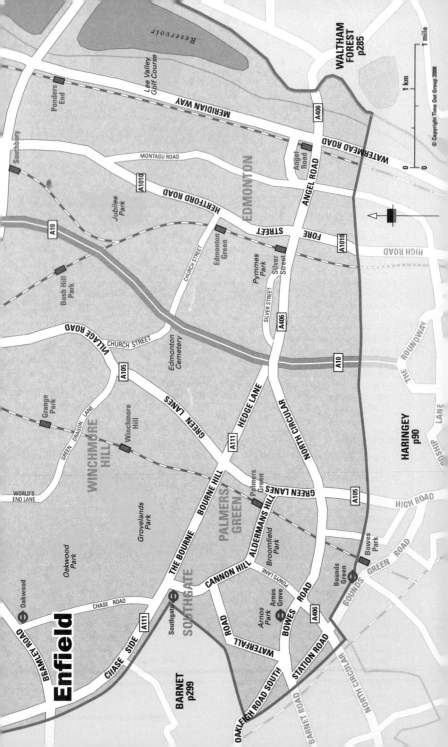

Similarly affluent, though much further north, is Hadley Wood. Discreetly nestling beside picturesque Monken Hadley Common, this is a small but affluent pocket of Enfield, noted for its high number of local aspirant millionaires. This is the place to find your detached ranch-style house, complete with spacious grounds, swimming pool and electronic gates. Key to the area's social life is Hadley Wood Golf Club, with its prestigious course and imposing clubhouse, a mansion built in 1781.

Restaurants & cafés

Chains dominate here, so you're never far from a McDonald's, Pizza Express or Starbucks. As a result independent gems really stand out – stylish, contemporary Dylan's in Cockfosters being the most aspirational of the area's restaurants. Cosy French restaurant Café Anjou in Palmers Green commands a loyal following, as does neighbouring Indian Bombay Spice. Southgate's Spanish eaterie La Paella holds fast, while Greek restaurant the Vine pulls in a lively Greek Cypriot crowd. As one might expect, affluent Winchmore Hill is particularly well served on the culinary front, with well-established favourites such as Italian restaurant Regatta and stylish fish restaurant Sargasso Sea.

Bombay Spice 396 Green Lanes, N13 5PD (8245 6095).
Café Anjou 394 Green Lanes, N13 5PD (8886 7267).
Dylan's Restaurant 21 Station Parade, Cockfosters Road, EN4 0DW (8275 1551/ www.dylansrestaurant.com).
La Paella 9 Broadway, N14 6PH (8882 7868).
Regatta 10-12 The Green, N21 1AX (8886 5471/www.regattarestaurant.co.uk).
Sargasso Sea 10 Station Road, N21 3RB (8360 0990/www.sargassosea.co.uk).
Vine 25 The Broadway, The Bourne, N14 6PH (8882 6007).

Bars & pubs

Many of Enfield Town's boozers have a brash, chav element to them. For those who like a peaceful pint, the picturesque Old Wheatsheaf is a friendly, old-fashioned Victorian pub with decent beer and a popular Thursday night pub quiz that brings in a crowd of regulars. For a more rural setting, try the King & Tinker, parts

of which date back to the 16th century. Today it offers decent ales, while the large beer garden makes it popular with families.

The Fox – a tarted-up old boozer in Palmers Green – pulls in the youngsters and is a popular meeting place. Unimaginative chain pubs include the Inn on the Green in Palmers Green and the New Crown in Southgate. Nicer is Ye Olde Cherry Tree, which draws a slightly older crowd. In Winchmore Hill, Jim Thompson at the Green Dragon is an immense old pub with a popular beer garden; it serves oriental grub. Also offering food and drink is the inviting Kings Head, in a grand Victorian building on Winchmore Hill Green. In Edmonton, the pubs that aren't chain joints tend to be intimidating backwater boozers – try the ones on Church Street if you're desperate, though these are often peopled by the barely legal from local schools.

The Fox 413 Green Lanes, N13 4JD (8886 9674).
Inn on the Green 295 Green Lanes, N13 4XS (8886 3760).
Jim Thompson at the Green Dragon 889 Green Lanes, N21 2QP (8360 0005).
King & Tinker Whitewebbs Lane, EN2 9HJ (8363 6411).
Kings Head 1 The Green, N21 1BB (8886 1988/www.geronimo-inns.co.uk).
New Crown 80-84 Chase Side, N14 5PH (8882 8758).
Old Wheatsheaf 3 Windmill Hill, EN2 6SE (8363 0516).
Ye Olde Cherry Tree 22 The Green, N14 6EN (8447 8022).

Enfield

LOCALS' TIPS

In summer take the kids to Parkside PYO Farm (8367 2035, www.parkside farmpyo.co.uk), where you can tug up beetroot and onions, and pick luscious raspberries. The kids love it, and you get to load them up on fresh air, exercise and fruit and veg, all in one go.
Don't schlep down to Ally Pally to see the fireworks on Bonfire Night. There's always a fabulous display at Hadley Wood recreation ground.
MoDA (Museum of Domestic Design & Architecture) runs really good craft workshops for adults and children.
Visit Forty Hall. It has a lovely old house, garden and grounds – it's a real tucked-away gem of a place.

Shops

Enfield Town's refurbished Palace Gardens and Palace Exchange shopping centres are the place to go for chain stores, especially clothes shops such as River Island, Monsoon and Next. For upmarket menswear, head to Winchmore Hill's Twenty-One The Green.

Book-lovers will enjoy browsing at the British Red Cross Shop dedicated to books on Palmers Green – it offers excellent, wide-ranging stock and the chance of a serendipitous find. Down the road, Palmers Green Antiques Centre is another spot for bargain hunters, a down-to-earth business selling miscellaneous antiques, from old china to furniture. For new furniture and homeware, head to IKEA in Edmonton, which, now the frenzy of opening is over, is generally less busy than its older sister store on the North Circular.

Winchmore Hill wins hands down in the individuality stakes, with interiors shop the House and the well-established Mistress

STATISTICS
BOROUGH MAKE-UP
Population 285,300
Average weekly pay £466.10
Ethnic origins
  White 72.37%
  Mixed 3.49%
  Asian or Asian British 8.79%
  Black or Black British 12.77%
  Chinese or other 2.58%
Students 9.33%
Retirees 11.23%

HOUSING STOCK
Borough size 81.2km²
No. of households 117,000

CRIME PER 1,000 OF POPULATION
(average for England and Wales in brackets)
Burglary 9 (5)
Robbery 5 (2)
Theft of vehicle 5 (4)
Theft from vehicle 10 (9)
Violence against the person 19 (19)
Sexual offences 1 (1)

MPs & COUNCIL
MPs *Edmonton* Andrew Love (Labour); *Enfield, Southgate* David Burrowes (Conservative)
CPA 3 stars; improving well

Appleby. Now in its 40th year, this charming shop sells a selection of contemporary, antique and bespoke jewellery.

British Red Cross Shop *383 Green Lanes, N13 4JG (8886 7467).*
The House *14 The Green, N21 1AY (8886 3800).*
IKEA *Glover Drive, N18 3HF (0845 355 2255/ www.ikea.co.uk).*
Mistress Appleby *20 The Green, N21 1AY (8886 1303).*
Palace Gardens Shopping Centre *Church Street, EN2 6SN (8367 1210).*
Palace Exchange Shopping Centre *Hatton Walk, EN2 6BP (8362 1934/ www.palace-exchange.com).*
Palmers Green Antiques Centre *472 Green Lanes, N13 5PA (8350 0878).*
Twenty-One The Green *21 The Green, N21 3NL (8882 4298).*

Arts & attractions

Cinemas & theatres
Chicken Shed *Theatre Chase Side, N14 4PE (8351 6161/www.chickenshed.org.uk).*
Cineworld Enfield *Southbury Leisure Park, 208 Southbury Road, EN1 1YQ (0871 200 2000/www.cineworld.co.uk).*
Millfield Theatre *Silver Street, N18 1PJ (8807 6680/www.millfieldtheatre.co.uk).*
Odeon Lee Valley *Lee Valley Leisure Complex, Picketts Lock Lane, N9 0AS (0871 224 4007/ www.odeon.co.uk).*

Galleries & museums
Artszone *1st floor, 54-56 Market Square, Edmonton Green Shopping Centre, N9 0TZ (8887 9500/www.enfieldartspartnership.org).* Gallery, studio space and theatre.
Museum of Domestic Design & Architecture (MoDA) *Middlesex University, Cat Hill, EN4 8HT (8411 5244/www.moda. mdx.ac.uk).* Past exhibitions have included outrageous wallpaper designs and an investigation into suburbia.

Other attractions
Forty Hall Estate *Forty Hill, EN2 9HA (8363 8196/www.enfield.gov.uk/fortyhall).* Henry VIII's hunting lodge dates back to the 13th century; it has a museum and appropriately regal grounds.

Sport & fitness

There's a decent spread of sports and leisure centres in Enfield. The opening of the Edmonton Leisure Centre in 2007 added another excellent facility. The borough also boasts the successful Southbury Leisure Centre and several good private centres.

Gyms & leisure centres

Albany Leisure Centre *505 Hertford Road, EN3 5XH (8804 4255/www.enfieldleisure centres.co.uk).*
Arnos Pool *Bowes Road, N11 0BD (8361 9336/www.enfieldleisurecentres.co.uk).*
David Lloyd *Caterhatch Lane, EN1 4LF (8364 5858/www.davidlloydleisure.co.uk).* Private.
Edmonton Leisure Centre *2 The Broadway, N9 0TR (8375 3750/www.enfieldleisurecentres. co.uk).*
Esporta *Tower Point, Sydney Road, EN2 6SZ (8370 4100/www.esporta.com).* Private.
Island Fitness *57 Island Centre Way, EN3 6GS (01992 762107/www.islandfitness.co.uk).* Private.
LA Fitness *www.lafitness.co.uk; 15 East Barnet Road, EN4 8RW (8440 2796); Winchmore Hill Road, N14 6AA (8886 8883).* Private.
Park Health & Fitness Club *Southgate Hockey Centre, Trent Park, Snakes Lane, EN4 0PS (8441 5855).* Private.
Southbury Leisure Centre *192 Southbury Road, EN1 1YP (8245 3201).*
Southgate Leisure Centre *Winchmore Hill Road, N14 6AD (8882 7963/www.enfieldleisure centres.co.uk).*

Other facilities

Lee Valley Athletics Centre *61 Meridian Way, Picketts Lock, N9 0AR (8344 7230/www. leevalleypark.org.uk).* Opened in January 2007 at a cost of £16 million, this centre will be the training base for many of Britain's 2012 Olympic hopefuls. It will also be the new home for the Enfield & Haringey Athletics Club, which counts Seb Coe and Geoff Capes as former members.
Southgate Hockey Centre *Trent Park, Snakes Lane, EN4 0PS (8440 7574/www. southgatehc.org.uk).*
Trent Park Equestrian Centre *Trent Park Stables, Bramley Road, N14 4XS (8363 8630/ www.trentpark.com).* One of the largest riding schools in London.
Trent Park Golf Club *Bramley Road, N14 4UW (8367 4653/www.trentparkgolf.com).*

Schools

WHAT THE PARENTS SAY:

❛There are many good primaries in Enfield, which makes it a popular borough for families. These include a couple of Ofsted-classified 'outstanding' schools: Cuckoo Hall and Eastfield. Walker, Grange Park and Eversley are also good, and good faith schools include St Paul's (which my nine-year-old daughter attends), St Monica's, St George's and St Andrew's. As the faith schools tend to do very well, they are often oversubscribed, so you get quite a lot of fair-weather church attendance. Some schools, especially in the east of the borough, have quite poor reputations, but many of them are improving.

Secondary comprehensive schools in Enfield aren't bad, and reflect the mixed abilities you'd expect in an outer London borough. The recently built Highlands is still proving itself, but with a strong new head and very good feeder schools it is likely to get better and better. Southgate has massive parental support and loyalty, and very strong leadership.

In Edmonton, the Latymer School (where my older daughter goes) is one of a handful of selective state schools in London – its results at GCSE and A level are excellent. To the affluent west of the borough, quite a few families send their children to private schools in Hertfordshire or the City.❜
Natalia Marshall, mother of two, Enfield

Primary

There are 59 state primary schools in the borough of Enfield, including 16 church schools and one Jewish school. There are also six independent primary schools. See www.enfield.gov.uk, www.edubase.gov.uk and www.ofsted.gov.uk for more information.

TRANSPORT

Tube stations *Piccadilly* Arnos Grove, Southgate, Oakwood, Cockfosters
Rail stations *one* Silver Street, Edmonton Green, Bush Hill Park, Southbury, Turkey Street; Angel Road, Ponders End, Brimsdown, Enfield Lock; *First Capital Connect Great Northern* Palmers Green, Winchmore Hill, Grange Park, Enfield Chase, Gordon Hill, Crews Hill
Main bus routes *into central London* 29, 141, 149, 259; *night buses* N29, N91, N279; *24-hour buses* 149

RECYCLING

No. of bring sites 110 (for nearest, visit www.recycleforlondon.com)
Household waste recycled 16.92%
Main recycling centre Barrowell Green Recycling Centre, Barrowell Green, Winchmore Hill, N21 3AR
Other recycling services green waste collection; home composting; furniture and white goods collection; washable nappies refund promotion
Council contact Waste Services, Civic Centre, Silver Street, EN1 3XY (8379 1000)

COUNCIL TAX

A	up to £40,000	£891.27
B	£40,001-£52,000	£1,039.81
C	£52,001-£68,000	£1,188.36
D	£68,001-£88,000	£1,336.90
E	£88,001-£120,000	£1,633.99
F	£120,001-£160,000	£1,931.08
G	£160,001-£320,000	£2,228.17
H	over £320,000	£2,673.80

Secondary

Albany School *Bell Lane, EN3 5PA (8804 1648).*
Gladys Aylward School *Windmill Road, N18 1NB (8803 1738).*
Bishop Stopford's School *Brick Lane, EN1 3PU (8804 1906/www.bishop-stopfords-school.co.uk).*
Broomfield School *Wilmer Way, N14 7HY (8368 4710).*
Chace Community School *Churchbury Lane, EN1 3HQ (8363 7321/www.chace.enfield.sch.uk).*
Edmonton County *Great Cambridge Road, EN1 1HQ (8360 3158).*
Enfield County School *Holly Walk, EN2 6QG (8363 3030/www.enfieldcs.enfield.sch.uk).* Girls only; mixed sixth form.
Enfield Grammar School *Market Place, EN2 6LN (8363 1095).* Boys only.
Highlands School *148 Worlds End Lane, N21 1QQ (8370 1100/www.highlands.enfield.sch.uk).*
Kingsmead School *Southbury Road, EN1 1YQ (8363 3037/www.kingsmead.org).*
Latymer School *Haselbury Road, N9 9TN (8807 4037/www.latymer.co.uk).*
Lea Valley High School *Bullsmoor Lane, EN3 6TW (01992 763666/www.lvhs.org.uk).*
Oasis Academy Enfield *Kinetic Crescent, Innova Park, Mollison Avenue, EN3 7XH (01992 655 400/www.oasisacademyenfield. org).* Opened September 2007.
St Anne's Catholic High School for Girls *Oakthorpe Road, N13 5TY (8886 2165/www.st-annes.enfield.sch.uk).* Girls only.
St Ignatius College *Turkey Street, EN1 4NP (0199 271 7835/www.st-ignatius.enfield.sch.uk).* Boys only.
Salisbury School *Turin Road, N9 8DQ (8372 5678).*
Southgate School *Sussex Way, EN4 0BL (8449 9583/www.southgate.enfield.sch.uk).*
Winchmore School *Laburnum Grove, N21 3HS (8360 7773/www.winchmore.enfield.sch.uk).*

Property

WHAT THE AGENTS SAY:

‘Palmers Green is becoming more and more multicultural – a lot of Eastern Europeans, Poles especially, are moving here. It used to be known as a Greek area, but I think that's changed recently as many from that community have moved further out. I wouldn't say the area's got wonderful bars and restaurants, but Marks & Spencer opened here recently, which shows it's on the up. Winchmore Hill is a lot more upmarket, with a village feel, and good secondary schools. A lot of families from Palmers Green move there for the schools. Edmonton is the bottom of the barrel, to be honest. They're trying to improve it – more bars and shops in the shopping centre – but it's generally a place people are trying to get away from.’
Martin McKelvey, Anthony Webb Estate Agents, Palmers Green

Average property prices

Detached £678,712
Semi-detached £354,790
Terraced £258,532
Flat £191,366

Local estate agents

Anthony Webb Estate Agents *348 Green Lanes, N13 5TL (8882 7888/www.anthony webb.co.uk).*
Brien Firmin *www.brienfirmin.com; 2 offices in the borough (Green Lanes 8889 9944/ Winchmore Hill 8360 9696).*
James Hayward *181 Chase Side, EN2 0PT (8367 4000/www.james-hayward.co.uk).*
Lanes *www.lanesproperty.co.uk; 4 offices in the borough (Enfield Town 8342 0101/Enfield Southbury Road 8362 7680/Enfield Highway 8804 2253/Palmers Green 8882 8068).*
Peter Barry *946 Green Lanes, N21 2AD (8360 4777/www.peterbarry.co.uk).*
Townends *913 Green Lanes, N21 2QP (8360 8111/www.townends.co.uk).*

Other information

Council

Enfield Council *Civic Centre, Silver Street, EN1 3XY (8379 1000/www.enfield.gov.uk).*

Legal services

Enfield CAB *10 Little Park Gardens, EN2 6PQ (0870 126 4664/www.adviceguide.org.uk).*
Palmers Green CAB *Southgate Town Hall, Green Lanes, N13 4XD (0870 126 4664/ www.adviceguide.org.uk).*

Local newspapers

Enfield Advertiser/Gazette *8364 4040/ www.icnorthlondononline.co.uk.*

Allotments & open spaces

Allotments Contact the council's Parks Business Unit (8379 3722/www.enfield.gov.uk) for assistance with local allotment sites.
Open spaces *www.enfield.gov.uk/nav2/ 200073.asp.*

Barnet

For London living with an edge, look elsewhere – Barnet's attractions are distinctly suburban. The borough takes in traffic-clogged Hendon, Jewish Golders Green, East, Central and North Finchley, wealthy and leafy Totteridge and, at the northern edge, self-sufficient High Barnet, offering oodles of 1930s semis, golf courses, excellent schools and plentiful parkland along the way.

Neighbourhoods

Golders Green and Hendon

In a classic story of the suburbs, Golders Green was transformed by the introduction of the tube in 1907. The Golders Green Northern line station and a busy bus terminus lie at the neighbourhood's core, by a major junction that sees Golders Green Road crossing Finchley Road. Nearby is the majestic-looking Golders Green Hippodrome, now the El-Shaddai International Christian Centre. Signs at the station point the way to Golders Green Crematorium (opened 1902) where the likes of Sigmund Freud, George Bernard Shaw and Marc Bolan were cremated.

The area has become synonymous with Jewish London, hence the presence of numerous kosher businesses (particularly along Golders Green Road and the stretch of Finchley Road by Temple Fortune). In order to observe the Jewish Shabbat, many of the district's businesses close from sunset on Friday to sunset on Saturday. The weekly reopening on Saturday night sees Golders Green buzzing with young people hanging out in the cafés and local bakeries doing a roaring trade in salmon and cream cheese bagels. Sunday too is a busy shopping day.

Heading up the hill towards Hampstead, you'll find Golders Hill Park, a popular and nicely laid-out patch of greenery. A little further up the hill is the London Jewish Cultural Centre, attractively housed in Ivy House (where ballerina Anna Pavlova once lived).

It's hard to imagine it, but neighbouring Hendon was once a land of fields and stables. These days, brutally bisected by traffic-choked Watford Way (A41) and adjacent to the start of the M1, Hendon's local identity lacks strong definition. In a *Time Out* article in 2006, local writer Naomi Alderman described Hendon's Jewish community, for example, as 'hidden, intentionally half-submerged so as to be almost invisible to outsiders.'

The proximity of the UK's first large enclosed shopping centre, Brent Cross (opened in 1976), has had a draining effect on Hendon's local shops, with Brent Street, the area's supposed high street, a surprisingly down-at-heel affair. Still, the area functions well in practical terms, with an excellent library just by the imposing Town Hall, a pleasantly formal green space in Hendon Park and the Barnet Copthall Leisure Centre.

Hampstead Garden Suburb

Bordered by arterial Falloden Way (A1) and Finchley Road, Hampstead Garden Suburb remains a relatively well-kept secret, although it's growing in popularity. Founded in 1907 by heiress Dame Henrietta Barnett, HGS was an idealistic piece of social engineering that aimed to provide housing for all social classes, from workers' cottages to grand residences for the toffs. Gardens and green spaces played a central part in Dame Barnett's vision: an average density of eight dwellings to an acre allowed for ample gardens. The attractive Arts and Crafts-style houses are much sought after – and, not surprisingly, command premium prices.

The buildings on the central square and at 140-142 Hampstead Way are frequently visited by fans of classic architecture, but, despite the appealing exteriors, there is something stand-offish about the neighbourhood. Even the central

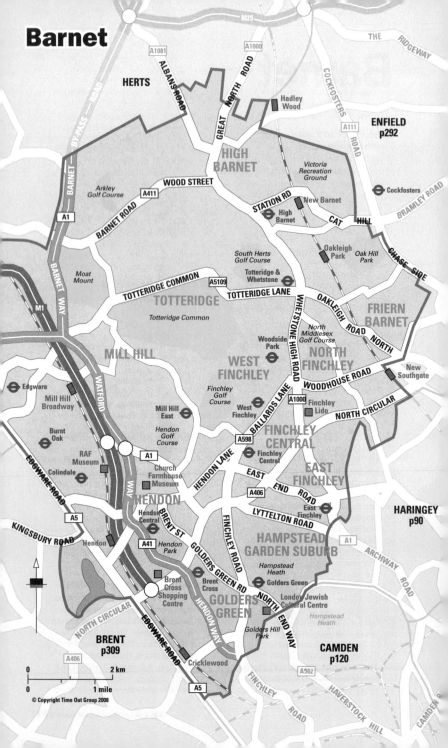

Barnet

HERTS

HADLEY WOOD

ENFIELD p292

THE RIDGEWAY

COCKFOSTERS ROAD

BRAMLEY ROAD

HIGH BARNET

Victoria Recreation Ground

Cockfosters

GREAT NORTH ROAD

A1081

ALBANS ROAD

A1000

M25

BARNET BY-PASS ROAD

Arkley Golf Course

WOOD STREET

A411

BARNET ROAD

STATION RD

High Barnet

New Barnet

CAT HILL

HILL

CHASE SIDE

A1

M1

BARNET WAY

Moat Mount

TOTTERIDGE COMMON

A5109

Oakleigh Park

Oak Hill Park

South Herts Golf Course

Totteridge & Whetstone

TOTTERIDGE

TOTTERIDGE LANE

FRIERN BARNET

Totteridge Common

WHETSTONE HIGH ROAD

OAKLEIGH ROAD NORTH

North Middlesex Golf Course

MILL HILL

Woodside Park

WEST FINCHLEY

NORTH FINCHLEY

New Southgate

WOODHOUSE ROAD

Edgware

WATFORD WAY

Mill Hill Broadway

Finchley Golf Course

West Finchley

BALLARDS LANE

A1000

Finchley Lido

NORTH CIRCULAR

Burnt Oak

Mill Hill East

A1

FINCHLEY CENTRAL

RAF Museum

Hendon Golf Course

Church Farmhouse Museum

HENDON LANE

A598

Finchley Central

EAST FINCHLEY

Colindale

EDGWARE ROAD

A5

HENDON

Hendon Central

BRENT ST

EAST END ROAD

A406

East Finchley

HARINGEY p90

KINGSBURY ROAD

Hendon

A41

Hendon Park

FINCHLEY ROAD

LYTTELTON ROAD

A1

ARCHWAY ROAD

GOLDERS GREEN RD

HAMPSTEAD GARDEN SUBURB

Hampstead Heath

Brent Cross Shopping Centre

Brent Cross

Golders Green

London Jewish Cultural Centre

NORTH CIRCULAR

GOLDERS GREEN

HENDON WAY

Golders Hill Park

NORTH END WAY

Hampstead Heath

BRENT p309

A406

EDGWARE ROAD

Cricklewood

A5

CAMDEN p120

A502

FINCHLEY ROAD

HAVERSTOCK HILL

CAMDEN

0   2 km

0   1 mile

© Copyright Time Out Group 2008

square's great Lutyens churches bear stern notices forbidding ball games against their walls. There are no shops within Hampstead Garden Suburb (let alone pubs or cafés), but residents are well catered for by nearby Temple Fortune.

East Finchley and Finchley Central

Of the several Finchleys, East Finchley offers the strongest sense of place, retaining its identity, local community and even an art deco tube station topped with a striking figure of an archer. Positioned cheek-by-jowl with Highgate and Muswell Hill, and with desirable Victorian and Edwardian housing stock, East Finchley appeals to a liberal arts crowd. Although the homely high street – part of the Great North Road – is often congested, it is also narrow enough to allow for life on a human scale. Local businesses include such London high-street rarities as a decent fishmonger, greengrocer and bookshop.

Adult learners are amply catered for by the Hampstead Garden Suburb Institute, with its new, purpose-built Arts Centre round the corner from East Finchley tube. The jewel in the district's crown, however, is the Phoenix Cinema. Opened in 1910 and thought to be the UK's oldest continuously operating picture house, this deco gem is one of the capital's few remaining independent cinemas and is loyally supported by locals. Families, especially those with toddlers, make a beeline for Cherry Tree Wood and its playground. The park hosts a community festival every summer.

The green fields of College Farm, formerly the showcase farm for Express Dairies, is a reminder of Finchley Central's rural past. Any pastoral feel, however, is long gone, with the area now seeing a high volume of traffic pass along its congested high street (Ballards Lane). Good transport links (both tube and buses) have attracted a mixed population, including a sizeable Jewish contingent, Japanese expats (catered for by Japanese food shop Atari-ya) and a recent influx of young Poles. For a much-needed breath of fresh air, residents head to the Victoria Recreation Ground.

West Finchley and North Finchley

Despite having its own tube station, West Finchley exists in Finchley Central's shadow. Primarily residential, it lacks a real shopping centre, but plus points include comparatively peaceful streets, views over the green belt and proximity to Finchley Golf Course.

North Finchley's most prominent landmark is the Artsdepot complex that towers over Tally Ho Corner. It houses a well-appointed arts centre, a bus depot and luxury apartments. For additional recreation, locals can head to nearby Finchley Lido. This redeveloped 1930s lido now houses a Vue cinema, fast-food outlets, a bowling alley and a swimming pool. The high street offers chains and a handful of down-to-earth independents, including a locksmith, a haberdashery shop and a school uniform store. The most desirable houses are tucked away in the peaceful streets around Woodside Park, location of the nearest tube station.

Totteridge and Whetstone

Drive into Whetstone from the south and it seems distinctly unprepossessing: a B&Q sits opposite a large timber merchant, with Barnet House – the tall, grim tower block that contains Barnet Council's offices – looming in the background. However, turn left into Totteridge Lane, towards Totteridge Village, and you're soon travelling tree-lined lanes between

Barnet

substantial houses. Home to the seriously wealthy (including footballers and their WAGs), the mansions here are discreetly set back from the road and boast fine greenbelt views. However, despite the area's prosperity, Whetstone High Road shows little sign of conspicuous consumption – unless you count the telltale branches of Waitrose and Marks & Spencer.

The prestigious South Herts Golf Club, its course designed by golf legend Harry Vardon, is among the area's hidden assets. Even further west, flanking Barnet Way, are Scratchwood and Moat Mount, a lovely nature reserve that comprises the largest area of woodland in Barnet.

Friern Barnet

During the 19th century, this part of north London was best known for Colney Hatch, its infamous mental hospital, correctly known as the Middlesex County Pauper Lunatic Asylum. Today, such is the driving force of the property market, the asylum has been reinvented as Princess Park Manor, a gated development of luxurious properties with gyms, a bar and tennis courts. The area's refurbishment, however, stops firmly at the gates. The immediate area is decidedly grim and down-at-heel, although Coppetts Wood on Colney Hatch

Hampstead Garden Suburb. *See p299.*

Lane and, west into North Finchley, the Glebelands Nature Reserve provide some relief. Local commuters head for New Southgate rail, as there's no tube nearby.

The picture improves, albeit along traditional suburban lines, as you head north towards Whetstone. The leafy roads around Friern Barnet Lane are lined with large houses and open on to North Middlesex Golf Course. Just south of the course lies Friary Park, which has landscaped grounds, a popular playground and a child-friendly café.

High Barnet

Once a staging post on the main road to London, High Barnet still has a bit of an old-fashioned, out-of-town feel, which is much relished by the residents. 'Barnet Church' (actually St John the Baptist) is the dominating local landmark. It marks the start of the high street, a narrow spot known appropriately as 'the squeeze'. The top of the church tower is meant to be the highest point between London and York; be that as it may, the tower certainly commands spectacular views. Historically, Barnet was famous for its fair, a major livestock trading event – 'Barnet (Fair)' became Cockney rhyming slang for 'hair'.

Even today Barnet has a sense of community to match its parochialism, with events like Scout parades, church fêtes and cricket on the green. There's even a professional football team (the Bees), which commands a passionate following. Barnet Market, granted a charter by King John in 1199, plied a thriving cattle trade; today the market's traders pull in the OAPs with good-value fish, meat, fresh fruit and veg, as well as flowers. At the end of 2007 the stalls were relocated to a much smaller site at a nearby open car park while the market site is developed into a covered market, with the inevitable flats overhead. Whether the market traders will survive this long-proposed development is moot. Easy access to green spaces is much appreciated by residents, who walk their dogs, cycle and fly kites on the Common and Hadley Green (where the Battle of Barnet was fought in 1471, during the War of the Roses).

On the downside, life in the suburbs here can be dull. Other than the flicks at the huge 1930s Odeon down the road, there is little cultural life on offer, and the fact that Barnet's yob element comes to the fore at night makes walking around after dark a depressing experience. Commuters working in central London and using the tube can rely on getting a seat in the morning, but with the Northern line's frequent signal problems, relying on the service itself can be problematic.

Barnet is, however, seeing a steady influx of families from other parts of north London drawn to the more affordable property prices and good schools.

Restaurants & cafés

With Golders Green home to a long-established Jewish community, it is no surprise to learn this is a great place to sample Jewish cuisine. Both Ashkenazi (Russian and east European) and Sephardi (Middle Eastern) food are generously represented. Bustling Dizengoff's offers a taste of Israeli cuisine, with generous portions of houmous, grilled meat and excellent salads; Solly's too specialises in Israeli-style food. For classic Ashkenazi fare, from salt beef to chopped liver, head to Bloom's, with its vintage staff and clientele. Other kosher options include La Fiesta (Argentinian) and Met Su Yan (Asian). Over in Hendon, Mr Baker pulls in a steady stream of customers for bagels and sweet pastries, while popular kosher restaurants include contemporary diner Eighty-Six Bistro Bar, Orli's café and homely Sami's.

Of course, it isn't all Jewish food round here. Café Japan has long had a loyal following, while newcomer H2O in Hendon is also good. Excellent Korean food can be found at Kimchee, while in Temple Fortune Beyoglu serves good traditional Turkish dishes. Fine fish and chips and traditional seafood are on offer at Leon and Tony Manzi's perpetually popular fish restaurant, the Two Brothers in Finchley Central. Indian restaurants range from Hendon's bustling Lahore Original Kebab House, offering robust Pakistani food, to sedate Gujarati vegetarian restaurant Rani in Finchley Central. A welcome addition to North Finchley is a new branch of Khoai Café, a good-quality Vietnamese restaurant. Joan Ferguson's Lavender Lady, meanwhile, is something of a North Finchley haven, serving up quality comfort food classics.

The Din Café at Temple Fortune is deservedly popular with local ladies who lunch. The menu takes in salads, burgers and South African specialities such as grilled boerewors sausages. In contrast, Dory's Café up in High Barnet serves great fry-ups to appreciative regulars.

Barnet is lacking in upmarket eateries. Whetstone's bar-cum-restaurant the Haven and North Finchley's N20 are as glamorous as it gets. Italian food is represented in Whetstone by perpetually bustling Al Fresco and the unreconstructed trattoria La Tavola. The cavernous and coyly named Coffee & Tease café does its bit for the area's harassed mothers, with a handy play area.

Barnet

Up in High Barnet, Indian newcomer Suruchi, despite many rival curry houses, has quickly become a firm favourite. Family-friendly noodle bar Emchai also pulls in a lively crowd. Head towards the picturesque Monken Hadley end of the high street and you'll find a branch of fish specialist Loch Fyne, as well as a recently opened outpost of brasserie Chez Gerard.

Al Fresco *1327 High Road, N20 9HR (8445 8880).*
Beyoglu *1031 Finchley Road, NW11 7ES (8455 4884).*
Bloom's *130 Golders Green Road, NW11 8HB (8455 1338).*
Brasserie Chez Gerard *238-240 High Street, EN5 5DT (8441 6112/www.brasseriechez gerard.co.uk).*
Café Japan *626 Finchley Road, NW11 7RR (8455 6854).*
Coffee & Tease *1379 High Road, N20 9LP (8492 3400).*
Din Café *816 Finchley Road, NW11 6YL (8731 8103/www.dincafe.co.uk).*
Dizengoff's *118 Golders Green Road, NW11 8HB (8458 7003).*
Dory's Café *3 St Albans Road, EN5 4LN (8440 1954).*
Eighty-Six Bistro Bar *86 Brent Street, NW4 2ES (8202 5575).*
Emchai *78 High Street, EN5 5SN (8364 9993).*
La Fiesta *235 Golders Green Road, NW11 9ES (8458 0444).*
Haven Bistro & Bar *1363 High Road, N20 9LN (8445 7419/www.haven-bistro.co.uk).*
H2O *33 Watford Way, NW4 35H (8203 2088).*
Isola Bella Café *63 Brent Street, NW4 2EA (8203 2000/www.isolabellacafe.com).*
Khoai Café *362 Ballards Lane, N12 0EE (8445 2039).*
Kimchee *887 Finchley Road, NW11 8RR (8455 1035).*
Lahore Original Kebab House *148-150 Brent Street, NW1 2DR (8203 6904).*

Lavender Lady *644 High Road, N12 0NL (8446 1713).*
Loch Fyne Restaurant *12 Hadley Highstone, EN5 4PU (8449 3674/www.lochfyne.com).*
Met Su Yan *134 Golders Green Road, NW11 8HP (8458 8088).*
Mr Baker *119-121 Brent Street, NW4 2DX (8202 6845).*
N20 *1111 High Road, N20 0PT (8445 8080).*
Orli *96 Brent Street, NW4 2HH (8203 7555).*
Rani *7 Long Lane, N3 2PR (8349 4386/ www.raniuk.com).*
Sami's Kosher Restaurant *157 Brent Street, NW4 4DJ (8203 8088).*
Solly's *148A Golders Green Road, NW11 8HE (ground floor & takeaway 8455 2121/ 1st floor 8455 0004).*
Suruchi *45 High Street, EN5 5UW (8447 1111).*
La Tavola *1357 High Road, N20 9HR (8445 0525).*
Two Brothers Fish Restaurant *297-303 Regents Park Road, N3 1DP (8346 0469).*

Bars & pubs

Barnet's drinking scene has a distinctly suburban vibe, lacking the variety, edge and glamour of more central London boroughs. It is, however, not short on pubs, be they trad locals or brash bars aimed at a younger crowd.

In Hendon, for example, tucked-away, traditional pub the Greyhound contrasts with the in-your-face Claddagh Ring, which attracts a boisterous crowd with its live music. The Gallery, a former pub reincarnated as a nightclub, bar and restaurant, is aimed at those wanting a West End-style night without the journey into town. Over in Finchley Central, the Catcher in the Rye, with football on its TV screens, reasonably priced pub grub and quiz nights, is also popular.

One of Totteridge's best-known pubs is the Orange Tree, which gets top marks for its picturesque location down tree-lined Totteridge Lane. On Whetstone High Road, the Black Bull offers a good range of beers and a peaceful atmosphere; cocktail drinkers should try restaurant-cum-bars N20 and the Haven (for both, *see above*).

Meanwhile, memories of High Barnet's past role as as a staging post linger in a number of traditional pubs: try Ye Olde Monken Holt or the White Lion. The refurbished Mitre (a name change that doesn't seem to have extended to the signage) offers a spruced-up trad pub vibe. Those who want a livelier atmosphere

TRANSPORT

Tube stations *Northern* Golders Green, Brent Cross, Hendon Central, Colindale, Burnt Oak, Edgware; East Finchley, Finchley Central, Mill Hill East, West Finchley, Woodside Park, Totteridge & Whetstone, High Barnet
Rail stations *Capital First Connect Thameslink* Cricklewood, Hendon, Mill Hill Broadway; *Great Northern* New Southgate, Oakleigh Park, New Barnet, Hadley Wood
Main bus routes *into central London* 13, 16, 82, 83, 113, 134, 189; *night buses* N13, N16; *24-hour buses* 83, 134, 189

have jazz bar After Office Hours, while the Sebright Arms is a firm local favourite.

After Office Hours *70 High Street, EN5 5SJ (8449 1142).*
Black Bull *1446 High Road, N20 9BJ (8445 3578).*
Catcher in the Rye *319 Regents Park Road, N3 1DP (8343 4369).*
Claddagh Ring *10 Church Road, NW4 4EA (8203 2600).*
Gallery *407-411 Hendon Way, NW4 3LH (8202 4000).*
Greyhound *Church End, NW4 4JT (8457 9730).*
Mitre *58 High Street, EN5 5SJ (8449 5701).*
Orange Tree *7 Totteridge Village, N20 8NX (8343 7031/www.theorangetreetotteridge.co.uk).*
Sebright Arms *9 Alston Road, EN5 4ET (8449 6869).*
White Lion *50 St Albans Road, EN5 4LA (8449 4560).*
Ye Olde Monken Holt *193 High Street, EN5 5SU (8449 4280/www.yeoldemonkenholt.com).*

Shops

The borough's shopping scene is, inevitably, dominated by Brent Cross Shopping Centre. The veteran shopping mall (home to some 110 shops and cafés) opened in 1976, harbinger of the countless out-of-town retail conglomerations that have opened since. Despite being near a tube station, Brent Cross has ample car parks, all heaving with vehicles – the car is very much king here. The centre is currently undergoing modernisation, however, with an increased focus on pedestrian access, improving the place's environmental credentials.

For those who prefer to shop on a more human scale, Golders Green offers quirky one-offs alongside chains and charity shops. Veterans of the days when Golders Green Road was a truly upmarket shopping street are florists Galton Flowers and old-fashioned clothing store Franks. In contrast, factory outlet Gold & Son, specialising in bargain suits, cheerfully advertises itself as 'the big red building on Golders Green Road'. Just up the road, genteel Temple Fortune boasts a number of small independents, including Brian's (kids' shoes), the Bookworm (kids' books) and Joseph's (more books).

High Barnet has the Spires, a pleasant, low-level shopping centre constructed around small open-air squares, which

offers the likes of Body Shop, Monsoon, Waterstone's and Tchibo. Down the Monken Hadley end of the high street, you'll find Bargain Buys (an Aladdin's cave of household goods), Wanders (chic footwear) and the Present (fancily wrapped gifts).

On the food front, the borough's most distinctive feature is the number of vintage Jewish food shops, including kosher wine specialist Amazing Grapes, classic Jewish deli Platters, fishmongers Sam Stoller and JA Corney, butcher La Boucherie and bustling bagel bakeries Carmelli, Daniel's and Hendon Bagel Bakery. Barnet's Japanese residents are catered for by branches of Atari-ya, and (just over the borough border in Brent) Oriental City shopping centre/food court; Asian food shops include Goodeats, Q Stores and Indian sweet specialist Chhappan Bhog.

Amazing Grapes *94 Brent Street, NW4 2ES (8202 2631/www.amazinggrapes.co.uk).*
Atari-ya Foods *www.atariya.co.uk: 595 High Road, N12 0DY (8446 6669); 15-16 Monkville Parade, Finchley Road, NW11 0AL (8458 7626).*
Bargain Buys *4 Hadley Parade, EN5 5SX (8440 7983).*
Black Gull Books *121 High Road, N2 8AC (8444 4717).*
The Bookworm *1177 Finchley Road, NW11 0AA (8201 9811/www.thebookworm.uk.com).*
La Boucherie *4 Cat Hill, EN4 85B (8449 9215).*

Brent Cross Shopping Centre *NW4 3FP (8202 8095/www.brentcross.co.uk).*
Brian's Shoes *2 Halleswelle Parade, Finchley Road, NW11 0DL (8455 7001/www.brians shoes.com).*
Carmelli Bakery *126-128 Golders Green Road, NW11 8HB (8455 2074/www.carmelli. co.uk).*
Chhappan Bhog *143-145 Ballards Lane, N3 1U (8371 8677/www.chhappanbhog.co.uk).*
Daniel's *12-13 Halleswelle Parade, Finchley Road, NW11 0DL (8455 5826).*
Franks *72-74 Golders Green Road, NW11 8LP (8455 2251).*
Galton Flowers *75 Golders Green Road, NW11 8EN (8455 5704).*
Gold & Son *110 Golders Green Road, NW11 8HB (8905 5721).*
Goodeats *124 Ballards Lane, N3 2PA (8349 2373).*
Hendon Bagel Bakery *55-57 Church Road, NW4 4DU (8203 6919).*
JA Corney *16 Halleswelle Parade, Finchley Road, NW11 0DL (8455 9588).*
Joseph's Book Store *2 Ashbourne Parade, 1257 Finchley Road, NW11 0AD (8731 7575/ www.josephsbookstore.com).*
Platters *10 Halleswelle Parade, Finchley Road, NW11 0DL (8455 7345).*
The Present *220-222 High Street, EN5 5SZ (8441 6400).*
Q Stores *19 Lodge Lane, N12 8JG (8446 2495).*
Sam Stoller & Son *28 Temple Fortune Parade, Finchley Road, NW11 0QS (8458 1429).*
Spires Shopping Centre *111 High Street, EN5 5XY (8449 7505).*
Wanders *180 High Street, EN5 5SZ (8449 2520).*

Arts & attractions

Cinemas & theatres
Artsdepot *5 Nether Street, N12 0GA (8369 5454/www.artsdepot.co.uk).* Multidisciplinary arts venue, featuring comedy, dance and theatre productions, plus lots of activities for kids.
Cineworld Staples Corner *Staples Corner Retail Park, Geron Way, NW2 6LW (0871 200 2000/www.cineworld.co.uk).*
Odeon Barnet *Great North Road, EN5 1AB (0871 224 4007/www.odeon.co.uk).*
Phoenix Cinema *52 High Road, N2 9PJ (8444 6789/www.phoenixcinema.co.uk).*
Vue North Finchley *Great North Leisure Park, Chaplin Square, N12 0GL (0871 224 0240/www.myvue.com).*

Galleries & museums
Artsdepot Gallery *5 Nether Street, N12 0GA (8369 5464/www.artsdepot.co.uk).*
Barnet Museum *31 Wood Street, EN5 4BE (8440 8066/www.barnetmuseum.co.uk).* Local history museum, holding everything from archaeological remains to a fine costume collection.

Church Farmhouse Museum *Greyhound Hill, NW4 4JR (8359 3942/www.churchfarm housemuseum.co.uk).* A 17th-century farmhouse with Victorian period rooms.
Royal Air Force Museum *Grahame Park Way, NW9 5LL (8205 2266/www.rafmuseum. org.uk).* More than 100 aircraft (including a Spitfire and a Lancaster bomber) are displayed on the site of the original London Aerodrome.

Other attractions
Hampstead Garden Suburb Institute Arts Centre *3 Beaumont Close, Bishop's Avenue, N2 0GA (8829 4229/www.hgsi.ac.uk).* New £6 million arts centre, launched in 2007 by the parent adult learning centre. There are facilities for art, photography and cookery sessions and other courses.
London Jewish Cultural Centre *Ivy House, 94-96 North End Road, NW11 7SX (8457 5000/www.ljcc.org.uk).* A Jewish hub, with a range of courses, exhibitions, films, music and lectures.

Sport & fitness
Barnet has a decent mix of clubs and centres, both public and private. Golfers will also be in their element: there are more golf courses in Barnet than any other London borough. For football fans, Barnet FC – at the time of writing – in Coca-Cola Football League 2, having been promoted from the Conference.

Gyms & leisure centres
Barnet Burnt Oak Leisure Centre *Watling Avenue, Middx HA8 0NP (8201 0982/www.gll.org).*
Barnet Copthall Leisure Centre *Champions Way, off Great North Way, NW4 1PX (8457 9900/www.gll.org).*
Church Farm Swimming Pool *Church Hill Road, EN4 8XE (8368 7070/www.gll.org).*
Compton Leisure Centre *Porters Way, off Summers Lane, N12 0RF (8361 8658/ www.gll.org).*
David Lloyd *Leisure Way, High Road, N12 0QZ (8492 2250/www.davidlloydleisure.co.uk).* Private.
Esporta *264 Princess Park Manor, Friern Barnet Road, N11 3BG (8362 8444/ www.esporta.com).* Private.
Finchley Lido Leisure Centre *Great North Leisure Park, Chaplin Square, N12 0GL (8343 9830/www.gll.org).*
Fitness First *Old Priory Road Shopping Centre, 706 High Road, N12 9QL (8492 2500/ www.fitnessfirst.com).* Private.
Hendon Leisure Centre *Marble Drive, NW2 1XQ (8455 0818/www.gll.org).*
Laboratory Spa & Health Club *1A Hall Lane, NW4 4TJ (8201 5500/spa 8201 5588/ www.labspa.co.uk).* Private.

LA Fitness *www.lafitness.co.uk; East End Road, N3 2TA (8346 7253); 152-154 Golders Green Road, NW11 8HE (8731 7312).* Private.
Oakleigh Park School of Swimming *100 Oakleigh Road North, N20 9EZ (8445 1911/www.swimoakleighpark.co.uk).*
Queen Elizabeth's Leisure Centre *Meadway, EN5 5RR (8441 2933/www.gll.org).*
Virgin Active *www.virginactive.co.uk; 108-110 Cricklewood Lane, NW2 2DS (8453 7200); 260 Hendon Way, NW4 3NL (8203 9421).* Private.

Other facilities

Arkley Golf Club *Rowley Green Road, Arkley, EN5 3HL (8449 0394/www.club-noticeboard.co.uk/arkley).*
Finchley Golf Club *Nether Court, Frith Lane, NW7 1PU (8346 2436/www.finchleygolfclub.co.uk).*
Hendon Golf Club *Ashley Walk, Devonshire Road, NW7 1DG (8346 6023/www.hendongolfclub.co.uk).*
Hollywood Bowl *Great North Leisure Park, High Road, N12 0QZ (8446 6667/www.hollywoodbowl.co.uk).*
Mill Hill Golf Club *100 Barnet Way, NW7 3AL (8959 2339/www.millhillgc.co.uk).*
North Middlesex Golf Course *Friern Barnet Lane, N20 0NL (8445 1604/www.northmiddlesexgc.co.uk).*
Old Fold Manor Golf Club *Old Fold Lane, Hadley Green, EN5 4QN (8440 9185/www.oldfoldmanor.co.uk).*
South Herts Golf Club *Links Drive, Totteridge, N20 8QU (8445 2035/www.southherts.co.uk).*

Spectator sports

Barnet FC *Underhill Stadium, Barnet Lane, EN5 2DN (8441 6932/tickets 8449 6325/www.barnetfc.premiumtv.co.uk).*

RECYCLING

No. of bring sites 14 (for nearest, visit www.recycleforlondon.com)
Household waste recycled 17.98%
Main recycling centre Summers Lane Civic Amenity & Recycling Centre, Summers Lane, Finchley, N12 0PD (8362 0752)
Other recycling services black box recyling service; green waste collection; home composting; 'block cleanse' service (free skip to take general waste and green garden waste, three times a year); white goods collection; hazardous waste collection
Council contact Waste & Sustainability, London Borough of Barnet, Building 4, North London Business Park, Oakleigh Road South, New Southgate, N11 1NP (8359 7400)

Schools

WHAT THE PARENTS SAY:

‘Barnet has good state primary provision. Our children have been very happy at East Finchley's Martin Primary, a medium-sized community school with a strong inclusive ethos and plenty of involved parents. Also in the area, St Theresa's and Holy Trinity are popular with church-going parents – Catholic and C of E respectively. If you are thinking of following this route, be aware that genuine letters from priests are expected.

Barnet has some excellent secondary schools, many of which select either on gender (Queen Elizabeth's Girls'), academic prowess (Mill Hill County) or both (such as Henrietta Barnett). There's lots of choice but some parents (particularly those with girls) feel poorly served.

Parents need to be canny. Schools not selecting in this manner include the well-regarded Compton (technology specialism) and up-and-coming Friern Barnet (performing arts). Many parents hop across the border to comprehensive Fortismere in neighbouring Haringey or high-achieving schools in Enfield.’

Kate Fuscoe, mother of two, East Finchley

Primary

There are 76 state primaries in Barnet, including 23 church schools and nine Jewish schools. There are also 18 independent primary schools, including nine faith schools and one international school. See www.edubase.gov.uk and www.ofsted.gov.uk for more information.

Secondary

Ashmole School *Cecil Road, N14 5RJ (8361 2703/www.ashmole.barnet.sch.uk).*
Bishop Douglass RC High School *Hamilton Road, N2 OSQ (8444 5211/www.bishopdouglass.barnet.sch.uk).*
Christ's College Finchley *East End Road, N2 OSE (8349 3581/www.christscollegefinchley.com).* Boys only; mixed sixth form.
Compton School *Summers Lane, N12 0QG (8368 1783/www.compton.barnet.lgfl.net).*
Copthall School *Pursley Road, NW7 2EP (8959 1937/www.copthall.barnet.lgfl.net).* Girls only.
East Barnet School *Chestnut Grove, EN4 8PU (8440 4162/www.eastbarnet.barnet.sch.uk).*
Finchley Catholic High School *Woodside Lane, N12 8TA (8445 0105/www.finchley catholic.org.uk).* Boys only.
Friern Barnet School *Hemington Avenue, N11 3LS (8368 2798/www.friern.barnet.sch.uk).*
Hasmonean High School Boys' site *Holders Hill Road, NW4 1NA (8203 1411/www.hasmonean.co.uk)*; Girls' site *2 Page Street, NW7 2EU (8203 4294/www.hasmonean.co.uk).* Jewish.

Hendon Foundation School *Golders Rise,
NW4 2HP (8202 9004/www.hendonschool.
co.uk).*
Henrietta Barnett School *Central Square,
NW11 7BN (8458 8999/www.hbschool.org.uk).*
Girls only.
London Academy *Spur Road, HA8 8DE
(8238 1100/www.londonacademy.org.uk).*
Mill Hill County High School *Worcester
Crescent, NW7 4LL (0844 477 2424/
www.mhchs.org.uk).*
Queen Elizabeth's Boys' School *Queen's
Road, EN5 4DQ (8441 4646/www.qebarnet.
co.uk).* Boys only.
Queen Elizabeth's Girls' School *High
Street, EN5 5RR (8449 2984/www.qegschool.
org.uk).* Girls only.
Ravenscroft School *Barnet Lane, N20
8AZ (8445 9205/www.ravenscroft.barnet.
sch.uk).*
St James' Catholic High School *Great
Strand, NW9 5PE (8358 2800/www.st-james.
barnet.sch.uk).*
St Mary's CE High School *Downage, NW4
1AB (8203 2827/www.stmaryshigh.barnet.
lgfl.net).*
St Michael's Catholic Grammar School
*Nether Street, N12 7NJ (8446 2256/
www.st-michaels.barnet.sch.uk).* Girls only.
Whitefield Community School *Claremont
Road, NW2 1TR (8455 4114/www.whitefield.
barnet.sch.uk).*

Property

WHAT THE AGENTS SAY:

'Finchley has a great mix of shops and green
spaces. Above all, it's got a fantastic education
record, which draws people in. Arts and leisure
have improved: we've now got the Artsdepot,
so there's always something on. I'd have to say
it isn't the most thrilling place to live in terms
of nightclubs and bars, but it's comfortable.
It has the highest representation of shops in
north London outside Brent Cross. In East
Finchley the properties are very similar to
nearby Muswell Hill and Highgate, but prices
are lower. The tube station is the last stop in
Zone 3, so it's attractive for younger people and
there's a more vibrant nightlife.'
Jeremy Leaf, Jeremy Leaf & Co, Finchley

Average property prices
Detached £915,681
Semi-detached £459,458
Terraced £334,283
Flat £247,485

Local estate agents
Douglas Martin *18 Central Circus, NW4
3AS (8202 6333/www.douglasmartin.co.uk).*

Ellis & Co *www.ellisandco.co.uk; 5 offices in
the borough (Barnet 8441 7700/Finchley 8349
3131/Golders Green 8455 1014/Hampstead
Garden Suburb 8458 8448/Mill Hill 8959 3281).*
Jeremy Leaf & Co *www.jeremyleaf.co.uk;
2 offices in the borough (East Finchley 8444
5222/North Finchley 8446 4295).*
Martyn Gerrard *www.martyngerrard.co.uk;
4 offices in the borough (East Finchley 8883
0077/Finchley Central 8346 0102/North
Finchley 8445 2222/Whetstone 8446 2111).*
Richard James *52A The Broadway, NW7
3LH (8959 9191/www.richardjames.biz).*

Other information

Council
Barnet Council *Hendon Town Hall,
The Burroughs, NW4 4BG (8359 2000/
www.barnet.gov.uk).*
Barnet Council First Contact Unit
8359 2277/first.contact@barnet.gov.uk.

Legal services
Finchley CAB *23 Hendon Lane, N3 1RT
(0870 128 8080/www.barnetcab.org.uk).*
Hendon CAB *40-42 Church End, NW4 4JT
(0870 128 8080/www.barnetcab.org.uk).*
New Barnet CAB *30 Station Road, New
Barnet, EN5 1PL (0870 128 8080/www.
barnetcab.org.uk).*

Local newspapers
The Archer *www.the-archer.co.uk.*
Community newspaper for East Finchley,
run entirely by volunteers.
Barnet Times *www.barnettimes.co.uk.*
Edgware & Mill Hill Times
www.edgwaretimes.co.uk.
Hendon & Finchley Times
www.hendontimes.co.uk.

Allotments & open spaces
London Borough of Barnet *Greenspaces
Officer, Building 4, North London Business
Park, Oakleigh Road South, N11 1NP (8359
7820/www.barnet.gov.uk).*
**Barnet Federation of Allotments
& Horticultural Societies**
www.kitchengardens.dial.pipex.com.
Open spaces *www.barnet.gov.uk/parks-and-
open-spaces.*

COUNCIL TAX		
A	up to £40,000	**£900.08**
B	£40,001-£52,000	**£1,050.09**
C	£52,001-£68,000	**£1,200.11**
D	£68,001-£88,000	**£1,350.12**
E	£88,001-£120,000	**£1,650.15**
F	£120,001-£160,000	**£1,950.18**
G	£160,001-£320,000	**£2,250.20**
H	over £320,000	**£2,700.24**

Barnet

Brent

With one foot firmly lodged in inner-city London, Brent also embraces smug suburbia. Upmarket media types wanting more bricks for their money rub shoulders with old-school Irish, Asian, Caribbean and Portuguese communities and newer eastern European ones. A vibrant microcosm of London living, Brent offers a mix of industrial and green landscapes plus great transport links.

Neighbourhoods

Kilburn and Brondesbury

Kilburn straddles the traffic-clogged thoroughfare of the A5, aka Kilburn High Road, an arterial route in and out of London since Roman times. This grotty but popular high street offers useful if uninspiring chains, such as Boots and Sainsbury's, alongside numerous pound shops and Kilburn Square Market. The area has been earmarked for development, although plans seem to have stalled for now.

Kilburn's long-standing sense of Irish identity is fast fading too – the St Patrick's Day Parade now starts in Willesden – as many older residents leave the area, cashing in on house prices as they go. Some Irish pubs remain, but there's been a definite sea change, typified by McGoverns Irish pub just north of Willesden Lane. Once occupying almost an entire block, McGoverns has shrunk to a quarter of its previous size, with the trendy Kilburn taking up the remaining space.

Despite the influx of coffee chains and other indicators of affluence, Kilburn retains a slightly down-at-heel vibe. The housing stock ranges from large estates to handsome Victorian terraces. The good news is that prices remain consistently less painful than those in nearby West Hampstead and Maida Vale – though the stream of young and middle-aged professionals taking advantage means things won't remain as such for long.

Residential Brondesbury stretches north and west of Kilburn, including Willesden Lane. It's another area with a varied ethnic mix, reflected in the many food shops proffering Indian, Polish and Persian specialities, alongside some generic greasy-spoon caffs. Historical precedence of the area's diversity can also be witnessed at peaceful and pretty Paddington Cemetery. House prices are fairly high, primarily due to the area's popularity with young families.

Kensal Rise and Kensal Green

Neighbouring Harlesden's edgy reputation helps amplify the laid-back feel of Kensal Green. The neighbourhood has an arty, bohemian feel (Kensal Green Cemetery, just over the Kensington & Chelsea border, was a fashionable final resting place for Victorian writers and artists) and its cosy, compact terraces appeal to young professionals who can't afford Notting Hill. In fact, estate agents often call this area 'Notting Hill borders', hence the dramatic increase in house prices in the last few years. At its southernmost tip, this part of Brent really is within spitting distance

Highs & Lows

▲ **Welsh Harp Reservoir** Sailing, birdwatching and dog walking, not far from Wembley Stadium and Brent Cross

Jubilee line Streamlined and speedy access to everything the city and the borough has to offer

Drab high streets Competition from Brent Cross shopping centre overshadows local retailers

Split personality The borough is vast and bisected by the North Circular – it can seem hard to find ▼ the gems amid the urban grime

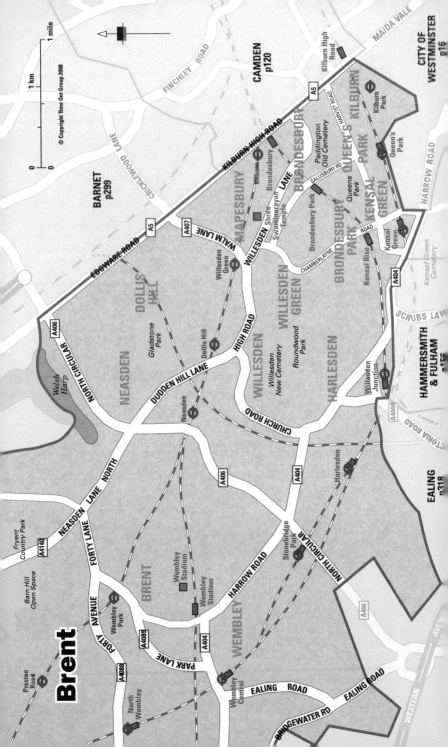

of Ladbroke Grove where housing stock ranges from swanky conversions and gated complexes to 1960s council estates, loft-style pads and terraces.

West of Kensal Green tube is a popular shopping area, with restaurants, takeaways, dumpling shacks and an old-style hardware shop. Transport links are decent and it's also possible to drive to Sainsbury's in Ladbroke Grove without entering the congestion charge zone (you only get charged if you stray south of the roundabout). The Kensal Rise end of Chamberlayne Road provides more local shopping options.

Kensal Rise itself has blossomed over the last couple of years – despite the shock tornado that hit the area in 2006. House prices are on the up, though it's still cheaper than Queen's Park. As a result it's a popular choice with young families. Property consists mainly of large Victorian terraces and 1930s houses, both large and small.

The north end of College Road is where most of the retail action happens. It has a bijou, middle-class vibe, with delis, alternative medicine treatment rooms and quirky boutiques. The revamp of Kensal Rise station, meanwhile, has made space for a gourmet café on the main road.

Harlesden, Stonebridge and Church End

Despite its often negative reputation, there's plenty to love about Harlesden. Around the famous clock tower is one of Brent's most vibrant shopping areas, with food stores catering for the local Caribbean, Asian and Brazilian communities, as well as discount shops and takeaways.

Brent grew and developed along with the arrival of the railways in the late 1880s and this is very much reflected in Harlesden's predominantly late Victorian properties. House sizes vary – north of the High Street, some are very large, and quite a few have (pleasingly) not yet been converted into flats. Prices reflect the area's long-standing notoriety and tend to be somewhat lower than you might expect.

Transport links (bus, tube and train) are good, though drivers have a hard time – Harlesden is a controlled parking zone and double-parking along the high street causes frequent gridlock at weekends. Locals can easily escape the hustle and bustle, though. Roundwood Park is a popular gated green space, with a café, play area and some award-winning flowerbeds.

West of Harlesden, Stonebridge has been transformed – at least from the outside. Demolition has started on the last of its grotty blocks, with new low-rise housing as a replacement. Recent investment has also included the development of colourful and contemporary £2.1 million family centre Stonebridge Nursery.

Neighbouring Church End is also getting a makeover and, with the new Central Middlesex Hospital in the middle of Park Royal, there's a note of optimism in a formerly bleak urban area. Church End sits between Harlesden, Willesden and Neasden, meeting Stonebridge on the other side of the railway tracks. Here, anonymous

Brent

prefabs have been replaced with modern low-rise estates. Plans are also afoot to add more trees and green spaces.

Willesden, Willesden Green and Cricklewood

Willesden High Road, which splits in two at Willesden Library, offers an array of restaurants, shops and takeaways. It is, however, a grimy thoroughfare, with frustratingly slow-moving traffic.

Long favoured by immigrant communities, Willesden has a large rental market as well as plenty of Victorian terraces that appeal to families and young professionals keen to get a foot on the property ladder. The area's Irish influence is less evident than it once was – nowadays eastern European and Antipodean voices are more likely to be heard on the high street than Irish ones. The library is a well-used local amenity; it's home to a bookshop, licensed café and cinema (the forecourt is occasionally used to hold markets too).

The Brent side of Cricklewood, meanwhile, shares many features with Kilburn; it's centred around the A5, grew up with the railways and was historically favoured by Irish immigrants. It has, however, a much more suburban feel, with wide roads and terraces. Transport links are good and it has its own bus station, but it's a walk to the nearest tube (Dollis Hill or Willesden Green). Family-friendly Cricklewood Library – repeatedly saved from closure by its many local fans – houses the Brent Archive.

Gladstone Park, which sits between Cricklewood, Willesden and Dollis Hill, recently won lottery funding to improve its sports grounds. This means that the park's southern half – it's split by the railway – will have new sports pitches available for club and school use by autumn 2008. The whole green space is much used by families and dog walkers, with two cafés and a friendly neighbourhood feel. To the south of the park are a number of popular cul-de-sacs with detached 1930s houses (these command a premium), while to the north are wide avenues of '30s semis. This isn't the most fashionable part of town – Jean Simmons grew up in Cricklewood, but used to say she came from Willesden to appear posher – but with its sizeable (and not entirely unreasonably

Harlesden's jubilee clock. *See p311*.

priced) houses and suburban vibe it's increasingly populated with young families.

Queen's Park, Brondesbury Park and Mapesbury

No longer undiscovered, Queen's Park has profited from the Notting Hill knock-on effect and is now beloved of creative folk. The houses around the park command the best views and the highest prices, while the southern end of Salusbury Road provides plenty of upmarket shopping and dining options. Around the park, houses vary in size, with the largest sitting either side of the railway line to the north. The Avenue boasts some desirable and spacious 1930s houses with large gardens front and back. There are still a few surviving areas of light industry, particularly Lonsdale Mews, although restaurants are fast replacing the spring manufacturers. Prices are lower the further you stray from the park.

Queen's Park itself is gated; dogs are not allowed to roam free, though children – and there are plenty of them in these parts – very much are. The café does brisk business, as does the crazy golf course and the tennis courts. It gets very crowded in summer, when the playground is packed.

At the top of Salusbury Road is another station, Brondesbury Park (North London line). This popular district offers appealing detached houses – many stone-clad and firmly gated – located around Mallorees School. Willesden Lane offers a slightly greyer version, with large Victorian piles, many of which have been turned into flats, and some new-builds and gated estates.

The Mapesbury conservation area, meanwhile, is a world of its own, with 'urban villas' situated on wide avenues. It's favoured by families and has a quiet, safe, suburban feel. Larger houses here have long since passed the £1 million price tag.

Dollis Hill and Neasden

North of Dollis Hill underground station congregates a selection of small Edwardian terraces and a 1930s estate. The area has a sedate but cosmopolitan feel and is popular with British Asian, English and Irish families. There's a marked contrast with nearby Willesden's grimy urban vibe. Local shops are limited to a smattering near the station (most residents scoot off to Willesden, Neasden or Brent Cross for serious supplies); other amenities include imposing Gladstone Park.

LOCALS' TIPS

Brent residents get discounted tickets for the theatre (Thursday, Friday) and cinema (Thursday and Friday matinées, Monday evening) at the Tricycle. **Arrive at the farmers' market at Salusbury School around 2pm on Sunday and get lots of bargains.** The Brent council website (www.brent. gov.uk) is a really useful resource. Unlike the parking restrictions and road humps, which are hellish and everywhere. **Get married at Brent Town Hall and have your wedding relayed live on webcam to friends and relatives all over the world. It's also got a lovely garden for photos.**

Neasden, long the butt of *Private Eye* jokes, was named after its nose-shaped hill, which is today lined with streets of '30s houses. More people are familiar with Neasden's traffic island than its shopping centre, which has become increasingly dilapidated in recent years. Outside the shopping centre, this is an area with a distinctly anonymous, suburban feel. For posh boutiques and fancy food you'll need to look elsewhere, but with the nearby North Circular, plenty of buses and the Jubilee line at residents' disposal, access to neighbouring areas is easy.

The magnificent Shri Swaminarayan Mandir Hindu temple is also in Neasden. To the north is the open green space of Welsh Harp Reservoir.

Wembley

Best known for its impressive new stadium, Wembley sits on the far side of the North Circular. A steady stream of stadium visitors means excellent transport links: locals have access to the Metropolitan and Jubilee lines (Wembley Park), Bakerloo line (Wembley Central and North Wembley), Piccadilly line (Alperton) and Central line (Hanger Lane in neighbouring Ealing).

Wembley High Road itself is a fairly unremarkable affair, dotted with banks, takeaways and chain shops like Boots, as well as some popular local restaurants (most specialising in South Indian cuisine). Deceptively quiet midweek, restaurants such as dosa specialist Sarashwathy Bavans become a hive of activity at weekends (you may well have to wait for a table at peak times). Also nearby is popular Copland School, which achieves good results, and, up Park Lane towards Wembley Park, is King Edward VII Park.

Wembley has a strong community feel, due largely to the extensive Gujarati and South Indian population. The area's housing stock includes plenty of good-sized family-friendly 1930s semis (particularly in North Wembley) and most residents seem to be in for the long haul, with many children of first- and second-generation immigrants choosing to remain in the area near their parents. A recent influx of eastern European residents has added another dimension to the cultural mix – shops like Polski Slep (on Mount Pleasant at the bottom of Ealing Road) are appearing fast.

Brent

Ealing Road – stunning by night when it's lit up for the Diwali festival – offers a bustling mix of restaurants, travel agents advertising great deals to Mumbai, and shops selling gold jewellery, fabulous sari fabrics, Bollywood hits, altars and huge piles of exotic fruit and veg. The road is also home to a small but well-used library, the Shree Sanatan Hindu Mandir temple, Wembley Central mosque and the Clay Oven banqueting suites, a popular venue for local wedding receptions. To the south is mainly residential Alperton.

Restaurants & cafés

Though not exactly a mecca of fine gastronomy, Brent has plenty to satisfy the average appetite. The borough's budget bistros, Little Star in Willesden and Small & Beautiful and Little Bay in Kilburn, are now established eateries and deservedly popular with bright young professional things.

In Willesden, Sushi-Say remains a big draw for sushi-lovers; chef Shimizu is a joy to watch. Kebab specialist Shish is another firm local favourite, while Vijay, Geeta and Kovalam are a pleasing cluster of South Indian specialists on Willesden Lane. For a classy coffee, pop into the café at the Tricycle Theatre (see p316); Kensal Rise caffeine needs are best fixed at family-friendly Gracelands.

As parts of the borough become increasingly fashionable, so too do its gastropubs. Paradise by Way of Kensal Green has benefited from a recent refurb and new energy in the kitchen; it's popular with the likes of Lily Allen and is often used as a venue for secret gigs. Nearby, the Regent offers excellent organic burgers and a calmer vibe. Also of note is Harrow Road's William IV.

Visit Behesht in Kensal Green for great Persian fare (grills, stews and salads) and Os Amigos in Harlesen for hearty Portuguese dishes and good tapas. In Queen's Park, Penk's (French/global) remains consistently charming, Hugo's has child-friendly brunching appeal, while the Salusbury satisfies those with gastropub leanings. There's also a branch of posh café Baker & Spice here.

New Kabana's North Indian dishes shine in Neasden, and Wembley is overrun with Indian restaurants; try Dadima and Sakonis

for Gujarati cuisine, Sanghaman for pan-Indian dishes and Sarashwathy Bavans for South Indian – all are vegetarian.

Baker & Spice 75 Salusbury Road, NW6 6NH (7604 3636/www.bakerandspice.com).
Behesht 1084 Harrow Road, NW10 5NL (8964 4477).
Dadima 228 Ealing Road, HA0 4QL (8902 1072).
Geeta 57-59 Willesden Lane, NW6 7RL (7624 1713).
Gracelands 118 College Road, NW10 5HD (8964 9161/www.gracelandscafe.com).
Hugo's 21 Lonsdale Road, NW6 6RA (7372 1232).
Kovalam 12 Willesden Lane, NW6 7SR (7625 4761/www.kovalamrestaurant.co.uk).
Little Bay 228 Belsize Road, NW6 4BT (7372 4699).
Little Star 26 Station Parade, NW2 4NH (8830 5221).
New Kabana 43 Blackbird Hill, NW9 8RS (8200 7094).
Os Amigos 25 Park Parade, NW10 4JG (8961 9161).
Paradise by Way of Kensal Green 19 Kilburn Lane, W10 4AE (8969 0098/www.theparadise.co.uk).
Penk's 79 Salusbury Road, NW6 6NH (7604 4484/www.penks.com).
Regent 5 Regent Street, NW10 5LG (8969 2184/www.theregentkensalgreen.com).
Sakonis 127-129 Ealing Road, HA0 4BP (8903 1058).
Salusbury 50-52 Salusbury Road, NW6 6NN (7328 3286/www.salusbury.com).

TRANSPORT

Tube stations *Bakerloo* Kilburn Park, Queen's Park, Kensal Green, Willesden Junction, Harlesden, Stonebridge Park, Wembley Central, North Wembley, South Kenton, Kenton; *Jubilee* Kilburn, Willesden Green, Dollis Hill, Neasden, Wembley Park, Kingsbury, Queensbury; *Metropolitan* Wembley Park, Preston Road, Northwick Park; *Piccadilly* Alperton, Sudbury Town

Rail stations *Chiltern Railways* Wembley Stadium, Sudbury & Harrow Road; *London Overground* Kilburn High Road, Queen's Park, Kensal Green, Brondesbury, Brondesbury Park, Kensal Rise, Willesden Junction, Harlesden, Stonebridge Park, Wembley Central, North Wembley, South Kenton, Kenton

Main bus routes *into central London* 6, 16, 18, 36, 43, 52, 98, 189; *night buses* N16, N18, N36, N52, N98; *24-hour buses* 6, 43, 189

Sanghaman *531 High Road, HA0 2DJ (8900 0777/www.sanghamam.co.uk).*
Sarashwathy Bavans *549 High Road, HA0 2DJ (8902 1515/www.sarashwathy.com).*
Shish *2-6 Station Parade, NW2 4NH (8208 9292).*
Small & Beautiful *351 Kilburn High Road, NW6 2QJ (7328 2637).*
Sushi-Say *33B Walm Lane, NW2 5SH (8459 2971).*
Vijay *49 Willesden Lane, NW6 7RF (7328 1087).*
William IV *786 Harrow Road, NW10 5LX (8969 5944).*

Bars & pubs

Brent's pubs reflect the changing faces of the borough. You can still find traditional Irish boozers on Kilburn High Road, but not as many as there once were. Some, such as the formerly old-school Kilburn, have taken a new tack – in this case an American diner vibe. The consistently excellent Black Lion, with its gorgeously ornate Victorian decor, is another must-visit for discerning drinkers, while the unpretentious, late-opening Good Ship draws a lively crowd to its DJ/music and comedy nights. In Willesden Green the Crown is a popular choice, especially with Antipodeans; bar-restaurant the Green, meanwhile, attracts a classy local crowd.

Kensal Green and Rise offer gastropubs the Greyhound, Paradise by Way of Kensal Green and the Regent (for both, *see p314*). In Queen's Park watch sports at Irish pub Corrib Rest or chill out at welcoming gastropub the Salusbury (*see p314*).

Harlesden's canalside Grand Junction Arms (just over the border in Ealing) is great in the summer. It's best to avoid Neasden's boozers unless you fancy a scrum as you head home. Towards Harrow in North Wembley is quirky Mumbai Junction pub/restaurant, where you can have Indian food with your pint.

Black Lion *274 Kilburn High Road, NW6 2BY (7625 1635/www.blacklionguesthouse.com).*
Crown *335-339 High Road, NW10 2JT (8459 4771).*
Corrib Rest *76 Salusbury Road, NW6 6PA (7625 9585/www.claddagh-ring.co.uk).*
Good Ship *289 Kilburn High Road, NW6 7JR (07949 008253/www.thegoodship.co.uk).*
Green *110 Walm Lane, NW2 4RS (8452 0909/www.thegreennw2.com).*
Greyhound *64-66 Chamberlayne Road, NW10 3JJ (8969 8080).*

Kilburn Bar & Kitchen *307-311 Kilburn High Road, NW6 7JR (7372 8668/www.thekilburn.com).*
Mumbai Junction *231 Watford Road, HA1 3TU (8904 2255).*

Shops

Brent residents often pop over the border to Barnet's Brent Cross Shopping Centre for supplies, though there's plenty of good retail action to be had here too. Kensal Rise maintains its new Crouch End status, with College Road at the helm. Popular café Gracelands (*see p314*) now offers alternative health treatments and workshops at adjoining Gracelands Yard, while, opposite, L'Angolo deli specialises in Italian fare. On Chamberlayne Road you'll find contemporary floristry courtesy of Flirty Flowers and a branch of children's clothes shop Their Nibs. Head south for Kuddyco (clothes, gifts and accessories sourced from Vietnam) and a number of decent furniture shops including Niche.

Cricklewood Broadway (on the borough border with Camden and Barnet) is home to modern furniture shop New Heights. Also near the borough border is the fabulous South-east Asian shopping and dining mall Oriental City. Redevelopment work, bringing shops, cafés, housing and a primary school, is due to start here in mid 2008 and, though it is promised that an Oriental City concept will remain, the future of the current tenants remains unclear. Alternatively, check out Chinese and Asian food superstore Wing Yip.

In Wembley you'll find standard high-street retailers and a thriving Sunday market around the stadium. Fruit Asia and Fruity Fresh offer top-notch fruit and veg, while Musik Zone proffers Bollywood tunes aplenty. Heading round the North Circular, local homeowners have IKEA on their doorsteps. Also a bonus for homeowners are the salvage yards at Park Royal and Willesden Green. Music fans should check out Hawkeye for reggae and Mandy's for Irish folk. Also in Willesden is Edward's Bakery, in business since 1908. Harlesden is buzzing: visit for some reggae vinyl, all things African and pound shops.

L'Angolo *120 College Road, NW10 5HD (8969 5757).*
Edward's Bakery *269 High Road, NW10 2RX (8459 3001).*

Flirty Flowers *98A Chamberlayne Road, NW10 3JN (8960 9191).*
Fruit Asia *196 Ealing Road, HA0 4QL (8903 2841).*
Fruity Fresh *111 Ealing Road, HA0 4BP (8902 9797).*
Hawkeye Record Store *2 Craven Park Road, NW10 4AB (8961 0866).*
IKEA *2 Drury Way, North Circular Road, NW10 0TH (0845 355 1141/www.ikea.co.uk).*
Kuddyco *117 Chamberlayne Road, NW10 3NS (8968 6617/www.kuddyco.com).*
Mandy's Irish Shop *161 High Road, NW10 2SG (8459 2842).*
Musik Zone *105A Ealing Road, HA0 4BP (8795 1266).*
New Heights *285-289 Cricklewood Broadway, NW2 6NX (8452 1500/ www.new-heights.co.uk).*
Niche *70 Chamberlayne Road, NW10 3JJ (3181 0081).*
Oriental City *399 Edgware Road, NW9 0JJ (8200 0009).*
Park Royal Salvage *Acton Lane, NW10 7AB (8961 3627).*
Their Nibs *79 Chamberlayne Road, NW10 3ND (8964 8444/www.theirnibs.com).*
Willesden Green Architectural Salvage *189 High Road, NW10 2SD (8459 2947).*
Wing Yip *395 Edgware Road, NW2 6LN (8450 0422/www.wingyip.com).*

COUNCIL TAX

A	up to £40,000	£866.31
B	£40,001-£52,000	£1,010.69
C	£52,001-£68,000	£1,155.08
D	£68,001-£88,000	£1,299.46
E	£88,001-£120,000	£1,588.23
F	£120,001-£160,000	£1,877.00
G	£160,001-£320,000	£2,165.77
H	over £320,000	£2,598.92

RECYCLING

No. of bring sites 50 (for nearest, visit www.recycleforlondon.com)
Household waste recycled 10.89%
Main recycling centre Brent Reuse & Recycling Centre, Abbey Road, Park Royal, NW10 (8965 5497)
Other recycling services green and kitchen waste collection; green bin recycling; home composting; collection of white goods and furniture; recycling electrical items
Council contact StreetCare, 1st floor (East), Brent House, 349-357 High Road, Wembley, Middx HA9 6BZ (8937 5050)

Arts & attractions

Cinemas & theatres

Tricycle Theatre & Cinema *269 Kilburn High Road, NW6 7JR (7328 1000/www.tricycle. co.uk).* As well as the titular theatre and cinema, there's a rehearsal studio, visual arts studio, café-bar and art gallery.
Willesden Green Belle Vue Cinema *Willesden Green Library Centre, 95 High Road, NW10 2SU (0871 223 6049).*

Galleries & museums

Brent Museum *Willesden Green Library Centre, 95 High Road, NW10 2SU (8937 3600/ www.brent.gov.uk/museum).* Local history museum (formerly the Grange Museum of Community History). There's also a library (8937 3400), café and cinema (*see above*).

Sport & fitness

Brent's four council-run sports centres are very popular, especially the newly rebuilt Willesden Sports Centre, which is often packed – parking can be a problem.

Gyms & leisure centres

Bridge Park Community Leisure Centre *Harrow Road, NW10 0RG (8937 3730/ www.brent.gov.uk).*

Cannons *Sidmouth Road, NW2 5JY (8451 7863/www.cannons.co.uk).* Private.
Charteris Road Sports Centre *24-30 Charteris Road, NW6 7ET (7625 6451/ www.brent.gov.uk).*
Fitness First *www.fitnessfirst.co.uk; The Atlip Centre, 197 Ealing Road, HA0 4LW (8903 6464); 1st floor, 632-640 Kingsbury Road, NW9 9HN (8204 5858); 105-109 Salusbury Road, NW6 6RG (7328 8333).* Private.
Genesis Gym *333 Athlon Road, HA0 1EF (8566 8687).* Private.
LivingWell *Wembley Plaza Hotel, Empire Way, HA9 8DS (8795 4118/www.livingwell.com).* Private.
The Manor Health & Leisure *307 Cricklewood Broadway, NW2 6PG (8450 6464/ www.themanorhealthandleisure.co.uk).* Private.
Vale Farm Sports Centre *Watford Road,HA0 3HG (8908 6545/www.leisureconnection.co.uk).*
Willesden Sports Centre *Donnington Road, NW10 3QX (8955 1120/www.leisureconnection. co.uk).*

Spectator sports

Wembley Stadium *HA9 0WS (stadium 0844 980 8001/box office 0845 676 2006/ www.wembleystadium.com).* The long-awaited new stadium, complete with illuminated arch, was finally completed in March 2007.
Wembley Arena *Arena Square, Engineers Way, HA9 0DH (8782 5566/www.livenation. co.uk/wembley).* Big-name bands, Dancing on Ice, snooker tournaments and more.

Schools

WHAT THE PARENTS SAY:

‶My daughter goes to Hampstead Comp (Camden) because it's the nearest secondary. I considered other schools, but the catchment areas limit choice, so Kingsbury High and Preston Manor were out of reach. My kids enjoyed Salusbury and Mora primary schools, and now Princess Frederica is in demand. There doesn't seem to be such an issue with transient families affecting learning any more.′

Sally Long, mother of three, Cricklewood

Primary

There are 51 state primary schools in Brent, 13 of which are church schools, three Jewish and one Muslim. There are also ten independent primaries, including two Muslim schools, one Montessori school, one Jewish school, one Hindu school and one Welsh school. See www.brent. gov.uk, www.edubase.gov.uk and www.ofsted. gov.uk for more information.

Secondary

Alperton Community School *Ealing Road, HA0 4PW (8902 2293).*

Capital City Academy *Doyle Gardens, NW10 3ST (8838 8700/www.capitalcity academy.org).*

Cardinal Hinsley Mathematics & Computing College *Harlesden Road, NW10 3RN (8965 3947/www.chmcc.brent.lgfl.net).* Boys only.

Claremont High School *Claremont Avenue, HA3 0UH (0870 350 0093/www.claremont-high.org.uk).*

Convent of Jesus & Mary Language College *Crownhill Road, NW10 4EP (8965 2986/www.cjmhs.brent.sch.uk).* Girls only.

Copland School *Cecil Avenue, HA9 7DU (8902 6362).*

Jewish Free School (JFS) *The Mall, HA3 9TE (8206 3100/www.jfs.brent.sch.uk).*

John Kelly Technology College *Crest Road, NW2 7SN (boys 8452 8700/girls 8452 4842).* Boys and girls taught separately.

Kingsbury High School *Princes Avenue, NW9 9JR (8204 9814/www.kingsburyhigh. org.uk).*

Preston Manor High School *Carlton Avenue East, HA9 8NA (8385 4040/www.pmanor. brent.sch.uk).*

Queen's Park Community School *Aylestone Avenue, NW6 7BQ (8438 1700/www.qpcs. brent.sch.uk).*

St Gregory's Catholic Science College *Donnington Road, HA3 0NB (8907 8828/ www.stgregorys.harrow.sch.uk).*

Wembley High Technology College *East Lane, HA0 3NT (8385 4800/www.whtc. co.uk).*

Property

WHAT THE AGENTS SAY:

‶Kensal Rise is just north of Ladbroke Grove. The houses are a mixture of Victorian and 1930s properties. In the last three years, the area has changed vastly, offering a wide range of pubs, bars and independent shops. There are also amenities such as Queen's Park, Willesden Sports Centre, many bus routes and the Bakerloo line into central London. It's community-spirited and very friendly. It's changed from being quite run-down to a desirable place to live.′

Steve Pickford, Margo's, Kensal Rise

Average property prices

Detached £608,446
Semi-detached £409,320
Terraced £386,213
Flat £240,457

Local estate agents

Camerons *90 Walm Lane, NW2 4QY (8459 0091/www.cameronslondon.com).*

Freshsteps *399 Kilburn High Road, NW6 7QE (7372 9000/www.freshsteps.co.uk).*

Hoopers *www.hoopersestateagents.co.uk; 2 offices in the borough (Kenton 8206 1484/ Neasden 8450 1633).*

Margo's *62 Chamberlayne Road, NW10 3JJ (8960 3030/www.margos.co.uk).*

Daniels *www.danielsestateagents.co.uk; 2 offices (Wembley 8900 2811/Neasden 8452 7000).*

Other information

Council

Brent Council *Town Hall, Forty Lane, Wembley, Middx HA9 9HD (switchboard 8937 1234/ customer services 8937 1200/www.brent.gov.uk).*

Legal services

Brent CAB *270-272 High Road, NW10 2EY (0845 050 5250/www.brentcab.co.uk).*

Brent Community Law Centre *8451 1122/www.lawcentres.org.uk.*

Local newspapers

Harrow Times *01923 216 343/ www.harrowtimes.co.uk.*

Harrow & Wembley Observer *8427 4404/www.icharrow.co.uk.*

Willesden & Brent Times *8962 6868/www.wbtimes.co.uk.*

Allotments & open spaces

Council Allotments *Barham Park Offices, 660 Harrow Road, HA0 2HB (Phil Bruce-Green 8937 5633).*

Open spaces *www.brent.gov.uk/parks.*

Brent

Ealing

It has been called the Queen of Suburbs, and on the whole Ealing is pleasant and leafy, with plenty of green spaces and a genteel feel. But the character of the borough is diverse. It also contains bustling, ethnically mixed spots like Southall and Acton and has its share of downtrodden housing estates.

Neighbourhoods

Acton

For many, Acton is just a place on the way to Heathrow, but get off the A40 and you'll find a thriving neighbourhood. Not all the area is prospering, though. North Acton is dominated by a business park-cum-industrial estate in Park Royal; this is also a road and rail spaghetti junction. The South Acton housing estate, meanwhile, is the largest in west London – one of its tower blocks was used to film *Only Fools and Horses*. But parts of the south and east are profiting from money squeezed out in Acton's direction by the prohibitive property prices of Chiswick and Fulham – hence the smart houses, parks, sports fields and upmarket private schools. An area known for its long-established Polish population, Acton has seen an influx of Somali and Iraqi immigrants and contains a rash of Antipodean pubs and a Japanese community in West Acton.

In Acton Town, the High Street, which is a conservation area, has all the usual banks, fast-food franchises and supermarkets, plus the imposing Acton Library and Town Hall. Pubs like the Redback Tavern cater to the large Australian population, while the Belvedere on the High Street is a Polish-owned pub. Halal tandoori places provide for the Pakistani community.

The district is swamped by 1930s mock-Tudor houses, but you can still find some impressive Victorian detached residences and brick terraces, particularly around Creffield Road. Other upmarket areas include South Acton, Acton Green and Bedford Park, which all benefit from being near the shops and restaurants of Chiswick High Road (in the borough of Hounslow). Further north, the streets around Acton Park are jammed with Clerkenwell-style office conversions, while East Acton has long rows of posh semis, sports grounds and the Saudi-sponsored independent school, the King Fahad Academy.

The north and west of Acton are the least attractive places to live in the borough. West Acton is dominated by train tracks and industrial estates, and North Acton is an unappealing jumble of industrial developments and retail parks, cut off from the rest of the district by the traffic mayhem on the A40 (Western Avenue). More pleasantly, Acton Green Common, near Turnham Green tube station, is a nice example of an old village green, though cut in half by a rail bridge. In an area not famous for its green spaces, there's also Acton Park, situated on the Vale.

This is one of the most ethnically mixed areas in west London and also one of the

Highs & Lows

Community unity With such a mix of nationalities in places like Greenford and Acton, integration is the pleasing result

Pitshanger Village It's hard to beat this neighbourhood for desirable property, nearby schools and transport convenience

Hub trouble Ealing's centre is losing its character as it gets busier and blander, with another shopping mall on the way

Road spaghetti It's great to have all the transport links, but the borough is shredded into pieces by roads, railway lines and a canal

best integrated. There is a panoply of churches and faith centres, all of which seem to pull in large congregations. The transport links are excellent too: numerous tube stops, overground train stations and the A40 and M4 right on the doorstep.

Ealing and Hanger Hill

By turns elegant, bijou and brash, Ealing has come a long way since Ealing Studios produced its famous comedies on the edge of Walpole Park. Sure, the area has its share of tower blocks and housing estates – most notably around Argyle Road – but Ealing is overwhelmingly upper middle class, and it shows. The district is ultra-suburban, with tree-lined avenues full of independent faith schools and stately detached homes with gravel drives.

From a resident's perspective, the main attractions (apart from the houses) are the schools and transport links. Ealing is packed with primary and secondary schools – mostly of the private, opted-out variety. Commuters have a choice of half a dozen train and tube stations, while the A40 and M4 provide easy access to Heathrow and the South-west.

There are numerous parks and sporting clubs too. Lammas Park is a large green lung, complete with playground and tennis courts. Walpole Park near the Broadway is child-friendly and hosts jazz and comedy festivals in summer. Right opposite, well-known Questors Theatre is an Ealing gem: a great venue for children and adults to get involved in the performing arts.

Ealing Green rivals Chiswick in terms of genteel affluence; the most extravagant houses are north of the Broadway towards Hanger Hill. The so-called Pitshanger Village area near the park of the same name boasts a villagey feel and a parade full of independent shops.

The main civic centre is on Ealing Broadway; the streets around the tube station are packed with banks, cafés, restaurants, chain pubs and shops. A new mixed-use development designed by Norman Foster's firm is planned between the Arcadia Centre and Haven Green; residents have been up in arms about it, but it looks like it's going ahead. There were also protests about the proposed West London Tram scheme along Uxbridge Road, which locals feared would displace

STATISTICS

BOROUGH MAKE-UP
Population 306,400
Average weekly pay £507
Ethnic origins
  White 58.88%
  Mixed 3.86%
  Asian or Asian British 23.29%
  Black or Black British 8.70%
  Chinese or other 5.23%
Students 9.49%
Retirees 9.11%

HOUSING STOCK
Borough size 55km^2
No. of households 122,000
Detached 4.4%
Semi-detached 23.5%
Terraced 29.6%
Flats (purpose-built) 28.2%
Flats (converted) 13.5%
Flats (both) 41.7%

CRIME PER 1,000 OF POPULATION
(average for England and Wales in brackets)
Burglary 9 (5)
Robbery 8 (2)
Theft of vehicle 6 (4)
Theft from vehicle 16 (9)
Violence against the person 25 (19)
Sexual offences 1 (1)

MPs & COUNCIL
MPs *Ealing, Acton & Shepherd's Bush*
Andrew Slaughter (Labour); *Ealing, Southall* Piara S Khabra (Labour)
CPA 3 stars; improving well

yet more traffic on to car-clogged residential avenues (the scheme has been abandoned in favour of Crossrail, which, at least, will be a long time coming).

Ealing has also been given a new lease of life by recent immigration from eastern Europe. As you can see from the delis and Polish-language signs in shops, the Polish community has long had a foothold in Ealing – ever since World War II, in fact, when Polish aircrew were based at nearby RAF Northolt.

Things get more residential as you head south, but South Ealing is still well-to-do. Houses may be mock-Tudor, but they're huge, and there are plenty of shops and restaurants along Ealing South Road. The grand housing extends to the streets around

Ealing

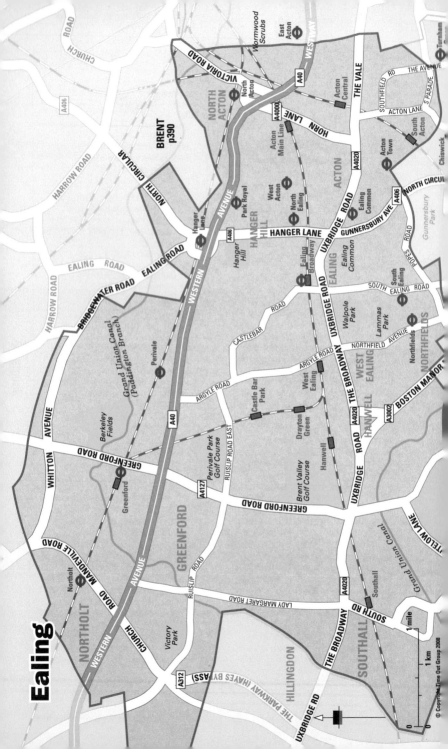

Ealing Common. This popular open space is divided in two by train tracks, but from here it's only a short stroll south to huge Gunnersbury Park (over the borough border in Hounslow). By contrast, Argyle Road in the north-west is dominated by retirement villages and uninspiring planned housing.

Greenford and Perivale

Greenford is a somewhat overlooked suburb sliced in half by the thundering A40, on either side of the art deco Hoover Building. Residents wanting to be near the shops and private schools of Ealing generally prefer West Ealing and Hanwell, where the property is similar; in Greenford, winding streets of mainly 1930s semis surround a down-at-heel town centre (the council is promising to 'revitalise' it). Greenford's 'other' town centre and residential area, north of the A40, is posher. The place feels like a backwater, though you wouldn't want to hang around on a street corner here at night: too many 'yoofs'. No single ethnicity dominates, though there are large Polish and Indian communities in the area.

Bonuses include Ravenor Park and Perivale Park. It's also blessed with low property prices and good transport links. But there's not much in the way of restaurants or nightlife. The area's best secret is that crossing the Grand Union Canal leads to Horsenden Hill, which has been compared to Hampstead Heath and feels like open countryside.

Perivale is a kind of satellite to Greenford, an out-of-the-way place that doesn't possess what you could call a proper town centre. But it's right next door to a Tesco superstore, the Westway shopping complex, and is even closer than Greenford to the Grand Union and Horsenden Hill.

Hanwell, Northfields and West Ealing

Bounded by Northfield Avenue and Boston Road, Hanwell is the poorer cousin of Ealing. As you travel west along the Uxbridge Road, from West Ealing to Hanwell to Southall, the area declines in status. Drayton Manor, a much-sought-after secondary school, is here, but it's all a bit grotty. Uxbridge Road cuts through the middle, providing the usual high-street amenities and a Rolls-Royce garage.

TRANSPORT

Tube stations *Central* East Acton, North Acton, West Acton, Ealing Broadway, Hanger Lane, Perivale, Greenford, Northolt; *District* Turnham Green, Chiswick Park, Acton Town, Ealing Common, Ealing Broadway; *Piccadilly* Acton Town, Ealing Common, North Ealing, Park Royal, South Ealing, Northfields, Boston Manor
Rail stations *First Great Western* Acton Main Line, Ealing Broadway, West Ealing, Hanwell, Southall, Drayton Green, Castle Bar Park, South Greenford, Greenford; *London Overground* Acton Central, South Acton
Main bus routes *into central London* 7, 70, 94; *night buses* N7, N11, N207; *24-hour buses* 94

Hanwell and Northfields (the next district south) both score highly for green open spaces; there are recreation grounds and sporting clubs galore. Uxbridge Road passes between the vast Kensington and City of Westminster cemeteries, final resting place for many of west London's wealthiest residents. For golfers, it's a short putt to the courses of Osterley Park and the Brent Valley. Brent Lodge Animal Centre in Hanwell is a small zoo, endearingly known locally as 'Bunny Park'.

The most appealing streets are east of Northfield Avenue in West Ealing. There are some huge detached houses here, notably around Lammas Park, while the south end of Northfield Avenue boasts an array of restaurants. For travelling to central London, there are tube stops at Boston Manor and Northfields, overland train stations at Hanwell and West Ealing, and the congested M4.

Southall

Southall is a residential area with a large south Asian population, originally due to its proximity to Heathrow (many Punjabis arrived as a source of cheap labour for the airport). The Commission for Racial Equality estimates that 55 per cent of residents are Indian/Pakistani, and there is also a large Somali community. The Punjabi population is sizeable, hence the Sri Guru Singh Sabha Southall, the largest Sikh temple outside India, the golden dome of which can be seen for miles.

Ealing

For a taste of the Punjab, visit Southall's lively street market.

As arguably a kind of capital for the UK's Indian community, Southall boasts a vibrant subculture: it has its own radio station, and is home territory to a number of writers, musicians and film directors, including Gurinder Chadha, director of *Bend it Like Beckham* (which was filmed locally) and playwright Kwame Kwei-Armah. The Chinese-style Himalaya Palace cinema (built 1929) caters for lovers of all things Bollywood, while the Glassy Junction, which was used as a location in the film *Dhan Dhana Dhan Goal*, was the first pub in Britain to accept rupees.

The Broadway running through the centre of Southall is a boisterous slice of the subcontinent. From wedding caterers to sari shops, wholesale grocers to pavement snack stalls, there's little you can't get here. There are also lots of restaurants, mainly Punjabi; even the McDonald's advertises itself as halal. The Broadway boasts a lively market, although its famous Wednesday horse auction (and Tuesday livestock market) finally closed in 2007 after 300 years of trading.

Restaurants & cafés

The highest concentration of restaurants is in Ealing, reflecting the division of disposable income in the borough. As well as the familiar list of chain options on and around the Broadway (Nando's, Carluccio's, Bella Italia), independent eateries covering a wide ethnic spread are thrown into the mix. Friendly Café Grove serves Polish specialities, while, to the south, the Ealing

Park Tavern is a huge and very popular gastropub with a great back garden. Café Chai serves excellent ice-cream and crêpes, and Joie de Vivre is a Mediterranean-style gaff that's both relaxed and romantic.

Southall is also a hub for gourmands, with numerous Indian restaurants and cafés. Notables include the New Asian Tandoori Centre (also known as Roxy's) and Madhu's; Giftos specialises in Karahi cuisine, while Moti Mahal is an all-rounder. Heading towards Acton, Sushi-Hiro may not look like much, but the sushi is swimmingly fresh. There's also accomplished Caribbean restaurant BB's.

Acton has a tiny but authentic Sichuan restaurant, Polish specialist Bohemia and a couple of pubs serving above-average fare on budding hotspot Churchfield Road, including the Rocket gastropub.

BB's *3 Chignell Place, off Uxbridge Road, W13 0TJ (8840 8322/www.bbscrabback.co.uk).*
Bohemia *265 High Street, W3 9BY (8993 5802).*
Café Chai *34 The Broadway, W5 2NP (8579 3696).*
Café Grove *65 The Grove, W5 5LL (8810 0364).*
Ealing Park Tavern *222 South Ealing Road, W5 4RL (8758 1879).*
Giftos Lahore Karahi *162 The Broadway, UB1 1NN (0871 971 6812).*
Joie de Vivre *12 St Mary's Road, W5 5ES (0871 971 7456).*
Madhu's *39 South Road, UB1 1SW (8574 1897/www.madhusonline.com).*
Moti Mahal *94 The Broadway, UB1 1QF (8574 7682/www.motimahal.co.uk).*
New Asian Tandoori Centre *114-118 The Green, UB2 4BQ (8574 2597).*

Rocket *11-13 Churchfield Road, W3 6BD*
(8993 6123/www.therocketw3.co.uk).
Sichuan Restaurant *116 Churchfield Road,*
W3 6BY (8992 9473).
Sushi-Hiro *1 Station Parade, Uxbridge Road,*
W5 3LD (8896 3175).

Bars & pubs

Ealing is not the best neighbourhood for a
pub crawl, but there are a handful of good
drinking holes. The area's oldest and most
attractive pubs tend to be found in South
Ealing – in the vicinity of St Mary's Road,
where the original Ealing village developed.
Thames Valley University is nearby, which
means that the pubs, for better or worse,
are often full of students. The cosy Red Lion
is a stone's throw from Ealing Film Studios;
a little further south is gastropub Ealing
Park Tavern (*see p322*).

The Broadway, with its chain shops,
coffee bars and fast-food joints, boasts the
usual names, All Bar One, Hog's Head and
O'Neills included. The North Star is a small
gem, while cocktail-lovers will enjoy the
sassy and good-humoured Baroque bar.
Further north, past West Ealing station,
is Drayton Court, where punters can relax
in the lounge area or landscaped garden,
or get rowdy in the sports bar.

Acton's contribution to the pub scene is,
at best, modest. The best pickings are to be
found near the Uxbridge Road/High Street
and adjoining Steyne Road, which offer a

slew of chain bars and pubs. A couple of
boozers on Churchfield Road have been
done up, including the Rocket (*see above*).
The Grand Junction Arms is an unexpected
find in an unpromising industrial area,
with seasonal ales and a large beer garden
overlooking the Grand Union Canal.

Unsurprisingly, neither Southall nor
Greenford contribute much to the drinking
scene. A decent pub away from the usual
spots is the Plough in Northfields, a friendly
local with reasonable food.

Baroque *94 Uxbridge Road, W13 8RA*
(8567 7346/www.baroque-ealing.co.uk).
Drayton Court *2 The Avenue, W13 8PH*
(8997 1019).
Grand Junction Arms *Canal Bridge, Acton*
Lane, NW10 7AD (8965 5670).
North Star *43 The Broadway, W5 5JN*
(8579 0863).
Plough *297 Northfields Avenue, W5 4XB*
(8567 1416).
Red Lion *13 St Mary's Road, W5 5RA*
(8567 2541).
Red Lion & Pineapple *281 High Street,*
W3 9PJ (8896 2248).

Shops

Although it's not an area you would travel
to for an afternoon's browse, Ealing has
sufficient retail resources for local needs.
Ealing Broadway is the borough's
undisputed shopping hub, site of the
Ealing Broadway Centre and smaller
Arcadia Centre, which contain a wide
array of chains (HMV, Morrisons, M&S,
Monsoon and TK Maxx, to name a few),
interspersed with smaller units. Outside,
there's Polish deli Parade and organic
food store As Nature Intended, alongside
various other independents – it's worth
exploring the streets around the back and
sides of the Broadway Centre.

Elsewhere, Stuff Boutique offers
women's clothes, while the Pitshanger
Village parade offers a choice of
independents, including the Pitshanger
Bookshop. A bus ride east towards
Hanwell is the well-established Ealing
Farmers' Market (9am-1pm Saturday).

Choice is rather more limited in Acton,
with a basic, chain-dominated high street
– although Churchfield Road is showing
early signs of a more interesting scene. The
Vintage Home Shop, whose owner also runs
a clothing emporium in Portobello Road,

Ealing

is well worth a look, as is contemporary florist Heart & Soul. Southall is strictly for those wanting an Indian-style shopping experience (think saris, henna and bangles), including the Ambala Sweet Centre. Greenford offers a Tesco superstore.

Ambala Sweet Centre *107 The Broadway, UB1 1LN (8843 9049/www.ambalafoods.com).*
Arcadia Centre *1-8 The Broadway, W5 2NH (8567 0854).*
As Nature Intended *17-21 High Street, W5 5DB (8840 1404/www.asnatureintended.uk.com).*
Ealing Broadway Centre *101 The Broadway, W5 5JY (8567 3453/www.ealingbroadway shopping.co.uk).*
Ealing Farmers' Market *Leeland Road, W13 (7833 0338/www.lfm.org.uk).*
Heart & Soul *73 Churchfield Road, W3 6AX (8896 3331/www.heart-n-soul.co.uk).*
Parade Delicatessen *8 Central Buildings, The Broadway, W5 2NT (8567 9066).*
Pitshanger Bookshop *141 Pitshanger Lane, W5 1RH (8991 8131/www.pitshanger books.co.uk).*
Stuff Boutique *7 The Green, W5 5DA (8567 1385).*
Vintage Home Store *105 Churchfield Road, W3 6AH (8993 4162).*

Arts & attractions

Cinemas & theatres

Empire Ealing *59-61 Uxbridge Road, New Broadway, W5 5AH (0871 471 4714/ www.empirecinemas.co.uk).*
Himalaya Palace *14 South Road, UB1 3RT (8813 8844/www.himalayapalacecinema.co.uk).* Grade II-listed art deco cinema designed by George Coles, showing Bollywood films.
Questors Theatre *12 Mattock Lane, W5 5BQ (8567 0011/www.questors.org.uk).* The largest local community theatre in Europe, presenting around 20 shows a year.
Vue Acton *Royale Leisure Park, Western Avenue, W3 0PA (0871 224 0240/www.myvue.co.uk).*

Galleries & museums

PM Gallery & House *Mattock Lane, W5 5EQ (8567 1227/www.ealing.gov.uk).* This grand manor house in Walpole Park, designed by John Soane in 1800, is west London's largest contemporary arts venue.

Sport & fitness

There is a broad choice of public leisure centres and plenty of private options, including three of the big-name chains – but if you really want to push the boat out, try the Park Club, a posh country club in the middle of Acton.

COUNCIL TAX

A	up to £40,000	**£896.07**
B	£40,001-£52,000	**£1,045.41**
C	£52,001-£68,000	**£1,194.76**
D	£68,001-£88,000	**£1,344.10**
E	£88,001-£120,000	**£1,642.79**
F	£120,001-£160,000	**£1,941.48**
G	£160,001-£320,000	**£2,240.17**
H	over £320,000	**£2,688.20**

RECYCLING

No. of bring sites 50 (for nearest, visit www.recycleforlondon.com)
Household waste recycled 15.36%
Main recycling centre Acton Reuse & Recycling Centre, Stirling Road, off Bollo Lane, W3 3DJ (8993 7580)
Other recycling services green waste, kitchen waste and plastics collections; home composting; white goods and furniture collection
Council contact Environmental Services, Winchester Room, Acton Town Hall, Winchester Street, W3 6NE (8825 6000)

Gyms & leisure centres

Acton Swimming Baths *Salisbury Street, W3 8NW (8992 8877/www.gll.org).*
David Lloyd *Greenford Road, UB6 0HX (8422 7777/www.davidlloydleisure.co.uk).* Private.
Dormers Wells Leisure Centre *Dormers Wells Lane, UB1 3HX (8571 7207/ www.gll.org).*
LA Fitness *Rowdell Road, UB5 6AG (8841 5611/www.lafitness.co.uk).* Private.
Elthorne Sports Centre *Westlea Road, off Boston Road, W7 2AD (8579 3226/ www.ealing.gov.uk).*
Featherstone Sports Centre *11 Montague Waye, UB2 5HF (8813 9886/www.featherstone-sportscentre.co.uk).*
Fitness First *The Oaks Shopping Centre, High Street, W3 6RD (8993 0364/www.fitness first.co.uk).* Private.
Greenford Sports Centre *Ruislip Road, UB6 9RX (8575 9157/www.ealing.gov.uk).*
Gurnell Leisure Centre *Ruislip Road East, W13 0AL (8998 3241/www.gll.org).*
Northolt Swimarama *Eastcote Lane North, UB5 4AB (8422 1176/www.gll.org).*
The Park Club *East Acton Lane, W3 7HB (8743 4321/www.theparkclub.co.uk).* Private.
Twyford Sports Centre *Twyford Crescent, W3 9PP (8993 9095/www.ealing.gov.uk).*
Virgin Active *5th floor, Ealing Broadway Centre, Town Square, W5 5JY (8579 9433/ www.virginactive.co.uk).* Private.

Schools

WHAT THE PARENTS SAY:

❝Drayton Manor is one of the country's best comprehensives. But its catchment area is shrinking all the time. Ealing is very good at coping with all the newly arrived kids. It has to be: this is one of the most ethnically mixed areas in Britain, with a shifting population. Ealing is also especially strong on music education.❞
Mother of three, South Ealing

Primary

There are 61 state primary schools in Ealing, including 12 church schools. There are also 13 independent primaries. See www.ealing.gov.uk, www.edubase.gov.uk and www.ofsted.gov.uk for more information.

Secondary

Acton High School Gunnersbury Lane, W3 8EY (3110 2400).
Brentside High School Greenford Avenue, W7 1JJ (8575 9162/www.brentsidehigh.ealing.sch.uk).
Cardinal Wiseman RC School Greenford Road, UB6 9AW (8575 8222/www.wiseman.ealing.sch.uk).
Dormers Wells High School Dormers Wells Lane, UB1 3HZ (8813 8671/www.dormers-wells.ealing.sch.uk).
Drayton Manor High School Drayton Bridge Road, W7 1EU (8357 1900/www.draytonmanor.ealing.sch.uk).
Ellen Wilkinson School for Girls Queen's Drive, W3 0HW (8752 1525/www.ellen-wilkinson-school.co.uk). Girls only.
Elthorne Park High School Westlea Road, W7 2AH (8566 1166/www.ephs.ealing.sch.uk).
Featherstone High School 11 Montague Waye, UB2 5HF (8843 0984/www.featherstonehigh.ealing.sch.uk).
Greenford High School Ruislip Road, UB6 9RX (8578 9152/www.greenford.ealing.sch.uk).
Northolt High School Eastcote Lane, UB5 4HP (8864 8544/www.northolthigh.org.uk).
Twyford CE High School Twyford Crescent, W3 9PP (8752 0141/www.twyford.ealing.sch.uk).
Villiers High School Boyd Avenue, UB1 3BT (8813 8001/www.villiers.ealing.sch.uk).
West London Academy Compton Crescent, UB5 5LQ (8841 4511/www.westlondonacademy.co.uk).

Property

WHAT THE AGENTS SAY:

❝I've lived and worked in Acton for about 25 years, and it's basically been the Cinderella surrounded by the ugly sisters of Ealing and Chiswick. But there's been a renaissance since the mid 1990s, with the schools improving year on year. The High Street is slowly getting better – more shops, cafés, bars – and more money is coming into the area. Generally, there's a movement west; for a terraced house in Chiswick you can get a semi here, with a large garden and an extra bedroom. And people in Acton don't walk around with their nose up their arse like in Chiswick and Fulham.❞
Phillip Harrison, Robertson Smith & Kempson, Acton

Average property prices

Detached £857,924
Semi-detached £411,096
Terraced £343,186
Flat £243,492

Local estate agents

Adams www.adamsproperty.co.uk; 2 offices in the borough (Ealing 8566 3738/Hanwell 8579 8070).
Churchill 18 Old Oak Common Lane, W3 7EL (8749 9798/www.churchillestateagents.co.uk).
Goodman Estate Agents 12 Market Place, W3 6QS (8993 0566/www.goodmanestates.co.uk).
Robertson Smith & Kempson www.rskhomes.co.uk; 4 offices in the borough (Acton 8896 3996/Ealing Broadway 8840 7677/7885/Hanway 8566 2339/Northfields 8566 2340).
Sinton Andrews www.sintonandrews.co.uk; 3 offices in the borough (Ealing 8566 1990/Hanwell 8567 3219/Northfields 8840 5151).

Other information

Council

Ealing Council Perceval House, 14-16 Uxbridge Road, W5 2HL (8825 5000/www.ealing.gov.uk).

Legal services

Ealing Legal Centre Church Avenue, UB2 4DF (8574 2434).
Law for All 191 The Vale, W3 7QS (8758 0668/www.lawforall.org.uk).
Southall Rights 54 High Street, UB1 3DB (8571 4920).

Local newspapers

Ealing Gazette/Ealing Informer 8579 3131/www.icealing.co.uk.
Ealing Times 01494 755000/www.ealingtimes.co.uk.

Allotments

Council Allotments www.ealing.gov.uk.
Ealing & Hanwell Allotment Association Nigel Sumner, Secretary, 66 Chatworth Gardens, W3 9LW.
Open spaces www.ealing.gov.uk/parks.

Hounslow

Leafy Chiswick has long been a favourite of affluent, middle-class families, but development in up-and-coming Brentford and culturally diverse Hounslow is bringing a new lease of life to the western reaches of the borough. Thames views are another local joy – if you're after a riverside pint there are few better places in London in which to sink one.

Neighbourhoods

Chiswick

This swanky part of west London offers easy access to the city centre alongside a tranquil, suburban feel. Two main thoroughfares divide Chiswick from west to east: bustling Chiswick High Road (A315), the main shopping hotspot, and the imposing, six-lane A4 (Great West Road), which runs through to Brentford, Isleworth and Hounslow in one direction and joins the M4. At the west of the A4 is Chiswick Roundabout, flanked by car dealerships and usually gridlocked. Some of the area's most affordable property is nearby. Chiswick Village, a collection of attractive 1930s flats, is popular and has a good sense of community – the residents' society is currently fighting proposals to build penthouses on top of the buildings.

Highs & Lows

▲ **Riverside locations** Chiswick, Brentford and Isleworth all have fine stretches next to the Thames, with beautiful views
Dining out Chiswick's eating options are numerous and high quality, while Brentford has a burgeoning restaurant scene

Flight path Hounslow proper is blighted by Heathrow noise. The opening of Terminal Five in 2008 means things can only get worse
Ugly commercial areas Brentford and Hounslow High Streets lack character and are in desperate need of a revamp ▼

The east side of the A4, meanwhile, is anchored by Hogarth Roundabout, named after 18th-century artist and satirist William Hogarth, who lived nearby (his house is open to the public). Also next to the roundabout is Fuller's, London's oldest (and now only) brewery.

Lined with upmarket shops, landmark restaurants and Parisian-style pavement cafés, Chiswick High Road is bustling by day and night. The traffic of sports cars, 4x4s and all-terrain buggies is testament to the predominance of wealthy, middle-class families. At the west end of the road is Chiswick Business Park, a glassy, high-tech, tree-lined office complex designed by Richard Rogers on the site of the old Gunnersbury bus depot, complete with its own pond and waterfall. Nearby is a triangular-shaped green space, confusingly called Turnham Green (Chiswick Common, meanwhile, can be found next to Turnham Green tube station). North of here – and just over the borough border in Ealing – is 19th-century Bedford Park, London's first garden suburb and still an exclusive area.

It's the southern half of Chiswick that is most sought after, however, with notable riverside stretches at Chiswick Mall – whose spectacular Georgian residences have mini-gardens across the road next to the Thames, facing Chiswick Eyot – and Strand-on-the-Green, whose waterside pubs are popular with walkers and cyclists heading along the Thames Path. Tiny Church Street is full of architectural gems, while Corney Reach, just to the south, is a more modern residential complex.

Also in great demand is the Grove Park area. Huge houses from all eras squat on a network of wide, tree-lined streets, with a smattering of shops around Chiswick rail station to break the residential norm.

Great Conservatory, **Syon House**.

Sutton Court Mansions on Fauconberg Road is popular with renters. To the south lies Dukes Meadows – largely inaccessible to the public unless you have an allotment, belong to the health club or can use the Civil Service sports fields – and beyond that Chiswick and Barnes Bridges. Elegant 18th-century Chiswick House, with its stunning grounds, is another local treasure.

Brentford

Though still very much playing catch-up with its more affluent W4 neighbour, Brentford has undergone significant redevelopment in the last five years. There's certainly plenty of potential: a riverside location, a 20-minute train ride to Waterloo, a strong community spirit and, the clincher, affordable housing. The most popular of several new schemes in Old Brentford (south of the A4) is Ferry Quays, located bang next to the Thames and containing assorted restaurants and Brentford's one and only nightclub (Copacabana) as well as swanky apartments. There are also some impressive canalside developments: the Island is an expensive gated community; Heron View is somewhat more affordable. Housing elsewhere consists mainly of Victorian two- and three-bed terraces. There are also two sizeable council estates.

Brentford has strong appeal for families, downsizers and young professionals wanting a foot on the property ladder. It also offers decent amenities. While Chiswick lacks a theatre and cinema, Brentford has both in the shape of the trusty riverside Watermans Centre, which offers everything from comedy to panto.

Other attractions include Kew Gardens (across the Thames, in the borough of Richmond) and spacious Syon Park. Then there's retro football stadium Griffin Park, home of Brentford FC, the Kew Bridge Steam Museum and the recently relocated Musical Museum.

Isleworth and Osterley

Isleworth and Osterley, separated by the thundering Great West Road, are largely residential, with lots of large 1930s homes – both areas are popular with families who find the prices in Chiswick too steep. New developments under way include the College Road site (previously a Brunel University campus) that is being turned into a luxury housing complex by mid 2008.

Isleworth's main shopping parade is on London Road, though it's not much to shout about: a few restaurants, a Spar, betting shops and takeaways – plus a new apartment complex, right next to Isleworth rail station, which links to Waterloo.

Osterley, home to gorgeous Osterley House and Park, is quieter than Isleworth and has a low-key, villagey feel. The nicest part of the area, however, is riverside Old Isleworth, where the landscape is dominated by the small Thames island of Isleworth Ait. The Ait opens once a year, offering visitors the opportunity to see rare wildlife in its natural habitat. Situated between Brentford and Isleworth is another local attraction, lion-topped Syon House.

Hounslow

If excellent transport links are high on your list of priorities, you'll find escape routes galore in Hounslow. Unfortunately, you may well feel the need to use them. What this area lacks in glamour, peace (the constant roar of planes overhead is an issue) and des res addresses, it makes up for in proximity to Heathrow and easy access to central London. Other pluses include cheap houses and a large Asian population that makes this the borough's most diverse corner.

The pedestrianised High Street is run-down, though a public consultation about the future of the town centre is on the agenda. Hints of regeneration are appearing, such as the Blenheim Centre, a huge glass shopping complex with luxury

Hounslow

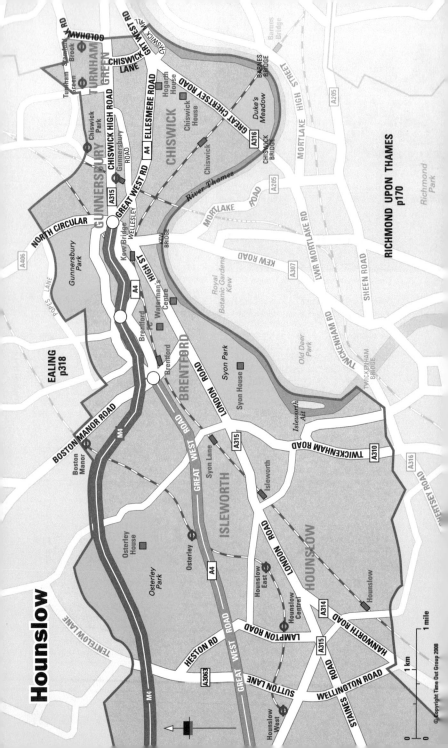

flats. In general, housing stock is not hugely exciting: 1930s and '60s semis and '80s flats. Green spaces include Hounslow Heath and Hounslow Urban Farm, one of the capital's largest community farms.

Restaurants & cafés

You're spoilt for choice when it comes to eating out in Chiswick. Family-friendly chains (ASK, Pizza Express, Nando's, Giraffe, Gourmet Burger Kitchen) abound on the High Road, alongside the likes of brasserie Balans, posh burger newcomer Ground and the High Road Brasserie (part of the High Road House hotel and members' club). Coffee chains are rife, but there's variety in the mix too, including photo-gallery-cum-café Classic Image and a branch of café/pâtisserie Maison Blanc.

Gordon Ramsay opened his second gastropub, the Devonshire, here in 2007, to compete with the Roebuck and the Pilot. Other new arrivals include Carvosso's at 210, where you can dine in the cells of the old police station it replaced; upmarket fish and chip restaurant the Catch; and, towards Gunnersbury, British restaurant Napa.

Still going strong are local favourites Frankie's (the brainchild of jockey Frankie Dettori and chef Marco Pierre White), swish Modern European restaurant Sam's, and Southwestern specialist Coyote. There's also fish specialist Fish Hook and a branch of the FishWorks chain. Chiswickians also have the choice of two of London's best French restaurants: the near-perfect La Trompette (part of the mini-empire of Nigel Platts-Martin and Bruce Poole) and revamped classic bistro Le Vacherin. Asian food is less well represented, with Boys (Thai/Malaysian) and Woodlands (South Indian vegetarian) the only notables. Tiffin Box is a good Indian takeaway.

The dining scene in Brentford is definitely on the up. The Ferry Quays development is host to three good outlets: Pappadums (Indian), San Marco (Italian) and Glistening Waters (Caribbean). The High Street itself has little to offer, though Italian La Rosetta is popular.

The number of restaurants starts to thin out as you delve further into the borough. Cheap and authentic Indian restaurant Dhaba (unlicensed, but you can BYO) and Le Bistro (Italian) are the standouts in

Isleworth. Slightly more upmarket is Memories of India in Osterley, also home to the much-loved Greedies (organic greasy spoon, café and deli). Hounslow is dominated by big-name chain restaurants and fast-food joints, including Pizza Hut, Nando's and, amusingly, a copycat rival Frangos – the Hounslow branch is halal. There are also plenty of Indian restaurants: the New Heathrow Tandoori has been voted the best of the bunch by the *Hounslow Guardian* for two years running.

Balans *214 Chiswick High Road, W4 1PD* *(8742 1435/www.balans.co.uk).*
Le Bistro *461 London Road, TW7 4BX* *(8568 0504).*
Boys *95 Chiswick High Road, W4 2EF* *(8995 7991).*
Carvosso's at 210 *210 Chiswick High Road, W4 1PD (8995 9121/www.carvossosat210.co.uk).*

The Catch *293 Chiswick High Road, W4 4HH*
(8747 9358).
Classic Image Café Gallery *15 Devonshire*
Road, W4 2EU (8995 9977).
Coyote *2 Fauconberg Road, W4 3JY*
(8742 8545/www.thecoyote.co.uk).
Devonshire *126 Devonshire Road, W4 2JJ*
(7592 7962/www.gordonramsay.com).
Dhaba *481 London Road, TW7 4BX*
(8568 5959).
Fish Hook *6-8 Elliott Road, W4 1PE*
(8742 0766).
FishWorks *6 Turnham Green Terrace,*
W4 1QP (8994 0086/www.fishworks.co.uk).
Frangos *55-67 Hounslow High Street, TW3*
1RB (8538 7779/www.frangosrestaurants.com).
Frankie's *66-68 Chiswick High Road, W4 1SY*
(8987 9988/www.frankiesitalianbarandgrill.com).
Glistening Waters *5 Ferry Lane, Ferry Quays,*
High Street, TW8 0AT (8758 1616).
Greedies *49 South Street, TW7 7AA*
(8560 8562).
Ground *217-221 Chiswick High Road, W4 2DW*
(8747 9113/www.groundrestaurants.com).
High Road Brasserie *162-166 Chiswick High*
Road, W4 1PR (8742 7474).
Memories of India *160-162 Thornbury Road,*
TW7 4QE (8758 1280).
Napa *Chiswick Moran Hotel, 626 Chiswick High*
Road, W4 5RY (8996 5200/www.chiswickhotel
london.co.uk).
New Heathrow Tandoori *482 Great West*
Road, TW5 0TA (8572 1772/8577 2145/
www.newheathrowtandoori.com).
Pappadums *Ferry Quays, Ferry Lane, TW8*
0BT (8847 1123/www.pappadums.co.uk).
Pilot *56 Wellesley Road, W4 4BZ (8994 0828).*
Roebuck *122 Chiswick High Road, W4 1PU*
(8995 4392).
La Rosetta *201 High Street, TW8 8AH*
(8560 3002).

Sam's Brasserie & Bar *11 Barley Mow*
Passage, W4 4PH (8987 0555/www.sams
brasserie.co.uk).
San Marco *5 Ferry Lane, Ferry Quays, TW8*
0AT (8569 9777/www.sanmarcoonthames.co.uk).
Tiffin Box *115 Chiswick High Road, W4 2ED*
(8747 3545).
La Trompette *5-7 Devonshire Road, W4 2EU*
(8747 1836/www.latrompette.co.uk).
Le Vacherin *76-77 South Parade, W4 5LF*
(8742 2121/www.levacherin.co.uk).
Woodlands *12-14 Chiswick High Road,*
W4 1TH (8994 9333/www.woodlands
restaurant.co.uk).

Bars & pubs

There's no excuse for wasting your time
on a below-par pint in Chiswick. The
proximity of the Fuller's brewery means
plenty of exemplary pubs, though barflies
are not quite as well catered for. Located on
riverside Strand-on-the-Green are the Bell
& Crown and the City Barge: both are child-
friendly, with decent pub grub, waterside
terraces and Fuller's ales. Also here is the
Bull's Head opposite Oliver's Island.

Chiswick High Road has plenty of options.
The George IV has the Headliners Comedy
Club, while the Packhorse & Talbot draws
a younger crowd. The Old Pack Horse (open
fires, leather sofas, Thai restaurant) is
one of the best, but for a pint of Chiswick
Bitter within barrel-rolling distance of the
brewery, head for the Mawson Arms, which
is also the start of the brewery tour. The
Bollo House has a good quiz night on
Wednesdays, while the Tabard has a tiny
(recently renovated) theatre above it.

In Brentford try excellent cocktail bar
the Old Fire Station or the Weir gastropub,
with its waterside garden. The Lord Nelson
in north Brentford is a cosy choice, while
Captain Morgan's river location means it's
always packed in summer.

Old Isleworth also has some fabulous
places to drink. The London Apprentice,
just outside Syon Park, opposite Isleworth
Ait, was once a favourite of Charles Dickens
– now it's a fine place to enjoy a drink by the
river in summer. Moving into new Isleworth
and Osterley, there's Young's pub the Coach
& Horses and the quaint Hare & Hounds.
Also of note is the Red Lion: it offers up to
nine real ales at any one time, as well as
live music, quiz nights and beer festivals.

Bell & Crown *11 13 Thames Road, Strand-*
on-the-Green, W4 3PL (8994 4164).

LOCALS' TIPS

Well-heeled residents mean Chiswick's
charity shops are real treasure troves.
The Cancer Research shop on the High
Road, opposite Turnham Green Church,
is great for vintage and designer stuff,
while the Oxfam shop on Turnham
Green Terrace is a winner for books.
**Going to central London and can't face
the grind of the tube? Hop on the 94
bus at Bath Road, by Turnham Green
station. On a good day this 24-hour
double-decker will get you to Oxford
Street in just over half an hour.**
If you're put off by Chiswick's sky-high
prices, investigate Brentford: a two-bed
house here might set you back
£300,000; metres away in Chiswick
you'd pay in excess of £700,000.

Bollo House *13-15 Bollo Lane, W4 5LR*
(8994 6037/www.thebollohouse.co.uk).
Bull's Head *15 Strand-on-the-Green, W4 3PQ*
(8994 1204).
Captain Morgan's *3 High Street, TW8 0DX*
(8560 5543).
City Barge *27 Strand-on-the-Green, W4 3PH*
(8994 2148).
Coach & Horses *183 London Road, TW7*
5BQ (8560 1447).
George IV *185 Chiswick High Road, W4 2DR*
(8994 4624/www.georgeiv.co.uk).
Hare & Hounds *Windmill Lane, Wyke Green,*
TW7 5PR (8560 5438).
London Apprentice *62 Church Street, TW7*
6BG (8560 1915).
Lord Nelson *9-11 Enfield Road, TW8 9NY*
(8568 1877).
Mawson Arms *110 Chiswick Lane South,*
W4 2QA (8994 2936).
Old Fire Station *55 High Street, TW8 0AH*
(8568 5999/www.the-firestation.co.uk).
Old Pack Horse *434 Chiswick High Road,*
W4 5TF (8994 2872).
Packhorse & Talbot *145 Chiswick High Road,*
W4 2DT (8994 0360).
Red Lion *92-94 Linkfield Road, TW7 6QJ*
(8560 1457).
Tabard *2 Bath Road, W4 1LW (8994 3492).*
Weir *22-24 Market Place, TW8 8EQ*
(8568 3600/www.theweirbar.co.uk).

Shops

Chiswick's retail action is predominantly
located on or near Chiswick High Road.
Devonshire Street and Turnham Green
Terrace – facing each other on opposite
sides of the High Road – also have notable
clusters of shops.

Matters domestic hold sway here, so
there's an abundance of interiors chains
(Cath Kidston has also opened a store here),
while the Old Cinema offers three floors
of antiques. Foodies are well catered for,
with a brace of fish shops (Covent Garden
Fishmongers and the wet fish counter at
FishWorks restaurant, *see p330*); lovely
continental deli Mortimer & Bennett;
Theobroma Cacao, one of London's best
chocolatiers; the Natural Food Store and
organic supermarket As Nature Intended.
One of the most exciting newcomers is
ecological destination store Eco, opened
in early 2008 and owned by local resident
Colin Firth.

Reproducing is a popular Chiswick
pastime and local tots are a well-dressed
lot, thanks to branches of JoJo Maman
Bébé and Petit Bateau, as well as one-offs
Shoe Tree and the Little Trading Company

TRANSPORT
Tube stations *District* Stamford
Brook, Turnham Green, Chiswick Park,
Gunnersbury; *Piccadilly* Boston Manor,
Osterley, Hounslow East, Hounslow
Central, Hounslow West
Rail stations *London Overground*
Gunnersbury; *South West Trains*
Barnes Bridge, Chiswick, Kew Bridge,
Brentford, Syon Lane, Isleworth,
Hounslow, Feltham
Main bus routes *into central London*
27, 94; *night buses* N9, N11;
24-hour buses 27, 94
River leisure boat services to/from
central London and Kew Pier

(second-hand). For adult clothing, women
fare much better than men, with various
upmarket chains (Sweaty Betty, Whistles)
and independent women's clothing and
jewellery shop Blink. Locals are also lucky
to have London's only Jurlique Day Spa on
their doorstep. Chiswick Farmers' Market is
held on Dukes Meadows on Sundays, and
the Chiswick Community School car boot
sale is popular (first Sunday of the month).

On Brentford High Street (A315) there's
excellent vintage clothing shop Butterfly
Girl and arty furniture shop Naked Grain.
Developers have their sights set on the
south side of the street – watch this space.
In Osterley there's the excellent second-hand
Osterley Bookshop, built on the site of the
old tube station; the owners also sell free-
range eggs from their own chickens and
homemade jam.

Hounslow High Street offers down-at-
heel chains as well as the outdated Treaty
Centre, which houses a Debenhams plus
various chains. A 24-hour Asda has opened
in the brand-new Blenheim Centre, but
locals generally prefer to get their groceries
from smaller independents. Try Ortadogu,
which offers Turkish, Greek and Middle
Eastern goodies, and Safa Supermarket.

As Nature Intended *201 Chiswick High Road,*
W4 2DR (8742 8838/www.asnatureintended.
uk.com).
Blenheim Centre *86-94 High Street, TW3*
1NH (8814 1516/www.blenheimcentre.com).
Blink *294 Chiswick High Road W4 1PA*
(8742 1313).
Butterfly Girl Vintage *116 High Street, TW8*
8AT (8569 9793/www.butterflygirlvintage.com).
Cath Kidston *125 Chiswick High Road, W4*
2ED (8995 8052/www.cathkidston.co.uk).

Covent Garden Fishmongers *37 Turnham Green Terrace, W4 1RG (8995 9273).*
Eco *213 Chiswick High Road, W4 2DW (www.eco-age.com).*
Jurlique Day Spa & Sanctuary *Holly House, 300-302 Chiswick High Road, W4 1NP (8995 2293/www.apotheke20-20.co.uk).*
Little Trading Company *7 Bedford Corner, The Avenue, W4 1LD (8742 3152).*
Mortimer & Bennett *33 Turnham Green Terrace, W4 1RG (8995 4145/www.mortimer andbennett.com).*
Naked Grain *192 High Street, TW8 8LB (8758 1456/www.nakedgrain.com).*
Natural Food Store *41 Turnham Green Terrace, W4 1RG (8995 4906).*
The Old Cinema *160 Chiswick High Road, W4 1PR (8995 4166/www.theoldcinema.co.uk).*
Ortadogu Supermarket *51-53 High Street, TW3 1RB (8814 1928).*
Osterley Bookshop *168A Thornbury Road, TW7 4QE (8560 6206).*
Safa Supermarket *96 High Street, TW3 1NH (8572 8591).*
Shoe Tree *1 Devonshire Road, W4 2EU (8987 0525).*
Theobroma Cacao *43 Turnham Green Terrace, W4 1RG (8996 0431/www.theobroma-cacao.co.uk).*
Treaty Centre *High Street, TW3 1RH (8572 3570/www.treatyshoppingcentre.co.uk).*

Arts & attractions

Cinemas & theatres
Cineworld Feltham *Leisure West, TW13 7EX (0871 200 2000/www.cineworld.co.uk).*
Watermans *40 High Street, TW8 0DS (8232 1010/www.watermans.org.uk).* Multi-purpose arts centre next to the river in Brentford.

Music & comedy venues
Headliners Comedy Club *George IV, 185 Chiswick High Road, W4 2DR (8566 4067/ www.headlinerscomedy.com).*

Galleries & museums
Gunnersbury Park Museum *Popes Lane, W3 8LQ (8992 1612).* Local history museum.
Kew Bridge Steam Museum *Green Dragon Lane, TW8 0EN (8568 4757/www.kbsm.org).* Lots of lovely steam engines, housed in a Victorian pumping station.
Musical Museum *399 High Street, TW8 0DU (8560 8108/www.musicalmuseum.co.uk).*

Other attractions
Chiswick House *Burlington Lane, W4 2RP (8995 0508/www.english-heritage.org.uk).* 1725 Palladian villa, with interiors by William Kent.
Hogarth's House *Hogarth Lane, Great West Road, W4 2QN (8994 6757).* Country home of the great 18th-century painter, engraver and satirist William Hogarth.
Osterley House & Park *Off Jersey Road,*

COUNCIL TAX

A	up to £40,000	**£929.69**
B	£40,001-£52,000	**£1,084.63**
C	£52,001-£68,000	**£1,239.59**
D	£68,001-£88,000	**£1,394.53**
E	£88,001-£120,000	**£1,704.43**
F	£120,001-£160,000	**£2,014.32**
G	£160,001-£320,000	**£2,324.22**
H	over £320,000	**£2,789.06**

RECYCLING
No. of bring sites 52 (for nearest, visit www.recycleforlondon.com).
Household waste recycled 15.74%
Main recycling centre Space Waye Civic Reuse & Recycling Centre, Pier Road, North Feltham Trading Estate, TW14 0TW (8890 0917)
Other recycling services green waste collection; home composting; collection of white goods and furniture
Council contact Recycling Team, Civic Centre, Lampton Road, Hounslow, Middx TW3 4DN (8583 5555)

TW7 4RB (8232 5050/www.nationaltrust. org.uk/osterley). Former Tudor house turned into a swish neo-classical villa by Robert Adam.
Syon House & Park *London Road, TW8 8JF (8560 0881/www.syonpark.co.uk).* Family seat of the Duke of Northumberland, with interiors by Robert Adam.

Sport & fitness

Hounslow has several public leisure facilities. There are also private clubs, particularly in well-heeled W4.

Gyms & leisure centres
Brentford Fountain Leisure Centre *658 Chiswick High Road, TW8 0HJ (0845 456 2935/www.hounslow.info).*
David Lloyd *Southall Lane, TW5 9PE (8573 9378/www.davidlloydleisure.co.uk).* Private.
Esporta *www.esporta.co.uk; Riverside Drive, Dukes Meadows, W4 2SX (8987 1800); Chiswick Business Park, 566 Chiswick High Road, W4 5YA (8987 5800).* Private.
Feltham Airparcs Leisure Centre *Uxbridge Road, TW13 5EG (0845 456 2865/ www.hounslow.info).*
Heston Pool *New Heston Road, TW5 0LW (8570 4396/www.hounslow.info).*
Heston Community Sports Hall *Heston Road, TW5 0QZ (0845 456 6675/ www.hounslow.info).*
Hogarth Health Club *1 Airedale Avenue, W4 2NW (8995 4600/www.thehogarth.co.uk).* Private.

Isleworth Recreation Centre *Twickenham Road, TW7 7EU (0845 456 2980/ www.hounslow.info).*
Lampton Sports Centre *Lampton Avenue, TW3 4EP (8814 0342/www.hounslow.info).*
New Chiswick Pool *Edensor Road, W4 2RG (8747 8811/www.hounslow.info).*
West 4 *10A Sutton Lane North, W4 4LD (8747 1713/www.west4healthclub.co.uk).* Private.

Other facilities
Chiswick Tennis Club *Burlington Lane, W4 3EU (07946 096933/www.chiswicktennis club.com).* Private.
Civil Service Sports Club *Riverside Drive, Dukes Meadow, W4 2SH (8994 1202/www. cssc-london.co.uk).* Private club for civil servants. Facilities include grass tennis courts, and football and cricket pitches.

Spectator sports
Brentford FC *Griffin Park, Braemar Road, TW8 0NT (0845 3456 442/www.brentfordfc.co.uk).*

Schools
WHAT THE PARENTS SAY:
'My three children all went to our nearest state primary, Green Dragon, and thrived in the inclusive, child-centred education it provided. At secondary level things are more difficult. With some perseverance on our part, our two older children attended Chiswick Community School, where they achieved well. Our youngest was keen to go with her friends to a different secondary, and is attending Lampton School, a specialist humanities school in Hounslow. This is another very inclusive school embracing the multicultural population of Hounslow, with very high academic and behavioural standards.'
Diana Oppe, mother of three, Brentford

Primary
There are 45 state primary schools in Hounslow, including eight church schools. There are also six independents, including one international school and one Muslim school. See www.hounslow.gov.uk, www.edubase.gov.uk and www.ofsted.gov.uk for more information.

Secondary
Hounslow has 14 secondary schools, of which ten are comprehensive (eight mixed, one boys only, one girls only) and four are voluntary-aided schools (two single-sex Roman Catholic schools, one mixed Roman Catholic school and one single-sex Church of England school). You can download a full list of addresses and contact details from the 'Education and learning' section of the borough of Hounslow's website, www.hounslow.gov.uk.

Property
WHAT THE AGENTS SAY:
'Chiswick is awesome. It's very family-oriented, but there's plenty to do at night, with lovely pubs and restaurants on the High Road. Brentford is very up and coming. It had a reputation for being a bit rough, but recent years have seen the arrival of lots of swish apartment blocks. There's no tube, but the train to Waterloo takes about 25 minutes from Kew Bridge or Brentford stations, and Gunnersbury tube is a 15-minute walk.'
Alan Maynard, Featherstone-Leigh, Chiswick

Average property prices
Detached £472,981
Semi-detached £355,777
Terraced £343,312
Flat £237,049

Local estate agents
Featherstone-Leigh *Chardin House, Chardin Road, W4 1RJ (8994 6567/www.featherstone-leigh.co.uk).*
Fletchers *58 Turnham Green Terrace, W4 1QP (8987 3000/www.fletcherestates.com).*
Riverhomes.co.uk *28 Thames Road, W4 3RJ (8996 0600/www.riverhomes.co.uk).*
Quilliam Property Services *206 High Street, TW8 8AH (8847 4737/www.quilliam.co.uk).*

Other information
Council
London Borough of Hounslow *Civic Centre, Lampton Road, TW3 4DN (8583 2000/out-of-hours 8583 2222/www.hounslow.gov.uk).*

Legal services
Brentford & Chiswick CAB *Old Town Hall, Heathfield Terrace, W4 4JN (0870 126 9500/ www.citizensadvice.org.uk).*
Hounslow CAB *2nd floor, 45 Treaty Centre, High Street, TW3 1ES (0870 126 9500).*
Hounslow Law Centre *51 Lampton Road, TW3 1LY (8570 9505/www.hounslowlaw centre.org.uk).*

Local newspapers
The Chiswick *www.thechiswick.co.uk.*
Brentford, Chiswick & Isleworth Times *www.rttimes.co.uk.*
Hounslow Guardian *www.hounslowguardian.co.uk.*

Allotments & open spaces
Council Allotments *Lettings Team, CIP, Treaty Centre, High Street, TW3 1ES (0845 456 2796/www.hounslow.info/allotments).*
Open spaces *www.hounslow.info/parks.*

Hounslow

Kingston upon Thames

The 'secret' side of south-west London, Kingston doesn't have the tube, so it doesn't get the hype that Richmond and Wimbledon do. Yet for shops, schools, security and river views it is well able to compete with its posher neighbours – and if you live on the right railway line, it's effectively 'closer' to Waterloo than Brixton.

Neighbourhoods

Kingston Town

Kingston loves pedestrians and hates drivers. Well, something has to explain why it takes 15 minutes to get round the town centre on what must be the worst bypass in outer London. The good thing, though, if you're moseying around Kingston's compact yet comprehensive shopping district, is that you'll barely see a bus or car all day.

Kingston was a market town in Saxon times: seven Saxon kings are said to have been crowned on the Coronation Stone, which stands to the right of the Guildhall on the High Street. Today Kingston and its immediate environs are a bustling, family-friendly shopping and leisure hub (David Mach's *Out of Order* phone box sculpture is worth a look on your way up Old London Road). Kingston University attracts a large number of foreign students, which gives a cosmopolitan air to what is largely a white, middle-class town. By night, however, the town centre can be lairy and noisy.

Property here, though more affordable than central London boroughs, can be pricey (especially the desirable riverside properties), with lots of big Victorian detached and semi-detached homes. There are a few sought-after new developments too, such as the Royal Quarter. Residents also benefit from easy access to the expansive greenery of neighbouring Richmond upon Thames (Bushy, Hampton Court and Richmond Parks) as well as spaces like Thames-side Canbury Gardens.

Norbiton, Coombe and Kingston Hill

Kingston Hospital sprawls around the centre of Norbiton, while the ring road and exit roads to the A3 hack into margins. It's not exactly a pretty place. Housing is a mix of Victorian and Edwardian properties and 1960s and '80s developments. As Kingston's 'inner city', Norbiton is also home to much of the borough's social housing.

In sharp contrast, just up the hill to the east is Coombe, a microcosm of modern, bourgeois gated life. Around the Coombe House conservation area – developed on the land of a demolished former manorial estate – it's all cul-de-sacs, CCTV, three

Highs & Lows

▲ **Riverside locations** Choose between the bars and restaurants in Kingston centre, pleasant parks to the north and Surbiton's serene footpath
Education Kingston University is one of the most ambitious ex-polys in the UK, and high-performing private and state secondaries make the borough a brainy one

Private roads Walking round Coombe's lanes and cul-de-sacs makes all but well-heeled residents feel like burglars on the prowl
Limited cultural offerings OK, there's an impressive brand-new theatre, but this isn't a borough at the ▼ cutting edge of culture

David Mach's **Out of Order**.

housing consists predominantly of Victorian and Edwardian terraces. Heading north on Coombe Road – later Traps Lane – things get immediately leafier.

Berrylands, the next stop on the trainline to Surbiton, is primarily residential. Apart from a smattering of shops – a florist, a laundrette, a picture framer – on Chiltern Drive, the neighbourhood is devoted entirely to 19th- and mid 20th-century housing. A good cycle path connects Surbiton, Berrylands and New Malden.

Surbiton

Much like Posh Spice and Simon Cowell, everybody has an opinion about Surbiton – and it's rarely positive. Residents have to put up with tedious ribbing about 1970s sitcom *The Good Life* (filmed in Northwood, but fictionally located here), the notion that it's just a railway junction (it isn't) and the stereotype that it is the definitive suburb (it isn't that, either).

Surbiton is 12 miles from central London, but is closer – in travelling minutes – than many places in Zone 2. Fast trains bound for Surrey and Hampshire stop here after Clapham Junction. The beautiful, white art deco station is a monument to the suburb's role as a commuter town, but conservation areas off Maple Road and along Claremont Road and the Crescent hint at a leafy graciousness that pre-dates the trains.

Surbiton's more sociable residents are happy with their handful of fine eateries and one cool cocktail bar (the Rubicon) – all on Maple Road. There is an excellent, if pricey gym on the riverside within a former Thames pumphouse, some good charity shops on Victoria Road (the high street) and a few decent pubs – but just as people go to London for work, they go to Kingston for shopping, to Home Park near Hampton Court for greenery and to Thames Ditton for bucolic boozing.

Mercs per garage and preened pampas grass beside the porch. The Coombe Hill Golf Course spreads its greens around the private lanes, and the one bus that runs through – the no.57 to Streatham – never needs to stop. The abutting district of Kingston Vale, while slightly less exclusive, is also leafy and stridently suburban – and also utterly bereft of pubs and amenities.

New Malden and Berrylands

New Malden's centre is spread out over Kingston Road, Malden Road, Burlington Road and New Malden High Street, with the great majority of shops and services on the latter. Crummy-looking discount stores, charity shops and chains dominate, with the only colour provided by the restaurants and shops that employ and serve the area's large and vibrant Korean community.

The word 'Seoul' features in many of the names of local businesses, but New Malden looks more like Pyongyang, with the grey hulks of the 16-storey Apex and CI Towers looming over the townscape and the A3 throbbing in the background. Developed around the railway station, the area's

Restaurants & cafés

When Kingston's riverside was redeveloped in the 1990s, the rent on units was set high, inviting in chains and making for a rather predictable dining experience. Fortunately, you'll also find fantastic Riverside Vegetaria, French brasserie Frère Jacques and friendly Italian Al Forno – all by the river, though Al Forno is a hop across the main road.

Kingston upon Thames

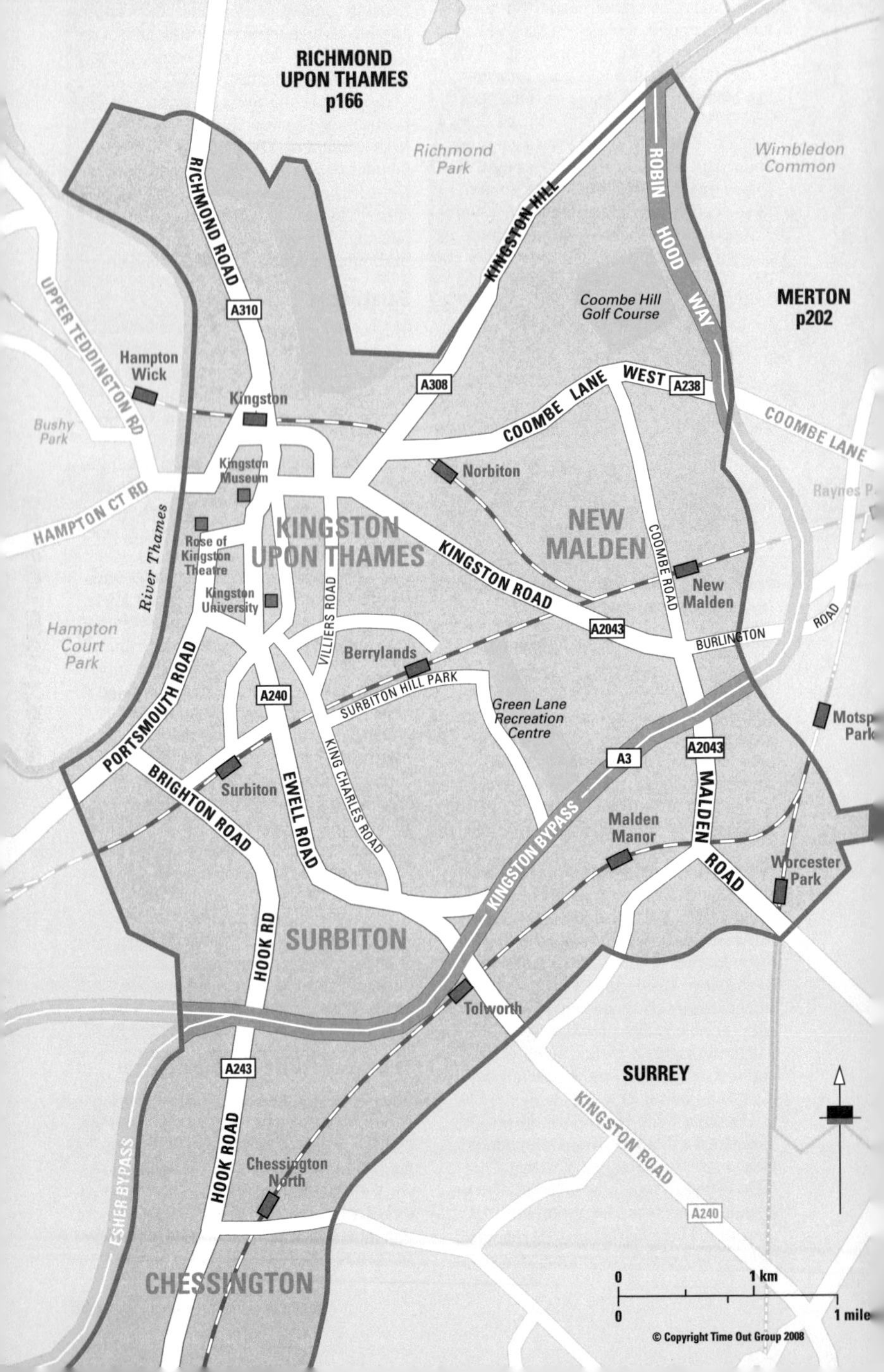

RICHMOND
UPON THAMES
p166

Richmond
Park

Wimbledon
Common

MERTON
p202

ROBIN HOOD WAY

KINGSTON HILL

Coombe Hill
Golf Course

UPPER TEDDINGTON RD

RICHMOND ROAD

A310

Hampton
Wick

Kingston

Bushy
Park

A308

COOMBE LANE WEST

A238

COOMBE LANE

Norbiton

HAMPTON CT RD

Kingston
Museum

Rose of
Kingston
Theatre

Kingston
University

KINGSTON
UPON THAMES

River Thames

KINGSTON ROAD

NEW
MALDEN

New
Malden

COOMBE ROAD

Raynes P.

Hampton
Court
Park

VILLIERS ROAD

Berrylands

A2043

BURLINGTON

ROAD

A240

SURBITON HILL PARK

KING CHARLES ROAD

Green Lane
Recreation
Centre

A3

A2043

Motsp
Park

PORTSMOUTH ROAD

Subiton

BRIGHTON ROAD

EWELL ROAD

HOOK RD

SURBITON

KINGSTON BYPASS

Malden
Manor

MALDEN ROAD

Worcester
Park

Tolworth

SURREY

A243

ESHER BYPASS

HOOK ROAD

Chessington
North

KINGSTON ROAD

A240

CHESSINGTON

0   1 km

0   1 mile

© Copyright Time Out Group 2008

For a laid-back meal, head to Surbiton where a handful of places on Maple Road offer something like chic suburbia. Well-priced Italian Da Lucio is good for a low-key bite, the French Table has long been praised by critics from uptown, and Gordon Bennett – somewhere between a gastropub and a bar-bistro – is always buzzing.

Elsewhere in the borough, it's hit and miss, though there are a few nice delis and restaurants near Norbiton railway station (classy fish and chippie fish! kitchen for one). There is also a slew of excellent Korean restaurants in New Malden: try Jee Cee Neh's tabletop barbecues and unusual specials, and sophisticated Su La's good-value set lunches and dinners.

Al Forno *1-3A Townsend Parade, High Street, KT1 1LY (8439 7555/www.alforno kingston.co.uk).*
Da Lucio *101 Maple Road, KT6 4AW (8399 5113/www.dalucio.local-restaurant.com).*
fish! kitchen *58 Coombe Road, KT2 7AF (8546 2886/www.fishkitchen.com).*
French Table *85 Maple Road, KT6 4AW (8399 2365/www.thefrenchtable.co.uk).*
Frère Jacques *10-12 Riverside Walk, Bishops Hall, KT1 1QN (8546 1332/ www.frerejacques.co.uk).*
Gordon Bennett *75 Maple Road, KT6 4AG (8390 7222).*
Jee Cee Neh *74 Burlington Road, KT3 4NU (8942 0682).*
Riverside Vegetaria *64 High Street, KT1 1HN (8546 0609/www.rsveg.plus.com).*
Su La *79-81 Kingston Road, KT3 3PB (8336 0121).*

Bars & pubs

Drinkers heading to Kingston town centre or the river have plenty of choice, though most venues get packed at weekends. Saturday night sees the place awash with drunken students and out-of-town youngsters. Locals after a quieter night tend to stay well away, though the Druid's Head is something of a refuge from shopping madness and the crawler circuit.

North of the town, the Richmond Park Tavern is a good local and the Wych Elm is a popular Fuller's pub. The Boater's Inn is one of the nicest places for a summer beer by the river.

In Surbiton, the Rubicon bar is always lively, while Brave New World has live music on Thursday nights, and the Lamb's beer garden makes a fine spot for summer

A taste of Korea: **Su La**.

boozing. The Grove, revamped in mid 2007, has a decent wine list. Or head for Woodies in New Malden for a great array of beers.

Boater's Inn *Canbury Gardens, Lower Ham Road, KT2 5AU (8541 4672).*
Brave New World *22-26 Berrylands Road, KT5 8QX (8399 0200).*
Druid's Head *3 Market Place, KT1 1JT (8546 0723).*
Grove *Grove Road, KT6 4BX (8399 1662).*
Lamb *73 Brighton Road, KT6 5NF (8390 9229).*
Richmond Park Tavern *178 Kings Road, KT2 5HU (8296 0894).*
Rubicon *97 Maple Road, KT6 4AW (8399 5055/www.rubiconbar.com).*
Woodies *Thetford Road, KT3 5DX (8949 5824/www.woodiesfreehouse.co.uk).*
Wych Elm *93 Elm Road, KT2 6HT (8546 3271).*

Shops

Kingston is the ultimate shopopolis: a stroll from the thriving Ancient Market to the Bentall Centre and then to the grand John Lewis by the river gives you the range. People come from Chessington, Hounslow and even Richmond to visit the upmarket chain stores, but there are plenty of smaller retailers too, especially along Fife Street and Castle Street. Health freaks can check out the running shoes, clothing and accessories at Lanson Running, while surfer types should head to Beachworks. Just outside the centre, Old London Road is home to around 90 antiques' dealers, courtesy of the Kingston Antiques Centre. Also here is homewares shop Under the Moon.

Pickings are much slimmer elsewhere in the borough. Heading up Coombe Road towards the golf courses, you'll find golf emporium American Golf. On the same road are Japanese food store Atari-Ya, wine merchant Wined Up Here, high-quality fish shop Jarvis and Sicilian deli Sud Ovest. New Malden has numerous Korean food shops, while Surbiton's Shoes at Last has a large local following.

American Golf *11-13 Coombe Road, KT2 7AB (08444 992159/www.americangolf.co.uk).*
Ancient Market *Market Place, KT1 1JS.*
Atari-Ya *44 Coombe Road, KT2 7AF (8547 9891/www.atariya.co.uk).*
Beachworks *28 Castle Street, KT1 1SS (8974 8973).*
Bentall Centre *Wood Street, KT1 1TP (8541 5066/www.thebentallcentre-shopping.com).*
Jarvis the Fishmonger *56-58 Coombe Road, KT2 7AF (8296 0139).*
Kingston Antiques Centre *29 Old London Road, KT2 6ND (8549 2004).*
Lanson Running *34 High Street, KT1 4DB (8943 4094/www.lansonrunning.com).*
Shoes at Last *81 Maple Road, KT6 4AW (8390 5673/www.shoesatlast.com).*
Sud Ovest *54 Coombe Road, KT2 7AF (8549 0084).*
Under the Moon *31 Old London Road, KT2 6ND (8974 9434/www.underthemoonltd.com).*
Wined Up Here *30 Coombe Road, KT2 7AG (8549 6622/www.wineduphere.co.uk).*

Arts & attractions

Cinemas & theatres

cornerHOUSE *Douglas Road, KT6 7SB (8296 9012/www.thecornerhouse.org).*
Green Theatre Company *Barton Green Theatre, Elm Road, KT3 3HU (8942 0155/www.greentheatre.com).*
Odeon Kingston *The Rotunda, Clarence Street, KT1 1QP (0871 224 4007/www.odeon.co.uk).* The Rotunda entertainment complex contains this 14-screen cinema, plus a bowling alley, fitness centre and several restaurants.
Rose of Kingston *24-26 High Street, KT1 1HL (0871 230 1552/www.kingstontheatre.org).* Impressive new theatre opened in January 2008.

Galleries & museums

Dorich House Museum *67 Kingston Vale, SW15 3RN (8547 7519/www.kingston.ac.uk/dorich).* 1930s house with a large collection of Russian art. Guided tours on certain days only.
Kingston Museum *Wheatfield Way, KT1 2PS (8547 6460/www.kingston.gov.uk/museum).* Local history museum.

Stanley Picker Gallery *Faculty of Art, Design & Architecture, Kingston University, Knights Park, KT1 2QJ (8547 8074/www.stanleypickergallery.org).*
Toilet Gallery *143-159 Clarence Street, KT1 1QT (07881 832291/www.toiletgallery.org).* Art gallery in a converted public toilet.

Music & comedy venues

Grey Horse *46 Richmond Road, KT2 5EE (8541 4328/www.www.grey-horse.co.uk).* Jazz, funk, blues and comedy nights take place at this venerable old boozer.
The Peel *160 Cambridge Road, KT1 3HH (8546 3516/www.peelmuzik.com).* Up and coming bands galore.

Other attractions

Coombe Conduit *Coombe Lane West (8541 3108/www.english-heritage.org.uk).* Two small

Tudor buildings connected by an underground passage that carried water to Hampton Court Palace. Open on the second Sunday of the month from April to September.

Chessington World of Adventures & Zoo
Leatherhead Road, KT9 2NE (0870 999 0045/ www.chessington.co.uk).

Sport & fitness

As well as plenty of public and private leisure facilities, Kingston also boasts a slew of golf courses (Coombe Hill, Coombe Wood and Surbiton, for example).

Gyms & leisure centres

Cannons *Simpson Way, KT6 4ER (8335 2900/ www.cannons.co.uk).* Private.

Chessington Sports Centre *Garrison Lane, KT9 2JS (8974 2277/www.ccc.kingston.sch.uk).*

David Lloyd *The Rotunda, Clarence Street, KT1 1QJ (8974 7440/www.davidlloyd.co.uk).* Private.

Esporta Health Club *Richmond Road, KT2 5EN (8481 6000/www.esporta.com).* Private.

Hawker Centre *Lower Ham Road, KT2 5BH (8296 9747).*

Kingfisher Leisure Centre *Fairfield Road, KT1 2PY (8546 1042/www.dcleisure centres.co.uk).*

Kingsmeadow Fitness & Athletics
422A Kingston Road, KT1 3PB (8547 2198/ www.dcleisurecentres.co.uk).

Malden Centre *Blagdon Road, KT3 4TA (8336 7770/www.dcleisurecentres.co.uk).*

Tiffin Girls Community Sports Centre
Richmond Road, KT2 5PL (8546 0773).

Tiffin Sports Centre *London Road, KT2 6RL (8541 3972).*

Tolworth Recreation Centre *Fullers Way, KT6 7LQ (8391 7910/www.dcleisurecentres.co.uk).*

Virgin Active *3rd floor, Bentall Centre, Wood Street, KT1 1TP (8549 7700/ www.virginactive.co.uk).* Private.

Other facilities

New Malden Tennis, Squash & Badminton Club *Somerset Close, KT3 5RG (8942 0539/www.newmaldenclub.co.uk).*

Spectator sports

AFC Wimbledon/Kingstonian FC
The Cherry Red Records Fans' Stadium, Kingsmeadow, Jack Goodchild Way, 422A

TRANSPORT

Rail stations *South West Trains* New Malden, Norbiton, Kingston; Berrylands, Surbiton; Malden Manor, Tolworth, Chessington North, Chessington South **Main bus routes** *into central London* no direct service; *night buses* N87

Kingston Road, KT1 3PB (8547 3528/www. afcwimbledon.co.uk/www.kingstonian.net). Now home to what many fans consider the real Wimbledon FC.

Schools

WHAT THE PARENTS SAY:

‘When it comes to primary schools we had the good fortune to have both our kids go to Latchmere – I couldn't rate it more highly. Secondary schools are a different kettle of fish, especially if you have a boy. Everybody wants to go to Tiffin: both the boys' and girls' schools have great reputations. The problem is they only take the best (based on 11-plus test results) – private tutoring is big business in Kingston.

If your child doesn't make it, Hollyfield in Surbiton is rapidly up and coming, but if you're out of the catchment area you might be offered Coombe Boys, Southborough or Grey Court (just over the border with Richmond). That's when many parents decide to go private. Girls fare better: if your daughter doesn't get into Tiffin, then Coombe Girls or Hollyfield are good choices.'

Dave Faulkner, father of two,
Kingston upon Thames

PRIMARY

There are 29 state primary schools in Kingston upon Thames (including 14 church schools), plus eight independent primaries. See www. kingston.gov.uk, www.edubase.gov.uk and www.ofsted.gov.uk for more information.

Secondary

Chessington Community College
Garrison Lane, KT9 2JS (8974 1156/ www.ccc.kingston.sch.uk).

LOCALS' TIPS

If you are new to the Surbiton area, the Rubicon on a Thursday or Friday night is definitely the place to meet people. **Only visitors walk on the Kingston side of the river. Cross over to the other bank for a gorgeous, completely car-free stroll from Kingston Bridge to Hampton Court.** In summer, the Ancient Market in Kingston town centre is fantastic fun, with gigs, microbreweries serving at improvised bars and great food stalls. **Tired of city life? Head for bucolic Thames Ditton between Kingston and Esher for a riverside village vibe.**

Coombe Boys' School *College Gardens, Blakes Lane, KT3 6NU (8949 1537/ www.coombeboysschool.org)*. Boys only.
Coombe Girls' School *Clarence Avenue, KT3 3TU (8942 1242/www.coombegirls school.org)*. Girls only.
Hollyfield School & Sixth Form Centre *Surbiton Hill Road, KT6 4TU (8339 4500/ www.hollyfield.kingston.sch.uk)*.
Holy Cross RC School *25 Sandal Road, KT3 5AR (8395 4225/www.holycross.kingston. sch.uk)*. Girls only.
Kingston Grammar School *70 London Road, KT2 6PY (8546 5875/www.kingston- grammar.surrey.sch.uk)*. Private.
Richard Challoner RC School *Manor Drive North, KT3 5PE (8330 5947/www.richard challoner.com)*. Boys only.
Southborough School *Hook Road, KT6 5AS (8391 4324/www.southborough.kingston. sch.uk)*. Boys only.
Tiffin Girls' School *Richmond Road, KT2 5PL (8546 0773/www.tiffingirls.kingston.sch.uk)*. Girls only.
Tiffin School *Queen Elizabeth Road, KT2 6RL (8546 4638/www.tiffin.kingston.sch.uk)*. Boys only.
Tolworth Girls' School *Fullers Way North, KT6 7LQ (8397 3854)*. Girls only.

Property

WHAT THE AGENTS SAY:

❛One of the main benefits of living here is the access to Richmond Park. Kingston is very popular with people who work in central London, but want green space and a suburban feel. The river is lovely in the summer, and the Bentall Centre is excellent for shopping. A lot of families are moving here too: the schools are brilliant. Plenty of people buy-to-let, especially as there are lots of students in the area. Parts of the borough that had a not-so-great reputation in the past have been redeveloped and are now desirable.❜
Corinne Watkyns, Carringtons, Kingston

Average property prices
Detached £735,353
Semi-detached £398,181
Terraced £316,630
Flat £251,765

Local estate agents
Carringtons *7 Kingston Hill, KT2 7PW (8549 3366/www.carringtonsproperty.co.uk)*.
Dexters *www.dexters.co.uk; 2 offices in the borough (Kingston 8546 3555/ Surbiton 8390 3939)*.
Hawes & Co *www.hawesandco.co.uk; 2 offices in the borough (Surbiton 8390 6565/New Malden 8949 5856)*.

Jeje Barons *5 Kingston Hill, KT2 7PW (8296 9800/www.jejebarons.co.uk)*.

Other information

Council
Royal Borough of Kingston upon Thames *The Guildhall Complex, High Street, KT1 1EU (8547 5757/www.kingston.gov.uk)*.

Legal services
Chessington & Hook CAB *The Hook Centre, Hook Road, KT9 1EJ (0870 126 4019)*.
Kingston CAB *Neville House, 55 Eden Street, KT1 1BW (0870 126 4019/www.kcabs.org.uk)*.
Kingston & Richmond Law Centre *Siddeley House, 50 Canbury Park Road, KT2 6LX (8547 2882)*.
Malden & Coombe CAB *New Malden Library, Kingston Road, KT3 3LY (0870 126 4019)*.

Local newspapers
Kingston Guardian *8646 6336/ www.kingstonguardian.co.uk*.
Kingston Informer *Informer House, 2 High Street, Teddington, TW11 8EW (8943 5171)*.

Allotments & open spaces
Council Allotments *Quadron Services, Recycling Centre, Chapel Mill Road, KT1 3GZ (8399 1274)*.
Kingston Federation of Allotment Gardeners *Gloria Wallis 8942 9686/www. e-voice.org.uk/kfag*.
Open spaces *www.kingston.gov.uk/parks*.

COUNCIL TAX
A	up to £40,000	**£1,014.67**
B	£40,001-£52,000	**£1,183.78**
C	£52,001-£68,000	**£1,352.89**
D	£68,001-£88,000	**£1,522.00**
E	£88,001-£120,000	**£1,860.22**
F	£120,001-£160,000	**£2,198.45**
G	£160,001-£320,000	**£2,536.67**
H	over £320,000	**£3,044.00**

RECYCLING
No. of bring sites 35 (for nearest, visit www.recycleforlondon.com)
Household waste recycled 17.41%
Main recycling centre Villers Road Recycling Centre, Kingston upon Thames, KT1 3BE
Other recycling services green waste and kitchen waste collection; collection of furniture and white goods
Council contact Guildhall, 2 High Street, Kingston upon Thames, KT1 1EU (8547 5560)

Advertisers' index

Please refer to relevant sections for addresses/telephone numbers

Image Credit: Charlie Pinder

Advertisers' index

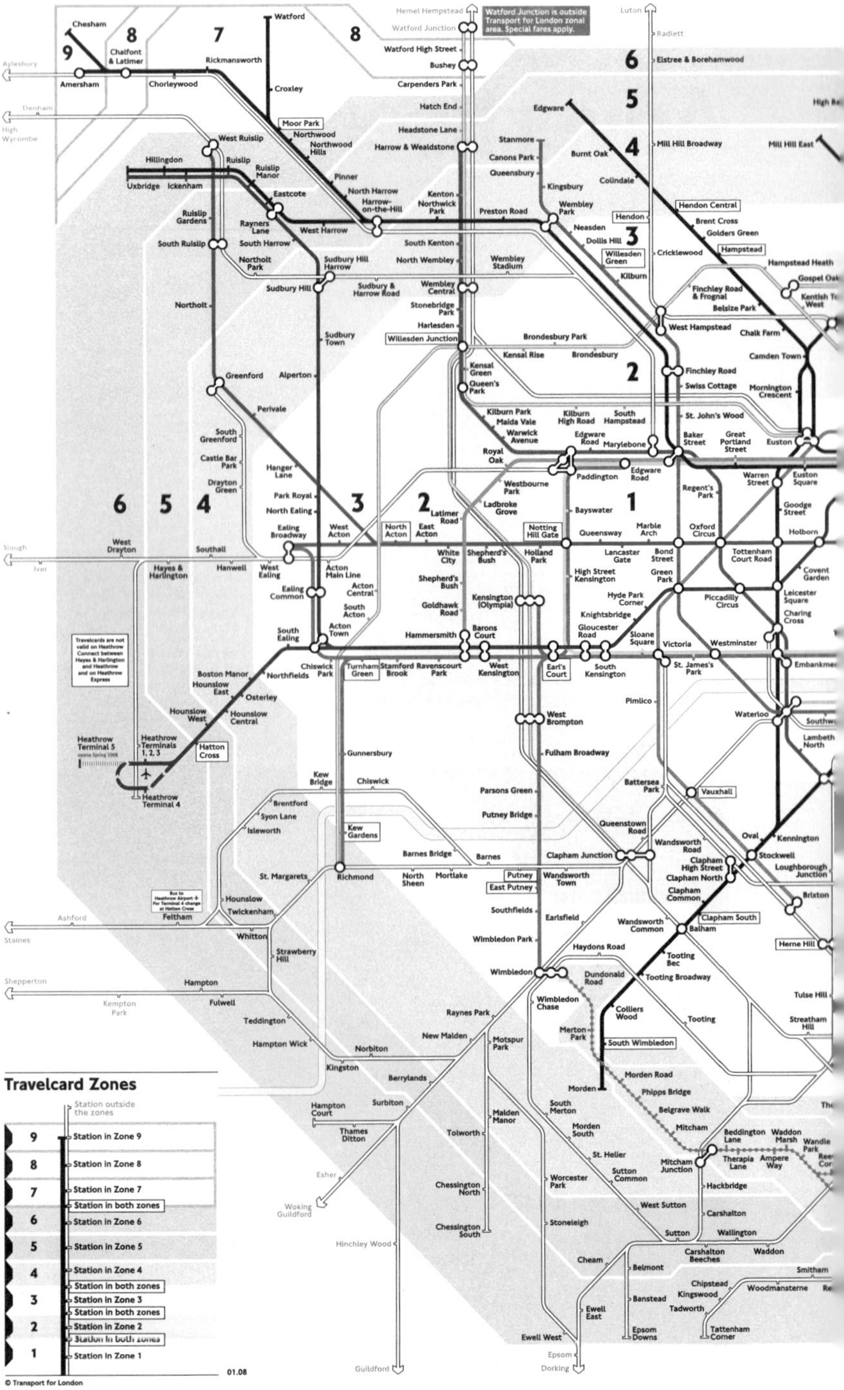

Tube & Rail Map

Watford Junction is outside Transport for London zonal area. Special fares apply.

Travelcard Zones

Station outside the zones

9	Station in Zone 9
8	Station in Zone 8
7	Station in Zone 7
	Station in both zones
6	Station in Zone 6
5	Station in Zone 5
4	Station in Zone 4
	Station in both zones
3	Station in Zone 3
	Station in both zones
2	Station in Zone 2
	Station in both zones
1	Station in Zone 1

© Transport for London   01.08

East London line is closed for major line extension work to become part of the London Overground network. Replacement bus services will be in operation.

Cutty Sark for Maritime Greenwich

Tramlink
Travelcards valid in Zones 3, or 4, or 5, or 6 (or combination of these Zones) and Bus Passes are available on Tramlink throughout the grey area

Key to lines

	Station	Interchange Station
Bakerloo		
Central		
Circle		
District		
East London		
Hammersmith & City		
Jubilee		
Metropolitan		
Northern		
Piccadilly		
Heathrow Terminal 5 opens Spring 2008		
Victoria		
Waterloo & City		
London Overground		
DLR		
Tramlink		
National Rail		

Some stations and lines have restricted opening times.

The routes shown on this map are a guide to weekday, off-peak services but do not guarantee direct trains between the stations shown.

Improvement works may affect your journey, particularly at weekends.
Check before you travel: look for publicity at stations, visit tfl.gov.uk/check or call 020 7222 1234

Correct at time of going to print

Reg. user No. 08/1095/LS

Useful Contacts

SERVICES & TRADESMEN

Directories 020 London www.020.co.uk.

118 www.118.com

BT Directory www.thephonebook.bt.com.

Tradesmens Directory www.thetradesmensdirectory.co.uk.

Yellow Pages www.yell.com.

Builders Federation of Master Builders www.findabuilder.co.uk.

Chimneys National Association of Chimney Sweeps 01785 811732/ www.nacs.org.uk.

Electricians Electrical Contractors' Association 7313 4800/www.eca.co.uk. Electrical engineering and building services.

National Inspection Council for Electrical Installation Contracting (NICEIC) 0870 013 0382/www.niceic.org.uk. NICEIC-approved electricians.

Glazing Glass & Glazing Federation www.ggf.org.uk. Database of registered glaziers.

Infestation British Pest Control Association 0870 609 2687/www.bpca.org.uk. For private pest control. Alternatively, local councils will address most common problems.

Plumbers Association of Plumbing & Heating Contractors 024 7647 0626/ www.aphc.co.uk.

Institute of Plumbing & Heating Engineering 01708 472791/www.iphe.org.uk.

Removals British Association of Removers 01923 699480/www.bar.co.uk.

HOME EMERGENCIES

Power cuts EDF ENERGY 0800 028 0247.

Electrical enquiries London Energy 0800 096 9000. 24hrs.

Gas leaks National Grid 0800 111999/non-emergencies 0845 605 6677/www.national grid.com.

Water leaks Thames Water leakline 0800 714614/ non-emergencies 0845 920 0800/www.thames-water.com.

Locksmiths Master Locksmiths Association 0800 783 1498/ www.locksmiths.co.uk.

ESTATE AGENTS

London-wide chains; locals are listed in each borough.

Adam Kennedy www.adamkennedy.co.uk

Bairstow Eves www.bairstoweves.co.uk

Barnard Marcus www.sequencehome.co.uk

Belvoir www.belvoirlettings.com

Dexters www.dexters.co.uk

Douglas Allen www.douglasallen.co.uk

Douglas & Gordon www.douglasandgordon.com

Ellis & Co www.ellisandco.co.uk

Faron Sutaria www.faronsutaria.co.uk

Felicity J Lord www.fjlord.co.uk

Foxtons www.foxtons.co.uk

Haart www.haart.co.uk

Hampton's International www.hamptons.co.uk

John D Wood & Co www.johndwood.co.uk

Keatons www.keatons.com

Kinleigh Folkard & Hayward www.kfh.co.uk

Ludlow Thompson www.ludlowthompson.com

Regents Estate Agent www.regents.co.uk

Wates Residential www.watesresidential.co.uk

Winkworth www.winkworth.co.uk

Your Move www.yourmove.co.uk

General websites: www.findaproperty.co.uk www.hotproperty.co.uk www.primelocation.com

HEALTH & SUPPORT

Complementary medicine British Homeopathic Association 0870 444 3950/ www.trusthomeopathy.org.

Institute for Complementary Medicine 7231 5855/www.i-c-m.org.uk.

Dentists Find a Dentist www.bda-findadentist.org.uk.

NHS services NHS Direct 0845 4647/www.nhsdirect. nhs.uk. Health information. Alternatively, find your nearest NHS health service at www.nhs.uk.

Helplines Alcoholics Anonymous 0845 769 7555/ www.alcoholicsanonymous. org.uk.

ChildLine 0800 1111/ www.childline.org.uk.

London Lesbian & Gay Switchboard 7837 7324/ www.queery.org.uk.

Narcotics Anonymous 0845 373 3366/www.ukna.org.

National Missing Persons Helpline 0500 700 700/ www.missingpersons.org.

Samaritans 08457 909090/ www.samaritans.org.uk.

Victim Support 0845 303 0900/www.victimsupport.com.

Pregnancy & birth British Pregnancy Advisory Service 08457 304030/ www.bpas.org.

National Childbirth Trust 0870 444 8707/www.nct.org.uk.

Sexual health Brook 7284 6040/helpline 0800 018 5023/www.brook.org.uk. Advice for young people.

Sexual Health Information Line 0800 567123/www. condomessentialwear.co.uk.

Terrence Higgins Trust/ Lighthouse helpline 0845 122 1200/www.tht.org.uk. Advice and counsel for those with HIV/AIDS.

CHILDREN

Childminding Sitters 7935 3000/www.babysitter.co.uk.

Universal Aunts 7738 8937/ www.universalaunts.co.uk.

Schools BBC Education www.bbc.co.uk/education.

Edubase www.edubase.gov.uk.

Ofsted www.ofsted.gov.uk.

CONGESTION CHARGE

Drivers coming into central London between 7am and 6pm Monday to Friday have to pay an £8 fee. The charging zone (extended west into Kensington & Chelsea in February 2007) is marked on the borough maps at the beginning of each chapter of this guide; red 'C' signs painted on the road indicate the zone. The scheme is enforced by CCTV cameras; expect a fine of £50 if you fail to pay (rising to £100 if you delay). You can pay by phone or online at any time during the day of entry. Payment is also accepted until midnight on the next charging day – but it rises to £10. Vauxhall Bridge Road, Grosvenor Place and Park Lane is the toll-free through-route. **0845 900 1234/www.cclondon.com**.

LEGAL SERVICES

Legal advice **Citizens' Advice Bureau** *www.citizensadvice.org.uk.*
Community Legal Service Direct *0845 345 4345/ www.clsdirect.org.uk.*
Legal Aid **Legal Services Commission** *7759 0000/ www.legalservices.gov.uk.*
Solicitors **Law Society** helpline *0870 606 2555/ www.lawsociety.org.uk.* Find a solicitor in your area.

PUBLIC TRANSPORT

Information **Transport for London** *7222 1234/www.tfl. gov.uk.* Information, maps and service updates for tubes, trains, buses, DLR and river services.
Journey Planner *www.journey planner.org.* Route advice.
National Rail Enquiries *0845 748 4950/www.national rail.co.uk.*
Oyster Card *0845 330 9876/ www.oystercard.com.*
Rail services **Chiltern Railways** *www.chiltern railways.co.uk.*
c2c *www.c2c-online.co.uk.*
Eurostar *www.eurostar.com.*
First Capital Connect *www.firstcapitalconnect.co.uk*
First Great Western *www.firstgreatwestern.co.uk.*
London Midland *www.londonmidland.com*
one *www.onerailway.com.*
Southern *www.southern railway.com.*
South Eastern Trains *www.setrains.co.uk.*
South West Trains *www.southwesttrains.co.uk.*
Coaches **Green Line Travel** *0870 608 7261/www.greenline. co.uk.*

National Express *0870 580 8080/www.nationalexpress.com.*
Complaints **Travel Watch** *7505 9000/www.londontravel watch.org.uk.*

DRIVING & CYCLING

Breakdown services **AA (Automobile Association)** information *0800 444999/* breakdown *0800 887766/ www.theaa.co.uk.*
ETA (Environmental Transport Association) *01932 828882/www.eta.co.uk.*
RAC (Royal Automobile Club) breakdown *0800 828282/office & membership 08705 722722/www.rac.co.uk.*
Cycling **London Cycle Network** *www.london cyclenetwork.org.uk.*
London Cycling Campaign *7234 9310/www.lcc.org.uk.*
OY Bike *www.oybike.com.* Bike hire by mobile phone.
Sustrans *www.sustrans.org.uk.* Promoting cycling.
Disabled services **Dial a Ride** *7027 5823/5824/ www.tfl.gov.uk.*
Wheelchair Travel & Access Mini Buses *01483 233640/ www.wheelchair-travel.co.uk.*
Parking **NCP** *0870 606 7050/ www.ncp.co.uk.*
Vehicle hire **Alamo** *0870 400 4508/www.alamo.com.*
Avis *0844 581 0147/ www.avis.co.uk.*
Easycar *www.easycar.com.*
Enterprise *0870 607 7757/ www.enterprise.com.*
HGB Motorcycles *01895 676 451/www.hgbmotorcycles.co.uk.*
Taxis Transport for London's website (www.tfl.gov.uk) has a licensed minicab database. Alternatively, text HOME to

60835 for firms in your area, or call 0800 666666.
Lady Cabs *7272 3300/ www.ladyminicabs.co.uk.* Women-only mini-cab drivers.
Radio Taxis *7272 0272.* For black cabs.
Scooterman *0870 242 6999/ www.scooterman.co.uk.* Be driven home in your own car.

SPORT

London Active Partnership *7815 7828/www.londonactive partnership.org.* Encouraging access to organised sport.
London Sports Forum for Disabled People *7717 1699/ www.londonsportsforum.org.uk.*
Sport England *08458 508508/ www.sportengland.org.* Find your local sports centre.

USEFUL WEBSITES

Time Out London *www.timeout.com/london.* Premier source of information about happenings in the capital.
BBC London *www.bbc.co.uk/ london.* Online news, weather, sport and entertainment.
Fix My Street *www.fixmy street.com.* Report, view or discuss problems in your area.
Greater London Authority *www.london.gov.uk.* See what the mayor and co are up to.
Gumtree *www.gumtree.com.* Online community noticeboard.
IAmMoving.com *www.iammoving.com.* Notify people of your new address.
Loot *www.loot.com.* Buy and sell in London.
London Farmers' Markets *www.lfm.org.uk.* Find your nearest market.
Meteorological Office *www.met-office.gov.uk.* Weather forecasts.
Post Office *www.postoffice. co.uk.* Find your nearest post office.
Streetmap *www.streetmap. co.uk.* Useful A-Z-like resource.
StreetSensation *www.street sensation.co.uk.* Panoramic 'streetscapes' of over 3,000 London streets.
This is London *www.thisis london.co.uk.* The *Evening Standard* online.
UpMyStreet.com *www.upmy street.com.* Services and info, broken down by neighbourhood.
Visit London *www.visitlondon.com.* The official tourist board website.

Useful Contacts

Index

Note: page numbers in **bold** indicate the section giving key information; *italics* indicate illustrations

Index

Index